Middle School 3-2
학교시험 완벽대비

2학기 전과정

적중 100 plus

영어 기출문제집

중 3

동아 | 이병민

Best Collection

구성과 특징

교과서의 주요 학습 내용을 중심으로 학습 영역별 특성에 맞춰 단계별로 다양한 학습 기회를 제공하여
단원별 학습능력 평가는 물론 중간 및 기말고사 시험 등에 완벽하게 대비할 수 있도록 내용을 구성

Words & Expressions

Step1 Key Words 단원별 핵심 단어 설명 및 풀이
       Key Expression 단원별 핵심 숙어 및 관용어 설명
       Word Power 반대 또는 비슷한 뜻 단어 배우기
       English Dictionary 영어로 배우는 영어 단어

Step2 실력평가 단원별 수시평가 대비 주관식, 객관식 문제풀이

Step3 서술형 대비 학업성취도 및 수행능력평가 대비 서술형 문제풀이

Conversation

Step1 핵심 의사소통 소통에 필요한 주요 표현 방법 요약
       핵심 Check 기본적인 표현 방법 및 활용능력 확인

Step2 대화문 익히기 교과서 대화문 심층 분석 및 확인

Step3 교과서 확인학습 빈칸 채우기를 통한 문장 완성 능력 확인

Step4 기본평가 시험대비 기초 학습 능력 평가

Step5 실력평가 단원별 수시평가 대비 주관식, 객관식 문제풀이

Step6 서술형 대비 학업성취도 및 수행능력평가 대비 서술형 문제풀이

Grammar

Step1 주요 문법 단원별 주요 문법 사항과 예문을 알기 쉽게 설명
       핵심 Check 기본 문법사항에 대한 이해 여부 확인

Step2 기본평가 시험대비 기초 학습 능력 평가

Step3 실력평가 단원별 수시평가 대비 주관식, 객관식 문제풀이

Step4 서술형 대비 학업성취도 및 수행능력평가 대비 서술형 문제풀이

Reading

Step1 구문 분석 단원별로 제시된 문장에 대한 구문별 분석과 내용 설명
       확인문제 문장에 대한 기본적인 이해와 인지능력 확인

Step2 확인학습A 빈칸 채우기를 통한 문장 완성 능력 확인

Step3 확인학습B 제시된 우리말을 영어로 완성하여 작문 능력 키우기

Step4 실력평가 단원별 수시평가 대비 주관식, 객관식 문제풀이

Step5 서술형 대비 학업성취도 및 수행능력평가 대비 서술형 문제풀이
       교과서 구석구석 교과서에 나오는 기타 문장까지 완벽 학습

Composition

|영역별 핵심문제|

단어 및 어휘, 대화문, 문법, 독해 등 각 영역별 기출문제의 출제 유형을 분석하여 실전에 대비하고 연습할 수 있도록 문제를 배열

|단원별 예상문제|

기출문제를 분석한 후 새로운 시험 출제 경향을 더하여 새롭게 출제될 수 있는 문제를 포함하여 시험에 완벽하게 대비할 수 있도록 준비

|서술형 실전 및 창의사고력 문제|

학교 시험에서 점차 늘어나는 서술형 시험에 집중 대비하고 고득점을 취득하는데 만전을 기하기 위한 학습 코너

|단원별 모의고사|

영역별, 단계별 학습을 모두 마친 후 실전 연습을 위한 모의고사

교과서 파헤치기

- 단어Test1~3 영어 단어 우리말 쓰기, 우리말을 영어 단어로 쓰기, 영영풀이에 해당하는 단어와 우리말 쓰기

- 대화문Test1~2 대화문 빈칸 완성 및 전체 대화문 쓰기

- 본문Test1~5 빈칸 완성, 우리말 쓰기, 문장 배열연습, 영어 작문하기 복습 등 단계별 반복 학습을 통해 교과서 지문에 대한 완벽한 습득

- 구석구석지문Test1~2 지문 빈칸 완성 및 전문 영어로 쓰기

Contents

Lesson

5

Believe in Yourself

🔊 의사소통 기능

- 기대 표현하기
  A: Are you going to travel to Jeju-do next week?
  B: Yes, I'm really looking forward to riding a horse.

- 거절하기
  A: Do you want to join me?
  B: I'd love to, but I can't. I have to do my homework.

🔊 언어 형식

- 가정법과거
  If I **were** a bird, I **would fly**.

- 의문사+to부정사
  We didn't know **how to read** music.

Words & Expressions

Key Words

- **afford** [əfɔ́ːrd] 동 ~할 형편이 되다
- **appear** [əpíər] 동 나타나다
- **award** [əwɔ́ːrd] 명 상
- **battle** [bǽtl] 명 전쟁, 전투
- **bored** [bɔːrd] 형 지루해하는
- **cheek** [tʃiːk] 명 볼, 뺨
- **cheer** [tʃiər] 동 응원하다
- **drone** [droun] 명 무인 항공기
- **educator** [édʒukèitər] 명 교육자
- **environmental** [invàiərənméntl] 형 환경의
- **excited** [iksáitid] 형 신이 난, 흥분한
- **giant** [dʒáiənt] 형 거대한
- **gym** [dʒim] 명 운동, 체육관
- **gym class** 체육 수업
- **journey** [dʒɔ́ːrni] 명 여행
- **landfill** [lǽndfil] 명 쓰레기 매립지
- **mostly** [móustli] 부 대부분, 일반적으로
- **musical instrument** 악기
- **none** [nʌn] 대 아무도 ~ 않다
- **ocean** [óuʃən] 명 바다
- **orchestra** [ɔ́ːrkəstrə] 명 오케스트라, 관현악단
- **parade** [pəréid] 명 퍼레이드, 가두 행진
- **patience** [péiʃəns] 명 인내심
- **performance** [pərfɔ́ːrməns] 명 공연
- **respect** [rispékt] 동 존경하다
- **roll** [roul] 동 구르다, 굴러가다
- **scared** [skɛərd] 형 무서워하는, 겁먹은
- **singing contest** 노래 경연 대회
- **speech** [spiːtʃ] 명 연설
- **stick** [stik] 동 붙이다
- **still** [stil] 부 아직도, 여전히
- **surprised** [sərpráizd] 형 놀란, 놀라는
- **talented** [tǽləntid] 형 재능 있는
- **thrilled** [θrild] 형 황홀해하는, 아주 신이 난
- **title** [táitl] 명 제목
- **trash** [træʃ] 명 쓰레기
- **tune** [tjuːn] 명 곡, 곡조, 선율
- **violinist** [vàiəlínist] 명 바이올린 연주자
- **worried** [wɔ́ːrid] 형 걱정하는

Key Expressions

- **a few+셀 수 있는 명사** 약간의, 몇 개의
- **be able to 동사원형** ~할 수 있다
- **be known as** ~로 알려지다
- **be made into** ~로 만들어지다
- **be made of** ~로 만들어지다
- **can't afford to 동사원형** ~할 형편이 못되다
- **cheer for** 응원하다
- **from then on** 그때부터 계속
- **give a big hand** 큰 박수를 보내다
- **give up** 포기하다
- **help with** ~를 돕다
- **how to 동사원형** ~하는 방법, 어떻게 ~할지
- **look forward to (동)명사** ~를 기대하다, 고대하다
- **one another** 서로
- **out of tune** 음이 맞지 않는
- **put ~ into practice** ~을 실행에 옮기다
- **step by step** 점차로, 차근차근, 하나씩
- **take care of** ~를 돌보다
- **take part in** ~에 참가하다
- **That's why ~.** 그것이 ~한 이유이다.
- **turn A into B** A를 B로 바꾸다

Word Power

※ 서로 비슷한 뜻을 가진 어휘

☐ **award** (상) – **prize** (상)

☐ **mostly** (대부분, 일반적으로) – **mainly** (주로, 대개는)

☐ **take part in** (~에 참가하다) – **participate in** (~에 참가하다)

☐ **journey** (여행) – **travel** (여행)

☐ **take care of** (~를 돌보다) – **look after** (~를 돌보다)

※ 감정을 나타내는 동사의 형용사 쓰임

주어가 감정을 느끼는 주체일 경우에는 감정을 나타내는 형용사로 과거분사 형태를 쓰고, 주어가 감정을 느끼게 하는 경우에는 현재분사(동사원형-ing) 형태를 쓴다.

(1) 주어가 감정을 느끼는 주체인 경우

☐ **thrilled** (아주 신이 난)

☐ **excited** (신이 난, 흥분한)

☐ **surprised** (놀란, 놀라는)

☐ **worried** (걱정하는)

☐ **scared** (무서워하는, 겁먹은)

☐ **bored** (지루해하는)

(2) 주어가 감정을 느끼게 하는 경우

☐ **thrilling** (아주 신나는)

☐ **exciting** (신나는, 흥분하게 하는)

☐ **surprising** (놀라운, 놀랄)

☐ **worrying** (걱정할 만한)

☐ **scaring** (겁주는, 위협적인)

☐ **boring** (재미없는, 지루한)

English Dictionary

☐ **afford** ~할 형편이 되다
→ to be able to pay for something
어떤 것의 비용을 지불할 수 있는

☐ **award** 상
→ a prize or certificate that a person is given for doing something well
어떤 것을 잘해서 누군가에게 주어지는 상이나 증명서

☐ **bored** 지루해하는
→ to feel tired and impatient because you have lost interest in something or because you have nothing to do
어떤 것에 흥미를 잃었거나 할 것이 없어져서 피곤함이나 짜증을 느끼는

☐ **cheek** 볼, 뺨
→ either side of the face below the eyes
얼굴의 눈 아래 양쪽

☐ **landfill** 쓰레기 매립지
→ an area where waste is buried under the ground
쓰레기가 땅 밑에 묻히는 지역

☐ **look forward to (동)명사** ~를 기대하다, 고대하다
→ to want it to happen because you think you will enjoy it
당신이 그것을 즐길 것이라 생각해서 그것이 일어나기를 바라다

☐ **patience** 인내심
→ the ability to stay calm and accept a delay or suffering without complaining
침착하고 불평 없이 지연이나 고통을 받아들이는 능력

☐ **practice** 실행, 실천
→ action rather than ideas
생각보다는 행동

☐ **scared** 무서워하는, 겁먹은
→ frightened of someone or something
어떤 사람이나 어떤 것에 대해 겁을 내는

☐ **step by step** 점차로, 차근차근, 하나씩
→ in a gradual manner
점진적인 방식으로

☐ **talented** 재능 있는
→ able or skillful
능력 있고 기술이 좋은

☐ **thrilled** 황홀해하는, 아주 신이 난
→ very excited and happy
매우 신이 나고 행복한

☐ **tune** 곡, 곡조, 선율
→ a series of musical notes that make a pleasing sound when played together
함께 연주되었을 때 유쾌한 소리를 내는 일련의 음표

01 빈칸에 'ing'나 'ed' 둘 중 하나가 들어갈 때 들어갈 말이 나머지와 다른 하나를 고르시오.

① They were frighten_____ of snakes.
② She was shock_____ to hear the news.
③ His stories are always interest_____.
④ I am thrill_____ to see him in person.
⑤ He was disappoint_____ at the test result.

02 밑줄 친 부분의 단어가 의미상 어색한 것을 고르시오.

① I was surprised that he won the game.
② She is bored not only with music but also with arts.
③ Everybody was scared at the news that they won the gold medal.
④ I'm worried about the English test tomorrow.
⑤ The children were excited about their presents.

03 주어진 문장에서 밑줄 친 still의 뜻으로 사용되지 않은 것을 고르시오.

I still haven't done my English homework.

① Your friend is still waiting for you there.
② They still live in that house.
③ The house was still being built.
④ The rain became still heavier.
⑤ I'm still looking for work.

04 주어진 두 문장이 같은 의미가 되도록 빈칸에 알맞은 말을 고르시오.

Who's going to look after the children while you're away?
= Who's going to _____ the children while you're away?

① look forward to   ② put off
③ look down on   ④ take after
⑤ take care of

05 다음 영영풀이에 해당하는 단어로 알맞은 것은?

very excited and happy

① bored   ② thrilled
③ worried   ④ talented
⑤ scared

06 빈칸 (A)와 (B)에 알맞은 말로 짝지어진 것을 고르시오.

• He soon turned his dreams (A)_____ reality.
• They went to Busan to take part (B)_____ the Busan International Film Festival.

　(A)　(B)　　　　　(A)　(B)
① into – in   ② into – from
③ in – from   ④ in – in
⑤ into – to

01 다음 문장들에서 쓰임이 자연스럽지 <u>않은</u> 것을 찾아 고치시오.

@ Can you show me how to do it?
ⓑ We can't afford to going abroad this summer.
ⓒ I'm really looking forward to work with you.

➡ _____

02 다음 괄호 안의 단어를 문맥에 맞게 고쳐 빈칸에 쓰시오.

(1) The show was very _____. (bore)
(2) The news was _____ to everyone. (shock)
(3) His new book is really _____! (amaze)
(4) Mike was too _____ to do bungee jumping. (scare)

03 다음 빈칸에 공통으로 들어갈 말을 쓰시오.

• The novel, *Beauty and the Beast*, has been made _____ a movie.
• Gwanghwamun Plaza in central Seoul has been turned _____ a skating rink.
• She's determined to put her new ideas _____ practice.

04 다음 우리말에 맞도록 빈칸에 알맞은 말을 쓰시오. (철자가 주어진 경우 주어진 철자로 시작할 것.)

(1) 나는 일을 서두르지 않고 차근차근 하는 중이다.
➡ I am not rushing things and I'm taking it _____ _____ _____.

(2) 그곳은 그 도시에서 가장 위험한 지역으로 알려져 있다.
➡ It's _____ _____ the most dangerous part of the city.

(3) 기타의 음이 맞지 않는다.
➡ The guitar is _____ of t_____.

(4) 그 이후 계속 그는 치아 관리를 잘 하게 됐어요.
➡ F_____ _____ _____, he started to _____ good care of his teeth.

(5) 야생동물 촬영은 많은 인내심을 필요로 한다.
➡ Wildlife photography requires a lot of _____.

(6) 그 여행이 얼마나 걸릴 것인지 추정하기가 어렵다.
➡ It's difficult to judge how long the j_____ will take.

05 빈칸을 주어진 영영풀이에 해당하는 말을 이용하여 채우시오.

to be able to pay for something

➡ I'm not sure how they are able to _____ such expensive holidays.

Conversation

1 기대 표현하기

> **A** Are you going to travel to Jeju-do next week? 다음 주에 제주도 여행을 갈 거니?
>
> **B** Yes, I'm really looking forward to riding a horse. 응. 나는 말 타기를 정말 고대하고 있어.

- 'I'm looking forward to (동)명사 ~.'는 '나는 ~하기를 기대한다.'라는 뜻으로, 기대를 나타낼 때 사용하는 표현이다. to는 전치사로 뒤에 명사 또는 동명사(-ing)를 쓴다. 간절히 고대하는 것은 'I'm really looking forward to (동)명사 ~.'로 표현한다.

- 'I'm looking forward to (동)명사 ~.' 대신 쓸 수 있는 표현으로, 'I can't wait to ~'가 있는데 'can't wait to' 다음에는 동사원형을 써야 한다.

기대 표현하기

- I'm looking forward to (동)명사 ~. (나는 ~하기를 기대한다.)
- I'm excited about (동)명사 ~. (나는 ~하는 것이 신이 나.)
- I can't wait to 동사원형 ~. (나는 ~하는 것이 기다려져.)

핵심 Check

1. 다음 우리말과 일치하도록 빈칸에 알맞은 말을 쓰시오.

    A: Are you going to Joohun's birthday party this Sunday?

    B: Yes, I am. I'm _____ _____ _____ it. (나는 그것을 기대하고 있어.)

2. 다음 대화의 괄호 안에서 알맞은 말을 고르시오.

    A: Are you going to go to the school festival next week?

    B: Yes. I'm really looking forward to (go / going) there.

3. 다음 주어진 문장 이후에 올 대화의 순서를 바르게 배열하시오.

    I'm looking forward to my school festival.

    (A) It's this Friday. Anyone can come and join the festival.

    (B) School festival? When is it?

    (C) Sounds interesting! I'll go there.

    ➡ _____

② 거절하기

A Do you want to join me? 너는 나랑 함께 하고 싶니?

B I'd love to, but I can't. I have to do my homework. 그러고 싶지만, 그럴 수 없어. 숙제해야 해.

- 'I'd love to, but I can't.'는 '그러고 싶지만, 할 수 없어.'라는 뜻으로 상대방의 제안을 거절할 때 사용할 수 있는 표현이다. but 뒤에 거절할 수밖에 없는 이유를 부연하여 상대방의 이해를 구할 수 있다.

- 'I'd love to, but I can't.' 대신에 'I'm sorry, but I can't.', 'I'm afraid I can't.' 등을 사용할 수 있다.

거절하기

- I'd love to, but I can't. (그러고 싶지만, 그럴 수 없어.)
- I'm sorry, but I can't. (미안하지만, 안 되겠어.)
- I'm afraid I can't. (안 될 것 같아.)
- I'll take a rain check. (다음에 할게.)
- I wish I could, but I have to ~. (할 수 있으면 좋겠는데, 하지만 나는 ~해야 해.)
- Your suggestion sounds great, but ~. (너의 제안은 좋아보여, 하지만 ~.)

핵심 Check

4. 다음 우리말과 일치하도록 주어진 단어를 알맞게 배열하여 문장을 만드시오.

A: Do you want to watch a movie after school?

B: 그러고 싶지만, 나는 숙제를 해야 해. (love, do, homework, I'd, to, my, have, but, I, to)

➡ _____

5. 다음 대화의 빈칸에 알맞은 말을 쓰시오.

A: I'm planning to go on a picnic. Do you want to join me?

B: I'd _____ _____, _____ _____ _____. I have to visit my grandparents.

6. 다음 대화의 순서를 바르게 배열하시오.

(A) I'd love to, but I can't. I have to go to the Spanish class on Sunday.

(B) Yes, I like them.

(C) Great! Let's go to the K-pop concert this Sunday.

(D) Tony, are you interested in Korean pop songs?

➡ _____

Listen and Speak 1 A

B: Hey, Bora. Welcome to our rock band.

G: Thanks. ❶I'm looking forward to playing in a concert with you.

B: We're ❷excited ❸to have a new guitar player.

G: Yeah. See you on Friday.

> B: 얘, 보라야. 우리 록 밴드에 온 걸 환영해.
> G: 고마워. 공연에서 너희들과 함께 연주할 게 기대돼.
> B: 우리는 새로운 기타 연주자를 갖게 되어서 신나.
> G: 잘됐다. 금요일에 봐.

❶ 'I'm looking forward to (동)명사 ~.'는 '~을 기대하다, 고대하다'라는 뜻으로, 어떤 일을 즐거운 마음으로 기대하는 상황에서 사용하는 표현이다.

❷ excited: 신난. 감정을 나타내는 동사의 형용사형으로 주어가 감정을 느끼는 주체일 경우에는 과거분사 형태를 쓰고, 주어가 감정의 대상인 경우에는 현재분사(동사원형-ing) 형태를 쓴다.

❸ to부정사의 부사적 용법 중 감정의 원인으로 '~하니까, ~해서'로 해석한다.

Check(√) True or False

(1) Bora is going to play in a concert.　　　　T ☐ F ☐

(2) They have practiced a lot for the concert.　　　　T ☐ F ☐

Listen and Speak 2 A

G: Minho, did you finish the math homework?

B: Not yet. Math is difficult.

G: Yes, but ❶it's interesting, too.

B: Then can you ❷help me with my math homework?

G: ❸I'd love to, but I can't. I ❹have to take care of my brother.

> G: 민호야, 너 수학 숙제 끝냈니?
> B: 아직. 수학은 어려워.
> G: 맞아, 그렇지만 재미있기도 해.
> B: 그럼 내 수학 숙제 좀 도와줄래?
> G: 그러고 싶지만, 안 돼. 내 남동생을 돌봐야 해.

❶ it은 앞에서 언급된 math를 지칭한다. interesting: 흥미로운, 재미있는

❷ help A with B: A가 B하는 것을 돕다

❸ 'I'd love to, but I can't.'는 '그러고 싶지만, 할 수 없어.'라는 뜻으로 상대방의 제안을 거절할 때 사용할 수 있는 표현이다. but 뒤에 거절할 수밖에 없는 이유를 부연하여 상대방의 이해를 구할 수 있다.

❹ have to 동사원형: ~해야 한다 take care of: ~를 돌보다

Check(√) True or False

(3) Minho finished the math homework.　　　　T ☐ F ☐

(4) The girl will help Minho with his homework.　　　　T ☐ F ☐

Listen and Speak 1 B

G: Jiho, what are you reading?

B: I'm reading a book about baseball player ❶named Jim Abbott.

G: Oh, the man ❷who was born without a right hand?

B: That's right. He tried really hard and even ❸won the MVP award.

G: Yeah. His story ❹was made into a movie. ❺I'm going to watch it this Saturday.

B: Really? What's the title?

G: *Our Hero.* ❻I'm really looking forward to watching it.

B: Can I join you?

G: Sure. See you on Saturday.

G: 지호야, 뭘 읽고 있니?

B: Jim Abbott이라는 이름의 야구 선수에 관한 책을 읽고 있어.

G: 오, 오른손이 없이 태어난 그 사람?

B: 맞아. 그는 정말 열심히 노력해서 최우수 선수상까지 받았어.

G: 그래. 그의 이야기가 영화로 만들어졌어. 난 이번 주 토요일에 그 영화를 볼 거야.

B: 정말? 제목이 뭐니?

G: 'Our Hero'야. 그 영화를 볼게 정말 기대돼.

B: 나도 너와 함께해도 될까?

G: 물론이지. 토요일에 봐.

❶ named는 동사 name(이름 짓다)의 과거분사형으로 '이름이 ～인'의 의미를 가지며, 앞의 명사 baseball player를 수식하고 있다.

❷ who는 주격 관계대명사로, 'who was born without a right hand'가 'the man'을 수식하고 있다. who 대신에 that을 사용할 수 있다. without: ～ 없이

❸ tried와 won은 접속사 and로 연결되어 있다.

❹ be made into ～: ～로 만들어지다

❺ 계획을 말할 때는 'be going to+동사원형'으로 말할 수 있다.

❻ 'I'm looking forward to ～.'는 앞으로 일어날 일에 대한 기대를 표현할 때 사용하는 표현으로, '나는 ～하기를 기대한다'의 의미이며 to 뒤에는 명사나 동명사가 온다. 비슷한 표현으로 'I'm excited about (동)명사 ～. (나는 ～하는 것이 신이 나.)', 'I can't wait to 동사원형 ～. (나는 ～하는 것이 기다려져.)' 등이 있다.

Check(√) True or False

(5) The movie, *Our Hero*, is about the man who was born without a left hand.   T ☐ F ☐

(6) They are going to see the movie this Saturday.   T ☐ F ☐

Listen and Speak 2 C

A: ❶What are you going to do this afternoon?

B: I'm going to ride my bike. Do you want to join me?

A: ❷I'd love to, but I can't. I have to ❸do my homework.

B: Okay, then next time.

A: 오늘 오후에 뭐 할 거니?

B: 나는 자전거를 탈 거야. 같이 탈래?

A: 그러고 싶지만, 안 돼. 나는 숙제를 해야 해.

B: 알겠어, 다음에 하자.

❶ 상대방에게 무엇을 할 계획인지(또는 어떤 계획이 있는지) 물어볼 때 'What are you planning[going] to+동사원형～?'을 사용할 수 있다.

❷ 'I'd love to, but I can't.'는 '그러고 싶지만, 할 수 없어.'라는 뜻으로 상대방의 제안을 거절할 때 사용할 수 있는 표현이다. but 뒤에 거절할 수밖에 없는 이유를 부연하여 상대방의 이해를 구할 수 있다.

❸ do one's homework: 숙제를 하다

Check(√) True or False

(7) A is going to ride a bike with B.   T ☐ F ☐

(8) A should do his or her homework this afternoon.   T ☐ F ☐

Listen and Speak 1 C

A: You ❶look happy today. ❷What's going on?

B: I'm so excited. I'm going to travel to Jeju-do.

A: That sounds great!

B: Yes, ❸I'm really looking forward to riding a horse.

❶ look+형용사: ～하게 보이다

❷ 'What's going on?'은 '무슨 일이야?'의 의미로, 여기에서는 상대방에게 행복해 보이는 이유를 물어보고 있다.

❸ 'I'm looking forward to (동)명사 ～.'는 '나는 ～하기를 기대한다.'라는 뜻으로, 기대를 나타낼 때 사용하는 표현이다. to는 전치사로 뒤에 명사 또는 동명사(-ing)를 쓴다. 간절히 고대하는 것은 'I'm really looking forward to (동)명사 ～.'로 표현한다.

Listen and Speak 2 B

G: Alex, ❶I'm going to take part in a singing contest next Monday.

B: That's great, Sumin!

G: You know ❷how to play the guitar, right?

B: Yes, ❸I've played the guitar for 3 years.

G: Great. Can you play the guitar ❹while I sing in the contest?

B: ❺I'd love to, but I can't. I hurt my hand in gym class yesterday.

G: Oh! ❻I'm sorry to hear that.

B: Thanks. But I'll be there to ❼cheer for you.

❶ be going to 동사원형: ～할 예정이다 take part in: ～에 참가하다

❷ '의문사+to부정사'는 주어, 목적어, 보어로 쓰인다. 여기서 'how to 동사원형(～하는 방법)'은 know의 목적어로 사용되었다.

❸ 'have p.p.'는 과거의 특정 시점에서 시작된 일이 현재까지 계속되고 있음을 나타내는 현재완료의 형태로, 여기서는 계속적 용법으로 사용되고 있다.

❹ while: ～하는 동안

❺ 'I'd love to, but I can't.', 'I'm sorry, but I can't.', 'I'm afraid I can't.' 등의 표현들은 상대방의 제안을 거절할 때 사용할 수 있다.

❻ 어떤 상황에 대하여 유감이나 동정을 표현할 때 'I'm sorry to hear that.'이라고 말할 수 있다

❼ cheer for: ～을 응원하다

Real Life Talk Watch a Video

Linda: Hi, Tony! ❶What are you going to do this weekend?

Tony: I'm going to watch the musical, *Billy Elliot*.

Linda: *Billy Elliot*? What is it about?

Tony: It's about a boy ❷who became a famous dancer. ❸I'm looking forward to watching it.

Linda: ❹Sounds interesting. Who is the main actor?

Tony: Jason Kim. He's a great dancer.

Linda: He's my favorite actor. I watched his musical last year.

Tony: Oh, really? Do you ❺want to join me?

Linda: ❻I'd love to, but I can't. I have volunteer work this weekend.

Tony: Okay. Maybe next time!

❶ 상대방에게 무엇을 할 계획인지(또는 어떤 계획이 있는지) 물어볼 때 'What are you planning[going] to+동사원형 ～?'을 사용할 수 있다.

❷ 선행사 'a boy'를 관계대명사절인 'who became a famous dancer'가 수식하고 있다.

❸ 'I'm looking forward to ～.'는 앞으로 일어날 일에 대한 기대를 표현할 때 사용하는 표현으로, '나는 ～하기를 기대한다.'의 의미이며 to 다음에는 명사나 동명사가 온다.

❹ sound+형용사: ～하게 들리다

❺ want는 to부정사를 목적어로 취하는 동사이다.

❻ 'I'd love to, but I can't.'는 '그러고 싶지만, 할 수 없어.'라는 뜻으로 상대방의 제안을 거절할 때 사용할 수 있는 표현이다. but 뒤에 거절할 수밖에 없는 이유를 부연하여 상대방의 이해를 구할 수 있다.

Real Life Talk Step 2

A: What are you going to do first?

B: I'm going to watch a parade at 10:30. ❷I'm really looking forward to watching it.

A: Sounds fun.

B: Do you want to join me?

A: ❷Yes, I'd love to. / I'd love to, but I can't. I'm going to get my face painted at that time.

❶ 'I'm looking forward to (동)명사 ～.'는 '나는 ～하기를 기대한다.'라는 뜻으로, 기대를 나타낼 때 사용하는 표현이다. to는 전치사로 뒤에 명사 또는 동명사(-ing)를 쓴다. 간절히 고대하는 것은 'I'm really looking forward to (동)명사 ～.'로 표현한다.

❷ 상대방의 제안에 응할 때는 'Yes, I'd love to.', 그렇지 않을 때는 'I'd love to, but I can't.'를 사용해서 대답할 수 있다. 거절할 때는 뒤에 거절할 수밖에 없는 이유를 부연하여 상대방의 이해를 구할 수 있다.

● 다음 우리말과 일치하도록 빈칸에 알맞은 말을 쓰시오.

Listen and Speak 1 A

B: Hey, Bora. Welcome _____ our rock band.

G: Thanks. I'm _____ _____ to playing in a concert with you.

B: We're _____ _____ have a new guitar player.

G: Yeah. _____ _____ _____ Friday.

B: 얘, 보라야. 우리 록 밴드에 온 걸 환영해.
G: 고마워. 공연에서 너희들과 함께 연주할 게 기대돼.
B: 우리는 새로운 기타 연주자를 갖게 되어서 신나.
G: 잘됐다. 금요일에 봐.

Listen and Speak 1 B

G: Jiho, _____ _____ you reading?

B: I'm _____ a book _____ baseball player _____ Jim Abbott.

G: Oh, the man _____ _____ _____ _____ a right hand?

B: That's right. He tried really hard and _____ _____ the MVP award.

G: Yeah. His story _____ _____ _____ a movie. I'm _____ _____ watch it this Saturday.

B: Really? What's the title?

G: *Our Hero.* _____ _____ _____ _____ _____ _____ watching it.

B: Can I join you?

G: Sure. See you _____ Saturday.

G: 지호야, 뭘 읽고 있니?
B: Jim Abbott이라는 이름의 야구 선수에 관한 책을 읽고 있어.
G: 오, 오른손이 없이 태어난 사람?
B: 맞아. 그는 정말 열심히 노력해서 최우수 선수상까지 받았어.
G: 그래. 그의 이야기가 영화로 만들어졌어. 난 이번 주 토요일에 그 영화를 볼 거야.
B: 정말? 제목이 뭐니?
G: 'Our Hero'야. 그 영화를 볼 게 정말 기대돼.
B: 나도 너와 함께해도 될까?
G: 물론이지. 토요일에 봐.

Listen and Speak 1 C

1. A: You look happy today. _____ going on?

   B: I'm so _____. _____ _____ _____ _____ _____ to Jeju-do.

   A: That sounds great!

   B: Yes. I'm _____ _____ _____ _____ riding a horse.

2. A: You _____ _____ today. What's going on?

   B: I'm so excited. I'm going to _____ _____ _____ a drone.

   A: That sounds great!

   B: Yes. _____ _____ _____ forward _____ _____ a drone in the park.

3. A: You look happy today. What's _____ _____?

   B: I'm _____. _____ _____ to see Jackson's concert.

   A: That sounds great!

   B: Yes. I'm really _____ _____ _____ _____ Jackson's performance.

1. A: 너 오늘 행복해 보인다. 무슨 일이야?
   B: 나는 아주 신나. 제주도로 여행을 갈 거야.
   A: 좋겠다!
   B: 응, 나는 말 타기를 정말 고대하고 있어.

2. A: 너 오늘 행복해 보인다. 무슨 일이야?
   B: 나는 아주 신나. 드론을 날리는 것을 배울 거야.
   A: 좋겠다!
   B: 응. 공원에서 드론을 날리는 것이 정말 기대돼.

3. A: 너 오늘 행복해 보인다. 무슨 일이야?
   B: 나는 아주 신나. Jackson의 콘서트를 볼 거야.
   A: 좋겠다!
   B: 응. Jackson의 공연을 보는 것이 정말 기대돼.

Listen and Speak 2 A

G: Minho, did you _____ the math homework?

B: Not yet. Math is _____.

G: Yes, but it's _____, _____.

B: Then can you _____ _____ _____ my math homework?

G: _____ _____ _____, but I can't. I _____ _____ _____ _____ _____ my brother.

G: 민호야, 너 수학 숙제 끝냈니?
B: 아직. 수학은 어려워.
G: 맞아, 그렇지만 재미있기도 해.
B: 그럼 내 수학 숙제 좀 도와줄래?
G: 그러고 싶지만, 안 돼. 내 남동생을 돌봐야 해.

Listen and Speak 2 B

G: Alex, I'm going to _____ _____ _____ a singing contest next Monday.

B: That's great, Sumin!

G: You know _____ _____ _____ the guitar, right?

B: Yes, _____ _____ the guitar for 3 years.

G: Great. _____ _____ _____ the guitar while I sing in the contest?

B: I'd love to, _____ _____ _____. I hurt my hand in gym class yesterday.

G: Oh! I'm _____ _____ _____ that.

B: Thanks. But I'll be there to _____ _____ you.

G: Alex, 나 다음 월요일에 노래 대회에 참가할 거야.
B: 대단하다, 수민아!
G: 너 기타 칠 줄 알지, 그렇지?
B: 응, 3년 동안 기타를 쳤어.
G: 잘됐다. 내가 대회에서 노래하는 동안 기타를 쳐 줄 수 있니?
B: 그러고 싶지만, 안 돼. 어제 체육 수업 중에 손을 다쳤어.
G: 오! 유감이다.
B: 고마워. 하지만 너를 응원하러 거기에 갈게.

Listen and Speak 2 C

1. A: What are you _____ _____ _____ this afternoon?

   B: I'm going to ride my bike. Do you _____ _____ join me?

   A: I'd love to, _____ _____ _____. I _____ _____ do my homework.

   B: Okay, then _____ _____.

2. A: What _____ _____ _____ _____ do this afternoon?

   B: I'm going to play soccer. Do you want to _____ _____?

   A: _____ _____ _____, but I can't. I have _____ _____ my grandparents.

   B: Okay, then _____ _____.

1. A: 오후에 뭐 할 거니?
   B: 나는 자전거를 탈 거야. 같이 할래?
   A: 그러고 싶지만, 안 돼. 나는 숙제를 해야 해.
   B: 알겠어, 다음에 하자.

2. A: 오후에 뭐 할 거니?
   B: 나는 축구를 할 거야. 같이 할래?
   A: 그러고 싶지만, 안 돼. 나는 조부모님 댁을 방문해야 해.
   B: 알겠어, 다음에 하자.

Real Life Talk Watch a Video

Linda: Hi, Tony! _____ _____ _____ _____ to do this weekend?

Tony: I'm going to _____ the musical, *Billy Elliot*.

Linda: *Billy Elliot*? What is _____ _____?

Tony: It's _____ _____ _____ _____ _____ a famous dancer. I'm _____ _____ _____ _____ it.

Linda: Sounds _____. Who is the main actor?

Tony: Jason Kim. He's a great dancer.

Linda: He's my favorite actor. I _____ his musical last year.

Tony: Oh, really? Do you _____ _____ _____ me?

Linda: I'd love to, _____ _____ _____. I have _____ work this weekend.

Tony: Okay. Maybe _____ time!

해석

Linda: 안녕, Tony! 이번 주말에 뭐 할 거니?

Tony: 나는 뮤지컬 'Billy Elliot'를 볼 거야.

Linda: 'Billy Elliot'? 무슨 내용이니?

Tony: 유명한 무용수가 된 한 소년에 관한 내용이야. 그 뮤지컬을 볼 게 기대돼.

Linda: 재미있겠다. 주연 배우가 누구니?

Tony: Jason Kim이야. 그는 훌륭한 무용수야.

Linda: 그는 내가 가장 좋아하는 배우야. 작년에 그의 뮤지컬을 봤어.

Tony: 오, 정말? 나와 함께 가고 싶니?

Linda: 그러고 싶지만, 안 돼. 이번 주말에 자원봉사 활동이 있어.

Tony: 알겠어. 다음에 같이 가자!

Real Life Talk Step 2

1. **A:** What are you going to do first?

   B: _____ _____ _____ _____ a parade at 10:30. I'm really looking forward _____ _____ it.

   A: Sounds _____.

   B: Do you want to join me?

   A: Yes, I'd _____ _____. / I'd love to, _____ _____ _____. I'm going to get _____ _____ _____ at that time.

2. **A:** What are you _____ _____ _____ _____?

   B: I'm going to play a water balloon game _____ 12:30. _____ _____ _____ forward to _____ _____.

   A: _____ fun.

   B: Do you want to join me?

   A: Yes, I'd love to. / _____ _____ _____, _____ I can't. I'm going to have the longest hot dog at that time.

1. **A:** 처음에 무엇을 할 거니?
   B: 10시 30분에 퍼레이드를 볼 거야. 퍼레이드 보는 것이 정말 기대돼.
   A: 재미있겠다.
   B: 너도 같이 할래?
   A: 응, 그래. / 그러고 싶지만, 안 돼. 나는 그 때 얼굴에 페이스 페인팅을 할 거야.

2. **A:** 다음에 무엇을 할 거니?
   B: 물풍선 게임을 12시 30분에 할 거야. 나는 그것을 하는 것이 정말 기대돼.
   A: 재미있겠다.
   B: 너도 같이 할래?
   A: 응, 그래. / 그러고 싶지만, 안 돼. 나는 그 때 가장 긴 핫도그를 먹을 거야.

[01~02] 다음 대화의 빈칸에 알맞은 것을 고르시오.

01

> G: Minho, did you finish the math homework?
>
> B: Not yet. Math is difficult.
>
> G: Yes, but it's interesting, too.
>
> B: Then can you help me with my math homework?
>
> G: _____ I have to take care of my brother.

① I'd love to, but I can't.　　② Sure, I can.

③ I don't know what you meant.　　④ Yes, I'd love to.

⑤ No, I am not.

02

> A: You look happy today. What's going on?
>
> B: I'm so excited. I'm going to learn to fly a drone.
>
> A: That sounds great!
>
> B: Yes, _____.

① I'm not interested in flying a drone in the park

② I'm really looking forward to flying a drone in the park

③ I don't want to fly a drone in the park

④ I didn't wait to fly a drone in the park

⑤ I'm not good at flying a drone in the park

03 다음 대화의 밑줄 친 부분과 바꿔 쓸 수 <u>없는</u> 것은? (2개)

> B: Hey, Bora. Welcome to our rock band.
>
> G: Thanks. I'm looking forward to playing in a concert with you.
>
> B: We're excited to have a new guitar player.
>
> G: Yeah. See you on Friday.

① I can't wait to play in a concert with you.

② I'm not interested in playing in a concert with you.

③ I really want to play in a concert with you.

④ I want to be good at playing in a concert with you.

⑤ I'm excited about playing in a concert with you.

[01~03] 다음 대화를 읽고 물음에 답하시오.

G: Jiho, what are you reading?
B: I'm reading a book about baseball player named Jim Abbott. (①)
G: Oh, the man who was born without a right hand?
B: That's right. (②) He tried really hard and even won the MVP award. (③)
G: Yeah. (④) I'm going to watch it this Saturday.
B: Really? What's the title?
G: *Our Hero.* (⑤) _____ (A)
B: Can I join you?
G: Sure. See you on Saturday.

01 위 대화의 ①~⑤ 중 주어진 문장이 들어갈 알맞은 곳은?

His story was made into a movie.

①   ②   ③   ④   ⑤

02 빈칸 (A)에 알맞은 말을 모두 고르시오.

① I'm really looking forward to watch it.
② I really want to watching it.
③ I can't wait to watching it.
④ I'm really looking forward to watching it.
⑤ I can't wait to watch it.

03 위 대화의 내용과 일치하는 것을 모두 고르시오.

① 지호와 소녀는 토요일에 만나서 영화를 같이 볼 것이다.
② 소녀는 Jim Abbott과 관련된 영화의 제목을 모르고 있다.
③ Jim Abbott은 오른손이 없는 야구 선수이다.
④ 지호는 토요일에 Jim Abbott에 관한 책을 읽을 것이다.
⑤ 소녀는 Jim Abbott이 누구인지 몰랐다.

[04~06] 다음 대화를 읽고 물음에 답하시오.

G: Minho, did you finish the math homework?
B: Not yet. Math is difficult.
G: Yes, _____ⓐ_____ it's interesting, too.
B: Then can you help me _____(A)_____ my math homework?
G: I'd love to, _____ⓑ_____ I can't. I have to take care of my brother.

04 빈칸 (A)에 알맞은 말을 고르시오.

① in   ② on   ③ with
④ off   ⑤ to

05 빈칸 ⓐ와 ⓑ에 공통으로 들어갈 말을 고르시오.

① and   ② so   ③ but
④ nor   ⑤ for

06 위 대화의 내용과 일치하는 것을 고르시오.

① Minho has a brother.
② The girl can't help Minho to do his homework.
③ Minho thinks that math is easy.
④ The girl thinks that math is not interesting but difficult.
⑤ Minho has finished his math homework.

07 다음 중 짝지어진 대화가 어색한 것은?

① A: I'm excited that we're going to high school next March.

　 B: Yeah. I can't wait to start high school.

② A: What are you looking forward to doing in high school?

　 B: I'm looking forward to making a lot of new friends.

③ A: I want to go skiing this winter. How about you?

　 B: I'm looking forward to taking a trip.

④ A: Could I ask you to give me a ride?

　 B: I'd love to, but I'm very busy now.

⑤ A: I'm going to visit Insa-dong this Sunday. Will you join me?

　 B: Sure. I'd love to, but I can't.

[08~10] 다음 대화를 읽고 물음에 답하시오.

> Linda: Hi, Tony! What are you going to do this weekend?
>
> Tony: I'm going to watch the musical, *Billy Elliot.*
>
> Linda: *Billy Elliot?* What is it about?
>
> Tony: It's about a boy who became a famous dancer. (a)I'm looking forward to watch it.
>
> Linda: Sounds interesting. Who is the main actor?
>
> Tony: Jason Kim. He's a great dancer.
>
> Linda: He's my favorite actor. I watched his musical last year.
>
> Tony: Oh, really? Do you want to join me?
>
> Linda: ＿＿＿＿＿(A)＿＿＿＿＿ I have volunteer work this weekend.
>
> Tony: Okay. Maybe next time!

08 〈보기〉에서 위 대화의 빈칸 (A)에 알맞은 말이 모두 몇 개인지 고르시오.

┌─── 보기 ───┐
ⓐ I'm afraid I can't.
ⓑ I wish I could, but
ⓒ Your suggestion sounds great. I would
ⓓ Of course.
ⓔ I'm sorry, but I can't.
ⓕ I'd love to, but I can't.
ⓖ Yes, I do.
└───────────┘

① 2개　② 3개　③ 4개　④ 5개　⑤ 6개

09 위 대화를 읽고 답할 수 없는 질문을 고르시오.

① What is the musical, *Billy Elliot*, about?

② How long has Linda had volunteer work?

③ When did Linda watch the musical in which Jason Kim acted?

④ What is Tony going to do this weekend?

⑤ Who is the main actor in *Billy Elliot*?

서답형

10 밑줄 친 (a)에서 어법상 어색한 것을 바르게 고치시오.

＿＿＿＿＿＿＿　➡　＿＿＿＿＿＿＿

01 주어진 단어를 알맞게 고쳐 빈칸에 써 넣으시오.

> G: Jiho, what are you reading?
> B: I'm reading a book about baseball player __(A)__ (name) Jim Abbott.
> G: Oh, the man who was born without a right hand?
> B: That's right. He tried really hard and even won the MVP award.
> G: Yeah. His story was made into a movie. I'm going to watch it this Saturday.
> B: Really? What's the title?
> G: *Our Hero*. I'm really looking forward __(B)__ (watch) it.
> B: Can I join you?
> G: Sure. See you on Saturday.

(A) _____
(B) _____ (2 단어)

[02~03] 다음 대화를 읽고 물음에 답하시오.

> G: Minho, did you finish the math homework?
> B: Not yet. Math is difficult.
> G: Yes, but it's interesting, too.
> B: Then can you help me with my math homework?
> G: I'd love to, __(A)__ . I have to take care __(B)__ my brother.

02 대화의 흐름상 빈칸 (A)에 들어갈 알맞은 말을 주어진 단어를 이용하여 쓰시오. (3 words)

(can)

➡ _____

03 빈칸 (B)에 알맞은 전치사를 쓰시오.

➡ _____

[04~05] 다음 대화를 읽고 물음에 답하시오.

> Linda: Hi, Tony! (A)What are you going to do this weekend?
> Tony: I'm going to watch the musical, *Billy Elliot*.
> Linda: *Billy Elliot*? What is it about?
> Tony: (B)It's about a boy who became a famous dancer. (a)그 뮤지컬을 볼 게 기대돼.
> Linda: Sounds interesting. Who is the main actor?
> Tony: Jason Kim. He's a great dancer.
> Linda: He's my favorite actor. (C)I watched his musical last year.
> Tony: Oh, really? (D)Do you want to join me?
> Linda: (E)Of course. I have volunteer work this weekend.
> Tony: Okay. Maybe next time!

04 밑줄 친 (A)~(E) 중 흐름상 어색한 것을 고르고 바르게 고치시오.

➡ _____

05 밑줄 친 (a)의 우리말을 주어진 단어를 이용하여 영작하시오.

look, watch, it

➡ _____

Grammar

① 가정법과거

> • **If** I **were** a bird, I **would fly.** 내가 새라면, 날아갈 텐데.

■ '만약 ~라면 …할 텐데'라는 뜻으로, 현재 사실을 반대로 가정하거나 실현 가능성이 없는 일에 대해서 가정할 때 쓰며, 'If+주어+were/동사의 과거형 ~, 주어+조동사의 과거형(would/should/could/might)+동사원형 …'의 형태로 나타낸다. 가정법이 사용된 문장이라는 표시로 if절에 과거 동사를 사용할 뿐이며, 의미상 과거를 나타내지 않는다.

■ 가정법과거 문장은 현재시제의 직설법으로 바꿔 쓸 수 있다.

  • If she **knew** how, she **would apply** to the university. 그녀가 방법을 알면 대학에 지원할 텐데.
  (가정법과거, 현재 사실의 반대 가정)

  = As she doesn't know how, she won't apply to the university.
  그녀는 방법을 모르기 때문에, 대학에 지원하지 않을 것이다.

   cf. If she knows how, she will apply to the university. 그녀가 방법을 안다면, 대학에 지원할 것이다.
   (조건문, 사실)

■ 'be'동사는 주어의 인칭 및 수와 무관하게 'were'를 쓰지만, 구어체에서는 주어가 'I' 또는 3인칭 단수인 경우 'was'를 쓰기도 한다.

  • If I **were**[**was**] rich enough, I **would buy** it. 내가 돈이 넉넉하면 그것을 살 텐데.

■ 가정법의 다양한 표현

  • As she is poor, she cannot buy that house. 그녀는 가난하기 때문에, 그 집을 살 수 없다. (직설법)

   = If she were not poor, she could buy that house. 그녀가 가난하지 않다면, 그 집을 살 수 있을 텐데. (가정법)

   = Were she not poor, she could buy that house. (가정법)

  • If it were not for the sun, we could not live at all. 만일 태양이 없다면, 우리는 전혀 살 수 없을 텐데.

   = Were it not for the sun, we could not live at all. (If 생략 후 도치)

   = Without the sun, we could not live at all. (without = if it were not for)

※ if절의 동사가 'were' 또는 'had'일 때 if를 생략하여 쓸 수 있으며, 이때 주어와 동사가 도치된다.

핵심 Check

1. 다음 우리말에 맞게 괄호 안의 단어를 바르게 배열하시오.

내가 너라면, 좀 더 오래 기다릴 텐데. (you, I, I, if, wait, would, were, longer, a little)

➡ _____

② 의문사+to부정사

- We didn't know **how to read** music. 우리는 악보를 읽는 방법을 알지 못했다.
- Don't tell me **what to do**! 나한테 이래라저래라 하지 말아요!

■ '의문사+to부정사'는 'what/when/where/how/which/who(m)+to부정사'의 형태로 쓰이며, 문장 속에서 주어, 목적어, 보어 역할을 하는 명사구로 사용되며, '~할지'라는 뜻을 나타낸다. 주로 동사의 목적어로 사용된다. 'why+to부정사'는 쓰이지 않는다.

- **How to save** money is very important. (주어) 돈을 저축하는 방법은 매우 중요하다.
- I don't know **how to save** money. (know의 목적어) 나는 돈을 저축하는 방법을 모르겠어.

의문사	to부정사	의미
what	to do	무엇을 해야 할지
when	to begin	언제 시작해야 할지
where	to go	어디로 가야 할지
how	to make	어떻게 만드는지(만드는 방법)
which	to select	어떤 것을 선택해야 할지
who(m)	to call	누구에게 전화를 해야 할지

■ 의문사가 의문형용사로 쓰여 '의문형용사+명사+to부정사'나 '의문부사+형용사+to부정사' 형태로도 사용된다.

- I hesitated over **which one to choose**. 난 어떤 것을 고를지 몰라 우물쭈물했다.
- I didn't know **how much to bring**. 나는 얼마나 많이 가져와야 할지 몰랐다.

■ '의문사+to부정사'는 '의문사+주어+should[can]+동사원형'으로 바꿔 쓸 수 있다.

- I can't decide **what to wear**. 무엇을 입을 것인지 결정할 수가 없어.
  = I can't decide **what I should wear**.
- She knows **how to persuade** her dad. 그녀는 자기 아빠를 설득시키는 법을 안다.
  = She knows **how she can persuade** her dad.

핵심 Check

2. 다음 우리말에 맞게 빈칸에 알맞은 말을 쓰시오.

(1) 이 팩스 사용할 줄 아세요?

➡ Do you know _____ _____ _____ this fax machine?

(2) 어디에 제 차를 주차해야 할지 제게 말해주시겠어요?

➡ Can you tell me _____ _____ _____ my car?

01 다음 가정법 문장에서 어법상 <u>어색한</u> 단어를 한 개씩 찾아 고치시오.

(1) If I have a lot of money, I would travel around the world.

＿＿＿＿＿＿＿＿＿＿ ➡ ＿＿＿＿＿＿＿＿＿＿

(2) If I were a teacher, I will not make my students do much homework.

＿＿＿＿＿＿＿＿＿＿ ➡ ＿＿＿＿＿＿＿＿＿＿

(3) If I know your address, I would send you a letter.

＿＿＿＿＿＿＿＿＿＿ ➡ ＿＿＿＿＿＿＿＿＿＿

(4) I will start looking for another job if I were you.

＿＿＿＿＿＿＿＿＿＿ ➡ ＿＿＿＿＿＿＿＿＿＿

02 다음 중 어법상 바르지 <u>않은</u> 것은?

① We didn't know how to make a kite.
② You will be instructed where to go as soon as the plane is ready.
③ I can't find why to stay here.
④ The problem lies in deciding when to start.
⑤ Nobody knew what to say.

03 다음 빈칸에 들어갈 말로 알맞은 것은?

> If I ＿＿＿＿＿ a famous movie star, I would hold many fan meetings.

① had   ② am   ③ have been
④ were   ⑤ be

04 다음 문장을 should를 이용하여 다시 쓰시오.

> I did not know whom to thank for the gift.

➡ ＿＿＿＿＿＿＿＿＿＿＿＿＿＿＿＿＿＿＿＿＿＿＿

01 다음 중 어법상 어색한 문장은?

① If I had wings, I could get out of this maze.
② If it were not for the expense, I would go.
③ If it were raining, I would put on the rain coat.
④ What will you do if another war occurred?
⑤ If the weather were nice, we would go outside.

02 다음 빈칸에 알맞은 것은?

> I don't know _____ to cook the eggs.

① how ② what ③ that
④ why ⑤ whom

03 다음 문장의 밑줄 친 단어들 중 어법상 어색한 단어는?

> ①If I ②have a time machine, I ③would ④go back to ⑤ancient Korea.

① ② ③ ④ ⑤

04 다음 중 어법상 바르지 않은 것은?

① Do you know how to make spaghetti?
② Let me know whom to ask about the problem.
③ Have you decided where to go?
④ I will contact you later to advise you when to come.
⑤ I don't know what to do it next.

05 다음 중 같은 뜻을 가진 문장끼리 짝지어진 것은?

① It is snowy, so she wants to make a snowman.
   = If it is snowy, she would want to make a snowman.
② Jim didn't have a car, so he couldn't drive.
   = If Jim had a car, he couldn't drive.
③ I don't have a computer, so I can't get better grades.
   = If I had a computer, I'd get better grades.
④ Mina doesn't have a smartphone, so she wants to have one.
   = Mina wants a smartphone if she had a smartphone.
⑤ I can't send an e-mail to her, so I don't know her address.
   = I could send an e-mail to her if I knew her address.

06 주어진 문장의 밑줄 친 부분과 용법이 다른 것은?

> Miranda doesn't know how to use the copy machine.

① People are pleased to use the copy machine.
② He told me when to use the copy machine.
③ We started to use the copy machine last month.
④ Can you teach me how to use the copy machine?
⑤ We plan to use the copy machine at our office.

[07~08] 다음 우리말을 바르게 영작한 것을 고르시오.

07 내가 타임머신이 있다면, 세종대왕을 만나러 갈 수 있을 텐데.

① If I have a time machine, I can go to meet King Sejong.
② If I have a time machine, I could go to meet King Sejong.
③ If I had a time machine, I could go to meet King Sejong.
④ If I had a time machine, I can go to meet King Sejong.
⑤ If I had had a time machine, I could have gone to meet King Sejong.

08 Alex는 그 책을 어디에서 사야 할지 알아냈다.

① Alex found out when to buy the book.
② Alex found out where to buy the book.
③ Alex found out to buy the book where.
④ Alex found out the book to buy where.
⑤ Alex found out to buy where the book.

서답형

09 다음 괄호 안에서 어법상 바른 것을 고르시오.

(1) If you (are / were) a doctor, what would you do?
(2) If I (have / had) a magic lamp, I would make three wishes.
(3) He knows (what / how) to ride a bicycle.
(4) I didn't know when (to go / going) to the station.

중요

10 다음 문장의 빈칸 (A)~(C)에 들어갈 말로 가장 적절한 것은?

- If there ____(A)____ more workers, the company could take better care of them.
- Were it not for water and air, what ____(B)____ become of us?
- If I ____(C)____ a lot of money, I would travel around the world.

	(A)	(B)	(C)
①	was	will	have
②	was	could	have
③	will be	could	had had
④	were	would	had
⑤	were	will	had

서답형

11 두 문장의 의미가 같도록 빈칸에 알맞은 말을 쓰시오.

(1) I sometimes teach them how to write Hangul.
  = I sometimes teach them _____ _____ _____ _____ Hangul.
(2) I don't know when to bring the birthday cake in.
  = I don't know _____ _____ the birthday cake in.
(3) Please tell me what to do.
  = Please tell me _____ _____ _____.

12 다음 문장과 같은 의미의 문장을 고르시오.

> If there were no air, we couldn't live.

① We can live so there is air.
② There is no air, so we can't live.
③ Though there is air, we can live.
④ As there is no air, we can't live.
⑤ As there is air, we can live.

13 다음 빈칸에 적절한 것을 <u>모두</u> 고르시오.

> They talked about _____ to meet again and said goodbye.

① what   ② where   ③ which
④ when   ⑤ why

14 다음 중 어법상 올바른 문장의 개수는?

> ⓐ If I have a million dollars, I would buy a driverless car.
> ⓑ If he were a policeman, he will help people.
> ⓒ I want to learn how to fly a drone.
> ⓓ Have you decided where going for your vacation?
> ⓔ David wanted to know where to send those goods.
> ⓕ My family is exciting about the trip to America.
> ⓖ The child was so scare at the big dog.

① 1개   ② 2개   ③ 3개   ④ 4개   ⑤ 5개

15 다음 우리말을 영작할 때, 바르지 <u>않은</u> 문장을 고르시오.

> 만일 컴퓨터가 없다면 우리 생활은 매우 불편할 텐데.

① But for no computers, our lives would be very inconvenient.
② If it were not for computers, our lives would be very inconvenient.
③ If there are no computers, our lives would be very inconvenient.
④ Were it not for computers, our lives would be very inconvenient.
⑤ Without computers, our lives would be very inconvenient.

서답형

16 다음 문장에서 <u>틀린</u> 것을 고쳐 다시 쓰시오.

(1) If it snows all night, I would not leave tomorrow morning.

➡ _____

_____

(2) My mom taught me to bake cookies how.

➡ _____

서답형

17 다음 문장에서 어법상 어색한 부분을 찾아서 한 단어만 고치시오.

(1) If I had the choice, I will stop working tomorrow.

_____ ➡ _____

(2) The man showed the girl what to play chess.

_____ ➡ _____

[01~02] 다음 우리말과 일치하도록 괄호 안에 주어진 단어들을 바르게 배열하시오.

01
> 그가 내 주소를 안다면, 내게 편지를 보낼 텐데.
> (he, he, me, a letter, my address, knew, send, would, if)

➡ _____

02
> 나는 언제 개에게 먹이를 줄지 그에게 말했다.
> (I, him, the dog, feed, told, when, to)

➡ _____

03 다음 문장과 같은 뜻이 되도록 괄호 안에 주어진 어휘를 활용하여 빈칸을 채우시오.

> Without injustice, men would not know justice.

(1) _____ _____ _____ _____
injustice, men would not know justice.
(it, be)

(2) _____ _____ _____ _____ injustice,
men would not know justice. (it, be)

(3) _____ _____ _____ _____ injustice,
men would not know justice. (there, no)

(4) _____ _____ injustice, men would
not know justice. (but)

(5) _____ _____ _____ injustice, men
will know justice.
(as, 직설법으로 쓸 것.)

04 다음 그림을 보고, 주어진 어휘를 이용하여 대화의 빈칸을 알맞게 채우시오.

> **A:** Did you decide _____ ?
>   (which, buy, 4 단어)
> **B:** Yeah. I'll buy the purple one.

➡ _____

05 다음 그림을 보고, 괄호 안에 주어진 단어를 빈칸에 알맞게 채우시오.

> If Linda _____ (sing) well, I would listen
> to her singing attentively.

➡ _____

06 우리말에 맞게 빈칸에 알맞은 말을 쓰시오.

> 그녀는 어디로 가야 할지를 몰랐다.
> ➡ She didn't know _____ _____
>   _____ .

07 다음 주어진 문장과 뜻이 같도록 빈칸을 알맞게 채우시오.

I don't speak 4 languages, so I can't be a good interpreter.

→ If I _____ 4 languages, I _____ _____ a good interpreter.

08 다음 우리말을 괄호 안에 주어진 단어들을 활용하여 영작하시오.

(1) 만약 내가 슈퍼맨이라면, 나는 위험에 처한 사람들을 구할 텐데.
(Superman, save, people in danger)
➡ _____

(2) 그가 감기에 걸리지 않았다면, 나와 함께 쇼핑을 갈 수 있을 텐데. (have a cold)
➡ _____

(3) 아무도 악기를 연주할 줄 몰랐다.
(no one, musical instruments)
➡ _____

(4) 어느 기차를 타야 할지 말해 줄 수 있니?
(can, which, take)
➡ _____

09 다음 글에서 어법상 잘못 쓰인 것을 찾아 알맞게 고치시오. (3곳)

It was amazed that you received a Nobel Peace Prize at the age of 17. If I am the president of your country, I will let girls go to school.

_____ ➡ _____
_____ ➡ _____
_____ ➡ _____

10 다음 직설법 문장을 가정법 문장으로 고쳐 쓰시오.

(1) As I am not a bird, I don't fly.
➡ _____

(2) It doesn't rain, so I won't put on the boots.
➡ _____

(3) Since she doesn't have enough eggs, she can't bake bread for her family.
➡ _____

(4) Because I don't have a magic carpet, I won't travel all around the world.
➡ _____

11 다음 문장을 바꿔 쓸 때, 빈칸에 알맞은 말을 쓰시오.

(1) Let me know where to put the eggs.
➡ Let me know _____.
(2) I don't know how to use this camera.
➡ I don't know _____.
(3) They have to decide when to take action.
➡ They have to decide _____.

12 다음 문장에서 어법상 어색한 부분을 찾아 고치시오.

(1) If he has enough time, he would visit us.
_____ ➡ _____

(2) He asked me when taking out the eggs.
_____ ➡ _____

From Trash to Music

Tears of joy are rolling down my cheeks. I'm so happy and thrilled.
_{주어가 감정을 느끼는 주체일 경우 과거분사 사용}
If I were a bird, I would fly. I look around. The other members in
_{가정법과거: 현재 사실에 반대되는 내용을 가정, '만약 ~라면, …할 텐데'}
my orchestra are hugging one another. Our concert has just finished
_{주어가 The other members이므로 동사는 are} _{현재완료 완료 용법}
and everyone is standing and giving us a big hand. None of us ever
_{everyone은 3인칭 단수로 취급하므로 is를 사용} _{우리에게 큰 박수를 보내다} _{부정의 의미로 '아무도 ~ 않다'}
expected that this day would come. It has been a long journey.
_{우리의 콘서트가 끝나고 모든 사람이 큰 박수를 보내는 날}
My name is Andrea and I'm a violinist in the Recycled Orchestra.

Why is it called the Recycled Orchestra? It's because our musical
_{오케스트라가 Recycled Orchestra로 불리는 이유를 묻는 수동태 문장}
instruments are made of objects from a landfill. That's why it's also
_{be made of는 '~로 만들어지다'. 물건들을 그대로 활용하여 악기를 만든 것을 의미.} _{그것이 ~한 이유이다}
known as the Landfill Harmonic Orchestra.
_{~로 알려지다} _{it과 the Landfill Harmonic Orchestra는 동일한 대상}
Most of us in the orchestra are from Cateura, a small town in
_{콤마(,)로 연결된 Cateura와 a small town in Paraguay는 동격 관계}
Paraguay. There is a huge landfill in our town. Some people even
_{'심지어'라는 뜻의 부사로 say를 수식}
say that Cateura itself is a giant landfill. Many of us are poor. There
_{재귀대명사로 주어 Cateura를 지칭}
weren't many hopes and dreams in our town. Everything began to

change, however, when we met Favio Chávez.

trash 쓰레기	
tear 눈물	
joy 기쁨	
roll 구르다, 굴러가다	
cheek 볼, 뺨	
thrilled 황홀해하는, 아주 신이 난	
one another 서로	
journey 여행	
orchestra 오케스트라, 관현악단	
musical instrument 악기	
landfill 쓰레기 매립지	

확인문제

● 다음 문장이 본문의 내용과 일치하면 T, 일치하지 <u>않으면</u> F를 쓰시오.

1 The other members in the orchestra are hugging one another. ☐

2 Everyone expected that this day would come. ☐

3 Andrea is a violinist in the Recycled Orchestra. ☐

4 Their musical instruments are bought from a landfill. ☐

5 Cateura is a small town in Paraguay. ☐

6 There were many hopes and dreams in Cateura. ☐

Favio was an environmental educator and a musician. He wanted to teach us music, but there was a big problem. There were only a few musical instruments in the whole town. We couldn't afford to buy new ones. But Favio didn't give up. He said that we could make musical instruments with objects from the landfill. A talented man named Nicholas was able to put this idea into practice. He made violins from oil drums. He turned water pipes into flutes.

We had another problem. No one knew how to play musical instruments. We didn't even know how to read music. Favio taught us with great patience. Step by step, we began to make some sounds on our instruments. I still remember the first piece of music that we played. It was very short and mostly out of tune. But it was the most beautiful music to us. We felt a new hope in our hearts. From then on, we gathered to practice every day. One day, Favio told us some great news. We were going to have a concert, a real concert!

And here we are now in front of hundreds of people. They love our music. The world sends us trash, but we send back music!

environmental 환경의
educator 교육자
afford ~할 형편이 되다
talented 재능 있는
be able to ~할 수 있다
put ~ into practice ~을 실행에 옮기다
patience 인내심
step by step 점차로, 차근차근, 하나씩
mostly 대부분, 일반적으로
out of tune 음이 맞지 않는

확인문제

● 다음 문장이 본문의 내용과 일치하면 T, 일치하지 않으면 F를 쓰시오.

1 Favio was an environmental educator and a musician. ☐

2 There were not a few musical instruments in the whole town. ☐

3 Nicholas made violins from oil drums. ☐

4 They began to make some sounds on their instruments quickly. ☐

5 The first piece of music that they played was very short and mostly out of tune. ☐

6 They gathered to practice every Sunday. ☐

● 우리말을 참고하여 빈칸에 알맞은 말을 쓰시오.

1 From _____ to _____

2 _____ _____ _____ are rolling down my cheeks.

3 I'm so happy and _____.

4 If I _____ a bird, I _____ _____.

5 I _____ _____.

6 _____ _____ _____ in my orchestra are hugging one another.

7 Our concert _____ _____ _____ and everyone is standing and _____ _____ _____ _____ _____.

8 None of us _____ _____ that this day would come.

9 _____ _____ a long journey.

10 My name is Andrea and _____ _____ _____ in the Recycled Orchestra.

11 _____ _____ _____ _____ the Recycled Orchestra?

12 It's because our musical instruments _____ _____ _____ objects _____ a landfill.

13 _____ _____ it's also known as the Landfill Harmonic Orchestra.

14 Most of us in the orchestra _____ _____ Cateura, a small town in Paraguay.

15 There is _____ _____ _____ in our town.

16 Some people even say that Cateura _____ is a giant landfill.

17 _____ _____ _____ are poor.

18 There weren't _____ _____ _____ _____ in our town.

19 Everything _____ _____ _____, however, when we met Favio Chávez.

20 Favio was _____ _____ _____ and a musician.

21 He wanted to _____ _____ _____, but there was a big problem.

22 There were _____ _____ _____ musical instruments in the whole town.

23 We _____ _____ buy new ones.

24 But Favio didn't _____ _____.

25 He said that we could make musical instruments _____ _____ _____ _____ _____.

26 A talented man _____ Nicholas was able to _____ this idea _____ _____.

27 He _____ violins _____ oil drums.

28 He _____ water pipes _____ flutes.

29 We had _____ _____.

30 No one knew _____ _____ _____ musical instruments.

31 We didn't even know _____ _____ _____ music.

32 Favio taught us _____ _____ _____.

33 _____ _____ _____, we began to make some sounds on our instruments.

34 I still remember _____ _____ _____ _____ that we played.

35 It was very short and mostly _____ _____ _____.

36 But it was _____ _____ _____ _____ to us.

37 We _____ _____ _____ _____ in our hearts.

38 _____ _____ _____, we gathered to practice every day.

39 One day, Favio told us _____ _____ _____.

40 We _____ _____ a concert, a real concert!

41 And here we are now in front of _____ _____ _____.

42 They love _____ _____.

43 The world _____ _____ _____, but we _____ _____ _____!

---

22 온 마을에 악기가 단지 몇 개뿐이었다.

23 우리는 새 악기를 살 형편도 아니었다.

24 그러나 Favio 선생님은 포기하지 않았다.

25 그는 우리가 쓰레기 매립지의 물건들로 악기를 만들 수 있다고 말했다.

26 재능이 많은 Nicholas 아저씨가 이 생각을 실행에 옮길 수 있었다.

27 그는 기름통으로 바이올린을 만들었다.

28 그는 수도관을 플루트로 바꾸었다.

29 우리에게 또 다른 문제가 있었다.

30 아무도 악기를 연주할 줄 몰랐다.

31 우리는 심지어 악보를 읽는 방법도 알지 못했다.

32 Favio 선생님은 엄청난 인내심으로 우리를 가르쳤다.

33 점차로, 우리는 악기로 어떤 소리를 만들어 내기 시작했다.

34 나는 아직도 우리가 연주했던 첫 곡을 기억한다.

35 그 곡은 매우 짧고 대부분은 음이 맞지 않았다.

36 그러나 그것은 우리에게 가장 아름다운 곡이었다.

37 우리는 마음속에 새로운 희망을 느꼈다.

38 그때부터, 우리는 매일 연습을 하기 위해 모였다.

39 어느 날, Favio 선생님은 우리에게 엄청난 소식을 말해 줬다.

40 우리는 공연을, 진짜 공연을 하게 될 것이었다!

41 그리고 여기 우리는 지금 수백 명의 사람들 앞에 있다.

42 그들은 우리의 음악을 사랑한다.

43 세상은 우리에게 쓰레기를 보내지만, 우리는 음악을 돌려보낸다!

● 우리말을 참고하여 본문을 영작하시오.

1 쓰레기를 음악으로
➡ _____

2 기쁨의 눈물이 내 볼에 흘러내리고 있다.
➡ _____

3 나는 정말 기쁘고 황홀하다.
➡ _____

4 내가 새라면, 날아오를 텐데.
➡ _____

5 나는 주변을 본다.
➡ _____

6 우리 오케스트라의 다른 단원들은 서로 껴안고 있다.
➡ _____

7 우리의 공연은 이제 막 끝났고 모든 사람들이 서서 우리에게 큰 박수를 보내고 있다.
➡ _____

8 우리 중 아무도 이 날이 올 거라고 예상하지 못했다.
➡ _____

9 긴 여정이었다.
➡ _____

10 내 이름은 Andrea이고 나는 Recycled Orchestra의 바이올리니스트이다.
➡ _____

11 오케스트라가 왜 Recycled Orchestra라고 불리냐고?
➡ _____

12 그것은 우리의 악기들이 쓰레기 매립지에서 나온 물건들로 만들어지기 때문이다.
➡ _____

13 그것이 오케스트라가 Landfill Harmonic Orchestra로도 알려진 이유이다.
➡ _____

14 오케스트라의 우리들 대부분은 파라과이의 작은 마을인 카테우라 출신이다.
➡ _____

15 우리 마을에는 거대한 쓰레기 매립지가 있다.
➡ _____

16 몇몇 사람들은 심지어 카테우라 자체가 거대한 쓰레기 매립지라고 말한다.
➡ _____

17 우리들 중 많은 이들이 가난하다.
➡ _____

18 우리 마을에는 꿈과 희망이 많지 않았다.
➡ _____

19 그러나 우리가 Favio Chávez 선생님을 만났을 때 모든 것이 바뀌기 시작했다.
➡ _____

20 Favio 선생님은 환경 교육가이자 음악가였다.
➡ _____

21 그는 우리에게 음악을 가르치고 싶어 했지만, 큰 문제가 있었다.
➡ _____

22 온 마을에 악기가 단지 몇 개뿐이었다.
➡ _____

23 우리는 새 악기를 살 형편도 아니었다.
➡ _____

24 그러나 Favio 선생님은 포기하지 않았다.
➡ _____

25 그는 우리가 쓰레기 매립지의 물건들로 악기를 만들 수 있다고 말했다.
➡ _____

26 재능이 많은 Nicholas 아저씨가 이 생각을 실행에 옮길 수 있었다.
➡ _____

27 그는 기름통으로 바이올린을 만들었다.
➡ _____

28 그는 수도관을 플루트로 바꾸었다.
➡ _____

29 우리에게 또 다른 문제가 있었다.
➡ _____

30 아무도 악기를 연주할 줄 몰랐다.
➡ _____

31 우리는 심지어 악보를 읽는 방법도 알지 못했다.
➡ _____

32 Favio 선생님은 엄청난 인내심으로 우리를 가르쳤다.
➡ _____

33 점차로, 우리는 악기로 어떤 소리를 만들어 내기 시작했다.
➡ _____

34 나는 아직도 우리가 연주했던 첫 곡을 기억한다.
➡ _____

35 그 곡은 매우 짧고 대부분은 음이 맞지 않았다.
➡ _____

36 그러나 그것은 우리에게 가장 아름다운 곡이었다.
➡ _____

37 우리는 마음속에 새로운 희망을 느꼈다.
➡ _____

38 그때부터, 우리는 매일 연습을 하기 위해 모였다.
➡ _____

39 어느 날, Favio 선생님은 우리에게 엄청난 소식을 말해 줬다.
➡ _____

40 우리는 공연을, 진짜 공연을 하게 될 것이었다!
➡ _____

41 그리고 여기 우리는 지금 수백 명의 사람들 앞에 있다.
➡ _____

42 그들은 우리의 음악을 사랑한다.
➡ _____

43 세상은 우리에게 쓰레기를 보내지만, 우리는 음악을 돌려보낸다!
➡ _____

[01~04] 다음 글을 읽고 물음에 답하시오.

Tears of joy are rolling down my cheeks. I'm so happy and (A)[thrilling / thrilled]. ⓐ 내가 새라면, 날아오를 텐데. I look around. The other members in my orchestra (B)[is / are] hugging one another. Our concert ⓑhas just finished and everyone is standing and (C) [gave / giving] us a big hand. None of us ever expected that this day would come. It has been a long journey.

서답형
01 위 글의 괄호 (A)~(C)에서 어법상 알맞은 낱말을 골라 쓰시오.

(A) _____ (B) _____ (C) _____

서답형
02 위 글의 밑줄 친 ⓐ의 우리말에 맞게 8 단어로 영작하시오.

➡ _____

03 위 글의 밑줄 친 ⓑ와 현재완료의 용법이 같은 것을 모두 고르시오.

① She has been sick since yesterday.
② Have you seen it already?
③ How many times have you read it?
④ I have lived here for 10 years.
⑤ She has not washed the dishes yet.

중요
04 According to the passage, which is NOT true?

① The writer is weeping for joy.
② The concert has just ended.
③ The writer saw the other members in the orchestra hugging one another.
④ Everyone is applauding.
⑤ The writer expected that this day would come.

[05~07] 다음 글을 읽고 물음에 답하시오.

My name is Andrea and I'm a violinist in the Recycled Orchestra. Why is it called the Recycled Orchestra? It's because our musical instruments are made of objects from a landfill. (A)That's why it's also known by the Landfill Harmonic Orchestra.

Most of us in the orchestra are from Cateura, a small town in Paraguay. There is a huge landfill in our town. Some people even say that Cateura itself is a giant landfill. Many of us are poor. There weren't many hopes and dreams in our town. Everything began to change, ___ⓐ___, when we met Favio Chávez.

05 위 글의 빈칸 ⓐ에 들어갈 알맞은 말을 고르시오.

① instead   ② therefore
③ that is   ④ however
⑤ in addition

서답형
06 위 글의 밑줄 친 (A)에서 어법상 틀린 부분을 찾아 고치시오.

_____ ➡ _____

중요
07 위 글의 주제로 알맞은 것을 고르시오.

① the description of the violinist of the Recycled Orchestra
② how to make musical instruments with objects from a landfill
③ the reason why the orchestra is called the Recycled Orchestra
④ the poor living condition of the people in Cateura
⑤ the way Favio Chávez changed everything

[08~11] 다음 글을 읽고 물음에 답하시오.

Favio was an environmental educator and a musician. He wanted to teach us music, but there was a big problem. There were only a few musical instruments in the whole town. We couldn't afford to buy new ⓐ . But Favio didn't give up. He said that ⓑ우리가 쓰레기 매립지의 물건들로 악기를 만들 수 있다. A talented man named Nicholas was able to put this idea into practice. He made violins from oil drums. He turned water pipes into flutes.

서답형

08 위 글의 빈칸 ⓐ에 들어갈 알맞은 대명사를 쓰시오.

➡ _____

서답형

09 위 글의 밑줄 친 ⓑ의 우리말에 맞게 주어진 어휘를 알맞게 배열하시오.

objects / musical instruments / from / we / the landfill / with / could make

➡ _____
_____

중요

10 위 글의 제목으로 알맞은 것을 고르시오.

① Favio, an Environmental Educator and a Musician
② How to Teach Music
③ Oops! A Few Musical Instruments in the Whole Town?
④ From Trash to Musical Instruments
⑤ A Talented Man Named Nicholas

11 위 글을 읽고 알 수 없는 것을 고르시오.

① Who was Favio?
② What did Favio want to teach?
③ What musical instruments were there in the town?
④ With what objects could they make musical instruments?
⑤ Who was able to put Favio's idea into practice?

[12~14] 다음 글을 읽고 물음에 답하시오.

We had another problem. No one knew how to play musical instruments. We didn't even know how to read music. Favio taught us ⓐ great patience. Step by step, we began to make some sounds ⓑ our instruments. I still remember the first piece of music that we played. It was very short and mostly out of tune. But it was the most beautiful music to us. We felt a new hope in our hearts. From then on, we gathered to practice every day. One day, Favio told us some great news. We were going to have a concert, a real concert!

And here we are now in front of hundreds of people. They love our music. The world sends us trash, but we send back music!

*We: the children of Cateura

12 위 글의 빈칸 ⓐ와 ⓑ에 들어갈 전치사가 바르게 짝지어진 것은?

	ⓐ	ⓑ		ⓐ	ⓑ
①	for	– at	②	with	– on
③	to	– on	④	for	– to
⑤	with	– at			

13 위 글의 앞에 올 내용으로 가장 알맞은 것을 고르시오.

① the problem of burying waste in landfill

② the challenge of having a concert in front of hundreds of people

③ the process of organizing the orchestra

④ the difficulty of reading music while they were practicing musical instruments

⑤ the difficulty of getting musical instruments

14 〔중요〕 Which question CANNOT be answered after reading the passage?

① Was there any one that knew how to play musical instruments?

② Was there any one that knew how to read music?

③ Who taught music to the children of Cateura?

④ What was the first piece of music that the children of Cateura played?

⑤ What did the children of Cateura think about their first piece of music that they played?

[15~17] 다음 글을 읽고 물음에 답하시오.

My name is Andrea and I'm a violinist in the Recycled Orchestra. (①) Why is it called the Recycled Orchestra? (②) That's why it's also known as the Landfill Harmonic Orchestra. (③) Most of us in the orchestra are from Cateura, a small town in Paraguay. (④) There is a huge landfill in our town. (⑤) Some people even say that Cateura ⓐitself is a giant landfill. Many of us are poor. There weren't many hopes and dreams in our town. Everything began to change, however, when we met Favio Chávez.

15 〔중요〕 위 글의 흐름으로 보아, 주어진 문장이 들어가기에 가장 적절한 곳은?

It's because our musical instruments are made of objects from a landfill.

①　　　②　　　③　　　④　　　⑤

〔서답형〕

16 주어진 영영풀이에 해당하는 단어를 본문에서 찾아 쓰시오.

a large deep hole in which very large amounts of trash are buried

➡ _____

17 〔중요〕 위 글의 밑줄 친 ⓐitself와 문법적 쓰임이 같은 것을 모두 고르시오.

① History repeats itself.

② We enjoyed ourselves very much.

③ I did it myself.

④ Please help yourself to the cake.

⑤ I saw Mr. Smith himself.

[18~20] 다음 글을 읽고 물음에 답하시오.

Favio was an environmental educator and a musician. He wanted to teach us music, but there was (A)a big problem. There were only a few musical instruments in the whole town. (B)We couldn't afford buying new ones. But Favio didn't give up. He said that we could make musical instruments with objects from the landfill. A talented man named Nicholas was able to put this idea ____ⓐ____ practice. He made violins from oil drums. He turned water pipes ____ⓑ____ flutes.

18 위 글의 빈칸 @와 ⓑ에 공통으로 들어갈 알맞은 전치사를 고르시오.

① by   ② on   ③ into

④ for   ⑤ at

서답형

19 위 글의 밑줄 친 (A)a big problem이 가리키는 것을 우리말로 쓰시오.

➡ _____

_____

서답형

20 위 글의 밑줄 친 (B)에서 어법상 틀린 부분을 찾아 고치시오.

_____ ➡ _____

[21~24] 다음 글을 읽고 물음에 답하시오.

We had another problem. No one knew how to play musical instruments. We didn't even know how to read music. Favio taught us with great patience. @Step by step, we began to make some sounds on our instruments. I still remember the first piece of music that we played. ⓑIt was very short and mostly in tune. But it was the most beautiful music to us. We felt a new hope in our hearts. From then on, we gathered ©to practice every day. One day, Favio told us some great news. We were going to have a concert, a real concert!

And here we are now in front of hundreds of people. They love our music. The world sends us trash, but we send back music!

*We: the children of Cateura

21 위 글의 밑줄 친 @Step by step과 바꿔 쓸 수 있는 말을 모두 고르시오.

① Gradually   ② Side by side

③ Time after time   ④ By degrees

⑤ Little by little

서답형

22 위 글의 밑줄 친 ⓑ에서 흐름상 어색한 부분을 찾아 고치시오.

_____ ➡ _____

23 아래 〈보기〉에서 위 글의 밑줄 친 ©to practice와 to부정사의 용법이 다른 것의 개수를 고르시오.

┌─ 보기 ┐

① This water is not good to drink.

② How to live is an important question in life.

③ She was very happy to get the birthday present.

④ He awoke to find himself famous.

⑤ My plan is to master English in a year.

① 1개   ② 2개   ③ 3개   ④ 4개   ⑤ 5개

24 위 글의 주제로 알맞은 것을 고르시오.

① many problems the children of Cateura experienced

② the patient lesson of Favio

③ the difficult process up to the performance of a concert

④ the first piece of music that the children of Cateura played

⑤ the deeply moved audience of a concert

[01~03] 다음 글을 읽고 물음에 답하시오.

Tears of joy are rolling down my cheeks. I'm so happy and thrilled. (A)If I were a bird, I would fly. I look around. The other members in my orchestra are hugging one another. Our concert has just finished and everyone is standing and ⓐgiving us _____ _____ _____. None of us ever expected that this day would come. It has been a long journey.

01 위 글의 밑줄 친 ⓐgiving us 다음에 이어지는 빈칸에 알맞은 세 단어를 넣어, 다음과 같은 뜻이 되도록 하시오.

> clapping his or her hands loudly and enthusiastically

➡ giving us _____ _____ _____

02 위 글의 밑줄 친 (A)를 직설법 문장으로 고치시오.

➡ _____

03 위 글의 내용을 다음과 같이 정리하고자 한다. 빈칸 (A)와 (B)에 들어갈 알맞은 단어를 본문에서 찾아 쓰시오.

> The concert has just finished and the writer is weeping for (A)_____ . The audience is applauding and (B)_____ of the members in the orchestra ever expected that this day would come.

[04~06] 다음 글을 읽고 물음에 답하시오.

My name is Andrea and I'm a violinist in the Recycled Orchestra. Why is it called the Recycled Orchestra? It's because our musical instruments are made of objects from a landfill. ⓐ그것이 오케스트라가 Landfill Harmonic Orchestra로도 알려진 이유이다.
ⓑMost of us in the orchestra is from Cateura, a small town in Paraguay. There is a huge landfill in our town. Some people even say that Cateura itself is a giant landfill. Many of us are poor. There weren't many hopes and dreams in our town. Everything began to change, however, when we met Favio Chávez.

04 위 글의 밑줄 친 ⓐ의 우리말에 맞게 주어진 어휘를 이용하여 10 단어로 영작하시오.

> why, also, as

➡ _____
_____

05 위 글의 밑줄 친 ⓑ에서 어법상 틀린 부분을 찾아 고치시오.

_____ ➡ _____

06 위 글의 내용을 다음과 같이 정리하고자 한다. 빈칸 (A)와 (B)에 들어갈 알맞은 단어를 본문에서 찾아 쓰시오.

> People call the orchestra (A)_____ _____ _____ or the Landfill Harmonic Orchestra because their musical instruments are made of objects from (B)_____ _____ .

[07~10] 다음 글을 읽고 물음에 답하시오.

Favio was an environmental educator and a musician. He wanted to teach us music, but there was a big problem. There were only a few musical instruments in the whole town. We couldn't afford to buy new ones. But Favio didn't give up. He said that we could make musical instruments with objects from the landfill. A talented man ⓐ Nicholas was able to put ⓑthis idea into practice. He made violins from oil drums. He turned water pipes into flutes.

07 위 글의 빈칸 ⓐ에 name을 알맞은 형태로 쓰시오.

➡ _____

08 위 글의 밑줄 친 ⓑthis idea가 가리키는 것을 본문에서 찾아 쓰시오.

➡ _____
_____

09 What objects did Nicholas use to make violins and flutes? Fill in the blanks (A) and (B) with suitable words.

He made violins from (A)_____ _____ and flutes from (B)_____ _____.

10 다음 빈칸 (A)와 (B)에 알맞은 단어를 넣어 Favio와 Nicholas에 대한 소개를 완성하시오.

Favio was an environmental educator and a musician who had an idea of making (A)_____ _____ with objects from the landfill, and Nicholas was a (B)_____ man who was able to put Favio's idea into practice.

[11~13] 다음 글을 읽고 물음에 답하시오.

We had another problem. No one knew how to play musical instruments. ⓐWe didn't even know how to read music. Favio taught us with great patience. Step by step, we began to make some sounds on our instruments. I still remember the first piece of music that we played. It was very short and mostly out of tune. But it was the most beautiful music to us. We felt a new hope in our hearts. From then on, we gathered to practice every day. One day, Favio told us ⓑ some great news. We were going to have a concert, a real concert!

ⓒAnd here we are now in front of hundred of people. They love our music. The world sends us trash, but we send back music!

*We: the children of Cateura

11 위 글의 밑줄 친 ⓐ를 다음과 같이 바꿔 쓸 때 빈칸에 들어갈 알맞은 말을 두 단어로 쓰시오.

We didn't even know how _____ _____ read music.

12 위 글의 밑줄 친 ⓑsome great news가 가리키는 것을 본문에서 찾아 쓰시오.

➡ _____

13 위 글의 밑줄 친 ⓒ에서 어법상 어색한 것을 고치시오.

_____ ➡ _____

구석구석

After You Read B

Reporter: Congratulations! How do you feel now?

Andrea: I feel thrilled. We just performed our first concert.
감정을 나타내는 동사는 수식받는 명사가 감정을 느끼게 되는 경우에 과거분사를 씀.

Reporter: Why is the orchestra called the Recycled Orchestra?

Andrea: That's because our musical instruments are made of objects from a
그것은 ~ 때문이다
landfill.

Reporter: That's amazing.
감정을 나타내는 동사는 감정을 유발할 때 현재분사를 씀.

Andrea: Yeah. None of us knew how to play musical instruments, but Favio
우리들 중 아무도 ~ 않다
taught us with great patience.
with patience = patiently: 인내심 있게

Reporter: That is a wonderful story.

구문해설 • thrilled: 황홀해하는, 아주 신이 난 • orchestra: 오케스트라, 관현악단
• musical instrument: 악기 • landfill: 쓰레기 매립지 • amazing: 놀라운

Think and Write

Dear Admiral Yi Sun-sin,

I'm Sumin. I really respect you because you never gave up in difficult
존경하다   이유를 나타내는 접속사   give up: 포기하다
situations. You saved the country and the people. It was amazing that you won
save: 구하다   가정법과거를 사용하여 현재 사실과 반대되는 것을 상상하여 말할 수 있다.
the battle with only 12 ships. If I had a time machine, I would go to meet you!
가정법과거의 형태는 'if+주어+과거동사, 주어+조동사의 과거형+동사원형'으로, '~하다면 …할 텐데.'라고 해석한다.
I'd like to ask you how to make geobukseon. You're my hero. Thank you.
how to 동사원형: ~하는 방법

Sincerely yours,

Sumin

구문해설 • admiral: 장군 • situation: 상황 • battle: 전투

Project Step 3

This is a bottle shaker. To make it, you need a bottle and buttons. Clean the
부사적 용법(목적)   명령문
bottle and put the buttons in the bottle. Close the bottle and decorate it. You
Clean과 병렬   = the bottle
can also put different things like rice or sand in it. Different items make
= such as   = the bottle
different sounds. Listen to my group's bottle shaker.

구문해설 • shaker: 흔드는 데 쓰는 용기, 셰이커 • decorate: 장식하다

리포터: 축하합니다! 지금 기분이 어떠세요?

Andrea: 나는 아주 황홀해요. 우리는 막 첫 번째 공연을 했어요.

리포터: 오케스트라가 왜 Recycled Orchestra라고 불립니까?

Andrea: 그것은 우리의 악기들이 쓰레기 매립지에서 나온 물건들로 만들어지기 때문입니다.

리포터: 그것은 놀랍군요.

Andrea: 네, 우리들 중 아무도 악기를 연주할 줄 몰랐지만, Favio 선생님은 엄청난 인내심으로 우리를 가르치셨어요.

리포터: 멋있는 이야기입니다.

이순신 장군님께,

저는 수민이에요. 저는 당신이 어려운 상황에서 결코 포기하지 않았기 때문에 당신을 정말 존경해요. 당신은 나라와 국민을 구했어요. 단지 12척의 배로 전투를 이긴 것은 놀라웠어요. 제게 타임 머신이 있다면, 저는 당신을 만나러 갈 텐데요! 저는 당신에게 거북선을 어떻게 만드는지를 묻고 싶어요. 당신은 제 영웅이에요. 감사합니다.

존경을 담아,

수민이가

이것은 병 셰이커야. 그것을 만들려면 너는 병 하나와 단추들이 필요해. 병을 씻고 단추들을 병 속에 넣어. 병을 닫고 그것을 장식해. 너는 또한 쌀이나 모래 같은 다른 것들을 안에 넣을 수 있어. 다른 물건들은 다른 소리들을 만들어 내. 내 모둠의 병 셰이커 소리를 들어 봐.

Words & Expressions

[01~02] 다음 빈칸에 가장 알맞은 말을 고르시오.

01

> She is a[an] _____ musician as well as a photographer.

① talented ② effective
③ accountable ④ extensive
⑤ individual

02

> They _____ for their favorite teams and players.

① apply ② discourage
③ cheer ④ ensure
⑤ prevent

03 두 문장이 같은 의미가 되도록 빈칸을 채우시오.

> They expected him to participate in the ceremony.
> = They expected him to _____ _____ in the ceremony.

04 다음 빈칸에 공통으로 들어갈 말을 쓰시오.

> • They're not _____ of stone the way ancient Greek temples were.
> • Her bestseller is soon to be _____ into a television mini-series.
> • Many products are _____ from machinery rather than by hand.

Conversation

[05~07] 다음 대화를 읽고 물음에 답하시오.

B: Hey, Bora. Welcome to our rock band.
G: Thanks. I'm looking forward (A)to playing in a concert with you.
B: We're (B)excite to have a new guitar player.
G: Yeah. See you on Friday.

05 밑줄 친 (A)와 성격이 다른 하나를 고르시오.

① What do you say to eating out tonight?
② I prefer walking to climbing.
③ What is to be used to clean the sinks?
④ It took her a while to adjust to living alone.
⑤ I'm a real coward when it comes to going to the dentist.

06 위 대화의 밑줄 친 (B)를 알맞은 형으로 고치시오.

➡ _____

07 위 대화의 내용으로 보아 알 수 없는 것은?

① Bora can play the guitar.
② They are going to meet on Friday.
③ Their rock band will play in a concert.
④ Bora is a new member of the rock band.
⑤ Bora has once played the guitar in a concert.

[08~09] 다음 대화를 읽고 물음에 답하시오.

> G: Jiho, what are you reading?
> B: I'm reading a book about baseball player named Jim Abbott. (①)
> G: Oh, 오른손이 없이 태어난 그 사람? (②)
> B: That's right. (③) He tried really hard and even won the MVP award.
> G: Yeah. His story was made into a movie. I'm going to watch it this Saturday.
> B: Really? What's the title?
> G: *Our Hero*. (④) I'm really looking forward to watching it.
> B: Can I join you?
> G: Sure. (⑤)

08 위 대화의 ①~⑤ 중 주어진 문장이 들어갈 곳은?

> See you on Saturday.

①   ②   ③   ④   ⑤

09 밑줄 친 우리말을 조건에 맞게 영작하시오.

> ┌ 보기 ┐
> • 전치사와 관계대명사를 사용할 것.
> • bear를 사용할 것. (형태 변화 가능)

➡ _____

[10~12] 다음 대화를 읽고 물음에 답하시오.

> G: Alex, I'm going to ___(A)___ part in a singing contest next Monday. (①)
> B: That's great, Sumin!
> G: You know how to play the guitar, right?
> B: Yes, I ___(B)___ the guitar for 3 years. (②)
> G: Great. (③) Can you play the guitar ___(C)___ I sing in the contest?

> B: I'd love to, but I can't. (④)
> G: Oh! I'm sorry to hear that. (⑤)
> B: Thanks. But I'll be there to cheer for you.

10 위 대화의 ①~⑤ 중 주어진 문장이 들어갈 곳은?

> I hurt my hand in gym class yesterday.

①   ②   ③   ④   ⑤

11 빈칸 (A)에 들어갈 말로 적절한 것을 고르시오

① make   ② do   ③ have
④ be   ⑤ take

12 빈칸 (B)와 (C)에 들어갈 말로 알맞게 짝지어진 것은?

	(B)		(C)
①	played	–	if
②	played	–	when
③	have played	–	while
④	have played	–	although
⑤	have been played	–	when

13 다음 대화가 자연스럽게 연결되도록 (A)~(D)를 순서대로 배열하시오.

> (A) I'd love to, but I can't. I have to visit my grandparents.
> (B) I'm going to play soccer. Do you want to join me?
> (C) What are you going to do this afternoon?
> (D) Okay, then next time.

➡ _____

Grammar

14 다음 중 밑줄 친 if의 쓰임이 나머지와 다른 하나를 고르시오.

① I would put it in the living room, if I were you.
② What would you do if you could win the lottery?
③ I wasn't sure if I could handle such a powerful car.
④ If he studied hard, he could pass the exam.
⑤ I would be happy if I could cut out junk food, like candy and potato chips.

15 다음 중 어법상 어색한 문장은?

① Would you tell me where to park the car?
② Could you tell me how to get to City Hall?
③ I'm hesitating about who to invite.
④ She asked her mother when to make spaghetti.
⑤ The writer couldn't decide what to wear the dress.

16 다음 주어진 문장을 가정법으로 바르게 고친 것은?

As it doesn't rain, I won't use my umbrella.

① If it rained, I won't use my umbrella.
② If it rained, I would use my umbrella.
③ If it rained, I wouldn't use my umbrella.
④ If it had rained, I would use my umbrella.
⑤ If it hadn't rained, I wouldn't use my umbrella.

[17~18] 우리말에 맞게 주어진 어휘를 이용하여 빈칸에 알맞은 말을 쓰시오.

17
내 문제는 모든 사람에게 어떻게 연락할지였다.
= My problem was _____ _____ _____ everyone. (contact)

18
내가 한국의 대통령이라면, 우리나라를 더 아름답게 만들 텐데.
= If I _____ the president of Korea, I _____ _____ my country more beautiful. (be, make)

19 다음 괄호 안에 주어진 단어를 어법에 맞게 빈칸에 쓰시오.

(1) We didn't even know how _____ _____ _____ music. (read)
(2) Please tell me what _____ _____ _____. (do)
(3) I don't have any idea who _____ _____. (contact)
(4) They didn't decide when _____ _____ for the station. (leave)
(5) If you ask three people _____ bus _____ _____ to reach a given place, you are sure to get three different answers. (take)

20 다음 그림을 보고, 괄호 안에 주어진 단어를 빈칸에 알맞게 채우시오.

If we _____ the music as we have practiced, we _____ _____ the contest. (play, win)

21 두 문장의 의미가 같도록 빈칸에 알맞은 말을 쓰시오.

(1) Please tell me when I can take out the eggs.
= Please tell me _____ the eggs.

(2) It's hard to choose which dress I should wear to the party.
= It's hard to choose _____ to the party.

(3) Did you decide whom you should meet at the meeting?
= Did you decide _____ at the meeting?

Reading

[22~23] 다음 글을 읽고 물음에 답하시오.

My name is Andrea and I'm a violinist in the Recycled Orchestra. Why is ①it called ②the Recycled Orchestra? ③It's because our musical instruments are made of objects from a landfill. That's why ④it's also known as ⑤the Landfill Harmonic Orchestra.

Most of us in the orchestra are from Cateura, a small town in Paraguay. There is a ⓐhuge landfill in our town. Some people even say that Cateura itself is a giant landfill. Many of us are poor. There weren't many hopes and dreams in our town. Everything began to change, however, when we met Favio Chávez.

22 밑줄 친 ①~⑤ 중에서 가리키는 대상이 나머지 넷과 다른 것은?

① ② ③ ④ ⑤

23 위 글의 밑줄 친 ⓐhuge의 반의어를 고르시오.

① giant   ② tiny
③ little   ④ large
⑤ rare

[24~26] 다음 글을 읽고 물음에 답하시오.

Favio was an environmental educator and a musician. He wanted to teach us music, but there was a big problem. ⓐ온 마을에 악기가 단지 몇 개뿐이었다. (①) We couldn't afford to buy new ones. (②) He said that we could make musical instruments with objects from the landfill. (③) A talented man named Nicholas was able to put this idea into practice. (④) He made violins from oil drums. (⑤) He turned water pipes into flutes.

*We: the children of Cateura

24 위 글의 흐름으로 보아, 주어진 문장이 들어가기에 가장 적절한 곳은?

But Favio didn't give up.

① ② ③ ④ ⑤

25 밑줄 친 ⓐ의 우리말에 맞게 주어진 어휘를 이용하여 11 단어로 영작하시오.

> there, only, whole town

➡ _____

_____

26 According to the passage, which is NOT true?

① Favio was an environmental educator and a musician.
② The children of Cateura couldn't afford to buy new musical instruments.
③ Favio didn't give up teaching music to the children of Cateura.
④ Nicholas was able to put Favio's idea into practice.
⑤ Nicholas made flutes from oil drums and violins from water pipes.

[27~29] 다음 글을 읽고 물음에 답하시오.

We had another problem. No one knew (A) how to play musical instruments. We didn't even know how to read music. Favio taught us with great patience. Step by step, we began to make some sounds on our instruments. I still remember the first piece of music that we played. It was very short and mostly out of tune. But it was the most beautiful music to us. We felt a new hope in our hearts. From then (B)on, we gathered to practice every day. One day, Favio told us some great news. We were going to have a concert, a real concert!

And here we are now in front of hundreds of people. They love our music. The world sends us trash, but we send back ___ⓐ___!

27 위 글의 빈칸 ⓐ에 들어갈 알맞은 말을 고르시오.

① dance　　　② music
③ stories　　　④ garbage
⑤ pictures

28 위 글의 밑줄 친 (A)how to play와 to부정사의 용법이 같은 것을 모두 고르시오.

① To hear him talk, you would think him a foreigner.
② I think it wrong to tell a lie.
③ I want something to write with.
④ He decided to buy new shoes.
⑤ I am sorry to give you much trouble.

29 위 글의 밑줄 친 (B)on과 같은 의미로 쓰인 것을 고르시오.

① Put it down on the table.
② He came on Sunday.
③ He worked on without a break.
④ On arriving home I discovered they had gone.
⑤ He is a reporter on the New York Times staff.

출제율 95%

01 다음 단어들의 관계가 <u>다른</u> 하나를 고르시오.

① bored : thrilled
② award : prize
③ journey : trip
④ mostly : mainly
⑤ take care of : look after

[02~03] 다음 빈칸에 알맞은 말을 고르시오.

출제율 95%

02

It was time to _____ their suggestion into practice.

① keep   ② make   ③ set
④ put   ⑤ bring

출제율 90%

03

Would you please _____ them a big hand?

① give   ② find   ③ take
④ do   ⑤ get

출제율 100%

04 다음 중 밑줄 친 부분의 뜻풀이가 바르지 <u>않은</u> 것은?

① Can we <u>afford</u> a new car? (~을 살[가질] 형편이 되다)
② I'll buy <u>a few</u> things at the store. (거의 없는)
③ The ball <u>rolled</u> into the net. (굴러갔다)
④ They discussed <u>environmental</u> issues. (환경의)
⑤ He had a scar running down his left <u>cheek</u>. (빰)

[05~08] 다음 대화를 읽고 물음에 답하시오.

Linda: Hi, Tony! _____(A)_____
Tony: (①) I'm going to watch the musical, *Billy Elliot*.
Linda: *Billy Elliot*? (②) _____(B)_____
Tony: It's about a boy ⓐ[who / what / how / why / that] became a famous dancer. I'm looking forward to watching it. (③)
Linda: Sounds interesting. _____(C)_____
Tony: Jason Kim. He's a great dancer. (④)
Linda: He's my favorite actor. I ⓑ[watched / played / have watched / have played] his musical last year.
Tony: Oh, really? _____(D)_____
Linda: (⑤) I have volunteer work this weekend.
Tony: Okay. Maybe next time!

출제율 90%

05 빈칸 (A)~(D)에 들어가지 <u>않는</u> 말을 고르시오.

① What is it about?
② What's the title?
③ Do you want to join me?
④ What are you going to do this weekend?
⑤ Who is the main actor?

출제율 100%

06 ①~⑤ 중 주어진 문장이 들어갈 곳은?

I'd love to, but I can't.

①   ②   ③   ④   ⑤

출제율 90%

07 위 대화에서 다음 영영풀이에 해당하는 어구를 찾아 쓰시오.

> to want it to happen because you think you will enjoy it

➡ _____

출제율 100%

08 위 대화의 괄호 ⓐ와 ⓑ에서 적절한 것을 고르시오.

ⓐ _____ ⓑ _____

출제율 95%

09 다음 대화의 빈칸에 기대를 표현하는 말을 주어진 단어를 이용하여 완성하시오.

> A: You look happy today. What's going on?
> B: I'm so excited. I'm going to learn to fly a drone.
> A: That sounds great!
> B: Yes. _____
> (the park, really, forward, in)

➡ _____

_____ (11 단어)

출제율 100%

10 주어진 문장 이후에 올 대화의 순서를 바르게 배열하시오.

> Minho, did you finish the math homework?

> (A) Then can you help me with my math homework?
> (B) Not yet. Math is difficult.
> (C) I'd love to, but I can't. I have to take care of my brother.
> (D) Yes, but it's interesting, too.

➡ _____

[11~12] 다음 대화를 읽고 물음에 답하시오.

> G: Jiho, what are you reading?
> B: I'm reading a book about baseball player named Jim Abbott.
> G: Oh, the man who was born without a right hand?
> B: That's right. He tried really hard and even won the MVP award.
> G: Yeah. His story was made into a movie. I'm going to watch it this Saturday.
> B: Really? What's the title?
> G: *Our Hero*. _____(A)_____ (it, forward, really, looking, watching, to, I'm)
> B: Can I join you?
> G: Sure. See you on Saturday.

출제율 90%

11 위 대화에서 다음 영영풀이에 해당하는 단어를 찾아 쓰시오.

> a prize or certificate that a person is given for doing something well

➡ _____

출제율 95%

12 빈칸 (A)를 괄호 안에 주어진 단어를 알맞게 배열하여 채우시오.

➡ _____

출제율 95%

13 다음 중 어법상 올바른 문장은?

① If I knew the truth, I will tell it to you.
② If there were no corn, there will be no frozen pizza.
③ Without your help, I could not succeed.
④ If were it not for trade unions, wages would not be so high as they are.
⑤ But for his idleness, he will be a good man.

출제율 90%

14 다음 우리말을 괄호 안에 주어진 조건대로 영작하시오.

(1) 그녀가 날아다니는 양탄자를 가지고 있다면, 전 세계를 여행할 수 있을 텐데. (if로 시작) (같은 뜻을 as로 시작)

➡ _____

_____

_____

(2) 만약 눈이 많이 내린다면, 나는 산에서 스키를 탈 텐데. (if로 시작) (같은 뜻을 since로 시작)

➡ _____

_____

_____

(3) 그는 우리에게 그 기계를 어떻게 사용해야 할지 가르쳐 주었다. (to부정사 이용) (should 이용)

➡ _____

_____

출제율 100%

15 다음 중 어법상 어색한 것을 모두 고르시오.

① He showed me how to open the safe.

② We must come to a decision about what to do next by tomorrow.

③ The message will tell you whom contacting.

④ Do you want to know what to make friends?

⑤ I am not sure where to put the key.

[16~18] 다음 글을 읽고 물음에 답하시오.

My name is Andrea and I'm a violinist in the Recycled Orchestra. Why is it called the Recycled Orchestra? It's because our musical instruments are made of ⓐobjects from a landfill. That's why it's also known as the Landfill Harmonic Orchestra.

Most of us in the orchestra are from Cateura, a small town in Paraguay. There is a huge landfill in our town. Some people even say that Cateura itself is a giant landfill. Many of us are poor. There weren't many hopes and dreams in our town. Everything began to change, however, when we met Favio Chávez.

출제율 90%

16 Why do they call it the Recycled Orchestra? Answer in English beginning with "Because".

➡ _____

_____

출제율 95%

17 위 글의 밑줄 친 ⓐobjects와 같은 의미로 쓰인 것을 고르시오.

① His objects in life are success and fame.

② She objects to your opinion.

③ He bought everyday objects such as cups and pots.

④ I learned about two kinds of objects in today's grammar class.

⑤ You must care for the objects of consideration.

출제율 100%

18 According to the passage, which is NOT true?

① Andrea is a violinist in the Recycled Orchestra.

② Andrea's violin is made of objects from a landfill.

③ The Recycled Orchestra is also known as the Landfill Harmonic Orchestra.

④ Cateura is a huge landfill.

⑤ There weren't many hopes and dreams in Cateura.

[19~20] 다음 글을 읽고 물음에 답하시오.

Favio was an ⓐenvironment educator and a musician. He wanted to teach us music, but there was a big problem. There were only a few musical instruments in the whole town. We couldn't afford to buy new ⓑones. But Favio didn't give up. He said that we could make musical instruments with objects from the landfill. A talented man named Nicholas was able to put this idea into practice. He made violins from oil drums. He turned water pipes into flutes.

🖉 출제율 95%
19 위 글의 밑줄 친 ⓐ를 알맞은 어형으로 고치시오.

➡ _____

🖉 출제율 90%
20 위 글의 밑줄 친 ⓑones가 가리키는 것을 본문에서 찾아 쓰시오.

➡ _____

[21~23] 다음 글을 읽고 물음에 답하시오.

We had another problem. ⓐ아무도 악기를 연주할 줄 몰랐다. We didn't even know how to read music. (①) Favio taught us with great patience. (②) I still remember the first piece of music ⓑthat we played. (③) It was very short and mostly out of tune. (④) But it was the most beautiful music to us. (⑤) We felt a new hope in our hearts. From then on, we gathered to practice every day. One day, Favio told us some great news. We were going to have a concert, a real concert!

And here we are now in front of hundreds of people. They love our music. The world sends us trash, but we send back music!

🖉 출제율 95%
21 위 글의 흐름으로 보아, 주어진 문장이 들어가기에 가장 적절한 곳은?

Step by step, we began to make some sounds on our instruments.

①   ②   ③   ④   ⑤

🖉 출제율 90%
22 위 글의 밑줄 친 ⓐ의 우리말에 맞게 주어진 어휘를 알맞게 배열하시오.

musical instruments / how / no one / to play / knew

➡ _____

🖉 출제율 100%
23 위 글의 밑줄 친 ⓑthat과 문법적 쓰임이 같은 것을 모두 고르시오.

① The people that I spoke to were very helpful.
② The fact that he's older than me is not true.
③ I was living with my parents at that time.
④ There was no hope that she would recover her health.
⑤ It's the best movie that I've ever watched.

01 다음 대화의 밑줄 친 문장 중 흐름상 또는 어법상 <u>어색한</u> 것을 찾아 바르게 고치시오.

> G: Jiho, what are you reading?
>
> B: (a)I'm reading a book about baseball player named Jim Abbott.
>
> G: Oh, the man who was born without a right hand?
>
> B: (b)That's right. He tried really hard and even won the MVP award.
>
> G: Yeah. (c)His story was made into a movie. (d)I'm going to watch it this Saturday.
>
> B: Really? What's the title?
>
> G: (e)*Our Hero*. I'm really looking forward to watching it.
>
> B: Can I join you?
>
> G: (f)I'd love to, but I can't. See you on Saturday.

➡ _____

[02~03] 밑줄 친 우리말과 일치하도록 주어진 단어를 사용하여 영작하시오.

02

> A: You look happy today. What's going on?
>
> B: I'm so excited. I'm going to travel to Jeju-do.
>
> A: That sounds great!
>
> B: Yes. 나는 말 타기를 정말 고대하고 있어.

(1) _____
   (look)

(2) _____
   (wait)

03

> A: What are you going to do this afternoon?
>
> B: I'm going to ride my bike. Do you want to join me?
>
> A: 그러고 싶지만, 안 돼. I have to do my homework.
>
> B: Okay, then next time.

(1) _____
   (can, love)

(2) _____
   (sorry, can)

04 다음 문장을 주어진 어휘를 이용하여 바꿔 쓰시오.

(1) If I had a time machine, I would go back in time and meet King Sejong. (as)

➡ _____

_____

(2) If I had a better camera, I could take better photos. (so)

➡ _____

_____

(3) As she is working, she can't go to a movie with Jack. (if)

➡ _____

_____

(4) Since he is not in Seoul today, he won't come to my house. (were)

➡ _____

_____

(5) There could be no government if there were no people to be governed. (without)

➡ _____

_____

05 다음 문장을 주어진 조건대로 바꿔 쓰시오.

(1) They want to know how people decide how much to eat. (can 이용)

➡ _____

_____

(2) I don't know which one to say first. (should 이용)

➡ _____

(3) The most important grammar rule to master is when we should use "I" and when we should use "me." (to부정사 이용)

➡ _____

_____

[06~08] 다음 글을 읽고 물음에 답하시오.

My name is Andrea and I'm a violinist in the Recycled Orchestra. ⓐWhy is it called the Recycled Orchestra? It's (A)[because / why] our musical instruments are made of (B)[objects / subjects] from a landfill. That's (C)[because / why] it's also known as the Landfill Harmonic Orchestra.

Most of us in the orchestra are from Cateura, a small town in Paraguay. There is a huge landfill in our town. Some people even say that Cateura ____ⓑ____ is a giant landfill. Many of us are poor. There weren't many hopes and dreams in our town. Everything began to change, however, when we met Favio Chávez.

06 위 글의 밑줄 친 ⓐ를 능동태로 고치시오.

➡ _____

_____

07 위 글의 빈칸 ⓑ에 it을 알맞은 형태로 쓰시오.

➡ _____

08 위 글의 괄호 (A)~(C)에서 문맥이나 어법상 알맞은 낱말을 골라 쓰시오.

(A) _____ (B) _____ (C) _____

[09~10] 다음 글을 읽고 물음에 답하시오.

We had another problem. No one knew how to play musical instruments. We didn't even know how to read music. Favio taught us with great patience. Step by step, we began to make some sounds on our instruments. I still remember the first piece of music that we played. ⓐIt was very short and mostly out of tune. But it was the most beautiful music to us. We felt a new hope in our hearts. From then on, ⓑwe gathered to practice every day. One day, Favio told us some great news. We were going to have a concert, a real concert!

And here we are now in front of hundreds of people. They love our music. The world sends us trash, but we send back music!

*We: the children of Cateura

09 위 글의 밑줄 친 ⓐIt이 가리키는 것을 본문에서 찾아 쓰시오.

➡ _____

10 위 글의 밑줄 친 ⓑ를 다음과 같이 바꿔 쓸 때 빈칸에 들어갈 알맞은 말을 쓰시오.

we gathered _____ _____ we _____ practice every day 혹은 we gathered _____ _____ _____ we _____ practice every day

01 다음은 Kate의 가족이 이번 주말에 할 계획이다. 이에 대한 정보와 주어진 〈조건〉에 맞게 글을 완성하시오.

> 조건
> - 기대 표현하기, 거절하기의 표현을 각각 1번씩 사용한다.
> - 주어진 단어를 이용하여 문장을 만든다.

> A: _____ this weekend. (look)
> B: Why? Do you have any special plans?
> A: I'm going to go to the music festival. Do you want to join me?
> B: _____ (can, love) I should study for the test.

02 다음 문장을 가정법을 사용하여 같은 의미가 되도록 바꿔 쓰시오.

(1) As he doesn't have enough time, he doesn't visit us.

➡ _____

(2) It's rainy, so I will not go swimming.

➡ _____

(3) Since I don't have a car, I have to walk.

➡ _____

(4) Flights are delayed because of the fog.

➡ _____

03 다음 대화를 읽고 대화의 내용과 일치하도록 빈칸을 완성하시오.

> Q1. Who is the person you respect most?
> A: Admiral Yi Sun-sin.
> Q2. Why do you respect that person?
> A: He never gave up in difficult situations.
> Q3. What did that person do?
> A: He saved the country and the people. He won the battle with only 12 ships.
> Q4. What would you like to ask/tell that person?
> A: I'd like to ask him how to make geobukseon.

> Dear (A)_____,
> I'm Sumin. I really respect you because (B)_____. You
> (C)_____ the country and the people. It was amazing that you won the battle
> (D)_____. If I had a time machine, I would go to meet you! I'd like to ask you
> (E)_____. You're my hero. Thank you.
>
> Sincerely yours,
Sumin

단원별 모의고사

01 밑줄 친 부분과 바꿔 쓸 수 있는 말을 고르시오.

> I've always been <u>frightened</u> of dogs.

① bored
② excited
③ angry
④ worried
⑤ scared

02 빈칸 (A)와 (B)에 들어갈 말로 알맞은 것끼리 짝지어진 것을 고르시오.

> • Simon loves you – that's ____(A)____ he wants to be with you.
> • Do you know ____(B)____ to use the coffee machine?

   (A)   (B)
① why – how
② why – what
③ why – why
④ how – how
⑤ how – what

03 다음 빈칸을 〈보기〉에 있는 어휘를 이용하여 채우시오. (형태 변형 가능)

> ┤ 보기 ├
> afford   look   take   turn

(1) I am _____ forward to working with him.

(2) The prince was _____ into a frog by the witch.

(3) We can't _____ to buy a new computer because it is too costly.

(4) I'm not worried about her — she can _____ care of herself.

04 다음 우리말에 맞도록 빈칸에 알맞은 말을 쓰시오. (철자가 주어진 경우 주어진 철자로 시작할 것.)

(1) 고래와 돌고래는 사람들이 말하면서 의사소통하는 것과 똑같이 서로 의사소통한다.
➡ Whales and dolphins communicate with o_____ _____ just like humans do – by talking.

(2) 한 팀이 이기도록 응원하는 것은 즐겁다.
➡ It is fun to c_____ _____ one team to win.

(3) 그녀는 키가 나보다 몇 인치 더 크다.
➡ She's a _____ inches taller than me.

(4) 그들은 경주에 참가할 것이다.
➡ They will _____ _____ in the race.

(5) 너 올 수 있겠니?
➡ Will you be _____ _____ come?

(6) 이 흥미로운 발견을 한 소년에게 큰 박수를 보내주세요!
➡ Let's _____ the boy _____ _____ _____ for this interesting discocery.

05 대화가 자연스럽게 연결되도록 (A)~(D)를 순서대로 배열하시오.

> (A) I'm so excited. I'm going to see Jackson's concert.
> (B) You look happy today. What's going on?
> (C) Yes. I'm really looking forward to watching Jackson's performance.
> (D) That sounds great!

➡ _____

[06~08] 다음 대화를 읽고 물음에 답하시오.

G: Jiho, what are you reading?

B: I'm reading a book about baseball player ⓐnamed Jim Abbott. (①)

G: Oh, the man who ⓑwas born without a right hand?

B: That's right. (②) He tried really hard and even ⓒwas won the MVP award.

G: Yeah. His story ⓓwas made into a movie. I'm going ⓔto watch it this Saturday. (③)

B: Really? (④)

G: *Our Hero*. (⑤) (A)I'm really looking forward to watching it.

B: Can I join you?

G: Sure. See you on Saturday.

---

06 ①~⑤ 중 주어진 문장이 들어갈 곳은?

> What's the title?

①   ②   ③   ④   ⑤

---

07 ⓐ~ⓔ 중 흐름상 또는 어법상 어색한 것을 고르시오.

① ⓐ   ② ⓑ   ③ ⓒ   ④ ⓓ   ⑤ ⓔ

---

08 밑줄 친 (A)와 바꿔 쓸 수 있는 문장을 주어진 단어를 이용하여 쓰시오.

➡ _____

(to, wait)

[09~11] 다음 대화를 읽고 물음에 답하시오.

G: Alex, I'm going to take part (A) a singing contest next Monday.

B: That's great, Sumin!

G: You know how to play the guitar, right?

B: Yes, I've played the guitar (B) 3 years.

G: Great. Can you play the guitar while I sing in the contest?

B: _____(C)_____ I hurt my hand in gym class yesterday.

G: Oh! I'm sorry to hear that.

B: Thanks. But I'll be there to cheer for you.

---

09 빈칸 (A)와 (B)에 들어갈 전치사를 쓰시오.

(A) _____ (B) _____

---

10 빈칸 (C)에 들어갈 말로 알맞은 것을 고르시오.

① Okay, then next time.

② Yes. I'm really looking forward to it.

③ Yeah. See you next Monday.

④ I'd love to, but I can't.

⑤ Sure, I can.

---

11 위 대화를 읽고 답할 수 없는 질문을 고르시오.

① Is Alex able to play the guitar?

② What time is Alex going to go to the contest to cheer for Sumin?

③ How long has Alex played the guitar?

④ What contest is Sumin going to participate in?

⑤ Why can't Alex play the guitar in the contest?

12 빈칸 (A)와 (B)에 들어갈 말로 알맞은 것끼리 짝지어진 것을 고르시오.

A: What are you going to do first?
B: I'm going to watch a parade at 10:30.
_____ (A) _____
A: Sounds fun.
B: Do you want to join me?
A: _____ (B) _____ I'm going to get my face painted at that time.

① I'm really looking forward to watching it. – Yes, I'd love to.
② I'm really looking forward to watching it. – I'd love to, but I can't.
③ I'm really looking forward to watching it. – I'm afraid I can.
④ I'm really looking forward to watch it. – I'd love to, but I can't.
⑤ I'm really looking forward to watch it. – I'm afraid I can.

13 다음 문장의 뜻이 나머지 넷과 다른 것은?

① If I were a doctor, I could help sick people.
② Were I a doctor, I could help sick people.
③ Since I am a doctor, I can help sick people.
④ As I am not a doctor, I can't help sick people.
⑤ I am not a doctor, so I can't help sick people.

14 다음 문장을 조동사를 이용하여 바꿔 쓰시오.

(1) Please tell me where to park my car.
➡ _____

(2) He hasn't decided when to leave for America.
➡ _____
_____

(3) I'm trying to decide what to take with me.
➡ _____

15 다음 중 밑줄 친 부분의 쓰임이 다른 것은?

① I don't know what she'd do if it rained.
② I had no idea if it would be possible or not.
③ If it were not for her mom, she would be in big trouble.
④ If I were a scientist, I would try to invent new medicines.
⑤ I could buy a house if I had one billion won.

16 다음 중 〈보기〉의 밑줄 친 부분과 바꿔 쓸 수 없는 것은?

┌─ 보기 ─┐
If there were no tests, I wouldn't study hard.

① If it were not for tests
② Without tests
③ But for tests
④ Had there no tests
⑤ Were it not for tests

17 다음 문장을 의문사나 조동사를 이용하여 바꿔 쓰시오.

(1) 그녀가 어른이라면, 전 세계를 여행할 텐데.
(an adult, travel, all around)

➡ _____

_____

(2) 만약 내가 왕이라면, 나는 사람들에게 선물을 줄 텐데. (people, presents, give)

➡ _____

(3) 어떻게 시작해야 할지가 전체에서 가장 중요한 부분이다. (start, part of all)

➡ _____

(4) 나는 건물에서 화재가 발생하면 무엇을 해야 할지 모르겠어. (know, a fire, to do, if, there)

➡ _____

_____

(5) 어디에 주차해야 할지 말해 주시겠습니까?
(could, tell, park)

➡ _____

[18~19] 다음 글을 읽고 물음에 답하시오.

My name is Andrea and I'm a violinist in the Recycled Orchestra. Why is it called the Recycled Orchestra? It's because our musical instruments are made of objects from ___ⓐ___. That's why it's also known ⓑas the Landfill Harmonic Orchestra.

18 위 글의 빈칸 ⓐ에 들어갈 알맞은 말을 고르시오.

① a factory   ② a marketplace
③ a workshop   ④ a landfill
⑤ a shop for musical instruments

19 위 글의 밑줄 친 ⓑas와 같은 의미로 쓰인 것을 고르시오.

① As he is honest, he is trusted by everyone.
② Some animals, as the fox and the squirrel, have bushy tails.
③ This is twice as large as that.
④ As one grows older, one becomes more silent.
⑤ He was famous as a statesman.

[20~22] 다음 글을 읽고 물음에 답하시오.

Favio was an environmental educator and a musician. He wanted to teach us music, but there was a big problem. There were only a few musical instruments in the whole town. We couldn't afford (A)to buy new ones. But Favio didn't give up. He said that we could make musical instruments with objects ___ⓐ___ the landfill. A talented man named Nicholas was able to put this idea into practice. He made violins ___ⓑ___ oil drums. He turned water pipes into flutes.

*We: the children of Cateura

20 위 글의 빈칸 ⓐ와 ⓑ에 공통으로 들어갈 알맞은 전치사를 고르시오.

① on   ② from   ③ for
④ by   ⑤ into

21 위 글의 밑줄 친 (A)to buy와 to부정사의 용법이 다른 것을 모두 고르시오.

① He is too young to read the book.
② I don't know where to go.
③ She has many children to look after.
④ He cannot be rich to ask you for some money.
⑤ It is difficult to know oneself.

22 본문의 내용과 일치하도록 다음 빈칸 (A)~(C)에 알맞은 단어를 쓰시오.

> Though there were (A)_____ _____ _____ musical instruments in the whole town and the children of Cateura couldn't afford to buy new ones, they could have musical instruments like (B)_____ and (C)_____ thanks to Favio and Nicholas.

23 위 글에 어울리는 속담으로 알맞지 <u>않은</u> 것을 고르시오.

① No pains, no gains.
② Sweet after bitter.
③ A stitch in time saves nine.
④ April showers bring May flowers.
⑤ Pain is gone, and pleasure is come.

24 위 글의 밑줄 친 ⓐ의 우리말에 맞게 주어진 어휘를 이용하여 10 단어로 영작하시오.

> trash, but, send back

➡ _____

_____

[23~25] 다음 글을 읽고 물음에 답하시오.

We had another problem. No one knew how to play musical instruments. We didn't even know how to read music. Favio taught us with great patience. Step by step, we began to make some sounds on our instruments. I still remember the first piece of music that we played. It was very short and mostly out of tune. But it was the most beautiful music to us. We felt a new hope in our hearts. From then on, we gathered to practice every day. One day, Favio told us some great news. We were going to have a concert, a real concert!

And here we are now in front of hundreds of people. They love our music. ⓐ<u>세상은 우리에게 쓰레기를 보내지만, 우리는 음악을 돌려보낸다!</u>

*We: the children of Cateura

25 According to the passage, which is NOT true?

① There was no one that knew how to play musical instruments.
② The children of Cateura didn't even know how to read music.
③ Step by step, the children of Cateura began to make some sounds on their instruments.
④ The first piece of music that they played was very short but in tune.
⑤ Favio told them that they were going to have a real concert.

MEMO

Lesson 6

Make the World Beautiful

의사소통 기능

- 감사하기
  A: Thank you for lending me the book.
  B: You're welcome.

- 금지하기
  A: You're not allowed to feed the birds here.
  B: I'm sorry. I didn't know that.

언어 형식

- so that
  The architect took the curved lines from nature **so that** city people could enjoy them.

- enough to부정사
  It is round and delicate, yet strong **enough to protect** its contents.

Words & Expressions

교과서

Key Words

- **actually** [ǽktʃuəli] 부 실제로, 정말로
- **allow** [əláu] 동 허락하다, 허가하다
- **architect** [á:rkətèkt] 명 건축가, 설계자
- **artwork** [á:rtwərk] 명 미술품, 예술품, 예술작품
- **basic** [béisik] 형 기본적인
- **beauty** [bjú:ti] 명 아름다움
- **book** [buk] 동 예약하다, 예매하다
- **capture** [kǽptʃər] 동 담아내다, 표현[포착]하다
- **check** [tʃek] 동 확인하다
- **choose** [tʃu:z] 동 선택하다
- **closely** [klóusli] 부 자세하게
- **column** [káləm] 명 기둥
- **contents** [kántents] 명 (복수형으로) 내용물, 안에 든 것
- **curved** [kə:rvd] 형 곡선 모양의, 굽은
- **delicate** [délikət] 형 섬세한, 부서지기 쉬운
- **design** [dizáin] 명 디자인
- **exhibit** [igzíbit] 동 전시하다
- **exist** [igzíst] 동 존재하다
- **expression** [ikspréʃən] 명 표현
- **feed** [fi:d] 동 먹이를 주다
- **flash** [flæʃ] 명 (카메라) 플래시
- **folk village** 민속 마을, 민속촌
- **giant** [dʒáiənt] 형 거대한 명 거인
- **imagination** [imædʒənéiʃən] 명 상상력
- **imitate** [ímətèit] 동 모방하다

- **indoors** [indɔ́:rz] 부 실내로, 실내에
- **inspiration** [ìnspəréiʃən] 명 영감
- **inspire** [inspáiər] 동 영감을 주다
- **invite** [inváit] 동 초대하다
- **lend** [lend] 동 빌려주다
- **natural** [nǽtʃərəl] 형 자연적인
- **nature** [néitʃər] 명 자연
- **obvious** [ábviəs] 형 분명한, 명백한
- **peel** [pi:l] 명 (과일·채소의) 껍질
- **pick** [pik] 동 (꽃을) 꺾다
- **pleasing** [plí:ziŋ] 형 즐거운, 기분 좋은
- **protect** [prətékt] 동 보호하다
- **recommend** [rèkəménd] 동 추천하다
- **remind** [rimáind] 동 상기시키다, 생각나게 하다
- **roof** [ru:f] 명 지붕
- **sailing boat** 돛단배, 범선
- **shape** [ʃeip] 명 형태
- **sign** [sain] 명 표지판
- **spaceship** [spéisʃip] 명 우주선
- **total** [tóutl] 형 총, 전체의
- **tourist attraction** 관광 명소
- **umbrella stand** 우산꽂이
- **wave** [weiv] 명 파도, 물결
- **wet** [wet] 형 젖은

Key Expressions

- **Am I allowed to ~?** ~해도 됩니까?
- **be allowed to ~** ~하도록 허가받다
- **be on sale** (할인) 판매중이다
- **Do you mind if ~?** ~해도 됩니까?
- **enough to ~** ~할 만큼 충분히
- **hear of ~** ~에 관하여 듣다
- **I can't wait to ~!** 너무 ~하고 싶다!
- **I'm glad to ~.** ~하게 되어 기뻐.

- **look like ~** ~처럼 보이다
- **(It's) My pleasure.** 천만에요.
- **Not at all.** 별말씀을요.
- **show A around B** A에게 B를 구경시켜 주다
- **take a picture of ~** ~의 사진을 찍다
- **Thank you for ~.** ~에 대하여 감사하다.
- **That's how ~.** 그런 식으로 ~하다.
- **try to ~** ~하려고 노력하다

Word Power

※ 서로 비슷한 뜻을 가진 어휘

- □ **actually** 실제로 – **really** 정말로
- □ **book** 예약하다 – **reserve** 예약하다
- □ **column** 기둥 – **post** 기둥
- □ **imitate** 모방하다 – **mimic** 모방하다
- □ **peel** (과일 · 채소의) 껍질 – **skin** 껍질

- □ **allow** 허락하다 – **permit** 허락하다
- □ **choose** 선택하다 – **select** 선택하다
- □ **exhibit** 전시하다 – **display** 전시하다
- □ **obvious** 분명한, 명백한 – **evident** 명백한
- □ **wet** 젖은 – **soaked** 젖은

※ 서로 반대의 뜻을 가진 어휘

- □ **allow** 허락하다, 허가하다 ↔ **forbid** 금하다
- □ **giant** 거대한, 거인 ↔ **dwarf** 왜소한, 난장이
- □ **lend** 빌려주다 ↔ **borrow** 빌리다
- □ **obvious** 분명한, 명백한 ↔ **obscure** 모호한

- □ **beauty** 아름다움 ↔ **ugliness** 추함
- □ **indoors** 실내로, 실내에 ↔ **outdoors** 야외에
- □ **natural** 자연적인 ↔ **artificial** 인공적인
- □ **pleasing** 즐거운, 기분 좋은 ↔ **unamusing** 재미없는

※ 동사 – 명사

- □ **choose** 선택하다 – **choice** 선택
- □ **exist** 존재하다 – **existence** 존재
- □ **imagine** 상상하다 – **imagination** 상상력
- □ **inspire** 영감을 주다 – **inspiration** 영감
- □ **protect** 보호하다 – **protection** 보호
- □ **attract** 끌다 – **attraction** 매력

- □ **exhibit** 전시하다 – **exhibition** 전시
- □ **express** 표현하다 – **expression** 표현
- □ **imitate** 모방하다 – **imitation** 모방
- □ **invite** 초대하다 – **invitation** 초대
- □ **recommend** 추천하다 – **recommendation** 추천

English Dictionary

- □ **architect** 건축가, 설계자
  → a person who designs buildings
  건물을 설계하는 사람

- □ **book** 예약하다, 예매하다
  → to make a reservation for a future time
  미래의 어떤 시간을 위해 예약하다

- □ **capture** 담아내다, 포착하다
  → to represent or describe something very accurately using words or image
  말이나 이미지를 이용하여 매우 정확하게 어떤 것을 묘사하거나 설명하다

- □ **column** 기둥
  → a long post made of steel, stone, etc., used to support a building
  건물을 지탱하기 위하여 사용되는 강철, 돌 등으로 만든 긴 기둥

- □ **contents** 내용물, 안에 든 것
  → the things that are inside something
  어떤 것 속에 들어 있는 것

- □ **curved** 곡선 모양의, 굽은
  → having the form of a curve
  곡선의 모양을 하고 있는

- □ **delicate** 부서지기 쉬운, 섬세한
  → easily broken or damaged
  쉽게 부서지거나 손상되는

- □ **exhibit** 전시하다
  → to show something in a public place so that people can see it
  사람들이 볼 수 있도록 공공장소에서 어떤 것을 보여주다

- □ **imagination** 상상력
  → the ability to form pictures or ideas in your mind
  마음속에 그림이나 생각을 형성하는 능력

- □ **imitate** 모방하다
  → to copy somebody or something
  어떤 사람이나 어떤 것을 베끼다

- □ **indoors** 실내로, 실내에
  → inside or into a building
  건물의 안이나 안쪽으로

- □ **peel** (과일 · 채소의) 껍질
  → the skin of a fruit
  과일의 껍질

- □ **spaceship** 우주선
  → a vehicle that travels in space, carrying people
  사람을 실어 나르며, 우주를 여행하는 운송 수단

- □ **wave** 파도, 물결
  → a raised line of water that moves across the surface of the sea
  바다의 표면을 가로질러 움직이는 수면의 도드라지는 선

01 접미사 -ion이나 -ation을 붙여 명사로 만들 수 <u>없는</u> 것을 고르시오.

① inspire ② express ③ attract
④ imagine ⑤ move

02 다음 밑줄 친 부분과 의미가 가장 가까운 것을 고르시오.

I'd like to <u>reserve</u> a table for two.

① book ② keep ③ pay
④ put in ⑤ charge

03 다음 밑줄 친 부분의 의미로 알맞지 <u>않은</u> 것은?

① The gallery will <u>exhibit</u> some of Monet's paintings. (전시하다)
② They think his music <u>inspires</u> and moves people. (영감을 주다)
③ They can't <u>exist</u> on the money he's earning. (살아가다)
④ These china plates have a lovely, <u>delicate</u> flower pattern. (섬세한)
⑤ The <u>obvious</u> way of reducing pollution is to use cars less. (불분명한, 모호한)

04 다음 제시된 단어를 사용하여 자연스러운 문장을 만들 수 <u>없는</u> 것은? (형태 변화 가능, 한 단어는 한 번만 사용 가능)

allow book capture protect

① You'll have to _____ by tomorrow if you want the lower price.
② _____ me to buy some milk tonight.
③ The cover _____ the machine from dust.
④ Are dictionaries _____ in the exam?
⑤ The robbery was _____ on police video cameras.

[05~06] 다음 빈칸에 알맞은 단어를 고르시오.

05
I left school in 1995, and _____ I've lived in London.

① when ② whereas ③ while
④ since then ⑤ therefore

06
The weather was good _____ to go on a picnic.

① else ② even ③ enough
④ still ⑤ quite

07 다음 영영풀이가 나타내는 말을 고르시오.

to represent or describe something very accurately using words or image

① capture ② stand for ③ force
④ catch ⑤ ignore

01 다음 짝지어진 단어의 관계가 같도록 빈칸에 알맞은 말을 쓰시오.

> imagine : imagination = inspire : _____

[02~03] 다음 빈칸에 공통으로 들어갈 말을 쓰시오.

02
> • Students are not allowed _____ eat in class.
> • She was trying not _____ cry.

03
> • _____ you had worked harder, you would have passed your exams.
> • Do you mind _____ I ask you one more thing?

04 다음 밑줄 친 부분과 바꿔 쓸 수 있는 말을 주어진 철자로 시작하여 쓰시오.

(1) His paintings have been <u>displayed</u> in the local art gallery.

➡ e_____

(2) It was <u>evident</u> that the company was in financial difficulties.

➡ o_____

05 다음 우리말에 맞게 주어진 단어를 바르게 배열하시오.

(1) 그녀는 그에게 그들이 지난번 만났던 때를 상기시켰다.

(reminded, met, the, had, she, time, of, they, last, him)

➡ _____

(2) 구경시켜 주시겠어요?

(around, show, me, would, you)

➡ _____

(3) 부산에 가까워지고 있으니, 어서 부모님을 보고 싶다.

(close, wait, parents, Busan, can't, my, getting, see, to, to, I)

➡ _____

(4) 너는 Edith에게 선물에 대해 감사했니?

(for, did, Edith, the, thank, you, present)

➡ _____

06 다음 빈칸에 알맞은 단어를 〈보기〉에서 골라 쓰시오.

> ┤ 보기 ├
> architect   column   content   sign

(1) The stone _____s support the temple.

(2) They swam in spite of all the danger _____s.

(3) The _____ is drawing up plans for the new offices.

(4) The narrator reads the _____s of the screen aloud for users who are blind.

Conructionation
교과서

Conversation

① 감사하기

> **A** Thank you for lending me the book. 책을 빌려줘서 고마워.
> **B** You're welcome. 천만에.

- 'Thank you for ~.'는 '~에 대하여 고마워.'라는 뜻으로 감사를 나타낼 때 사용하는 표현이다. 전치사 for 뒤에는 감사하는 이유를 명사나 동명사의 형태로 쓴다. 또한 'I'm very thankful/grateful to you for ~.(~에 대하여 감사하다.)', 'I can't tell you how much this means to me.(이것이 내게 얼마나 중요한 의미인지 어떻게 말해야 할지 모르겠어요.)'처럼 감사를 표현하기도 한다. 감사에 답하는 표현으로는 '천만에요.'라는 뜻으로 'You're welcome.' 또는 '(It's) My pleasure.' 등을 쓴다.

- 감사하는 표현은 아주 간단히 'Thank you.'로 할 수 있지만 좀 더 정중하게 표현할 때는 '감사하다'는 의미를 가지는 동사 appreciate를 사용하여 'I appreciate ~'로 표현할 수 있다. 이때 appreciate 뒤에는 감사의 내용이 바로 오면 된다. 예를 들어 '너의 친절이 감사하다'라고 할 때는 'I appreciate your kindness.'라고 쓰면 된다. '네가 ~해주면 고맙겠다.'라고 상대방에게 정중히 부탁할 때에는 'I would appreciate it if you ~.'라고 표현한다.

감사하기

- Thanks a lot. 대단히 감사합니다.
- Thank you for your help. 도와주셔서 고맙습니다.
- I am really grateful for ~. ~에 대하여 감사합니다.
- Thank you very[so] much. 매우 고맙습니다.
- I appreciate your help. 도와주셔서 고맙습니다.

감사에 답하기

- You're welcome. 천만에요.
- Don't mention it. 별말씀을요.
- Anytime. 언제든지요.
- It's my pleasure. 제 기쁨이에요.
- No problem. 뭘요.

핵심 Check

1. 다음 대화의 우리말 의미에 해당하는 적절한 문장을 쓰시오.

   B: Hi, Lisa. 생일 파티에 초대해 줘서 고마워.

   G: My pleasure. I'm glad you could come.

   B: These flowers are for you. Happy birthday!

   G: They are beautiful! Thank you.

   ➡ _____

❷ 금지하기

A You're not allowed to feed the birds here. 이곳에서 새에게 먹이를 주면 안 돼요.

B I'm sorry. I didn't know that. 죄송합니다. 몰랐어요.

■ 'You're not allowed to ~.(~해서는 안 된다.)'는 하지 말아야 할 행동을 말할 때 사용하는 표현이다. 미술관이나 도서관 등 공공장소에서의 금지 사항을 말할 때 자주 쓰이는 표현이다. 보통 'You're not allowed to park here.(이곳에 주차하는 것은 허용되지 않습니다.)'와 같이 금지하는 말을 들으면 'I'm sorry. I didn't know that.(죄송합니다. 그걸 몰랐어요.)'처럼 사과하며 몰랐다고 답을 하거나 'Okay, I see.(네, 알겠어요.)'와 같이 알겠다고 대답한다.

■ 보통 금지하는 표현은 '~하지 마세요.'의 의미로 'Don't ~.'라고 하거나 'You should not ~(~해서는 안 됩니다.)' 또는 'You had better not ~.(~하지 않는 것이 좋을 것이다.)'와 같은 표현으로 금지를 나타낸다. 'You are not supposed to ~.(~하면 안 됩니다.)'와 같은 표현도 금지를 나타낼 때 흔히 쓰인다.

금지하기

- You're not allowed to ~. ~하면 안 됩니다.
- You're not supposed to ~. ~하시면 안 됩니다.
- You must not ~. ~하지 마세요.
- You should not ~. ~하면 안 돼요.
- You'd better not ~. ~하지 않는 것이 좋을 겁니다.
- Don't ~. ~하지 마시오.

핵심 Check

2. 다음 대화의 밑줄 친 우리말을 주어진 단어를 이용하여 영작하시오.

A: 이곳에서 낚시를 하는 것은 허용되지 않습니다.(allow)

B: I'm sorry. I didn't know that.

➡ _____

3. 다음 대화의 순서를 바르게 배열하시오.

M: Excuse me. You're not allowed to bring your umbrella inside.

(A) Okay. I'll put it there. Thank you.

(B) Oh, where should I put it?

(C) There is an umbrella stand outside.

➡ _____

Listen and Speak 1 A

B: Hi, Lisa. ❶Thank you for ❷inviting me to your birthday party.

G: My pleasure. ❸I'm glad you could come.

B: These flowers are for you. Happy birthday!

G: ❹They are beautiful! Thank you.

B: 안녕, Lisa. 네 생일 파티에 나를 초대해 줘서 고마워.
G: 천만에. 네가 와서 기뻐.
B: 이 꽃들은 너를 위한 거야. 생일 축하해!
G: 꽃들이 아름다워! 고마워.

❶ 'Thank you for ～.'는 '～해 주셔서 감사합니다.'라는 뜻으로 고마움을 나타낼 때 사용하는 표현이다. 전치사 for 뒤에는 감사하는 이유가 오는데 보통 명사나 동명사의 형태로 쓴다. 감사에 답하는 표현으로는 'You're welcome.' 또는 'My pleasure.' 등을 쓴다.

❷ invite: 초대하다

❸ I'm glad 다음에는 접속사 that이 생략되었다.

❹ They는 앞 문장의 These flowers를 받는 대명사이다.

Check(√) True or False

(1) Today is Lisa's birthday. T ☐ F ☐

(2) The boy gives Lisa a flower for her birthday. T ☐ F ☐

Listen and Speak 2 A

M: Excuse me. ❶You're not allowed to bring your umbrella inside.

G: Oh, ❷where should I put it?

M: There is an ❸umbrella stand outside.

G: Okay. I'll put it there. Thank you.

M: 실례합니다. 우산을 안으로 가져오면 안 됩니다.
G: 아, 우산을 어디에 놓아야 하나요?
M: 밖에 우산꽂이가 있어요.
G: 알겠습니다. 그곳에 놓을게요. 감사합니다.

❶ 'You're not allowed to ～.'는 '～하는 게 허용되지 않는다.'라는 뜻으로 하지 말아야 할 행동을 말할 때 사용하는 표현이다. 미술관이나 도서관 등 공공장소에서의 금지 사항을 말할 때 자주 쓰이는 표현이다. 'You're not allowed to ～.'와 바꿔 쓸 수 있는 표현들로 'Don't 동사원형 ～.', 'You shouldn't 동사원형 ～.', 'You'd better not 동사원형 ～.' 등이 있다.

❷ 의무에 대해서 표현할 때 조동사 should를 사용하여 말할 수 있다. 'Where should I put it?'을 'Where do I have to put it?'으로 바꿔 말할 수 있다.

❸ umbrella stand: 우산꽂이

Check(√) True or False

(3) The girl can bring her umbrella inside. T ☐ F ☐

(4) The man suggests the girl put her umbrella in an umbrella stand which is outside. T ☐ F ☐

Listen and Speak 1 B

B: Sumin, my train ❶is leaving in five minutes.

G: ❷I hope you enjoyed your trip, Daniel.

B: Of course, I did.

G: ❸Which place did you like most in my town?

B: I liked the folk village most.

G: Yeah, it's ❹the most popular place here.

B: I really liked ❺walking around in hanbok. I ❻looked really cool.

G: ❼I'm glad to hear that.

B: ❽Thank you for showing me around.

G: It was my pleasure. Have a safe trip.

B: 수민아, 기차가 5분 후에 떠나.
G: 여행이 즐거웠기를 바라, Daniel.
B: 물론 즐거웠지.
G: 우리 마을에서 어느 장소가 가장 좋았니?
B: 민속촌이 가장 좋았어.
G: 응, 민속촌이 이곳에서 가장 인기 있는 곳이야.
B: 나는 한복을 입고 돌아다니는 게 정말 좋았어. 내가 정말 멋져 보였어.
G: 그 말을 들으니 기뻐.
B: 여기저기 구경시켜 줘서 고마워.
G: 천만에. 조심해서 가.

❶ 정해져 있는 가까운 미래에 대해서 말할 때 leave 동사의 경우 현재진행형을 사용할 수 있다. in+시간: (시간의 경과를 나타내어) ~ 후에

❷ 기원하거나 바랄 때 동사 hope를 사용하며, 뒤에는 to동사원형이나 that절이 온다. 여기서는 hope와 you 사이에 접속사 that이 생략되어 있다.

❸ 가장 좋아하는 것을 물어볼 때 최상급 the most를 사용해 'Which 명사 do you like most?(어떤 명사가 가장 좋아?)'로 물어 볼 수 있다. 여기에서는 과거형으로 do 대신 did를 질문에서 사용하고 있다.

❹ popular(인기 있는)의 최상급은 앞에 the most를 붙인다.

❺ like는 동명사(Ving)와 to부정사(to 동사원형) 둘 다 목적어로 취할 수 있다.

❻ look은 자동사로 보어인 형용사를 취할 수 있다. 여기서는 형용사 cool(멋진)을 보어로 사용하였다.

❼ 상대방이 한 말을 듣고 기쁨을 표현할 때 'I'm glad to hear that.'이나 'I'm happy to hear that.'을 사용할 수 있다.

❽ 'Thank you for ~.'는 '~해 주셔서 감사합니다.'라는 뜻으로 고마움을 나타낼 때 사용하는 표현이다. 바꿔 쓸 수 있는 표현으로 'I appreciate ~.'이 있는데 appreciate는 타동사로 목적어 자리에 고마워하는 내용을 쓴다.

Check(√) True or False

(5) The folk village is the most popular site in Sumin's town.　　T ☐ F ☐

(6) Daniel showed Sumin around.　　T ☐ F ☐

Listen and Speak 1 C

A: ❶How was the book?

B: It was great. ❷Thank you for ❸lending me the book.

A: ❹You're welcome. It was my pleasure.

A: 책은 어땠니?
B: 좋았어. 책을 빌려줘서 고마워.
A: 천만에. 오히려 내가 더 기뻤어.

❶ 묻는 사람이 상대방의 경험에 대해 알고자 할 때 쓰는 표현으로 'How was ~?'는 '~가 어땠니?'의 의미이며, 바꿔 쓸 수 있는 표현으로 'How did you like ~?'가 있다.

❷ 감사하는 표현은 간단히 'Thank you.'로 할 수 있지만 전치사 for를 뒤에 써서 감사하는 내용을 쓸 수 있다. for는 전치사이므로 뒤에 동명사나 명사가 올 수 있다.

❸ lend는 '~에게 …을 빌려주다'의 의미로 간접목적어와 직접목적어를 취할 수 있는 4형식 동사이다.

❹ 감사에 답하는 표현으로는 'You're welcome.(천만에요.)', 'Don't mention it.(별말씀을요.)', 'It's my pleasure.(제 기쁨이에요.)', 'Don't mention it.(별말씀을요.)' 등이 있다.

Check(√) True or False

(7) A borrowed the book from B.　　T ☐ F ☐

(8) B thinks that the book which A lent to B was not great.　　T ☐ F ☐

Listen and Speak 2 B

B: ❶The tickets for the World Music Concert are ❷on sale now.

G: Really? ❸Let's book the tickets online right away.

B: Okay. Let's see.... There are still tickets ❹left for November 5th.

G: Sounds good. Let's get two student tickets.

B: Oh, ❺do you mind if I bring my little brother?

G: ❻Not at all. But it says that ❼you are not allowed to bring children under 8.

B: No problem. He's 10.

G: Okay, I'll ❽add one child ticket. ❾The total price is 25 dollars.

B: Great.

G: ❿I can't wait to see the concert!

❶ The tickets가 복수주어로 복수동사인 are가 와야 한다. for the World Music Concert는 the tickets를 수식하고 있다.

❷ on sale은 '판매 중인, 할인 중인'의 2개의 뜻을 가지고 있는데 여기서는 '판매 중인'의 의미로 사용되었다.

❸ 'Let's 동사원형'은 '~하자'의 의미로, 권유할 때 사용한다. book: 예약하다, 예매하다 right away: 즉시, 당장

❹ left는 과거분사로 앞의 tickets를 수식하며 '남겨진'의 뜻이다.

❺ 'Do you mind if 주어 동사?'는 '내가 ~해도 될까?'라는 뜻으로 상대방에게 허락을 구하거나 요청할 때 사용하는 표현이다.

❻ mind는 '꺼리다'의 뜻이므로 Yes는 거절을 의미하고, No는 승낙을 의미한다. 승낙할 때 'No, I don't mind.', 'Not at all.', 'No, go ahead.', 'Of course not.' 등을 사용할 수 있다.

❼ 어떤 행동이 허락되지 않음을 알려 줄 때는 'You're not allowed to ~.'라고 표현하며 '~하는 게 허용되지 않는다.'라는 의미이다.

❽ add: 추가하다

❾ total price: 총 비용

❿ 기대를 표현할 때 'can't wait to 동사원형'을 사용하며, '~이 정말 기대돼'의 의미이다. 유사 표현으로 'can't wait for (동)명사'와 'be looking forward to (동)명사'가 있다.

Listen and Speak 2 C

A: Excuse me. ❶You're not allowed to feed the birds here.

B: I'm sorry. I didn't know that.

A: Please check ❷the sign over there.

B: Okay. Thank you.

❶ 'You're not allowed to ~.'는 '~하는 게 허용되지 않는다.'라는 뜻으로 하지 말아야 할 행동을 말할 때 사용하는 표현이다. feed: 먹이를 주다

❷ sign: 표지판

Real Life Talk Watch a Video

W: Hello, students! ❶Thank you for visiting our art museum. This museum ❷opened in 1995. ❸Since then, it has exhibited many famous artworks. Today, you will see some famous artworks from the art books. Before we begin the tour, ❹let me ❺remind you of a basic rule. You can ❻take pictures of the artworks, but ❼you're not allowed to touch them. Now let's start the tour.

❶ 'Thank you for ~.'는 '~해 주셔서 감사합니다.'라는 뜻으로 고마움을 나타낼 때 사용하는 표현이다. 전치사 for 뒤에는 감사하는 이유가 오는데 보통 명사나 동명사의 형태로 쓴다.

❷ 시간의 부사구 'in 1995'가 과거이므로, 과거형 동사 opened를 쓴다.

❸ since는 전치사로 '~ 이래로'의 뜻이며, 과거에 일어난 일이 현재까지 영향을 미칠 때 쓰는 현재완료(have+p.p)와 자주 쓰인다. since then: 그때부터 exhibit: 전시하다

❹ let은 사역동사로 목적어와 목적격보어의 관계가 능동이면 목적격보어로 동사원형을 사용해야 한다.

❺ remind A of B: A에게 B를 상기시키다

❻ take pictures of: ~의 사진을 찍다

❼ 'You're not allowed to ~.'는 '~하는 게 허용되지 않는다.'라는 뜻으로 하지 말아야 할 행동을 말할 때 사용하는 표현이다.

Real Life Talk Step 2

A: Excuse me. Can I ❶ask you a question?

B: Sure, what is it?

A: ❷Am I allowed to drink soda?

B: Sorry. ❸You're not allowed to drink soda here.

A: Okay, I see.

B: ❹Thank you for understanding.

❶ ask가 수여동사로 간접목적어인 you와 직접목적어인 a question을 취하고 있다.

❷ 'Am I allowed to 동사원형 ~?'은 '내가 ~하는 것이 허용될까요?'의 의미로, 어떤 행동을 하기 전에 허가 여부를 물을 때 쓰는 표현이다. 허가를 묻는 다른 표현으로 'Do you mind if I ~?', 'Can I ~?', 'Is it okay if I ~?' 등이 있다.

❸ 어떤 행동이 허락되지 않음을 알려 줄 때는 'You're not allowed to ~.'라고 표현하며 '~하는 게 허용되지 않는다.'라는 의미이다. soda: 탄산음료

❹ 'Thank you for ~.'는 '~해 주셔서 감사합니다.'라는 뜻으로 고마움을 나타낼 때 사용하는 표현이다. 바꿔 쓸 수 있는 표현으로 'I appreciate ~.'이 있는데 appreciate는 타동사로 목적어 자리에 고마워하는 내용을 쓴다.

• 다음 우리말과 일치하도록 빈칸에 알맞은 말을 쓰시오.

Listen and Speak 1 A

B: Hi, Lisa. Thank you _____ _____ _____ _____ your birthday party.

G: My pleasure. I'm _____ you could come.

B: These flowers _____ for you. Happy birthday!

G: They are beautiful! Thank you.

Listen and Speak 1 B

B: Sumin, my train _____ _____ _____ five minutes.

G: I _____ you enjoyed your trip, Daniel.

B: Of course, I did.

G: _____ place did you like _____ in my town?

B: I liked the folk village _____.

G: Yeah, it's _____ _____ popular place here.

B: I really _____ _____ around in hanbok. I looked really _____.

G: I'm _____ _____ _____ that.

B: Thank you _____ _____ _____ _____.

G: It was my _____. _____ a safe trip.

Listen and Speak 1 C

1. A: How was the book?
   B: It was great. _____ _____ _____ lending me the book.
   A: You're _____. It was my _____.

2. A: _____ was the movie?
   B: It was great. Thank you _____ _____ the movie.
   A: You're _____. It was my _____.

3. A: _____ _____ your mom's birthday party?
   B: It was great. Thank you _____ _____ _____ _____ a cake.
   A: You're welcome. It was _____ _____.

Listen and Speak 2 A

M: Excuse me. _____ _____ _____ _____ bring your umbrella inside.

G: Oh, _____ should I put it?

M: There is an umbrella _____ outside.

G: Okay, _____ _____ _____ there. Thank you.

Listen and Speak 2 B

B: The tickets _____ the World Music Concert _____ _____ _____ now.

G: Really? Let's _____ the tickets online right _____.

B: Okay. Let's see.... There are still tickets _____ for November 5th.

G: Sounds good. _____ _____ two student tickets.

B: Oh, _____ _____ _____ _____ I bring my little brother?

G: Not at all. But it _____ _____ you are _____ _____ _____ _____ children _____ 8.

B: No _____. He's 10.

G: Okay, I'll _____ one child ticket. The total price _____ 25 dollars.

B: Great.

G: I _____ _____ _____ _____ the concert!

Listen and Speak 2 C

1. A: Excuse me. _____ _____ _____ to feed the birds here.

   B: I'm sorry. I didn't know that.

   A: Please check the _____ over there.

   B: Okay. Thank you.

2. A: Excuse me. You're _____ _____ _____ _____ a drone.

   B: I'm sorry. I didn't know that.

   A: Please _____ _____ _____ over there.

   B: Okay. Thank you.

3. A: Excuse me. _____ _____ _____ _____ pick flowers.

   B: I'm sorry. I didn't know that.

   A: Please _____ _____ _____ over there.

   B: Okay. Thank you.

 해석

M: 실례합니다. 우산을 안으로 가져오면 안 됩니다.
G: 아, 우산을 어디에 놓아야 하나요?
M: 밖에 우산꽂이가 있어요.
G: 알겠습니다. 그곳에 놓을게요. 감사합니다.

B: '세계 음악 콘서트'의 표가 지금 판매 중이야.
G: 정말? 지금 당장 온라인으로 표를 예매하자.
B: 좋아. 어디 보자···. 11월 5일에 표가 아직 남아 있어.
G: 잘됐다. 학생 표 두 장을 예매하자.
B: 오, 내 남동생을 데려가도 될까?
G: 물론이지. 하지만 8세 미만의 어린이들을 데려오지 못한다고 쓰여 있어.
B: 문제없어. 남동생은 열 살이야.
G: 그래, 어린이 표 한 장을 추가할게. 총액이 25달러야.
B: 좋아.
G: 콘서트를 볼 게 정말 기대돼!

1. A: 실례합니다. 여기서 새에게 먹이를 주면 안 됩니다.
   B: 죄송합니다. 몰랐어요.
   A: 저기에 있는 표지판을 확인하세요.
   B: 알겠습니다. 감사합니다.

2. A: 실례합니다. 여기서 드론을 날리면 안 됩니다.
   B: 죄송합니다. 몰랐어요.
   A: 저기에 있는 표지판을 확인하세요.
   B: 알겠습니다. 감사합니다.

3. A: 실례합니다. 여기서 꽃을 꺾으면 안 됩니다.
   B: 죄송합니다. 몰랐어요.
   A: 저기에 있는 표지판을 확인하세요.
   B: 알겠습니다. 감사합니다.

Real Life Talk Watch a Video

W: Hello, students! _____ _____ _____ _____ our art museum. This museum _____ in 1995. Since then, it _____ _____ many famous artworks. Today, you will see some _____ _____ from the art books. Before we begin the tour, let me _____ _____ _____ a basic rule. You can _____ _____ _____ the artworks, but _____ _____ _____ _____ touch them. Now _____ _____ the tour.

W: 안녕하세요, 학생 여러분! 우리 미술 관을 방문해 주셔서 감사합니다. 이 미술관은 1995년에 문을 열었습니 다. 그때부터 많은 유명한 작품을 전 시했습니다. 오늘, 여러분은 미술 책 에 실린 유명한 작품 몇 개를 보게 될 것입니다. 관람을 시작하기 전에 기본 규칙을 상기시켜 드리겠습니 다. 작품의 사진을 찍을 수는 있지만 만져서는 안 됩니다. 이제 관람을 시 작해 봅시다.

Real Life Talk Step 2

1. A: Excuse me. _____ _____ _____ you a question?
   B: Sure, what is it?
   A: _____ _____ _____ _____ drink soda?
   B: Sorry. _____ _____ _____ _____ _____ soda here.
   A: Okay, I see.
   B: Thank you _____ understanding.

2. A: Excuse me. _____ _____ _____ _____ _____ _____ _____?
   B: Sure, what is it?
   A: _____ _____ _____ _____ _____ the artwork?
   B: Sorry. _____ _____ _____ _____ _____ the artwork here.
   A: Okay, I see.
   B: Thank you _____ _____.

1. A: 실례합니다. 뭐 좀 물어봐도 될까요?
   B: 물론이죠. 뭔데요?
   A: 제가 탄산음료를 먹어도 되나요?
   B: 죄송합니다. 여기서 탄산음료 마 시면 안 돼요.
   A: 네, 알겠습니다.
   B: 이해해 주셔서 감사합니다.

2. A: 실례합니다. 뭐 좀 물어봐도 될까요?
   B: 물론이죠. 뭔데요?
   A: 제가 미술작품 만져도 되나요?
   B: 죄송합니다. 여기서 미술작품 만 지면 안 돼요.
   A: 네, 알겠습니다.
   B: 이해해 주셔서 감사합니다.

Check up Dialogue Champion

A: Thank you _____ _____ _____ _____ my project.
B: You're welcome. It was my _____.

A: 내 과제를 끝나게 나를 도와줘서 고 마워.
B: 천만에. 오히려 내가 더 기뻤어.

01 다음 빈칸에 알맞은 말을 모두 고르시오.

> B: Hi, Lisa. _____
> G: My pleasure. I'm glad you could come.
> B: These flowers are for you. Happy birthday!
> G: They are beautiful! Thank you.

① I'm looking forward to inviting you to my birthday party.

② I appreciate your preparing for my birthday party.

③ Thank you for inviting me to your birthday party.

④ I'm very grateful to you for the invitation.

⑤ I'm happy to invite you to my birthday party.

[02~03] 다음 대화를 읽고 물음에 답하시오.

> B: The tickets for the World Music Concert are on sale now.
> G: Really? Let's book the tickets online right away.
> B: Okay. Let's see.... There are still tickets ⓐleave for November 5th.
> G: Sounds good. Let's get two student tickets.
> B: Oh, do you mind if I bring my little brother?
> G: _____(A)_____ But it says that you are not allowed to bring children under 8.
> B: No problem. He's 10.
> G: Okay, I'll add one child ticket. The total price is 25 dollars.
> B: Great.
> G: I can't wait to see the concert!

02 위 대화의 밑줄 친 ⓐleave를 알맞은 형으로 고치시오.

➡ _____

03 위 대화의 빈칸 (A)에 적절한 것은?

① Sure.   ② Yes, I do.   ③ Certainly.

④ Not at all.   ⑤ Of course.

[01~03] 다음 대화를 읽고 물음에 답하시오.

B: Sumin, my train is leaving in five minutes.
G: I hope you enjoyed your trip, Daniel.
B: Of course, I did.
G: _____(A)_____
B: I liked the folk village most.
G: Yeah, it's the most popular place here.
B: I really liked walking around in hanbok. I looked really cool.
G: I'm glad to hear that.
B: Thank you _____(B)_____.
G: It was my pleasure. Have a safe trip.

01 빈칸 (A)에 알맞은 말을 고르시오.

① Do you know where the folk village is?
② How did you like the folk village?
③ Which place did you like most in my town?
④ Where would you like to go most in my town?
⑤ Where should I go?

02 빈칸 (B)에 알맞은 말을 고르시오.

① for having around
② to have around
③ in showing me around
④ for showing me around
⑤ to show me around

03 위 대화를 읽고 답할 수 없는 질문을 고르시오.

① 누가 Daniel에게 마을을 구경시켜 주었는가?
② Daniel은 며칠 동안 여행했는가?
③ Daniel은 마을에서 어디를 가장 좋아했는가?
④ 언제 기차가 떠나는가?
⑤ 수민이는 민속촌을 갔는가?

04 ⓐ~ⓔ의 대화 중 어색한 것끼리 짝지어진 것을 고르시오.

ⓐ A: Am I allowed to ride a bike here?
   B: Yes, it's OK.
ⓑ A: Excuse me, am I allowed to bring my own food?
   B: I'm sorry. No food or drink from outside is allowed in the museum.
ⓒ A: Am I allowed to use your phone?
   B: You're right.
ⓓ A: Do you mind if I try it on?
   B: Of course. Go ahead.
ⓔ A: Do you mind if I use your computer?
   B: I'm afraid, but I should use it now.

① ⓐ, ⓑ   ② ⓑ, ⓒ   ③ ⓒ, ⓓ
④ ⓓ, ⓔ   ⑤ ⓐ, ⓔ

05 다음 대화가 자연스럽게 연결되도록 (A)~(C)를 순서대로 가장 적절하게 배열한 것은?

(A) It was great. Thank you for recommending the movie.
(B) How was the movie?
(C) You're welcome. It was my pleasure.

① (A) – (C) – (B)   ② (B) – (A) – (C)
③ (B) – (C) – (A)   ④ (C) – (A) – (B)
⑤ (C) – (B) – (A)

[06~07] 다음 대화를 읽고 물음에 답하시오.

M: Excuse me. (①) You're not allowed to bring your umbrella inside. (②)
G: Oh, _____ (③)
M: There is an umbrella stand outside. (④)
G: Okay. (⑤) Thank you.

06 위 대화의 ①~⑤ 중 주어진 문장이 들어갈 곳은?

| I'll put it there. |

①   ②   ③   ④   ⑤

07 위 대화의 빈칸에 들어갈 말로 알맞은 것을 고르시오.

① how was the concert?
② what should I bring?
③ where can I bring it?
④ do you mind if I bring it inside?
⑤ where should I put it?

[08~11] 다음 대화를 읽고 물음에 답하시오.

B: The tickets for the World Music Concert are on sale now. (①)
G: Really? Let's book the tickets online right away.
B: Okay. Let's see.... There are still tickets (a) left for November 5th. (②)
G: Sounds good. Let's get two student tickets.
B: Oh, do you mind ___(A)___ I bring my little brother?
G: Not at all. (③)
B: No problem. He's 10.
G: Okay, I'll add one child ticket. (④) The total price is 25 dollars.
B: Great. (⑤)
G: I can't wait to see the concert!

08 위 대화의 ①~⑤ 중 주어진 문장이 들어갈 곳은?

| But it says that you are not allowed to bring children under 8. |

①   ②   ③   ④   ⑤

09 빈칸 (A)에 알맞은 말을 고르시오.

① what   ② that   ③ if
④ how   ⑤ why

10 밑줄 친 (a)left와 다른 의미로 쓰인 것은?

① People left behind are unable to survive the low oxygen and will die.
② They still have six games left to play.
③ The experience left her scarred for life.
④ Are there any problems left?
⑤ He's got plenty of money left.

11 위 대화를 읽고 답할 수 없는 질문을 고르시오.

① Is it possible that the boy who is 10 years old enters the World Music Concert?
② When can they see the World Music Concert?
③ How many of them will go to the World Music Concert?
④ How much is the ticket for a student?
⑤ What tickets are they going to buy?

01 빈칸 (A)와 (B)에 공통으로 들어갈 말을 쓰시오.

> B: Hi, Lisa. Thank you ___(A)___ inviting me to your birthday party.
> G: My pleasure. I'm glad you could come.
> B: These flowers are ___(B)___ you. Happy birthday!
> G: They are beautiful! Thank you.

➡ _____

[02~03] 다음 대화를 읽고 물음에 답하시오.

> B: Sumin, my train (A)[left / is leaving / has left] in five minutes.
> G: I hope you enjoyed your trip, Daniel.
> B: (B)[Of course / Of course not], I did.
> G: Which place did you like most in my town?
> B: I liked the folk village most.
> G: Yeah, it's the most popular place here.
> B: I really liked walking around in hanbok. I looked really cool.
> G: I'm glad to hear that.
> B: 여기저기 구경시켜 줘서 고마워.
> G: It was my pleasure. Have a safe trip.

02 위 대화의 괄호 (A)와 (B)에서 적절한 것을 고르시오.

(A) _____ (B) _____

03 밑줄 친 우리말을 주어진 단어를 이용해 영작하시오.

> (for)

➡ _____

04 밑줄 친 (A)의 우리말을 대화에 나온 단어를 이용해 영작하시오.

> A: Excuse me. Can I ask you a question?
> B: Sure, what is it?
> A: (A)제가 미술작품 만져도 되나요?
> B: Sorry. You're not allowed to touch the artwork here.
> A: Okay, I see.
> B: Thank you for understanding.

➡ _____

05 빈칸 (A)를 괄호 안에 주어진 어휘를 알맞게 배열하여 문장을 완성하시오.

> A: How was your mom's birthday party?
> B: It was great. ___(A)___ (for, a, thank, helping, me, you, cake, make)
> A: You're welcome. It was my pleasure.

➡ _____

06 다음 괄호 안의 단어를 문맥에 맞게 고쳐 빈칸을 채우시오.

> M: Excuse me. You're not allowed _____(bring) your umbrella inside.
> G: Oh, where should I put it?
> M: There is an umbrella stand outside.
> G: Okay. I'll put it there. Thank you.

➡ _____

Grammar

1 so that

> • The architect took the curved lines from nature **so that** city people could enjoy them. 그 건축가는 도시 사람들이 즐길 수 있도록 자연에서 곡선을 가져왔다.

- 형태: '주절+so that+주어+can/could 또는 may/might+동사원형'
  의미: '~하기 위해서', '~하고자', '~하도록'

- so that이 이끄는 절은 '목적'이나 '의도'를 나타내며 일반적으로 so that이 이끄는 절의 동사는 주로 'can/could 또는 may/might'와 함께 쓰거나 현재 시제로 쓴다.
  - Bend the wire **so that** it forms a 'V'. 전선을 구부려 V자 모양을 만들어라.
  - I'll give you a key **so that** you can let yourself in. 네가 들어갈 수 있게 내가 열쇠를 줄게.

- 'so that ~ can/may …'는 'in order that ~ can/may …'로 바꿔 쓸 수 있으며, 주절과 종속절의 주어가 같은 경우 '(in order[so as]) to부정사'로 바꿔 쓸 수 있다.
  - I turned on the TV **so that** I could watch the news. 나는 뉴스를 보려고 TV를 켰다.
    = I turned on the TV **in order that** I could watch the news.
    = I turned on the TV **to watch** the news. (to부정사의 부사적 용법 – 목적)
    = I turned on the TV **in order[so as] to** watch the news.

- 'so (that)'은 '결과'의 부사절을 이끌어 '그래서, 그 결과'의 의미를 갖는 접속사로 쓰이기도 하는데, 대개 앞에 쉼표(,)가 온다.
  - I couldn't sleep well last night, **so that** I was late for school today.
    난 어젯밤에 잠을 잘 잘 수 없어서, 오늘 학교에 늦었다.

- so that을 기준으로 앞과 뒤의 동사의 시제를 일치시킨다.
  - He saved money **so that** he might buy a house. 그는 집을 사기 위하여 돈을 모았다.
  - He saves money **so that** he may buy a house. 그는 집을 사기 위하여 돈을 모은다.

핵심 Check

1. 다음 괄호 안에서 알맞은 것을 고르시오.
   (1) I moved my legs out of the way so (that / which) she could get past.
   (2) Can you work it (in that / so that) we get free tickets?

② enough to + 동사원형

> • It is round and delicate, yet strong **enough to protect** its contents.
> 그것은 둥글고 부서지기 쉽지만 내용물을 보호할 만큼 충분히 튼튼하다.

- 형태: 형용사/부사+enough to+동사원형
  의미: '~하기에 충분히 …한[하게]'

- '형용사/부사+enough to+동사원형'은 '~하기에 충분히 …한[하게]'이라는 의미로 어떤 일을 하기에 충분한 정도를 나타낼 때 쓴다.

  • She was lucky **enough to be** chosen for the team. 그녀는 아주 운 좋게도 그 팀에 선발되었다.

- to부정사의 의미상 주어가 문장의 주어와 다를 경우 to부정사 앞에 'for+목적격'을 쓴다.

  • This computer is small **enough** for me **to carry**. 이 컴퓨터는 내가 휴대할 수 있을 정도로 무척 작다.

- '형용사+enough to …(…할 정도로 충분히 ~한)'는 'so+형용사[부사]+that+주어+can …(매우 ~해서 …할 수 있는)'으로 바꿔 쓸 수 있다. 또한 'so+형용사[부사]+that+주어+can't …(너무 ~해서 …할 수 없는)'는 'too+형용사[부사]+to부정사(…하기에 너무 ~한)'로 바꿔 쓸 수 있다.

  • I was **so** foolish **that** I could believe what Jeff told me. 나는 어리석게도 Jeff가 내게 한 말을 믿었다.

  = I was foolish **enough to believe** what Jeff told me.

  • The pain was **so** great **that** I couldn't endure it. 그 통증은 너무 심해서 거의 참을 수가 없을 정도였다.

  = The pain was **too** great for me **to** endure.

핵심 Check

2. 다음 괄호 안에서 알맞은 것을 고르시오.

(1) She's (enough old / old enough) to decide for herself.

(2) I couldn't get close enough (seeing / to see) the bird.

(3) Is the book easy enough (for you / of you) to read?

01 다음 우리말에 맞게 빈칸에 알맞은 것은?

> Emily는 일찍 일어날 수 있도록 일찍 잠자리에 들었다.
> = Emily went to bed early so _____ she could get up early.

① if   ② when   ③ what
④ whether   ⑤ that

02 다음 괄호 안에서 알맞은 말을 고르시오.

(1) Eric is (enough smart / smart enough) to solve difficult math problems.

➡ _____

(2) My little brother is old (so / enough) to go to school.

➡ _____

(3) We collected old clothes (though / so that) we could donate them.

➡ _____

(4) I did my best, (because / so that) I could pass the test.

➡ _____

03 다음 빈칸에 들어갈 말로 알맞은 것은?

> The box is big _____ to carry 20 books.

① enough   ② so   ③ as
④ too   ⑤ very

04 다음 우리말에 맞게 주어진 어휘를 바르게 배열하시오.

(1) 신선한 상태가 유지되도록 우유를 냉장고 안에 넣어야 한다.

(you, it, a fridge, milk, that, should, stays, keep, fresh, so, in)

➡ _____

(2) 그 쥐는 그 구멍을 통과할 만큼 충분히 작다.

(the hole, the mouse, small, is, go, enough, through, to)

➡ _____

01 다음 중 어법상 <u>어색한</u> 것은?

① We grow some vegetables there so that we can have fresh food.
② He noted every detail so to fix the scene in his mind.
③ We had saved enough money to buy the house.
④ Come early in order that you may see him.
⑤ We stood up in order to get a better view.

02 다음 중 어법상 <u>어색한</u> 것은?

① She is not old enough to drive a car.
② Mike is clever enough to solve the problems.
③ I was enough foolish to spend the money I had saved.
④ The box is big enough to put a cake in.
⑤ Would you be kind enough to close the window?

03 다음 빈칸에 알맞은 말이 바르게 짝지어진 것은?

• He plays soccer _____ that he can relieve his stress.
• I couldn't get close enough _____ the sight.

① so – to see　　② for – to see
③ so – seeing　　④ for – seeing
⑤ in – see

04 주어진 두 문장을 한 문장으로 바꿀 때 옳지 <u>않은</u> 것은?

• I'll give you a key.
• You can let yourself in.

① I'll give you a key so that you can let yourself in.
② I'll give you a key in order that you can let yourself in.
③ I'll give you a key in order for you to let yourself in.
④ I'll give you a key so as for you to let yourself in.
⑤ I'll give you a key enough for you to let yourself in.

서답형

05 다음 괄호 안에서 알맞은 말을 고르시오.

(1) Ann saved money so (that / to) she could buy a new bicycle.
(2) We went early so (as / that) to get good seats.
(3) I worked hard in (order / condition) that I might succeed.
(4) The box is big (too / enough) to carry 20 books.
(5) The desk is (too / enough) small to put a computer.
(6) Be humble (so / enough) to learn from your mistakes.

06 다음 문장의 밑줄 친 부분 중 어법상 어색한 것은?

> That box ⓐisn't ⓑstrong ⓒso ⓓto sit ⓔ on.

① ⓐ   ② ⓑ   ③ ⓒ
④ ⓓ   ⑤ ⓔ

07 빈칸 (A)와 (B)에 알맞은 것으로 바르게 짝지어진 것은?

> • Come early ___(A)___ as to have plenty of time.
> • The rope is ___(B)___ long that it can reach the ground.

	(A)	(B)
①	so	too
②	so	so
③	too	so
④	too	too
⑤	enough	as

08 다음 밑줄 친 부분과 바꿔 쓸 수 있는 것은?

> I left home early <u>so that</u> I could catch the bus.

① for that   ② so as to   ③ to
④ in order   ⑤ in order that

09 다음 두 문장을 한 문장으로 바꿔 쓸 때 빈칸에 들어갈 한 단어를 쓰시오.

> • We're old.
> • We can look after ourselves.
> = We're old _____ to look after ourselves.

★ 중요
10 다음 우리말을 바르게 영작한 것을 고르시오.

> 그녀는 건강을 유지할 수 있도록 매일 수영을 한다.

① She swims every day in that she can stay healthy.
② She swims every day so that she can stay healthy.
③ She swims every day so what she can stay healthy.
④ She swims every day so as she can stay healthy.
⑤ She swims every day so as to she can stay healthy.

11 우리말과 의미가 같도록 빈칸에 들어갈 말로 알맞은 것을 고르시오.

> 불은 물을 빨리 끓일 수 있을 만큼 충분히 강했다.
> = The fire was _____ the water quickly.

① enough to boil strong
② strong to boil enough
③ enough strong to boil
④ strong enough to boil
⑤ to boil enough strong

12 다음 두 문장의 의미가 같도록 빈칸에 알맞은 말을 쓰시오.

(1) Harry saved money to buy the house.
  = Harry saved money so _____ he _____ buy the house.

(2) Because I laughed very hard, I had tears in my eyes.
  = I laughed _____ _____ _____ I had tears in my eyes.

13 다음 문장의 <u>틀린</u> 부분을 찾아 바르게 고친 것을 고르시오.

> She has become too weak that she can't even move her own body.

① She has become weak in that she can't even move her own body.
② She has become weak so to she can't even move her own body.
③ She has become so weak that can't even move her own body.
④ She has become so weak that she can't even move her own body.
⑤ She has become too weak to she can't even move her own body.

서답형

14 다음 문장에서 어법상 <u>어색한</u> 것을 바르게 고쳐 다시 쓰시오.

(1) We must improve the work environment in order for everyone can work efficiently.

➡ _____
_____
_____
_____

(2) Jihun saved money so as that he could donate it to the poor.

➡ _____
_____

(3) He is enough fast to cross the finish line first.

➡ _____

(4) I don't think she's smart enough for getting a job.

➡ _____

 15 다음 중 어법상 <u>어색한</u> 것을 <u>모두</u> 고르시오. (2개)

① He came in quietly so as not to wake the child.
② The drill is enough strong to bore through solid rock.
③ I blend tea so as that obtain a nice flavor.
④ Yumi drinks warm milk so that she can sleep well.
⑤ They wanted to be very diligent so that they could be successful.

16 다음 우리말을 바르게 영작한 것을 고르시오.

> 그 사다리는 선반 꼭대기에 닿을 만큼 길다.

① The ladder is too long to reach the top shelf.
② The ladder is long to reach the top shelf.
③ The ladder is so long to reach the top shelf.
④ The ladder is enough long to reach the top shelf.
⑤ The ladder is long enough to reach the top shelf.

17 다음 두 문장을 'so that'을 이용하여 한 문장으로 바꿔 쓰시오.

> • We deliver lunch to the elderly on Sundays.
> • They can feel happy.

➡ _____
_____

Grammar 서술형 시험대비

01 다음 문장을 'to부정사'를 이용하여 바꿔 쓰시오.

(1) He drinks plenty of water so that he can stay healthy.

　➡ _____

　_____

(2) Go early in order that you may get a good seat.

　➡ _____

(3) The story touched her so softly that it filled her with happiness.

　➡ _____

　_____

(4) Is it so late that I can't cancel my order?

　➡ _____

(5) This book is so difficult that I can't read it.

　➡ _____

02 'so that'을 이용하여 다음 두 문장을 한 문장으로 바꿔 쓰시오.

(1) • Yumi swims every morning.

　• She can stay healthy.

　➡ _____

　_____

(2) • We wore running shoes.

　• We could go jogging together.

　➡ _____

　_____

03 다음 우리말에 맞게 주어진 단어를 바르게 배열하시오.

(1) 그 소년은 선반의 맨 위에 닿을 만큼 충분히 키가 크지 않다. (the boy, enough, the top shelf, reach, is, tall, not, to)

　➡ _____

(2) 그의 연설은 그의 관점을 전달하기에 충분히 명확했다. (his speech, his point of view, enough, was, convey, clear, to)

　➡ _____

　_____

(3) 그녀는 너무 열심히 공부해서 종종 코피를 쏟았다. (she, she, hard, studied, had, so, often, that, nosebleeds)

　➡ _____

(4) 모든 자재가 준비되어서 우리는 즉각 일을 시작할 수 있었다. (we, the materials, all, could, work, so, were, start, ready, that, immediately, to)

　➡ _____

　_____

04 다음 문장에서 어법상 어색한 부분을 'to부정사'를 이용하여 바르게 고치시오.

(1) You walk so fast for me following.

　_____ ➡ _____

(2) He was so generous to he could forgive me.

　_____ ➡ _____

05 다음 그림을 보고, 주어진 어휘를 이용하여 빈칸을 알맞게 채우시오.

(1) Narae was _____ me make a cake for my mom's birthday party. (can, that, kind, help)

➡ _____

(2) Narae was _____ me make a cake for my mom's birthday party. (kind, help, to)

➡ _____

06 다음 그림을 보고, 괄호 안에 주어진 단어를 빈칸에 알맞게 채우시오.

(1) Hannah held her umbrella _____ in the rain. (get wet, to, not)

➡ _____

(2) Hannah held her umbrella _____ in the rain. (get wet, that, not, so, did, she)

➡ _____

(3) Hannah held her umbrella _____ in the rain. (get wet, to, not, so, as)

➡ _____

07 다음 우리말을 괄호 안의 지시대로 영작하시오.

(1) 그녀는 그 문제를 풀 수 있을만큼 충분히 영리하다.

➡ _____

(to부정사를 써서)

(2) John은 새 자전거를 사기 위해서 돈을 저축했다.

➡ _____

_____

(to부정사를 써서)

➡ _____

_____

(접속사를 써서)

(3) 그는 모든 사람들이 들을 수 있도록 큰 소리로 말했다.

➡ _____

_____

(접속사를 써서)

08 다음 문장에서 잘못된 것을 알맞게 고쳐 다시 쓰시오.

(1) Mina is smart enough that solve the math problem.

➡ _____

_____

(2) She learned French so as to she could help her husband with his work.

➡ _____

_____

_____

Reading

Nature Meets City

Have you heard of the expression, "Art imitates nature"? Many
Have you+과거분사 ~?: ~해 본 적이 있니?(경험)

artists get their ideas and inspirations from the world around them.

This is because the natural world is a beautiful place. The shapes in
This = Many artists ~ around them. This is because+이유: 이것은 ~이기 때문이다.

nature are very pleasing to the eye. For example, look at the egg on
사물이 주어 pleased: 사람이 주어

the left. Isn't it beautiful? It is round and delicate, yet strong enough to
달걀 형용사+enough to+동사원형: ~할 만큼 충분히 ···한

protect its contents. Can you imagine a building that looks like an egg?
주격 관계대명사

Such a building actually exists in London.

Nature has inspired many architects around the world. This is the
과거부터 현재까지 계속 영감을 주어 왔다는 의미를 나타내기 위한 현재완료 시제

Sagrada Familia in Spain. It is one of the most famous churches in
사그라다 파밀리아 성당 one of the+최상급+복수 명사: 가장 ~한 ··· 중의 하나

the world. Look at the beautiful tall columns inside the church. They
= the beautiful tall columns

look like trees, don't they? The famous architect, Antoni Gaudi, used
look like+명사: ~처럼 보이다 부가의문문으로 앞의 문장이 긍정문이면 부가의문문은 부정문으로 쓴다.

the shape of trees in the Sagrada Familia. That's how he brought the

beauty of nature indoors.

---

imitate 모방하다

inspiration 영감

pleasing 즐거운, 기분 좋은

delicate 부서지기 쉬운, 섬세한

contents (복수형으로) 내용물, 안에 든 것

actually 실제로, 정말로

exist 존재하다

architect 건축가, 설계자

column 기둥

indoors 실내로, 실내에

📎 확인문제

● 다음 문장이 본문의 내용과 일치하면 T, 일치하지 않으면 F를 쓰시오.

1 Many artists get their ideas and inspirations from the world around them. ☐

2 The egg is round and delicate, yet strong enough to protect its contents. ☐

3 Nature has discouraged many architects around the world. ☐

4 The Sagrada Familia in Spain is one of the most famous churches in the world. ☐

5 The famous architect, Antoni Gaudi, used the shape of other churches in the
Sagrada Familia. ☐

In the first two examples, we can easily see what inspired the architect. But in the next example from Australia, this is not so obvious. Jørn Utzon, the architect of the Sydney Opera House, took a shape from nature and added his imagination. Can you guess what inspired him? Many people think that it is the waves in the ocean or a sailing boat. But interestingly, the inspiration came from an orange. Look at the roof closely. Can you see the peels of an orange? When orange lights are shone on the building, you can see the peels more clearly.

What about Korea? Have you ever been to Dongdaemun Design Plaza in Seoul? Many people think that the building looks like a giant spaceship. But the architect, Zaha Hadid, took the curved lines from nature so that city people could enjoy them. Thanks to its special design, it has become a popular tourist attraction in Seoul.

As you can see, many buildings try to capture the beauty of nature in their design. They are perfect examples of "Nature meets city." If you were an architect, what would you choose from nature?

easily 쉽게
environmental 환경의
obvious 분명한, 명백한
add 더하다, 추가하다
imagination 상상력
wave 파도, 물결
spaceship 우주선
curved 곡선 모양의, 굽은
thanks to ~ 덕분에
tourist attraction 관광 명소
capture 담아내다, 표현하다, 포착하다

확인문제

● 다음 문장이 본문의 내용과 일치하면 T, 일치하지 <u>않으면</u> F를 쓰시오.

1 Jørn Utzon is the architect of the Sydney Opera House. ☐

2 Jørn Utzon took a shape from his imagination. ☐

3 What inspired Jørn Utzon was an orange. ☐

4 Many people think that Dongdaemun Design Plaza in Seoul looks like a giant balloon. ☐

5 Zaha Hadid took the curved lines from nature for city people to enjoy them. ☐

6 Many buildings try to capture the beauty of the cities in their design. ☐

● 우리말을 참고하여 빈칸에 알맞은 말을 쓰시오.

1 Nature _____ City

2 Have you heard of the expression, "_____ _____ _____"?

3 Many artists get their _____ and _____ from the world around them.

4 This is because _____ _____ _____ is a beautiful place.

5 The shapes in nature are very _____ _____ _____ _____.

6 _____ _____, look at the egg on the left.

7 _____ _____ beautiful?

8 It is round and delicate, yet _____ _____ _____ _____ its contents.

9 Can you imagine a building that _____ _____ _____ _____?

10 _____ _____ _____ actually exists in London.

11 Nature _____ _____ many architects around the world.

12 This is the Sagrada Familia _____ _____.

13 It is _____ _____ _____ _____ _____ _____ in the world.

14 Look at the _____ _____ inside the church.

15 They look like trees, _____ _____?

16 The famous architect, Antoni Gaudi, _____ _____ _____ _____ _____ in the Sagrada Familia.

17 That's how he _____ the beauty of nature _____.

1 자연이 도시를 만나다

2 "예술은 자연을 모방한다"라는 표현을 들어 본 적이 있는가?

3 많은 예술가들이 그들의 아이디어와 영감을 그들 주변의 세상에서 얻는다.

4 이것은 자연계가 아름다운 곳이기 때문이다.

5 자연의 형태는 눈에 보기에 매우 좋다.

6 예를 들면 왼쪽의 달걀을 봐라.

7 아름답지 않은가?

8 그것은 둥글고 부서지기 쉽지만 내용물을 보호할 만큼 충분히 튼튼하다.

9 달걀처럼 생긴 건물을 상상할 수 있는가?

10 이러한 형태의 건물이 런던에는 실제로 존재한다.

11 자연은 세계의 많은 건축가에게 영감을 주어 왔다.

12 이것은 스페인에 있는 사그라다 파밀리아 성당이다.

13 그것은 세계에서 가장 유명한 성당 중의 하나이다.

14 교회 안에 있는 아름다운 높은 기둥을 봐라.

15 기둥은 나무처럼 보인다. 그렇지 않은가?

16 유명한 건축가인 Antoni Gaudi는 사그라다 파밀리아 성당에 나무의 형태를 사용했다.

17 그것이 그가 자연의 아름다움을 실내로 가져온 방법이다.

18 In the first two examples, we can easily see _____ _____ the architect.

19 But in the next example from Australia, this is not _____ _____.

20 Jørn Utzon, the architect of the Sydney Opera House, took a shape from nature and _____ _____ _____.

21 Can you guess _____ _____ _____?

22 Many people think that it is _____ _____ _____ _____ _____ or _____ _____ _____.

23 But interestingly, the inspiration _____ _____ an orange.

24 Look at the roof _____.

25 Can you see _____ _____ of an orange?

26 When orange lights _____ _____ on the building, you can see the peels _____ _____.

27 _____ _____ Korea?

28 _____ you ever _____ _____ Dongdaemun Design Plaza in Seoul?

29 Many people think that the building _____ _____ a giant spaceship.

30 But the architect, Zaha Hadid, took _____ _____ _____ from nature _____ _____ city people could enjoy them.

31 _____ _____ its special design, it has become a popular _____ _____ in Seoul.

32 _____ you can see, many buildings try to _____ _____ _____ of nature in their design.

33 They are perfect examples of "_____ _____ _____."

34 If you _____ an architect, what _____ you _____ from nature?

18	앞의 두 예시에서 우리는 무엇이 건축가에게 영감을 주었는지 쉽게 알 수 있다.
19	하지만 호주의 다음 예시에서는 이것이 그다지 명확하지 않다.
20	시드니 오페라 하우스의 건축가인 Jørn Utzon은 자연에서 형태를 가져와 자신의 상상력을 더했다.
21	무엇이 그에게 영감을 주었는지 추측할 수 있는가?
22	많은 사람들은 그것이 바다의 파도나 돛단배라고 생각한다.
23	하지만 흥미롭게도, 그 영감은 오렌지에서 비롯되었다.
24	지붕을 자세히 봐라.
25	오렌지의 껍질 형태가 보이는가?
26	오렌지색 조명이 건물을 비추면, 껍질 이미지를 더 명확하게 볼 수 있다.
27	한국은 어떤가?
28	서울의 동대문 디자인 플라자에 가 본 적이 있는가?
29	많은 사람들은 이 건물이 거대한 우주선처럼 보인다고 생각한다.
30	하지만 건축가인 Zaha Hadid는 도시 사람들이 즐길 수 있도록 자연에서 곡선을 가져왔다.
31	이 특별한 디자인 덕분에, 동대문 디자인 플라자는 서울의 인기 있는 관광 명소가 되었다.
32	보는 바와 같이 많은 건물들이 디자인에 자연의 아름다움을 담아내려고 한다.
33	이 건물들은 '자연이 도시를 만나다'의 완벽한 예이다.
34	만약 당신이 건축가라면, 자연에서 무엇을 선택할 것인가?

• 우리말을 참고하여 본문을 영작하시오.

1 자연이 도시를 만나다
➡ _____

2 "예술은 자연을 모방한다"라는 표현을 들어 본 적이 있는가?
➡ _____

3 많은 예술가들이 그들의 아이디어와 영감을 그들 주변의 세상에서 얻는다.
➡ _____

4 이것은 자연계가 아름다운 곳이기 때문이다.
➡ _____

5 자연의 형태는 눈에 보기에 매우 좋다.
➡ _____

6 예를 들면 왼쪽의 달걀을 봐라.
➡ _____

7 아름답지 않은가?
➡ _____

8 그것은 둥글고 부서지기 쉽지만 내용물을 보호할 만큼 충분히 튼튼하다.
➡ _____

9 달걀처럼 생긴 건물을 상상할 수 있는가?
➡ _____

10 이러한 형태의 건물이 런던에는 실제로 존재한다.
➡ _____

11 자연은 세계의 많은 건축가에게 영감을 주어 왔다.
➡ _____

12 이것은 스페인에 있는 사그라다 파밀리아 성당이다.
➡ _____

13 그것은 세계에서 가장 유명한 성당 중의 하나이다.
➡ _____

14 교회 안에 있는 아름다운 높은 기둥을 봐라.
➡ _____

15 기둥은 나무처럼 보인다, 그렇지 않은가?
➡ _____

16 유명한 건축가인 Antoni Gaudi는 사그라다 파밀리아 성당에 나무의 형태를 사용했다.
➡ _____

17 그것이 그가 자연의 아름다움을 실내로 가져온 방법이다.
➡ _____

18 앞의 두 예시에서 우리는 무엇이 건축가에게 영감을 주었는지 쉽게 알 수 있다.
➡ _____

19 하지만 호주의 다음 예시에서는 이것이 그다지 명확하지 않다.
➡ _____

20 시드니 오페라 하우스의 건축가인 Jørn Utzon은 자연에서 형태를 가져와 자신의 상상력을 더했다.
➡ _____
_____

21 무엇이 그에게 영감을 주었는지 추측할 수 있는가?
➡ _____

22 많은 사람들은 그것이 바다의 파도나 돛단배라고 생각한다.
➡ _____

23 하지만 흥미롭게도, 그 영감은 오렌지에서 비롯되었다.
➡ _____

24 지붕을 자세히 봐라.
➡ _____

25 오렌지의 껍질 형태가 보이는가?
➡ _____

26 오렌지색 조명이 건물을 비추면, 껍질 이미지를 더 명확하게 볼 수 있다.
➡ _____

27 한국은 어떤가?
➡ _____

28 서울의 동대문 디자인 플라자에 가 본 적이 있는가?
➡ _____

29 많은 사람들은 이 건물이 거대한 우주선처럼 보인다고 생각한다.
➡ _____

30 하지만 건축가인 Zaha Hadid는 도시 사람들이 즐길 수 있도록 자연에서 곡선을 가져왔다.
➡ _____
_____

31 이 특별한 디자인 덕분에, 동대문 디자인 플라자는 서울의 인기 있는 관광 명소가 되었다.
➡ _____

32 보는 바와 같이 많은 건물들이 디자인에 자연의 아름다움을 담아내려고 한다.
➡ _____

33 이 건물들은 '자연이 도시를 만나다'의 완벽한 예이다.
➡ _____

34 만약 당신이 건축가라면, 자연에서 무엇을 선택할 것인가?
➡ _____

[01~03] 다음 글을 읽고 물음에 답하시오.

Have you heard of the expression, "Art imitates nature"? Many artists get their ideas and inspirations from the world around them. (A)This is because the natural world is a beautiful place. The shapes in nature are very pleasing to the eye. ___ⓐ___, look at the egg on the left. Isn't it beautiful? It is round and delicate, yet strong enough to protect its contents. Can you imagine a building that looks like an egg? Such a building actually exists in London.

01 위 글의 빈칸 ⓐ에 들어갈 알맞은 말을 고르시오.

① However ② Therefore
③ That is ④ For example
⑤ In addition

서답형

02 위 글의 밑줄 친 (A)This가 가리키는 것을 본문에서 찾아 쓰시오.

➡ _____

_____

According to the passage, which is NOT true?

① Many artists' ideas and inspirations come from the world around them.
② The shapes in nature give pleasure and satisfaction to the eye.
③ The shape of an egg isn't beautiful.
④ Though the egg is round and delicate, it's strong enough to protect its contents.
⑤ A building that looks like an egg actually exists in London.

[04~06] 다음 글을 읽고 물음에 답하시오.

ⓐWhat about Korea? Have you ever been to Dongdaemun Design Plaza in Seoul? Many people think that the building looks like a giant spaceship. But the architect, Zaha Hadid, took the curved lines from nature so that city people could enjoy them. Thanks to its special design, it has become a popular tourist attraction in Seoul.

ⓑAs you can see, many buildings try to capture the beauty of nature in their design. They are perfect examples of "Nature meets city." If you were an architect, what would you choose from nature?

서답형

04 위 글의 밑줄 친 ⓐWhat about Korea?와 바꿔 쓸 수 있는 말을 쓰시오. (3 words)

➡ _____

05 위 글의 밑줄 친 ⓑAs와 같은 의미로 쓰인 것을 고르시오.

① She sang as she walked.
② Try as he might, he couldn't open the door.
③ As you are leaving last, lock the door.
④ As you know, Tom is very honest.
⑤ Her anger grew as she talked.

서답형

06 다음 문장에서 위 글의 내용과 다른 부분을 찾아서 고치시오.

The architect of Dongdaemun Design Plaza took the curved lines from nature so that people living in the country could enjoy them.

➡ _____

_____

[07~10] 다음 글을 읽고 물음에 답하시오.

Nature has inspired many architects around the world. This is the Sagrada Familia in Spain. ⓐ그것은 세계에서 가장 유명한 성당 중의 하나이다. Look at the beautiful tall columns inside the church. They look like trees, don't they? The famous architect, Antoni Gaudi, used the shape of trees in the Sagrada Familia. ⓑThat's how he brought the beauty of nature outdoors.

서답형

07 위 글의 밑줄 친 ⓐ의 우리말에 맞게 주어진 어휘를 이용하여 11 단어로 영작하시오.

> It, one, churches

➡ _____

_____

서답형

08 위 글의 밑줄 친 ⓑ에서 흐름상 어색한 부분을 찾아 고치시오.

_____ ➡ _____

서답형

09 By what have many architects around the world been inspired? Fill in the blank with a suitable word.

> Many architects around the world have been inspired by _____ .

서답형

10 본문의 내용과 일치하도록 다음 빈칸 (A)와 (B)에 알맞은 단어를 쓰시오.

> The beautiful tall (A)_____ inside the Sagrada Familia look like trees because Antoni Gaudi used (B)_____ _____ _____ _____ in the church.

[11~13] 다음 글을 읽고 물음에 답하시오.

Have you heard of the expression, "Art imitates nature"? (①) Many artists get their ideas and inspirations from the world around them. (②) The shapes in nature are very pleasing to the eye. (③) For example, look at the egg on the left. (④) Isn't it beautiful? (⑤) It is round and delicate, yet strong enough ⓐto protect its contents. Can you imagine a building that looks like an egg? Such a building actually exists in London.

11 위 글의 흐름으로 보아, 주어진 문장이 들어가기에 가장 적절한 곳은?

> This is because the natural world is a beautiful place.

① ② ③ ④ ⑤

12 위 글의 밑줄 친 ⓐto protect와 to부정사의 용법이 같은 것을 모두 고르시오.

① I got up early to get ready for the game.
② I don't know what to do for him.
③ Do you have something interesting to read?
④ I'm too nervous to sleep.
⑤ It is very good to see you again.

13 위 글의 주제로 알맞은 것을 고르시오.

① Various objects inspire artists.
② There are many ways the artists get their ideas.
③ Art imitates nature.
④ The natural world is a beautiful place to live in.
⑤ Nature copies art.

[14~16] 다음 글을 읽고 물음에 답하시오.

What about Korea? Have you ever been to Dongdaemun Design Plaza in Seoul? Many people think that the building looks like a giant spaceship. But the architect, Zaha Hadid, took the curved lines from nature so that city people could enjoy ⓐthem. Thanks to its special design, it has become a popular tourist attraction in Seoul.

As you can see, many buildings try to capture the beauty of nature in their design. They are perfect examples of "Nature meets city." If you were an architect, what would you choose from nature?

서답형

14 위 글의 밑줄 친 ⓐthem이 가리키는 것을 본문에서 찾아 쓰시오.

➡ _____

서답형

15 다음 빈칸 (A)~(D)에 알맞은 단어를 넣어 서울의 동대문 디자인 플라자를 소개하는 글을 완성하시오.

Location: (A)_____
• Architect: (B)_____ _____
• The architect took the curved lines
  (C)_____ _____.
• It is a (D)_____ _____ _____ in Seoul.

중요

16 Which question CANNOT be answered after reading the passage?

① What do many people think Dongdaemun Design Plaza in Seoul looks like?
② Who is the architect of Dongdaemun Design Plaza in Seoul?
③ Where did the architect of Dongdaemun Design Plaza in Seoul take the curved lines?
④ When did Dongdaemun Design Plaza become a popular tourist attraction in Seoul?
⑤ What do many buildings try to capture in their design?

[17~19] 다음 글을 읽고 물음에 답하시오.

ⓐ앞의 두 예시에서, we can easily see what inspired the architect. But in the next example from Australia, this is not so obvious. Jørn Utzon, the architect of the Sydney Opera House, took a shape from nature and added his imagination. Can you guess what inspired him? Many people think that it is the waves in the ocean or a sailing boat. But interestingly, the inspiration came from an orange. Look at the roof ⓑclosely. Can you see the peels of an orange? When orange lights are shone on the building, you can see the peels more clearly.

서답형

17 위 글의 밑줄 친 ⓐ의 우리말에 맞게 5 단어로 영작하시오.

➡ _____

18 위 글의 밑줄 친 ⓑclosely와 바꿔 쓸 수 없는 말을 고르시오.

① carefully   ② precisely
③ roughly   ④ thoroughly
⑤ in detail

서답형

19 본문의 내용과 일치하도록 다음 빈칸 (A)와 (B)에 알맞은 단어를 쓰시오.

> Jørn Utzon, the architect of the Sydney Opera House, took a shape from nature and added (A)_____ _____ and what inspired him was (B)_____ _____.

[20~22] 다음 글을 읽고 물음에 답하시오.

> Nature has inspired many architects around the world. This is the Sagrada Familia in Spain. It is one of the most famous churches in the world. Look at the beautiful tall columns inside the church. (A)They look like trees, don't they? The famous architect, Antoni Gaudi, used the shape of trees in the Sagrada Familia. That's ____ⓐ____ he brought the beauty of nature indoors.

20 위 글의 빈칸 ⓐ에 들어갈 수 없는 말을 고르시오.

① the way
② the way how
③ how
④ the way that
⑤ the way in which

서답형

21 위 글의 밑줄 친 (A)They가 가리키는 것을 본문에서 찾아 쓰시오.

➡ _____

22 위 글을 읽고 사그라다 파밀리아 성당에 대해 알 수 없는 것을 고르시오.

① Where is it?
② Who is the architect?
③ What do its beautiful tall columns look like?
④ When was it built?
⑤ What shape did the architect use in the Sagrada Familia?

[23~25] 다음 글을 읽고 물음에 답하시오.

> In the first two examples, we can easily see what inspired the architect. But in the next example from Australia, this is not so obvious. Jørn Utzon, the architect of the Sydney Opera House, took a shape from nature and added his imagination. Can you guess what inspired him? Many people think that it is the waves in the ocean or a sailing boat. But interestingly, the inspiration came ____ⓐ____ an orange. Look at the roof closely. Can you see the peels of an orange? When orange lights are shone ____ⓑ____ the building, you can see the peels more clearly.

23 위 글의 빈칸 ⓐ와 ⓑ에 들어갈 전치사가 바르게 짝지어진 것은?

	ⓐ	ⓑ		ⓐ	ⓑ
①	in	on	②	from	by
③	in	from	④	for	from
⑤	from	on			

24 위 글의 앞에 올 내용으로 가장 알맞은 것을 고르시오.

① the way we can easily see what inspired the architect
② two examples which obviously show what inspired the architect
③ the thing which inspired Jørn Utzon
④ how to get inspiration from the waves in the ocean or a sailing boat
⑤ Jørn Utzon's creative imagination

서답형

25 How can you see the peels of an orange more clearly when you look at the roof of the Sydney Opera House? Fill in the blanks with suitable words.

> You can see its peels more clearly when _____ _____ _____ _____ on the building.

[01~03] 다음 글을 읽고 물음에 답하시오.

Have you heard of the expression, "Art imitates nature"? Many artists get their ideas and inspirations from the world around them. This is because the natural world is a beautiful place. The shapes in nature are very pleasing to the eye. For example, look at the egg on the left. Isn't it beautiful? ⓐIt is round and delicate, yet enough strong to protect its contents. Can you imagine a building that looks like an egg? ⓑSuch a building actually exists in London.

01 위 글의 밑줄 친 ⓐ에서 어법상 틀린 것을 찾아 고치시오.

_____ ➡ _____

02 위 글의 밑줄 친 ⓑSuch a building이 가리키는 것을 본문에서 찾아 쓰시오.

➡ _____

03 본문의 내용과 일치하도록 다음 빈칸 (A)와 (B)에 알맞은 단어를 쓰시오.

The natural world is a (A)_____ place, so it gives (B)_____ _____ the ideas and inspirations.

[04~06] 다음 글을 읽고 물음에 답하시오.

Nature has inspired many architects around the world. This is the Sagrada Familia in Spain. It is one of the most famous churches in the world. Look at the beautiful tall

_____ⓐ_____ inside the church. They look like trees, _____ⓑ_____? The famous architect, Antoni Gaudi, used the shape of trees in the Sagrada Familia. That's how he brought the beauty of nature indoors.

04 주어진 영영풀이를 참고하여 빈칸 ⓐ에 철자 c로 시작하는 단어를 쓰시오.

(architecture) tall vertical cylindrical structures standing upright and used to support a structure

➡ _____

05 위 글의 빈칸 ⓑ에 들어갈 알맞은 부가의문문을 쓰시오.

➡ _____

06 How did Antoni Gaudi bring the beauty of nature indoors? Fill in the blanks (A) and (B) with suitable words.

He brought the beauty of nature indoors by (A)_____ _____ _____ _____ _____ and then making the beautiful tall columns inside the Sagrada Familia (B)_____ _____ _____.

[07~10] 다음 글을 읽고 물음에 답하시오.

In the first two examples, we can easily see what inspired the architect. (A)But in the next example from Australia, this is not so vague. Jørn Utzon, the architect of the

Sydney Opera House, took a shape from nature and added his imagination. Can you guess what inspired him? Many people think that it is the waves in the ocean or a sailing boat. But interestingly, the ⓐ＿＿＿ came from an orange. Look at the roof closely. Can you see the peels of an orange? When orange lights are shone on the building, you can see the peels more clearly.

07 본문의 한 단어를 변형하여 위 글의 빈칸 ⓐ에 알맞은 형태로 쓰시오.

➡ ＿＿＿＿＿＿＿＿＿＿＿＿

08 위 글의 밑줄 친 (A)에서 흐름상 어색한 부분을 찾아 고치시오.

＿＿＿＿＿＿ ➡ ＿＿＿＿＿＿

09 위 글을 읽고, Jøm Utzon가 시드니 오페라 하우스를 건축할 때 그에게 영감을 준 것이라고 사람들이 생각하는 것을 우리말로 쓰시오.

➡ ＿＿＿＿＿＿＿＿＿＿＿＿

10 다음 빈칸 (A)~(C)에 알맞은 단어를 넣어 시드니 오페라 하우스를 소개하는 글을 완성하시오.

Location: (A)＿＿＿＿＿
• Architect: (B)＿＿＿＿ ＿＿＿＿
• The architect was inspired by (C)＿＿＿＿
＿＿＿＿.

[11~14] 다음 글을 읽고 물음에 답하시오.

What about Korea? Have you ever (A)[been / gone] to Dongdaemun Design Plaza in Seoul? Many people think that the building (B)[looks / looks like] a giant spaceship. But

the architect, Zaha Hadid, took the curved lines from nature so that city people could enjoy them. ⓐ이 특별한 디자인 덕분에, 동대문 디자인 플라자는 서울의 인기 있는 관광 명소가 되었다.

As you can see, many buildings try to (C) [capture / release] the beauty of nature in their design. They are perfect examples of "Nature meets city." ⓑIf you were an architect, what will you choose from nature?

11 위 글의 괄호 (A)~(C)에서 문맥이나 어법상 알맞은 낱말을 골라 쓰시오.

(A) ＿＿＿＿ (B) ＿＿＿＿ (C) ＿＿＿＿

12 위 글의 밑줄 친 ⓐ의 우리말에 맞게 주어진 어휘를 알맞게 배열하시오.

it / in Seoul / thanks to / a popular tourist attraction / has become / its special design / ,

➡ ＿＿＿＿＿＿＿＿＿＿＿＿

＿＿＿＿＿＿＿＿＿＿＿＿

13 위 글의 밑줄 친 ⓑ에서 어법상 틀린 부분을 찾아 고치시오.

＿＿＿＿＿＿ ➡ ＿＿＿＿＿＿

14 본문의 내용과 일치하도록 다음 빈칸 (A)와 (B)에 알맞은 단어를 쓰시오.

Many buildings which try to catch (A)＿＿＿＿ ＿＿＿＿ ＿＿＿＿ ＿＿＿＿
in their design are perfect examples of "(B)＿＿＿＿ ＿＿＿＿ ＿＿＿＿."

구석구석

After You Read

The Sagrada Familia

• Location: Spain   • Architect: Antoni Gaudi

• Its beautiful tall columns <u>look like</u> trees.
    look like+명사: ~처럼 보이다
• The architect <u>brought</u> the beauty of nature indoors.
    bring–brought–brought
The Sydney Opera House

• Location: Australia   • Architect: Jørn Utzon

• The architect <u>was inspired by</u> an orange.
    be inspired by: ~에서 영감을 얻다
Dongdaemun Design Plaza

• Location: Korea   • Architect: Zaha Hadid

• The architect <u>took</u> the curved lines from nature.
    take A from B: B로부터 A를 가져오다
• It is a popular tourist attraction in Seoul.

구문해설 • architect: 건축가, 설계자 • indoors: 실내로, 실내에 • be inspired by: ~에서 영감을 얻다
• curved: 곡선 모양의, 굽은 • tourist attraction: 관광 명소

해석 (오른쪽)

사그라다 파밀리아 성당
• 위치: 스페인
• 건축가: Antoni Gaudi
• 그것의 아름다운 높은 기둥은 나무처럼 보인다.
• 그 건축가는 자연의 아름다움을 실내로 가져왔다.

시드니 오페라 하우스
• 위치: 호주
• 건축가: Jørn Utzon
• 그 건축가는 '오렌지'에서 영감을 얻었다.

동대문 디자인 플라자
• 위치: 한국
• 건축가: Zaha Hadid
• 그 건축가는 자연에서 곡선을 가져왔다.
• 그곳은 서울의 인기 있는 관광 명소이다.

Word Power

• The store has many interesting items, so it <u>attracts</u> many people.

• Namsan is a popular tourist <u>attraction</u> in Seoul.

• I can't <u>imagine</u> a world without water.

• She used her <u>imagination</u> to write the story.
    to 부정사의 부사적 용법 중 목적으로 '~하기 위해서'의 의미로 사용했다.

접미사는 독립된 단어 뒤에 붙어서
그 단어의 의미와 품사를 변형시킨다.
'-ion'과 '-ation'은 명사형 접미
사로 특정 동사 뒤에 붙으면 그 단
어는 명사로 의미와 품사가 바뀐다.

구문해설 • attract: 끌다 • attraction: 매력 • imagine: 상상하다 • imagination: 상상

해석 (오른쪽)

• 그 가게는 재미있는 물품이 많아서, 많은 사람들을 끈다.
• 남산은 서울의 인기 있는 관광 명소이다.
• 나는 물이 없는 세상은 상상할 수 없다.
• 그녀는 그 이야기를 쓰기 위해 상상력을 발휘했다.

Think and Write

I go to Boram Middle School in Suwon. <u>My school has a 4-story building.</u> It
        = There is a 4-story building in my school.
also has a large playground, a gym and a small garden. The garden is on top of

the school building. We grow some vegetables there <u>so that we can</u> have fresh
                              주절+so that+주어+can: ~하기 위해서, ~하도록
food. My favorite place is the bench under the big tree. I love <u>sitting</u> there and
                                        동명사 목적어 1
<u>talking</u> with my friends. I like my school very much.
동명사 목적어 2

구문해설 • story: 층 • on top of: ~ 위에

해석 (오른쪽)

나는 수원에 있는 보람 중학교에 다닌다. 우리 학교는 4층짜리 건물을 가지고 있다. 우리 학교에는 또한 넓은 운동장, 체육관, 작은 정원이 있다. 정원은 학교 건물 옥상에 있다. 우리는 신선한 음식을 먹을 수 있도록 그곳에 채소를 기른다. 내가 가장 좋아하는 장소는 커다란 나무 아래에 있는 벤치이다. 나는 그곳에 앉아서 친구들과 이야기하는 것을 아주 좋아한다. 나는 우리 학교를 아주 좋아한다.

Words & Expressions

01 다음 짝지어진 단어의 관계가 〈보기〉와 <u>다른</u> 것은?

┤ 보기 ├
arrive – arrival

① inspire – inspiration
② attract – attraction
③ refuse – refusal
④ nature – natural
⑤ imitate – imitation

02 다음 영영풀이가 나타내는 말을 고르시오.

a raised line of water that moves across the surface of the sea

① wave   ② frame   ③ storm
④ shore   ⑤ border

03 다음 밑줄 친 부분과 바꿔 쓸 수 있는 말을 고르시오.

The detective watched him <u>very carefully</u>, waiting for a reply.

① highly   ② relatively   ③ closely
④ lately   ⑤ shortly

04 다음 빈칸에 알맞은 단어를 고르시오.

Stephen King's new novel will go _____ sale next week.

① on   ② in   ③ by
④ with   ⑤ up

Conversation

[05~06] 다음 대화를 읽고 물음에 답하시오.

B: The tickets for the World Music Concert are on sale now.
G: Really? Let's ⓐ<u>booking</u> the tickets online right away.
B: Okay. Let's see.... There are still tickets ⓑ<u>leaving</u> for November 5th.
G: Sounds good. Let's get two student tickets.
B: Oh, 내 남동생을 데려가도 될까?
G: Not at all. But it says ⓒ<u>if</u> you are not allowed ⓓ<u>bringing</u> children under 8.
B: No problem. He's 10.
G: Okay, I'll add one child ticket. The total price is 25 dollars.
B: Great.
G: I can't wait ⓔ<u>to see</u> the concert!

05 ⓐ~ⓔ 중 흐름상 또는 어법상 올바른 것을 고르시오.

① ⓐ   ② ⓑ   ③ ⓒ   ④ ⓓ   ⑤ ⓔ

06 밑줄 친 우리말과 일치하도록 주어진 단어를 사용해 영작하시오.

(if, bring)

➡ _____

[07~10] 다음 글을 읽고 물음에 답하시오.

W: Hello, students! Thank you __(A)__ visiting our art museum. (①) Since then, it has exhibited many famous artworks. Today, you will see some famous artworks from the art books. (②) Before we begin the tour, let me remind you __(B)__ a basic rule. (③) You can take pictures of the artworks, but you're not allowed to touch them. (④) Now let's start the tour. (⑤)

07 위 글의 ①~⑤ 중 주어진 문장이 들어갈 곳은?

> This museum opened in 1995.

①   ②   ③   ④   ⑤

08 위 글의 빈칸 (A)에 알맞은 전치사를 쓰시오.

➡ _____

09 위 글의 빈칸 (B)에 알맞은 말을 고르시오.

① for   ② to   ③ in
④ from   ⑤ of

10 위 글을 읽고 답할 수 <u>없는</u> 질문을 고르시오.

① How many artworks are exhibited in this art museum?
② Where are the students?
③ Can the students take pictures of the artworks?
④ What are the students going to see in the art museum?
⑤ When did this art museum open?

[11~12] 다음 대화를 읽고 물음에 답하시오.

A: Excuse me. Can I ask you a question?
B: _____
A: _____
B: _____
A: _____
B: 이해해 주셔서 감사합니다.

11 위 대화의 빈칸에 들어갈 말을 <보기>에서 골라 순서대로 옳게 배열한 것은?

(A) Sorry. You're not allowed to drink soda here.
(B) Sure, what is it?
(C) Am I allowed to drink soda?
(D) Okay, I see.

① (B) – (A) – (C) – (D)
② (B) – (C) – (A) – (D)
③ (C) – (A) – (B) – (D)
④ (C) – (B) – (A) – (D)
⑤ (C) – (D) – (B) – (A)

12 밑줄 친 우리말과 일치하도록 영작하시오. (4 단어)

➡ _____

Grammar

13 다음 문장을 바꾸어 쓸 때 가장 적절한 것은?

> This car is too small to carry four people.

① This car is so small that it can carry four people.
② This car is so small that it can't carry four people.
③ This car is small enough to carry four people.
④ This car is enough small to carry four people.
⑤ This car is very small so it can carry four people.

14 다음 밑줄 친 부분과 바꿔 쓸 수 있는 것은?

> Yuna takes baking classes <u>so that</u> she can bake a cake.

① in order that   ② in order to
③ such that   ④ so as to
⑤ so which

15 다음 문장 중에서 어법상 어색한 것을 고르시오.

① She chose the window seat so that she could see the nice view.
② I turned off the radio so that I could concentrate on studying math.
③ Speak clearly so that we may understand you.
④ You've studied so hard that I am sure you won't fail the exam again.
⑤ I went to Seoul Station in the heavy rain so as that I could meet my mother.

16 다음 두 문장을 괄호 안의 단어를 이용하여 한 문장으로 만드시오.

(1) • Sumi is brave.
     • She can go into the Ghost House. (enough)
     ➡ _____

(2) • The dog is very big.
     • He can't get through the small window. (too)
     ➡ _____

(3) • Tom went to bed early.
     • Tom wanted to get up early. (so that)
     ➡ _____
     _____

(4) • Minsu turned on the radio.
     • He could listen to the baseball game. (so as)
     ➡ _____
     _____

(5) • The training must be planned systematically.
     • It should be effective. (order that)
     ➡ _____
     _____

[17~19] 다음 주어진 우리말을 바르게 영작한 것은?

17
> 나는 잊지 않도록 그의 이름을 내 일기장에 썼다.

① I wrote his name in my diary so as to I wouldn't forget it.
② I wrote his name in my diary so what I wouldn't forget it.
③ I wrote his name in my diary so that I wouldn't forget it.
④ I wouldn't forget it so that I wrote his name in my diary.
⑤ I wouldn't forget it so as that I wrote his name in my diary.

18 나는 열심히 공부했기 때문에 시험에 통과할 수 있었다.

① I studied hard that I could pass the test.
② I studied hard, so that I could pass the test.
③ I studied so hard what I could pass the test.
④ I could study hard so that I passed the test.
⑤ I passed the test so as to study hard.

19 그 상자는 20권의 책을 담을 만큼 충분히 크다.

① The box is so big can't carry 20 books.
② The box is big so that to carry 20 books.
③ The box is so big to carry 20 books.
④ The box is big enough to carry 20 books.
⑤ The box is too big to carry 20 books.

Reading

[20~22] 다음 글을 읽고 물음에 답하시오.

ⓐHave you heard of the expression, "Art imitates nature"? Many artists get their ideas and inspirations from the world around them. This is (A)[because / because of] the natural world is a beautiful place. The shapes in nature are very (B)[pleasing / pleased] to the eye. For example, look at the egg on the left. Isn't it beautiful? It is round and delicate, yet (C)[strong enough / too strong] to protect its contents. Can you imagine a building that looks like an egg? Such a building actually exists in London.

20 아래 〈보기〉에서 위 글의 밑줄 친 문장 ⓐ에 쓰인 현재완료와 용법이 같은 것의 개수를 고르시오.

┤ 보기 ├
① I have known him for 20 years.
② She has never heard such a moving speech.
③ He has already written a letter.
④ How long have you been in Korea?
⑤ I have met him before.

① 1개 ② 2개 ③ 3개 ④ 4개 ⑤ 5개

21 위 글의 괄호 (A)~(C)에서 문맥이나 어법상 알맞은 낱말을 골라 쓰시오.

(A) _____ (B) _____
(C) _____

22 According to the text, what gives many artists the ideas and inspirations? Answer in English. (4 words)

➡ _____

[23~25] 다음 글을 읽고 물음에 답하시오.

In the first two examples, we can easily see what inspired the architect. But in the next example from Australia, this is not so obvious. Jørn Utzon, the architect of the Sydney Opera House, took a shape from nature and added his imagination. Can you guess what inspired him? Many people think that ⓐit is the waves in the ocean or a sailing boat. But interestingly, the inspiration came from an orange. ⓑLook at the roof close. Can you see the peels of an orange? When orange lights are shone on the building, you can see the peels more clearly.

23 위 글의 밑줄 친 ⓐit이 가리키는 것을 본문에서 찾아 쓰시오.

➡ _____

24 위 글의 밑줄 친 ⓑ에서 어법상 틀린 부분을 찾아 고치시오.

_____ ➡ _____

25 According to the passage, which is NOT true?

① It is not so obvious what inspired Jørn Utzon.
② Jørn Utzon was the architect of the Sydney Opera House.
③ Jørn Utzon took a shape from nature and added his imagination.
④ What actually inspired Jørn Utzon was the waves in the ocean or a sailing boat.
⑤ It's possible to see the peels of an orange more clearly when orange lights are shone on the building.

[26~27] 다음 글을 읽고 물음에 답하시오.

What about Korea? Have you ever been to Dongdaemun Design Plaza in Seoul? Many people think that the building looks like a giant spaceship. (①) But the architect, Zaha Hadid, took the curved lines from nature so that city people could enjoy them. (②) Thanks to its special design, it has become a popular tourist attraction in Seoul. (③)

As you can see, many buildings try to capture the beauty of nature in their design. (④) If you were an architect, what would you choose from nature? (⑤)

26 위 글의 흐름으로 보아, 주어진 문장이 들어가기에 가장 적절한 곳은?

> They are perfect examples of "Nature meets city."

①   ②   ③   ④   ⑤

27 위 글의 제목으로 알맞은 것을 고르시오.

① Visit Dongdaemun Design Plaza, a Popular Tourist Attraction in Seoul
② Many Buildings Trying to Capture the Beauty of Nature in Their Design
③ Zaha Hadid, the Architect of Dongdaemun Design Plaza
④ The Reason City People Enjoy the Curved Lines from Nature
⑤ Various Ways That Nature Meets City

[28~29] 다음 글을 읽고 물음에 답하시오.

I go to Boram Middle School in Suwon. My school has ⓐ4층짜리 건물. It also has a large playground, a gym and a small garden. The garden is on top of the school building. We grow some vegetables there so that we can have fresh food. My favorite place is the bench under the big tree. I love sitting there and talking with my friends. I like my school very much.

28 위 글의 밑줄 친 ⓐ의 우리말에 맞게 3 단어로 영작하시오.

➡ _____

29 Which question CANNOT be answered after reading the passage?

① Where is Boram Middle School?
② Where is the garden of Boram Middle School?
③ What vegetables do they grow in the garden of Boram Middle School?
④ Why do they grow some vegetables in the garden of Boram Middle School?
⑤ What does the writer love to do on the bench under the big tree?

출제율 95%

01 다음 짝지어진 단어의 관계가 〈보기〉와 같은 것끼리 짝지어진 것을 고르시오.

┌─ 보기 ┤
indoors – outdoors

ⓐ lend – borrow
ⓑ delicate – fragile
ⓒ actually – indeed
ⓓ allow – permit
ⓔ natural – artificial

① ⓐ, ⓑ   ② ⓑ, ⓒ   ③ ⓒ, ⓓ
④ ⓓ, ⓔ   ⑤ ⓐ, ⓔ

출제율 90%

02 다음 영영풀이에 해당하는 말을 문장의 빈칸에 주어진 철자로 시작하여 쓰시오.

the things that are inside something
➡ The textbook covers basic c_____.

출제율 95%

03 빈칸 (A)와 (B)에 들어갈 말이 바르게 짝지어진 것을 고르시오.

• Visitors can touch the figures and ____(A)____ pictures of them.
• We need to start doing something right ____(B)____, before we lose any more of our market share.

(A) (B)   (A) (B)
① take – on   ② take – out
③ take – away   ④ allow – out
⑤ allow – away

출제율 95%

04 빈칸에 공통으로 들어갈 말을 주어진 철자로 시작하여 쓰시오.

• The hotel was p_____ as the best small hotel in the area.
• Amy p_____ a bunch of wild flowers yesterday.

[05~06] 다음 대화를 읽고 물음에 답하시오.

B: Hi, Lisa. Thank you for ____(A)____ me to your birthday party.
G: (①) My pleasure. (②) I'm ____(B)____ you could come. (③)
B: (④) Happy birthday!
G: They are beautiful! (⑤) Thank you.

출제율 100%

05 ①~⑤ 중 주어진 문장이 들어갈 곳은?

These flowers are for you.

①   ②   ③   ④   ⑤

출제율 90%

06 다음 빈칸 (A)와 (B)에 들어갈 말로 알맞게 짝지어진 것은?

(A)   (B)
① invitation   sorry
② invitation   glad
③ inviting   sorry
④ inviting   glad
⑤ inviting   sad

[07~11] 다음 대화를 읽고 물음에 답하시오.

B: The tickets for the World Music Concert ⓐ is on sale now.

G: Really? (①) Let's book the tickets ⓑonline right away.

B: Okay. Let's see.... (②) ©There are still tickets left for November 5th.

G: Sounds good. (③)

B: Oh, ⓓdo you mind if I bring my little brother?

G: ⓔNot at all. But _____(A)_____ (that, under, allowed, bring, 8, it, not, you, children, to, says, are). (④)

B: No problem. He's 10. (⑤)

G: Okay, I'll add one child ticket. The total price is 25 dollars.

B: Great.

G: (B)콘서트를 볼 게 정말 기대돼!

출제율 100%
07 ①~⑤ 중 주어진 문장이 들어갈 곳은?

> Let's get two student tickets.

①   ②   ③   ④   ⑤

출제율 95%
08 빈칸 (A)를 괄호 안에 주어진 단어를 알맞게 배열하여 채우시오.

➡ _____

_____

출제율 90%
09 위 대화에서 다음 영영풀이에 해당하는 단어를 찾아 쓰시오.

> to make a reservation for a future time

➡ _____

출제율 95%
10 ⓐ~ⓔ 중 흐름상 또는 어법상 어색한 것을 고르시오.

① ⓐ   ② ⓑ   ③ ©   ④ ⓓ   ⑤ ⓔ

출제율 100%
11 밑줄 친 (B)의 우리말과 일치하도록 주어진 단어를 이용해 영작하시오.

> (to, wait)

➡ _____

출제율 95%
12 대화가 자연스럽게 연결되도록 (A)~(D)를 순서대로 가장 적절하게 배열한 것은?

> (A) I'm sorry. I didn't know that.
> (B) Excuse me. You're not allowed to fly a drone.
> (C) Please check the sign over there.
> (D) Okay. Thank you.

① (B) – (A) – (C) – (D)
② (B) – (C) – (A) – (D)
③ (C) – (A) – (B) – (D)
④ (C) – (B) – (A) – (D)
⑤ (C) – (D) – (B) – (A)

출제율 90%
13 다음 중 어법상 어색한 문장을 고르시오.

① It is round and delicate, yet strong enough to protect its contents.
② Sora saved money so that she could donate it.
③ The problem is so difficult that you can't solve.
④ The ball is not small enough to fit in the hand.
⑤ Yumi studies hard in order to pass the exam.

14 다음을 접속사를 이용한 문장으로 바꿔 쓰시오.

(1) She studies several languages to be a tour guide.

➡ _____

_____

(2) Sumin is tall enough to get on the ride.

➡ _____

(3) The sand was too hot for me to walk on.

➡ _____

15 다음 중 의미가 다른 문장을 고르시오.

① My father went to the airport so that he could pick up my sister.
② My father went to the airport so as to pick up my sister.
③ My father went to the airport to pick up my sister.
④ My father went to the airport, so he could pick up my sister.
⑤ My father went to the airport in order that he could pick up my sister.

[16~18] 다음 글을 읽고 물음에 답하시오.

Nature has inspired many architects around the world. This is the Sagrada Familia in Spain. It is one of the most famous churches in the world. Look at the beautiful tall ⓐcolumns inside the church. They look like trees, don't they? The famous architect, Antoni Gaudi, used the shape of trees in the Sagrada Familia. That's how he brought the beauty of nature indoors.

16 위 글의 밑줄 친 ⓐcolumns와 같은 의미로 쓰인 것을 모두 고르시오.

① I always read advertisement columns in the local paper.
② The temple is supported by marble columns.
③ There were long columns of troops and tanks on the street.
④ He has several regular columns in many weekly newspapers.
⑤ Look at the columns of the Corinthian style.

17 위 글의 제목으로 알맞은 것을 고르시오.

① Nature Meets City around the World
② The Sagrada Familia, the Most Famous Church in the World
③ Antoni Gaudi, the Famous Architect in Spain
④ Gaudi Brought the Beauty of Nature Indoors
⑤ Let's Visit a Popular Tourist Attraction in Spain!

18 According to the passage, which is NOT true?

① Nature has given inspiration to many architects around the world.
② The Sagrada Familia is in Spain.
③ The Sagrada Familia is the most famous church in the world.
④ The beautiful tall columns inside the Sagrada Familia look like trees.
⑤ Antoni Gaudi used the shape of trees in the Sagrada Familia.

[19~21] 다음 글을 읽고 물음에 답하시오.

In the first two examples, we can easily see what inspired the architect. (①) But in the next example from Australia, this is not so obvious. (②) Jørn Utzon, the architect of the Sydney Opera House, took a shape from nature and added his imagination. (③) Many people think that it is the waves in the ocean or a sailing boat. (④) But interestingly, the inspiration came from an orange. (⑤) Look at the roof closely. Can you see the peels of an orange? ⓐ When orange lights are shined on the building, you can see the peels more clearly.

출제율 95%

19 위 글의 흐름으로 보아, 주어진 문장이 들어가기에 가장 적절한 곳은?

Can you guess what inspired him?

①   ②   ③   ④   ⑤

출제율 90%

20 위 글의 밑줄 친 ⓐ에서 어법상 틀린 부분을 찾아 고치시오.

_____ ➡ _____

출제율 100%

21 위 글을 읽고 알 수 없는 것을 고르시오.

① Is it easy to see what inspired the architect of the Sydney Opera House?
② Who is the architect of the Sydney Opera House?
③ When did the architect add his imagination to the shape of the Sydney Opera House?
④ What do many people think inspired the architect of the Sydney Opera House?
⑤ Where did the inspiration of the Sydney Opera House come from?

[22~24] 다음 글을 읽고 물음에 답하시오.

What about Korea? ⓐHave you ever been to Dongdaemun Design Plaza in Seoul? Many people think that the building looks like a giant spaceship. But the architect, Zaha Hadid, took the curved lines from nature so that city people could enjoy them. Thanks to its special design, it has become a popular tourist attraction in Seoul.

As you can see, many buildings try to capture the beauty of nature in ⓑtheir design.

출제율 90%

22 주어진 영영풀이에 해당하는 단어를 본문에서 찾아 쓰시오.

a place of interest where tourists visit

➡ _____

출제율 100%

23 위 글의 밑줄 친 문장 ⓐ에 쓰인 현재완료와 용법이 같은 것을 모두 고르시오.

① Have you solved the problem yet?
② He has been ill since yesterday.
③ How many times have you seen it?
④ She has never eaten such a delicious cake.
⑤ I have just finished doing the dishes.

출제율 95%

24 위 글의 밑줄 친 ⓑtheir가 가리키는 것을 본문에서 찾아 쓰시오.

➡ _____

01 그림을 보고 주어진 단어를 이용해 빈칸에 알맞은 말을 쓰시오.

A: Excuse me. _____
B: I'm sorry. I didn't know that.
A: Please check the sign over there.
B: Okay. Thank you.

➡ _____
　(allow, 6 단어)

02 다음 대화에서 흐름상 <u>어색한</u> 것을 찾아 바르게 고치시오.

B: ①The tickets for the World Music Concert are on sale now.
G: Really? ②Let's book the tickets online right away.
B: Okay. Let's see.... ③There are still tickets left for November 5th.
G: Sounds good. Let's get two student tickets.
B: Oh, do you mind if I bring my little brother?
G: ④Of course. But it says that you are not allowed to bring children under 8.
B: No problem. He's 10.
G: Okay, I'll add one child ticket. The total price is 25 dollars.
B: Great.
G: ⑤I can't wait to see the concert!

_____ ➡ _____

03 접속사가 있는 것은 to부정사를, to부정사가 있는 것은 접속사를 이용하여 바꿔 쓰시오.

(1) We collected old clothes so that we could donate them.

　➡ _____
　_____

(2) He practices singing very hard in order to be a singer.

　➡ _____
　_____

(3) The ladder is tall enough for me to reach the shelf.

　➡ _____

(4) Mike is too weak to lift the box.

　➡ _____

04 다음 문장을 같은 뜻을 갖는 문장으로 바꿔 쓰려고 한다. 빈칸을 알맞게 채우시오.

(1) Yumi swims every morning so that she can stay healthy.
　= Yumi swims every morning _____ _____ _____ she can stay healthy.
(2) Tom saved money so that he could travel with his friends.
　= Tom saved money _____ _____ _____ travel with his friends.
(3) The doll is so small that it can fit into the pocket.
　= The doll is small _____ _____ fit into the pocket.
(4) In the summer, it is so hot that we can't wear a coat.
　= In the summer, it is _____ _____ _____ wear a coat.

In the first two examples, we can easily see what inspired the architect. But in the next example from Australia, ⓐthis is not so obvious. Jørn Utzon, the architect of the Sydney Opera House, took a shape from nature and added his imagination. ⓑ무엇이 그에게 영감을 주었는지 추측할 수 있는가? Many people think that it is the waves in the ocean or a sailing boat. But interestingly, the inspiration came from an orange. Look at the roof closely. Can you see the peels of an orange? When orange lights are shone on the building, you can see the peels more clearly.

05 위 글의 밑줄 친 ⓐthis가 가리키는 것을 본문에서 찾아 쓰시오.

➡ _____

06 위 글의 밑줄 친 ⓑ의 우리말에 맞게 주어진 어휘를 알맞게 배열하시오.

> what / him / you / can / inspired / guess

➡ _____

07 본문의 내용과 일치하도록 다음 빈칸 (A)와 (B)에 알맞은 단어를 쓰시오.

> The architect of the Sydney Opera House was inspired by an orange, not by (A)_____
> _____ _____ _____ _____ or
> (B)_____ _____ _____ .

What about Korea? Have you ever been to Dongdaemun Design Plaza in Seoul? Many people think that the building looks like a giant spaceship. But the architect, Zaha Hadid, took the curved lines from nature (A) so that city people could enjoy them. Thanks to its special design, it has become a popular tourist attraction in Seoul.

As you can see, many buildings try to capture the beauty of ___ⓐ___ in their design. They are perfect examples of " ___ⓑ___ meets city." If you were an architect, what would you choose from nature?

08 위 글의 빈칸 ⓐ와 ⓑ에 공통으로 들어갈 알맞은 단어를 쓰시오. (대 · 소문자 무시)

➡ _____

09 위 글의 밑줄 친 (A)를 다음과 같이 바꿔 쓸 때 빈칸에 들어갈 알맞은 말을 두 단어로 쓰시오.

> for city people _____ _____ them

10 What makes Dongdaemun Design Plaza in Seoul a popular tourist attraction in Seoul? Fill in the blanks with suitable words.

> _____ _____ _____ makes Dongdaemun Design Plaza in Seoul a popular tourist attraction in Seoul.

01 외출해서 친구와 영화를 보고 싶어하는 딸과 방 청소를 하라는 엄마의 대화이다. 주어진 표현과 조건을 보고 대화를 완성하시오.

조건

- 허락을 요청하는 질문과 금지하는 표현을 반드시 사용할 것.
- 완벽한 문장으로 답할 것.

A: Mom, _____? (allow)
B: Sure, but when are you going to clean your room?
A: Well... Can you clean my room for me? I'll go out right now, and cleaning is tiring.
B: What? I can't stand it. _____!(allow)

02 〈보기〉에 주어진 표현과 to부정사를 이용하여 3 문장 이상 쓰시오.

보기

this bag / big / carry many books	go to bed / get up early
study hard / pass the exam	the coffee / hot / drink

(1) _____
(2) _____
(3) _____

03 다음 내용을 바탕으로 우리 학교를 소개하는 글을 쓰시오.

- I go to Boram Middle School in Suwon.
- What does your school have?
  4-story building, large playground, gym, small garden
- What is special about your school?
  The garden is on top of the school building. We grow some vegetables there.
- What is your favorite place?
  My favorite place is the bench under a big tree.

I go to (A)_____ in Suwon. My school has a (B)_____ building. It also has a large playground, a gym and a (C)_____. The garden is on top of the school building. We grow (D)_____ there so that we can have fresh food. My favorite place is (E)_____ under the tree. I love sitting there and talking with my friends. I like my school very much.

단원별 모의고사

01 다음 영영풀이가 나타내는 말을 고르시오.

> a person who designs buildings

① mechanic ② architect
③ construction ④ structure
⑤ designer

02 밑줄 친 부분과 바꿔 쓸 수 있는 말을 고르시오.

> Be careful. The forest is full of extremely big snakes and spiders.

① special ② serious
③ entire ④ amazing
⑤ giant

03 다음 〈보기〉의 단어를 사용하여 자연스러운 문장을 만들 수 없는 것은? (형태 변화 가능, 한 단어는 한 번만 사용 가능.)

┌─── 보기 ───┐
  add check choose imitate
└────────────┘

① He has a unique ability to _____ any sound he has heard.
② He _____ his words carefully as he spoke.
③ My sister _____ the cats when we are away.
④ _____ 10% to the total.
⑤ The first rule in solving any mystery is to _____ the facts.

04 다음 우리말에 맞도록 빈칸에 알맞은 말을 쓰시오. (철자가 주어진 경우 주어진 철자로 시작할 것.)

(1) 비행기 날개의 윗부분은 곡선 모양이고, 밑부분은 평평하다.
➡ An airplane wing is _____ on top and flat on the bottom.

(2) 표현의 자유는 기본적인 인권이다.
➡ Freedom of e_____ is a basic human right.

(3) 저에게 식당을 좀 추천해 주시겠어요?
➡ Could you r_____ a restaurant for me?

(4) 그는 항상 나에게 영감의 원천이다.
➡ He has always been a source of i_____ for me.

[05~08] 다음 대화를 읽고 물음에 답하시오.

B: Sumin, my train is leaving (a)in five minutes.
G: I hope you enjoyed your trip, Daniel.
B: Of course, I did.
G: Which place did you like ⓐ in my town?
B: I liked the folk village ⓑ .
G: Yeah, it's the most popular place here.
B: I really liked walking ⓒ in hanbok. I looked really cool.
G: I'm glad to hear that.
B: Thank you for showing me ⓓ .
G: _____(A)_____ Have a safe trip.

05 빈칸 (A)에 알맞은 말이 〈보기〉에서 모두 몇 개인지 고르시오.

> • It was my pleasure. • I appreciate it.
> • Don't mention it. • You're welcome.
> • No problem. • Anytime.

① 2개 ② 3개 ③ 4개 ④ 5개 ⑤ 6개

06 빈칸 ⓐ와 ⓑ에 공통으로 들어갈 말을 대화에서 찾아 쓰시오.

➡ _____

07 빈칸 ⓒ와 ⓓ에 공통으로 들어갈 말을 고르시오.

① from　　② in　　③ over
④ for　　⑤ around

08 밑줄 친 (a)in과 같은 의미로 쓰인 것을 모두 고르시오.

① The play starts in a few hours.
② Bright yellow flowers appear in late summer.
③ We'll be back in an hour.
④ Shaw first visited Russia in 1927.
⑤ He retired in October.

[09~11] 다음 글을 읽고 물음에 답하시오.

W: Hello, students! 우리 미술관을 방문해 주셔서 감사합니다. This museum opened in 1995. ___(A)___ then, it has exhibited many famous artworks. Today, you will see some famous artworks from the art books. Before we begin the tour, ___ⓐ___. (a, remind, let, basic, of, rule, you, me) You can take pictures of the artworks, ___(B)___ you're not allowed to touch them. Now let's start the tour.

09 빈칸 (A)와 (B)에 들어갈 말로 알맞게 짝지어진 것은?

(A)　　(B)　　　　(A)　　(B)
① While – although　② While – so
③ Since – although　④ Since – so
⑤ Since – but

10 빈칸 ⓐ를 괄호 안에 주어진 단어를 알맞게 배열하여 채우시오.

➡ _____

11 밑줄 친 우리말과 일치하도록 주어진 단어를 이용해 영작하시오.

（for, visit, 7 단어）

➡ _____

12 다음 대화에서 흐름상 또는 어법상 어색한 것을 골라 바르게 고치시오.

M: Excuse me. You're allowed to bring your umbrella inside.
G: Oh, where should I put it?
M: There is an umbrella stand outside.
G: Okay. I'll put it there. Thank you.

➡ _____
_____

13 다음 문장에서 어법상 어색한 것을 바르게 고쳐 다시 쓰시오.

(1) We planted some trees in a park so as to they could keep the air clean.

➡ _____
_____

(2) I saved money in order to I could buy a present for my grandma.

➡ _____

_____

_____

(3) The bag is enough big to carry two soccer balls.

➡ _____

14 다음 우리말을 주어진 어휘를 이용하여 영작하시오.

(1) 그녀는 그 대회를 준비하기 위해서 열심히 연습한다. (the contest, prepare, hard, practice, can, that, for, 11 단어)

➡ _____

_____

(2) 차가 너무 뜨거워서 마실 수 없다. (the tea, hot, to)

➡ _____

15 Which is grammatically WRONG?

① The architect took the curved lines from nature so that city people could enjoy them.

② Please speak louder in order for everyone to hear you.

③ Additional funding will be required in order to the bridge be completed.

④ The book is so difficult that children can't understand it.

⑤ Jiho is strong enough to lift the heavy box.

16 다음 중 어법상 옳은 문장을 모두 고르시오.

① I went to bed early so that I could catch the first train.

② I went to bed early, as that I could get up early.

③ She is not strong enough to lift the box.

④ He valued his team too much to quit.

⑤ It was so hot as to we couldn't go out.

⑥ He's too young that he can't take care of himself.

⑦ Minho's English is good enough talking with a foreigner.

17 다음 두 문장을 해석하고 그 차이를 설명하시오.

(1) She jogged regularly so that she could stay healthy.

➡ _____

➡ _____

_____

(2) She jogged so regularly that she could stay healthy.

➡ _____

➡ _____

_____

[18~20] 다음 글을 읽고 물음에 답하시오.

Have you heard of the expression, "Art ____ⓐ____ nature"? Many artists get their ideas and inspirations from the world around them. ⓑ<u>This is why the natural world is a beautiful place.</u> The shapes in nature are very pleasing to the eye. For example, look at the egg on the left. Isn't it beautiful? It is round and delicate, ____ⓒ____ strong enough to protect its contents. Can you imagine a building that looks like an egg? Such a building actually exists in London.

18 위 글의 빈칸 ⓐ에 알맞은 것을 고르시오.

① inspires　　② imitates
③ produces　　④ influences
⑤ encourages

19 위 글의 밑줄 친 ⓑ에서 흐름상 어색한 부분을 찾아 고치시오.

_____ ➡ _____

20 위 글의 빈칸 ⓒ에 알맞은 것을 고르시오.

① yet　　② so
③ for　　④ while
⑤ because

[21~23] 다음 글을 읽고 물음에 답하시오.

Nature has inspired many architects around the world. (①) This is the Sagrada Familia in Spain. (②) It is one of the most famous churches in the world. (③) Look at the beautiful tall columns inside the church. (④) The famous architect, Antoni Gaudi, used the ____ⓐ____ of trees in the Sagrada Familia. (⑤) ⓑ<u>That's</u> how he brought the beauty of nature indoors.

21 위 글의 흐름으로 보아, 주어진 문장이 들어가기에 가장 적절한 곳은?

They look like trees, don't they?

①　　②　　③　　④　　⑤

22 위 글의 빈칸 ⓐ에 알맞은 것을 고르시오.

① nature　　② shade
③ height　　④ pattern
⑤ shape

23 위 글의 밑줄 친 ⓐThat이 가리키는 것을 본문에서 찾아 쓰시오.

➡ _____

_____

[24~25] 다음 글을 읽고 물음에 답하시오.

In the first two examples, we can easily see what inspired the architect. But in the next example from Australia, this is not so obvious. Jørn Utzon, the architect of the Sydney Opera House, took a shape from nature and added his imagination. Can you guess what inspired him? Many people think that it is the waves in the ocean or a sailing boat. But interestingly, the inspiration came from an orange. Look at the roof closely. Can you see the peels of an orange? When orange lights are shone on the building, you can see the peels more clearly.

24 위 글의 주제로 알맞은 것을 고르시오.

① What is the reason why we can easily see what inspired the architect?
② Who is the architect of the Sydney Opera House?
③ How much imagination do we need to take a shape from nature?
④ Why did the waves in the ocean or a sailing boat inspire the architect?
⑤ What inspired the architect of the Sydney Opera House?

25 다음 문장에서 위 글의 내용과 <u>다른</u> 부분을 찾아서 고치시오.

> Jørn Utzon, the architect of the Sydney Opera House, took a shape from nature such as the waves in the ocean or a sailing boat.

➡ _____

_____

[26~27] 다음 글을 읽고 물음에 답하시오.

What about Korea? Have you ever been to Dongdaemun Design Plaza in Seoul? Many people think that the building looks like a giant spaceship. But the architect, Zaha Hadid, took the curved lines from nature so that city people could enjoy them. ____ⓐ____ its special design, it has become a popular tourist attraction in Seoul.

As you can see, many buildings try to capture the beauty of nature in their design. They are perfect examples of "Nature meets city." If you were an architect, what would you choose from nature?

26 위 글의 빈칸 ⓐ에 들어갈 알맞은 말을 고르시오.

① In spite of   ② In addition to
③ Instead of   ④ Thanks to
⑤ Besides

27 According to the passage, which is NOT true?

① Many people think that Dongdaemun Design Plaza in Seoul looks like a giant spaceship.
② Zaha Hadid is the architect of Dongdaemun Design Plaza in Seoul.
③ Zaha Hadid took the curved lines from nature for city people to enjoy them.
④ Dongdaemun Design Plaza has become a popular tourist attraction in Seoul.
⑤ Many buildings try to capture the beauty of cities in their design.

MEMO

Lesson 7

Feel the Wonder

 의사소통 기능

- 궁금함 표현하기
  A: I wonder where the bus stop is.
  B: It's in front of the police station.

- 보고하기
  A: Is there anything interesting?
  B: This article says scientists have discovered
     a new planet.

언어 형식

- 소유격 관계대명사 whose
  This small fish **whose** favorite food is clams
  uses a tool to open them.

- 시간을 나타내는 접속사
  Humpback whales stand on their tails **while**
  they sleep.

Words & Expressions

Key Words

- **abroad** [əbrɔ́ːd] 부 해외에, 해외로
- **against** [əgénst] 전 ~에 대고, ~에 반대하여
- **Arctic** [áːrktik] 명 북극 (지방)
- **article** [áːrtikl] 명 기사
- **average** [ǽvəridʒ] 형 평균의, 보통의
- **blood** [blʌd] 명 피
- **blow** [blou] 동 (입으로) 불다
- **breathe** [briːð] 동 숨을 쉬다
- **calculate** [kǽlkjulèit] 동 계산하다
- **camel** [kǽməl] 명 낙타
- **careful** [kéərfəl] 형 조심스러운
- **clam** [klæm] 명 조개
- **communicate** [kəmjúːnəkèit] 동 소통하다
- **complete** [kəmplíːt] 동 완성하다
- **completely** [kəmplíːtli] 부 완전히
- **cute** [kjuːt] 형 귀여운
- **desert** [dézərt] 명 사막
- **discover** [diskʌ́vər] 동 발견하다
- **distance** [dístəns] 명 거리
- **dive** [daiv] 동 뛰어들다, 다이빙하다
- **enemy** [énəmi] 명 적
- **fat** [fæt] 명 지방
- **finally** [fáinəli] 부 마침내
- **fool** [fuːl] 동 속이다, 기만하다 명 바보
- **forecast** [fɔ́ːrkæst] 명 예측, 예보
- **friendly** [fréndli] 형 친절한
- **guess** [ges] 동 추측하다
- **hide** [haid] 동 숨다
- **join** [dʒɔin] 동 합류하다
- **million** [míljən] 명 100만 형 100만의, 수많은
- **monster** [mánstər] 명 괴물
- **mop** [map] 동 대걸레로 닦다
- **nearby** [nìərbái] 형 인근의, 가까운 곳의 부 인근에, 가까운 곳에
- **ocean** [óuʃən] 명 대양, 바다
- **octopus** [áktəpəs] 명 문어
- **planet** [plǽnit] 명 행성
- **probably** [prábəbli] 부 아마
- **rainy** [réini] 형 비가 내리는
- **scenery** [síːnəri] 명 경치, 풍경
- **serve** [səːrv] 동 (음식을) 제공하다, 차려 주다
- **smash** [smæʃ] 동 때려 부수다, 깨뜨리다
- **snowy** [snóui] 형 눈이 내리는
- **species** [spíːʃiːz] 명 (분류상의) 종
- **spot** [spat] 동 발견하다, 찾아내다
- **solar** [sóulər] 형 태양의
- **sunny** [sʌ́ni] 형 화창한
- **surface** [sɔ́ːrfis] 명 수면, 표면
- **surround** [səráund] 동 둘러싸다
- **temperature** [témpərətʃər] 명 온도, 기온
- **the South Pole** 남극
- **tightly** [táitli] 부 단단히, 꽉
- **tool** [tuːl] 명 도구
- **vacuum** [vǽkjuəm] 동 진공청소기로 청소하다
- **weather forecast** 일기 예보
- **whale** [hweil] 명 고래
- **wonder** [wʌ́ndər] 명 경이, 경탄, 놀라움 동 궁금하다

Key Expressions

- **be covered with** ~로 덮여 있다
- **be different from** ~와 다르다
- **be full of** ~로 가득 차다
- **check out** (흥미로운 것을) 살펴보다, 확인하다
- **fall asleep** 잠들다
- **give up** 포기하다
- **go on a picnic** 소풍가다
- **go without** ~ 없이 지내다
- **grow up** 자라다, 성장하다
- **How about -ing?** ~하는 것이 어떠니?
- **in a line** 한 줄로
- **in the end** 마침내, 결국
- **in front of** ~ 앞에
- **keep -ing** 계속 ~하다
- **millions of** 수백만의
- **melt away** 차츰 사라지다
- **smash A against B** A를 B에 내리치다
- **this time of year** 연중 이맘때는, 연중 이맘때쯤이면

Word Power

※ 서로 비슷한 뜻을 가진 어휘

- □ **abroad** 해외에 – **overseas** 해외에
- □ **calculate** 계산하다 – **count** 세다
- □ **complete** 완성하다 – **finish** 끝내다
- □ **forecast** 예측 – **prediction** 예측
- □ **scenery** 경치, 풍경 – **landscape** 풍경
- □ **tightly** 단단히 – **firmly** 단단히

- □ **article** 기사 – **column** 기사
- □ **careful** 조심스러운 – **thoughtful** 사려 깊은
- □ **finally** 마침내 – **lastly** 마지막으로
- □ **probably** 아마 – **perhaps** 아마
- □ **smash** 때려 부수다 – **shatter** 산산이 조각내다

※ 서로 반대의 뜻을 가진 어휘

- □ **against** ~에 반대하여 ↔ **for** ~에 찬성하여
- □ **careful** 조심스러운 ↔ **careless** 부주의한
- □ **enemy** 적 ↔ **friend** 친구
- □ **nearby** 인근의 ↔ **faraway** 멀리 떨어진

- □ **Arctic** 북극 (지방) ↔ **Antarctic** 남극 지방
- □ **discover** 발견하다 ↔ **hide** 숨기다
- □ **friendly** 친절한 ↔ **unfriendly** 불친절한
- □ **probably** 아마 ↔ **improbably** 있음직 하지 않게

※ 동사 – 명사

- □ **bleed** 피를 흘리다 – **blood** 피
- □ **calculate** 계산하다 – **calculation** 계산
- □ **complete** 완성하다 – **completion** 완성

- □ **breathe** 숨을 쉬다 – **breath** 호흡
- □ **communicate** 소통하다 – **communication** 소통
- □ **discover** 발견하다 – **discovery** 발견

※ 명사 – 형용사

- □ **care** 조심 – **careful** 조심스러운, **careless** 부주의한
- □ **friend** 친구 – **friendly** 친절한
- □ **rain** 비 – **rainy** 비가 내리는
- □ **sun** 태양 – **sunny** 맑은

- □ **cloud** 구름 – **cloudy** 구름 낀
- □ **monster** 괴물 – **monstrous** 괴물 같은
- □ **snow** 눈 – **snowy** 눈이 내리는
- □ **wonder** 경이, 경탄, 놀라움 – **wonderful** 놀라운

English Dictionary

- □ **Arctic** 북극 (지방)
  → the area around the North Pole
  북극의 주변 지역

- □ **blow** (입으로) 불다
  → to send out air from the mouth
  입에서 공기를 내보내다

- □ **breathe** 숨을 쉬다
  → to move air into and out of your lungs
  공기를 폐 안팎으로 움직이다

- □ **distance** 거리
  → the amount of space between two places or things
  두 개의 장소나 물건 사이에 있는 공간의 양

- □ **dive** 뛰어들다, 다이빙하다
  → to jump into water, especially with your arms and head going in first
  특히 머리와 팔이 먼저 가도록하여 물속으로 뛰어들다

- □ **forecast** 예측, 예보
  → a statement about what you think is going to happen in the future
  당신이 생각하기에 미래에 무엇이 일어날지에 대한 언급

- □ **million** 100만
  → the number 1,000,000
  1,000,000이라는 수

- □ **smash** 때려 부수다, 깨뜨리다
  → to break something into many pieces
  무언가를 많은 조각으로 깨뜨리다

- □ **species** (분류상의) 종
  → a set of animals or plants that have similar characteristics to each other
  서로 유사한 특성을 가진 동물이나 식물의 집합

- □ **surface** 수면, 표면
  → the upper layer of an area of land or water
  땅이나 물의 위층

- □ **tool** 도구
  → a piece of equipment you use with your hands for a particular task
  특정한 일을 위하여 손으로 사용하는 기구

- □ **whale** 고래
  → a very large mammal that lives in the sea
  바다에 사는 거대한 포유동물

01 다음 밑줄 친 부분의 의미가 다른 하나를 고르시오.

① The plane landed at the airport.

② The bird landed on the water.

③ The pilot managed to land the aircraft safely.

④ The land in this town is good for farming.

⑤ There's a plane coming in to land now.

02 다음 밑줄 친 부분의 의미로 알맞지 않은 것은?

① People are looking at the camel in the zoo. (낙타)

② Students must complete the course. (경쟁하다)

③ Katya will make her first trip abroad next month. (해외로)

④ My parents sometimes seem to treat me as if I were their enemy. (적)

⑤ I cut this article out of the newspaper. (기사)

03 다음 제시된 단어를 사용하여 자연스러운 문장을 만들 수 없는 것은?

> away   from   up   with

① London was different _____ most European capitals.

② We spent half an hour looking for the keys, but eventually gave _____ and went home.

③ The ice hotel will melt _____ completely and flow into the river.

④ His desk was covered _____ books and papers.

⑤ They were stuck _____ a line of traffic.

04 다음 밑줄 친 부분과 의미가 가장 가까운 것을 고르시오.

> From the hill, he looked down on the peaceful landscape.

① horizon   ② local   ③ climate
④ scenery   ⑤ environment

05 다음 영영풀이가 어색한 것은?

① Arctic: the area around the South Pole

② surface: the upper layer of an area of land or water

③ whale: a very large mammal that lives in the sea

④ dive: to jump into water, especially with your arms and head going in first

⑤ breathe: to move air into and out of your lungs

01 빈칸을 주어진 영영풀이에 해당하는 말을 이용하여 채우시오.

> to break something into many pieces

➡ They repeatedly _____ the shellfish against the rock until it breaks open.

02 다음 우리말에 맞도록 빈칸에 알맞은 말을 쓰시오. (철자가 주어진 경우 주어진 철자로 시작할 것)

(1) 너 근처에 사니?
　➡ Do you live n_____?
(2) 지금부터 10년 후의 회사 판매에 대한 정확한 예측을 하는 것은 불가능하다.
　➡ It is impossible to give an accurate f_____ of company sales 10 years from now.
(3) 마침내 우리가 빚을 다 청산했다.
　➡ We are _____ clear of debt.
(4) Marie는 아기를 그녀의 팔로 단단히 잡았다.
　➡ Marie held the baby _____ in her arms.

[03~04] 다음 빈칸에 공통으로 들어갈 말을 쓰시오. (철자가 주어진 경우 주어진 철자로 시작할 것)

03
> • She is _____ing her new song in the studio.
> • She set an Olympic _____.

04
> • Anyone who thinks TV news gives you enough information is a f_____.
> • You can't f_____ me. I know he's already given you the money.

05 다음 빈칸에 들어갈 말을 〈보기〉에서 찾아 쓰시오. (필요하면 어형을 바꿀 것)

> ┤ 보기 ├
> blow　dive　serve　spot

(1) I _____ a police car behind us a moment ago.
(2) I saw her _____ onto her coffee to cool it down.
(3) _____ off the cliffs is dangerous.
(4) Teacakes should be _____ hot with butter.

06 우리말 해석에 맞게 주어진 단어를 알맞게 배열하시오.

(1) 연중 이맘때는 날씨가 변덕이 아주 심하다.
　(at, very, of, year, this, the weather, time, changeable, is)
　➡ _____
　_____
(2) 학부모들이 학교를 둘러볼 기회가 있을 것이다.
　(there, to, around, parents, school, chance, the, be, look, a, will, for)
　➡ _____
　_____

Converstion

1 궁금함 표현하기

> **A** I wonder where the bus stop is. 나는 버스 정류소가 어디인지 궁금해.
>
> **B** It's in front of the police station. 그것은 경찰서 앞에 있어.

- 어떤 것에 대한 궁금증을 표현할 때는 wonder(궁금하다), curious(궁금한, 호기심이 많은), want to know(알고 싶다) 등의 표현을 이용하여 'I wonder ~.(나는 ~이 궁금하다.)' 또는 'I'm curious about ~.(나는 ~이 궁금해.)'라고 말한다. 또한 궁금한 내용을 알고 싶다는 의미를 'I would like to know ~.', 'I want to know ~.', 'I don't know why ~.' 등으로 표현할 수도 있다.

- 'I wonder ~'를 사용할 때의 어순은 'I wonder+의문사+주어+동사 ~.', 'I wonder+if/whether+주어+동사 ~.'이고, 명사(구)와 함께 나타낼 때는 'I wonder+명사(구)'이다. 궁금함을 나타내는 'I'm curious'와 명사구를 같이 쓸 때는 'I'm curious about+명사구'이고, 명사절과 함께 쓸 때는 'I'm curious if/whether ~.' 또는 'I'm curious 의문사(+주어)+동사.'이다.

- 궁금한 점에 대하여 알고 싶을 때는 'Can you tell me about ~?(~에 대하여 이야기해 줄 수 있니?)', 'I'm interested to know ~.(나는 ~를 아는 것에 관심 있어.)'와 같이 표현할 수 있고, 'Can I ~?', 'Can/Could you ~?' 등과 같이 요구/요청을 나타내는 조동사 표현을 사용하여 'Can I ask you ~?' 또는 'Can you tell me ~?'와 같이 궁금한 점에 대하여 물어볼 수 있다. 그 외에 궁금증을 나타낼 때는 'Do you know ~?' 등을 사용할 수도 있다.

궁금함 표현하기

- I wonder+의문사/if/whether 주어+동사 ~. ~인지 궁금하다.
- I would like/want to know ~. 나는 ~이 알고 싶다.
- I am curious about ~. 나는 ~이 궁금하다.
- I'm curious if/whether 주어+동사 ~. 나는 ~가 궁금하다.
- Can you tell me about ~? ~에 대해 말해 줄 수 있니?
- I want to know 명사구/명사절. 나는 ~을 알고 싶다.

핵심 Check

1. 괄호 안에 주어진 말을 바르게 배열하여 대화를 완성하시오.

(1) **B:** (where, wonder, is, the museum, I).

G: It is next to the bank.

➡ _____

(2) **B:** (wonder, long, the Amazon River, I, how, is).

G: It's about 7,000km long.

➡ _____

2 보고하기

A Is there anything interesting? 재미있는 뭔가가 있니?

B This article says scientists have discovered a new planet.
이 기사에 따르면 과학자들이 새로운 행성을 발견했어.

- 'This article says ~.(이 기사에 따르면 ~이다.)'처럼 '~ says (that) ...(~에 따르면 …이다)'는 어딘가에서 보거나 들은 내용을 상대방에게 보고하거나 전달할 때 사용하는 표현이다. 동사 'say'는 '~라고 말하다'라는 뜻으로 흔히 사용되지만, 여기에서는 '~라고 되어[쓰여] 있다, ~라고 나와 있다, (글, 표지판 등이) ~을 나타내다, ~에 따르면 …이다' 등의 의미로 사용되었다.

- 무엇을 통해서 보고 들은 내용을 상대방에게 보고하는가에 따라서 'This article says ~.' 형태의 표현에서 This article 대신 The Internet, The book, People, Someone 등을 쓸 수 있다. 어떤 사람이 전해준 말일 때는 'He[She] said ~'의 형태로 상대방에게 보고하거나 전달한다. 전달자에 따라 he를 people, someone, my friend 등으로 바꿔 말할 수 있으며, He told me ~., I've heard ~ from him. 등으로 말할 수도 있다.

- '~에 따르면'이라는 뜻으로 'according to'를 사용할 수 있다. 'according to'는 전치사구 취급하여 명사(구)를 목적어로 가져서 'according to 명사(구)'의 형태가 된다.

보고하기

- This article says ~. 이 기사에 따르면 ~.
- The book says ~. 그 책에 따르면 ~.
- Someone says/said ~. 누군가 ~라고 한다.
- The Internet says ~. 인터넷에 따르면 ~.
- People say/said ~. 사람들이 ~라고 한다.
- According to ~, ... ~에 따르면 …이다.

핵심 Check

2. 다음 우리말과 일치하도록 빈칸에 알맞은 말을 쓰시오.

(1) 인터넷에 따르면 목성은 지구보다 11배 이상 더 크다고 한다.

➡ _____ Jupiter is over 11 times bigger than Earth.

(2) 그 책에 따르면 남극의 평균 기온은 약 영하 49℃라고 한다.

➡ _____ the average temperature of the South Pole is about -49℃.

3. 다음 대화의 밑줄 친 부분의 의도로 알맞은 것을 고르시오.

A: Can you check the weather?

B: Oh, no! The weather forecast says it'll be rainy in the afternoon.

① 당부하기   ② 동의하기   ③ 보고하기

④ 거절하기   ⑤ 감사하기

Listen and Speak 1 A

B: ❶We're almost at the top of the mountain.

G: ❷I wonder how high this mountain is.

B: It's ❸about 2,000m high.

G: Wow! This is a really high mountain.

B: Yes, it is. Let's ❹keep going.

B: 우리는 산 정상에 거의 다 왔어.
G: 나는 이 산이 얼마나 높은지 궁금해.
B: 이 산은 높이가 약 2,000미터야.
G: 우와! 정말 높은 산이구나.
B: 응, 맞아. 계속 올라가자.

❶ almost: 거의, 장소 앞에 전치사 at을 사용할 수 있다. at the top of: ~의 맨 위에
❷ 'I wonder ~.'는 '나는 ~이 궁금하다.'라는 뜻으로 어떤 것에 대해 궁금할 때 사용하는 표현이다. wonder 다음에는 의문사절이나 if/whether절이 온다. wonder: 궁금해하다
❸ about: 대략, 약
❹ keep 동사ing: 계속해서 ~하다

Check(√) True or False

(1) They already reached the top of the mountain.   T ☐ F ☐

(2) The girl wants to know how high the mountain is.   T ☐ F ☐

Listen and Speak 2 A

B: The weather is so nice outside.

G: Yeah. ❶How about going on a picnic this afternoon?

B: Good idea. Can you ❷check the weather?

G: Oh, no! ❸The weather forecast says ❹it'll be rainy in the afternoon.

B: Let's go another time, ❺then.

B: 바깥 날씨가 아주 좋아.
G: 응. 오늘 오후에 소풍 갈래?
B: 좋은 생각이야. 날씨를 확인해 주겠니?
G: 오, 안 돼! 일기 예보에 따르면 오후에 비가 올 거래.
B: 그러면 다음에 가자.

❶ How about 다음에 동사구를 ~ing 형태로 사용하여 상대방에게 제안·권유할 수 있다. go on a picnic: 소풍 가다
❷ check: 확인하다
❸ '~가 …라고 말하다'라는 의미의 '주어+say(s)+that+주어+동사 ~.' 구문을 이용해 주어가 한 말인 that절의 내용을 상대방에게 보고하거나 전해줄 수 있다. 이때 접속사 that은 생략 가능하다. 정보 제공자에 따라 'The weather forecast' 대신에 'The Internet', 'The book', 'People', 'Someone' 등을 쓸 수 있다.
❹ 시간, 거리, 계절, 요일, 명암, 날씨, 날짜 등을 이야기할 때 비인칭 주어 it을 사용한다. 여기서는 '날씨'로 비인칭 주어 it을 사용했다.
❺ then: (논리적인 결과를 나타내어) 그러면[그렇다면]

Check(√) True or False

(3) It is fine now, but is going to be rainy in the afternoon.   T ☐ F ☐

(4) They are going to go on a picnic this afternoon.   T ☐ F ☐

Listen and Speak 1 C

A: We're finally here.

B: Yes, I'm so excited. Let's ❶look around.

A: ❷I wonder where the bus stop is.

B: It's ❸in front of the police station.

A: You're right. Let's go.

A: 마침내 다 왔어.
B: 맞아. 매우 신나. 주위를 둘러보자.
A: 나는 버스 정류장이 어디에 있는지 궁금해.
B: 경찰서 앞에 있어.
A: 맞아. 가자.

❶ look around: 둘러보다

❷ 'I wonder ~.'는 '나는 ~이 궁금하다.'라는 뜻으로 어떤 것에 대해 궁금할 때 사용하는 표현이다. wonder 다음에는 의문사절이나 if/whether절이 온다. 여기서는 '의문사(where)+주어(the bus stop)+동사(is)'인 의문사절을 wonder의 목적어로 사용했다. 궁금증을 나타내는 다른 표현으로 '어떤 일에 대해 호기심이 생기다, 궁금해지다'라는 의미는 'be[become] curious about+명사'로 나타낼 수 있으며, 'be interested in ~, want to know ~' 등으로도 표현할 수도 있다. 위의 문장인 'I wonder where the bus stop is.'를 'I'm curious where the bus stop is.', 'I'm interested in where the bus stop is.', 'I want to know where the bus stop is.'로 바꿔 쓸 수 있다.

❸ in front of ~: ~ 앞에

Check(√) True or False

(5) They are looking for the police station. T ☐ F ☐

(6) A wants to know where the bus stop is. T ☐ F ☐

Real Life Talk Step 2

A: Where is ❶the coldest place on Earth?

B: I thinks it's ❷the South Pole.

A: ❸I wonder ❹how cold it is.

B: ❺The book says ❻the average temperature of the South Pole is about -49°C.

A: ❼That's amazing!

A: 지구에서 가장 추운 곳이 어디니?
B: 남극이라고 생각해.
A: 얼마나 추울지 궁금해.
B: 책에 따르면 남극의 평균 온도가 영하 49도래.
A: 굉장하다!

❶ the coldest는 형용사 cold의 최상급으로 '가장 추운'의 의미이다.
❷ the South Pole: 남극 (the North Pole, the Arctic: 북극)
❸ I wonder+의문사절 또는 if/whether 주어 동사: 나는 ~이 궁금하다.
❹ how 뒤에 형용사나 부사가 오면 how는 '얼마나'의 의미로 사용된다.
❺ 'The book says ~.'는 '책에 따르면 ~.'이라는 뜻으로 어딘가에서 보거나 들은 내용을 상대방에게 보고하거나 전달할 때 사용하는 표현이다. average: 평균; 평균의
❻ says와 the average temperature 사이에 접속사 that이 생략되어 있다. the average temperature가 단수 주어이므로 단수동사인 is가 사용되었다.
❼ 놀람을 표현할 때는 'That's amazing.' 'That's surprising.' 'I can't believe it.' 등으로 말할 수 있다.

Check(√) True or False

(7) B searches the temperature of the South Pole in the book. T ☐ F ☐

(8) There is a place colder than the South Pole. T ☐ F ☐

Listen and Speak 1 B

B: Look at the baby penguins on TV. They're so cute.

G: Yes, but they ❶look very cold out there.

B: Yeah, the South Pole is the coldest place ❷on Earth.

G: ❸I wonder how cold it is there.

B: The average temperature is ❹about -58℃ in July and -26℃ in December.

G: Oh, then, July is ❺colder than December there. Interesting!

B: Yes. ❻Although it's very cold there, it doesn't snow much.

G: That's interesting, too!

❶ look+형용사: ~하게 보이다
❷ on Earth: 지구상에서
❸ 궁금증을 표현할 때 '~를 궁금해하다'라는 의미를 가진 동사 wonder를 이용하여 'I wonder ~.'라고 말한다. I wonder 뒤에는 간접의문문의 어순인 '의문사(how cold)+주어(it)+동사(is)'의 순서로 문장을 쓴다.
❹ about: 대략, 약. 연도나 달 앞에는 전치사 in을 사용한다.
❺ colder than ~: ~보다 더 추운(cold의 비교급)
❻ although는 접속사로 '비록 ~일지라도', '~이긴 하지만'의 의미로 뒤에 주어와 동사가 나온다.

 Listen and Speak 2 B

B: Sumin, ❶what are you going to do on Sunday?

G: I'm going to go hiking. Do you want to join me?

B: I'd love to. Where do you want to go?

G: ❷I'm thinking of going to Namsan.

B: Oh, the ❸scenery there is so beautiful ❹this time of year.

G: Right. ❺I heard that it's covered with red autumn leaves now.

B: Great. How long does the shortest hiking course ❻take?

G: ❼The Internet says it takes about two hours.

B: Okay, see you on Sunday!

❶ 상대방에게 무엇을 할 계획인지(또는 어떤 계획이 있는지) 물어볼 때 'What are you planning[going] to+동사원형 ~?'을 사용할 수 있다.
❷ 'I'm thinking of ~.'는 '나는 ~할까 생각 중이다.'라는 뜻으로 of 뒤에 동명사를 취해 의도나 계획을 나타낼 때 쓰는 표현이다. 'I'm considering ~ing.' 또는 'I intend to ~.'와 바꿔 쓸 수 있다.
❸ scenery: 경치, 풍경

❹ this time of year: 이맘때는, 이맘때쯤이면
❺ 어떤 내용을 들어서 알고 있음을 표현할 때 'I heard that+주어+동사 ~.'의 형태로 말할 수 있다. heard 대신에 현재완료형의 형태인 have heard를 사용할 수도 있다. be covered with: ~로 덮여 있다 autumn leaves: 단풍
❻ take: (얼마의 시간이) 걸리다
❼ 'The Internet says ~.'는 '인터넷에 따르면 ~.'이라는 뜻으로 어딘가에서 보거나 들은 내용을 상대방에게 보고하거나 전달할 때 사용하는 표현이다.

 Listen and Speak 2 C

A: What are you doing?

B: I'm reading the newspaper.

A: Is there ❶anything interesting?

B: ❷This article says scientists have discovered a new planet.

❶ -thing, -body, -one으로 끝나는 부정대명사는 형용사가 뒤에 나온다.
❷ 'This article says ~.'는 '이 기사에 따르면 ~.'이라는 뜻으로 어딘가에서 보거나 들은 내용을 상대방에게 보고하거나 전달할 때 사용하는 표현이다. 정보 제공자에 따라 This article 대신 The Internet, The book, People, Someone 등을 쓸 수 있다.

 Real Life Talk Watch a Video

Suji: ❶Check out this picture!

Tony: Wow! ❷The camels are walking in a line in the desert.

Suji: Yeah. The desert ❸looks very hot and dry.

Tony: ❹I wonder how long camels can go without water in the desert.

Suji: Let's ❺find out ❻on the Internet.

Tony: Okay. ❼The Internet says they can go about two weeks without water.

Suji: Wow, that's amazing! Camels are really ❽ interesting animals.

Tony: ❾I want to travel with them in the desert someday.

❶ check out: (흥미로운 것을) 살펴보다, 확인하다
❷ camel: 낙타 in a line: 한 줄로 desert: 사막
❸ look+형용사: ~하게 보이다
❹ 궁금증을 표현할 때 '~를 궁금해하다'라는 의미를 가진 동사 wonder를 이용하여 'I wonder ~.'라고 말한다. wonder 다음에는 의문사절이나 if/whether절이 온다. without: ~ 없이
❺ find out: 찾아내다, (조사하여) 발견하다
❻ on the Internet: 인터넷에서
❼ '~가 …라고 말하다'라는 의미의 '주어+say(s)+that+주어+동사 ~.' 구문을 이용해 주어가 한 말인 that절의 내용을 상대방에게 보고하거나 전해줄 수 있다. 이때 접속사 that은 생략 가능하다.
❽ interesting은 '흥미로운'의 뜻으로 animals가 감정을 유발함을 나타내기 때문에 현재분사형으로 사용했다.
❾ want는 to부정사를 목적어로 취하는 동사이다. travel: 여행하다 someday: 언젠가, 훗날

● 다음 우리말과 일치하도록 빈칸에 알맞은 말을 쓰시오.

 해석

Listen and Speak 1 A

B: We're _____ _____ the top of the mountain.

G: I _____ _____ _____ this mountain is.

B: _____ _____ 2,000m high.

G: Wow! This is a really high mountain.

B: Yes, it is. Let's _____ _____.

B: 우리는 산 정상에 거의 다 왔어.
G: 나는 이 산이 얼마나 높은지 궁금해.
B: 이 산은 높이가 약 2,000미터야.
G: 우와! 정말 높은 산이구나.
B: 응, 맞아. 계속 올라가자.

Listen and Speak 1 B

B: Look _____ the baby penguins _____ TV. They're so cute.

G: Yes, but they _____ very cold out there.

B: Yeah, the South Pole _____ _____ _____ _____ _____ Earth.

G: I wonder _____ _____ _____ _____ _____ there.

B: The _____ temperature _____ about -58℃ _____ July and -26℃ _____ December.

G: Oh, _____, July is _____ _____ December there. Interesting!

B: Yes. _____ _____ very cold there, it _____ snow much.

G: That's _____, too!

B: TV에 나온 아기 펭귄들을 봐. 아주 귀여워.
G: 응, 하지만 그들은 저곳에서 매우 추워 보여.
B: 응, 남극은 지구에서 가장 추운 곳이야.
G: 그곳이 얼마나 추운지 궁금해.
B: 평균 기온이 7월에는 약 섭씨 영하 58도이고, 12월에는 약 섭씨 영하 26도야.
G: 오, 그러면 그곳은 12월보다 7월이 더 춥구나. 흥미롭다!
B: 응. 비록 그곳은 매우 춥지만 눈은 많이 내리지 않아.
G: 그것도 흥미롭다!

Listen and Speak 1 C

1. A: We're _____ here.

   B: Yes, I'm so _____. Let's _____ _____.

   A: I _____ _____ the bus stop is.

   B: It's _____ _____ _____ the police station.

   A: You're right. Let's go.

2. A: We're _____ _____.

   B: Yes, I'm so excited. Let's look around.

   A: I _____ _____ _____ _____ _____ is.

   B: It's _____ the library.

   A: You're right. Let's go.

3. A: We're finally here.

   B: Yes, I'm so excited. Let's look around.

   A: _____ _____ _____ Green Park _____.

   B: It's _____ _____ the school.

   A: You're right. Let's go.

1. A: 마침내 다 왔어.
   B: 맞아, 매우 신나. 둘러보자.
   A: 나는 버스 정류장이 어디에 있는지 궁금해.
   B: 경찰서 앞에 있어.
   A: 맞아. 가자.

2. A: 마침내 다 왔어.
   B: 맞아, 매우 신나. 둘러보자.
   A: 나는 안내 센터가 어디에 있는지 궁금해.
   B: 도서관 뒤에 있어.
   A: 맞아. 가자.

3. A: 마침내 다 왔어.
   B: 맞아, 매우 신나. 둘러보자.
   A: 나는 Green Park가 어디에 있는지 궁금해.
   B: 학교 옆에 있어.
   A: 맞아. 가자.

Listen and Speak 2 A

B: The weather is _____ nice outside.

G: Yeah. How _____ _____ _____ _____ _____ this afternoon?

B: Good idea. Can you _____ the weather?

G: Oh, no! The weather _____ _____ _____ _____ _____ in the afternoon.

B: Let's go _____ _____, then.

B: 바깥 날씨가 아주 좋아.
G: 응. 오늘 오후에 소풍 갈래?
B: 좋은 생각이야. 날씨를 확인해 주겠니?
G: 오, 안 돼! 일기 예보에 따르면 오후에 비가 올 거래.
B: 그러면 다음에 가자.

Listen and Speak 2 B

B: Sumin, what are you going _____ _____ on Sunday?

G: I'm going to go hiking. Do you want to _____ _____?

B: I'd love to. _____ _____ _____ _____ _____ go?

G: I'm _____ _____ _____ to Namsan.

B: Oh, the _____ there is so beautiful _____ _____ _____ year.

G: Right. _____ _____ _____ _____ _____ _____ red autumn leaves now.

B: Great. _____ _____ does the shortest hiking course _____?

G: _____ _____ _____ _____ _____ about two hours.

B: Okay, see you _____ Sunday!

B: 수민아, 일요일에 무엇을 할 거니?
G: 나는 등산을 갈 거야. 나와 함께 가겠니?
B: 그러고 싶어. 어디로 가고 싶니?
G: 나는 남산에 가려고 생각 중이야.
B: 오, 매년 이맘때 그곳 경치는 아주 아름다워.
G: 맞아. 지금 빨간 단풍잎으로 덮여 있다고 들었어.
B: 좋아. 가장 짧은 등산 코스는 얼마나 걸리니?
G: 인터넷 정보에 따르면 약 두 시간 정도 걸린대.
B: 알겠어, 일요일에 봐!

Listen and Speak 2 C

1. A: _____ are you _____?

   B: I'm reading the newspaper.

   A: Is there _____ _____?

   B: _____ _____ _____ _____ _____ _____ _____ a new planet.

2. A: What are you doing?

   B: I'm reading _____ _____.

   A: Is there _____ _____?

   B: _____ _____ _____ a whale family _____ _____ _____ _____ _____.

1. A: 뭐 하고 있니?
   B: 신문을 읽는 중이야.
   A: 흥미로운 것이 있니?
   B: 이 기사에 따르면 과학자들이 새로운 행성을 발견했대.

2. A: 뭐 하고 있니?
   B: 신문을 읽는 중이야.
   A: 흥미로운 것이 있니?
   B: 이 기사에 따르면 고래 가족이 동해에서 발견됐대.

Real Life Talk Watch a Video

Suji: _____ _____ this picture!

Tony: Wow! The _____ are walking _____ _____ _____ _____ the desert.

Suji: Yeah. The desert looks very hot and dry.

Tony: I _____ _____ _____ _____ _____ _____ without water in the desert.

Suji: Let's find _____ on the Internet.

Tony: Okay. _____ _____ _____ they can go about two weeks without water.

Suji: Wow, that's amazing! _____ _____ really _____ animals.

Tony: I want to _____ _____ _____ in the desert someday.

해석

수지: 이 사진을 봐!
Tony: 우와! 낙타들이 사막에서 한 줄로 걸어가고 있네.
수지: 응. 사막은 매우 덥고 건조해 보여.
Tony: 낙타들이 사막에서 물 없이 얼마나 오래 지낼 수 있는지 궁금해.
수지: 인터넷에서 찾아보자.
Tony: 그래. 인터넷 정보에 따르면 낙타는 물 없이 2주 정도 지낼 수 있대.
수지: 우와, 굉장하다! 낙타는 정말 흥미로운 동물이구나.
Tony: 나는 언젠가 사막에서 그들과 함께 여행하고 싶어.

Real Life Talk Step 2

1. **A:** _____ is the coldest place on Earth?

   B: I thinks it's the South Pole.

   A: _____ _____ _____ _____ it is.

   B: The book _____ the _____ _____ of the South Pole is _____ -49℃.

   A: That's _____!

2. **A:** Which planet is the biggest in the _____ _____?

   B: I thinks it's Jupiter.

   A: _____ _____ _____ _____ it is.

   B: _____ _____ _____ Jupiter is over 11 _____ _____ _____ Earth.

   A: That's amazing!

3. **A:** Where is the hottest desert _____ Earth?

   B: I thinks it's the Sahara Desert.

   A: I wonder _____ _____ _____ _____.

   B: The newspaper _____ the temperature of the Sahara Desert can _____ _____ _____ 50℃.

   A: That's amazing!

1. A: 지구에서 가장 추운 곳이 어디니?
   B: 남극이라고 생각해.
   A: 나는 그곳이 얼마나 추운지 궁금해.
   B: 책에 따르면 남극의 평균 온도가 섭씨 영하 49도래.
   A: 굉장하다!

2. A: 태양계에서 가장 큰 행성이 어느 것이니?
   B: 목성이라고 생각해.
   A: 나는 그것이 얼마나 큰지 궁금해.
   B: 인터넷에 따르면 목성은 지구보다 11배 이상 크다고 해.
   A: 굉장하다!

3. A: 지구에서 가장 더운 사막이 어디게?
   B: 사하라 사막이라고 생각해.
   A: 나는 그곳이 얼마나 더운지 궁금해.
   B: 신문에 따르면 사하라 사막 온도가 섭씨 50도까지 이룰 수 있다고 해.
   A: 굉장하다!

01 다음 대화의 밑줄 친 부분과 바꿔 쓸 수 있는 것을 고르시오.

> B: We're almost at the top of the mountain.
> G: <u>I wonder how high this mountain is.</u>
> B: It's about 2,000m high.
> G: Wow! This is a really high mountain.
> B: Yes, it is. Let's keep going.

① I know exactly how high this mountain is.
② I'm curious how high this mountain is.
③ Do you know if this mountain is high?
④ I'd like to know whether this mountain is high.
⑤ Can you check whether this mountain is high?

02 다음 대화의 빈칸에 알맞은 것을 고르시오.

> B: The weather is so nice outside.
> G: Yeah. How about going on a picnic this afternoon?
> B: Good idea. Can you check the weather?
> G: Oh, no! The weather forecast _____ it'll be rainy in the afternoon.
> B: Let's go another time, then.

① hears   ② heard   ③ have heard
④ says   ⑤ is said

03 다음 대화의 밑줄 친 부분과 바꿔 쓸 수 <u>없는</u> 것은?

> A: Which planet is the biggest in the solar system?
> B: I thinks it's Jupiter.
> A: <u>I wonder how big it is.</u>
> B: The Internet says Jupiter is over 11 times bigger than Earth.
> A: That's amazing!

① I'm sure how big it is.
② Can you tell me how big it is?
③ I want to know how big it is.
④ I'd be very interested to know how big it is.
⑤ I'm curious about how big it is.

[01~03] 다음 대화를 읽고 물음에 답하시오.

> B: We're almost at the top of the mountain.
> G: I ___(A)___ how high this mountain is.
> B: It's about 2,000m high.
> G: Wow! This is a really high mountain.
> B: Yes, it is. Let's keep ___(B)___ (go).

01 빈칸 (A)에 알맞은 말을 고르시오.

① wonder ② know ③ curious

④ strange ⑤ create

02 괄호 안의 단어를 문맥에 맞게 고쳐 빈칸 (B)를 채우시오.

➡ _____

03 위 대화의 내용과 일치하는 것을 고르시오.

① To get to the top of the mountain, they have to climb for about 2 hours.
② The boy doesn't know how high the mountain is.
③ They think that the mountain which they are climbing up is not high.
④ They have just reached the top of the mountain.
⑤ The girl wants to know how high the mountain is.

04 다음 빈칸에 알맞은 말을 고르시오.

> A: I wonder what the highest mountain in the world is.
> B: It's Mt. Everest. _____

① The weather forecast says it'll be rainy in the afternoon.
② The Internet says that it's about 8,850m high.
③ The Internet says they can go about two weeks without water.
④ This article says scientists have discovered a new planet.
⑤ This article says a whale family was seen in the East Sea.

05 다음 중 짝지어진 대화가 어색한 것은?

① A: How did Ann become a member of the orchestra?
  B: She said she played the violin 8 hours a day.
② A: My grandma said that a brand-new computer was so expensive.
  B: Really? How much is it?
③ A: I wonder who sang this song.
  B: The Internet says Jack wrote it.
④ A: I wonder where noodles come from.
  B: The book says they are from China.
⑤ A: Websites are very useful for doing homework, aren't they?
  B: Yes, they are. I wonder how people did their homework before the Internet.

06 다음 빈칸 (A)와 (B)에 알맞은 말을 쓰시오.

> A: Mina, is there anything interesting in the newspaper?
> B: The newspaper ___(A)___ the Arctic ice is melting ___(B)___.

(A) _____ (B) _____

[07~10] 다음 대화를 읽고 물음에 답하시오.

B: Look at the baby penguins on TV. They're so cute. (①)

G: Yes, but they look very cold out there. (②)

B: Yeah, the South Pole is the coldest place ___(a)___ Earth.

G: _____(A)_____

B: The average temperature is about -58℃ in July and -26℃ in December. (③)

G: Oh, then, July is colder ___(b)___ December there. Interesting! (④)

B: Yes. (⑤)

G: That's interesting, too!

07 위 대화의 ①~⑤ 중 주어진 문장이 들어갈 알맞은 곳은?

> Although it's very cold there, it doesn't snow much.

①   ②   ③   ④   ⑤

08 위 대화의 빈칸 (A)에 알맞지 <u>않은</u> 말을 고르시오.

① I'm curious about how cold it is there.

② Can you tell me how cold it is there?

③ I wonder how cold it is there.

④ I heard how cold it is there.

⑤ I would like to know how cold it is there.

서답형

09 위 대화의 빈칸 (a)와 (b)에 알맞은 말을 쓰시오.

(a) _____ (b) _____

중요

10 위 대화를 읽고 답할 수 <u>없는</u> 질문을 고르시오.

① How cold is it in the South Pole?

② What are they watching on TV?

③ What is the average temperature for the year in the South Pole?

④ Where is the coldest place on Earth?

⑤ Does it snow much in the South Pole?

11 다음 대화의 빈칸에 들어갈 말을 〈보기〉에서 골라 순서대로 옳게 배열한 것은?

> B: Sumin, what are you going to do on Sunday?
>
> G: _____
>
> B: _____
>
> G: _____
>
> B: _____
>
> G: Right. I heard that it's covered with red autumn leaves now.
>
> B: Great. How long does the shortest hiking course take?
>
> G: The Internet says it takes about two hours.
>
> B: Okay, see you on Sunday!

> (A) Oh, the scenery there is so beautiful this time of year.
>
> (B) I'm thinking of going to Namsan.
>
> (C) I'm going to go hiking. Do you want to join me?
>
> (D) I'd love to. Where do you want to go?

① (B) – (A) – (C) – (D)

② (B) – (C) – (A) – (D)

③ (C) – (A) – (B) – (D)

④ (C) – (B) – (A) – (D)

⑤ (C) – (D) – (B) – (A)

[01~03] 다음 대화를 읽고 물음에 답하시오.

Suji: Check ___(A)___ this picture!

Tony: Wow! The camels are walking in a line in the desert.

Suji: Yeah. The desert looks very hot and dry.

Tony: I wonder _____ⓐ_____ camels can go without water in the desert.

Suji: Let's find ___(B)___ on the Internet.

Tony: Okay. The Internet says they can go about two weeks without water.

Suji: Wow, that's amazing! Camels are really interesting animals.

Tony: I want to travel with ⓑthem in the desert someday.

01 빈칸 (A)와 (B)에 공통으로 들어갈 말을 쓰시오.

➡ _____

02 빈칸 ⓐ에 들어갈 말을 쓰시오.

➡ _____

03 밑줄 친 ⓑthem이 가리키는 것을 대화에서 찾아 쓰시오.

➡ _____

[04~05] 다음 대화를 읽고 물음에 답하시오.

B: Sumin, what are you going to do on Sunday?

G: I'm going to go hiking. Do you want to join me?

B: I'd love to. Where do you want to go?

G: I'm thinking of going to Namsan.

B: Oh, the scenery there is so beautiful this time of year.

G: Right. 지금 빨간 단풍잎으로 덮여 있다고 들었어. (heard, leaves, covered, I, red, that, autumn, is, now, with, it)

B: Great. How long does the shortest hiking course take?

G: The Internet ___(A)___ it ___(B)___ about two hours.

B: Okay, see you on Sunday!

04 빈칸 (A)와 (B)에 들어갈 말을 〈보기〉에서 찾아 어법에 맞게 쓰시오.

┌─── 보기 ────┐

get   know   make   say

speak   take

(A) _____ (B) _____

05 밑줄 친 우리말과 일치하도록 괄호 안에 주어진 단어를 알맞게 배열하시오.

➡ _____

_____

06 다음 밑줄 친 우리말과 일치하도록 주어진 단어를 이용하여 영작하시오.

┌──────────────────────────┐

A: We're finally here.

B: Yes, I'm so excited. Let's look around.

A: 나는 Green Park가 어디에 있는지 궁금해.

B: It's next to the school.

A: You're right. Let's go.

└──────────────────────────┘

➡ _____ (be, wonder)

Grammar
교과서

① 소유격 관계대명사 whose

> • This small fish **whose** favorite food is clams uses a tool to open them.
> 가장 좋아하는 먹이가 조개인 이 작은 물고기는 조개를 열기 위해 도구를 사용한다.

■ 관계대명사의 소유격은 선행사가 그 뒤에 나오는 문장에서 소유격 형태로 나올 때 두 문장을 하나로 이어주어 '접속사'와 '대명사의 소유격'의 역할을 한다. 소유격 관계대명사는 생략할 수 없으며, 관계대명사절은 형용사 역할을 하여 바로 앞의 선행사를 꾸며준다.

- He's a man. I respect his opinion.
  = He's a man, and I respect his opinion.
  = He's a man **whose** opinion I respect. 그는 내가 그의 의견을 존중하는 남자이다.
- It's the house. Its door is painted red.
  = It's the house, and its door is painted red.
  = It's the house **whose** door is painted red. 그것은 문이 빨간색 페인트로 칠해진 집이다.

■ 관계대명사의 소유격은 선행사가 사람 또는 사물인 경우에 whose를 쓸 수 있으며, 선행사가 사물일 경우에는 of which로 바꿔 쓸 수 있으며 사람일 경우에는 of which를 쓸 수 없다. of which를 쓸 경우 of which가 받는 명사 앞에는 정관사 the를 써야 한다.

- The desk did not burn. Its top was made of metal.
  = The desk did not burn and its top was made of metal.
  = The desk, **whose** top was made of metal, did not burn.
  = The desk, **of which** the top was made of metal, did not burn.
  = The desk, the top **of which** was made of metal, did not burn. 그 책상은 표면이 금속제여서 타지 않았다.

■ 소유격을 대신하기 때문에 whose 뒤에 명사가 오고, 관계사절은 완전한 절이 나온다.

- I saw a sick animal. Its life was in danger.
  = I saw a sick animal **whose** life was in danger. 나는 생명이 위태로운 아픈 동물을 보았다.

■ 의문사 whose(누구의)와 혼동하지 않도록 유의한다.

- He **whose** walk is upright fears the Lord. 걸음이 올바른 사람은 하나님을 두려워한다. (소유격 관계대명사)
- **Whose** house is that? 저것이 누구의 집이죠? (의문사)

핵심 Check

1. 다음 괄호 안에서 알맞은 단어를 고르시오.

   (1) I have several friends (whose / who) jobs are doctors.

   (2) I'd rather work for a company (which / of which) the products I trust.

② 시간을 나타내는 접속사

- **Humpback whales stand on their tails while they sleep.**
  혹동고래는 잠을 자는 동안 꼬리로 서 있다.

■ 시간을 나타내는 접속사의 종류와 쓰임: 시간의 접속사는 종속절을 이끌며 주절과 종속절을 이어주는 역할을 한다.

when	~할 때	while	~하는 동안에
before	~하기 전에	until	~할 때까지
after	~한 후에	as soon as	~하자마자

- It hurts **when** I bend my knee. 저는 무릎을 구부리면 아파요.
- It began to rain **before** I got home. 내가 집에 도착하기 전에 비가 내리기 시작했다.
- I've got into the habit of turning on the TV **as soon as** I get home.
  나는 집에 오자마자 TV를 켜는 것이 버릇이 되었다.

■ 시간의 접속사가 이끄는 종속절은 주절의 앞이나 뒤에 모두 올 수 있다. 주절의 앞에 올 경우 보통 종속절 끝에 콤마(,)를 찍어 준다.

- We waited inside **until** things calmed down.
  = **Until** things calmed down, we waited inside. 우리는 사태가 진정될 때까지 안에서 기다렸다.

■ 시간의 접속사가 이끄는 부사절에서는 미래의 의미일지라도 현재 시제를 쓴다.

- I will look after your affairs **while** you are away. (○)
  I will look after your affairs **while** you will be away. (×) 내가 당신이 없는 동안 당신의 일을 돌보겠습니다.

핵심 Check

2. 다음 우리말에 맞게 괄호 안의 어구를 바르게 배열하시오.

(1) 우리는 성질이 가라앉을 때까지 기다려야 할 것 같아. (I, we, think, wait, have, should, cooled, tempers, until)

   ➡ _____

(2) 도로를 건널 때는 내 손을 잡아라. (we, me, the road, your hand, give, cross, while)

   ➡ _____

01 다음 빈칸에 들어갈 말로 알맞은 것은?

> This small fish _____ favorite food is clams uses a tool to open them.

① which　　　　② of which　　　　③ who
④ whose　　　　⑤ whom

02 다음 두 문장을 한 문장으로 바꾸어 쓸 때 알맞게 표현한 것을 고르시오.

> • What happened? • I was out.

① What happened while I was out?
② What happened because I was out?
③ What happened although I was out?
④ What happened since I was out?
⑤ What happened if I was out?

03 다음 두 문장을 관계대명사를 이용하여 하나의 문장으로 바르게 쓴 것을 고르시오.

> • I know the woman. • Her last name is Johnson.

① I know the woman who last name is Johnson.
② I know the woman whose last name is Johnson.
③ I know the woman whom last name is Johnson.
④ I know the woman which last name is Johnson.
⑤ I know the woman of which last name is Johnson.

04 다음 괄호 안에서 알맞은 말을 고르시오.

(1) I got a surprise (until / when) I saw the bill.

　➡ _____

(2) I felt so lonesome (after / although) she left.

　➡ _____

(3) He repeated it several times over (as soon as / until) he could remember it.

　➡ _____

01 다음 문장의 밑줄 친 부분 중 어법상 어색한 것은?

> The documentary ①caused ②a lot of bad feeling among the workers ③of which lives ④it ⑤described.

①   ②   ③   ④   ⑤

02 다음 중 어법상 어색한 문장은?

① I learned French after I moved to Paris.
② There was a long pause before she answered.
③ I recognized him as soon as he came in the room.
④ Mr. Cho met many foreigners while he was abroad.
⑤ The female sits on the eggs after they hatch.

서답형

[03~04] 다음 우리말과 일치하도록 괄호 안에 주어진 어구를 바르게 배열하시오.

03
> 나는 나와 이름이 같은 소녀를 만났다.
> (I, a girl, name, the same, mine, whose, met, is, as)

➡ _____

04
> 내가 말하는 동안 조용히 해라.
> (I'm, be, while, quiet, speaking)

➡ _____

[05~06] 다음 우리말과 일치하도록 바르게 영작한 것을 고르시오.

05
> 미술관에 그의 그림이 있는 남자는 나의 삼촌이다.

① The man whose painting is in the museum is my uncle.
② The man who painting is in the museum is my uncle.
③ The man whom painting is in the museum is my uncle.
④ The man which painting is in the museum is my uncle.
⑤ The man of which painting is in the museum is my uncle.

06
> 그는 점심 식사 후에, 친구들과 야구를 했다.

① He played baseball with his friends before he had lunch.
② He played baseball with his friends when he had lunch.
③ He played baseball with his friends after he had lunch.
④ He played baseball with his friends while he had lunch.
⑤ He played baseball with his friends until he had lunch.

서답형

07 다음 문장에서 어법상 어색한 것을 바르게 고치시오.

> This is the picture of which price is unbelievably high.

_____ ➡ _____

08 다음 중 빈칸 ⓐ~ⓕ에 같은 단어가 들어가는 것끼리 바르게 짝지어진 것은?

> • I know a boy ⓐ_____ dad is a history teacher.
> • The book the cover ⓑ_____ is blue is mine.
> • There is a student ⓒ_____ favorite subject is music.
> • There was a big house the garden ⓓ_____ was very beautiful.
> • She's an artist ⓔ_____ work I really admire.

① ⓐ, ⓒ, ⓓ
② ⓐ, ⓒ, ⓔ
③ ⓑ, ⓒ, ⓔ
④ ⓑ, ⓓ, ⓔ
⑤ ⓒ, ⓓ

09 다음 중 밑줄 친 접속사의 쓰임이 어색한 것은?

① When he was a child, he lived in Busan.
② I was listening to the radio while my husband was taking a shower.
③ He came up as she was speaking.
④ Eddie bought a bottle of water until he was thirsty.
⑤ We'll leave in the morning as soon as it's light.

10 다음 중 밑줄 친 부분의 쓰임이 나머지와 다른 것은?

① The boy whose T-shirt is red is Homin.
② I have several friends whose jobs are doctors.
③ There is a frog whose length is longer than a pencil.
④ A man whose name I didn't know lived there.
⑤ Will you tell me whose side are you on?

11 다음 중 밑줄 친 부분의 쓰임이 어색한 것은?

① We have ten minutes before the train leaves.
② Just ring for the nurse if you need her.
③ I usually go to the gym while my lunch hour.
④ She felt disappointed since she hadn't been invited.
⑤ Strange though it may sound, I was pleased it was over.

12 다음 중 어법상 옳은 문장은?

① Look at the house of which roof is red.
② My favorite sea animal is the beluga whale whose body is white all over.
③ Veronica, of which the hobby is playing the piano, finally received the first prize last week.
④ Teachers tend to be more generous to those students whose the work is neat and tidy.
⑤ We came to a small circular apartment roof of which was a perfect arched dome.

[13~14] 주어진 두 문장을 관계대명사를 사용해서 하나의 문장으로 바르게 고친 것을 고르시오.

13

- She met the man.
- His name is Mark.

① She met the man the name of which is Mark.
② She met the man who the name is Mark.
③ She met the man whose the name is Mark.
④ She met the man whom the name is Mark.
⑤ She met the man whose name is Mark.

- War must be a word.
- Its meaning has to disappear from our understanding.

① War must be a word the meaning of which has to disappear from our understanding.
② War must be a word whose the meaning has to disappear from our understanding.
③ War must be a word of which meaning has to disappear from our understanding.
④ War must be a word the meaning of what has to disappear from our understanding.
⑤ War must be a word who the meaning has to disappear from our understanding.

15 다음 괄호 안에서 알맞은 말을 고르시오.

(1) I have a watch (whose / of which) price is 9,000 won.
(2) I have a brother (that / whose) name is Tony.
(3) Look at the dog (of which / whose) the tail is very long.
(4) Please make yourself comfortable (while / during) I get some coffee.
(5) I hope you will have a housewarming party when you (are / will be) settled.
(6) I'll wait outside (until / that) the meeting's over.

16 다음 우리말을 영작할 때, 어법상 어색한 문장을 고르시오. (2개)

> 유명한 작가의 소설은 잘 팔린다.
> *readily: 즉시, 쉽사리, 순조롭게

① Novels of which the authors are famous sell readily.
② Novels the authors of which are famous sell readily.
③ Novels whose authors are famous sell readily.
④ Novels whose the authors are famous sell readily.
⑤ Novels of which authors are famous sell readily.

중요

01 다음 우리말과 일치하도록 괄호 안에 주어진 어구를 알맞게 배열하시오.

(1) Tony는 머리가 빨간색인 그 소녀를 본 적이 있다. (Tony, the girl, red, hair, has, is, seen, whose)

➡ _____

(2) 그것들은 개인 사업이기 때문에 주요 목적이 돈을 버는 것이다. (businesses, focus, they, money, is, are, private, whose, main, making)

➡ _____
_____

(3) 혹등고래는 잠을 자는 동안 꼬리로 서 있다. (humpback whales, tails, they, their, sleep, stand, while, on)

➡ _____
_____

(4) 우리는 그 섬에 도착하자마자 간절히 탐사가 하고 싶었다. (As, as, we, we, the island, explore, were, arrived, eager, soon, to, on)

➡ _____
_____

02 다음 괄호 안에 주어진 접속사를 사용하여 두 문장을 한 문장으로 바꿔 쓰시오. (주절을 앞에 쓸 것.)

(1) • I met my friend.
• I was on my way to school. (while)

➡ _____

(2) • You will be instructed where to go.
• The plane is ready. (as soon as)

➡ _____
_____

(3) • He grew and grew.
• He was taller than his father. (until)

➡ _____
_____

(4) • You must be careful.
• You are handling chemicals. (when)

➡ _____
_____

고난이도

03 다음 두 문장을 which를 이용하여 한 문장으로 쓰시오.

(1) • I have a cup.
• The color of the cup is blue.

➡ _____
_____

(2) • I could not solve the science problem.
• Its solution was very difficult.

➡ _____
_____

(3) • I want to enter an international school.
• The students of the school come from many countries.

➡ _____
_____
_____

(4) • Years ago I happened to get a very old-looking jar.
• The owner of the jar is not known up to now.

➡ _____
_____
_____

04 다음 각 문장에서 어법상 <u>어색한</u> 단어를 한 개씩만 찾아 고치시오.

> (1) I know a boy whose the hobby is collecting stamps.
> (2) I used to take care of a cat of which owner went away frequently on business.
> (3) Andy lives in a house which the windows were covered with roses.
> (4) Look at the boy who dog is bigger than him.
> (5) He wanted to honor people whose made the world better.
> (6) Shrek is a friendly monster who body is green.

(1) _____ ➡ _____
(2) _____ ➡ _____
(3) _____ ➡ _____
(4) _____ ➡ _____
(5) _____ ➡ _____
(6) _____ ➡ _____

[05~06] 다음 우리말과 일치하도록 괄호 안에 주어진 단어와 조건을 활용하여 문장을 완성하시오.

05

> 꼭대기가 눈으로 덮인 저 산을 보아라.
> ➡ Look at the mountain _____ snow.
> (the top, cover, with, 어형 변화 가능)

➡ _____

06

> Jinsu가 Mark와 이야기를 하고 있는 동안 Ann은 그녀의 개를 산책시키고 있었다.
> ➡ _____, Ann was walking her dog.
> (talk with, 6 단어, 어형 변화 가능)

➡ _____

07 다음 우리말을 괄호 안에 주어진 어휘를 사용하여 영작하시오. (필요시 단어를 추가할 수 있으나, 변형은 하지 말 것.)

> (1) 'tuskfish'는 조개가 나타날 때까지 모래에 입김을 분다. (a clam, the tuskfish, the sand, blows, appears, on)
>
> ➡ _____

> (2) 당신은 표지를 변경하고 싶은 앨범을 선택할 수 있습니다. (you, you'd, the album, cover of, select, like, can, change, to)
>
> ➡ _____

> (3) 인류는 세상을 다른 시각으로 보는 사람들에게 아주 냉담할 수 있다. (Humanity, eyes, those, be, can, see the world differently, quite cold to)
>
> ➡ _____

Under the Sea

Two-thirds of our planet is covered by oceans. They are full of
3분의 2 (분자는 기수, 분모는 서수)   = oceans   ~로 가득 차다
wonder and are home to millions of species. Every day, we are learning
수많은   매일, 날마다(부사) everyday: 일상의, 매일의
new things about them. Let's find out about some interesting sea
animals.

Sweet Dreams

Can you guess what these whales are doing in the picture? It looks
'의문사+주어+동사'의 어순으로 쓰인 간접의문문   ~처럼 보이다
like they are standing up in a group. But they are actually sleeping!
한 무리를 이루어
Humpback whales stand on their tails while they sleep. They sleep near
혹등고래   '~하는 동안에', 동작이나 상태가 계속됨을 나타냄.(접속사)
the surface. Since they are not fish, they need to come up to breathe.
'~이기 때문에', 이유의 부사절을 이끄는 접속사   목적을 나타내는 to부정사의 부사적 용법
Also, they don't fall asleep completely. When they wake up, they come

out of the water for a deep breath and dive back into the sea.
'~을 위해, ~하러', 목적의 의미를 나타내는 전치사   이전 장소나 상태로 다시 돌려놓는다는 의미를 나타냄.(부사)
*humpback whale: 혹등고래라고 불리며, 북극해를 제외한 모든 대양에서 서식한다.

---

planet 행성
wonder 경이, 경탄, 놀라움
millions of 수많은
species (분류상의) 종
whale 고래
tail 꼬리
surface 수면, 표면
breathe 숨을 쉬다
breath 숨, 호흡

📎 확인문제

● 다음 문장이 본문의 내용과 일치하면 T, 일치하지 않으면 F를 쓰시오.

1 Two-thirds of our planet is covered by oceans. ☐

2 Humpback whales stand on their heads while they sleep. ☐

3 Humpback whales sleep near the surface. ☐

4 Humpback whales don't need to come up to breathe. ☐

5 Humpback whales don't fall asleep completely. ☐

6 When humpback whales sleep, they come out of the water and dive back into the
   sea. ☐

Enjoy Your Meal

If you think fish are not smart, take a look at the tuskfish. This small
<small>fish는 단수형과 복수형이 동일한 단어로 뒤에 나온 are를 근거로 fish가 복수임을 알 수 있다.</small>
fish whose favorite food is clams uses a tool to open them. Clams
<small>소유격 관계대명사   목적을 나타내는 to부정사의 부사적 용법 = clams</small>
usually hide under the sand, so they cannot be easily discovered. The
<small>'그래서, 그 결과'(접속사)   조동사가 포함된 수동태: '조동사(cannot)+be+과거분사'의 형태</small>
tuskfish blows on the sand until a clam appears. The clam is closed
tightly, so the fish cannot eat it. But the tuskfish doesn't give up. It
<small>= the tuskfish</small>
smashes the clam against a rock. In the end, the clam opens and dinner
<small>   smash A against B: A를 B에 내리치다   마침내, 결국</small>
is served.

*tuskfish: 놀래깃과의 물고기로 서태평양과 인도양에서 주로 서식한다.

One, Two, Three, Jump!

You have probably seen a bird fly down to the sea to catch a fish.
<small>지각동사 see+목적어+동사원형: (목적어)가 ~하는 것을 보다   to부정사의 부사적 용법(목적)</small>
But have you ever seen a fish jump out of the water to catch a bird?

Well, birds have to be careful when a giant trevally is around. This fish
<small>Well은 감탄사로 실제로 말하고자 하는 것을 소개하기 위해 씀</small>
can grow up to 170cm and 80kg. But don't let its size fool you. This
<small>   '~까지', 숫자, 정도, 위치 등과 함께 사용   사역동사(let)+목적어+동사원형: (목적어)가 ~하도록 허락하다</small>
fish is quick and smart. It can spot a flying bird and calculate its speed
<small>quick(빠른)과 smart(똑똑한)는 형용사로 주격보어   spot (V1)   현재분사 · 등위접속사 and를 써서 대등하게 연결 calculate (V2)</small>
and distance. When the bird flies nearby, the giant trevally jumps out
<small>   근처에, 가까운 곳에(부사)</small>
of the water and catches it.
<small>out of+명사: ~의 밖으로</small>

*giant trevally: 전갱잇과의 물고기로 서태평양과 인도양에서 서식한다.

clam 조개
tool 도구
discover 발견하다
blow (입으로) 불다
tightly 단단히, 꽉
smash 때려 부수다, 깨뜨리다
serve (음식을) 제공하다, 차려 주다
fool 속이다, 기만하다
spot 발견하다, 찾아내다
calculate 계산하다
distance 거리

 확인문제

- 다음 문장이 본문의 내용과 일치하면 T, 일치하지 않으면 F를 쓰시오.

1 The favorite food of the tuskfish is clams. ☐

2 Clams usually hide under the rock. ☐

3 The tuskfish smashes the clam against a rock. ☐

4 It is impossible for a bird to fly down to the sea to catch a fish. ☐

5 A giant trevally can grow up to 170cm and 80kg. ☐

6 A giant trevally can't calculate the speed and distance of a flying bird. ☐

● 우리말을 참고하여 빈칸에 알맞은 말을 쓰시오.

1 _____ the Sea

2 _____ of our planet is covered by oceans.

3 They are full of wonder and are home to _____ _____ _____.

4 Every day, we are learning _____ _____ about them.

5 _____ _____ _____ about some interesting sea animals.

6 _____ Dreams

7 Can you guess _____ _____ _____ _____ _____ in the picture?

8 It looks like they are standing up _____ _____ _____.

9 But they are _____ sleeping!

10 Humpback whales _____ _____ _____ _____ while they sleep.

11 They sleep _____ _____ _____.

12 Since they are not fish, they _____ _____ _____ to breathe.

13 Also, they don't _____ _____ completely.

14 When they wake up, they come out of the water _____ _____ _____ _____ and dive back into the sea.

15 _____ Your Meal

16 If you think fish are not smart, _____ _____ _____ _____ the tuskfish.

1	바다 아래에
2	우리 행성의 3분의 2는 대양들로 덮여 있다.
3	대양들은 신기한 것으로 가득 차 있고 수많은 종의 서식지이다.
4	매일 우리는 그들에 관한 새로운 것들을 배우고 있다.
5	몇몇 흥미로운 바다 동물들을 알아보자.
6	좋은 꿈 꿔라
7	여러분은 그림 속 이 고래들이 무엇을 하고 있는지 추측할 수 있는가?
8	그들이 무리를 지어 서 있는 것처럼 보인다.
9	그러나 그들은 실제로는 잠을 자고 있다!
10	혹등고래들은 잠을 자는 동안 꼬리로 서 있다.
11	그들은 수면 근처에서 잠을 잔다.
12	그들은 물고기가 아니기 때문에 숨을 쉬기 위해 위로 나올 필요가 있다.
13	또한 그들은 완전히 잠들지 않는다.
14	그들은 잠에서 깨면 심호흡을 하러 물 밖으로 나왔다가 바다로 다시 뛰어든다.
15	맛있게 먹어라
16	만약 물고기가 똑똑하지 않다고 생각한다면 'tuskfish'를 보아라.

17 This small fish _____ _____ _____ is clams uses a tool to open them.

18 Clams usually hide under the sand, so they _____ _____ _____ _____.

19 The tuskfish blows on the sand _____ a clam _____.

20 The clam _____ _____ _____, so the fish cannot eat it.

21 But the tuskfish doesn't _____ _____.

22 It _____ the clam _____ a rock.

23 In the end, the clam opens and dinner _____ _____.

24 One, Two, Three, _____!

25 You have probably seen a bird _____ _____ to the sea to catch a fish.

26 But have you ever seen a fish _____ _____ _____ _____ to catch a bird?

27 Well, birds have to be careful when a giant trevally _____ _____.

28 This fish can grow _____ _____ 170cm and 80kg.

29 But don't _____ its size _____ you.

30 This fish is _____ _____ _____.

31 It can _____ a flying bird and _____ its speed and distance.

32 When the bird flies _____, the giant trevally _____ out of the water and _____ it.

---

17 가장 좋아하는 먹이가 조개인 이 작은 물고기는 조개를 열기 위해 도구를 사용한다.

18 조개는 대개 모래 아래에 숨어 있어서 쉽게 발견할 수 없다.

19 'tuskfish'는 조개가 나타날 때까지 모래에 입김을 분다.

20 조개가 단단히 닫혀 있어서 물고기는 이것을 먹을 수 없다.

21 그러나 'tuskfish'는 포기하지 않는다.

22 'tuskfish'는 돌에 조개를 내리친다.

23 마침내 조개가 열리고 밥상이 차려진다.

24 하나, 둘, 셋. 뛰어라!

25 여러분은 아마 새가 물고기를 잡기 위해 바다로 날아 내려가는 것을 본 적이 있을 것이다.

26 그러나 물고기가 새를 잡기 위해 물 밖으로 뛰어오르는 것을 본 적이 있는가?

27 자, 새들은 'giant trevally'가 주변에 있을 때 조심해야 한다.

28 이 물고기는 170센티미터에 80킬로그램까지 자랄 수 있다.

29 그러나 그 크기에 속지 마라.

30 이 물고기는 빠르고 똑똑하다.

31 이것은 날고 있는 새를 발견하고 그 새의 속도와 거리를 계산할 수 있다.

32 새가 근처에 날고 있을 때, 'giant trevally'는 물 밖으로 뛰어올라 새를 잡는다.

● 우리말을 참고하여 본문을 영작하시오.

1 바다 아래에

➡ _____

2 우리 행성의 3분의 2는 대양들로 덮여 있다.

➡ _____

3 대양들은 신기한 것으로 가득 차 있고 수많은 종의 서식지이다.

➡ _____

4 매일 우리는 그들에 관한 새로운 것들을 배우고 있다.

➡ _____

5 몇몇 흥미로운 바다 동물들을 알아보자.

➡ _____

6 좋은 꿈 꿔라

➡ _____

7 여러분은 그림 속 이 고래들이 무엇을 하고 있는지 추측할 수 있는가?

➡ _____

8 그들이 무리를 지어 서 있는 것처럼 보인다.

➡ _____

9 그러나 그들은 실제로는 잠을 자고 있다!

➡ _____

10 혹등고래들은 잠을 자는 동안 꼬리로 서 있다.

➡ _____

11 그들은 수면 근처에서 잠을 잔다.

➡ _____

12 그들은 물고기가 아니기 때문에 숨을 쉬기 위해 위로 나올 필요가 있다.

➡ _____

13 또한 그들은 완전히 잠들지 않는다.

➡ _____

14 그들은 잠에서 깨면 심호흡을 하러 물 밖으로 나왔다가 바다로 다시 뛰어든다.

➡ _____

15 맛있게 먹어라

➡ _____

16 만약 물고기가 똑똑하지 않다고 생각한다면 'tuskfish'를 보아라.

➡ _____

17 가장 좋아하는 먹이가 조개인 이 작은 물고기는 조개를 열기 위해 도구를 사용한다.

➡ _____

18 조개는 대개 모래 아래에 숨어 있어서 쉽게 발견할 수 없다.

➡ _____

19 'tuskfish'는 조개가 나타날 때까지 모래에 입김을 분다.

➡ _____

20 조개가 단단히 닫혀 있어서 물고기는 이것을 먹을 수 없다.

➡ _____

21 그러나 'tuskfish'는 포기하지 않는다.

➡ _____

22 'tuskfish'는 돌에 조개를 내리친다.

➡ _____

23 마침내 조개가 열리고 밥상이 차려진다.

➡ _____

24 하나, 둘, 셋, 뛰어라!

➡ _____

25 여러분은 아마 새가 물고기를 잡기 위해 바다로 날아 내려가는 것을 본 적이 있을 것이다.

➡ _____

26 그러나 물고기가 새를 잡기 위해 물 밖으로 뛰어오르는 것을 본 적이 있는가?

➡ _____

27 자, 새들은 'giant trevally'가 주변에 있을 때 조심해야 한다.

➡ _____

28 이 물고기는 170센티미터에 80킬로그램까지 자랄 수 있다.

➡ _____

29 그러나 그 크기에 속지 마라.

➡ _____

30 이 물고기는 빠르고 똑똑하다.

➡ _____

31 이것은 날고 있는 새를 발견하고 그 새의 속도와 거리를 계산할 수 있다.

➡ _____

32 새가 근처에 날고 있을 때, 'giant trevally'는 물 밖으로 뛰어올라 새를 잡는다.

➡ _____

[01~03] 다음 글을 읽고 물음에 답하시오.

ⓐTwo-thirds of our planet are covered by oceans. ⓑThey are full of wonder and are home to millions of species. Every day, we are learning new things about them. Let's find out about some interesting sea animals.

서답형

01 위 글의 밑줄 친 ⓐ에서 어법상 틀린 부분을 찾아 고치시오.

_____ ➡ _____

서답형

02 위 글의 밑줄 친 ⓑThey가 가리키는 것을 본문에서 찾아 쓰시오.

➡ _____

03 위 글의 뒤에 올 내용으로 가장 알맞은 것을 고르시오.

① the oceans which cover two-thirds of our planet
② the stories about our planet which is full of wonder
③ millions of species living in oceans
④ the stories about some interesting sea animals
⑤ many new things we are learning about every day

[04~07] 다음 글을 읽고 물음에 답하시오.

Enjoy Your Meal

If you think fish are not smart, ①take a look at the tuskfish. This small fish whose favorite food is clams uses a tool to open them. Clams usually hide under the sand, so (A)they cannot be easily discovered. The tuskfish blows on the sand until a clam ② appears. The clam ____ⓐ____ tightly, so the fish cannot eat it. But the tuskfish doesn't give up. ③It smashes the clam against a rock. ④In the end, the clam opens and dinner ⑤is served.

*tuskfish: 놀래깃과의 물고기로 서태평양과 인도양에서 주로 서식한다.

서답형

04 위 글의 빈칸 ⓐ에 close를 알맞은 형태로 쓰시오.

➡ _____

서답형

05 위 글의 밑줄 친 (A)they가 가리키는 것을 본문에서 찾아 쓰시오.

➡ _____

서답형

06 다음 문장에서 위 글의 내용과 다른 부분을 찾아서 고치시오.

When the clam is closed tightly and the tuskfish cannot eat it, the fish gives up eating it.

➡ _____

07 다음 중 위 글의 밑줄 친 ①~⑤에 대한 설명이 옳지 않은 것을 고르시오.

① have a look at이나 look at으로 바꿔 쓸 수 있다.
② '조개가 나타날 때까지'라고 해야 하므로, is appeared로 고쳐야 한다.
③ the tuskfish를 가리킨다.
④ Finally로 바꿔 쓸 수 있다.
⑤ is ready로 바꿔 쓸 수 있다.

[08~10] 다음 글을 읽고 물음에 답하시오.

Enjoy Your Meal

If you think fish (A)[is / are] not smart, take a look at the tuskfish. This small fish whose favorite food is clams (B)[use / uses] ⓐa tool to open them. Clams usually hide under the sand, so they cannot be easily discovered. The tuskfish blows on the sand until a clam appears. ⓑThe clam is closed tightly, so the fish cannot eat it. But the tuskfish doesn't (C)[give up / keep trying]. It smashes the clam against a rock. In the end, the clam opens and dinner is served.

*tuskfish: 놀래깃과의 물고기로 서태평양과 인도양에서 주로 서식한다.

서답형

08 위 글의 괄호 (A)~(C)에서 문맥이나 어법상 알맞은 낱말을 골라 쓰시오.

(A) _____ (B) _____ (C) _____

서답형

09 위 글의 밑줄 친 ⓐa tool의 예에 해당하는 것을 본문에서 찾아 쓰시오.

➡ _____

서답형

10 위 글의 밑줄 친 ⓑ를 다음과 같이 바꿔 쓸 때 빈칸에 들어갈 알맞은 접속사를 쓰시오.

> _____ the clam is closed tightly, the fish cannot eat it.

[11~13] 다음 글을 읽고 물음에 답하시오.

One, Two, Three, Jump!

You have probably seen a bird fly down to the sea to catch a fish. But have you ever seen a fish jump out of the water to catch a bird? Well, birds have to be careful when a giant trevally is around. This fish can grow up to 170cm and 80kg. But don't let its size fool you. This fish is quick and smart. It can spot a ⓐflying bird and calculate its speed and distance. When the bird flies nearby, the giant trevally jumps out of the water and catches it.

*giant trevally: 전갱잇과의 물고기로 서태평양과 인도양에서 서식한다.

11 위 글의 밑줄 친 ⓐflying과 문법적 쓰임이 같은 것을 모두 고르시오.

① I saw the smoke coming out of the house.
② Do you mind turning down the volume?
③ The boy sleeping under the tree is my brother.
④ She answered smiling at me.
⑤ Did you practice playing the cello?

12 위 글의 주제로 알맞은 것을 고르시오.

① Birds can fly down to the sea to catch a fish.
② A giant trevally is a fish that jumps out of the water to catch a bird.
③ How big can a giant trevally grow?
④ How can a giant trevally spot a flying bird?
⑤ What can a giant trevally calculate?

13 Why do birds have to be careful when a giant trevally is around? Fill in the blanks (A) and (B) with suitable words.

> Because the giant trevally (A)_____ out of the water and (B)_____ a bird when a bird flies nearby.

[14~16] 다음 글을 읽고 물음에 답하시오.

Enjoy Your Meal

If you think fish are not smart, take a look at the tuskfish. This small fish whose favorite food is clams uses a tool to open ⓐthem. Clams usually hide under the sand, so they cannot be easily discovered. The tuskfish blows on the sand until a clam appears. The clam is closed tightly, so the fish cannot eat it. But the tuskfish doesn't give up. ⓑ그것은 돌에 조개를 내리친다. In the end, the clam opens and dinner is served.

*tuskfish: 놀래깃과의 물고기로 서태평양과 인도양에서 주로 서식한다.

서답형

14 위 글의 밑줄 친 ⓐthem이 가리키는 것을 본문에서 찾아 쓰시오.

➡ _____

서답형

15 위 글의 밑줄 친 ⓑ의 우리말에 맞게 주어진 어휘를 이용하여 7 단어로 영작하시오.

> smashes, rock

➡ _____

서답형

16 How does the tuskfish discover a clam in the sand? Answer in English in a full sentence beginning with "It". (9 words)

➡ _____

[17~19] 다음 글을 읽고 물음에 답하시오.

Sweet Dreams

Can you guess what these whales are doing in the picture? It looks like they are standing up _____ⓐ_____ a group. But they are actually sleeping! Humpback whales stand _____ⓑ_____ their tails while they sleep. They sleep near the surface. Since they are not fish, they need to come up ⓒto breathe. ⓓAlso, they don't fall sleepy completely. When they wake up, they come out of the water for a deep breath and dive back into the sea.

*humpback whale: 혹등고래라고 불리며, 북극해를 제외한 모든 대양에서 서식한다

17 위 글의 빈칸 ⓐ와 ⓑ에 들어갈 전치사가 바르게 짝지어진 것은?

	ⓐ	ⓑ		ⓐ	ⓑ
①	by	– from	②	for	– on
③	in	– on	④	for	– to
⑤	in	– from			

18 위 글의 밑줄 친 ⓒto breathe와 to부정사의 용법이 같은 것을 모두 고르시오.

① He worked hard only to fail.
② She encouraged me to try once again.
③ She must be a fool to say like that.
④ There is no one to do it.
⑤ I want to be busy again.

서답형

19 위 글의 밑줄 친 ⓓ에서 어법상 틀린 부분을 찾아 고치시오.

_____ ➡ _____

[20~22] 다음 글을 읽고 물음에 답하시오.

_____ⓐ_____

You have probably seen a bird fly down to the sea to catch a fish. But have you ever seen a fish jump out of the water to catch a bird? Well, birds have to be careful when a giant trevally is around. This fish can grow

ⓑup to 170cm and 80kg. But don't let its size fool you. This fish is quick and smart. It can spot a flying bird and calculate its speed and distance. When the bird flies nearby, the giant trevally jumps out of the water and catches it.

*giant trevally: 전갱잇과의 물고기로 서태평양과 인도양에서 서식한다.

20 위 글의 빈칸 ⓐ에 들어갈 제목으로 가장 알맞은 것을 고르시오.

① Under the Sea
② Birds Flying Down to the Sea to Catch Fish
③ One, Two, Three, Jump!
④ Sweet Dreams
⑤ Don't Let the Great Speed Fool You!

21 위 글의 밑줄 친 ⓑup to와 같은 의미로 쓰인 것을 고르시오.

① What have you been up to?
② It's up to the manager to make the decision.
③ Are you up to this job?
④ Up to now, I believe he's innocent.
⑤ This room can hold up to 200 people.

22 Which question CANNOT be answered after reading the passage?

① Is there a bird which can fly down to the sea to catch a fish?
② How big can a giant trevally grow?
③ Is a giant trevally a quick and smart fish?
④ What can a giant trevally spot?
⑤ How can a giant trevally calculate the speed and distance of a flying bird?

[23~25] 다음 글을 읽고 물음에 답하시오.

_____ ⓐ

Can you guess what these whales are doing in the picture? (①) It looks like they are standing up in a group. (②) Humpback whales stand on their tails while they sleep. (③) They sleep near the surface. (④) Since they are not fish, they need to come up to breathe. (⑤) Also, they don't fall asleep completely. When they wake up, they come out of the water for a deep breath and dive back into the sea.

*humpback whale: 혹등고래라고 불리며, 북극해를 제외한 모든 대양에서 서식한다.

23 위 글의 빈칸 ⓐ에 들어갈 제목으로 가장 알맞은 것을 고르시오.

① One, Two, Three, Jump!
② Sweet Dreams
③ Under the Sea
④ Enjoy Your Meal
⑤ Don't Fall Asleep Completely

24 위 글의 흐름으로 보아, 주어진 문장이 들어가기에 가장 적절한 곳은?

But they are actually sleeping!

①　　②　　③　　④　　⑤

25 According to the passage, which is NOT true?

① Humpback whales stand on their tails while they sleep.
② Humpback whales sleep near the surface.
③ Humpback whales are not fish, so they need to come up to breathe.
④ Humpback whales fall asleep completely.
⑤ When humpback whales wake up, they come out of the water for a deep breath.

[01~03] 다음 글을 읽고 물음에 답하시오.

ⓐ우리 행성의 3분의 2는 is covered by oceans. ⓑThey are full of wonder and are home to millions of species. Every day, we are learning new things about ⓒthem. Let's find out about some interesting sea animals.

중요

01 위 글의 밑줄 친 ⓐ의 우리말에 맞게 영작하시오.

➡ _____

02 위 글의 밑줄 친 ⓑ를 다음과 같이 바꿔 쓸 때 빈칸에 들어갈 알맞은 전치사를 쓰시오.

They are filled _____ wonder and are home to millions of species.

03 위 글의 밑줄 친 ⓒthem이 가리키는 것을 본문에서 찾아 쓰시오.

➡ _____

[04~06] 다음 글을 읽고 물음에 답하시오.

Sweet Dreams
ⓐ여러분은 그림 속 이 고래들이 무엇을 하고 있는지 추측할 수 있는가? It looks like they are standing up in a group. But they are actually sleeping! Humpback whales stand on their tails (A)[during / while] they sleep. They sleep (B)[near / nearby] the surface. Since they are not fish, they need to come up (C)[to breathe / breathing]. Also, they don't fall asleep completely. When they wake up, they come out of the water for a deep breath and dive back into the sea.
*humpback whale: 혹등고래라고 불리며, 북극해를 제외한 모든 대양에서 서식한다.

중요

04 위 글의 밑줄 친 ⓐ의 우리말에 맞게 주어진 어휘를 알맞게 배열하시오.

what / can / in the picture / you / are doing / these whales / guess

➡ _____
_____

05 위 글의 괄호 (A)~(C)에서 어법상 알맞은 낱말을 골라 쓰시오.

(A) _____ (B) _____ (C) _____

고난이도

06 본문의 내용과 일치하도록 다음 빈칸 (A)와 (B)에 알맞은 단어를 쓰시오.

Humpback whales are not fish, so they come (A)_____ _____ _____ _____ for a deep breath when they wake up, and (B)_____ _____ into the sea.

[07~10] 다음 글을 읽고 물음에 답하시오.

One, Two, Three, Jump!
ⓐYou have probably seen a bird fly down to the sea to catch a fish. ⓑBut have you ever seen a fish to jump out of the water to catch a bird? Well, birds have to be careful when a giant trevally is around. This fish can grow up to 170cm and 80kg. ⓒBut don't let its size fool you. This fish is quick and smart. It can spot a flying bird and calculate its speed and distance. When the bird flies nearby, the giant trevally jumps out of the

water and catches ⓓit.
*giant trevally: 전갱잇과의 물고기로 서태평양과 인도양에서 서식한다.

07 위 글의 밑줄 친 ⓐ를 복문으로 고칠 때 빈칸에 들어갈 알맞은 말을 (1)에는 세 단어로, (2)에는 두 단어로 각각 쓰시오.

(1) You have probably seen a bird fly down to the sea _____ _____ _____ it can catch a fish.

(2) You have probably seen a bird fly down to the sea _____ _____ it can catch a fish.

08 위 글의 밑줄 친 ⓑ에서 어법상 틀린 부분을 찾아 고치시오.

_____ ➡ _____

09 다음 빈칸 (A)와 (B)에 알맞은 단어를 넣어 위 글의 밑줄 친 ⓒ처럼 말한 이유를 완성하시오.

Though the giant trevally can grow up to 170cm and 80kg, it is (A)_____ _____ _____. So, you had better not be fooled by its (B)_____ because when a bird flies nearby, it spots the flying bird, calculates its speed and distance, and jumps out of the water to catch it.
*had better 동사원형: (~하는 것이) 좋을 것이다

10 위 글의 밑줄 친 ⓓit이 가리키는 것을 본문에서 찾아 쓰시오.

➡ _____

[11~14] 다음 글을 읽고 물음에 답하시오.

Enjoy Your Meal

If you think fish are not smart, take a look at the tuskfish. This small fish ___ⓐ___ favorite food is clams uses a tool to open them. Clams usually hide under the sand, so (A)they cannot be easily discovered. The tuskfish blows on the sand until a clam appears. The clam is closed tightly, so the fish cannot eat it. But the tuskfish doesn't give up. It smashes the clam against a rock. In the end, the clam opens and dinner ___ⓑ___.
*tuskfish: 놀래깃과의 물고기로 서태평양과 인도양에서 주로 서식한다.

11 위 글의 빈칸 ⓐ에 들어갈 알맞은 관계대명사를 쓰시오.

➡ _____

12 위 글의 빈칸 ⓑ에 serve를 알맞은 형태로 쓰시오.

➡ _____

13 위 글의 밑줄 친 (A)를 능동태로 고치시오.

➡ _____

14 다음 빈칸 (A)와 (B)에 알맞은 단어를 넣어, tuskfish가 자신이 가장 좋아하는 먹이인 조개를 열기 위해 도구를 사용하는 방법을 완성하시오.

When a clam appears from the sand, it is closed tightly. Then, the tuskfish (A)_____ the clam (B)_____ a rock to open it.

After You Read A. Read and Correct

I learned about oceans today. <u>Two-thirds</u> of our planet <u>is covered by oceans.</u>
Two-thirds: '3분의 2'를 나타내는 분수 표현, 분자는 기수로, 분모는 서수로 씀.   be covered by: '~로 덮여 있다'(수동태)
They are home to <u>millions of</u> species. There are many interesting facts about
수많은
sea animals. For example, humpback whales stand on their tails while they

sleep, and they sleep <u>near the surface.</u>
수면 근처에서

구문해설 • **millions of**: 수많은 • **species**: (분류상의) 종 • **whale**: 고래 • **surface**: 수면, 표면

나는 오늘 바다에 대해 배웠다. 우리 행성의 3분의 2는 대양들로 덮여 있다. 그것들은 수많은 종의 서식지이다. 바다 동물들에 관한 많은 흥미로운 사실들이 있다. 예를 들어, 혹등고래들은 잠을 자는 동안 꼬리로 서 있고, 그들은 수면 근처에서 잠을 잔다.

Word Power

• He found a good spot <u>to park the car.</u>
to부정사의 형용사적 용법(앞의 명사 spot을 수식)
• I can spot you in the audience.

• Don't <u>be fooled</u> by his cute looks.
수동태
• Experience makes even <u>fool wise.</u>
make가 5형식 동사로 쓰여 fool이 목적어, wise가 목적격보어로 사용되고 있다.

구문해설 • **spot**: 장소, 위치, 발견하다, 찾아내다 • **audience**: 관중 • **fool**: 속이다; 바보

• **look**: 외모, 모습

• 그는 차를 주차하기 좋은 장소를 발견했다.
• 나는 관중 속에서 너를 발견할 수 있다.
• 그의 귀여운 외모에 속지 마라.
• 경험은 바보조차도 현명하게 만든다.

Think and Write Step 3

My Fun Animal: Beluga whale

I will introduce the beluga whale. It lives in the Arctic Ocean. It has a round

head. It usually eats fish and clams. An interesting fact about the beluga whale
감정동사: 감정을 유발할 때 현재분사
is <u>that</u> it is white all over. <u>That's why</u> people <u>call it</u> the white whale. <u>When</u> it is
보어절을 이끄는 접속사   그것이 ~한 이유이다.   call A B: A를 B라고 부르다   시간을 나타내는 접속사
born, it is gray. But when it grows up, its body becomes white! I want to see

this animal with <u>my own</u> eyes!
나 자신의

구문해설 • **Arctic**: 북극 • **clam**: 조개 • **all over**: 곳곳에

나의 재미있는 동물: 벨루가 고래

저는 벨루가 고래를 소개할게요. 벨루가 고래는 북극해에 살아요. 둥근 머리를 가졌어요. 벨루가 고래는 주로 물고기와 조개를 먹어요. 벨루가 고래에 관한 흥미로운 사실은 온몸이 하얗다는 거예요. 그것이 사람들이 벨루가 고래를 흰고래라고 부르는 이유예요. 벨루가 고래는 태어날 때, 회색이에요. 그러나 다 자라면, 몸은 하얀색이 돼요! 저는 제 눈으로 이 동물을 보고 싶어요!

Words & Expressions

01 ⓐ~ⓔ에서 밑줄 친 spot이 같은 의미로 쓰인 것끼리 바르게 짝지어진 것을 <u>모두</u> 고르시오.

> ⓐ If you <u>spot</u> Mom and Dad coming, warn me.
> ⓑ It took me about twenty minutes to find a parking <u>spot</u>.
> ⓒ This looks like a good <u>spot</u> to stop and rest.
> ⓓ If you are lucky, you will also <u>spot</u> a deer or two.
> ⓔ These ants are often relatively easy to <u>spot</u>.

① ⓐ, ⓑ   ② ⓑ, ⓒ
③ ⓒ, ⓓ   ④ ⓓ, ⓔ
⑤ ⓐ, ⓔ

02 다음 빈칸에 공통으로 들어갈 말을 쓰시오.

> • Sometimes he _____ed why his father hated him.
> • The sight of the Taj Mahal filled us with _____.

03 빈칸에 가장 알맞은 말을 고르시오.

> The _____ of 3, 8, and 10 is 7.

① average   ② individual
③ standard   ④ usual
⑤ certain

04 빈칸 (A)와 (B)에 들어갈 말로 알맞은 것끼리 짝지어진 것을 고르시오.

> • The kitchen was full (A)_____ smoke.
> • Boston is so beautiful this time (B)_____ year.

  (A) (B)   (A) (B)
① with – of   ② with – in
③ of – of   ④ of – in
⑤ of – for

Conversation

[05~07] 다음 대화를 읽고 물음에 답하시오.

> B: We're almost at the top of the mountain. (①)
> G: _____(A)_____ (how, is, wonder, this, I, high, mountain) (②)
> B: It's ___(B)___ 2,000m high. (③)
> G: Wow! (④)
> B: Yes, it is. (⑤) Let's keep going.

05 빈칸 (A)를 괄호 안에 주어진 단어를 알맞게 배열하여 채우시오.

➡ _____

06 빈칸 (B)에 알맞은 말을 고르시오.

① about   ② on   ③ in
④ for   ⑤ over

07 ①~⑤ 중 주어진 문장이 들어갈 곳은?

> This is a really high mountain.

①   ②   ③   ④   ⑤

[08~10] 다음 대화를 읽고 물음에 답하시오.

> B: The weather is so nice outside. (①)
> G: Yeah. (②) How about going on a picnic this afternoon?
> B: Good idea. (③)
> G: Oh, no! (④) The weather forecast says it'll be rainy in the afternoon. (⑤)
> B: Let's go another time, then.

08 위 대화의 ①~⑤ 중 주어진 문장이 들어갈 곳은?

> Can you check the weather?

①   ②   ③   ④   ⑤

09 위 대화에서 다음 영영풀이에 해당하는 단어를 찾아 쓰시오.

> a statement about what you think is going to happen in the future

➡ _____

10 위 대화를 읽고 답할 수 있는 질문을 모두 고른 것은?

> ⓐ How is the weather this afternoon?
> ⓑ Who checked the weather forecast?
> ⓒ What day are they going to go on a picnic?
> ⓓ Is it nice outside now?
> ⓔ Who suggest going on a picnic?

① ⓐ, ⓑ   ② ⓐ, ⓑ, ⓓ
③ ⓐ, ⓑ, ⓒ, ⓓ   ④ ⓐ, ⓑ, ⓒ, ⓔ
⑤ ⓐ, ⓑ, ⓓ, ⓔ

[11~12] 다음 대화를 읽고 물음에 답하시오.

> Suji: Check out this picture!
> Tony: Wow! The camels are walking __(A)__ a line __(B)__ the desert.
> Suji: Yeah. The desert looks very hot and dry.
> Tony: I wonder how long camels can go without water in the desert.
> Suji: Let's find out on the Internet.
> Tony: Okay. 인터넷 정보에 따르면 낙타는 물 없이 2주 정도 지낼 수 있대.
> Suji: Wow, that's amazing! Camels are really interesting animals.
> Tony: I want to travel with them in the desert someday.

11 위 대화의 빈칸 (A)와 (B)에 공통으로 들어갈 말을 쓰시오.

➡ _____

12 밑줄 친 우리말과 일치하도록 주어진 단어를 이용하여 영작하시오.

➡ _____
_____ (can, say)

Grammar

[13~14] 다음 중 밑줄 친 부분의 쓰임이 〈보기〉와 같은 것은?

13
> ┤ 보기 ├
> I drink a lot of water when I'm thirsty.

① Sunday is the only day when I can relax.
② He got interested in politics when he was in college.
③ When did she promise to meet him?
④ Since when have you got interested in collecting stamps?
⑤ He told me the when and the where of the event.

14

┌─ 보기 ─┐
I like the girl whose hobby is playing the piano.
└──────────┘

① The girl whose dog is very big is Ann.
② Do you know whose ball this is?
③ Kate asked me whose team I was on.
④ The detective was wondering whose fingerprint it was.
⑤ They have to decide whose computer they should use.

[15~16] 다음 주어진 두 문장을 관계대명사를 사용해서 하나의 문장으로 바르게 고친 것을 고르시오.

15

• I have a friend.
• Her father is a famous actor.

① I have a friend which father is a famous actor.
② I have a friend which of father is a famous actor.
③ I have a friend of which father is a famous actor.
④ I have a friend that father is a famous actor.
⑤ I have a friend whose father is a famous actor.

16

• Look at the dog.
• Its tail is very short.

① Look at the dog whom tail is very short.
② Look at the dog which tail is very short.
③ Look at the dog of which tail is very short.
④ Look at the dog of which the tail is very short.
⑤ Look at the dog that tail is very short.

17 다음 그림을 보고 빈칸에 맞는 단어를 채우시오.

시드니에는 밤의 경치가 아름다운 오페라 하우스가 있다.

➡ There is the Opera House _____

_____ _____ _____ _____

in Sydney.

(night view, wonderful, 5 단어)

18 다음 주어진 두 문장을 한 문장으로 가장 적절하게 바꾼 것은?

• Let's wait here.
• The rain stops.

① Let's wait here while the rain stops.
② Let's wait here when the rain stops.
③ Let's wait here until the rain stops.
④ Let's wait here as soon as the rain stops.
⑤ Let's wait here that the rain stops.

19 다음 중 어법상 어색한 문장은?

① After he had lunch, he played baseball with his friends.
② Linda lost her husband while she was 40.
③ She did a lot of acting when she was at college.
④ They didn't arrive at the hotel until very late.
⑤ As soon as he went to bed, he fell asleep.

20 빈칸 (A)~(C)에 들어갈 말로 알맞은 것끼리 짝지어진 것을 고르시오.

> • He wrote a book (A)_____ he was on his journey.
> • He ran away (B)_____ he saw me.
> • His mom put flowers on the table (C)_____ they finished cleaning.

  (A)   (B)   (C)
① after – while – as soon as
② until – after – until
③ after – as soon as – until
④ while – as soon as – after
⑤ as soon as – while – after

Reading

[21~23] 다음 글을 읽고 물음에 답하시오.

Sweet Dreams

Can you guess what these whales are doing in the picture? It looks like they are standing up in a group. But they are actually sleeping! Humpback whales stand on their tails while they sleep. They sleep near the surface. (A) Since they are not fish, they need to come up to breathe. Also, they don't fall asleep completely. When they wake up, they come out of the water for a deep ⓐ and dive back into the sea.

*humpback whale: 혹등고래라고 불리며, 북극해를 제외한 모든 대양에서 서식한다.

21 본문의 한 단어를 변형하여 위 글의 빈칸 ⓐ에 들어갈 알맞은 단어를 쓰시오.

➡ _____

22 위 글의 밑줄 친 (A)Since와 같은 의미로 쓰인 것을 모두 고르시오.

① I have known her since she was a child.
② I have not seen him since.
③ Let's do our best, since we can expect no help from others.
④ Since we're not very busy now, we can get away from the office.
⑤ It has been two years since I left school.

23 Why do humpback whales sleep near the surface? Fill in the blanks with suitable words.

> They do so in order that they can come out of the water _____ _____ when they wake up.

[24~26] 다음 글을 읽고 물음에 답하시오.

> _____ ⓐ _____
>
> If you think fish are not smart, take a look at the tuskfish. ⓑ가장 좋아하는 먹이가 조개인 이 작은 물고기는 조개를 열기 위해 도구를 사용한다. Clams usually hide under the sand, so they cannot be easily discovered. The tuskfish blows on the sand until a clam appears. The clam is closed tightly, so the fish cannot eat it. But the tuskfish doesn't give up. It smashes the clam against a rock. In the end, the clam opens and dinner is served.
>
> *tuskfish: 놀래깃과의 물고기로 서태평양과 인도양에서 주로 서식한다.

24 위 글의 빈칸 ⓐ에 들어갈 제목으로 알맞은 것을 고르시오.

① Under the Sea
② Clams Which Hide under the Sand
③ One, Two, Three, Jump!
④ Sweet Dreams
⑤ Enjoy Your Meal

25 위 글의 밑줄 친 ⓑ의 우리말에 맞게 주어진 어휘를 알맞게 배열하시오.

> a tool / this small fish / uses / clams /
> whose / is / them / favorite food / to open

➡ _____

_____

26 According to the passage, which is NOT true?

① The tuskfish's favorite food is clams.

② The tuskfish is a large fish.

③ Clams cannot be easily discovered because they usually hide under the sand.

④ The tuskfish discovers a clam in the sand by blowing on the sand until a clam appears.

⑤ The tuskfish smashes the clam against a rock.

[27~28] 다음 글을 읽고 물음에 답하시오.

One, Two, Three, Jump!

You have probably seen a bird fly down to the sea to catch a fish. But ⓐhave you ever seen a fish jump out of the water to catch a bird? Well, birds have to be careful when a giant trevally is around. ①This fish can grow up to 170cm and 80kg. But don't let ②its size fool you. This fish is quick and smart. ③It can spot a flying bird and calculate ④its speed and distance. When the bird flies nearby, ⑤ the giant trevally jumps out of the water and catches it.

*giant trevally: 전갱잇과의 물고기로 서태평양과 인도양에서 서식한다.

27 위 글의 밑줄 친 ⓐ의 현재완료와 용법이 같은 것을 모두 고르시오.

① I have played tennis three times.

② How long have you played the piano?

③ She has gone to Paris.

④ They have just finished it.

⑤ I have been to America before.

28 밑줄 친 ①~⑤ 중에서 가리키는 대상이 나머지 넷과 다른 것은?

①   ②   ③   ④   ⑤

[29~30] 다음 글을 읽고 물음에 답하시오.

My Fun Animal: Beluga whale

I will introduce the beluga whale. It lives in the Arctic Ocean. It has a round head. It usually eats fish and clams. An interesting fact about the beluga whale is that it is white all over. ⓐThat's because people call it the white whale. When it is born, it is gray. But when it grows up, its body becomes white! I want to see this animal with my own eyes!

29 위 글의 밑줄 친 ⓐ에서 흐름상 어색한 부분을 찾아 고치시오.

_____ ➡ _____

30 다음 빈칸 (A)와 (B)에 알맞은 단어를 넣어 벨루가 고래의 몸의 색깔 변화를 완성하시오.

> The beluga whale is born (A)_____,
> but when it grows up, its body becomes
> (B)_____.

01 ⓐ~ⓔ에서 밑줄 친 land의 의미가 같은 것끼리 짝지으시오.

> ⓐ It shows where the balls land.
> ⓑ Their journey took them to many foreign lands.
> ⓒ They moved to the country and bought some land.
> ⓓ He didn't hear the plane land.
> ⓔ It isn't clear whether the plane went down over land or sea.

➡ _____

02 밑줄 친 부분과 바꿔 쓸 수 있는 말을 고르시오.

> The front door is locked and all the windows are firmly shut.

① obviously　　② nearly
③ clearly　　④ highly
⑤ tightly

03 다음 우리말에 맞도록 빈칸에 알맞은 말을 쓰시오.

(1) 북극 지방에서는 생물을 거의 볼 수 없다.
　➡ There is very little life to be seen in the _____.
(2) 공기가 너무 차서 우리는 숨을 쉬기도 어려웠다.
　➡ The air was so cold that we could hardly _____.

04 다음 빈칸에 공통으로 들어갈 말을 쓰시오.

> • Check _____ the prices at our new store!
> • Can you find _____ what time the meeting starts?
> • Don't lean _____ of the window.

[05~06] 다음 대화를 읽고 물음에 답하시오.

> A: Where is the coldest place on Earth?
> B: I thinks it's the South Pole.
> A: 그곳이 얼마나 추울지 궁금해.
> B: The book says the average ___(A)___ of the South Pole is about -49°C.
> A: That's amazing!

05 위 글의 빈칸 (A)에 알맞은 말을 고르시오.

① weather　　② temperature
③ amount　　④ surface
⑤ climate

06 밑줄 친 우리말과 일치하도록 주어진 단어를 이용해 영작하시오.

> (wonder, it)

➡ _____

[07~09] 다음 대화를 읽고 물음에 답하시오.

> B: Look at the baby penguins on TV. They're so cute.
> G: Yes, ___(A)___ they look very cold out there.
> B: Yeah, the South Pole is the coldest place on Earth.

G: I wonder how cold is it there.

B: The average temperature is about -58℃ in July and -26℃ in December.

G: Oh, then, __ⓐ__ is colder than __ⓑ__ there. Interesting!

B: Yes. __(B)__ it's very cold there, it doesn't snow much.

G: That's interesting, too!

✏️ 출제율 90%

07 빈칸 (A)와 (B)에 들어갈 말로 알맞은 것끼리 짝지어진 것을 고르시오.

① but – Therefore   ② but – Unless

③ but – Although   ④ since – Unless

⑤ since – Although

✏️ 출제율 95%

08 위 대화에 나온 단어를 이용해 빈칸 ⓐ, ⓑ에 알맞은 말을 쓰시오.

ⓐ _____   ⓑ _____

✏️ 출제율 95%

09 밑줄 친 부분에서 어법상 어색한 것을 골라 바르게 고치시오.

➡ _____

[10~12] 다음 대화를 읽고 물음에 답하시오.

B: Sumin, what are you going to do on Sunday?

G: I'm going to go hiking. (①) Do you want to join me?

B: I'd love to. (②)

G: I'm thinking __(A)__ going to Namsan.

B: Oh, the scenery there is so beautiful this time of year. (③)

G: Right. (④) I __(B)__ that it's covered __(C)__ red autumn leaves now. (⑤)

B: Great. How long does the shortest hiking course take?

G: 인터넷에 따르면 약 두 시간 정도 걸린대.

B: Okay, see you on Sunday!

✏️ 출제율 100%

10 ①~⑤ 중 주어진 문장이 들어갈 곳은?

> Where do you want to go?

①   ②   ③   ④   ⑤

✏️ 출제율 90%

11 빈칸 (A)~(C)에 들어갈 말로 알맞은 것끼리 짝지어진 것을 고르시오.

① of – heard – with   ② of – said – of

③ of – heard – of   ④ to – said – with

⑤ to – heard – with

✏️ 출제율 90%

12 밑줄 친 우리말과 일치하도록 주어진 단어를 이용해 8 단어로 영작하시오. (say, it, about)

➡ _____

✏️ 출제율 100%

13 다음 중 어법상 어색한 것을 고르시오.

① Tom sang a song while he washed the dishes.

② After Jenny mopped the floor, it looked very shiny.

③ He won't rest until he will find her.

④ Buy now before it's too late.

⑤ Call me when you arrive!

14 다음 빈칸에 들어갈 알맞은 말을 〈보기〉에서 골라 써 넣으시오.

출제율 90%

┌─── 보기 ───┐
who   whose   which   of which
└──────────┘

(1) I know a girl _____ favorite number is 7.

(2) Pinocchio is a cute doll _____ the wish is to become a boy.

(3) The people _____ called yesterday want to buy the house.

(4) Rapunzel is a beautiful princess _____ hair is very long.

(5) I have a piggy bank _____ the color is pink.

(6) I'm afraid the position for _____ you applied has been filled.

[15~16] 다음 글을 읽고 물음에 답하시오.

My Fun Animal: Octopus

I will introduce the octopus. It lives on the ocean floor. It has no bones so it can move around easily in the ocean. It usually eats small fish. An interesting fact about the octopus is ⓐ<u>that</u> it can change the color of its skin to hide from its enemies. When it meets an enemy, it shoots out dark black ink and swims away. I want to see this animal with my own eyes!

출제율 95%

15 위 글의 밑줄 친 ⓐthat과 문법적 쓰임이 같은 것을 고르시오.

① What is <u>that</u> loud noise?

② Are you sure she's <u>that</u> young?

③ The trouble is <u>that</u> we are short of money.

④ This is my sister and <u>that</u> is my cousin.

⑤ He is the greatest novelist <u>that</u> has ever lived.

출제율 100%

16 위 글을 읽고 문어에 대해서 알 수 <u>없는</u> 것을 고르시오.

① Where does it live?

② What does it usually eat?

③ What is an interesting fact about it?

④ How can it change the color of its skin?

⑤ When it meets an enemy, what does it do?

[17~18] 다음 글을 읽고 물음에 답하시오.

One, Two, Three, Jump!

You have probably seen a bird fly down to the sea to catch a fish. But have you ever seen a fish jump out of the water to catch a bird? Well, birds have to be careful when a giant trevally is around. This fish can grow up to 170cm and 80kg. But ⓐ<u>그 크기에 속지 마라</u>. This fish is quick and smart. It can spot a flying bird and calculate its speed and distance. When the bird flies nearby, the giant trevally jumps out of the water and catches it.

*giant trevally: 전갱잇과의 물고기로 서태평양과 인도양에서 서식한다.

출제율 90%

17 위 글의 밑줄 친 ⓐ의 우리말에 맞게 주어진 어휘를 이용하여 6 단어로 영작하시오.

┌────────────────────┐
│   its, fool   │
└────────────────────┘

➡ _____

---

18 According to the passage, which is NOT true?

① It's impossible for a bird to fly down to the sea to catch a fish.

② There is a fish which can jump out of the water to catch a bird.

③ When a giant trevally is around, it will be better for birds to be careful.

④ A giant trevally can grow up to 170cm and 80kg.

⑤ A giant trevally is quick and smart.

[19~20] 다음 글을 읽고 물음에 답하시오.

Sweet Dreams

Can you guess what these whales are doing in the picture? It looks like they are standing up in a group. But they are actually sleeping! Humpback whales stand on their tails while they sleep. They sleep near the surface. Since they are not fish, they need to come up to breathe. Also, they don't fall asleep completely. When they wake up, they come ____ⓐ____ the water for a deep breath and dive back ____ⓑ____ the sea.

19 위 글의 빈칸 ⓐ와 ⓑ에 들어갈 전치사가 바르게 짝지어진 것은?

① out of – into   ② into – on

③ into – for   ④ out of – on

⑤ to – into

20 위 글의 주제로 알맞은 것을 고르시오.

① Why do humpback whales stand on their tails while they sleep?

② Where do humpback whales sleep?

③ When do humpback whales breathe?

④ How do humpback whales sleep and breathe?

⑤ Why do humpback whales dive back into the sea?

[21~23] 다음 글을 읽고 물음에 답하시오.

Enjoy Your Meal

If you think fish are not smart, take a look at the tuskfish. (①) This small fish whose favorite food is clams uses a tool ⓐto open them. (②) Clams usually hide under the sand, so they cannot be easily discovered. (③) The tuskfish blows on the sand until a clam appears. (④) The clam is closed tightly, so the fish cannot eat it. (⑤) It smashes the clam against a rock. In the end, the clam opens and dinner is served.

21 위 글의 흐름으로 보아, 주어진 문장이 들어가기에 가장 적절한 곳은?

But the tuskfish doesn't give up.

①   ②   ③   ④   ⑤

22 아래 〈보기〉에서 위 글의 밑줄 친 ⓐto open과 to부정사의 용법이 다른 것의 개수를 고르시오.

┌─── 보기 ───┐
① I am happy to hear that.
② He has a few books to read.
③ His wealth enabled him to go abroad.
④ He can't be rich to ask me for some money.
⑤ His job is to sing songs.
└────────────┘

① 1개   ② 2개   ③ 3개   ④ 4개   ⑤ 5개

23 Which question CANNOT be answered after reading the passage?

① What is the tuskfish's favorite food?

② Where do clams usually hide?

③ How does the tuskfish discover a clam in the sand?

④ How long does it take for the tuskfish to open the clam?

⑤ Why does the tuskfish smash the clam against a rock?

01 다음 문장을 주어진 〈조건〉에 맞춰 바꿔 쓰시오.

How long does the shortest hiking course take?

┤ 조건 ├

(1) wonder를 이용하여 궁금증을 표현할 것.
(2) curious를 이용하여 궁금증을 표현할 것.

(1) _____

_____

(2) _____

_____

02 밑줄 친 우리말과 일치하도록 주어진 단어를 사용하여 두 가지 문장으로 만드시오.

A: Is there anything interesting?
B: 이 기사에 따르면 과학자들이 새로운 행성을 발견했대.

(1) _____

_____

(say, 9 단어)

(2) _____

_____

(according, 10 단어)

03 다음 대화의 밑줄 친 문장 중 문맥상 또는 어법상 어색한 것을 찾아 바르게 고치시오.

Suji: Check out this picture!
Tony: Wow! The camels are walking in a line in the desert.
Suji: Yeah. The desert looks very hot and dry.

Tony: I wonder how long can camels go without water in the desert.
Suji: Let's find out on the Internet.
Tony: Okay. The Internet says they can go about two weeks without water.
Suji: Wow, that's amazing! Camels are really interesting animals.
Tony: I want to travel with them in the desert someday.

➡ _____

_____

_____

04 다음 주어진 두 문장을 관계대명사를 사용해서 하나의 문장으로 쓰시오.

(1) • I interviewed a man.
    • His dream is to climb Baekdusan.

    ➡ _____

    _____

(2) • The cat is sitting on the table.
    • The name of the cat is Molly.

    ➡ _____

    _____

05 다음 두 문장을 주어진 접속사를 사용해서 하나의 문장으로 쓰시오.

(1) • You have to finish your homework.
    • You go to bed. (before)

    ➡ _____

    _____

(2) • Tom waited in front of the door.
    • Someone came out. (until)

    ➡ _____

    _____

[06~08] 다음 글을 읽고 물음에 답하시오.

Sweet Dreams

Can you guess what these whales are doing in the picture? It looks like they are standing up in a group. But they are actually sleeping! Humpback whales stand on their tails while they sleep. They sleep near the surface. Since they are not fish, they need to come up to breathe. Also, ⓐ그들은 완전히 잠들지 않는다. When they wake up, they come out of the water for a deep breath and dive back into the sea.

*humpback whale: 혹등고래라고 불리며, 북극해를 제외한 모든 대양에서 서식한다.

06 위 글의 밑줄 친 ⓐ의 우리말에 맞게 주어진 어휘를 이용하여 5 단어로 영작하시오.

> fall, completely

➡ _____

07 다음 문장에서 위 글의 내용과 다른 부분을 찾아서 고치시오.

> Humpback whales sleep near the bottom of the sea.

_____ ➡ _____

08 Why do humpback whales need to come out of the water when they wake up? Fill in the blanks (A) and (B) with suitable words.

> Since they are not (A)_____, they need to come out of the water for (B)_____ _____ _____.

[09~11] 다음 글을 읽고 물음에 답하시오.

One, Two, Three, Jump!

You have probably seen a bird (A)[fly / to fly] down to the sea to catch a fish. But have you ever seen a fish jump out of the water to catch a bird? Well, birds have to be careful when a giant trevally is around. This fish can grow up to 170cm and 80kg. ⓐBut don't let its size fool you. This fish is quick and smart. It can spot a flying bird and calculate its speed and distance. When the bird flies (B)[nearby / nearly], the giant trevally jumps (C)[into / out of] the water and catches it.

*giant trevally: 전갱잇과의 물고기로 서태평양과 인도양에서 서식한다.

09 위 글의 괄호 (A)~(C)에서 문맥이나 어법상 알맞은 낱말을 골라 쓰시오.

(A) _____ (B) _____ (C) _____

10 위 글의 밑줄 친 ⓐ를 다음과 같이 바꿔 쓸 때 빈칸에 들어갈 알맞은 말을 두 단어로 쓰시오.

> But don't allow its size _____ _____ you.

11 주어진 영영풀이에 해당하는 단어를 본문에서 찾아 쓰시오.

> to notice something or someone

➡ _____

창의사고력 서술형 문제

01 다음 사진을 보고, 〈조건〉에 맞게 대화를 완성하시오.

조건

• 궁금증 표현하기 2번, 보고하기의 표현을 1번 사용한다.
• 주어진 단어를 이용하여 문장을 만든다.

A: _____ (wonder)
B: _____ Machu Picchu.(Internet)
A: _____ (curious)
B: It is in Peru.

02 다음 내용을 바탕으로 바다 동물 보고서를 쓰시오.

• Animal: Beluga whale
• Where does it live?   It lives in the Arctic Ocean.
• What does it look like?   It has a round head.
• What does it eat?   It usually eats fish and clams.
• Interesting facts   It is white all over. When it is born, it is gray. But when it grows up, its body becomes white.

My Fun Animal: Beluga whale

I will introduce the beluga whale. It lives (A)_____. It has (B)_____. It usually eats (C)_____. An interesting fact about the beluga whale is that (D)_____. That's why people call it the white whale. When it is born, it is (E)_____. But when it grows up, its body becomes (F)_____! I want to see this animal with my own eyes!

단원별 모의고사

01 빈칸 (A)와 (B)에 들어갈 말로 알맞은 것끼리 짝지어진 것을 고르시오.

> • I drank a lot of coffee earlier and now I can't (A)_____ asleep.
> • The important thing is to (B)_____ trying.

　　(A)　(B)　　　　　(A)　(B)
① go – take　　　② turn – take
③ turn – keep　　④ fall – take
⑤ fall – keep

02 다음 빈칸을 〈보기〉에 있는 어휘를 이용하여 채우시오. (한 단어는 한 번만 사용)

> ┤ 보기 ├
> completely　friendly　nearby　finally

(1) I went to a small store _____.
(2) The hotel staff were very _____ and helpful.
(3) I _____ forgot that it's his birthday today.
(4) We _____ arrived home at midnight.

03 다음 제시된 단어를 사용해서 자연스러운 문장을 만들 수 없는 것은? (형태 변화 가능)

> calculate　hide　surround　take

① How long is this going to _____?
② You are _____! Put down your weapons!
③ He found it difficult to _____ his disappointment when she didn't arrive.

④ Several cups fell to the floor and were _____ to pieces.
⑤ No matter how many times I _____, I'm missing 3,000 won.

04 다음 우리말에 맞도록 빈칸에 알맞은 말을 쓰시오. (철자가 주어진 경우 주어진 철자로 시작할 것.)

(1) 하늘에는 밝은 불꽃들이 가득했다.
　➡ The sky _____ _____ of brightly colored fireworks.

(2) 내일 소풍 가지 않을래?
　➡ Would you like to _____ _____ _____ _____ tomorrow?

(3) 비만아들은 어른이 되어서도 비만일 수 있습니다.
　➡ Overweight children _____ _____ _____ become overweight adults.

(4) 이번 지진으로 수백만 명의 이재민이 발생했다.
　➡ The earthquake left _____ _____ people homeless.

05 대화가 자연스럽게 연결되도록 (A)~(D)를 순서대로 적절하게 배열하시오.

> (A) What are you doing?
> (B) This article says a whale family was seen in the East Sea.
> (C) I'm reading the newspaper.
> (D) Is there anything interesting?

➡ _____

[06~07] 다음 대화를 읽고 물음에 답하시오.

A: We're finally here.
B: Yes, I'm so excited. Let's look around.
A: _____(A)_____
B: It's ____(B)____ the police station.
A: You're right. Let's go.

06 빈칸 (A)에 wonder를 이용해, 동그라미 친 부분의 위치에 대해 궁금증을 표현하는 문장을 쓰시오.

➡ _____

07 빈칸 (B)에 들어갈 말을 쓰시오.

➡ _____

[08~09] 다음 대화를 읽고 물음에 답하시오.

B: The weather is so nice outside.
G: Yeah. How about ____(A)____ (go) on a picnic this afternoon?
B: Good idea. Can you check the weather?
G: Oh, no! 일기 예보에 따르면 오후에 비가 올 거래.
B: Let's go another time, then.

08 다음 괄호 안의 단어를 문맥에 맞게 고쳐 빈칸 (A)를 채우시오.

➡ _____

09 밑줄 친 우리말과 일치하도록 주어진 단어를 사용하여 두 가지 문장으로 쓰시오.

(1) (say, rainy)
➡ _____
_____

(2) (according, rainy)
➡ _____
_____

[10~12] 다음 대화를 읽고 물음에 답하시오.

B: Sumin, what are you going to do on Sunday?
G: I'm going to go hiking. Do you want to join me?
B: I'd love to. Where do you want to go?
G: I'm thinking of going to Namsan.
B: Oh, _____(A)_____. (is, of, the, so, year, scenery, this, there, time, beautiful)
G: Right. I heard that it's ____(B)____ with red autumn leaves now.
B: Great. How long does the shortest hiking course take?
G: The Internet says it takes about two hours.
B: Okay, see you on Sunday!

10 빈칸 (A)를 괄호 안에 주어진 단어를 알맞게 배열하여 채우시오.

➡ _____

11 빈칸 (B)에 들어갈 말을 고르시오.

① related   ② filled
③ covered   ④ located
⑤ contained

12 위 대화를 읽고 답할 수 있는 질문의 개수를 고르시오.

> ⓐ Where are Sumin planning to go on Sunday?
> ⓑ How many hiking courses are there in Namsan?
> ⓒ Where does B find the information about the shortest course of the Han River?
> ⓓ What day are they going to meet on?
> ⓔ What is Sumin doing this Sunday?

① 1개　② 2개　③ 3개　④ 4개　⑤ 5개

13 다음 중 어법상 <u>어색한</u> 것을 고르시오.

① I took her classes for her during she was sick.
② Sue didn't stop practicing until she could play the instrument.
③ While you were out, you had two phone calls.
④ He didn't get married until he was well into his forties.
⑤ Turn the sweater inside out before you wash it.

14 다음 중 어법상 올바른 것을 고르시오.

① I have a friend who dog won the Fastest Dog contest.
② I met a girl of which mother writes novels.
③ The boy of whose hair is red is Mark.

④ She was in a large stone-chamber of which window was usually open.
⑤ The mountain of which the summit you can see over there is Mt. Namsan.

[15~16] 다음 우리말에 맞도록 괄호 안에 주어진 어휘를 이용하여 영작하시오.

15
> 나는 취미가 농구인 친구가 있다. (to play basketball, a friend, hobby, have, 10 단어)

➡ _____

16
> 그가 집에 돌아오면, 그는 아버지에게 전화할 것이다. (come back home, call his father, when)

➡ _____
　_____

17 다음 문장에서 어법상 <u>어색한</u> 것을 찾아 바르게 고치시오.

(1) Charlotte is a wise spider which best friend is Wilbur.
➡ _____
　_____

(2) The girl of which dress is yellow is Bora.
➡ _____

(3) I'll take care of your dog while you will be away.
➡ _____

18 다음 중 어법상 옳은 것을 고르시오.

① The boy whose the backpack is blue is Jinsu.

② I have a watch of which price is 9,000 won.

③ She will wait here until the contest will be over.

④ You should wait on the sidewalk as soon as the traffic light changes to green.

⑤ Mike called her back as soon as he saw her message.

[19~22] 다음 대화를 읽고 물음에 답하시오.

Sweet Dreams

Can you guess what these whales are doing in the picture? It looks like they are standing up in a group. But they are ⓐactually sleeping! Humpback whales stand on their tails while they sleep. They sleep near the surface. Since they are not fish, they need to come up to breathe. Also, they don't fall asleep completely. ⓑWhen they wake up, they come out of the water for a deep breathe and dive back into the sea.

*humpback whale: 혹등고래라고 불리며, 북극해를 제외한 모든 대양에서 서식한다.

19 위 글의 밑줄 친 ⓐactually와 바꿔 쓸 수 없는 말을 고르시오.

① in truth ② in fact

③ exactly ④ in reality

⑤ indeed

20 본문의 내용과 일치하도록 다음 빈칸 (A)~(C)에 알맞은 단어를 쓰시오.

Humpback whales sleep near (A)_____ _____ standing on (B)_____ _____, and they don't fall asleep (C)_____.

21 위 글의 밑줄 친 ⓑ에서 문맥상 어색한 단어를 고치시오.

_____ ➡ _____

22 위 글을 읽고 알 수 없는 것을 고르시오.

① Do humpback whales sleep on their side?

② Are humpback whales fish?

③ Why do humpback whales need to come up to breathe?

④ When humpback whales wake up, what do they do?

⑤ How often do humpback whales come out of the water for a deep breath?

[23~24] 다음 글을 읽고 물음에 답하시오.

Enjoy Your Meal

If you think fish are not smart, take a look at the tuskfish. This small fish whose favorite food is clams uses a tool to open them. Clams usually hide under the sand, so they cannot be easily discovered. The tuskfish blows on the sand until a clam appears. The clam is closed tightly, so the fish cannot eat ⓐit. But the tuskfish doesn't give up. It smashes the clam against a rock. In the end, the clam opens and dinner is served.

*tuskfish: 놀래깃과의 물고기로 서태평양과 인도양에서 주로 서식한다.

23 위 글의 주제로 알맞은 것을 고르시오.

① It's unclear why people think fish are not smart.
② The tuskfish is a smart fish which uses a tool to open clams.
③ The place where clams usually hide is under the sand.
④ It is not easy to discover clams.
⑤ The clams appear when the tuskfish blows on the sand.

24 위 글의 밑줄 친 ⓐit이 가리키는 것을 본문에서 찾아 쓰시오.

➡ _____

[25~27] 다음 글을 읽고 물음에 답하시오.

One, Two, Three, Jump!

You have probably seen a bird fly down to the sea to catch a fish. But ⓐ물고기가 새를 잡기 위해 물 밖으로 뛰어오르는 것을 본 적이 있는가? Well, birds have to be careful when a giant trevally is around. (①) This fish can grow up to ⓑ170cm and 80kg. (②) This fish is quick and smart. (③) It can spot a flying bird and calculate its speed and distance. (④) When the bird flies nearby, the giant trevally jumps out of the water and catches it. (⑤)

*giant trevally: 전갱잇과의 물고기로 서태평양과 인도양에서 서식한다.

25 위 글의 밑줄 친 ⓐ의 우리말에 맞게 주어진 어휘를 알맞게 배열하시오.

> to catch / ever / a fish / jump / seen / you / out of the water / a bird / have

➡ _____
_____

26 위 글의 흐름으로 보아, 주어진 문장이 들어가기에 가장 적절한 곳은?

> But don't let its size fool you.

①   ②   ③   ④   ⑤

27 위 글의 밑줄 친 ⓑ를 읽는 법을 영어로 쓰시오.

➡ _____
_____

MEMO

Lesson 8

Up to You

의사소통 기능

- 후회 표현하기
  A: Oh, no! You got caught in the rain.
  B: I should have taken an umbrella.

- 기원하는 말 하기
  A: I'm going to sing in the school festival.
  B: I hope you move the audience.

언어 형식

- 분사구문
  Reading the article, he dropped his cup in surprise.

- 과거완료
  The article said Alfred Nobel **had died** in France from a heart attack.

Words & Expressions

Key Words

- **active** [ǽktiv] 휑 활동적인, 적극적인
- **actually** [ǽktʃuəli] 뷔 사실
- **appreciate** [əprí:ʃièit] 동 고맙게 생각하다
- **article** [á:rtikl] 명 기사
- **audience** [ɔ́:diəns] 명 관객
- **award** [əwɔ́:rd] 명 상, 시상
- **chain** [tʃein] 동 사슬로 묶다(매다)
- **clothes** [klouz] 명 옷
- **contribute** [kəntríbju:t] 동 기여하다, 공헌하다
- **create** [kriéit] 동 창조하다, 만들어 내다
- **decide** [disáid] 동 결정하다
- **deeply** [dí:pli] 뷔 몹시, 깊이, 매우
- **describe** [diskráib] 동 기술하다, 묘사하다
- **disappointed** [dìsəpɔ́intid] 휑 실망한, 낙담한
- **drop** [drɑp] 동 떨어뜨리다
- **due** [dju:] 휑 ~하기로 되어 있는, 예정된
- **dynamite** [dáinəmàit] 명 다이너마이트
- **even** [í:vən] 뷔 훨씬
- **fault** [fɔ:lt] 명 잘못
- **graduate** [grǽdʒuet] 동 졸업하다
- **graduation** [grædʒuéiʃən] 명 졸업(식)
- **grandparents** [grǽndpɛ̀ərənts] 명 조부모
- **habit** [hǽbit] 명 습관
- **headline** [hédlain] 명 (신문 기사 등의) 표제
- **heart attack** 심장 마비
- **including** [inklú:diŋ] 전 ~을 포함해서

- **invention** [invénʃən] 명 발명품
- **inventor** [invéntər] 명 발명가
- **merchant** [mɔ́:rtʃənt] 명 상인
- **mistake** [mistéik] 명 실수, 잘못
- **mistakenly** [mistéikənli] 뷔 실수로
- **moment** [móumənt] 명 (정확한 시점을 나타내는) 순간
- **move** [mu:v] 동 감동시키다
- **normal** [nɔ́:rməl] 휑 보통의, 정상적인
- **opinion** [əpínjən] 명 의견
- **originally** [ərídʒənəli] 뷔 원래는, 처음에는
- **participate** [pɑ:rtísəpèit] 동 참가하다
- **perfect** [pɔ́:rfikt] 휑 완벽한
- **plan** [plæn] 명 계획 동 계획을 세우다
- **protect** [prətékt] 동 보호하다, 지키다
- **regret** [rigrét] 명 후회 동 후회하다
- **report** [ripɔ́:rt] 동 보도하다 명 기사, 보도
- **satisfied** [sǽtisfàid] 휑 만족한
- **score** [skɔ:r] 동 득점하다
- **shocked** [ʃɑkt] 휑 충격을 받은
- **spill** [spil] 동 쏟아지다, 흐르다, 쏟다
- **step** [step] 동 밟다
- **stomachache** [stʌ́məkeik] 명 복통
- **trust** [trʌst] 동 신뢰하다, 믿다
- **unbelievable** [ənbilívəbəl] 휑 믿을 수 없는, 믿기 어려운
- **vacation** [veikéiʃən] 명 휴가, 방학
- **voice** [vɔis] 명 목소리

Key Expressions

- **be late for** ~에 지각하다
- **be over** 끝나다
- **catch one's breath** 숨을 고르다
- **catch one's eye** 눈길을 끌다
- **describe A as B** A를 B로 기술하다, 묘사하다
- **get caught** 잡히다
- **give it a try** 시도하다
- **give up** 포기하다
- **hang out** 많은 시간을 보내다
- **in surprise** 놀라서

- **keep in touch** 연락하고 지내다
- **keep -ing** 계속해서 ~하다
- **make a mistake** 실수하다
- **put off** 미루다, 연기하다
- **rather than** ~보다는
- **stay up** 안 자다, 깨어 있다
- **take eyes off** 눈을 떼다
- **take part in** ~에 참가하다
- **thanks to** ~ 덕분에
- **think of A as B** A를 B라고 생각하다

Word Power

※ 서로 비슷한 뜻을 가진 어휘

- □ **active** 활동적인 – **dynamic** 역동적인
- □ **decide** 결정하다 – **determine** 결정하다
- □ **merchant** 상인 – **trader** 무역상
- □ **normal** 보통의 – **ordinary** 보통의
- □ **protect** 보호하다 – **defend** 방어하다

- □ **appreciate** 감사하다 – **be grateful** 감사하다
- □ **fault** 잘못 – **blunder** 잘못, 실수
- □ **move** 감동시키다 – **touch** 감동을 주다
- □ **participate** 참가하다 – **engage in** 참가하다
- □ **trust** 신뢰하다, 믿다 – **rely on** 의존하다

※ 서로 반대의 뜻을 가진 어휘

- □ **active** 활동적인 ↔ **inactive** 활동이 없는
- □ **normal** 정상적인 ↔ **abnormal** 비정상인
- □ **perfect** 완벽한 ↔ **imperfect** 불완전한
- □ **trust** 신뢰하다, 믿다 ↔ **distrust** 불신하다

- □ **including** 포함해서 ↔ **excluding** 제외하고
- □ **opinion** 의견 ↔ **fact** 사실
- □ **satisfied** 만족한 ↔ **dissatisfied** 불만족한

※ 동사 – 명사

- □ **appreciate** 감사하다 – **appreciation** 감사
- □ **describe** 묘사하다 – **description** 묘사
- □ **participate** 참가하다 – **participation** 참가

- □ **decide** 결정하다 – **decision** 결정
- □ **graduate** 졸업하다 – **graduation** 졸업(식)

※ 동사 – 명사 – 행위자

- □ **contribute** 기여하다 – **contribution** 기여 – **contributor** 기여자
- □ **create** 창조하다 – **creation** 창조 – **creator** 창조자
- □ **educate** 교육하다 – **education** 교육 – **educator** 교육자
- □ **invent** 발명하다 – **invention** 발명품 – **inventor** 발명가
- □ **protect** 보호하다 – **protection** 보호 – **protector** 보호자

English Dictionary

- □ **appreciate** 고맙게 생각하다
  → to be grateful for something
  어떤 것에 대해 감사하다

- □ **contribute** 기여하다, 공헌하다
  → to help to cause something to happen
  어떤 일이 발생하도록 돕다

- □ **describe** 기술하다, 묘사하다
  → to explain about something
  어떤 것에 관하여 설명하다

- □ **due** ~하기로 되어 있는, 예정된
  → expected at or planned for a certain time
  어떤 시간에 예정되어 있거나 계획된

- □ **dynamite** 다이너마이트
  → a powerful explosive
  강력한 폭약, 폭발물

- □ **graduation** 졸업(식)
  → a ceremony at which degrees or diplomas are given out
  학위나 졸업장이 주어지는 의식

- □ **headline** (신문 기사 등의) 표제
  → the title written in large letters over a story in a newspaper
  신문 기사에 큰 글씨로 쓰여진 제목

- □ **merchant** 상인
  → a person who sells products in large amounts
  대량으로 상품을 파는 사람

- □ **regret** 후회하다
  → to feel sorry or unhappy about something
  무엇인가에 대하여 유감스럽거나 불행하다고 느끼다

- □ **report** 보도하다
  → to give information about something via newspaper, TV or radio
  신문, TV 또는 라디오를 통해서 무언가에 관한 정보를 주다

- □ **score** 득점하다
  → to gain a goal or point in a sport or game
  운동 또는 경기에서 점수를 얻다

- □ **spill** 쏟아지다, 흐르다, 쏟다
  → to flow over the edge of a container
  용기의 가장자리 너머로 흐르다

- □ **unbelievable** 믿을 수 없는, 믿기 어려운
  → difficult or impossible to believe
  믿기 어렵거나 불가능한

01 접미사 -or를 붙여 명사로 만들 수 <u>없는</u> 것을 <u>모두</u> 고르시오.

① produce   ② invent   ③ protect

④ educate   ⑤ collect

02 다음 밑줄 친 부분의 의미로 알맞지 <u>않은</u> 것은?

① We hope everyone will <u>contribute</u> to the discussion. (기여하다)

② He <u>should have been</u> more careful. (~해야 한다)

③ The cost is $150 per night, <u>including</u> buffet breakfast. (포함해서)

④ She plays an <u>active</u> part in local politics. (적극적인)

⑤ It would be hard to <u>describe</u> my feelings. (묘사하다)

03 다음 영영풀이가 나타내는 말을 고르시오.

> to give information about something via newspaper, TV or radio

① research   ② inspect   ③ report

④ review   ⑤ examine

04 다음 〈보기〉의 밑줄 친 단어와 같은 의미로 쓰인 것을 <u>모두</u> 고르시오.

> ┤ 보기 ├
> I'm deeply <u>moved</u> by such kindness.

① They <u>move</u> house fairly frequently.

② She <u>moved</u> quickly towards the door.

③ Could you <u>move</u> your car, please?

④ These stories surprised and <u>moved</u> me.

⑤ His speech <u>moved</u> the audience to tears.

05 다음 밑줄 친 부분과 의미가 가장 가까운 것을 고르시오.

> I <u>am grateful for</u> all your help.

① enjoy   ② increase

③ appreciate   ④ am aware of

⑤ deal with

[06~07] 다음 빈칸에 알맞은 것을 고르시오.

06

> They arrived early, _____ good weather.

① such as   ② in spite of

③ thanks to   ④ depending on

⑤ by means of

07

> He decided to quit _____ accept the new rules.

① as if   ② as well as

③ in addition to   ④ rather than

⑤ by the time

01 다음 짝지어진 단어의 관계가 같도록 빈칸에 알맞은 말을 쓰시오.

> act : actor = win : _____

02 밑줄 친 부분과 바꿔 쓸 수 있는 말을 주어진 철자로 시작하여 쓰시오.

> All the students at the school must <u>engage</u> in volunteer work.

➡ p_____

[03~04] 다음 빈칸에 공통으로 들어갈 말을 쓰시오.

03
> • Clark had to sit down to _____ his breath.
> • There are some paintings that _____ my eye.

04
> • Do you _____ in touch with him?
> • Why do you _____ talking that way?

05 다음 제시된 의미에 맞는 단어를 주어진 철자로 시작하여 빈칸에 쓰고, 알맞은 것을 골라 문장을 완성하시오.

> • d_____ : a powerful explosive
> • h_____ : the title written in large letters over a story in a newspaper
> • m_____ : a person who sells products in large amounts

(1) Have you seen the _____ in today's paper?

(2) The _____ paid customs on what he had bought in China.

(3) They used _____ to break big stones.

06 다음 우리말에 맞게 주어진 단어를 바르게 배열하시오.

(1) 그의 새 책은 내년에 출판될 예정이다.
   (next, new, year, his, published, is, book, be, to, due)
   ➡ _____

(2) 그 영화는 매우 자극적인 스릴러물로 묘사되고 있다.
   (film, a, thriller, charged, the, described, highly, is, as)
   ➡ _____

(3) 나는 같은 실수를 다시 하지 않을 거야.
   (make, the, mistake, won't, I, same, again)
   ➡ _____

(4) 소풍에서 비를 만나기 전까지는 좋았지.
   (until, the, the, at, was, in, fine, picnic, we, caught, it, rain, got)
   ➡ _____
   _____

① 후회 표현하기

> **A** Oh, no! You got caught in the rain. 오, 저런! 너 비를 맞았구나.
> **B** I should have taken an umbrella. 나는 우산을 가져갔어야 했어.

- 'I should have+과거분사 ~.'는 '나는 ~했어야 했는데 (하지 못해 유감이다)'의 의미로 과거 사실에 대한 후회, 안타까움, 유감 등을 나타낼 때 사용하는 표현이다. 'I should not/shouldn't have+과거분사 ~.'는 '나는 ~하지 말았어야 했다.'라는 뜻을 나타낸다. 이 표현에서는 'should'를 'ought to'로 바꾸어 'I ought to have+과거분사'로 표현할 수 있다. '~하지 말았어야 했는데 (했다)'는 의미의 'I should not have+과거분사'는 'I ought not to have+과거분사'로 나타낼 수 있다.

- 안타까움, 후회를 나타내는 비슷한 표현으로 'I had to ~, but I didn't.', 'I (really) regret ~.' 등이 있고, sorry를 사용하여 'I'm sorry that 주어+과거동사 ~.'로 나타내기도 한다. 'should have+과거분사'는 과거 사실에 대한 가정의 표현으로 '~했어야 했는데 (하지 않았다)'의 의미를 나타내는 과거에 하지 않은 일에 대해 후회하는 표현이다. should 대신 could를 사용하여 'could have+과거분사'가 되면 '~할 수 있었는데'의 의미가 될 수 있다.

- 'should have p.p.'는 과거에 했어야 하는 일 또는 하지 못한 일에 대한 후회, 유감, 안타까움을 표현하며 '~했어야 했는데 (못했다)'의 의미로 사용되고, 'could/would have p.p.'는 과거의 일에 대한 유감을 의미하여 '~할 수 있었는데 (못했다), ~했어야 했는데 (못했다)'의 의미로 가정법에 주로 사용된다. 'must have p.p.'는 과거에 대한 강한 추측을 나타내어 '~이었음에 틀림없다'의 의미로 사용되고, 'cannot have p.p.'는 과거에 대한 강한 부정의 추측을 나타내어 '~이었을 리가 없다'의 의미로 사용되며, 'may have p.p.'는 과거에 대한 약한 추측을 나타내어 '~했을지도 모른다'의 의미로 사용된다.

후회 표현하기

- I should[shouldn't] have 과거분사 나는 ~했어야[하지 말았어야] 했는데
- I ought (not) to have 과거분사 나는 ~했어야(하지 말았어야) 했는데
- I (really) regret (that) 주어+과거동사 ~한 것이 유감이다/후회한다
- I'm sorry that 주어+과거동사 ~한 것이 유감이다

핵심 Check

1. 우리말에 맞게 괄호 안의 단어들을 바르게 배열하시오.

   (1) 나는 열심히 공부했어야 했다. (should, I, hard, studied, have)

   ➡ _____

   (2) 나는 학교에 늦지 말았어야 했다. (have, I, school, for, should, not, late, been)

   ➡ _____

2 기원하는 말 하기

A I'm going to sing in the school festival. 나는 학교 축제에서 노래를 할 예정이야.

B I hope you move the audience. 네가 관객들을 감동시키기를 바라.

- 상대에게 좋은 일이 생기도록 기원하는 표현은 'I hope ~.'를 사용한다. I hope 뒤에 접속사 that은 보통 생략하고, 기원하고자 하는 내용의 '주어+동사 ~'를 넣어 'I hope you succeed.(네가 성공하기를 기원해.)'처럼 말한다. hope 이외에도 wish, pray 등을 사용하여 'I wish ~.' 또는 'I pray ~.'라고 하기도 한다.

- 상대가 하는 일이 잘 되기를 기원하면서 '행운을 빌어!'라고 할 때 'I'll keep my fingers crossed (for you)!'라고 한다. 'keep one's fingers crossed'란 집게손가락 위에 가운데 손가락을 교차시켜서 소원이 이루어지도록(= hope for something) 행운을 비는 동작을 묘사한 말로 'I'll keep my fingers crossed (for you).(행운을 빌어.)'처럼 사용한다.

- 상대의 구체적인 행동을 언급하지 않고 단순히 상대에게 행운이 깃들기를 기원하는 의미로 '행운을 빌어.'와 같은 표현으로 'Good luck to you.(행운을 빌어.)', 'I hope everything goes well with you.(다 잘되기를 희망해.)' 등을 사용하기도 한다. 'Have a nice ~!'도 상대에게 행운을 기원하는 말이다. 'Break a leg!(행운을 빌어!)'라는 표현은 주로 공연이나, 행사, 경기 등을 앞두고 있는 사람에게 '행운을 빌어!'라고 격려할 때 자주 쓰인다.

기원하기

- I hope ~. ~하기를 희망한다.
- I would like you to ~. 나는 네가 ~하기를 원한다.
- What I really want is ~. 내가 정말로 원하는 것은 ~하는 것이다.
- I really want you to ~. 나는 정말로 네가 ~하기를 원한다.
- I hope everything goes well with you. 너의 일이 다 잘되기를 희망해.
- I'll keep my fingers crossed (for you). 행운을 빌어.
- Good luck to you. / Break a leg. 행운을 빌어.

핵심 Check

2. 다음 대화의 빈칸에 알맞은 것을 고르시오.

A: I'm planning to visit my grandparents in Busan.

B: Sounds great. I _____ you have a wonderful vacation.

① try   ② hope   ③ decide

④ remember   ⑤ break

Listen and Speak 1 A

> G: Mike, why ❶were you late for class?
>
> B: I had a bad ❷stomachache.
>
> G: Oh, no! Are you okay now?
>
> B: Yeah. ❸I should have eaten ❹less last night.

G: Mike, 왜 수업에 늦었니?
B: 배가 많이 아팠어.
G: 오, 저런! 지금은 괜찮니?
B: 응. 어젯밤 덜 먹었어야 했어.

❶ be late for ~: ~에 늦다
❷ stomachache: 복통, 위통
❸ 'I should have+과거분사 ~.'는 '나는 ~했어야 했다.'라는 뜻으로 과거 사실에 대한 후회를 표현할 때 사용하는 표현이다.
❹ less: 더 적게, 덜하게

Check(√) True or False

(1) Mike ate less last night.   T ☐ F ☐

(2) Mike was late for class due to a bad stomachache.   T ☐ F ☐

Listen and Speak 2 B

> G: Jaemin, ❶are you ready for the singing contest?
>
> B: Well, ❷I'm thinking of giving up, Tina.
>
> G: Why? I thought you really wanted to ❸take part in the contest.
>
> B: I don't think I'm a good singer.
>
> G: Come on. You're ❹the best singer I know.
>
> B: ❺Do you really think so?
>
> G: Of course. You have a really nice voice.
>
> B: ❻Thank you for saying so. I'll ❼do my best.
>
> G: ❽I hope you win the contest.

G: 재민아, 노래 경연 대회에 나갈 준비는 됐니?
B: 음, 포기할까 생각 중이야, Tina.
G: 왜? 나는 네가 그 대회에 정말로 참가하고 싶어 한다고 생각했어.
B: 나는 내가 노래를 잘하는 것 같지 않아.
G: 그러지 말고. 너는 내가 아는 가장 노래를 잘하는 사람이야.
B: 정말로 그렇게 생각하니?
G: 물론이지. 너는 정말 멋진 목소리를 가졌어.
B: 그렇게 말해 줘서 고마워. 최선을 다해 볼게.
G: 네가 대회에서 우승하기를 바라.

❶ be ready for ~: ~할 준비가 되다
❷ 'I'm thinking of ~.'는 '나는 ~을 할까 생각 중이다.'라는 뜻으로 of 뒤에 동명사를 취해 의도나 계획을 나타낼 때 쓰는 표현이며 'I'm considering ~ing' 또는 'I intend to 동사원형 ~.'과 바꿔 쓸 수 있다. 전치사 of 대신 about을 사용하여 'I'm thinking about ~.'으로도 표현한다.
❸ take part in: ~에 참가하다
❹ the best singer와 I know 사이에 목적격 관계대명사 who(m)나 that이 생략되어 있다.
❺ 'Do you really think so?'는 상대방의 말이 확실한지를 묻는 표현으로 'Are you sure?'로 바꿔 말할 수 있다.
❻ thank you 다음에 전치사 for를 사용해서 감사의 이유를 덧붙여 말할 수 있다.
❼ do one's best: 최선을 다하다
❽ 'I hope you ~.'는 '나는 네가 ~하기를 바란다[희망한다].'라는 뜻으로 상대방에게 기원하는 말을 할 때 쓸 수 있는 표현이다.

Check(√) True or False

(3) Tina hopes Jaemin wins the contest.   T ☐ F ☐

(4) Jaemin will take part in the singing contest.   T ☐ F ☐

Listen and Speak 1 B

G: Jiho, what's up? You look tired.

B: Yeah. I ❶stayed up ❷late last night.

G: Did you play computer games again?

B: No, not this time. I ❸had to finish my history project.

G: Is it ❹due today?

B: Yeah. I ❺shouldn't have ❻put it off until the last moment.

G: Hmm, I understand. I often have the same problem.

B: Really? Well, ❼let's try to change our bad habits.

G: 지호야, 무슨 일이니? 너 피곤해 보여.
B: 응. 어젯밤에 늦게까지 깨어 있었어.
G: 너 또 컴퓨터 게임을 했니?
B: 아니, 이번엔 아니야. 나는 역사 과제를 끝내야 했어.
G: 그 과제가 오늘까지니?
B: 응. 나는 마지막 순간까지 미루지 말았어야 했어.
G: 음, 이해해. 나도 종종 같은 문제를 겪어.
B: 정말? 음, 우리의 나쁜 습관을 바꾸도록 노력하자.

❶ stay up: 안 자다, 깨어 있다
❷ late는 동사인 stay up을 꾸며주고 있으므로 부사로 '늦게'의 의미로 사용되었다.
❸ had to는 'have to(~해야 한다)'의 과거형으로 '~해야만 했다'로 해석한다.
❹ due: ~하기로 되어 있는, 예정된
❺ 'should not have+과거분사'는 '~하지 말았어야 했는데 (했다)'의 의미로, 말하는 시점보다 과거의 일에 대한 유감이나 후회를 나타낼 때 사용한다.
❻ put off: 미루다, 연기하다 until은 전치사로 '~까지'의 뜻이다.
❼ Let's+동사원형: ~하자 try to 동사원형: ~하는 것을 노력하다

Check(√) True or False

(5) Jiho doesn't know the due date of the history project. T ☐ F ☐

(6) Jiho stayed up late last night playing computer games. T ☐ F ☐

Listen and Speak 2 C

A: ❶What are you going to do tomorrow?

B: I'm going to sing in the school festival.

A: Great! ❷I hope you ❸move the audience.

B: Thanks. I hope so, too.

A: 너는 내일 무엇을 할 계획이니?
B: 학교 축제에서 노래 부를 거야.
A: 멋지네! 나는 네가 청중을 감동시키기를 바라.
B: 고마워. 나도 그러길 바라.

❶ 상대방에게 무엇을 할 계획인지(또는 어떤 계획이 있는지) 물어볼 때 'What are you planning[going] to+동사원형?'을 사용할 수 있다.
❷ 'I hope you ~.'는 '나는 네가 ~하기를 바란다[희망한다].'라는 뜻으로 상대방에게 기원하는 말을 할 때 쓸 수 있는 표현이다.
❸ move: (남을) 감동시키다 audience: 청중

Check(√) True or False

(7) B is planning to sing in the school festival. T ☐ F ☐

(8) A hopes to move the audience. T ☐ F ☐

Listen and Speak 1 C

A: ❶What's wrong?

B: I ❷got caught in the rain.

A: Oh, ❸I'm sorry to hear that.

B: ❹I should have taken an umbrella.

❶ 상대방이 뭔가에 불만족하거나 실망하고 있는 것을 보고 그 원인을 물을 때 'What's wrong?'이라고 물을 수 있다. 비슷한 표현으로 'What's the matter?' 혹은 'What's the problem?'도 있다.

❷ get caught in the rain: 비를 만나다

❸ 슬픔, 불만족, 실망에 대해 위로할 때 'I'm sorry to hear that.'을 사용하며 '안 됐구나.'로 해석한다.

❹ 'I should have+과거분사 ~.'는 '나는 ~했어야 했다.'라는 뜻으로 과거 사실에 대한 후회를 표현할 때 사용하는 표현이다. should 대신에 ought to를 사용하기도 한다.

Listen and Speak 2 A

G: Jinsu, what are you going to do ❶during the vacation?

B: I'm going to read ❷lots of books. What about you?

G: I'm planning to visit my grandparents in Busan.

B: Sounds great. ❸I hope you have a wonderful vacation.

❶ during+명사: ~ 동안에

❷ lots of: 많은

❸ 'I hope that 주어+동사 ~.'는 기원하고자 할 때 사용하는 표현으로 'I hope' 뒤에 기원하고자 하는 내용을 넣어 말한다.

Real Life Talk Watch a Video

Minho: Linda, what are you reading?

Linda: I'm reading ❶graduation messages from my classmates.

Minho: Oh, it looks like they had ❷a lot to say to you.

Linda: Many of them wrote ❸that they like my smile.

Minho: That's nice. What else?

Linda: Some of them said I didn't ❹hang out enough with them.

Minho: That's not your fault. You were always busy.

Linda: Yeah, but ❺I should have spent more time with my classmates.

Minho: ❻You still have time after graduation.

Linda: You're right.

Minho: ❼I hope you ❽keep in touch with your classmates ❾after graduation.

Linda: Thanks. I hope so, too.

❶ graduation: 졸업

❷ lot이 '많음'이라는 뜻의 명사로 사용되고 있다. to say to you는 명사 lot을 수식하는 형용사적 용법이다.

❸ that은 wrote의 목적어(명사절)를 이끄는 접속사이다.

❹ hang out: 많은 시간을 보내다

❺ 'should have 과거분사'는 '~했어야 했는데 (하지 못했다.)'의 의미로 후회를 표현할 때 사용하는 표현이다. 비슷한 표현으로 'I regret that 주어+과거동사 ~.', 'I feel sorry that 주어+과거동사 ~.', 'I ought to have 과거분사 ~.', 'I wish I had 과거분사 ~.'가 있다.

❻ still: 아직(도) graduation: 졸업

❼ 'I hope you ~.'는 '나는 네가 ~하기를 바란다[희망한다].'라는 뜻으로 상대방에게 기원하는 말을 할 때 쓸 수 있는 표현이다. 바꿔 쓸 수 있는 표현으로 'I would like you to 동사원형 ~.', 'I really want you to 동사원형 ~.', 'What I really want is for you to 동사원형 ~.' 등이 있다.

❽ keep in touch with: ~와 연락하고 지내다

❾ 'after'는 전치사로 '~ 후에'의 뜻이며 뒤에 명사가 올 수 있다.

Real Life Talk Step 2

A: ❶I can't believe we're ❷graduating soon.

B: Yeah. Is there anything ❸you regret about your middle school life?

A: Yes. ❹I should have been active in classes.

B: Well, you have a second ❺chance in high school.

A: ❻I guess you're right.

B: ❼I hope you are active in classes in high school.

❶ 어떤 사실에 대해 놀라움을 나타낼 때에는 'I can't believe 주어+동사 ~.', 'I was surprised that 주어+동사 ~.' 등과 같은 표현을 이용해 말할 수 있다.

❷ graduate: 졸업하다

❸ anything과 you regret about your middle school life 사이에 목적격 관계대명사 that이 생략되어 있다. regret: 후회하다

❹ 'I should have+과거분사 ~.'는 '나는 ~했어야 했다.'라는 뜻으로 과거 사실에 대한 후회를 표현할 때 사용하는 표현이다. active: 적극적인

❺ chance: 기회

❻ 'I guess you're right.'는 '네 말이 맞는 것 같아.'의 의미로, 상대방의 말에 동의하는 표현이다.

❼ 'I hope that 주어+동사 ~.'는 기원하고자 할 때 사용하는 표현으로 'I hope' 뒤에 기원하고자 하는 내용을 넣어 말한다.

● 다음 우리말과 일치하도록 빈칸에 알맞은 말을 쓰시오.

Listen and Speak 1 A

G: Mike, why _____ _____ _____ _____ class?

B: I had a bad _____.

G: Oh, no! _____ you okay now?

B: Yeah. I _____ _____ _____ less last night.

Listen and Speak 1 B

G: Jiho, what's _____? You look _____.

B: Yeah. I _____ _____ _____ last night.

G: Did you play computer games _____?

B: No, _____ this time. I _____ _____ finish my history project.

G: Is it _____ today?

B: Yeah. I _____ _____ _____ _____ _____ _____ the last moment.

G: Hmm, I understand. I often have _____ _____ problem.

B: Really? Well, let's _____ _____ _____ our bad _____.

Listen and Speak 1 C

1. A: What's _____?

   B: I _____ _____ _____ the rain.

   A: Oh, I'm _____ _____ hear that.

   B: I should _____ _____ an umbrella.

2. A: _____ wrong?

   B: I _____ the test.

   A: Oh, I'm sorry to _____ _____.

   B: I _____ _____ _____ _____.

3. A: What's wrong?

   B: I _____ my bike.

   A: Oh, I'm sorry to hear that.

   B: _____ _____ _____ _____ it.

4. A: What's wrong?

   B: I _____ _____ _____ school.

   A: Oh, I'm sorry to hear that.

   B: I _____ _____ _____ _____ _____.

해석

G: Mike, 왜 수업에 늦었니?
B: 배가 많이 아팠어.
G: 오, 저런! 지금은 괜찮니?
B: 응. 어젯밤 덜 먹었어야 했어.

G: 지호야, 무슨 일이니? 너 피곤해 보여.
B: 응. 어젯밤에 늦게까지 깨어 있었어.
G: 너 또 컴퓨터 게임을 했니?
B: 아니, 이번엔 아니야. 나는 역사 과제를 끝내야 했어.
G: 그 과제가 오늘까지니?
B: 응. 나는 마지막 순간까지 미루지 말았어야 했어.
G: 음, 이해해. 나도 종종 같은 문제를 겪어.
B: 정말? 음, 우리의 나쁜 습관을 바꾸도록 노력하자.

1. A: 무슨 일 있니?
   B: 오, 비를 맞았어.
   A: 오, 안됐구나.
   B: 나는 우산을 가져왔어야 했어.

2. A: 무슨 일 있니?
   B: 시험에 떨어졌어.
   A: 오, 안됐구나.
   B: 나는 공부를 열심히 했어야 했어.

3. A: 무슨 일 있니?
   B: 자전거를 잃어버렸어.
   A: 오, 안됐구나.
   B: 나는 사슬로 묶어놨어야 했어.

4. A: 무슨 일 있니?
   B: 학교에 늦었어.
   A: 오, 안됐구나.
   B: 나는 일찍 일어났어야 했어.

Listen and Speak 2 A

G: Jinsu, what are you _____ _____ _____ _____ the vacation?

B: I'm going to read _____ _____ books. What _____ you?

G: I'm planning to _____ my grandparents in Busan.

B: Sounds great. I _____ _____ _____ a wonderful vacation.

G: 진수야, 방학 동안 무엇을 할 거니?
B: 나는 책을 많이 읽을 거야. 너는 어떠니?
G: 나는 부산에 계신 조부모님을 방문할 계획이야.
B: 좋구나. 멋진 방학을 보내길 바라.

Listen and Speak 2 B

G: Jaemin, are you _____ _____ the singing contest?

B: Well, _____ _____ _____ _____ _____ _____, Tina.

G: Why? I thought you really _____ _____ _____ _____ _____ the contest.

B: I don't think I'm a _____ _____.

G: Come on. You're _____ _____ _____ _____ _____ _____.

B: Do you really _____ _____?

G: Of course. You have a really nice _____.

B: Thank _____ _____ _____ so, I'll _____ _____ _____.

B: _____ _____ _____ _____ the contest.

G: 재민아, 노래 경연 대회에 나갈 준비는 됐니?
B: 음, 포기할까 생각 중이야, Tina.
G: 왜? 나는 네가 그 대회에 정말로 참가하고 싶어 한다고 생각했어.
B: 나는 내가 노래를 잘하는 것 같지 않아.
G: 그러지 말고. 너는 내가 아는 노래를 가장 잘하는 사람이야.
B: 정말로 그렇게 생각하니?
G: 물론이지. 너는 정말 멋진 목소리를 가졌어.
B: 그렇게 말해 줘서 고마워. 최선을 다해 볼게.
G: 네가 대회에서 우승하기를 바라.

Listen and Speak 2 C

1. **A:** What are you going to do tomorrow?
   B: I'm _____ _____ _____ in the school festival.
   A: Great! I _____ _____ _____ the _____.
   B: Thanks. I _____ _____, too.

2. **A:** What are you going to do tomorrow?
   B: I'm going to play soccer.
   A: Great! I _____ _____ _____ _____ _____ _____.
   B: Thanks. I hope so, too.

3. **A:** What are you going to do tomorrow?
   B: I'm going to _____ _____ the speech contest.
   A: Great! _____ _____ _____ _____ the contest.
   B: Thanks. _____ _____ _____, too.

1. A: 너는 내일 무엇을 할 계획이니?
   B: 학교 축제에서 노래 부를 거야.
   A: 멋지네! 나는 네가 청중을 감동시키기를 바라.
   B: 고마워. 나도 그러길 바라.

2. A: 너는 내일 무엇을 할 계획이니?
   B: 축구를 할 거야.
   A: 멋지네! 나는 네가 득점하기를 바라.
   B: 고마워. 나도 그러길 바라.

3. A: 너는 내일 무엇을 할 계획이니?
   B: 연설 대회에 참가할 거야.
   A: 멋지네! 나는 네가 대회에서 우승하기를 바라.
   B: 고마워. 나도 그러길 바라.

Real Life Talk Watch a Video

Minho: Linda, what are you reading?

Linda: I'm reading _____ messages from my classmates.

Minho: Oh, it _____ _____ they had _____ _____ _____ to you.

Linda: Many of them _____ _____ they like my smile.

Minho: That's nice. What _____?

Linda: _____ _____ _____ said I didn't _____ _____ _____ _____ them.

Minho: That's not your _____. You were always busy.

Linda: Yeah, but I _____ _____ _____ _____ my classmates.

Minho: You still have time _____ _____.

Linda: You're right.

Minho: I _____ _____ _____ _____ your classmates after graduation.

Linda: Thanks. _____ _____ _____, too.

해석

Minho: Linda, 무엇을 읽고 있니?
Linda: 나는 학급 친구들에게 받은 졸업 메시지를 읽고 있어.
Minho: 오, 친구들이 너에게 할 말이 많은 것 같구나.
Linda: 그들 중 많은 친구들이 나의 미소를 좋아한다고 적었어.
Minho: 멋지네. 그 외에는?
Linda: 그들 중 몇몇은 내가 그들과 충분히 어울리지 않았다고 말했어.
Minho: 그건 네 잘못이 아니야. 너는 항상 바빴잖아.
Linda: 응, 하지만 나는 학급 친구들과 더 많은 시간을 보냈어야 했어.
Minho: 졸업 후에도 여전히 시간이 있어.
Linda: 네 말이 맞아.
Minho: 네가 졸업 후에도 학급 친구들과 계속 연락하기를 바라.
Linda: 고마워. 나도 그러길 바라.

Real Life Talk Step 2

1. A: I _____ _____ we're graduating soon.

   B: Yeah. Is _____ _____ you _____ about your middle school life?

   A: Yes. I _____ _____ _____ _____ in classes.

   B: Well, you _____ _____ _____ _____ in high school.

   A: I _____ you're right.

   B: I _____ _____ _____ _____ in classes in high school.

2. A: I can't _____ _____ _____ soon.

   B: Yeah. Is there _____ _____ _____ _____ your middle school life?

   A: Yes. I _____ _____ _____ part in many school events.

   B: Well, you have a second chance in high school.

   A: I _____ you're _____.

   B: I _____ _____ _____ _____ _____ many school events in high school.

1. A: 우리가 곧 졸업하는 것을 믿을 수 없어.
   B: 응. 중학교 생활에서 네가 후회하는 것이 있니?
   A: 응. 나는 수업에서 적극적이었어야 했어.
   B: 음, 너는 고등학교에서 다시 한 번 기회가 있어.
   A: 네 말이 맞는 것 같아.
   B: 고등학교에서는 네가 수업에서 적극적이기를 바라.

2. A: 우리가 곧 졸업하는 것을 믿을 수 없어.
   B: 응. 중학교 생활에서 네가 후회하는 것이 있니?
   A: 응. 나는 학교 행사에 많이 참여했어야 했어.
   B: 음, 너는 고등학교에서 다시 한 번 기회가 있어.
   A: 네 말이 맞는 것 같아.
   B: 고등학교에서는 네가 많은 학교 행사에 참여하기를 바라.

01 다음 대화의 빈칸에 알맞은 것을 고르시오.

> A: What are you going to do tomorrow?
> B: I'm going to sing in the school festival.
> A: Great! I hope _____.
> B: Thanks. I hope so, too.

① you do better next time
② you move the audience
③ you have a chance to visit the school festival
④ you take part in the school festival
⑤ you read the book about the festival

02 다음 대화의 밑줄 친 문장과 같은 의미의 문장을 고르시오.

> G: Mike, why were you late for class?
> B: I had a bad stomachache.
> G: Oh, no! Are you okay now?
> B: Yeah. <u>I should have eaten less last night.</u>

① I regret that I didn't eat less last night.
② I forgot not to eat less last night.
③ I feel sorry that I ate less last night.
④ I didn't know if I ate less last night.
⑤ I don't think that I had to eat less last night.

03 대화가 자연스럽게 연결되도록 (A)~(D)를 순서대로 적절하게 배열한 것은?

> (A) I'm going to participate in the speech contest.
> (B) Great! I hope you win the contest.
> (C) What are you going to do tomorrow?
> (D) Thanks. I hope so, too.

① (B) – (A) – (C) – (D)
② (B) – (C) – (A) – (D)
③ (C) – (A) – (B) – (D)
④ (C) – (B) – (A) – (D)
⑤ (C) – (D) – (B) – (A)

[01~03] 다음 대화를 읽고 물음에 답하시오.

> G: Jiho, what's up? You look tired.
> B: Yeah. I stayed up late last night. (①)
> G: (②) Did you play computer games again?
> B: No, not this time. (③)
> G: Is it due today?
> B: Yeah. I _____(A)_____ until the last moment. (④)
> G: Hmm, I understand. I often have the same problem. (⑤)
> B: Really? Well, _____(B)_____ .

01 ①~⑤ 중 주어진 문장이 들어갈 곳으로 가장 알맞은 것은?

> I had to finish my history project.

①   ②   ③   ④   ⑤

02 위 대화의 빈칸 (A)에 알맞은 말을 고르시오.

① should have put it off
② shouldn't have put it off
③ must have put it off
④ must not have put it off
⑤ may not have put it off

03 위 대화의 빈칸 (B)에 알맞은 말을 고르시오.

① let's get up early in the morning
② let's prepare the midterm exam
③ let's play the computer games
④ let's finish the history project
⑤ let's try to change our bad habits

04 다음 대화의 빈칸에 들어갈 말을 〈보기〉에서 골라 바르게 배열한 것은?

> A: I can't believe we're graduating soon.
> B: _____
> A: _____
> B: _____
> A: _____
> B: I hope you are active in classes in high school.

> (A) Yes. I should have been active in classes.
> (B) Well, you have a second chance in high school.
> (C) Yeah. Is there anything you regret about your middle school life?
> (D) I guess you're right.

① (B) – (A) – (C) – (D)
② (B) – (C) – (A) – (D)
③ (C) – (A) – (B) – (D)
④ (C) – (B) – (A) – (D)
⑤ (C) – (D) – (B) – (A)

[05~06] 다음 대화를 읽고 물음에 답하시오.

> G: Jaemin, are you ready for the singing contest? (①)
> B: Well, I'm thinking of giving _____(A)_____, Tina. (②)
> G: Why? I thought you really wanted to take part in the contest.
> B: I don't think I'm a good singer. (③)
> G: Come on. (④)
> B: Do you really think so?
> G: Of course. You have a really nice voice.
> B: Thank you for saying so. (⑤) I'll do my best.
> G: I hope you win the contest.

05 위 대화의 ①~⑤ 중 주어진 문장이 들어갈 곳은?

> You're the best singer I know.

①   ②   ③   ④   ⑤

06 빈칸 (A)에 알맞은 말을 고르시오.

① on   ② up   ③ in
④ for   ⑤ with

07 다음 중 짝지어진 대화가 <u>어색한</u> 것은?

① A: This is my first visit to Busan.
　B: Oh, really? I hope you have a good time in Busan.
② A: I've practiced a lot, but I lost the game.
　B: I'm sorry to hear that. I hope you will win next time.
③ A: My grandmother is sick in bed with a cold.
　B: That's too bad. I hope she'll get well soon.
④ A: I have been to Sydney many times.
　B: Oh, I hope you can visit there sometime.
⑤ A: My bag is too heavy.
　B: You shouldn't have bought too much.

[08~10] 다음 대화를 읽고 물음에 답하시오.

Minho: Linda, what are you reading?
Linda: I'm reading graduation messages from my classmates. (①)
Minho: Oh, it looks like they had a lot to say to you.

Linda: Many of (A)them wrote that they like my smile.
Minho: That's nice. What else?
Linda: Some of them said I didn't hang out enough with them. (②)
Minho: (③) You were always busy.
Linda: Yeah, but I should have spent more time with my classmates. (④)
Minho: You still have time after graduation.
Linda: You're right.
Minho: I hope you keep in touch with your classmates after graduation. (⑤)
Linda: Thanks. I hope so, too.

08 위 대화의 ①~⑤ 중 주어진 문장이 들어갈 곳은?

> That's not your fault.

①   ②   ③   ④   ⑤

[서답형]

09 밑줄 친 (A)them이 가리키는 것을 두 단어로 쓰시오.

➡ _____

10 위 대화의 내용과 일치하지 <u>않는</u> 것을 고르시오.

① Linda의 친구들은 Linda의 미소를 좋아한다.
② Linda는 졸업 후에도 친구들과 계속 연락하기를 바란다.
③ Linda는 항상 바빴다.
④ Linda는 지금 학급 친구들에게 받은 졸업 메시지를 읽고 있는 중이다.
⑤ Linda의 친구들은 Linda가 그들과 많은 시간을 보냈다고 생각한다.

01 밑줄 친 문장과 같은 의미가 되도록 주어진 단어를 이용하여 쓰시오.

> B: Mike, why were you late for class?
> B: I had a bad stomachache.
> G: Oh, no! Are you okay now?
> B: Yeah. I should have eaten less last night.

➡ _____ (not)

[02~03] 다음 대화를 읽고 물음에 답하시오.

> G: Jaemin, are you ready ___(A)___ the singing contest?
> B: Well, I'm thinking ___(B)___ giving up, Tina.
> G: Why? I thought you really wanted to take part in the contest.
> B: I don't think I'm a good singer.
> G: Come on. You're the best singer I know.
> B: Do you really think so?
> G: Of course. You have a really nice voice.
> B: Thank you for saying so. I'll do my best.
> G: (C)네가 대회에서 우승하기를 바라.

02 위 대화의 빈칸 (A)와 (B)에 들어갈 말을 〈보기〉에서 골라 쓰시오.

> ┌ 보기 ┐
> as   for   from   in   of   to

(A) _____ (B) _____

03 밑줄 친 (C)의 우리말을 주어진 단어를 이용하여 영작하시오. (6 words)

➡ _____ (hope)

[04~05] 다음 대화를 읽고 물음에 답하시오.

> G: Jiho, what's up? You look tired.
> B: Yeah. I stayed ___(A)___ late last night.
> G: ⓐDid you play computer games again?
> B: No, not this time. ⓑI had to finish my history project.
> G: ⓒIs it due today?
> B: Yeah. ⓓI shouldn't put it off until the last moment.
> G: Hmm, I understand. I often have the same problem.
> B: Really? ⓔWell, let's try to change our bad habits.

04 빈칸 (A)에 알맞은 말을 쓰시오.

➡ _____

05 밑줄 친 ⓐ~ⓔ 중 흐름상 또는 어법상 어색한 것을 고르고 바르게 고치시오.

➡ _____
_____

06 후회하는 표현과 대화에 나오는 단어를 이용하여 빈칸을 채우시오. (7 words)

> A: I can't believe we're graduating soon.
> B: Yeah. Is there anything you regret about your middle school life?
> A: Yes. _____
> B: Well, you have a second chance in high school.
> A: I guess you're right.
> B: I hope you are active in classes in high school.

➡ _____

교과서

Grammar

① 분사구문

> • **Reading the article**, he dropped his cup in surprise.
>
> 기사를 읽으며 그는 놀라서 컵을 떨어뜨렸다.

■ 분사가 이끄는 구를 분사구문이라고 하며, 이유, 조건, 시간, 동시동작, 양보 등의 뜻을 나타낸다. 분사구문은 '접속사+주어+동사'로 이루어진 부사절의 주어가 주절의 주어와 일치할 때 접속사와 주어를 생략하고 동사를 분사로 만들어 부사구로 표현한 것이다. 이때 생략되는 접속사에 따라 뜻이 달라진다.

- I panicked when I saw smoke coming out of the engine.
  → I panicked **seeing** smoke coming out of the engine. (시간)
  나는 엔진에서 연기가 나는 것을 보고 겁에 질렸다.

■ 부사절과 주절의 주어가 다를 때는 부사절의 주어를 생략하지 않고 사용하며 이것을 독립분사구문이라고 한다. 일반인이 주어일 경우에는 생략한다. (비인칭 독립분사구문)

- As it was dark, we quickened our pace.
  → It **being** dark, we quickened our pace. 날이 어두웠기 때문에 우리는 발걸음을 재촉했다.

■ 분사구문의 부정은 분사 앞에 'not'이나 'never'를 쓴다.

- Because he didn't pass the exam, he was feeling down.
  → Not **passing** the exam, he was feeling down. 그는 시험에 떨어져서 기분이 우울했다.

■ 분사구문의 의미를 분명히 하기 위해 분사 앞에 접속사를 쓰는 경우도 있다. 이 경우는 부사절에서 '주어+be동사'를 생략한 것과 같은 형태가 된다.

- I have just dropped in while **taking** a walk. 산책하다가 잠깐 들렀습니다.

■ 부사절의 시제가 주절보다 앞선 경우에는 완료분사구문(having+과거분사)으로 쓴다.

- After I had finished the work, I went home directly.
  = **Having finished** the work, I went home directly. 일을 끝내고 바로 집으로 갔다.

■ 분사구문에서 Being이나 Having been은 대부분 생략하지만, 보어가 명사일 경우나 분사가 아닌 경우에 보통 접속사 없이 being을 생략하지 않는다.

- Though she was nervous, she said it was a good experience.
  → Though (**being**) nervous, she said it was a good experience.
  그녀는 긴장되기는 했지만, 좋은 경험이었다고 말했다.

■ 과거분사로 시작되는 분사구문은 being이 생략된 것으로 수동의 의미를 갖는다.

- (Being) **Seen** from above, the cars looked tiny. 위에서 보니 차들이 아주 조그마했다.

핵심 Check

1. 다음 괄호 안에서 알맞은 단어를 고르시오.

(1) (Live / Living) next door, I seldom see her.

(2) (Feeling / Felt) tired, he took a nap.

② 과거완료

> • The article said Alfred Nobel **had died** in France from a heart attack.
> 기사에는 Alfred Nobel이 심장 마비로 프랑스에서 죽었다고 쓰여 있었다.

■ 과거완료는 'had+과거분사'의 형태로, 과거 이전에 일어난 일이 과거의 어느 시점까지 영향을 미칠 때 쓴다. 과거완료도 현재완료처럼 경험, 계속, 완료, 결과의 용법이 있다. 또한 과거의 어느 시점보다 먼저 일어난 일이나 상태를 나타낼 때도 쓰이며 이것을 보통 '대과거'라고 한다.

- She **had** never **been** greatly concerned about her appearance. (경험)
  그녀는 자기 외모에 크게 신경을 쓰지 않았었다.
- He **had been** fat since he was in elementary school. (계속) 그는 초등학교 때부터 뚱뚱했었습니다.
- The child **had** just **wakened**. (완료) 아이는 방금 잠을 깬 참이었다.
- He **had gone** to America leaving his family in Korea. (결과) 그는 가족을 한국에 남겨 두고 미국으로 가버렸다.
- She remembered everything that **had happened** long before. (대과거)
  그녀는 오래 전의 일들을 모두 기억하고 있었다.

■ 한 문장에 두 가지 과거의 일이 나올 때, 두 동작이 거의 동시에 일어났거나 시간차가 거의 없이 연속적으로 일어났을 경우에는 단순과거로 표현한다. 또, 접속사 after나 before가 쓰여 두 동작의 전후 관계가 명백할 때도 단순과거로 표현할 수 있다.

- She **smiled** at him and he **smiled** back. (시간차가 거의 없는 연속 동작)
  그녀가 그를 보고 웃자 그도 마주 보고 웃어 주었다.
- **Did** she leave a message before she **went**? (전후 관계가 명백함)
  그녀가 가기 전에 전갈을 남겼어요?

핵심 Check

2. 다음 괄호 안에서 알맞은 말을 고르시오.

(1) I asked him whether he (had done / does) it all himself.

(2) Later, Terry found that she (had not turned / did not turn) off the light.

(3) The airplane (has / had) just taken off when she arrived at the airport.

01 다음 빈칸에 들어갈 말로 알맞은 것은?

> _____ late, I had to hurry.

① Being ② Been ③ Am
④ Was ⑤ Be

02 다음 괄호 안에서 알맞은 말을 고르시오.

(1) (Read / Reading) the article, he dropped his cup in surprise.
(2) (Knowing not / Not knowing) the library was closed, I made the trip in vain.
(3) When you arrived, he (has / had) only just left.
(4) I had never (visiting / visited) there before.

03 다음 우리말에 맞게 빈칸에 알맞은 것은?

> 그가 그 돈을 가져갔다고 나에게 실토했다.
> = He confessed to me that he _____ the money.

① takes ② taking ③ took
④ has taken ⑤ had taken

04 다음 우리말에 맞게 주어진 어휘를 바르게 배열하시오.

(1) 텔레비전을 보면서 그녀는 저녁을 먹었다.
   (ate, watching, she, dinner, TV)
   ➡ _____

(2) 기사에는 Alfred Nobel이 프랑스에서 심장 마비로 죽었다고 쓰여 있었다.
   (a heart attack, Alfred Nobel, France, the article, said, died, had, from, in)
   ➡ _____

01 다음 중 어법상 어색한 문장은?

① Talking on the phone, she watched TV.
② Turning to the right, you will find the post office.
③ She washes away the fatigue of the day listens to music.
④ While walking home from work, I found this bakery.
⑤ Catching his breath, Nobel kept reading.

02 다음 주어진 문장의 밑줄 친 부분과 용법이 같은 것은?

> Lucy had gone to Seattle when I reached Boston.

① Jacob had studied on the subject for two months.
② Mary had been on a diet since last month.
③ Howard had met her several times.
④ I knew someone had stolen my purse on the subway.
⑤ I had finished my homework when my friend came to my house.

03 다음 문장의 밑줄 친 부분 중 어법상 어색한 것은?

> Alfred, ⓐthought ⓑthat he shouldn't be ⓒacting ⓓthis way, ⓔquickly left the place.

① ⓐ   ② ⓑ   ③ ⓒ   ④ ⓓ   ⑤ ⓔ

04 다음 빈칸에 알맞은 말이 바르게 짝지어진 것은?

> • Not _____ tired, she took out her book and read until 2:00 A.M.
> • The roads were wet because it _____ during the night.

① feeling – has rained
② feeling – had rained
③ feel – has rained
④ felt – had rained
⑤ felt – rained

서답형

05 다음 괄호 안에서 알맞은 말을 고르시오.

(1) When I arrived at the station, the train (already left / had already left).
(2) He begged forgiveness for what he (did / had done).
(3) Until last week, Emily (never went / had never been) to a soccer match.
(4) (Run / Running) to the bus stop, we sat down to catch our breath.
(5) While (talk / talking) on the phone, he cleaned his room.
(6) I felt so awkward, (knowing not / not knowing) where to look.

06 다음 주어진 두 문장을 한 문장으로 바꿀 때 <u>어색한</u> 것은?

> • The thief saw the police.
> • He ran away.

① When the thief saw the police, he ran away.

② Seeing the police, the thief ran away.

③ As the thief saw the police, he ran away.

④ As soon as the thief saw the police, he ran away.

⑤ When saw the police, the thief ran away.

07 다음 중 어법상 <u>어색한</u> 것은?

① When I woke up this morning, the snow had already stopped.

② We talked about what happened the previous week.

③ I watched TV after I did my science homework.

④ The team found thousands of interesting creatures that had never been seen before.

⑤ My family had lived in Baghdad for several generations.

서답형

08 다음 두 문장을 한 문장으로 바꿔 쓸 때 빈칸에 들어갈 한 단어를 쓰시오.

> • I was nervous.
> • I forgot my lines at the school musical.
> ➡ _____ nervous, I forgot my lines at the school musical.

➡ _____

[09~10] 다음 우리말을 바르게 영작한 것을 고르시오.

09

> Sam이 공원에 도착했을 때, Kate는 집에 가고 없었다.

① When Sam arrives at the park, Kate goes home.

② When Sam arrived at the park, Kate went home.

③ When Sam arrived at the park, Kate had gone home.

④ When Sam had arrived at the park, Kate went home.

⑤ When Sam had arrived at the park, Kate had gone home.

10

> 피곤하기 때문에 그녀는 일찍 집에 돌아왔다.

① Because tired, she came back home early.

② Because she tired, she came back home early.

③ Being she tired, she came back home early.

④ Being tired, she came back home early.

⑤ Being she was tired, she came back home early.

서답형

11 시간 흐름에 따른 사건 전개에 맞게 빈칸을 채워 문장을 완성하시오.

> • Mom bought a cellphone for me last week.
> ➡ I lost the cellphone.
> ➡ I don't have the cellphone now.
> ➡ I lost the cellphone that _____.

➡ _____

[12~13] 다음 밑줄 친 부분의 쓰임이 주어진 문장과 같은 것은?

12

> <u>Being</u> sick, I went to see a doctor.

① <u>Having</u> no partner, he danced with grace.
② <u>Being</u> honest, she was liked by many people.
③ <u>Walking</u> along the street, I met Jake's sister.
④ He kept on reading while <u>eating</u>.
⑤ <u>Going</u> out now, you'll get wet.

13

> When David arrived at the station, the train <u>had</u> already <u>left</u>.

① She <u>had</u> never <u>been</u> greatly concerned about her appearance.
② Mike <u>had lost</u> the power of speech because of the operation.
③ I <u>had visited</u> Madrid three times until then.
④ I was in a hotel, and I <u>had</u> just <u>finished</u> shaving.
⑤ My grandmother <u>had lived</u> on the farm for two years when I was born.

서답형
[14~15] 다음 문장에서 생략할 수 있는 것을 찾아 쓰시오.

14

> (1) While he was listening to music, he did his homework.
> (2) Though she was lonely, Maryanne was good-humored.

➡ (1) _____ (2) _____

15

> He had lived in Alabama before he moved to Texas.

➡ _____

[16~17] 다음 밑줄 친 우리말을 참고하여 주어진 문장의 틀린 부분을 찾아 바르게 고친 것을 고르시오.

16

> <u>어제만큼 해가 빛나지는 않지만 그리 쌀쌀하지는 않다.</u>
> Not shining as much as it did yesterday, it isn't that chilly.

① Shining not as much as it did yesterday, it isn't that chilly.
② Not shining the sun as much as it did yesterday, it isn't that chilly.
③ The sun not shining as much as it did yesterday, it isn't that chilly.
④ Though not shining as much as it did yesterday, it isn't that chilly.
⑤ The sun didn't shining as much as it did yesterday, it isn't that chilly.

17

> <u>그 소녀는 열쇠를 집에 두고 온 것을 알아차렸다.</u>
> The girl had found that she left her key at home.

① The girl found that she had left her key at home.
② The girl found that she left her key at home.
③ The girl had found that she had left her key at home.
④ The girl finds that she had left her key at home.
⑤ The girl found that she leaves her key at home.

01 주어진 문장을 분사구문으로 바꿔 쓰시오.

(1) Because I got up too late, I missed the school bus.

➡ _____

(2) As he was talking on the phone, he watered the plants.

➡ _____

(3) If you have a problem, ask the teacher.

➡ _____

(4) Although she knew it was wrong, she wouldn't change it.

➡ _____

(5) Because I didn't have any money, I couldn't buy a bike.

➡ _____

(6) If the weather is good, we'll eat out.

➡ _____

02 적절한 접속사와 과거완료를 이용하여 다음 두 문장을 한 문장으로 바꿔 쓰시오.

(1) • They couldn't find the treasure.

• Mr. Joe hid it under the sea.

➡ _____

_____

(2) • I arrived at home.

• Lucky already fell asleep.

➡ _____

_____

03 다음 우리말에 맞게 주어진 어구를 바르게 배열하시오.

(1) 산에서 바라보니 경치는 푸르고 아름답다.
(the landscape, the mountains, green and beautiful, seen, is, from)

➡ _____

_____

(2) 아파서 나는 하루 종일 집에 있어야 했다.
(I, home, all day, had, being, stay, sick, to)

➡ _____

(3) 선생님이 들어왔을 때 그녀는 일을 막 끝마쳤다.
(she, her task, the teacher, when, finished, came, had, just, in)

➡ _____

_____

(4) 그들이 플랫폼으로 달려갔지만 기차는 막 출발해 버렸다. (the train, the platform, they, had, ran, gone, but, just, to)

➡ _____

_____

04 다음 문장에서 어법상 어색한 부분을 분사구문을 이용하여 바르게 고치시오. (생략하지 말 것.)

(1) Deeply disappointing at the news, Nobel decided to change people's opinions about him.

_____ ➡ _____

(2) Taking his holiday, he came back refreshed.

_____ ➡ _____

[05~06] 그림을 보고 주어진 어휘를 이용하여 빈칸을 알맞게 채우시오.

05

Emma _____ to the sea up to last week. It was her first visit. (be, never)

06

_____ at the station, David found that the train had already left. (arrive)

07 다음 우리말을 괄호 안의 지시대로 영작하시오.

(1) 지금 곧 떠나면, 그 기차를 놓치지 않을 겁니다. (right, leave, miss)

➡ _____

(분사구문을 써서)

➡ _____

(접속사를 써서)

(2) 그녀는 내게 뛰어오면서 손을 흔들었다. (as, wave)

➡ _____

(분사구문을 써서)

➡ _____

(접속사를 써서)

(3) 그는 중국에 가기 전에 2년 동안 중국어를 공부했다. (study)

➡ _____

08 다음 문장에서 어법상 어색한 것을 바르게 고쳐 다시 쓰시오.

(1) My grandmother was ill for five days when I visited her.

➡ _____

(2) The ground had been covered with snow because it snowed during the night.

➡ _____

(3) Walked in the park, he met an old friend.

➡ _____

(4) Getting so cold outside, the rain changed into snow.

➡ _____

(5) Making of thick trees, the doors looked unbreakable.

➡ _____

(6) Eaten dinner, he was not hungry.

➡ _____

How Will You Be Remembered?

It was just a normal morning. Alfred Nobel sat in his chair to read
시간을 나타내는 비인칭 주어   부사적 용법의 to부정사(목적): ~하기 위해서
the newspaper. While he was drinking his coffee, a headline caught his
     ~하는 동안(접속사)   catch one's eye: 눈길을 끌다
eye: *The Merchant of Death, Alfred Nobel, Is Dead.*

"What? What is this?"
앞 문장의 'The Merchant of Death. Alfred Nobel. Is Dead'라고 적힌 headline을 가리킨다.
Reading the article, he dropped his cup in surprise. His coffee spilled
   = As he read the article   놀라서
all over his clothes and desk, but he couldn't take his eyes off the
                can't take one's eyes off: ~에서 눈을 뗄 수 없다
newspaper.

↓ The article
The article was about his own death! It said Nobel had died in France
          기사가 쓰인 것보다 죽음이 더 먼저 일어난 일이므로 과거완료 had died로 표현
from a heart attack.

"Oh my goodness! Am I dead?"
어머나!. 아이고!. 놀람을 나타낼 때 사용하는 표현
Catching his breath, Nobel kept reading. Soon, he became even
= After he caught his breath   keep+동사-ing: 계속 ~하다   훨씬(비교급 강조)
more shocked. The article described him as the inventor of dynamite
          describe A as B: A를 B로 기술하다(묘사하다)
and other dangerous objects for war. It said that he had become rich
         It = The article / 기사가 쓰여진 것보다 부유해진 것이 더 먼저 일어난 일이므로 과거완료 시제로 표현
from the deaths of others. He couldn't believe his eyes. It was true that
                               가주어   that 이하: 진주어
dynamite was one of his many inventions. But he never imagined that
          one of+복수 명사: ~ 중 하나
the world would think of him as "the merchant of death."
         think of A as B: A를 B로 생각하다

headline (신문 기사 등의) 표제
catch one's eye 눈길을 끌다
merchant 상인
spill 쏟아지다, 흐르다, 쏟다
heart attack 심장 마비
catch one's breath 숨을 고르다
shocked 충격을 받은
describe 기술하다, 묘사하다
dynamite 다이너마이트

 확인문제

● 다음 문장이 본문의 내용과 일치하면 T, 일치하지 <u>않으면</u> F를 쓰시오.

1   Alfred Nobel sat in his chair to read the newspaper. ☐

2   Alfred Nobel couldn't continue reading the article in surprise. ☐

3   The article said that Alfred Nobel had become rich from the deaths of others. ☐

4   Alfred Nobel expected that the world would think of him as "the merchant of death." ☐

Nobel was deeply disappointed.
몹시, 깊이, 매우

"How could this be? This is unbelievable! I'm not a merchant of death. I want to be remembered in a different way. I want to be
to부정사의 수동태
remembered as a person who made the world better."
~로 기억되다   주격 관계대명사

He decided to change people's opinions about him.

In 1888, a French newspaper mistakenly reported Alfred Nobel's death. The person who had actually died was his brother, Ludvig.
주격 관계대명사
Thanks to the report, however, Nobel decided to do something to
~ 덕분에. 다음에 명사(구)가 이어짐   decide: to부정사를 목적어로 취하는 동사
contribute to the world. In 1895, he decided to use his money to create
부사적 용법의 to부정사(목적): ~하기 위해서
the Nobel Prize. Originally, there were only five awards. A sixth award
was added in 1968. Today, when we think of Alfred Nobel, we think of
수동태
the Nobel Prize, rather than dynamite.

deeply 몹시, 깊이, 매우

disappointed 실망한, 낙담한

unbelievable 믿을 수 없는, 믿기 어려운

mistakenly 실수로

thanks to ~ 덕분에

contribute 기여하다, 공헌하다

rather than ~보다는

 확인문제

- 다음 문장이 본문의 내용과 일치하면 T, 일치하지 않으면 F를 쓰시오.

1   Nobel wanted to be remembered as a person who made the world better. ☐

2   In 1888, a French newspaper reported Alfred Nobel's death on purpose. ☐

3   It was Nobel's brother, Ludvig, who had actually died. ☐

4   Nobel had already decided to do something to contribute to the world before reading the report. ☐

5   In 1895, Nobel decided to use his money to create the Nobel Prize. ☐

6   Today, when we think of Alfred Nobel, we think of dynamite, rather than the Nobel Prize. ☐

● 우리말을 참고하여 빈칸에 알맞은 말을 쓰시오.

1 _____ Will You _____ _____?

2 It was just a _____ _____.

3 Alfred Nobel _____ _____ _____ _____ to read the newspaper.

4 While he was drinking his coffee, a headline _____ _____ _____ : *The Merchant of Death, Alfred Nobel, Is Dead.*

5 "What? What is this?"

6 Reading the article, he dropped his cup _____ _____.

7 His coffee spilled all over his clothes and desk, but he couldn't _____ _____ _____ _____ the newspaper.

8 The article was about _____ _____ _____!

9 It said Nobel had died in France _____ _____ _____ _____.

10 "Oh _____ _____! Am I dead?"

11 _____ _____ _____, Nobel kept reading.

12 Soon, he became _____ _____ _____.

13 The article _____ him _____ the inventor of dynamite and other dangerous objects for war.

14 It said that he _____ _____ _____ from the deaths of others.

15 He _____ _____ his eyes.

16 It was true that dynamite was _____ _____ _____ _____ _____.

1 당신은 어떻게 기억될까요?

2 그저 평범한 아침이었다.

3 Alfred Nobel은 신문을 읽기 위해 의자에 앉았다.

4 커피를 마시는 동안 한 기사 제목이 그의 눈길을 끌었다. "죽음의 상인, Alfred Nobel 사망하다"

5 "뭐라고? 이게 뭐지?"

6 기사를 읽으며 그는 놀라서 컵을 떨어뜨렸다.

7 커피가 그의 옷과 책상 온 곳에 쏟아졌지만 그는 신문에서 눈을 뗄 수 없었다.

8 기사는 그 자신의 죽음에 관한 것이었다!

9 기사에는 Nobel이 심장 마비로 프랑스에서 죽었다고 쓰여 있었다.

10 "오, 이럴 수가! 내가 죽었다고?"

11 숨을 고른 후, Nobel은 계속 읽었다.

12 곧, 그는 훨씬 더 충격을 받게 되었다.

13 기사는 그를 전쟁에 쓰이는 다이너마이트와 다른 위험한 물건의 발명가로 기술했다.

14 기사에는 그가 다른 사람들의 죽음으로 인해 부유해졌다고 쓰여 있었다.

15 그는 자신의 눈을 믿을 수 없었다.

16 다이너마이트가 그의 많은 발명품 중 하나인 것은 사실이었다.

17 But he never imagined that the world would _____ _____ him _____ "the merchant of death."

18 Nobel was deeply _____.

19 "_____ could this be?

20 This is _____!

21 I'm not a _____ _____ _____.

22 I want to be remembered _____ _____ _____ _____.

23 I want to _____ _____ as a person who made _____ _____ _____."

24 He decided _____ _____ _____ _____ about him.

25 In 1888, a French newspaper _____ reported Alfred Nobel's death.

26 The person _____ _____ _____ _____ was his brother, Ludvig.

27 _____ _____ the report, however, Nobel decided to do something to _____ _____ the world.

28 In 1895, he decided to use his money _____ _____ the Nobel Prize.

29 Originally, there were _____ _____ _____.

30 A _____ _____ was added in 1968.

31 Today, when we think of Alfred Nobel, we think of the Nobel Prize, _____ _____ dynamite.

17 하지만 그는 세상이 그를 '죽음의 상인'으로 생각할 거라고는 결코 상상하지 못했다.

18 Nobel은 몹시 실망했다.

19 "어떻게 이럴 수가 있지?

20 이건 믿을 수 없어!

21 나는 죽음의 상인이 아니야.

22 나는 다르게 기억되고 싶어.

23 나는 세상을 더 좋게 만든 사람으로 기억되고 싶어."

24 그는 자신에 대한 사람들의 견해를 바꾸기로 결심했다.

25 1888년에, 한 프랑스 신문에서 실수로 Alfred Nobel의 죽음을 보도했다.

26 실제로 죽은 사람은 Alfred Nobel의 형인 Ludvig였다.

27 하지만 그 보도 덕분에, Nobel은 세상에 공헌하기 위해 무언가를 하기로 결심했다.

28 1895년에, 그는 자신의 돈을 노벨상을 만드는 데 사용하기로 결정했다.

29 원래 다섯 종류의 상만 있었다.

30 여섯 번째 상은 1968년에 추가되었다.

31 오늘날 우리가 Alfred Nobel을 생각할 때, 우리는 다이너마이트보다는 노벨상을 떠올린다.

● 우리말을 참고하여 본문을 영작하시오.

1 당신은 어떻게 기억될까요?

➡ _____

2 그저 평범한 아침이었다.

➡ _____

3 Alfred Nobel은 신문을 읽기 위해 의자에 앉았다.

➡ _____

4 커피를 마시는 동안 한 기사 제목이 그의 눈길을 끌었다. "죽음의 상인, Alfred Nobel 사망하다"

➡ _____

_____

5 "뭐라고? 이게 뭐지?"

➡ _____

6 기사를 읽으며 그는 놀라서 컵을 떨어뜨렸다.

➡ _____

7 커피가 그의 옷과 책상 온 곳에 쏟아졌지만 그는 신문에서 눈을 뗄 수 없었다.

➡ _____

8 기사는 그 자신의 죽음에 관한 것이었다!

➡ _____

9 기사에는 Nobel이 심장 마비로 프랑스에서 죽었다고 쓰여 있었다.

➡ _____

10 "오, 이럴 수가! 내가 죽었다고?"

➡ _____

11 숨을 고른 후, Nobel은 계속 읽었다.

➡ _____

12 곧, 그는 훨씬 더 충격을 받게 되었다.

➡ _____

13 기사는 그를 전쟁에 쓰이는 다이너마이트와 다른 위험한 물건의 발명가로 기술했다.

➡ _____

14 기사에는 그가 다른 사람들의 죽음으로 인해 부유해졌다고 쓰여 있었다.

➡ _____

15 그는 자신의 눈을 믿을 수 없었다.

➡ _____

16 다이너마이트가 그의 많은 발명품 중 하나인 것은 사실이었다.

➡ _____

17 하지만 그는 세상이 그를 '죽음의 상인'으로 생각할 거라고는 결코 상상하지 못했다.

➡ _____

18 Nobel은 몹시 실망했다.

➡ _____

19 "어떻게 이럴 수가 있지?

➡ _____

20 이건 믿을 수 없어!

➡ _____

21 나는 죽음의 상인이 아니야.

➡ _____

22 나는 다르게 기억되고 싶어.

➡ _____

23 나는 세상을 더 좋게 만든 사람으로 기억되고 싶어."

➡ _____

24 그는 자신에 대한 사람들의 견해를 바꾸기로 결심했다.

➡ _____

25 1888년에, 한 프랑스 신문에서 실수로 Alfred Nobel의 죽음을 보도했다.

➡ _____

26 실제로 죽은 사람은 Alfred Nobel의 형인 Ludvig였다.

➡ _____

27 하지만 그 보도 덕분에, Nobel은 세상에 공헌하기 위해 무언가를 하기로 결심했다.

➡ _____

28 1895년에, 그는 자신의 돈을 노벨상을 만드는 데 사용하기로 결정했다.

➡ _____

29 원래 다섯 종류의 상만 있었다.

➡ _____

30 여섯 번째 상은 1968년에 추가되었다.

➡ _____

31 오늘날 우리가 Alfred Nobel을 생각할 때, 우리는 다이너마이트보다는 노벨상을 떠올린다.

➡ _____

[01~03] 다음 글을 읽고 물음에 답하시오.

It was just a normal morning. Alfred Nobel sat in his chair to read the newspaper. ⓐ While he was drinking his coffee, a headline caught his eye: *The Merchant of Death, Alfred Nobel, Is Dead.*

"What? What is this?"

Reading the article, he dropped his cup in surprise. His coffee spilled all over his clothes and desk, but he couldn't take his eyes off the newspaper.

01 위 글의 밑줄 친 ⓐWhile과 같은 의미로 쓰인 것을 고르시오.

① It took him a while to calm down.

② I've read fifty pages, while he's read only twenty.

③ He didn't while away his holidays on the beach.

④ She came to the door while I was ringing the bell.

⑤ Some are rich, while others are poor.

02 위 글에서 알 수 있는 Alfred Nobel의 심경으로 가장 알맞은 것을 고르시오.

① nervous and anxious

② embarrassed and confused

③ disappointed and depressed

④ excited and satisfied

⑤ surprised and ashamed

03 According to the passage, which is NOT true?

① It was just like any other morning.

② Alfred Nobel sat in his chair to read the newspaper drinking his coffee.

③ A headline attracted the attention of Alfred Nobel.

④ The article was about Alfred Nobel's own death.

⑤ Alfred Nobel ignored the article about his own death.

[04~07] 다음 글을 읽고 물음에 답하시오.

The article was about his own death! ⓐIt said Nobel had died in France from a heart attack.

"Oh my goodness! Am I dead?"

Catching his breath, Nobel kept reading. Soon, he became ⓑeven more shocked. The article described him as the inventor of dynamite and other dangerous objects for war. It said that he ⓒhad become rich from the deaths of others. He couldn't believe his eyes. It was true that dynamite was one of his many inventions. But he never imagined that the world would think of him as "the merchant of death."

서답형

04 위 글의 밑줄 친 ⓐIt이 가리키는 것을 본문에서 찾아 쓰시오.

➡ _____

05 위 글의 밑줄 친 ⓑeven과 바꿔 쓸 수 없는 말을 고르시오.

① much   ② very

③ far   ④ still

⑤ a lot

06 위 글의 밑줄 친 ⓒhad become과 과거완료의 용법이 같은 것을 고르시오.

① I recognized him well because I had often seen him before.
② He had lived there for ten years when his father died.
③ I lost the book which I had bought the day before.
④ When we called on her, she had been ill in bed for a week.
⑤ I had never seen such a strange animal before.

서답형

07 본문의 내용과 일치하도록 다음 빈칸 (A)와 (B)에 알맞은 단어를 쓰시오.

> Nobel became rich by inventing (A)_____ and other dangerous objects for war, but they could kill lots of people, so the article described him as "(B)_____ _____ _____ _____."

[08~10] 다음 글을 읽고 물음에 답하시오.

Nobel was deeply disappointed.
"How could this be? This is unbelievable! I'm not a merchant of death. I want to be remembered ⓐin a different way. I want to be remembered as a person who made the world better."
ⓑ그는 자신에 대한 사람들의 견해를 바꾸기로 결심했다.

서답형

08 위 글의 밑줄 친 ⓐin a different way가 구체적으로 가리키는 것을 본문에서 찾아 쓰시오.

➡ _____

서답형

09 위 글의 밑줄 친 ⓑ의 우리말에 맞게 주어진 어휘를 이용하여 8 단어로 영작하시오.

> decided, people's opinions

➡ _____
_____

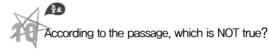

중요

10 According to the passage, which is NOT true?

① Nobel was extremely disappointed.
② Nobel couldn't believe that he was a merchant of a death.
③ Nobel didn't think he was a merchant of death.
④ Nobel wanted to be remembered as a person who made the world better, not as a merchant of death.
⑤ People remembered Nobel as a person who made the world better.

[11~12] 다음 글을 읽고 물음에 답하시오.

In 1888, a French newspaper mistakenly reported Alfred Nobel's death. The person who had actually died was his brother, Ludvig. Thanks to the report, however, Nobel decided to do something to contribute to the world. In 1895, he decided to use his money to create the Nobel Prize. Originally, there were only five awards. A sixth award ____ⓐ____ in 1968. Today, when we think of Alfred Nobel, we think of the Nobel Prize, rather than dynamite.

서답형

11 위 글의 빈칸 ⓐ에 add를 알맞은 형태로 쓰시오.

➡ _____

12 위 글의 제목으로 가장 알맞은 것을 고르시오.

① A Mistaken Report about Alfred Nobel's Death

② A Mistake Led to the Precious Result!

③ Actually Alfred Nobel Was Not Dead!

④ Originally, There Were Only Five Awards!

⑤ What Do You think of Alfred Nobel?

[13~15] 다음 글을 읽고 물음에 답하시오.

The article was about his own death! It said Nobel had died in France ___ⓐ___ a heart attack.

"Oh my goodness! Am I dead?"

(A)Catching his breath, Nobel kept reading. Soon, he became even more shocked. The article described him as the inventor of dynamite and other dangerous objects for war. It said that he had become rich ___ⓑ___ the deaths of others. He couldn't believe his eyes. It was true that dynamite was one of his many inventions. But he never imagined that the world would (B)think of him as "the merchant of death."

서답형

13 위 글의 빈칸 ⓐ와 ⓑ에 공통으로 들어갈 전치사를 쓰시오.

➡ _____

14 위 글의 밑줄 친 (A)Catching과 문법적 쓰임이 같은 것을 모두 고르시오.

① My hobby is reading books.

② The girl sat by the window, listening to music.

③ Smiling brightly, he welcomed her.

④ Being healthy is the most important.

⑤ John answered the phone, watching TV.

15 위 글의 밑줄 친 (B)think of와 바꿔 쓸 수 없는 말을 고르시오. (2개)

① regard   ② respect

③ discuss   ④ look upon

⑤ see

[16~19] 다음 글을 읽고 물음에 답하시오.

(A)Nobel was deeply disappointing.

"How could this be? This is unbelievable! I'm not a merchant of death. I want to be remembered in a different way. I want to be remembered (B)as a person ___ⓐ___ made the world better."

He decided to change people's opinions about him.

서답형

16 위 글의 빈칸 ⓐ에 들어갈 알맞은 관계대명사를 쓰시오.

➡ _____

서답형

17 위 글의 밑줄 친 (A)에서 어법상 틀린 부분을 찾아 고치시오.

_____ ➡ _____

18 위 글의 밑줄 친 (B)as와 의미가 다른 것을 고르시오.

① He lives as a saint.

② I don't like a position as an assistant music teacher.

③ This can be used as a knife.

④ He was famous as a statesman.

⑤ Some animals, as the fox and the squirrel, have bushy tails.

19 위 글의 앞에 올 내용으로 가장 알맞은 것을 고르시오.

① People deeply respected Nobel.

② Nobel expected to be remembered as a person who made the world better.

③ Nobel tried to change people's opinions about him.

④ Nobel was mentioned as a merchant of death.

⑤ People changed their opinions about Nobel.

[20~21] 다음 글을 읽고 물음에 답하시오.

It was just a normal morning. (①) While he was drinking his coffee, a headline caught his eye: The Merchant of Death, Alfred Nobel, Is Dead. (②)

"What? What is this?" (③)

Reading the article, he dropped his cup _____ ⓐ surprise. (④) His coffee spilled all over his clothes and desk, but he couldn't take his eyes _____ ⓑ the newspaper. (⑤)

20 위 글의 빈칸 ⓐ와 ⓑ에 들어갈 전치사가 바르게 짝지어진 것은?

	ⓐ	ⓑ		ⓐ	ⓑ
①	at	from	②	at	off
③	in	off	④	to	from
⑤	in	for			

21 위 글의 흐름으로 보아, 주어진 문장이 들어가기에 가장 적절한 곳은?

Alfred Nobel sat in his chair to read the newspaper.

① ② ③ ④ ⑤

[22~24] 다음 글을 읽고 물음에 답하시오.

In 1888, a French newspaper (A)[mistakenly / purposely] reported Alfred Nobel's death. The person who had (B)[accidentally / actually] died was his brother, Ludvig. Thanks to the report, _____ ⓐ , Nobel decided to do something to contribute to the world. In 1895, he decided to use his money to create the Nobel Prize. Originally, there were only five awards. (C)[A sixth award was added / Six awards were added] in 1968. Today, when we think of Alfred Nobel, we think of the Nobel Prize, rather than dynamite.

22 위 글의 빈칸 ⓐ에 들어갈 알맞은 말을 고르시오.

① therefore ② as a result

③ however ④ that is

⑤ in addition

23 위 글의 괄호 (A)~(C)에서 문맥이나 어법상 알맞은 낱말을 골라 쓰시오.

(A) _____ (B) _____

(C) _____

24 위 글을 읽고 알 수 <u>없는</u> 것을 고르시오.

① When did a French newspaper report Alfred Nobel's death?

② Was the article that the French newspaper reported true?

③ What did Nobel decide to do in 1895?

④ Originally, how many awards were there?

⑤ Why did they add one more award?

[01~04] 다음 글을 읽고 물음에 답하시오.

It was just a normal morning. Alfred Nobel sat in his chair to read the newspaper. While he was drinking his coffee, a headline caught his eye: ⓐ*The Merchant of Death, Alfred Nobel, Are Dead.*

"What? What is ⓑthis?"

ⓒReading the article, he dropped his cup in surprise. His coffee spilled all over his clothes and desk, but he couldn't take his eyes off the newspaper.

01 위 글의 밑줄 친 ⓐ에서 어법상 **틀린** 부분을 찾아 고치시오.

_____ ➡ _____

02 위 글의 밑줄 친 ⓑthis가 가리키는 것을 우리말로 쓰시오.

➡ _____

위 글의 밑줄 친 분사구문 ⓒ를 부사절로 고치시오.

➡ _____

04 Why did Alfred Nobel drop his cup while reading the article? Fill in the blank with a suitable word.

Because he was surprised to read the _____ of the newspaper.

[05~07] 다음 글을 읽고 물음에 답하시오.

The article was about his own death! It said Nobel had died in France from a heart attack. "Oh my goodness! Am I dead?"

Catching his breath, Nobel kept reading. Soon, he became even more shocked. The article described him as the inventor of dynamite and other dangerous objects for war. It said that he had become rich from the deaths of others. He couldn't believe his eyes. It was true that dynamite was one of his many inventions. But he never imagined that ⓐ세상이 그를 '죽음의 상인'으로 생각할 거라고는."

05 위 글의 밑줄 친 ⓐ의 우리말에 맞게 주어진 어휘를 이용하여 11 단어로 영작하시오.

think of, the merchant

➡ _____

_____

06 다음 문장에서 위 글의 내용과 **다른** 부분을 찾아서 고치시오.

The article said Nobel's brother had died in France from a heart attack.

_____ ➡ _____

07 본문의 내용과 일치하도록 다음 빈칸 (A)와 (B)에 알맞은 단어를 쓰시오.

Nobel became even (A)_____ _____ because the article described him as the inventor of dynamite and other dangerous objects for war saying that he had become rich from (B)_____ _____ _____ _____.

[08~11] 다음 글을 읽고 물음에 답하시오.

Nobel was (A)[deep / deeply] disappointed. "How could this be? This is (B)[reasonable / unbelievable]! I'm not a merchant of death. I want to ___ⓐ___ in a different way. I want to ___ⓑ___ as a person who made the world better."

He decided (C)[changing / to change] people's opinions about him.

08 위 글의 빈칸 ⓐ와 ⓑ에 공통으로 들어갈 remember의 알맞은 형태를 쓰시오.

➡ _____

09 위 글의 괄호 (A)~(C)에서 문맥이나 어법상 알맞은 낱말을 골라 쓰시오.

(A) _____ (B) _____ (C) _____

10 주어진 영영풀이에 해당하는 단어를 본문에서 찾아 쓰시오.

a person who buys or sells goods in large quantities, especially one who imports and exports them

➡ _____

11 본문의 내용과 일치하도록 다음 빈칸 (A)와 (B)에 알맞은 단어를 쓰시오.

Nobel was extremely (A)_____ because he was mentioned as a merchant of death. So he wanted people to remember him as a person who made (B)_____ _____ _____.

[12~14] 다음 글을 읽고 물음에 답하시오.

In ⓐ1888, a French newspaper mistakenly reported Alfred Nobel's death. The person who had actually died was his brother, Ludvig. Thanks to the report, however, Nobel decided to do something to contribute to the world. In ⓑ1895, he decided to use his money to create the Nobel Prize. Originally, there were only five awards. A sixth award was added in ⓒ1968. ⓓToday, when we think of Alfred Nobel, we think of the Nobel Prize, rather than dynamite.

12 위 글의 밑줄 친 ⓐ~ⓒ를 읽는 법을 영어로 쓰시오.

ⓐ _____
ⓑ _____
ⓒ _____

13 위 글의 밑줄 친 ⓓ를 다음과 같이 바꿔 쓸 때 빈칸 (A)~(B)에 들어갈 알맞은 단어를 쓰시오.

Today, when we think of Alfred Nobel, we think of (A)_____ _____ _____ more than (B)_____.

14 Who had actually died? Fill in the blank with a suitable word.

It was Alfred Nobel's brother, _____, who had actually died.

구석구석

After You Read A. Read and Correct

WORLD NEWS

APRIL 13, 1888

The Merchant of Death, Alfred Nobel, Is Dead
The Merchant of Death와 Alfred Nobel은 동격

Alfred Nobel <u>died</u> yesterday in France <u>from</u> a heart attack. He invented
die from: ~으로 죽다

dynamite and <u>other</u> dangerous <u>objects</u> for war. He became rich <u>from</u> the deaths
다른   물건들   [원인·이유] ~으로 인해

of <u>others</u>. He is responsible for the deaths of thousands of people. The world
다른 사람들

will remember him <u>as</u> "the merchant of death."
[역할·자격·기능·성질 따위를 나타내어] ~으로

구문해설 • heart attack: 심장마비   • invent: 발명하다   • dynamite: 다이너마이트
• be responsible for: ~에 대해 책임이 있다, ~의 원인이 되다   • thousands of: 수천의
• merchant: 상인

• Tim <u>invented</u> special shoes for the beach.
'-ion'과 '-or'은 명사형 접미사로 특정 동사 뒤에 붙이면 해당 동사가 명사로 품사와 뜻이 바뀐다.
'-or'은 '~하는 사람(행위자)'이라는 의미를 만들어 주는 접미사이다. 동사가 'e'로 끝나는 경우 'e'를 빼고 접미사를 붙인다.

• Thomas Edison made over 1,000 <u>inventions</u> in his life.
= more than

• Who is the <u>inventor of the plane</u>?
발명품 앞에는 정관사 the를 붙인다.

구문해설 • invent: 발명하다   • invention: 발명, 발명품   • inventor: 발명가

Think and Write Step 2

<u>Looking back this year</u>, I'm glad that I donated money to children in Africa.
분사구문 (= When I look back this year)

I did <u>this</u> because I wanted to make a difference for children in need. To save
아프리카의 아이들에게 돈을 기부한 것   부사적 용법(목적)

money, I didn't buy snacks <u>for</u> a month. I donated the money to UNICEF.
~ 동안

Before I donated, I sometimes left food on my plate. Now I really appreciate

my meals. I'm proud of <u>myself</u>.
주어와 목적어가 같은 대상일 때 쓰인 재귀대명사

구문해설 • donate: 기부하다   • make a difference: 변화를 가져오다, 차이를 낳다, 영향을 주다, 중요하다
• in need: 어려움에 처한[하여], 궁핍한[하여]   • appreciate: 고맙게 여기다

해석

세계 뉴스
1888년 4월 13일
죽음의 상인, Alfred Nobel
사망하다

Alfred Nobel이 어제 프랑스에서 심장마비로 사망했다. 그는 전쟁에 쓰이는 다이너마이트와 다른 위험한 물건들을 발명했다. 그는 다른 사람들의 죽음으로 인해 부유해졌다. 그는 수천 명의 사람들의 죽음에 대해 책임이 있다. 세상은 그를 "죽음의 상인"으로 기억할 것이다.

• Tim은 특별한 해변용 신발을 발명했다.
• Thomas Edison은 일생 동안 천 개 이상의 발명품을 만들었다.
• 비행기의 발명가는 누구인가?

올해를 뒤돌아보니, 나는 아프리카의 아이들에게 돈을 기부해서 기쁘다. 나는 어려움에 처한 아이들의 상황을 변화시키고 싶었기 때문에 기부를 했다. 돈을 모으기 위해, 나는 한 달 동안 간식을 사지 않았다. 나는 그 돈을 유니세프에 기부했다. 나는 기부하기 전에는 가끔 접시에 음식을 남겼다. 이제 나는 내 음식을 정말 고맙게 여긴다. 나는 내 자신이 자랑스럽다.

Words & Expressions

[01~02] 다음 빈칸에 가장 알맞은 단어를 고르시오.

01

> I am _____ that I am negative.

① disappointed   ② satisfied

③ excited   ④ proud

⑤ confident

02

> The new factory is expected to _____ more than 400 new jobs.

① describe   ② reduce   ③ prevent

④ create   ⑤ complete

03 다음 빈칸 (A)와 (B)에 들어갈 말로 알맞게 짝지어진 것은?

> • It seems difficult, but I'll (A)_____ it a try.
> • The match has been (B)_____ off until tomorrow because of bad weather.

① give – got   ② give – put

③ give – done   ④ put – got

⑤ put – put

04 다음 괄호 안의 단어를 문맥에 맞게 고쳐 쓰시오.

> We had an _____ time in Paris. (believe)

Conversation

[05~07] 다음 대화를 읽고 물음에 답하시오.

G: Jaemin, are you ready for the singing contest?

B: Well, 포기할까 생각 중이야, Tina.

G: Why? I thought you really wanted to __(A)__ part in the contest.

B: I don't think I'm a good singer.

G: Come on. You're the best singer I know.

B: Do you really think so?

G: Of course. You have a really nice voice.

B: Thank you for saying so. I'll ___(B)___ my best.

G: _____(C)_____

05 밑줄 친 우리말과 일치하도록 주어진 단어를 이용해 영작하시오.

➡ _____ (give, of, 5 단어)

06 빈칸 (A)와 (B)에 알맞은 말을 〈보기〉에서 골라 쓰시오.

┌─ 보기 ─────────────────────┐
│   do   get   keep   put   take   │
└──────────────────────────────┘

(A) _____   (B) _____

07 빈칸 (C)에 알맞은 말을 고르시오.

① I hope I participate in the singing contest.

② I hope you put off the contest.

③ I hope you win the contest.

④ I hope you'll join the contest again.

⑤ I hope I have the chance to win.

[08~10] 다음 대화를 읽고 물음에 답하시오.

G: Jiho, what's up? You look tired.

B: Yeah. I stayed up (A)[late / lately] last night.

G: Did you play computer games again?

B: No, not this time. I had to finish my history project.

G: Is it due today?

B: Yeah. 나는 마지막 순간까지 미루지 말았어야 했어.

G: Hmm, I understand. I often have the same problem.

B: Really? Well, let's try (B)[changing / to change] our bad habits.

08 위 대화의 괄호 (A)와 (B)에서 적절한 것을 골라 쓰시오.

(A) _____ (B) _____

09 위 대화에서 다음 영영풀이에 해당하는 단어를 찾아 쓰시오.

> expected at or planned for a certain time

➡ _____

10 위 대화의 밑줄 친 우리말과 일치하도록 괄호 안에 주어진 단어를 알맞게 배열하여 영작하시오.

> (put, until, off, shouldn't, moment, the, I, last, have, it)

➡ _____

[11~12] 다음 대화를 읽고 물음에 답하시오.

Minho: Linda, what are you reading?

Linda: I'm reading graduation messages from my classmates. (①)

Minho: Oh, it looks like they had a lot to say to you. (②)

Linda: Many of them wrote that they like my smile.

Minho: That's nice. (③)

Linda: Some of them said I didn't hang out enough with them.

Minho: That's not your fault. (④) You were always busy.

Linda: Yeah, but 나는 학급 친구들과 더 많은 시간을 보냈어야 했어. (⑤)

Minho: You still have time after graduation.

Linda: You're right.

Minho: I hope you keep in touch with your classmates after graduation.

Linda: Thanks. I hope so, too.

11 위 대화의 ①~⑤ 중 주어진 문장이 들어갈 곳은?

> What else?

① ② ③ ④ ⑤

12 위 대화의 밑줄 친 우리말을 영작하시오.

➡ _____

_____ (9 단어)

Grammar

13 다음 중 어법상 어색한 문장을 고르시오.

① She had lived in Busan for 15 years before she got married.

② Mike had stayed up until his dad returned.

③ When I had got up, she already went to work.

④ Nathalie lost the cell phone that her mom had bought for her.

⑤ When Tom opened the door, Kate had already eaten an apple.

14 다음 문장을 바꾸어 쓸 때 가장 적절한 것은?

> Being late for school, Ann ran to catch the school bus.

① She was late for school, Ann ran to catch the school bus.

② If she was late for school, Ann ran to catch the school bus.

③ Though she was late for school, Ann ran to catch the school bus.

④ Ann ran to catch the school bus, and she was late for school.

⑤ Because she was late for school, Ann ran to catch the school bus.

15 그림을 보고 주어진 어휘를 이용하여 빈칸을 알맞게 채우시오.

_____ _____ sunny, I decided to go hiking. (be)

16 다음 중 어법상 <u>어색한</u> 문장을 고르시오.

① Not knowing where he was, Helen just wanted to know how to get to him.

② Looking back this year, I'm glad that I donated money to children in Africa.

③ Doing this work every day, you will soon improve.

④ Being very tall, she became a basketball player.

⑤ Not telling the truth the previous day, he fell in danger.

17 다음 두 문장을 when으로 시작하여 한 문장으로 연결하되, 두 사건의 시간차가 드러나도록 고쳐 쓰시오.

(1) • Mina returned home.
   • Her brother ate all her cookies.

➡ _____
_____

(2) • The waiter finally arrived with the food.
   • The guests already left the restaurant.

➡ _____
_____

18 다음 문장을 바꿔 쓸 때 빈칸에 알맞은 말을 쓰시오.

(1) Being a thrilling movie, it lacks reality.

➡ _____, it lacks reality.

(2) Feeling hungry, I ate some cookies.

➡ _____, I ate some cookies.

(3) Turning left, you will find the police station on your right.

➡ _____, you will find the police station on your right.

19 다음 ⓐ～ⓖ 중 어법상 옳은 것을 <u>모두</u> 고르시오.

> ⓐ Read the book, I drank a cup of tea.
> ⓑ Being not late for school, Amy walked to school.
> ⓒ Seeing from a distance, it has a beautiful rainbow design.
> ⓓ Not knowing what to do, she asked him for help.
> ⓔ Using a saw, you should wear gloves.
> ⓕ When I arrived there, the meeting has

already begun.

ⓖ He stayed up late until his mom had returned.

ⓗ Mina couldn't buy the book because she had spent all her money.

➡ _____

Reading

[20~21] 다음 글을 읽고 물음에 답하시오.

WORLD NEWS

APRIL 13, 1888

The Merchant of Death, Alfred Nobel, Is Dead

Alfred Nobel died yesterday in France from a heart attack. He invented dynamite and other dangerous objects for war. He became rich from the deaths of others. He is responsible for the ___ⓐ___ of thousands of people. The world will remember him as "the merchant of death."

20 위 글의 빈칸 ⓐ에 들어갈 알맞은 말을 본문에서 찾아 쓰시오.

➡ _____

21 위 글의 종류로 알맞은 것을 고르시오.

① e-mail   ② article
③ essay   ④ diary
⑤ review

[22~24] 다음 글을 읽고 물음에 답하시오.

In 1888, a French newspaper mistakenly reported Alfred Nobel's death. ⓐ실제로 죽은 사람은 Alfred Nobel의 형인 Ludvig였다. Thanks to the report, however, Nobel decided ⓑto do something to contribute to the world. In 1895, he decided to use his money to create the Nobel Prize. Originally, there were only five awards. A sixth award was added in 1968. Today, when we think of Alfred Nobel, we think of the Nobel Prize, rather than dynamite.

22 위 글의 밑줄 친 ⓐ의 우리말에 맞게 주어진 어휘를 알맞게 배열하시오.

who / was / Ludvig / the person / his brother / had actually died / , /

➡ _____
_____

23 위 글의 밑줄 친 ⓑto do와 to부정사의 용법이 같은 것을 모두 고르시오.

① It's time to go home.
② It is not difficult to read this book.
③ They came here to see you.
④ Give me something to eat.
⑤ My hobby is to collect stamps.

24 위 글의 내용을 다음과 같이 정리하고자 한다. 빈칸 (A)와 (B)에 들어갈 알맞은 단어를 본문에서 찾아 쓰시오.

Thanks to the incorrect report of a French newspaper, Nobel decided to do something to (A)_____ _____ the world and decided to use his money to create (B)_____ _____ _____.

[25~26] 다음 글을 읽고 물음에 답하시오.

ⓐLooking back this year, I'm glad that I donated money to children in Africa. I did this because I wanted to make a difference for children in need. To save money, I didn't buy snacks for a month. I donated the money to UNICEF. Before I donated, I sometimes left food on my plate. Now I really appreciate my meals. I'm proud of myself.

25 위 글의 밑줄 친 ⓐ와 분사구문의 용법이 같은 것을 고르시오.

① Drinking lots of water, you will get healthier.
② Feeling sick, I couldn't take a rest.
③ Having no money, I had to go home on foot.
④ Living near the sea, I cannot swim.
⑤ Walking down the street, I happened to meet Tony.

26 Which question CANNOT be answered after reading the passage?

① What did the writer do?
② Why did the writer do it?
③ How did the writer do it?
④ How much money did the writer donate to UNICEF?
⑤ How did it make the writer different?

[27~29] 다음 글을 읽고 물음에 답하시오.

The article was about his own death! It said Nobel had died in France from a heart attack.
"Oh my goodness! Am I dead?"
Catching his breath, Nobel kept reading.

(①) Soon, he became even more shocked. (②) The article described him as the inventor of dynamite and other dangerous objects for war. (③) He couldn't believe his eyes. (④) It was true that dynamite was one of his many inventions. (⑤) But he never imagined that the world would think of him as "the merchant of death."

27 위 글의 흐름으로 보아, 주어진 문장이 들어가기에 가장 적절한 곳은?

It said that he had become rich from the deaths of others.

①   ②   ③   ④   ⑤

28 위 글의 제목으로 알맞은 것을 고르시오.

① Nobel Died in France from a Heart Attack
② Oh My Goodness! Am I "the Merchant of Death?"
③ A Man Who Became Rich from the Deaths of Others
④ Nobel, the Inventor of Dynamite
⑤ Dynamite, One of Nobel's Many Inventions

29 According to the passage, which is NOT true?

① The article said Nobel had died in France from a heart attack.
② Because of the shocking news, Nobel couldn't read the article any more.
③ The article said that Nobel had become rich from the deaths of others.
④ Dynamite was one of Nobel's many inventions.
⑤ Nobel never imagined that the world would think of him as "the merchant of death."

01 다음 짝지어진 단어의 관계가 〈보기〉와 같은 것끼리 짝지어진 것을 고르시오.

출제율 90%

┌─ 보기 ─┐

move – touch

ⓐ active – inactive
ⓑ including – excluding
ⓒ normal – ordinary
ⓓ decide – determine
ⓔ satisfied – dissatisfied

① ⓐ, ⓑ   ② ⓑ, ⓒ   ③ ⓒ, ⓓ
④ ⓓ, ⓔ   ⑤ ⓐ, ⓔ

출제율 95%

02 다음 빈칸 (A)와 (B)에 들어갈 말로 알맞은 것끼리 짝지어진 것을 고르시오.

• By the time we arrived, the meeting was (A)_____.
• If we get caught (B)_____ a traffic jam, it'll take 3 hours.

(A)   (B)   (A)   (B)
① on – in   ② on – on
③ over – in   ④ over – on
⑤ in – in

출제율 95%

03 빈칸에 공통으로 들어갈 말을 쓰시오. (주어진 철자로 시작할 것.)

• She t_____ her eyes off the road to glance at me.
• About 24,000 people t_____ part in the marathon.

출제율 90%

04 다음 괄호 안의 단어를 문맥에 맞게 고쳐 빈칸을 채우시오.

(1) It was my first job after _____ from Oxford in 2019. (graduate)
(2) He's the art _____ of this movie. (direct)

출제율 90%

05 밑줄 친 문장과 같은 의미가 되도록 빈칸을 채우시오.

A: What's wrong?
B: I was late for school.
A: Oh, I'm sorry to hear that.
B: I should have got up early.

➡ I _____ late.

출제율 100%

06 대화가 자연스럽게 연결되도록 (A)~(D)를 순서대로 적절하게 배열한 것은?

(A) Sounds great. I hope you have a wonderful vacation.
(B) I'm planning to visit my grandparents in Busan.
(C) Jinsu, what are you going to do during the vacation?
(D) I'm going to read lots of books. What about you?

① (B) – (A) – (C) – (D)
② (B) – (C) – (A) – (D)
③ (C) – (A) – (B) – (D)
④ (C) – (B) – (A) – (D)
⑤ (C) – (D) – (B) – (A)

Minho: Linda, what are you reading?

Linda: I'm reading graduation messages from my classmates.

Minho: Oh, it looks like they had a lot to say to you.

Linda: Many of them wrote (A)[that / what] they like my smile.

Minho: That's nice. What else?

Minho: Some of them said I didn't hang _____ⓐ_____ enough with them.

Minho: That's not your fault. You were always busy.

Linda: Yeah, but I _____ⓑ_____ more time with my classmates.

Minho: You still have time (B)[after / before] graduation.

Linda: You're right.

Minho: I hope you keep in touch with your classmates after graduation.

Linda: Thanks. I hope so, too.

출제율 90%

07 위 대화의 빈칸 ⓐ에 알맞은 말을 쓰시오.

➡ _____

출제율 95%

08 위 대화의 빈칸 ⓑ에 알맞은 말을 고르시오.

① shouldn't have taken

② should have left

③ shouldn't have left

④ should have spent

⑤ shouldn't have spent

출제율 95%

09 위 대화의 괄호 (A)와 (B)에서 적절한 것을 골라 쓰시오.

(A) _____ (B) _____

G: Jiho, what's up? You look tired.

B: Yeah. (①) I stayed up late last night.

G: Did you play computer games again? (②)

B: No, not this time. (③) I had ____(A)____ (finish) my history project.

G: Is it due today?

B: Yeah. I shouldn't ____(B)____ (put off, it) until the last moment. (④)

G: Hmm, I understand. (⑤)

B: Really? Well, let's try to change our bad habits.

출제율 100%

10 위 대화의 ①~⑤ 중 주어진 문장이 들어갈 곳은?

> I often have the same problem.

① ② ③ ④ ⑤

출제율 95%

11 주어진 괄호 안의 단어를 문맥에 맞게 고쳐 빈칸 (A)와 (B)를 채우시오.

(A) _____ (B) _____

출제율 100%

12 위 대화를 읽고 답할 수 없는 질문을 고르시오.

① How will they change their bad habits?

② When is the due date of the history project?

③ How does Jiho look like?

④ What is the bad habit which they have to change?

⑤ What did Jiho do last night?

13 다음 중 어법상 어색한 문장을 고르시오. (2개)

① While I was walking on the street, I saw a famous movie star.

② Walked on the street, I saw a famous movie star.

③ Walking on the street, I saw a famous movie star.

④ I walking on the street, I saw a famous movie star.

⑤ While walking on the street, I saw a famous movie star.

14 그림을 보고 주어진 어휘를 이용하여 빈칸을 알맞게 채우시오.

When Ann ran to the bus stop, the bus _____ _____ _____ . (just, leave)

15 다음 중 어법상 어색한 문장을 고르시오.

① She came earlier than I had expected.

② When Tom had opened the door, Alex already watered the plants.

③ I watched TV after I did my homework.

④ An article said that he had died!

⑤ The person who had actually died was his brother, Ludvig.

[16~18] 다음 글을 읽고 물음에 답하시오.

The article was about his own death! It said Nobel had died in France from a heart attack.

"Oh my goodness! Am I (A)[died / dead]?" Catching his breath, Nobel kept reading. Soon, he became even more (B)[shocking / shocked]. The article described him as the inventor of dynamite and other dangerous (C)[objects / subjects] for war. It said that he _____ⓐ rich from the deaths of others. He couldn't believe his eyes. ⓑIt was true that dynamite was one of his many inventions. But he never imagined that the world would think of him as "the merchant of death."

16 위 글의 빈칸 ⓐ에 become을 알맞은 형태로 쓰시오.

➡ _____

17 위 글의 괄호 (A)~(C)에서 문맥이나 어법상 알맞은 낱말을 골라 쓰시오.

(A) _____ (B) _____ (C) _____

18 위 글의 밑줄 친 ⓑIt과 문법적 쓰임이 같은 것을 고르시오.

① I make it a rule to get up early.

② It is 2 miles from here to the airport.

③ Did you see it?

④ It is important for you to choose good friends.

⑤ How's it going with you?

[19~21] 다음 글을 읽고 물음에 답하시오.

The Man Behind the Nobel Prize
ⓐAlfred Nobel decided to use his money to create the Nobel Prize. He wanted to honor people who made the world better. The Nobel Prize is given to people for great work in physics, chemistry, medicine, literature and the promotion of peace.

19 위 글의 밑줄 친 ⓐ를 복문으로 고칠 때 빈칸에 들어갈 알맞은 말을 쓰시오.

> Alfred Nobel decided to use his money
> _____ _____ _____ he _____
> _____ the Nobel Prize.

20 Why did Alfred Nobel create the Nobel Prize? Answer in English beginning with "Because".

➡ _____

_____

21 다음 중 위 글에서 설명한 노벨상 수상 부문에 해당하지 않는 것을 고르시오.

① 물리학 ② 경제학 ③ 의학
④ 문학 ⑤ 평화

[22~24] 다음 글을 읽고 물음에 답하시오.

In 1888, a French newspaper mistakenly reported Alfred Nobel's death. The person who had actually died was his brother, Ludvig. ___ⓐ___ the report, however, Nobel decided to do something to contribute to the world. In 1895, he decided to use his money to create the Nobel Prize. Originally, there were only five awards. A sixth award was added in 1968. Today, when we think of Alfred Nobel, we think of the Nobel Prize, rather than dynamite.

22 위 글의 빈칸 ⓐ에 들어갈 알맞은 말을 모두 고르시오.

① Instead of ② In spite of
③ Thanks to ④ In addition to
⑤ Because of

23 위 글의 주제로 알맞은 것을 고르시오.

① A French newspaper mistakenly reported Alfred Nobel's death.
② The incorrect report made Nobel decide to contribute to the world.
③ The person who had actually died was not Nobel but his brother, Ludvig.
④ The incorrect report can cause the harmful effect.
⑤ We should think of the Nobel Prize, rather than dynamite.

24 According to the passage, which is NOT true?

① In 1888, a French newspaper reported Alfred Nobel's death on purpose.
② It was Alfred Nobel's brother, Ludvig, who had actually died.
③ Nobel decided to use his money to create the Nobel Prize.
④ In 1968, the number of the awards increased to six.
⑤ Today, when we think of Alfred Nobel, the Nobel Prize rather than dynamite comes to our mind first.

01 다음 대화의 흐름상 빈칸에 들어갈 말을 주어진 〈조건〉에 맞춰 쓰시오.

조건
- 기원하는 말 하기
- 대화에 나와 있는 어휘 이용하기
- 9 단어

A: I can't believe we're graduating soon.
B: Yeah. Is there anything you regret about your middle school life?
A: Yes. I should have taken part in many school events.
B: Well, you have a second chance in high school.
A: I guess you're right.
B: _____ in high school.

➡ _____

02 다음 문장과 바꿔 쓸 수 있는 문장을 주어진 단어를 이용하여 바꿔 쓰시오.

I should have eaten less last night.

(1) _____ (ought)
(2) _____ (regret)
(3) _____ (sorry)

03 다음 대화의 밑줄 친 문장 중 문맥상 또는 어법상 어색한 것을 찾아 바르게 고치시오.

Minho: Linda, what are you reading?
Linda: ①I'm reading graduation messages from my classmates.
Minho: Oh, it looks like they had a lot to say to you.

Linda: ②Many of them wrote that they like my smile.
Minho: That's nice. What else?
Linda: ③Some of them said I didn't hang out enough with them.
Minho: That's not your fault. You were always busy.
Linda: Yeah, but ④I must have spent more time with my classmates.
Minho: You still have time after graduation.
Linda: You're right.
Minho: ⑤I hope you keep in touch with your classmates after graduation.
Linda: Thanks. I hope so, too.

➡ _____

04 분사구문은 부사절로, 부사절은 분사구문으로 바꿔 쓰시오.

(1) Being sick, he went to see a doctor.
  ➡ _____

(2) You will get a perfect result, following these instructions.
  ➡ _____
  _____

(3) As there was no bus left, I had to walk home.
  ➡ _____

(4) He goes to work by train every morning and comes home the same way.
  ➡ _____
  _____

05 다음 두 문장을 that을 이용하여 한 문장으로 연결할 때 두 사건의 시간차가 드러나도록 빈칸을 알맞게 채우시오.

(1) • The article said.
   • He became rich from the deaths of others.
   = The article said that he _____ rich from the deaths of others.

(2) • When he returned to Korea after twenty years' absence, he found it.
   • Everything changed completely.
   = When he returned to Korea after twenty years' absence, he found that everything _____ completely.

[06~08] 다음 글을 읽고 물음에 답하시오.

The article was about his own death! It said Nobel ⓐ _____ in France from a heart attack. "Oh my goodness! Am I dead?"

ⓑCatching his breath, Nobel kept reading. Soon, he became even more shocked. The article described him as the inventor of dynamite and other dangerous objects for war. It said that he had become rich from the deaths of others. He couldn't believe his eyes. It was true that dynamite was one of his many inventions. But he never imagined that the world would think of ⓒhim as "the merchant of death."

06 위 글의 빈칸 ⓐ에 die를 알맞은 형태로 쓰시오.

➡ _____

07 위 글의 밑줄 친 분사구문 ⓑ를 부사절로 고치시오.

➡ _____

08 위 글의 밑줄 친 ⓒhim이 가리키는 것을 본문에서 찾아 쓰시오.

➡ _____

[09~11] 다음 글을 읽고 물음에 답하시오.

In 1888, a French newspaper mistakenly reported Alfred Nobel's death. The person who had actually died was his brother, Ludvig. Thanks to the report, however, ⓐNobel decided to do something to contribute to the world. In 1895, he decided to use his money to create the Nobel Prize. Originally, there were only five awards. A sixth award was added in 1968. Today, when we think of Alfred Nobel, ⓑ우리는 다이너마이트보다는 노벨상을 떠올린다.

09 위 글의 밑줄 친 ⓐ를 다음과 같이 바꿔 쓸 때 빈칸에 들어갈 알맞은 말을 세 단어로 쓰시오.

Nobel _____ _____ _____ to do something to contribute to the world.

10 위 글의 밑줄 친 ⓑ의 우리말에 맞게 주어진 어휘를 알맞게 배열하시오.

rather than / think of / dynamite / the Nobel Prize / we / , /

➡ _____

11 본문의 내용과 일치하도록 다음 빈칸 (A)와 (B)에 알맞은 단어를 쓰시오.

In 1888, a French newspaper mistakenly reported that _____ _____ died, but the person who had actually died was his brother, Ludvig.

창의사고력 서술형 문제

01 〈보기〉에 주어진 표현과 분사구문을 이용하여 3 문장 이상 쓰시오.

> 보기
>
> have nothing to do / go for a walk
>
> tired / come back home early
>
> they are not fish / they need to come up to breathe
>
> walk on the street / saw a famous movie star

(1) _____

(2) _____

(3) _____

02 다음 내용을 바탕으로 보람을 느꼈던 일에 관해 쓰시오.

> • What did you do?
>
>   I donated money to children in Africa.
>
> • Why did you do it?
>
>   I wanted to make a difference for children in need.
>
> • How did you do it?
>
>   I didn't buy snacks for a month.
>
> • How did it make you different?
>
>   Now I really appreciate my meals.
>
> • How do you feel about yourself?
>
>   I'm proud of myself.

> Looking back this year, I'm glad that I (A)_____. I did this because I wanted to (B)_____. To save money, I didn't (C)_____. I donated the money to UNICEF. Before I donated, I sometimes left food on my plate. Now I really appreciate (D)_____. I'm proud of (E)_____.

단원별 모의고사

01 다음 빈칸에 공통으로 들어갈 말을 고르시오.

• She's late _____ work every day.
• After the long walk, we were all ready _____ a drink.

① to   ② for   ③ of
④ from   ⑤ on

02 다음 괄호 안의 단어를 문맥에 맞게 고쳐 쓰시오.

They were equally amazed at her. It was _____(believe) that she was only the same age as many of them.

03 다음 빈칸을 〈보기〉에 있는 어휘를 이용하여 채우시오.

┌─ 보기 ─────────────────┐
│   catch   get   give   hang   │
│   keep   stay   spend   │
└──────────────────────┘

(1) We _____ half an hour looking for the keys, but eventually _____ up and went home.
(2) I often _____ out in coffee shops.
(3) Josh could _____ up all night without getting tired.

04 다음 우리말에 맞도록 빈칸에 알맞은 말을 쓰시오. (철자가 주어진 경우 주어진 철자로 시작할 것)

(1) 그녀는 기대하지 못했다는 듯 놀라서 외쳤다.
➡ She shouted _____ surprise as if she weren't expecting it.

(2) 우리가 계속 연락하고 지내기를 바라.
➡ I h_____ we'll _____ in _____.

(3) 그들에게 나의 전화번호를 주는 바보 같은 실수를 저질렀다.
➡ I stupidly _____ the _____ of giving them my phone number.

(4) 나는 이곳을 나의 고향으로 생각한다.
➡ I t_____ _____ this place _____ my home.

[05~06] 다음 대화를 읽고 물음에 답하시오.

G: Jiho, what's up? You look (A)[angry / excited / tired].
B: Yeah. I stayed up late last night.
G: Did you play computer games again?
B: No, not this time. I had to finish my history project.
G: Is it (B)[due / plan / work] today?
B: Yeah. 나는 마지막 순간까지 미루지 말았어야 했어.
G: Hmm, I understand. I often have the same problem.
B: Really? Well, let's try to (C)[change / keep / make] our bad habits.

05 위 대화의 괄호 (A)~(C)에서 적절한 것을 골라 쓰시오.

(A) _____ (B) _____ (C) _____

06 위 글의 밑줄 친 우리말과 일치하도록 주어진 단어를 이용해 영작하시오.

┌──────────────────────┐
│   put, should, it, until, 10 단어   │
└──────────────────────┘

➡ _____

[07~09] 다음 대화를 읽고 물음에 답하시오.

> G: Jaemin, are you ready ⓐ the singing contest?
>
> B: Well, I'm thinking ⓑ giving ⓒ , Tina.
>
> G: Why? I thought you really wanted to take part ⓓ the contest.
>
> B: ①I don't think I'm a good singer.
>
> G: Come on. ②You're the best singer I know.
>
> B: ③Do you really think so?
>
> G: ④Of course not. You have a really nice voice.
>
> B: Thank you ⓔ saying so. I'll do my best.
>
> G: ⑤I hope you win the contest.

07 위 대화의 빈칸 ⓐ~ⓔ에 들어가지 <u>않는</u> 말을 고르시오.

① for　　② in　　③ of　　④ on　　⑤ up

08 위 대화의 밑줄 친 ①~⑤ 중 흐름상 또는 어법상 <u>어색한</u> 것을 고르시오.

①　　　②　　　③　　　④　　　⑤

09 질문에 답할 수 <u>없는</u> 것을 <u>모두</u> 고르시오.

① 재민이는 무슨 종류의 노래를 잘하는가?

② Tina는 재민이가 대회에서 무엇을 하기를 바라는가?

③ 노래 대회는 언제 있는가?

④ 왜 재민이는 대회를 포기할까 생각 중이었는가?

⑤ 재민이는 노래 대회에 나갈 것인가?

[10~12] 다음 대화를 읽고 물음에 답하시오.

> Minho: Linda, what are you reading?
>
> Linda: _____
>
> Minho: _____
>
> Linda: _____
>
> Minho: _____
>
> Linda: Some of them said I didn't hang out enough with them.
>
> Minho: That's not your fault. You were always busy.
>
> Linda: Yeah, but I should have spent more time with my classmates.
>
> Minho: You still have time after graduation.
>
> Linda: You're right.
>
> Minho: <u>네가 졸업 후에도 학급 친구들과 계속 연락하기를 바라.</u>
>
> Linda: Thanks. I hope so, too.

10 위 대화의 빈칸에 들어갈 말을 바르게 배열하시오.

> (A) Oh, it looks like they had a lot to say to you.
>
> (B) Many of them wrote that they like my smile.
>
> (C) I'm reading graduation messages from my classmates.
>
> (D) That's nice. What else?

➡ _____

11 위 대화에서 다음 영영풀이에 해당하는 단어를 찾아 쓰시오.

> a ceremony at which degrees or diplomas are given out

➡ _____

12 밑줄 친 우리말과 일치하도록 주어진 단어를 이용해 영작하시오. (hope, touch, after) (11 words)

➡ _____

_____

13 다음 문장에서 어법상 <u>어색한</u> 것을 바르게 고쳐 다시 쓰시오.

(1) When I woke up this morning, the rain already stopped.

➡ _____

_____

(2) The article said Alfred Nobel died in France from a heart attack.

➡ _____

_____

(3) Ann was late for school, Ann ran to catch the school bus.

➡ _____

_____

14 다음 우리말을 주어진 어휘를 이용하여 영작하시오.

(1) 내가 집에 갔을 때, 나는 누군가 우리 집에 침입했었다는 것을 알았다. (got, found, break into, someone, 12 단어)

➡ _____

_____

(2) 그들은 친구들이 도착하기 전에 피자를 다 먹었다. (the pizza, their friends, arrive, finish, 9 단어)

➡ _____

_____

(3) 팝콘을 먹으면서 그는 TV를 보았다. (eat, watch, popcorn, 5 단어)

➡ _____

(4) 오른쪽으로 돌면, 너는 꽃 가게를 발견할 수 있을 것이다. (the flower shop, to the right, find, turn, 10 단어)

➡ _____

15 Which is grammatically WRONG? Select ALL.

① Be nervous on the stage, the actor forgot his lines.

② While listening to music, he washed the dishes.

③ Losing the game, she felt disappointed.

④ Jimmy had borrowed some money because he lost his bag.

⑤ I went to bed after I watched my favorite TV show.

[16~18] 다음 글을 읽고 물음에 답하시오.

The article was about his own death! It said Nobel had died in France from a heart attack. "Oh my goodness! Am I dead?"

ⓐ숨을 고른 후, Nobel은 계속 읽었다. Soon, he became even more shocked. The article described him as the inventor of dynamite and other dangerous objects for war. It said that he had become rich from the deaths of others. He couldn't believe his eyes. It was true ⓑthat dynamite was one of his many inventions. But he never imagined that the world would think of him as "the merchant of death."

16 위 글의 밑줄 친 ⓐ의 우리말에 맞게 주어진 어휘를 이용하여 6 단어로 영작하시오. (분사구문을 사용하시오.)

kept

➡ _____

17 위 글의 밑줄 친 ⓑthat과 문법적 쓰임이 같은 것을 고르시오.

① The trouble is that we are short of money.
② She warned me that I should be more careful.
③ It's true that we were a little late.
④ I heard that you've been abroad.
⑤ There was no hope that she would recover her health.

18 Why did Nobel become even more shocked as he continued to read the article? Fill in the blanks (A) and (B) with suitable words.

> Because he realized that the world would think of him as "the merchant of (A)_____" after he died and he never (B)_____ it.

[19~21] 다음 글을 읽고 물음에 답하시오.

> In 1888, a French newspaper mistakenly reported Alfred Nobel's death. (①) Thanks to the report, however, Nobel decided to do something to contribute to the world. (②) In 1895, he decided to use his money ⓐto create the Nobel Prize. (③) Originally, there were only five awards. (④) A sixth award was added in 1968. (⑤) Today, when we think of Alfred Nobel, we think of the Nobel Prize, rather than dynamite.

19 위 글의 흐름으로 보아, 주어진 문장이 들어가기에 가장 적절한 곳은?

> The person who had actually died was his brother, Ludvig.

①   ②   ③   ④   ⑤

20 다음 〈보기〉에서 위 글의 밑줄 친 ⓐto create와 to부정사의 용법이 다른 것의 개수를 고르시오.

┌─ 보기 ─┐
① He promised never to be late again.
② He grew up to be a cook.
③ I don't have any friends to talk with.
④ All he can do is to support himself.
⑤ I'm glad to meet you.

① 1개   ② 2개   ③ 3개   ④ 4개   ⑤ 5개

21 When was a sixth award added? Answer in English in a full sentence beginning with "It". (5 words)

➡ _____

[22~23] 다음 글을 읽고 물음에 답하시오.

> Looking back this year, I'm glad that I participated in the tree planting program. I ⓐdid this because I wanted to do something for the environment. To get more people to join this program, I put up some posters and encouraged my friends to join. I didn't care about trees before I participated in this program. Now I know they are really important for us. I feel proud of myself.

22 위 글의 밑줄 친 ⓐdid this가 가리키는 것을 본문에서 찾아 쓰시오.

➡ _____

23 According to the passage, which is NOT true?

① This year, the writer participated in the tree planting program.
② The writer wanted to do something for the environment.
③ The writer put up some posters.
④ The writer encouraged his or her friends to join the program.
⑤ The writer doesn't care about trees.

Lesson

Special

Picture the Future

Words & Expressions

Key Words

- **after**[ǽftər] 전 ~ 후에
- **appear**[əpíər] 동 나타나다
- **bathroom**[bǽθrùːm] 명 욕실
- **brightly**[bráitli] 부 밝게
- **clear**[kliər] 동 맑게[투명하게] 하다 형 투명한, 맑은
- **comfortable**[kʌ́mfərtəbl] 형 편안한, 안락한
- **drawer**[drɔːr] 명 서랍
- **driverless**[dráivərlis] 형 운전자가 필요 없는
- **future**[fjúːtʃər] 명 미래
- **grocery**[gróusəri] 명 식료품 및 잡화
- **health condition** 건강 상태
- **land**[lænd] 동 내려앉다, 착륙하다 명 육지, 땅
- **press**[pres] 동 누르다
- **remind**[rimáind] 동 상기시키다

- **rub**[rʌb] 동 문지르다, 비비다
- **scan**[skæn] 동 정밀 검사[촬영]하다
- **select**[silékt] 동 선택하다
- **sensor**[sénsər] 명 센서, 감지기
- **shake**[ʃeik] 동 흔들리다, 흔들다
- **shine**[ʃain] 동 빛나다, 비추다
- **shower**[ʃáuər] 명 샤워실, 샤워
- **solution**[səlúːʃən] 명 해결책
- **special**[spéʃəl] 형 특별한
- **story**[stɔ́ːri] 명 (건물의) 층
- **usual**[júːʒuəl] 형 일상의, 늘 하는 명 늘 먹던 것
- **whisper**[hwíspər] 동 속삭이다
- **yell**[jel] 동 소리치다, 외치다

Key Expressions

- **be tired of** ~에 싫증이 나다
- **by 동사ing** ~함으로써
- **come back** 돌아오다
- **don't have to 동사원형** ~할 필요가 없다
- **feel like** ~인 것처럼 느끼다
- **give a presentation** 발표를 하다
- **on top of** ~의 꼭대기에

- **pay for** ~의 값을 지불하다
- **print out** (프린트로) 출력하다
- **remind A to 동사원형** A에게 ~할 것을 상기시키다
- **send A to B** A를 B에게 보내다
- **step in** ~에 발을 디디다
- **stop 동명사** ~하기를 멈추다
- **thanks to 명사** ~ 덕분에

Word Power

※ 명사+less: ~이 없는

□ **careless** 부주의한

□ **driverless** 운전자가 필요 없는

□ **endless** 끝없는

□ **harmless** 해롭지 않은

□ **homeless** 집 없는

□ **useless** 쓸모없는

□ **wireless** 선이 없는

※ 서로 비슷한 뜻을 가진 어휘

□ **press** 누르다 – **push down** ~을 꽉 누르다

□ **rub** 문지르다, 비비다 – **stroke** 쓰다듬다

□ **select** 선택하다 – **choose** 고르다, 선택하다

□ **story** (건물의) 층 – **floor** 층

※ 서로 반대의 뜻을 가진 어휘

□ **appear** 나타나다 ↔ **disappear** 사라지다

□ **comfortable** 편안한 ↔ **uncomfortable** 불편한

□ **future** 미래 ↔ **past** 과거

□ **usual** 일상의 ↔ **unusual** 특이한, 흔치 않은

□ **special** 특별한 ↔ **general** 일반적인

English Dictionary

□ **appear** 나타나다
→ to start to be seen, to arrive, or to exist in a place, especially suddenly
특히 갑자기 보이거나, 도착하거나, 어느 장소에 존재하기 시작하다

□ **press** 누르다
→ to push a button, switch, etc. to make a machine start, a bell ring, etc.
기계가 시작하거나, 종이 울리도록 하기 위해서 버튼이나 스위치 등을 누르다

□ **remind** 상기시키다
→ to make someone remember something that they must do
누군가가 그들이 해야만 하는 것을 기억하게 만들다

□ **rub** 문지르다, 비비다
→ to move your hand, or something such as a cloth, backwards and forwards over a surface while pressing firmly
꽉 누른 채 손이나 천 같은 어떤 것을 표면 위로 앞뒤로 움직이다

□ **select** 선택하다
→ to choose something or someone by thinking carefully about which is the best, most suitable, etc.
어떤 것 또는 누군가를 무엇이 최선인지, 가장 적절한지 등에 관해 조심스러운 생각으로 고르다

□ **shake** 흔들리다, 흔들다
→ to move suddenly from side to side or up and down usually with a lot of force, or to make something or someone do this
보통 큰 힘으로 위아래나 옆으로 갑자기 움직이거나 어떤 것이나 누군가를 이렇게 하도록 만들다

□ **shine** 빛나다, 비추다
→ to produce bright light
밝은 빛이 생기게 하다

□ **whisper** 속삭이다
→ to speak or say something very quietly, using your breath rather than your voice
목소리보다는 숨을 사용해서 매우 조용하게 말하다

□ **yell** 소리치다, 외치다
→ to shout or say something very loudly, especially because you are frightened, angry, or excited
특히 겁이 나거나, 화가 나거나, 흥분해서 매우 크게 소리치거나 말하다

Reading

Picture the Future

It's 7 a.m. The bed <u>shakes</u> and Minji Kim yells, "Five more minutes!"
'흔들리다'(자동사)
The bed <u>stops shaking</u>. Suddenly, Minji's mom appears on a screen on
stop ~ing: ~하기를 그만두다. stop+to부정사: ~하기 위해 멈추다(부사적 용법 목적)
the wall and says, "You're going to be late for school!" Minji rubs her
eyes and says, "Clear the windows." The dark windows become clear
and the sun shines brightly through them.

In the bathroom, a red light scans Minji's body. A voice says, "54
kilograms. Your health condition is excellent." When she steps in the
shower, water comes out from the top and sides. <u>After</u> her shower,
~ 후에(전치사)+명사(구)
warm air comes out and dries her. When she gets out, <u>a drawer opens</u>
서랍이 열리며 그 안에 오늘 입을 옷이 들어 있다
<u>with today's clothes.</u>

In the kitchen, her father says, "Good morning, Honey. What do you
want for breakfast?" Minji says, "The usual, please." Mr. Kim presses
a few buttons on the cooking machine. The machine prints out some
문맥상 음식을 찍어 내는 삼차원 프린터(3–D printer)를 의미
bacon, eggs and bread. Mr. Kim says goodbye and rushes out the door.

A few minutes <u>later</u>, Minji's father appears on a screen and shouts,
후에
"I forgot my glasses!" Ms. Kim smiles and answers, "No problem. I'll
send a drone to your office." Mr. Kim says, "Thanks a million!"

shake 흔들리다, 흔들다
yell 소리치다, 외치다
appear 나타나다
rub 문지르다, 비비다
clear 맑게[투명하게] 하다; 투명한, 맑은
shine 빛나다, 비추다
brightly 밝게
bathroom 욕실
scan 정밀 검사[촬영]하다
health condition 건강 상태
step in ~에 발을 디디다
shower 샤워실, 샤워
drawer 서랍
usual 일상의, 늘 하는; 늘 먹던 것
press 누르다
print out (프린터로) 출력하다

 확인문제

● 다음 문장이 본문의 내용과 일치하면 T, 일치하지 <u>않으면</u> F를 쓰시오.

1 Minji's mom appears on a screen on the wall and says, "You're going to be late for
school!" ☐

2 When Minji steps in the shower, water comes out from the bottom. ☐

3 The cooking machine prints out some bacon, eggs and bread. ☐

4 Mr. Kim will send a drone to Ms. Kim's office. ☐

Ms. Kim and Minji get into a driverless flying car. They sit in comfortable chairs around a table. Ms. Kim touches the car window to select the groceries for this week. She pays for them by putting her finger on a sensor. They will be delivered to her house.

The car lands at Minji's school on top of a 150-story building. Today Minji will give a presentation with Dona, a student in America. But Minji doesn't have to go to America. Thanks to a VR classroom, they will feel like they are in the same classroom.

When Minji's family comes back home, dinner is ready. They eat and talk about their day. After a delicious dinner, the cleaning robot clears the table and washes the dishes. Minji says, "I learned a game called chess today. Do you want to play?" Everyone agrees.

A 3-D chess board appears on the table. They have lots of fun.

Right before Minji goes to bed, she whispers to her watch.

"Remind Daddy to take his glasses tomorrow."

driverless 운전자가 필요 없는

comfortable 편안한, 안락한

select 선택하다

grocery 식료품 및 잡화

pay for ~의 값을 지불하다

sensor 센서, 감지기

land 내려앉다, 착륙하다

story (건물의) 층

give a presentation 발표를 하다

whisper 속삭이다

확인문제

● 다음 문장이 본문의 내용과 일치하면 T, 일치하지 않으면 F를 쓰시오.

1 Ms. Kim and Minji get into a driverless flying car. ☐

2 Ms. Kim touches the smartphone to select the groceries for this week. ☐

3 Ms. Kim and Minji's flying car lands on the playground of Minji's school. ☐

4 Minji's school is located on top of a 150-story building. ☐

5 After a delicious dinner, Minji clears the table and washes the dishes. ☐

● 우리말을 참고하여 빈칸에 알맞은 말을 쓰시오.

1 _____ the Future

2 _____ 7 a.m.

3 The bed _____ and Minji Kim yells, "_____ _____ _____!"

4 The bed _____ _____.

5 Suddenly, Minji's mom _____ on a screen on the wall and says, "You're going to _____ _____ _____ school!"

6 Minji rubs her eyes and says, "_____ the windows."

7 The dark windows _____ _____ and the sun shines brightly through them.

8 In the bathroom, a red light _____ _____ _____.

9 A voice says, "54 kilograms. Your _____ _____ is excellent."

10 When she steps in the shower, water _____ _____ _____ the top and sides.

11 After her shower, warm air _____ out and _____ her.

12 When she gets out, a drawer opens _____ _____ _____.

13 In the kitchen, her father says, "Good morning, Honey. What do you want _____ _____?"

14 Minji says, "_____ _____, please."

15 Mr. Kim _____ a few buttons _____ the cooking machine.

16 The machine _____ _____ some bacon, eggs and bread.

17 Mr. Kim says goodbye and _____ _____ the door.

1 미래를 상상하다

2 오전 7시이다.

3 침대가 흔들리고 김민지가 "5분만 더!"라고 소리를 지른다.

4 침대가 흔들기를 멈춘다.

5 갑자기, 민지의 엄마가 벽 스크린에 나타나 말한다. "학교에 늦겠구나!"

6 민지는 눈을 비비며 "창문을 투명하게 해 줘."라고 말한다.

7 어두운 창문이 투명해지며 창문으로 햇살이 밝게 비춘다.

8 욕실에서 빨간 빛이 민지의 몸을 정밀 검사한다.

9 목소리가 "54킬로그램. 건강 상태가 매우 좋습니다."라고 말한다.

10 그녀가 샤워실 안에 발을 디디자, 물이 위와 양측에서 나온다.

11 샤워 후에, 따뜻한 공기가 나와 그녀를 말린다.

12 그녀가 나가자, 서랍이 열리며 오늘의 옷이 나타난다.

13 부엌에서 민지의 아빠가 "좋은 아침이구나, 얘야. 아침으로 무엇을 먹고 싶니?"라고 말한다.

14 민지는 "늘 먹던 걸로 주세요."라고 말한다.

15 아빠가 요리 기계의 버튼 몇 개를 누른다.

16 기계는 베이컨, 달걀, 빵을 만들어 낸다.

17 아빠는 작별 인사를 하고 문 밖으로 급히 나간다.

18 _____ _____ _____ _____, Minji's father appears on a screen and shouts, "I forgot my glasses!"

19 Ms. Kim smiles and answers, "No problem. I'll _____ _____ _____ _____ your office."

20 Mr. Kim says, "Thanks _____ _____!"

21 Ms. Kim and Minji get into a _____ _____ _____.

22 They sit _____ _____ _____ around a table.

23 Ms. Kim touches the car window _____ _____ the groceries for this week.

24 She pays for them _____ _____ her finger _____ _____ _____.

25 They _____ _____ _____ _____ to her house.

26 The car lands at Minji's school on top of a _____ building.

27 Today Minji will _____ _____ _____ _____ _____ Dona, a student in America.

28 But Minji _____ _____ _____ go to America.

29 _____ _____ a VR classroom, they will _____ _____ they are in the same classroom.

30 When Minji's family comes back home, dinner _____ _____.

31 They eat and _____ _____ their day.

32 After a delicious dinner, the cleaning robot clears the table and _____ _____ _____.

33 Minji says, "I learned a game _____ _____ today. Do you want to play?"

34 Everyone _____.

35 A _____ _____ _____ appears on the table.

36 They have _____ _____ _____.

37 Right before Minji goes to bed, she _____ _____ her watch.

38 "_____ Daddy _____ _____ his glasses tomorrow."

18 몇 분 후에, 민지의 아빠가 스크린에 나타나 소리친다. "안경을 깜빡했어요!"

19 민지의 엄마가 미소 지으며 답한다. "괜찮아요. 드론을 당신의 사무실로 보낼게요."

20 민지의 아빠가 "정말 고마워요!"라고 말한다.

21 민지의 엄마와 민지는 운전자가 필요 없는 비행 자동차에 탄다.

22 두 사람은 탁자 주변의 편안한 의자에 앉는다.

23 민지의 엄마가 이번 주 식료품을 선택하기 위해 자동차 창문을 터치한다.

24 그녀는 센서에 손가락을 대서 식료품 값을 지불한다.

25 식료품은 집으로 배달될 것이다.

26 자동차는 150층 빌딩의 꼭대기에 있는 민지의 학교에 내린다.

27 오늘 민지는 미국에 있는 학생 Dona와 함께 발표를 할 것이다.

28 하지만 민지가 미국에 갈 필요는 없다.

29 VR(가상 현실) 교실 덕분에, 그들은 같은 교실에 있는 것처럼 느낄 것이다.

30 민지의 가족이 집에 돌아오자 저녁이 준비된다.

31 그들은 식사를 하며 그 날에 관해 이야기한다.

32 맛있는 저녁 식사 후에, 청소 로봇이 식탁을 치우고 설거지를 한다.

33 민지가 "오늘 체스라고 불리는 놀이를 배웠어요. 해 보실래요?"라고 말한다.

34 모두가 동의한다.

35 탁자 위에 삼차원 체스판이 나타난다.

36 그들은 아주 즐거운 시간을 보낸다.

37 민지는 자러 가기 직전에, 자신의 손목시계에 속삭인다.

38 "아빠께 내일 안경을 가져가시라고 상기시켜 드려."

● 우리말을 참고하여 본문을 영작하시오.

1 미래를 상상하다
➡ _____

2 오전 7시이다.
➡ _____

3 침대가 흔들리고 김민지가 "5분만 더!"라고 소리를 지른다.
➡ _____

4 침대가 흔들기를 멈춘다.
➡ _____

5 갑자기, 민지의 엄마가 벽 스크린에 나타나 말한다. "학교에 늦겠구나!"
➡ _____
_____

6 민지는 눈을 비비며 "창문을 투명하게 해 줘."라고 말한다.
➡ _____

7 어두운 창문이 투명해지며 창문으로 햇살이 밝게 비춘다.
➡ _____

8 욕실에서 빨간 빛이 민지의 몸을 정밀 검사한다.
➡ _____

9 목소리가 "54킬로그램. 건강 상태가 매우 좋습니다."라고 말한다.
➡ _____

10 그녀가 샤워실 안에 발을 디디자, 물이 위와 양측에서 나온다.
➡ _____

11 샤워 후에, 따뜻한 공기가 나와 그녀를 말린다.
➡ _____

12 그녀가 나가자, 서랍이 열리며 오늘의 옷이 나타난다.
➡ _____

13 부엌에서 민지의 아빠가 "좋은 아침이구나, 얘야. 아침으로 무엇을 먹고 싶니?"라고 말한다.
➡ _____

14 민지는 "늘 먹던 걸로 주세요."라고 말한다.
➡ _____

15 아빠가 요리 기계의 버튼 몇 개를 누른다.
➡ _____

16 기계는 베이컨, 달걀, 빵을 만들어 낸다.
➡ _____

17 아빠는 작별 인사를 하고 문 밖으로 급히 나간다.
➡ _____

18 몇 분 후에, 민지의 아빠가 스크린에 나타나 소리친다. "안경을 깜빡했어요!"
➡ _____

19 민지의 엄마가 미소 지으며 답한다. "괜찮아요. 드론을 당신의 사무실로 보낼게요."
➡ _____

20 민지의 아빠가 "정말 고마워요!"라고 말한다.
➡ _____

21 민지의 엄마와 민지는 운전자가 필요 없는 비행 자동차에 탄다.
➡ _____

22 두 사람은 탁자 주변의 편안한 의자에 앉는다.
➡ _____

23 민지의 엄마가 이번 주 식료품을 선택하기 위해 자동차 창문을 터치한다.
➡ _____

24 그녀는 센서에 손가락을 대서 식료품 값을 지불한다.
➡ _____

25 식료품은 집으로 배달될 것이다.
➡ _____

26 자동차는 150층 빌딩의 꼭대기에 있는 민지의 학교에 내린다.
➡ _____

27 오늘 민지는 미국에 있는 학생 Dona와 함께 발표를 할 것이다.
➡ _____

28 하지만 민지가 미국에 갈 필요는 없다.
➡ _____

29 VR(가상 현실) 교실 덕분에, 그들은 같은 교실에 있는 것처럼 느낄 것이다.
➡ _____

30 민지의 가족이 집에 돌아오자 저녁이 준비된다.
➡ _____

31 그들은 식사를 하며 그 날에 관해 이야기한다.
➡ _____

32 맛있는 저녁 식사 후에, 청소 로봇이 식탁을 치우고 설거지를 한다.
➡ _____

33 민지가 "오늘 체스라고 불리는 놀이를 배웠어요. 해 보실래요?"라고 말한다.
➡ _____

34 모두가 동의한다.
➡ _____

35 탁자 위에 삼차원 체스판이 나타난다.
➡ _____

36 그들은 아주 즐거운 시간을 보낸다.
➡ _____

37 민지는 자러 가기 직전에, 자신의 손목시계에 속삭인다.
➡ _____

38 "아빠께 내일 안경을 가져가시라고 상기시켜 드려."
➡ _____

[01~02] 다음 빈칸에 공통으로 들어갈 말을 쓰시오.

01

- She made all the u_____ excuses.
- I'll have the u_____, please.

02

- We were tired _____ waiting for him to call.
- The house is located on top _____ a hill.

03 다음 빈칸에 알맞은 단어를 〈보기〉에서 골라 쓰시오.

┌─── 보기 ───┐
clear   comfortable   story
└─────────────┘

(1) His office is on the top floor of a thirty-_____ building.
(2) I was so _____ and warm in bed that I didn't want to get up.
(3) Will you please help me _____ the table?

04 우리말에 맞게 주어진 단어를 알맞게 배열하시오.

(1) 그의 좋지 않은 건강 때문에 그는 대학을 마치지 못했다. (finish, condition, of, he, bad, his, couldn't, college, because, health)

➡ _____

(2) 한 남자가 나무 뒤에서 갑자기 나타났다. (a, a, tree, suddenly, from, man, behind, appeared)

➡ _____

(3) 달이 하늘에서 밝게 빛났다. (shone, in, the, sky, moon, the, brightly)

➡ _____

05 주어진 영영풀이를 보고 빈칸에 알맞은 단어를 주어진 철자로 시작하여 쓰시오.

to make someone remember something that they must do

R_____ me to buy some milk tonight.

06 다음 밑줄 친 부분 중 그 쓰임이 어색한 것을 모두 찾아 고치시오.

ⓐ I stopped to read and turned out the light.
ⓑ The drought is over, thanks to the recent heavy rains.
ⓒ By use the Internet you can do your shopping from home.

➡ _____

07 다음 우리말에 맞게 괄호 안의 단어를 알맞게 바꿔 빈칸에 쓰시오.

Google says the _____(driver) cars are safer than those with human drivers.
(구글은 운전자가 없는 자동차가 사람이 운전하는 자동차보다 안전하다고 말하고 있다.)

08 다음 문장을 수동태로 고쳤을 때 알맞은 것은?

> We cannot see the island from here.

① The island cannot see from here.
② The island is not seen from here.
③ The island not be seen from here.
④ The island cannot see from here.
⑤ The island cannot be seen from here.

09 다음 문장의 밑줄 친 부분을 강조하여 쓰시오.

(1) Right before Minji goes to bed, she whispers to her watch.

➡ _____

_____

(2) Water comes out from the top and sides.

➡ _____

(3) Mr. Kim presses a few buttons on the cooking machine.

➡ _____

_____

(4) The car lands on top of a 150-story building.

➡ _____

_____

10 다음 우리말을 괄호 안에 주어진 어휘를 이용하여 영작하시오.

> 당신에게 Peters라는 이름을 가진 고객이 있습니까? (a client, name, 7 단어)

➡ _____

[11~13] 다음 글을 읽고 물음에 답하시오.

A few minutes later, Minji's father appears on a screen and shouts, "I forgot my glasses!" Ms. Kim smiles and answers, "No problem. I'll send a drone to your office." Mr. Kim says, "Thanks a million!"

Ms. Kim and Minji get into a driverless flying car. They sit in comfortable chairs around a table. Ms. Kim touches the car window to select the groceries for this week. (A)그녀는 센서에 손가락을 대서 식료품 값을 지불한다. They will ___ⓐ___ to her house.

11 위 글의 빈칸 ⓐ에 deliver를 알맞은 형태로 쓰시오.

➡ _____

12 How will Mr. Kim get his glasses that he left at home? Fill in the blanks (A) and (B) with suitable words.

> Ms. Kim will send (A)_____ _____ to (B)_____ _____ with his glasses.

13 위 글의 밑줄 친 (A)의 우리말에 맞게 주어진 어휘를 알맞게 배열하시오.

> on / them / pays / putting / she / a sensor / by / her finger / for

➡ _____

_____

[14~16] 다음 글을 읽고 물음에 답하시오.

ⓐThe car lands at Minji's school on top of a 150-stories building. Today Minji will give a presentation with Dona, a student in America. ⓑBut Minji doesn't have to go to America. Thanks to a VR classroom, they will feel like they are in the same classroom.

14
위 글의 밑줄 친 ⓐ에서 어법상 <u>틀린</u> 부분을 찾아 고치시오.

_____ ➡ _____

15
위 글의 밑줄 친 ⓑ를 다음과 같이 바꿔 쓸 때 빈칸에 들어갈 알맞은 말을 두 단어로 쓰시오.

> But Minji _____ _____ go to America.

16
How will it be possible for Minji and Dona, a student in America, to feel like they are in the same classroom? Fill in the blanks with suitable words.

> Thanks to _____ _____ _____, it will be possible for them to feel like they are in the same classroom.

[17~18] 다음 글을 읽고 물음에 답하시오.

> It's 7 a.m. The bed shakes and Minji Kim yells, "Five more minutes!" ⓐThe bed stops to shake. Suddenly, Minji's mom appears on a screen on the wall and says, "You're going to be late for school!" Minji rubs her eyes and says, "Clear the windows." The dark windows become clear and the sun shines brightly through ⓑthem.

17
위 글의 밑줄 친 ⓐ에서 어법상 <u>틀린</u> 부분을 찾아 고치시오.

➡ _____

18
위 글의 밑줄 친 ⓑthem이 가리키는 것을 본문에서 찾아 쓰시오.

➡ _____

[19~21] 다음 글을 읽고 물음에 답하시오.

> In the bathroom, a red light (A)[scans / skips] Minji's body. A voice says, "54 kilograms. Your health condition is excellent." When she steps in the shower, water comes out from the top and sides. After her shower, warm air comes out and dries her. When she gets out, a drawer opens with today's (B)[cloths / clothes].
>
> In the kitchen, her father says, "Good morning, Honey. What do you want for breakfast?" Minji says, "The usual, please." Mr. Kim presses (C)[a few / a little] buttons on the cooking machine. The machine prints out some bacon, eggs and bread. Mr. Kim says goodbye and rushes out the door.

19
위 글의 괄호 (A)~(C)에서 문맥이나 어법상 알맞은 낱말을 골라 쓰시오.

(A) _____ (B) _____ (C) _____

20
What happens when Minji finishes her shower? Answer in English in a full sentence.

➡ _____

21
주어진 영영풀이에 해당하는 단어를 본문에서 찾아 쓰시오.

> part of a desk, chest, or other piece of furniture that is shaped like a box and is designed for putting things in

➡ _____

01 다음 빈칸에 알맞은 단어를 〈보기〉에서 골라 쓰시오

┌─── 보기 ───
│ for   on   out   to
└─────────

(1) The tower is located _____ top of a hill.

(2) The reality is that there is not enough money to pay _____ this project.

(3) Could you please print _____ this document?

(4) He sent a dozen red roses _____ his girlfriend on her birthday.

02 다음 주어진 단어의 영영풀이가 <u>잘못된</u> 것을 고르시오.

① select: to choose something or someone by thinking carefully about which is the best, most suitable etc

② whisper: to shout or say something very loudly, especially because you are frightened, angry, or excited

③ press: to push a button, switch etc to make a machine start, a bell ring etc

④ shine: to produce bright light

⑤ appear: to start to be seen, to arrive, or to exist in a place, especially suddenly

03 다음 밑줄 친 부분과 바꿔 쓸 수 있는 말을 고르시오.

It's important that parents <u>select</u> the right school for a child with learning difficulties.

① collect   ② create

③ require   ④ include

⑤ choose

04 빈칸에 들어갈 접미사가 나머지와 <u>다른</u> 하나를 고르시오.

① It only takes one care_____ driver to cause an accident.

② The company is currently testing a driver_____ car.

③ Smoking has a harm_____ effect on people's health.

④ It's use_____ worrying about it.

⑤ Music is a source of end_____ pleasure to many people.

05 다음 우리말에 맞도록 빈칸에 알맞은 말을 쓰시오. (철자가 주어진 것도 있음.)

(1) 나는 그것을 설명하는 것에 싫증이 난다.
   ➡ I'm t_____ _____ explaining it.

(2) Jenny가 올 때 그녀의 노트북을 가져오라고 상기시켜라.
   ➡ _____ Jenny _____ bring her laptop when she comes.

(3) 갑자기 모두가 말하는 것을 멈췄다.
   ➡ Suddenly everyone _____ t_____ .

06 출제율 95%

다음 빈칸 (A)와 (B)에 들어갈 말로 알맞은 것끼리 짝지어진 것을 고르시오.

> • I always ask how much time I have to (A)_____ my presentation.
> • The front door opens automatically when you (B)_____ in front of it.

(A)	(B)		(A)	(B)
① give	– attach		② give	– avoid
③ give	– step		④ take	– avoid
⑤ take	– step			

07 출제율 100%

다음 중 어법상 어색한 것은?

① A few minutes later, Minji's father appears on a screen and shouts, "I forgot my glasses!"
② I tried to offer a few word of comfort.
③ Very few of his books are worth reading.
④ He has very little sight in his right eye.
⑤ I have a little money in the bank to fall back on.

08 출제율 90%

그림을 보고 주어진 어휘를 이용하여 빈칸을 알맞게 채우시오.

_____ _____ _____, the cleaning starts. (press, the button)

09 출제율 90%

그림을 보고, 주어진 어휘를 이용하여 빈칸을 알맞게 채우시오.

> The table _____ _____ _____ with flowers by my mom. (will, decorate)

10 출제율 95%

다음 문장에서 어법상 어색한 것을 바르게 고치시오.

> Tiring after a long walk, Minji went to bed early.

➡ _____

11 출제율 95%

다음의 부사절은 분사구문으로, 분사구문은 부사절로 바꿔 쓰시오.

(1) Minji's mom appears on a screen on the wall and says, "You're going to be late for school!"

➡ _____

(2) Being late, she hurried to work.

➡ _____

(3) Being an architect, what will you choose from nature?

➡ _____

✏️ 출제율 95%

12 다음 문장을 수동태로 바꿔 쓰시오.

(1) Many teens will love this movie.

➡ _____

(2) We should not destroy the environment.

➡ _____

(3) They can make the fruit into delicious jam.

➡ _____

(4) You have to deliver what you promised.

➡ _____

✏️ 출제율 95%

13 다음 ⓐ~ⓕ 중 어법상 옳은 것을 <u>모두</u> 고르시오.

ⓐ Personal calls must be taken outside of the office area.
ⓑ After today heavy snow, many roads are still blocked.
ⓒ Minji's father is appeared on a screen and shouts, "I forgot my glasses!"
ⓓ Being delicate, the egg is strong enough to protect its contents.
ⓔ It is from oil drums that Nicholas made violins.
ⓕ As he climbed the hill, the old man had to stop catching his breath every few minutes.

➡ _____

[14~15] 다음 글을 읽고 물음에 답하시오.

(①) Ms. Kim and Minji get into a driverless flying car. (②) They sit in comfortable chairs around a table. (③) She pays for them by putting her finger on a sensor. (④) ⓐThey will be delivered to her house. (⑤)

✏️ 출제율 95%

14 위 글의 흐름으로 보아, 주어진 문장이 들어가기에 가장 적절한 곳은?

> Ms. Kim touches the car window to select the groceries for this week.

①　　　②　　　③　　　④　　　⑤

✏️ 출제율 90%

15 위 글의 밑줄 친 ⓐThey가 가리키는 것을 본문에서 찾아 쓰시오.

➡ _____

[16~17] 다음 글을 읽고 물음에 답하시오.

When Minji's family comes back home, dinner is ready. They eat and talk about their day. After a delicious dinner, the cleaning robot clears the table and washes the dishes. Minji says, "ⓐI learned a game called chess today. Do you want to play?" Everyone agrees. A 3-D chess board appears on the table. They have lots of fun.

Right before Minji goes to bed, she whispers to her watch. "Remind Daddy to take his glasses tomorrow."

✏️ 출제율 95%

16 위 글의 밑줄 친 문장 ⓐ에서 생략된 부분을 넣어 문장을 다시 쓰시오.

➡ _____

✏️ 출제율 100%

17 위 글의 주제로 알맞은 것을 고르시오.

① the difficulties people will experience in the future
② a scene of the life in the future
③ the development of the cleaning robot
④ how to play chess on a 3-D chess board
⑤ how to use the watch to remind something

[18~20] 다음 글을 읽고 물음에 답하시오.

In the bathroom, a red light scans Minji's body. A voice says, "54 kilograms. Your health condition is excellent." When she steps in the shower, water comes out from the top and sides. After her shower, warm air comes out and dries her. When she gets out, a drawer opens with today's clothes.

In the kitchen, her father says, "Good morning, Honey. What do you want ⓐ breakfast?" Minji says, "(A)늘 먹던 걸로 주세요." Mr. Kim presses a few buttons ⓑ the cooking machine. The machine prints out some bacon, eggs and bread. Mr. Kim says goodbye and rushes out the door.

18 위 글의 빈칸 ⓐ와 ⓑ에 들어갈 전치사가 바르게 짝지어진 것은?

	ⓐ	ⓑ		ⓐ	ⓑ
①	for	on	②	in	by
③	in	on	④	for	to
⑤	on	to			

19 위 글의 밑줄 친 (A)의 우리말에 맞게 3 단어로 영작하시오.

➡ _____

20 According to the passage, which is NOT true?

① Minji's health condition is excellent.
② When Minji steps in the shower, water comes out from the top and sides.
③ Minji opens a drawer to choose today's clothes.
④ The cooking machine prints out some bacon, eggs and bread.
⑤ Minji's father says goodbye and rushes out the door.

[21~23] 다음 글을 읽고 물음에 답하시오.

It's 7 a.m. The bed shakes and Minji Kim yells, "Five more minutes!" The bed stops ⓐshaking. ⓑSuddenly, Minji's mom is appeared on a screen on the wall and says, "You're going to be late for school!" Minji rubs her eyes and says, "Clear the windows." The dark windows become clear and the sun shines brightly through them.

21 위 글의 밑줄 친 ⓐshaking과 문법적 쓰임이 같은 것을 모두 고르시오.

① I heard him singing a song.
② Who is the girl playing the piano?
③ Taking a walk every day is very good for the health.
④ She is learning English now.
⑤ Why did you go there without saying anything?

22 위 글의 밑줄 친 ⓑ에서 어법상 틀린 부분을 찾아 고치시오.

_____ ➡ _____

23 Which question CANNOT be answered after reading the passage?

① How does the bed wake Minji up?
② Does Minji get up instantly in the morning?
③ How does Minji's mom wake Minji up?
④ What does Minji say to her mom?
⑤ What does Minji do to make the dark windows become clear?

MEMO

MEMO

중간 + 기말

적중100 plus

영어 기출문제집

영어 중 3

동아 | 이병민

Best Collection

내용문의 중등영어발전소 적중100 편집부 TEL 070-7707-0457

INSIGHT
on the textbook

교과서 파헤치기

영어 기출 문제집

적중100 plus

2학기 전과정

영어 중 3

동아 | 이병민

INSIGHT
on the textbook
교과서 파헤치기

※ 다음 영어를 우리말로 쓰시오.

01	none		22	patience
02	ocean		23	award
03	afford		24	musical instrument
04	talented		25	performance
05	bored		26	respect
06	roll		27	giant
07	scared		28	cheek
08	worried		29	stick
09	excited		30	title
10	cheer		31	trash
11	speech		32	gym
12	journey		33	drone
13	landfill		34	orchestra
14	mostly		35	cheer for
15	appear		36	from then on
16	surprised		37	take care of
17	thrilled		38	give up
18	battle		39	take part in
19	tune		40	one another
20	educator		41	give a big hand
21	environmental		42	put ~ into practice
			43	out of tune

※ 다음 우리말을 영어로 쓰시오.

01	무인 항공기	22	붙이다
02	교육자	23	구르다, 굴러가다
03	공연	24	무서워하는, 겁먹은
04	존경하다	25	환경의
05	거대한	26	응원하다
06	쓰레기 매립지	27	신이 난, 흥분한
07	대부분, 일반적으로	28	연설
08	~할 형편이 되다	29	아직도, 여전히
09	나타나다	30	곡, 곡조, 선율
10	아무도 ~않다	31	체육 수업
11	볼, 뺨	32	여행
12	상	33	퍼레이드, 가두 행진
13	전쟁, 전투	34	악기
14	바이올린 연주자	35	포기하다
15	황홀해하는, 아주 신이 난	36	~로 알려지다
16	걱정하는	37	~에 참가하다
17	놀란, 놀라는	38	응원하다
18	재능 있는	39	그때부터
19	지루해하는	40	서로
20	쓰레기	41	~로 만들어지다
21	인내심	42	~을 돌보다
		43	~을 실행에 옮기다

※ 다음 영영풀이에 알맞은 단어를 <보기>에서 골라 쓴 후, 우리말 뜻을 쓰시오.

1 _____ : able or skillful: _____

2 _____ : to be able to pay for something: _____

3 _____ : very excited and happy: _____

4 _____ : in a gradual manner: _____

5 _____ : either side of the face below the eyes: _____

6 _____ : action rather than ideas: _____

7 _____ : frightened of someone or something: _____

8 _____ : to move along a surface by turning over and over: _____

9 _____ : an area where waste is buried under the ground: _____

10 _____ : things that you throw away because you no longer want or need them:
    _____

11 _____ : a prize or certificate that a person is given for doing something well:
    _____

12 _____ : to want it to happen because you think you will enjoy it:
    _____

13 _____ : the ability to stay calm and accept a delay or suffering without
    complaining: _____

14 _____ : a series of musical notes that make a pleasing sound when played together:
    _____

15 _____ : a large group of people who play various musical instruments together,
    led by a conductor: _____

16 _____ : to feel tired and impatient because you have lost interest in something or
    because you have nothing to do: _____

보기			
tune	roll	scared	patience
trash	thrilled	afford	step by step
practice	orchestra	award	talented
landfill	look forward to	bored	cheek

※ 다음 우리말과 일치하도록 빈칸에 알맞은 말을 쓰시오.

Listen and Speak 1 A

B: Hey, Bora. _____ _____ our rock band.

G: Thanks. I'm _____ _____ _____ _____ in a concert with you.

B: We're _____ _____ have a new guitar player.

G: Yeah. _____ _____ _____ Friday.

Listen and Speak 1 B

G: Jiho, _____ _____ you _____?

B: I'm _____ a book _____ baseball player _____ Jim Abbott.

G: Oh, the man _____ _____ _____ _____ a right hand?

B: That's right. He tried really hard and _____ _____ the MVP award.

G: Yeah. His story _____ _____ _____ a movie. I'm _____ _____ _____ it this Saturday.

B: Really? What's the _____?

G: Our Hero. _____ _____ _____ _____ _____ it.

B: Can I _____ you?

G: Sure. See you _____ Saturday.

Listen and Speak 1 C

1. A: You look happy today. _____ going _____?

   B: I'm so _____. _____ _____ _____ _____ _____ to Jeju-do.

   A: That _____ great!

   B: Yes. I'm _____ _____ _____ _____ _____ riding a horse.

2. A: You _____ _____ today. What's going on?

   B: I'm so _____. I'm going to _____ _____ _____ a drone.

   A: That sounds great!

   B: Yes. _____ _____ _____ forward _____ _____ a drone in the park.

3. A: You _____ _____ today. What's _____ _____?

   B: I'm _____ _____. _____ _____ _____ to see Jackson's concert.

   A: That sounds great!

   B: Yes. I'm really _____ _____ _____ _____ _____ Jackson's _____.

B: 얘, 보라야. 우리 록 밴드에 온 걸 환영해.

G: 고마워. 공연에서 너희들과 함께 연주할 게 기대돼.

B: 우리는 새로운 기타 연주자를 갖게 되어서 신나.

G: 잘됐다. 금요일에 봐.

G: 지호야, 뭘 읽고 있니?

B: Jim Abbott이라는 이름의 야구 선수에 관한 책을 읽고 있어.

G: 오, 오른손이 없이 태어난 사람?

B: 맞아. 그는 정말 열심히 노력해서 최우수 선수상까지 받았어.

G: 그래. 그의 이야기가 영화로 만들어졌어. 난 이번 주 토요일에 그 영화를 볼 거야.

B: 정말? 제목이 뭐니?

G: 'Our Hero'야. 그 영화를 볼 게 정말 기대돼.

B: 나도 너와 함께해도 될까?

G: 물론이지. 토요일에 봐.

1. A: 너 오늘 행복해 보인다. 무슨 일이야?

   B: 나는 아주 신나. 제주도로 여행을 갈 거야.

   A: 좋겠다!

   B: 응, 나는 말 타기를 정말 고대하고 있어.

2. A: 너 오늘 행복해 보인다. 무슨 일이야?

   B: 나는 아주 신나. 드론을 날리는 것을 배울 거야.

   A: 좋겠다!

   B: 응. 공원에서 드론을 날리는 것이 정말 기대돼.

3. A: 너 오늘 행복해 보인다. 무슨 일이야?

   B: 나는 아주 신나. Jackson의 콘서트를 볼 거야.

   A: 좋겠다!

   B: 응. Jackson의 공연을 보는 것이 정말 기대돼.

G: Minho, did you _____ the _____ _____?

B: Not yet. Math is _____.

G: Yes, but it's _____, _____.

B: Then can you _____ _____ _____ my math homework?

G: _____ _____ _____, but I can't. I _____ _____ _____ _____ _____ my brother.

G: Alex, I'm _____ _____ _____ _____ _____ a singing contest next Monday.

B: That's great, Sumin!

G: You know _____ _____ _____ the guitar, _____?

B: Yes, _____ _____ the guitar _____ 3 years.

G: Great. _____ _____ _____ the guitar _____ I sing in the contest?

B: I'd love to, _____ _____ _____. I _____ my hand in _____ _____ yesterday.

G: Oh! I'm _____ _____ _____ that.

B: Thanks. But I'll be there to _____ _____ you.

1. **A:** What are you _____ _____ _____ this afternoon?

   B: I'm going to ride my bike. Do you _____ _____ join me?

   A: I'd love to, _____ _____ _____. I _____ _____ do my homework.

   B: Okay, then _____ _____.

2. **A:** What _____ _____ _____ _____ do this afternoon?

   B: I'm _____ _____ play soccer. Do you want to _____ _____?

   A: _____ _____ _____, but I can't. I have _____ _____ my grandparents.

   B: Okay, then _____ _____.

G: 민호야, 너 수학 숙제 끝냈니?
B: 아직. 수학은 어려워.
G: 맞아, 그렇지만 재미있기도 해.
B: 그럼 내 수학 숙제 좀 도와줄래?
G: 그러고 싶지만, 안 돼. 내 남동생을 돌봐야 해.

G: Alex, 나 다음 월요일에 노래 대회에 참가할 거야.
B: 대단하다, 수민아!
G: 너 기타 칠 줄 알지, 그렇지?
B: 응, 3년 동안 기타를 쳤어.
G: 잘됐다. 내가 대회에서 노래하는 동안 기타를 쳐 줄 수 있니?
B: 그러고 싶지만, 안 돼. 어제 체육 수업 중에 손을 다쳤어.
G: 오! 유감이다.
B: 고마워. 하지만 너를 응원하러 거기에 갈게.

1. A: 오후에 뭐 할 거니?
   B: 나는 자전거를 탈 거야. 같이 할래?
   A: 그러고 싶지만, 안 돼. 나는 숙제를 해야 해.
   B: 알겠어, 다음에 하자.

2. A: 오후에 뭐 할 거니?
   B: 나는 축구를 할 거야. 같이 할래?
   A: 그러고 싶지만, 안 돼. 나는 조부모님 댁을 방문해야 해.
   B: 알겠어, 다음에 하자.

Real Life Talk Watch a Video

Linda: Hi, Tony! _____ _____ _____ _____ to do this weekend?

Tony: I'm _____ _____ _____ the musical, *Billy Elliot*.

Linda: *Billy Elliot*? What is _____ _____?

Tony: It's _____ _____ _____ _____ _____ a famous dancer. I'm _____ _____ _____ _____ it.

Linda: Sounds _____. Who is the _____ _____?

Tony: Jason Kim. He's a great dancer.

Linda: He's my favorite actor. I _____ his musical _____ _____.

Tony: Oh, really? Do you _____ _____ _____ me?

Linda: I'd love to, _____ _____ _____. I have _____ work this weekend.

Tony: Okay. Maybe _____ time!

Linda: 안녕, Tony! 이번 주말에 뭐 할 거니?
Tony: 나는 뮤지컬 'Billy Elliot'를 볼 거야.
Linda: 'Billy Elliot'? 무슨 내용이니?
Tony: 유명한 무용수가 된 한 소년에 관한 내용이야. 그 뮤지컬을 볼 게 기대돼.
Linda: 재미있겠다. 주연 배우가 누구니?
Tony: Jason Kim이야. 그는 훌륭한 무용수야.
Linda: 그는 내가 가장 좋아하는 배우야. 작년에 그의 뮤지컬을 봤어.
Tony: 오, 정말? 나와 함께 가고 싶니?
Linda: 그러고 싶지만, 안 돼. 이번 주말에 자원봉사 활동이 있어.
Tony: 알겠어. 다음에 같이 가자!

Real Life Talk Step 2

1. **A:** What _____ you _____ _____ do first?

   B: _____ _____ _____ _____ _____ a parade at 10:30. I'm really _____ _____ _____ _____ it.

   A: Sounds _____.

   B: Do you want to join me?

   A: Yes, I'd _____ _____. / I'd love to, _____ _____ _____. I'm going to get _____ _____ _____ at that time.

2. **A:** What are you _____ _____ _____ _____ _____?

   B: I'm going to play a water balloon game _____ 12:30. _____ _____ _____ to _____ _____.

   A: _____ fun.

   B: Do you want _____ _____ me?

   A: Yes, I'd love to. / _____ _____ _____ _____, _____ I can't. I'm going to have the _____ hot dog at that time.

1. A: 처음에 무엇을 할 거니?
   B: 10시 30분에 퍼레이드를 볼 거야. 퍼레이드 보는 것이 정말 기대돼.
   A: 재미있겠다.
   B: 너도 같이 할래?
   A: 응, 그래. / 그러고 싶지만, 안 돼. 나는 그 때 얼굴에 페이스 페인팅을 할 거야.

2. A: 다음에 무엇을 할 거니?
   B: 물풍선 게임을 12시 30분에 할 거야. 나는 그것을 하는 것이 정말 기대돼.
   A: 재미있겠다.
   B: 너도 같이 할래?
   A: 응, 그래. / 그러고 싶지만, 안 돼. 나는 그 때 가장 긴 핫도그를 먹을 거야.

※ 다음 우리말에 맞도록 대화를 영어로 쓰시오.

Listen and Speak 1 A

B: _____

G: _____

B: _____

G: _____

B: 얘, 보라야. 우리 록 밴드에 온 걸 환영해.
G: 고마워. 공연에서 너희들과 함께 연주할 게 기대돼.
B: 우리는 새로운 기타 연주자를 갖게 되어서 신나.
G: 잘됐다. 금요일에 봐.

Listen and Speak 1 B

G: _____

B: _____

G: _____

B: _____

G: _____

B: _____

G: _____

B: _____

G: _____

G: 지호야, 뭘 읽고 있니?
B: Jim Abbott이라는 이름의 야구 선수에 관한 책을 읽고 있어.
G: 오, 오른손이 없이 태어난 사람?
B: 맞아. 그는 정말 열심히 노력해서 최우수 선수상까지 받았어.
G: 그래. 그의 이야기가 영화로 만들어졌어. 난 이번 주 토요일에 그 영화를 볼 거야.
B: 정말? 제목이 뭐니?
G: 'Our Hero'야. 그 영화를 볼 게 정말 기대돼.
B: 나도 너와 함께해도 될까?
G: 물론이지. 토요일에 봐.

Listen and Speak 1 C

1. A: _____

   B: _____

   A: _____

   B: _____

2. A: _____

   B: _____

   A: _____

   B: _____

3. A: _____

   B: _____

   A: _____

   B: _____

1. A: 너 오늘 행복해 보인다. 무슨 일이야?
   B: 나는 아주 신나. 제주도로 여행을 갈 거야.
   A: 좋겠다!
   B: 응, 나는 말 타기를 정말 고대하고 있어.

2. A: 너 오늘 행복해 보인다. 무슨 일이야?
   B: 나는 아주 신나. 드론을 날리는 것을 배울 거야.
   A: 좋겠다!
   B: 응. 공원에서 드론을 날리는 것이 정말 기대돼.

3. A: 너 오늘 행복해 보인다. 무슨 일이야?
   B: 나는 아주 신나. Jackson의 콘서트를 볼 거야.
   A: 좋겠다!
   B: 응. Jackson의 공연을 보는 것이 정말 기대돼.

Listen and Speak 2 A

G: _____

B: _____

G: _____

B: _____

G: _____

G: 민호야, 너 수학 숙제 끝냈니?
B: 아직. 수학은 어려워.
G: 맞아, 그렇지만 재미있기도 해.
B: 그럼 내 수학 숙제 좀 도와줄래?
G: 그러고 싶지만, 안 돼. 내 남동생을 돌봐야 해.

Listen and Speak 2 B

G: _____

B: _____

G: _____

B: _____

G: _____

B: _____

G: _____

B: _____

G: Alex, 나 다음 월요일에 노래 대회에 참가할 거야.
B: 대단하다, 수민아!
G: 너 기타 칠 줄 알지, 그렇지?
B: 응, 3년 동안 기타를 쳤어.
G: 잘됐다. 내가 대회에서 노래하는 동안 기타를 쳐 줄 수 있니?
B: 그러고 싶지만, 안 돼. 어제 체육 수업 중에 손을 다쳤어.
G: 오! 유감이다.
B: 고마워. 하지만 너를 응원하러 거기에 갈게.

Listen and Speak 2 C

1. A: _____

   B: _____

   A: _____

   B: _____

2. A: _____

   B: _____

   A: _____

   B: _____

1. A: 오후에 뭐 할 거니?
   B: 나는 자전거를 탈 거야. 같이 할래?
   A: 그러고 싶지만, 안 돼. 나는 숙제를 해야 해.
   B: 알겠어, 다음에 하자.

2. A: 오후에 뭐 할 거니?
   B: 나는 축구를 할 거야. 같이 할래?
   A: 그러고 싶지만, 안 돼. 나는 조부모님 댁을 방문해야 해.
   B: 알겠어, 다음에 하자.

Real Life Talk Watch a Video

Linda: _____

Tony: _____

Linda: _____

Tony: _____

_____

Linda: _____

Tony: _____

Linda: _____

Tony: _____

Linda: _____

Tony: _____

Linda: 안녕, Tony! 이번 주말에 뭐 할 거니?

Tony: 나는 뮤지컬 'Billy Elliot'를 볼 거야.

Linda: 'Billy Elliot'? 무슨 내용이니?

Tony: 유명한 무용수가 된 한 소년에 관한 내용이야. 그 뮤지컬을 볼 게 기대돼.

Linda: 재미있겠다. 주연 배우가 누구니?

Tony: Jason Kim이야. 그는 훌륭한 무용수야.

Linda: 그는 내가 가장 좋아하는 배우야. 작년에 그의 뮤지컬을 봤어.

Tony: 오, 정말? 나와 함께 가고 싶니?

Linda: 그러고 싶지만, 안 돼. 이번 주말에 자원봉사 활동이 있어.

Tony: 알겠어. 다음에 같이 가자!

Real Life Talk Step 2

1. A: _____

B: _____

_____

A: _____

B: _____

A: _____

_____

2. A: _____

B: _____

_____

A: _____

B: _____

A: _____

_____

1. A: 처음에 무엇을 할 거니?
   B: 10시 30분에 퍼레이드를 볼 거야. 퍼레이드 보는 것이 정말 기대돼.
   A: 재미있겠다.
   B: 너도 같이 할래?
   A: 응, 그래. / 그러고 싶지만, 안 돼. 나는 그 때 얼굴에 페이스 페인팅을 할 거야.

2. A: 다음에 무엇을 할 거니?
   B: 물풍선 게임을 12시 30분에 할 거야. 나는 그것을 하는 것이 정말 기대돼.
   A: 재미있겠다.
   B: 너도 같이 할래?
   A: 응, 그래. / 그러고 싶지만, 안 돼. 나는 그 때 가장 긴 핫도그를 먹을 거야.

※ 다음 우리말과 일치하도록 빈칸에 알맞은 것을 골라 쓰시오.

1 From _____ _____ _____
A. Music   B. to   C. Trash

2 _____ of _____ are _____ _____ my cheeks.
A. down   B. joy   C. rolling   D. tears

3 I'm _____ _____ and _____ .
A. happy   B. so   C. thrilled

4 If I _____ a bird, I _____ _____ .
A. would   B. were   C. fly

5 I _____ _____ .
A. around   B. look

6 The _____ members in my orchestra are _____
_____ .
A. another   B. other   C. hugging   D. one

7 Our concert _____ just _____ and everyone is standing and
_____ us a big _____ .
A. finished   B. hand   C. has   D. giving

8 _____ of us _____ _____ that this day _____ come.
A. expected   B. none   C. ever   D. would

9 It _____ _____ a _____ _____ .
A. journey   B. long   C. been   D. has

10 My _____ is Andrea and I'm _____ _____ _____ the
Recycled Orchestra.
A. in   B. violinist   C. name   D. a

11 _____ _____ _____ _____ _____ the Recycled Orchestra?
A. it   B. why   C. called   D. it

12 It's _____ our musical instruments are _____ _____
objects _____ a landfill.
A. made   B. because   C. from   D. of

13 That's _____ it's _____ _____ _____ the Landfill
Harmonic Orchestra.
A. as   B. why   C. known   D. also

14 _____ of _____ in the orchestra _____ _____ Cateura, a
small town in Paraguay.
A. most   B. from   C. us   D. are

1 쓰레기를 음악으로

2 기쁨의 눈물이 내 볼에 흘러내리고 있다.

3 나는 정말 기쁘고 황홀하다.

4 내가 새라면, 날아오를 텐데.

5 나는 주변을 본다.

6 우리 오케스트라의 다른 단원들은 서로 껴안고 있다.

7 우리의 공연은 이제 막 끝났고 모든 사람들이 서서 우리에게 큰 박수를 보내고 있다.

8 우리 중 아무도 이 날이 올 거라고 예상하지 못했다.

9 긴 여정이었다.

10 내 이름은 Andrea이고 나는 Recycled Orchestra의 바이올리니스트이다.

11 오케스트라가 왜 Recycled Orchestra라고 불리냐고?

12 그것은 우리의 악기들이 쓰레기 매립지에서 나온 물건들로 만들어지기 때문이다.

13 그것이 오케스트라가 Landfill Harmonic Orchestra로도 알려진 이유이다.

14 오케스트라의 우리들 대부분은 파라과이의 작은 마을인 카테우라 출신이다.

15 _____ is a _____ _____ in our _____.

A. landfill   B. huge   C. town   D. there

16 Some people _____ say that Cateura _____ is a _____
_____.

A. itself   B. giant   C. even   D. landfill

17 _____ of _____ are _____.

A. us   B. many   C. poor

18 There _____ _____ _____ and _____ in our town.

A. many   B. dreams   C. hopes   D. weren't

19 Everything _____ to _____, _____, when we _____
Favio Chávez.

A. change   B. met   C. began   D. however

20 Favio was _____ _____ _____ and a _____.

A. environment   B. musician   C. educator   D. an

21 He wanted to _____ _____ _____, but there was a big
_____.

A. teach   B. problem   C. music   D. us

22 There were _____ a _____ musical _____ in the
_____ town.

A. whole   B. few   C. only   D. instruments

23 We _____ _____ _____ buy new _____.

A. to   B. afford   C. couldn't   D. ones

24 But Favio _____ _____ _____.

A. give   B. didn't   C. up

25 He said that we could make musical instruments _____
_____ _____ the _____.

A. objects   B. landfill   C. with   D. from

26 A talented man _____ Nicholas was able to _____ this idea
_____ _____.

A. put   B. practice   C. named   D. into

27 He _____ violins _____ oil _____.

A. from   B. made   C. drums

15 우리 마을에는 거대한 쓰레기 매립지가 있다.

16 몇몇 사람들은 심지어 카테우라 자체가 거대한 쓰레기 매립지라고 말한다.

17 우리들 중 많은 이들이 가난하다.

18 우리 마을에는 꿈과 희망이 많지 않았다.

19 그러나 우리가 Favio Chávez 선생님을 만났을 때 모든 것이 바뀌기 시작했다.

20 Favio 선생님은 환경 교육가이자 음악가였다.

21 그는 우리에게 음악을 가르치고 싶어 했지만, 큰 문제가 있었다.

22 온 마을에 악기가 단지 몇 개뿐이었다.

23 우리는 새 악기를 살 형편도 아니었다.

24 그러나 Favio 선생님은 포기하지 않았다.

25 그는 우리가 쓰레기 매립지의 물건들로 악기를 만들 수 있다고 말했다.

26 재능이 많은 Nicholas 아저씨가 이 생각을 실행에 옮길 수 있었다.

27 그는 기름통으로 바이올린을 만들었다.

28 He _____ water pipes _____ _____.

A. into   B. turned   C. flutes

29 We _____ _____ _____.

A. problem   B. had   C. another

30 _____ one knew _____ _____ _____ musical instruments.

A. no   B. to   C. how   D. play

31 We didn't _____ know _____ _____ _____ music.

A. to   B. even   C. read   D. how

32 Favio taught us _____ _____ _____.

A. great   B. with   C. patience

33 Step _____ _____, we began to make some _____ on our _____.

A. sounds   B. step   C. by   D. instruments

34 I still _____ the first _____ of _____ that we _____.

A. piece   B. played   C. remember   D. music

35 It was very _____ and _____ _____ of _____.

A. tune   B. mostly   C. short   D. out

36 But it was _____ _____ _____ _____ to us.

A. beautiful   B. the   C. music   D. most

37 We _____ a _____ _____ in our _____.

A. hearts   B. new   C. hope   D. felt

38 _____ _____ _____, we _____ to practice every day.

A. gathered   B. then   C. from   D. on

39 _____ day, Favio told us _____ _____ _____.

A. great   B. one   C. news   D. some

40 We _____ _____ _____ _____ a concert, a real concert!

A. have   B. going   C. were   D. to

41 And here we are now in _____ of _____ _____ _____.

A. front   B. of   C. people   D. hundreds

42 They _____ _____ _____.

A. our   B. love   C. music

43 The world _____ _____ _____, but we send _____ music!

A. trash   B. back   C. us   D. sends

---

28 그는 수도관을 플루트로 바꾸었다.

29 우리에게 또 다른 문제가 있었다.

30 아무도 악기를 연주할 줄 몰랐다.

31 우리는 심지어 악보를 읽는 방법도 알지 못했다.

32 Favio 선생님은 엄청난 인내심으로 우리를 가르쳤다.

33 점차로, 우리는 악기로 어떤 소리를 만들어 내기 시작했다.

34 나는 아직도 우리가 연주했던 첫 곡을 기억한다.

35 그 곡은 매우 짧고 대부분은 음이 맞지 않았다.

36 그러나 그것은 우리에게 가장 아름다운 곡이었다.

37 우리는 마음속에 새로운 희망을 느꼈다.

38 그때부터, 우리는 매일 연습을 하기 위해 모였다.

39 어느 날, Favio 선생님은 우리에게 엄청난 소식을 말해 줬다.

40 우리는 공연을, 진짜 공연을 하게 될 것이었다!

41 그리고 여기 우리는 지금 수백 명의 사람들 앞에 있다.

42 그들은 우리의 음악을 사랑한다.

43 세상은 우리에게 쓰레기를 보내지만, 우리는 음악을 돌려보낸다!

※ 다음 우리말과 일치하도록 빈칸에 알맞은 것을 골라 쓰시오.

1 From _____ to _____

2 _____ _____ _____ are _____ _____ my cheeks.

3 I'm so happy and _____.

4 If I _____ a bird, I _____ _____.

5 I _____ _____.

6 _____ _____ _____ in my orchestra are hugging _____ _____.

7 Our concert _____ _____ _____ and everyone is standing and _____ _____ _____ _____ _____.

8 _____ of us _____ _____ that this day would come.

9 _____ _____ _____ a long _____.

10 My name is Andrea and _____ _____ _____ in the Recycled Orchestra.

11 _____ _____ _____ _____ the Recycled Orchestra?

12 It's _____ our musical instruments _____ _____ _____ objects _____ a _____.

13 _____ _____ it's also _____ _____ the Landfill Harmonic Orchestra.

14 _____ _____ us in the orchestra _____ _____ Cateura, a small town in Paraguay.

1 쓰레기를 음악으로

2 기쁨의 눈물이 내 볼에 흘러내리고 있다.

3 나는 정말 기쁘고 황홀하다.

4 내가 새라면, 날아오를 텐데.

5 나는 주변을 본다.

6 우리 오케스트라의 다른 단원들은 서로 껴안고 있다.

7 우리의 공연은 이제 막 끝났고 모든 사람들이 서서 우리에게 큰 박수를 보내고 있다.

8 우리 중 아무도 이 날이 올 거라고 예상하지 못했다.

9 긴 여정이었다.

10 내 이름은 Andrea이고 나는 Recycled Orchestra의 바이올리니스트이다.

11 오케스트라가 왜 Recycled Orchestra라고 불리냐고?

12 그것은 우리의 악기들이 쓰레기 매립지에서 나온 물건들로 만들어지기 때문이다.

13 그것이 오케스트라가 Landfill Harmonic Orchestra로도 알려진 이유이다.

14 오케스트라의 우리들 대부분은 파라과이의 작은 마을인 카테우라 출신이다.

15 There is _____ _____ _____ in our town.

16 Some people even say that Cateura _____ is a _____ _____.

17 _____ _____ _____ are _____.

18 There weren't _____ _____ _____ _____ in our town.

19 Everything _____ _____ _____, _____, when we met Favio Chávez.

20 Favio was _____ _____ and a _____.

21 He wanted to _____ _____ _____, but there was a big problem.

22 There were _____ _____ _____ musical instruments in the _____ _____.

23 We _____ _____ _____ buy new ones.

24 But Favio didn't _____ _____.

25 He said that we could make musical instruments _____ _____ _____ _____ _____.

26 A talented man _____ Nicholas _____ _____ _____ this idea _____ _____.

27 He _____ violins _____ oil drums.

---

15 우리 마을에는 거대한 쓰레기 매립지가 있다.

16 몇몇 사람들은 심지어 카테우라 자체가 거대한 쓰레기 매립지라고 말한다.

17 우리들 중 많은 이들이 가난하다.

18 우리 마을에는 꿈과 희망이 많지 않았다.

19 그러나 우리가 Favio Chávez 선생님을 만났을 때 모든 것이 바뀌기 시작했다.

20 Favio 선생님은 환경 교육가이자 음악가였다.

21 그는 우리에게 음악을 가르치고 싶어 했지만, 큰 문제가 있었다.

22 온 마을에 악기가 단지 몇 개뿐이었다.

23 우리는 새 악기를 살 형편도 아니었다.

24 그러나 Favio 선생님은 포기하지 않았다.

25 그는 우리가 쓰레기 매립지의 물건들로 악기를 만들 수 있다고 말했다.

26 재능이 많은 Nicholas 아저씨가 이 생각을 실행에 옮길 수 있었다.

27 그는 기름통으로 바이올린을 만들었다.

28 He _____ water pipes _____ flutes.

29 We had _____ _____.

30 No one knew _____ _____ _____ musical instruments.

31 We didn't even know _____ _____ _____ music.

32 Favio _____ us _____ _____ _____.

33 _____ _____ _____, we began to make some sounds on our instruments.

34 I still remember _____ _____ _____ _____ _____ that we _____.

35 It was very short and _____ _____ _____ _____.

36 But it was _____ _____ _____ to us.

37 We _____ _____ _____ _____ in our hearts.

38 _____ _____ _____, we _____ _____ _____ every day.

39 One day, Favio told us _____ _____ _____.

40 We _____ _____ _____ _____ a concert, a real concert!

41 And here we are now in _____ of _____ _____ _____.

42 They love _____ _____.

43 The world _____ _____ _____, but we _____ _____ _____!

28 그는 수도관을 플루트로 바꾸었다.

29 우리에게 또 다른 문제가 있었다.

30 아무도 악기를 연주할 줄 몰랐다.

31 우리는 심지어 악보를 읽는 방법도 알지 못했다.

32 Favio 선생님은 엄청난 인내심으로 우리를 가르쳤다.

33 점차로, 우리는 악기로 어떤 소리를 만들어 내기 시작했다.

34 나는 아직도 우리가 연주했던 첫 곡을 기억한다.

35 그 곡은 매우 짧고 대부분은 음이 맞지 않았다.

36 그러나 그것은 우리에게 가장 아름다운 곡이었다.

37 우리는 마음속에 새로운 희망을 느꼈다.

38 그때부터, 우리는 매일 연습을 하기 위해 모였다.

39 어느 날, Favio 선생님은 우리에게 엄청난 소식을 말해 줬다.

40 우리는 공연을, 진짜 공연을 하게 될 것이었다!

41 그리고 여기 우리는 지금 수백 명의 사람들 앞에 있다.

42 그들은 우리의 음악을 사랑한다.

43 세상은 우리에게 쓰레기를 보내지만, 우리는 음악을 돌려보낸다!

※ 다음 문장을 우리말로 쓰시오.

1 ▸ From Trash to Music

➡ _____

2 ▸ Tears of joy are rolling down my cheeks.

➡ _____

3 ▸ I'm so happy and thrilled.

➡ _____

4 ▸ If I were a bird, I would fly.

➡ _____

5 ▸ I look around.

➡ _____

6 ▸ The other members in my orchestra are hugging one another.

➡ _____

7 ▸ Our concert has just finished and everyone is standing and giving us a big hand.

➡ _____

8 ▸ None of us ever expected that this day would come.

➡ _____

9 ▸ It has been a long journey.

➡ _____

10 ▸ My name is Andrea and I'm a violinist in the Recycled Orchestra.

➡ _____

11 ▸ Why is it called the Recycled Orchestra?

➡ _____

12 ▸ It's because our musical instruments are made of objects from a landfill.

➡ _____

13 ▸ That's why it's also known as the Landfill Harmonic Orchestra.

➡ _____

14 ▸ Most of us in the orchestra are from Cateura, a small town in Paraguay.

➡ _____

15 There is a huge landfill in our town.

➡ _____

16 Some people even say that Cateura itself is a giant landfill.

➡ _____

17 Many of us are poor.

➡ _____

18 There weren't many hopes and dreams in our town.

➡ _____

19 Everything began to change, however, when we met Favio Chávez.

➡ _____

20 Favio was an environmental educator and a musician.

➡ _____

21 He wanted to teach us music, but there was a big problem.

➡ _____

22 There were only a few musical instruments in the whole town.

➡ _____

23 We couldn't afford to buy new ones.

➡ _____

24 But Favio didn't give up.

➡ _____

25 He said that we could make musical instruments with objects from the landfill.

➡ _____

26 A talented man named Nicholas was able to put this idea into practice.

➡ _____

27 He made violins from oil drums.

➡ _____

28 He turned water pipes into flutes.

➡ _____

29 We had another problem.

➡ _____

30 No one knew how to play musical instruments.

➡ _____

31 We didn't even know how to read music.

➡ _____

32 Favio taught us with great patience.

➡ _____

33 Step by step, we began to make some sounds on our instruments.

➡ _____

34 I still remember the first piece of music that we played.

➡ _____

35 It was very short and mostly out of tune.

➡ _____

36 But it was the most beautiful music to us.

➡ _____

37 We felt a new hope in our hearts.

➡ _____

38 From then on, we gathered to practice every day.

➡ _____

39 One day, Favio told us some great news.

➡ _____

40 We were going to have a concert, a real concert!

➡ _____

41 And here we are now in front of hundreds of people.

➡ _____

42 They love our music.

➡ _____

43 The world sends us trash, but we send back music!

➡ _____

※ 다음 괄호 안의 단어들을 우리말에 맞도록 바르게 배열하시오.

1 (Trash / From / Music / to)
➡ _____

2 (of / tears / are / joy / down / rolling / cheeks. / my)
➡ _____

3 (so / I'm / thrilled. / and / happy)
➡ _____

4 (I / if / were / bird, / a / would / I / fly.)
➡ _____

5 (look / I / around.)
➡ _____

6 (other / the / in / members / orchestra / my / hugging / are / another. / one)
➡ _____

7 (concert / our / just / as / finished / and / is / everyone / standing / giving / and / a / us / hand. / big)
➡ _____

8 (of / none / us / expected / ever / this / that / day / come. / would)
➡ _____

9 (has / it / a / been / journey. / long)
➡ _____

10 (name / my / Andrea / is / and / a / I'm / in / violinist / the / Orchestra. / Recycled)
➡ _____

11 (is / why / called / it / Recycled / the / Orchestra?)
➡ _____

12 (because / it's / musical / our / are / instruments / of / made / from / objects / landfill. / a)
➡ _____

13 (why / that's / also / it's / as / known / the / Harmonic / Landfill / Orchestra.)
➡ _____

14 (of / most / in / us / the / are / orchestra / Cateura, / from / small / a / town / Paraguay. / in)
➡ _____

1 쓰레기를 음악으로

2 기쁨의 눈물이 내 볼에 흘러내리고 있다.

3 나는 정말 기쁘고 황홀하다.

4 내가 새라면, 날아오를 텐데.

5 나는 주변을 본다.

6 우리 오케스트라의 다른 단원들은 서로 껴안고 있다.

7 우리의 공연은 이제 막 끝났고 모든 사람들이 서서 우리에게 큰 박수를 보내고 있다.

8 우리 중 아무도 이 날이 올 거고 예상하지 못했다.

9 긴 여정이었다.

10 내 이름은 Andrea이고 나는 Recycled Orchestra의 바이올리니스트이다.

11 오케스트라가 왜 Recycled Orchestra라고 불리냐고?

12 그것은 우리의 악기들이 쓰레기 매립지에서 나온 물건들로 만들어지기 때문이다.

13 그것이 오케스트라가 Landfill Harmonic Orchestra로도 알려진 이유이다.

14 오케스트라의 우리들 대부분은 파라과이의 작은 마을인 카테우라 출신이다.

15 (is / there / huge / a / landfill / our / in / town.)

➡ _____

16 (people / some / say / even / that / itself / Cateura / a / is / landfill. / giant)

➡ _____

17 (of / many / us / poor. / are)

➡ _____

18 (weren't / there / hopes / many / and / in / dreams / town. / our)

➡ _____

19 (began / everything / change, / to / however, / we / when / Favio / met / Chávez)

➡ _____

20 (Favio / an / was / educator / environmental / and / musician. / a)

➡ _____

21 (wanted / he / teach / to / music, / us / there / but / a / was / problem. / big)

➡ _____

22 (were / there / a / only / musical / few / in / instruments / the / town. / whole)

➡ _____

23 (couldn't / we / to / afford / new / buy / ones.)

➡ _____

24 (Favio / but / give / didn't / up.)

➡ _____

25 (said / he / we / that / make / could / instruments / musical / objects / with / the / from / landfill.)

➡ _____

26 (talented / a / named / man / was / Nicholas / to / able / put / idea / this / practice. / into)

➡ _____

27 (made / he / from / violins / drums. / oil)

➡ _____

15 우리 마을에는 거대한 쓰레기 매립지가 있다.

16 몇몇 사람들은 심지어 카테우라 자체가 거대한 쓰레기 매립지라고 말한다.

17 우리들 중 많은 이들이 가난하다.

18 우리 마을에는 꿈과 희망이 많지 않았다.

19 그러나 우리가 Favio Chávez 선생님을 만났을 때 모든 것이 바뀌기 시작했다.

20 Favio 선생님은 환경 교육가이자 음악가였다.

21 그는 우리에게 음악을 가르치고 싶어 했지만, 큰 문제가 있었다.

22 온 마을에 악기가 단지 몇 개뿐이었다.

23 우리는 새 악기를 살 형편도 아니었다.

24 그러나 Favio 선생님은 포기하지 않았다.

25 그는 우리가 쓰레기 매립지의 물건들로 악기를 만들 수 있다고 말했다.

26 재능이 많은 Nicholas 아저씨가 이 생각을 실행에 옮길 수 있었다.

27 그는 기름통으로 바이올린을 만들었다.

28 (turned / he / pipes / water / flutes. / into)

➡ _____

29 (had / we / problem. / another)

➡ _____

30 (one / no / how / knew / play / to / instruments. / musical)

➡ _____

31 (didn't / we / know / even / to / how / music. / read)

➡ _____

32 (taught / Favio / with / us / patience. / great)

➡ _____

33 (by / step / we / step, / to / began / make / sounds / some / our / on / instruments.)

➡ _____

34 (still / I / the / remember / piece / first / music / of / we / that / played.)

➡ _____

35 (was / it / short / very / and / out / mostly / tune. / of)

➡ _____

36 (it / but / the / was / beautiful / most / music / us. / to)

➡ _____

37 (felt / we / new / a / in / hope / hearts. / our)

➡ _____

38 (then / from / on, / gathered / we / practice / to / day. / every)

➡ _____

39 (day, / one / told / Favio / some / us / news. / great)

➡ _____

40 (were / we / to / going / a / have / concert, / real / a / concert!)

➡ _____

41 (here / and / are / we / in / now / front / hundreads / of / people. / of)

➡ _____

42 (love / they / music. / our)

➡ _____

43 (world / the / us / sends / trash, / we / but / back / send / music!)

➡ _____

28 그는 수도관을 플루트로 바꾸었다.

29 우리에게 또 다른 문제가 있었다.

30 아무도 악기를 연주할 줄 몰랐다.

31 우리는 심지어 악보를 읽는 방법도 알지 못했다.

32 Favio 선생님은 엄청난 인내심으로 우리를 가르쳤다.

33 점차로, 우리는 악기로 어떤 소리를 만들어 내기 시작했다.

34 나는 아직도 우리가 연주했던 첫 곡을 기억한다.

35 그 곡은 매우 짧고 대부분은 음이 맞지 않았다.

36 그러나 그것은 우리에게 가장 아름다운 곡이었다.

37 우리는 마음속에 새로운 희망을 느꼈다.

38 그때부터, 우리는 매일 연습을 하기 위해 모였다.

39 어느 날, Favio 선생님은 우리에게 엄청난 소식을 말해 줬다.

40 우리는 공연을, 진짜 공연을 하게 될 것이었다!

41 그리고 여기 우리는 지금 수백 명의 사람들 앞에 있다.

42 그들은 우리의 음악을 사랑한다.

43 세상은 우리에게 쓰레기를 보내지만, 우리는 음악을 돌려보낸다!

※ 다음 우리말을 영어로 쓰시오.

1 쓰레기를 음악으로

➡ _____

2 기쁨의 눈물이 내 볼에 흘러내리고 있다.

➡ _____

3 나는 정말 기쁘고 황홀하다.

➡ _____

4 내가 새라면, 날아오를 텐데.

➡ _____

5 나는 주변을 본다.

➡ _____

6 우리 오케스트라의 다른 단원들은 서로 껴안고 있다.

➡ _____

7 우리의 공연은 이제 막 끝났고 모든 사람들이 서서 우리에게 큰 박수를 보내고 있다.

➡ _____

8 우리 중 아무도 이 날이 올 거라고 예상하지 못했다.

➡ _____

9 긴 여정이었다.

➡ _____

10 내 이름은 Andrea이고 나는 Recycled Orchestra의 바이올리니스트이다.

➡ _____

11 오케스트라가 왜 Recycled Orchestra라고 불리냐고?

➡ _____

12 그것은 우리의 악기들이 쓰레기 매립지에서 나온 물건들로 만들어지기 때문이다.

➡ _____

13 그것이 오케스트라가 Landfill Harmonic Orchestra로도 알려진 이유이다.

➡ _____

14 오케스트라의 우리들 대부분은 파라과이의 작은 마을인 카테우라 출신이다.

➡ _____

15 우리 마을에는 거대한 쓰레기 매립지가 있다.

➡ _____

16 몇몇 사람들은 심지어 카테우라 자체가 거대한 쓰레기 매립지라고 말한다.

➡ _____

17 우리들 중 많은 이들이 가난하다.

➡ _____

18 우리 마을에는 꿈과 희망이 많지 않았다.

➡ _____

19 그러나 우리가 Favio Chávez 선생님을 만났을 때 모든 것이 바뀌기 시작했다.

➡ _____

20 Favio 선생님은 환경 교육가이자 음악가였다.

➡ _____

21 그는 우리에게 음악을 가르치고 싶어 했지만, 큰 문제가 있었다.

➡ _____

22 온 마을에 악기가 단지 몇 개뿐이었다.

➡ _____

23 우리는 새 악기를 살 형편도 아니었다.

➡ _____

24 그러나 Favio 선생님은 포기하지 않았다.

➡ _____

25 그는 우리가 쓰레기 매립지의 물건들로 악기를 만들 수 있다고 말했다.

➡ _____

26 재능이 많은 Nicholas 아저씨가 이 생각을 실행에 옮길 수 있었다.

➡ _____

27 그는 기름통으로 바이올린을 만들었다.

➡ _____

28 그는 수도관을 플루트로 바꾸었다.

➡ _____

29 우리에게 또 다른 문제가 있었다.

➡ _____

30 아무도 악기를 연주할 줄 몰랐다.

➡ _____

31 우리는 심지어 악보를 읽는 방법도 알지 못했다.

➡ _____

32 Favio 선생님은 엄청난 인내심으로 우리를 가르쳤다.

➡ _____

33 점차로, 우리는 악기로 어떤 소리를 만들어 내기 시작했다.

➡ _____

34 나는 아직도 우리가 연주했던 첫 곡을 기억한다.

➡ _____

35 그 곡은 매우 짧고 대부분은 음이 맞지 않았다.

➡ _____

36 그러나 그것은 우리에게 가장 아름다운 곡이었다.

➡ _____

37 우리는 마음속에 새로운 희망을 느꼈다.

➡ _____

38 그때부터, 우리는 매일 연습을 하기 위해 모였다.

➡ _____

39 어느 날, Favio 선생님은 우리에게 엄청난 소식을 말해 줬다.

➡ _____

40 우리는 공연을, 진짜 공연을 하게 될 것이었다!

➡ _____

41 그리고 여기 우리는 지금 수백 명의 사람들 앞에 있다.

➡ _____

42 그들은 우리의 음악을 사랑한다.

➡ _____

43 세상은 우리에게 쓰레기를 보내지만, 우리는 음악을 돌려보낸다!

➡ _____

※ 다음 우리말과 일치하도록 빈칸에 알맞은 말을 쓰시오.

After You Read B

1. Reporter: Congratulations! How do you _____ now?
2. Andrea: I _____ _____. We _____ _____ our _____ _____.
3. Reporter: _____ is the orchestra _____ the Recycled Orchestra?
4. Andrea: _____ _____ our _____ _____ _____ _____ _____ objects _____ _____ _____ _____.
5. Reporter: That's _____.
6. Andrea: Yeah. _____ _____ us knew _____ _____ _____ _____ _____, but Favio taught us _____ _____ _____.
7. Reporter: That is a _____ _____.

Think and Write

1. _____ _____ Yi Sun-sin,
2. I'm Sumin. I really _____ you _____ you never _____ _____ _____ _____ _____ _____.
3. You _____ the _____ and the people.
4. _____ was amazing _____ you _____ the battle _____ _____ _____ _____.
5. _____ I _____ a time machine, I _____ _____ you!
6. I'd _____ _____ _____ you _____ _____ _____ geobukseon.
7. You're _____ _____. Thank you.
8. _____ yours,

　　　　　　　　　　　　　　　　　　　　　Sumin

Project Step 3

1. This is a _____ _____.
2. _____ _____ it, you need _____ _____ and _____.
3. _____ the bottle and _____ the buttons _____ _____ _____.
4. _____ the bottle and _____ _____ _____.
5. You _____ _____ _____ _____ _____ _____ _____ rice or sand in _____.
6. _____ items make _____ _____.
7. _____ _____ my _____ _____ _____.

---

1. 리포터: 축하합니다. 지금 기분이 어떠세요?
2. Andrea: 나는 아주 황홀해요. 우리는 막 첫 번째 공연을 했어요.
3. 리포터: 오케스트라가 왜 Recycled Orchestra라고 불립니까?
4. Andrea: 그것은 우리의 악기들이 쓰레기 매립지에서 나온 물건들로 만들어지기 때문입니다.
5. 리포터: 그것은 놀랍군요.
6. Andrea: 네, 우리들 중 아무도 악기를 연주할 줄 몰랐지만, Favio 선생님은 엄청난 인내심으로 우리를 가르치셨어요.
7. 리포터: 멋있는 이야기입니다.

1. 이순신 장군님께,
2. 저는 수민이에요. 저는 당신이 어려운 상황에서 결코 포기하지 않았기 때문에 당신을 정말 존경해요.
3. 당신은 나라와 국민을 구했어요.
4. 단지 12척의 배로 전투를 이긴 것은 놀라웠어요.
5. 제게 타임머신이 있다면, 저는 당신을 만나러 갈 텐데요!
6. 저는 당신에게 거북선을 어떻게 만드는지를 묻고 싶어요.
7. 당신은 제 영웅이에요. 감사합니다.
8. 존경을 담아,

　　　　　　　　　　수민이가

1. 이것은 병 셰이커야.
2. 그것을 만들려면 너는 병 하나와 단추들이 필요해.
3. 병을 씻고 단추들을 병 속에 넣어.
4. 병을 닫고 그것을 장식해.
5. 너는 또한 쌀이나 모래 같은 다른 것들을 안에 넣을 수 있어.
6. 다른 물건들은 다른 소리들을 만들어 내.
7. 내 모둠의 병 셰이커 소리를 들어 봐.

구석구석 지문 Test

※ **다음 우리말을 영어로 쓰시오.**

After You Read B

1. 리포터: 축하합니다. 지금 기분이 어떠세요?
   ➡ _____

2. Andrea: 나는 아주 황홀해요. 우리는 막 첫 번째 공연을 했어요.
   ➡ _____

3. 리포터: 오케스트라가 왜 Recycled Orchestra라고 불립니까?
   ➡ _____

4. Andrea: 그것은 우리의 악기들이 쓰레기 매립지에서 나온 물건들로 만들어지기 때문입니다.
   ➡ _____

5. 리포터: 그것은 놀랍군요.
   ➡ _____

6. Andrea: 네, 우리들 중 아무도 악기를 연주할 줄 몰랐지만, Favio 선생님은 엄청난 인내심으로 우리를 가르치셨어요.
   ➡ _____

7. 리포터: 멋있는 이야기입니다.
   ➡ _____

Think and Write

1. 이순신 장군님께,
   ➡ _____

2. 저는 수민이에요. 저는 당신이 어려운 상황에서 결코 포기하지 않았기 때문에 당신을 정말 존경해요.
   ➡ _____

3. 당신은 나라와 국민을 구했어요.
   ➡ _____

4. 단지 12척의 배로 전투를 이긴 것은 놀라웠어요.
   ➡ _____

5. 제게 타임머신이 있다면, 저는 당신을 만나러 갈 텐데요!
   ➡ _____

6. 저는 당신에게 거북선을 어떻게 만드는지를 묻고 싶어요.
   ➡ _____

7. 당신은 제 영웅이에요. 감사합니다.
   ➡ _____

8. 존경을 담아,   수민이가
   ➡ _____

Project Step 3

1. 이것은 병 셰이커야.
   ➡ _____

2. 그것을 만들려면 너는 병 하나와 단추들이 필요해.
   ➡ _____

3. 병을 씻고 단추들을 병 속에 넣어.
   ➡ _____

4. 병을 닫고 그것을 장식해.
   ➡ _____

5. 너는 또한 쌀이나 모래 같은 다른 것들을 안에 넣을 수 있어.
   ➡ _____

6. 다른 물건들은 다른 소리들을 만들어 내.
   ➡ _____

7. 내 모둠의 병 셰이커 소리를 들어 봐.
   ➡ _____

※ 다음 영어를 우리말로 쓰시오.

01 total _____

02 expression _____

03 feed _____

04 tourist attraction _____

05 wave _____

06 protect _____

07 remind _____

08 architect _____

09 lend _____

10 inspiration _____

11 artwork _____

12 closely _____

13 pleasing _____

14 column _____

15 delicate _____

16 actually _____

17 beauty _____

18 exhibit _____

19 natural _____

20 obvious _____

21 peel _____

22 exist _____

23 imitate _____

24 basic _____

25 giant _____

26 contents _____

27 curved _____

28 imagination _____

29 shape _____

30 book _____

31 capture _____

32 inspire _____

33 roof _____

34 recommend _____

35 try to ~ _____

36 show A around B _____

37 I can't wait to ~! _____

38 enough to ~ _____

39 be on sale _____

40 look like ~ _____

41 That's how ~. _____

42 Thank you for ~. _____

43 Do you mind if ~? _____

※ 다음 우리말을 영어로 쓰시오.

01	빌려주다	22	상상력
02	표현	23	예약하다, 예매하다
03	예술품, 예술작품	24	거대한; 거인
04	기본적인	25	파도, 물결
05	실제로, 정말로	26	담아내다, 포착하다
06	존재하다	27	우주선
07	먹이를 주다	28	자연
08	민속 마을, 민속촌	29	보호하다
09	건축가, 설계자	30	형태
10	전시하다	31	분명한, 명백한
11	추천하다	32	(과일·채소의) 껍질
12	아름다움	33	총, 전체의
13	섬세한, 부서지기 쉬운	34	영감을 주다
14	상기시키다, 생각나게 하다	35	~에 관하여 듣다
15	곡선 모양의, 굽은	36	~하도록 허가되다
16	모방하다	37	~할 만큼 충분히
17	영감	38	(할인) 판매중이다
18	자세하게	39	그런 식으로 ~하다.
19	(꽃을) 꺾다	40	~하려고 노력하다
20	젖은	41	너무 ~하고 싶다!
21	붙이다	42	A에게 B를 구경시켜 주다
		43	~해도 됩니까?

※ 다음 영영풀이에 알맞은 단어를 <보기>에서 골라 쓴 후, 우리말 뜻을 쓰시오.

1 _____ : a person who designs buildings: _____

2 _____ : inside or into a building: _____

3 _____ : having the form of a curve: _____

4 _____ : to be present in a place or situation: _____

5 _____ : to make a reservation for a future time: _____

6 _____ : easily broken or damaged: _____

7 _____ : to copy somebody or something: _____

8 _____ : a raised line of water that moves across the surface of the sea: _____

9 _____ : the things that are inside something: _____

10 _____ : a vehicle that travels in space, carrying people: _____

11 _____ : the ability to form pictures or ideas in your mind: _____

12 _____ : to choose someone to do a particular job by voting for them: _____

13 _____ : to show something in a public place so that people can see it: _____

14 _____ : a long post made of steel, stone, etc., used to support a building: _____

15 _____ : to take flowers, fruit, etc. from the plant or the tree where they are growing:
_____

16 _____ : to represent or describe something very accurately using words or image:
_____

보기			
elect	exist	spaceship	delicate
capture	curved	exhibit	indoors
contents	imitate	imagination	book
column	pick	wave	architect

※ 다음 우리말과 일치하도록 빈칸에 알맞은 말을 쓰시오.

Listen and Speak 1 A

B: Hi, Lisa. Thank you _____ _____ _____ your birthday party.

G: My _____. I'm _____ you could come.

B: These flowers _____ for you. Happy birthday!

G: They are _____! Thank you.

B: 안녕, Lisa. 네 생일 파티에 나를 초대해 줘서 고마워.
G: 천만에. 네가 와서 기뻐.
B: 이 꽃들은 너를 위한 거야. 생일 축하해!
G: 꽃들이 아름다워! 고마워.

Listen and Speak 1 B

B: Sumin, my train _____ _____ _____ five minutes.

G: I _____ you enjoyed your trip, Daniel.

B: Of _____, I did.

G: _____ _____ did you like _____ in my town?

B: I liked the _____ _____ _____.

G: Yeah, it's _____ _____ _____ _____ here.

B: I really _____ _____ around in hanbok. I looked really _____.

G: I'm _____ _____ _____ that.

B: Thank you _____ _____ _____ _____.

G: It was my _____. _____ a safe trip.

B: 수민아, 기차가 5분 후에 떠나.
G: 여행이 즐거웠기를 바라, Daniel.
B: 물론 즐거웠지.
G: 우리 마을에서 어느 장소가 가장 좋았니?
B: 민속촌이 가장 좋았어.
G: 응, 민속촌이 이곳에서 가장 인기 있는 곳이야.
B: 나는 한복을 입고 돌아다니는 게 정말 좋았어. 내가 정말 멋져 보였어.
G: 그 말을 들으니 기뻐.
B: 여기저기 구경시켜 줘서 고마워.
G: 천만에. 조심해서 가.

Listen and Speak 1 C

1. A: How was the book?

   B: It was great. _____ _____ _____ _____ me the book.

   A: You're _____. It was my _____.

2. A: _____ was the movie?

   B: It was great. Thank you _____ _____ the movie.

   A: You're _____. It was my _____.

3. A: _____ _____ your mom's birthday party?

   B: It was great. Thank you _____ _____ _____ _____ a cake.

   A: You're _____. It was _____ _____.

1. A: 책은 어땠니?
   B: 좋았어. 책을 빌려줘서 고마워.
   A: 천만에. 오히려 내가 더 기뻤어.

2. A: 영화는 어땠니?
   B: 좋았어. 영화를 추천해 줘서 고마워.
   A: 천만에. 오히려 내가 더 기뻤어.

3. A: 엄마 생일 파티는 어땠니?
   B: 좋았어. 케이크를 만드는 것을 도와줘서 고마워.
   A: 천만에. 오히려 내가 더 기뻤어.

M: Excuse me. _____ _____ _____ _____ _____ your umbrella inside.

G: Oh, _____ should I _____ it?

M: There is an umbrella _____ _____.

G: Okay, _____ _____ _____ there. Thank you.

M: 실례합니다. 우산을 안으로 가져오면 안 됩니다.
G: 아, 우산을 어디에 놓아야 하나요?
M: 밖에 우산꽂이가 있어요.
G: 알겠습니다. 그곳에 놓을게요. 감사합니다.

Listen and Speak 2 B

B: The tickets _____ the World Music Concert _____ _____ _____ now.

G: Really? _____ _____ the tickets online right _____.

B: Okay. Let's see.... There are still tickets _____ for November 5th.

G: Sounds good. _____ _____ two student tickets.

B: Oh, _____ _____ _____ _____ I bring my little brother?

G: Not at all. But it _____ _____ you are _____ _____ _____ children _____ 8.

B: No _____. He's 10.

G: Okay, I'll _____ one child ticket. The _____ _____ _____ 25 dollars.

B: Great.

G: I _____ _____ _____ _____ the concert!

B: '세계 음악 콘서트'의 표가 지금 판매 중이야.
G: 정말? 지금 당장 온라인으로 표를 예매하자.
B: 좋아. 어디 보자…. 11월 5일에 표가 아직 남아 있어.
G: 잘됐다. 학생 표 두 장을 예매하자.
B: 오, 내 남동생을 데려가도 될까?
G: 물론이지. 하지만 8세 미만의 어린이들을 데려오지 못한다고 쓰여 있어.
B: 문제없어. 남동생은 열 살이야.
G: 그래, 어린이 표 한 장을 추가할게. 총액이 25달러야.
B: 좋아.
G: 콘서트를 볼 게 정말 기대돼!

Listen and Speak 2 C

1. **A:** Excuse me. _____ _____ _____ _____ _____ the birds here.

   B: I'm sorry. I didn't know that.

   A: Please check the _____ _____ _____.

   B: Okay. Thank you.

2. **A:** Excuse me. You're _____ _____ _____ _____ a drone.

   B: I'm sorry. I didn't know that.

   A: Please _____ _____ _____ over there.

   B: Okay. Thank you.

3. **A:** Excuse me. _____ _____ _____ _____ _____ flowers.

   B: I'm sorry. I didn't know that.

   A: Please _____ _____ _____ over there.

   B: Okay. Thank you.

1. **A:** 실례합니다. 여기서 새에게 먹이를 주면 안 됩니다.
   B: 죄송합니다. 몰랐어요.
   A: 저기에 있는 표지판을 확인하세요.
   B: 알겠습니다. 감사합니다.

2. **A:** 실례합니다. 여기서 드론을 날리면 안 됩니다.
   B: 죄송합니다. 몰랐어요.
   A: 저기에 있는 표지판을 확인하세요.
   B: 알겠습니다. 감사합니다.

3. **A:** 실례합니다. 여기서 꽃을 꺾으면 안 됩니다.
   B: 죄송합니다. 몰랐어요.
   A: 저기에 있는 표지판을 확인하세요.
   B: 알겠습니다. 감사합니다.

Real Life Talk Watch a Video

W: Hello, students! _____ _____ _____ _____ our art museum. This museum _____ in 1995. _____ then, it _____ _____ many _____ _____. Today, you will see some _____ _____ from the art books. Before we begin the tour, _____ me _____ _____ _____ a basic rule. You can _____ _____ the artworks, but _____ _____ _____ _____ them. Now _____ _____ the tour.

W: 안녕하세요, 학생 여러분! 우리 미술관을 방문해 주셔서 감사합니다. 이 미술관은 1995년에 문을 열었습니다. 그때부터 많은 유명한 작품을 전시했습니다. 오늘, 여러분은 미술 책에 실린 유명한 작품 몇 개를 보게 될 것입니다. 관람을 시작하기 전에 기본 규칙을 상기시켜 드리겠습니다. 작품의 사진을 찍을 수는 있지만 만져서는 안 됩니다. 이제 관람을 시작해 봅시다.

Real Life Talk Step 2

1. A: Excuse me. _____ _____ _____ you a question?

   B: Sure, what is it?

   A: _____ _____ _____ _____ drink soda?

   B: Sorry. _____ _____ _____ _____ _____ soda here.

   A: Okay, I see.

   B: Thank you _____ _____.

2. A: Excuse me. _____ _____ _____ _____ _____ _____ _____ _____?

   B: Sure, what is it?

   A: _____ _____ _____ _____ _____ the artwork?

   B: Sorry. _____ _____ _____ _____ _____ the artwork here.

   A: Okay, I see.

   B: Thank you _____ _____.

1. A: 실례합니다. 뭐 좀 물어봐도 될까요?
   B: 물론이죠. 뭔데요?
   A: 제가 탄산음료를 먹어도 되나요?
   B: 죄송합니다. 여기서 탄산음료 마시면 안 돼요.
   A: 네, 알겠습니다.
   B: 이해해 주셔서 감사합니다.

2. A: 실례합니다. 뭐 좀 물어봐도 될까요?
   B: 물론이죠. 뭔데요?
   A: 제가 미술작품 만져도 되나요?
   B: 죄송합니다. 여기서 미술작품 만지면 안 돼요.
   A: 네, 알겠습니다.
   B: 이해해 주셔서 감사합니다.

Check up Dialogue Champion

A: Thank you _____ _____ _____ _____ my project.

B: You're _____. It was my _____.

A: 내 과제를 끝나게 나를 도와줘서 고마워.
B: 천만에. 오히려 내가 더 기뻤어.

※ 다음 우리말에 맞도록 대화를 영어로 쓰시오.

 해석

Listen and Speak 1 A

B: _____

G: _____

B: _____

G: _____

B: 안녕, Lisa. 네 생일 파티에 나를 초대해 줘서 고마워.
G: 천만에. 네가 와서 기뻐.
B: 이 꽃들은 너를 위한 거야. 생일 축하해!
G: 꽃들이 아름다워! 고마워.

Listen and Speak 1 B

B: _____

G: _____

B: _____

G: _____

B: _____

G: _____

B: _____

G: _____

B: _____

G: _____

B: 수민아, 기차가 5분 후에 떠나.
G: 여행이 즐거웠기를 바라, Daniel.
B: 물론 즐거웠지.
G: 우리 마을에서 어느 장소가 가장 좋았니?
B: 민속촌이 가장 좋았어.
G: 응, 민속촌이 이곳에서 가장 인기 있는 곳이야.
B: 나는 한복을 입고 돌아다니는 게 정말 좋았어. 내가 정말 멋져 보였어.
G: 그 말을 들으니 기뻐.
B: 여기저기 구경시켜 줘서 고마워.
G: 천만에. 조심해서 가.

Listen and Speak 1 C

1. A: _____
   B: _____
   A: _____

2. A: _____
   B: _____
   A: _____

3. A: _____
   B: _____
   A: _____

1. A: 책은 어땠니?
   B: 좋았어. 책을 빌려줘서 고마워.
   A: 천만에. 오히려 내가 더 기뻤어.

2. A: 영화는 어땠니?
   B: 좋았어. 영화를 추천해 줘서 고마워.
   A: 천만에. 오히려 내가 더 기뻤어.

3. A: 엄마 생일 파티는 어땠니?
   B: 좋았어. 케이크를 만드는 것을 도와줘서 고마워.
   A: 천만에. 오히려 내가 더 기뻤어.

Listen and Speak 2 A

M: _____

G: _____

M: _____

G: _____

M: 실례합니다. 우산을 안으로 가져오면 안 됩니다.
G: 아, 우산을 어디에 놓아야 하나요?
M: 밖에 우산꽂이가 있어요.
G: 알겠습니다. 그곳에 놓을게요. 감사합니다.

Listen and Speak 2 B

B: _____

G: _____

B: _____

G: _____

B: _____

G: _____

B: _____

G: _____

B: _____

G: _____

B: '세계 음악 콘서트'의 표가 지금 판매 중이야.
G: 정말? 지금 당장 온라인으로 표를 예매하자.
B: 좋아. 어디 보자…. 11월 5일에 표가 아직 남아 있어.
G: 잘됐다. 학생 표 두 장을 예매하자.
B: 오, 내 남동생을 데려가도 될까?
G: 물론이지. 하지만 8세 미만의 어린이들을 데려오지 못한다고 쓰여 있어.
B: 문제없어. 남동생은 열 살이야.
G: 그래, 어린이 표 한 장을 추가할게. 총액이 25달러야.
B: 좋아.
G: 콘서트를 볼 게 정말 기대돼!

Listen and Speak 2 C

1. A: _____
   B: _____
   A: _____
   B: _____

2. A: _____
   B: _____
   A: _____
   B: _____

3. A: _____
   B: _____
   A: _____
   B: _____

1. A: 실례합니다. 여기서 새에게 먹이를 주면 안 됩니다.
   B: 죄송합니다. 몰랐어요.
   A: 저기에 있는 표지판을 확인하세요.
   B: 알겠습니다. 감사합니다.

2. A: 실례합니다. 여기서 드론을 날리면 안 됩니다.
   B: 죄송합니다. 몰랐어요.
   A: 저기에 있는 표지판을 확인하세요.
   B: 알겠습니다. 감사합니다.

3. A: 실례합니다. 여기서 꽃을 꺾으면 안 됩니다.
   B: 죄송합니다. 몰랐어요.
   A: 저기에 있는 표지판을 확인하세요.
   B: 알겠습니다. 감사합니다.

Real Life Talk Watch a Video

W: _____
_____
_____
_____
_____

W: 안녕하세요, 학생 여러분! 우리 미술관을 방문해 주셔서 감사합니다. 이 미술관은 1995년에 문을 열었습니다. 그때부터 많은 유명한 작품을 전시했습니다. 오늘, 여러분은 미술 책에 실린 유명한 작품 몇 개를 보게 될 것입니다. 관람을 시작하기 전에 기본 규칙을 상기시켜 드리겠습니다. 작품의 사진을 찍을 수는 있지만 만져서는 안 됩니다. 이제 관람을 시작해 봅시다.

Real Life Talk Step 2

1. A: _____
   B: _____
   A: _____
   B: _____
   A: _____
   B: _____

2. A: _____
   B: _____
   A: _____
   B: _____
   A: _____
   B: _____

1. A: 실례합니다. 뭐 좀 물어봐도 될까요?
   B: 물론이죠. 뭔데요?
   A: 제가 탄산음료를 먹어도 되나요?
   B: 죄송합니다. 여기서 탄산음료 마시면 안 돼요.
   A: 네, 알겠습니다.
   B: 이해해 주셔서 감사합니다.

2. A: 실례합니다. 뭐 좀 물어봐도 될까요?
   B: 물론이죠. 뭔데요?
   A: 제가 미술작품 만져도 되나요?
   B: 죄송합니다. 여기서 미술작품 만지면 안 돼요.
   A: 네, 알겠습니다.
   B: 이해해 주셔서 감사합니다.

Check up Dialogue Champion

A: _____
B: _____

A: 내 과제를 끝내게 나를 도와줘서 고마워.
B: 천만에. 오히려 내가 더 기뻤어.

※ 다음 우리말과 일치하도록 빈칸에 알맞은 것을 골라 쓰시오.

1 _____ _____ City
A. Meets   B. Nature

2 Have you _____ of the _____, "_____ _____ nature"?
A. expression   B. imitates   C. heard   D. art

3 Many _____ get their _____ and _____ from the world _____ them.
A. inspirations   B. around   C. artists   D. ideas

4 This is _____ the _____ is a beautiful _____.
A. place   B. natural   C. because   D. world

5 The _____ in nature are very _____ the _____.
A. pleasing   B. shapes   C. eye   D. to

6 _____ _____, _____ at the egg on the _____.
A. example   B. look   C. left   D. for

7 _____ _____ beautiful?
A. it   B. isn't

8 It is round and _____, yet strong _____ to _____ its _____.
A. protect   B. delicate   C. contents   D. enough

9 Can you _____ a building that _____ _____ an _____?
A. like   B. imagine   C. looks   D. egg

10 _____ _____ building _____ _____ in London.
A. exists   B. a   C. actually   D. such

11 Nature _____ _____ many _____ _____ the world.
A. around   B. inspired   C. architects   D. has

12 _____ is the Sagrada Familia _____ _____.
A. Spain   B. in   C. this

13 It is _____ of the _____ _____ _____ in the world.
A. churches   B. one   C. most   D. famous

14 Look at the _____ _____ _____ _____ the church.
A. tall   B. beautiful   C. columns   D. inside

15 They _____ _____ trees, _____ _____?
A. they   B. like   C. don't   D. look

16 The _____ _____, Antoni Gaudi, _____ the _____ of trees in the Sagrada Familia.
A. shape   B. famous   C. used   D. architect

17 That's _____ he _____ the _____ of nature _____.
A. indoors   B. brought   C. beauty   D. how

---

1 자연이 도시를 만나다

2 "예술은 자연을 모방한다"라는 표현을 들어 본 적이 있는가?

3 많은 예술가들이 그들의 아이디어와 영감을 그들 주변의 세상에서 얻는다.

4 이것은 자연계가 아름다운 곳이기 때문이다.

5 자연의 형태는 눈에 보기에 매우 좋다.

6 예를 들면 왼쪽의 달걀을 봐라.

7 아름답지 않은가?

8 그것은 둥글고 부서지기 쉽지만 내용물을 보호할 만큼 충분히 튼튼하다.

9 달걀처럼 생긴 건물을 상상할 수 있는가?

10 이러한 형태의 건물이 런던에는 실제로 존재한다.

11 자연은 세계의 많은 건축가에게 영감을 주어 왔다.

12 이것은 스페인에 있는 사그라다 파밀리아 성당이다.

13 그것은 세계에서 가장 유명한 성당 중의 하나이다.

14 교회 안에 있는 아름다운 높은 기둥을 봐라.

15 기둥은 나무처럼 보인다. 그렇지 않은가?

16 유명한 건축가인 Antoni Gaudi는 사그라다 파밀리아 성당에 나무의 형태를 사용했다.

17 그것이 그가 자연의 아름다움을 실내로 가져온 방법이다.

18 In the first two _____, we can _____ see _____ _____ the architect.

    A. inspired   B. examples   C. what   D. easily

19 But in the next _____ _____ Australia, this is not _____.

    A. obvious   B. example   C. so   D. from

20 Jørn Utzon, the architect of the Sydney Opera House, _____ a _____ from nature and _____ his _____.

    A. shape   B. imagination   C. took   D. added

21 Can you _____ _____ _____ him?

    A. inspired   B. guess   C. what

22 Many people think that it is the _____ in the _____ or a _____.

    A. waves   B. sailing   C. ocean   D. boat

23 But _____, the _____ _____ _____ an orange.

    A. inspiration   B. interestingly   C. from   D. came

24 _____ at the _____ _____.

    A. roof   B. closely   C. look

25 Can you _____ the _____ of an _____?

    A. orange   B. see   C. peels

26 When orange lights are _____ on the building, you can see the _____ _____.

    A. clearly   B. shone   C. more   D. peels

27 _____ _____ Korea?

    A. about   B. what

28 _____ you _____ _____ _____ Dongdaemun Design Plaza in Seoul?

    A. to   B. have   C. been   D. ever

29 Many people think that the building _____ _____ a _____.

    A.like   B. spaceship   C. looks   D. giant

30 But the architect, Zaha Hadid, took the _____ _____ from nature _____ _____ _____ city people could enjoy them.

    A. that   B. so   C. lines   D. curved

31 _____ _____ its special design, it has become a popular _____ _____ in Seoul.

    A. attraction   B. to   C. tourist   D. thanks

32 _____ you can see, many buildings try to _____ the _____ of _____ in their design.

    A. capture   B. as   C. nature   D. beauty

33 They are _____ _____ of " _____ _____ city."

    A. meets   B. examples   C. perfect   D. nature

34 If you _____ an architect, what _____ you _____ from _____?

    A. choose   B. were   C. nature   D. would

---

18 앞의 두 예시에서 우리는 무엇이 건축가에게 영감을 주었는지 쉽게 알 수 있다.

19 하지만 호주의 다음 예시에서는 이것이 그다지 명확하지 않다.

20 시드니 오페라 하우스의 건축가인 Jørn Utzon은 자연에서 형태를 가져와 자신의 상상력을 더했다.

21 무엇이 그에게 영감을 주었는지 추측할 수 있는가?

22 많은 사람들은 그것이 바다의 파도나 돛단배라고 생각한다.

23 하지만 흥미롭게도, 그 영감은 오렌지에서 비롯되었다.

24 지붕을 자세히 봐라.

25 오렌지의 껍질 형태가 보이는가?

26 오렌지색 조명이 건물을 비추면, 껍질 이미지를 더 명확하게 볼 수 있다.

27 한국은 어떤가?

28 서울의 동대문 디자인 플라자에 가 본 적이 있는가?

29 많은 사람들은 이 건물이 거대한 우주선처럼 보인다고 생각한다.

30 하지만 건축가인 Zaha Hadid는 도시 사람들이 즐길 수 있도록 자연에서 곡선을 가져왔다.

31 이 특별한 디자인 덕분에, 동대문 디자인 플라자는 서울의 인기 있는 관광 명소가 되었다.

32 보는 바와 같이 많은 건물들이 디자인에 자연의 아름다움을 담아내려고 한다.

33 이 건물들은 '자연이 도시를 만나다'의 완벽한 예이다.

34 만약 당신이 건축가라면, 자연에서 무엇을 선택할 것인가?

※ 다음 우리말과 일치하도록 빈칸에 알맞은 것을 골라 쓰시오.

1 _____ _____ City

2 _____ you _____ of the expression, " _____ _____ _____ "?

3 Many artists get their _____ and _____ from the world _____ them.

4 This is because _____ _____ _____ is a beautiful place.

5 The shapes in nature are very _____ _____ _____ _____ .

6 _____ _____ , _____ _____ the egg on the left.

7 _____ _____ beautiful?

8 It is round and delicate, yet _____ _____ _____ _____ its contents.

9 Can you _____ a building that _____ _____ _____ _____ ?

10 _____ _____ _____ actually _____ in London.

11 Nature _____ _____ many _____ around the world.

12 This is the Sagrada Familia _____ _____ .

13 It is _____ _____ _____ _____ _____ _____ in the world.

14 Look at the _____ _____ _____ the church.

15 They _____ _____ trees, _____ _____ ?

16 The _____ _____ , Antoni Gaudi, _____ _____ _____ _____ _____ in the Sagrada Familia.

17 That's _____ he _____ the _____ of nature _____ .

---

1 자연이 도시를 만나다

2 "예술은 자연을 모방한다"라는 표현을 들어 본 적이 있는가?

3 많은 예술가들이 그들의 아이디어와 영감을 그들 주변의 세상에서 얻는다.

4 이것은 자연계가 아름다운 곳이기 때문이다.

5 자연의 형태는 눈에 보기에 매우 좋다.

6 예를 들면 왼쪽의 달걀을 봐라.

7 아름답지 않은가?

8 그것은 둥글고 부서지기 쉽지만 내용물을 보호할 만큼 충분히 튼튼하다.

9 달걀처럼 생긴 건물을 상상할 수 있는가?

10 이러한 형태의 건물이 런던에는 실제로 존재한다.

11 자연은 세계의 많은 건축가에게 영감을 주어 왔다.

12 이것은 스페인에 있는 사그라다 파밀리아 성당이다.

13 그것은 세계에서 가장 유명한 성당 중의 하나이다.

14 교회 안에 있는 아름다운 높은 기둥을 봐라.

15 기둥은 나무처럼 보인다. 그렇지 않은가?

16 유명한 건축가인 Antoni Gaudi는 사그라다 파밀리아 성당에 나무의 형태를 사용했다.

17 그것이 그가 자연의 아름다움을 실내로 가져온 방법이다.

18 In the first two _____, we can easily see _____ _____ the architect.

19 But in the next example from Australia, this is not _____ _____.

20 Jørn Utzon, the _____ of the Sydney Opera House, took a shape from nature and _____ _____ _____.

21 Can you guess _____ _____ _____?

22 Many people think that it is _____ _____ _____ _____ _____ or _____ _____ _____.

23 But _____, the inspiration _____ _____ an orange.

24 Look at the _____ _____.

25 Can you see _____ _____ of an orange?

26 When orange lights _____ _____ on the building, you can see the _____ _____ _____.

27 _____ _____ Korea?

28 _____ you ever _____ _____ Dongdaemun Design Plaza in Seoul?

29 Many people think that the building _____ _____ a _____.

30 But the architect, Zaha Hadid, took _____ _____ _____ from nature _____ _____ city people could enjoy them.

31 _____ _____ its special design, it has become a _____ _____ _____ in Seoul.

32 _____ you can see, many buildings try to _____ _____ of nature in their design.

33 They are perfect examples of "_____ _____ _____."

34 If you _____ an _____, what _____ you _____ from nature?

18 앞의 두 예시에서 우리는 무엇이 건축가에게 영감을 주었는지 쉽게 알 수 있다.

19 하지만 호주의 다음 예시에서는 이것이 그다지 명확하지 않다.

20 시드니 오페라 하우스의 건축가인 Jørn Utzon은 자연에서 형태를 가져와 자신의 상상력을 더했다.

21 무엇이 그에게 영감을 주었는지 추측할 수 있는가?

22 많은 사람들은 그것이 바다의 파도나 돛단배라고 생각한다.

23 하지만 흥미롭게도, 그 영감은 오렌지에서 비롯되었다.

24 지붕을 자세히 봐라.

25 오렌지의 껍질 형태가 보이는가?

26 오렌지색 조명이 건물을 비추면, 껍질 이미지를 더 명확하게 볼 수 있다.

27 한국은 어떤가?

28 서울의 동대문 디자인 플라자에 가 본 적이 있는가?

29 많은 사람들은 이 건물이 거대한 우주선처럼 보인다고 생각한다.

30 하지만 건축가인 Zaha Hadid는 도시 사람들이 즐길 수 있도록 자연에서 곡선을 가져왔다.

31 이 특별한 디자인 덕분에, 동대문 디자인 플라자는 서울의 인기 있는 관광 명소가 되었다.

32 보는 바와 같이 많은 건물들이 디자인에 자연의 아름다움을 담아내려고 한다.

33 이 건물들은 '자연이 도시를 만나다'의 완벽한 예이다.

34 만약 당신이 건축가라면, 자연에서 무엇을 선택할 것인가?

※ 다음 문장을 우리말로 쓰시오.

1　Nature Meets City

➡ _____

2　Have you heard of the expression, "Art imitates nature"?

➡ _____

3　Many artists get their ideas and inspirations from the world around them.

➡ _____

4　This is because the natural world is a beautiful place.

➡ _____

5　The shapes in nature are very pleasing to the eye.

➡ _____

6　For example, look at the egg on the left.

➡ _____

7　Isn't it beautiful?

➡ _____

8　It is round and delicate, yet strong enough to protect its contents.

➡ _____

9　Can you imagine a building that looks like an egg?

➡ _____

10　Such a building actually exists in London.

➡ _____

11　Nature has inspired many architects around the world.

➡ _____

12　This is the Sagrada Familia in Spain.

➡ _____

13　It is one of the most famous churches in the world.

➡ _____

14　Look at the beautiful tall columns inside the church.

➡ _____

15　They look like trees, don't they?

➡ _____

16　The famous architect, Antoni Gaudi, used the shape of trees in the Sagrada Familia.

➡ _____

17　That's how he brought the beauty of nature indoors.

➡ _____

18 In the first two examples, we can easily see what inspired the architect.

➡ _____

19 But in the next example from Australia, this is not so obvious.

➡ _____

20 Jørn Utzon, the architect of the Sydney Opera House, took a shape from nature and added his imagination.

➡ _____

21 Can you guess what inspired him?

➡ _____

22 Many people think that it is the waves in the ocean or a sailing boat.

➡ _____

23 But interestingly, the inspiration came from an orange.

➡ _____

24 Look at the roof closely.

➡ _____

25 Can you see the peels of an orange?

➡ _____

26 When orange lights are shone on the building, you can see the peels more clearly.

➡ _____

27 What about Korea?

➡ _____

28 Have you ever been to Dongdaemun Design Plaza in Seoul?

➡ _____

29 Many people think that the building looks like a giant spaceship.

➡ _____

30 But the architect, Zaha Hadid, took the curved lines from nature so that city people could enjoy them.

➡ _____

31 Thanks to its special design, it has become a popular tourist attraction in Seoul.

➡ _____

32 As you can see, many buildings try to capture the beauty of nature in their design.

➡ _____

33 They are perfect examples of "Nature meets city."

➡ _____

34 If you were an architect, what would you choose from nature?

➡ _____

※ 다음 괄호 안의 단어들을 우리말에 맞도록 바르게 배열하시오.

1 (Meets / Nature / City)
➡ _____

2 (you / have / of / heard / expression, / the / imitates / nature"? / "art)
➡ _____

3 (artists / many / their / get / and / ideas / from / inspirations / world / the / them. / around)
➡ _____

4 (is / this / the / because / natural / is / world / beautiful / a / place.)
➡ _____

5 (shapes / the / nature / in / very / are / to / pleasing / eye. / the)
➡ _____

6 (example, / for / at / look / egg / the / the / on / left.)
➡ _____

7 (it / beautiful? / isn't)
➡ _____

8 (is / it / and / round / delicate, / strong / yet / to / enough / protect / contents. / its)
➡ _____

9 (you / can / a / imagine / that / building / like / looks / egg? / an)
➡ _____

10 (a / such / actually / building / in / exists / London.)
➡ _____

11 (has / nature / many / inspired / architects / the / around / world.)
➡ _____

12 (is / this / Sagrada / the / in / Familia / Spain.)
➡ _____

13 (is / it / of / one / most / the / famous / in / churches / world. / the)
➡ _____

14 (at / look / beautiful / the / columns / tall / the / inside / church.)
➡ _____

15 (look / they / trees, / like / they? / don't)
➡ _____

16 (famous / the / architect, / Gaudi, / Antoni / the / used / of / shape / trees / the / in / Familia. / Sagrada)
➡ _____

17 (how / that's / brought / he / beauty / the / nature / of / indoors.)
➡ _____

---

1 자연이 도시를 만나다

2 "예술은 자연을 모방한다"라는 표현을 들어 본 적이 있는가?

3 많은 예술가들이 그들의 아이디어와 영감을 그들 주변의 세상에서 얻는다.

4 이것은 자연계가 아름다운 곳이기 때문이다.

5 자연의 형태는 눈에 보기에 매우 좋다.

6 예를 들면 왼쪽의 달걀을 봐라.

7 아름답지 않은가?

8 그것은 둥글고 부서지기 쉽지만 내용물을 보호할 만큼 충분히 튼튼하다.

9 달걀처럼 생긴 건물을 상상할 수 있는가?

10 이러한 형태의 건물이 런던에는 실제로 존재한다.

11 자연은 세계의 많은 건축가에게 영감을 주어 왔다.

12 이것은 스페인에 있는 사그라다 파밀리아 성당이다.

13 그것은 세계에서 가장 유명한 성당 중의 하나이다.

14 교회 안에 있는 아름다운 높은 기둥을 봐라.

15 기둥은 나무처럼 보인다, 그렇지 않은가?

16 유명한 건축가인 Antoni Gaudi는 사그라다 파밀리아 성당에 나무의 형태를 사용했다.

17 그것이 그가 자연의 아름다움을 실내로 가져온 방법이다.

18 (the / in / two / first / examples, / can / we / see / easily / what / the / inspired / architect.)
➡ _____

19 (in / but / next / the / from / example / Australia, / is / this / so / not / obvious.)
➡ _____

20 (Utzon, / Jørn / architect / the / the / of / Opera / Sydney / House, / a / took / from / shape / nature / and / his / added / imagination.)
➡ _____
_____

21 (you / can / what / guess / him? / inspired)
➡ _____

22 (people / many / that / think / is / it / waves / the / the / in / ocean / a / or / boat. / sailing)
➡ _____

23 (interstingly, / but / inspiration / the / from / came / orange. / an)
➡ _____

24 (at / look / roof / the / closely.)
➡ _____

25 (you / can / the / see / peels / an / of / orange?)
➡ _____

26 (orange / when / are / lights / on / shone / building, / the / can / you / see / peels / the / clearly. / more)
➡ _____

27 (about / what / Korea?)
➡ _____

28 (you / have / been / ever / Dongdaemun / to / Plaza / Design / Seoul? / in)
➡ _____

29 (people / many / that / think / building / the / like / looks / giant / a / spaceship.)
➡ _____

30 (the / but / Zaha / architect, / Hadid, / the / took / lines / curved / nature / from / that / so / people / city / could / them. / enjoy)
➡ _____

31 (to / thanks / special / its / design, / has / it / a / become / popular / attraction / tourist / Seoul. / in)
➡ _____

32 (you / as / see, / can / buildings / many / to / try / the / capture / beauty / nature / of / their / in / design.)
➡ _____

33 (are / they / examples / perfect / of / meets / city." / "nature)
➡ _____

34 (you / if / an / were / architect, / would / what / choose / you / nature? / from)
➡ _____

18 앞의 두 예시에서 우리는 무엇이 건축가에게 영감을 주었는지 쉽게 알 수 있다.

19 하지만 호주의 다음 예시에서는 이것이 그다지 명확하지 않다.

20 시드니 오페라 하우스의 건축가인 Jørn Utzon은 자연에서 형태를 가져와 자신의 상상력을 더했다.

21 무엇이 그에게 영감을 주었는지 추측할 수 있는가?

22 많은 사람들은 그것이 바다의 파도나 돛단배라고 생각한다.

23 하지만 흥미롭게도, 그 영감은 오렌지에서 비롯되었다.

24 지붕을 자세히 봐라.

25 오렌지의 껍질 형태가 보이는가?

26 오렌지색 조명이 건물을 비추면, 껍질 이미지를 더 명확하게 볼 수 있다.

27 한국은 어떤가?

28 서울의 동대문 디자인 플라자에 가 본 적이 있는가?

29 많은 사람들은 이 건물이 거대한 우주선처럼 보인다고 생각한다.

30 하지만 건축가인 Zaha Hadid는 도시 사람들이 즐길 수 있도록 자연에서 곡선을 가져왔다.

31 이 특별한 디자인 덕분에, 동대문 디자인 플라자는 서울의 인기 있는 관광 명소가 되었다.

32 보는 바와 같이 많은 건물들이 디자인에 자연의 아름다움을 담아내려고 한다.

33 이 건물들은 '자연이 도시를 만나다'의 완벽한 예이다.

34 만약 당신이 건축가라면, 자연에서 무엇을 선택할 것인가?

※ 다음 우리말을 영어로 쓰시오.

1 자연이 도시를 만나다

➡ _____

2 "예술은 자연을 모방한다"라는 표현을 들어 본 적이 있는가?

➡ _____

3 많은 예술가들이 그들의 아이디어와 영감을 그들 주변의 세상에서 얻는다.

➡ _____

4 이것은 자연계가 아름다운 곳이기 때문이다.

➡ _____

5 자연의 형태는 눈에 보기에 매우 좋다.

➡ _____

6 예를 들면 왼쪽의 달걀을 봐라.

➡ _____

7 아름답지 않은가?

➡ _____

8 그것은 둥글고 부서지기 쉽지만 내용물을 보호할 만큼 충분히 튼튼하다.

➡ _____

9 달걀처럼 생긴 건물을 상상할 수 있는가?

➡ _____

10 이러한 형태의 건물이 런던에는 실제로 존재한다.

➡ _____

11 자연은 세계의 많은 건축가에게 영감을 주어 왔다.

➡ _____

12 이것은 스페인에 있는 사그라다 파밀리아 성당이다.

➡ _____

13 그것은 세계에서 가장 유명한 성당 중의 하나이다.

➡ _____

14 교회 안에 있는 아름다운 높은 기둥을 봐라.

➡ _____

15 기둥은 나무처럼 보인다, 그렇지 않은가?

➡ _____

16 유명한 건축가인 Antoni Gaudi는 사그라다 파밀리아 성당에 나무의 형태를 사용했다.

➡ _____

17 그것이 그가 자연의 아름다움을 실내로 가져온 방법이다.

➡ _____

18 앞의 두 예시에서 우리는 무엇이 건축가에게 영감을 주었는지 쉽게 알 수 있다.
➡ _____

19 하지만 호주의 다음 예시에서는 이것이 그다지 명확하지 않다.
➡ _____

20 시드니 오페라 하우스의 건축가인 Jørn Utzon은 자연에서 형태를 가져와 자신의 상상력을 더했다.
➡ _____
_____

21 무엇이 그에게 영감을 주었는지 추측할 수 있는가?
➡ _____

22 많은 사람들은 그것이 바다의 파도나 돛단배라고 생각한다.
➡ _____

23 하지만 흥미롭게도, 그 영감은 오렌지에서 비롯되었다.
➡ _____

24 지붕을 자세히 봐라.
➡ _____

25 오렌지의 껍질 형태가 보이는가?
➡ _____

26 오렌지색 조명이 건물을 비추면, 껍질 이미지를 더 명확하게 볼 수 있다.
➡ _____

27 한국은 어떤가?
➡ _____

28 서울의 동대문 디자인 플라자에 가 본 적이 있는가?
➡ _____

29 많은 사람들은 이 건물이 거대한 우주선처럼 보인다고 생각한다.
➡ _____

30 하지만 건축가인 Zaha Hadid는 도시 사람들이 즐길 수 있도록 자연에서 곡선을 가져왔다.
➡ _____
_____

31 이 특별한 디자인 덕분에, 동대문 디자인 플라자는 서울의 인기 있는 관광 명소가 되었다.
➡ _____

32 보는 바와 같이 많은 건물들이 디자인에 자연의 아름다움을 담아내려고 한다.
➡ _____

33 이 건물들은 '자연이 도시를 만나다'의 완벽한 예이다.
➡ _____

34 만약 당신이 건축가라면, 자연에서 무엇을 선택할 것인가?
➡ _____

※ 다음 우리말과 일치하도록 빈칸에 알맞은 말을 쓰시오.

After You Read

The Sagrada Familia

1. _____ : Spain / _____ : Antoni Gaudi

2. _____ _____ _____ _____ look _____ trees.

3. The architect _____ the _____ _____ _____ _____ .

The Sydney Opera House

4. Location: _____ / _____ : Jørn Utzon

5. The architect _____ _____ _____ an orange.

Dongdaemun Design Plaza

6. _____ : Korea / _____ : Zaha Hadid

7. The architect _____ _____ _____ _____ _____ nature.

8. It is _____ _____ _____ _____ in Seoul.

사그라다 파밀리아 성당
1. 위치: 스페인 / 건축가: Antoni Gaudi
2. 그것의 아름다운 높은 기둥은 나무처럼 보인다.
3. 그 건축가는 자연의 아름다움을 실내로 가져왔다.
시드니 오페라 하우스
4. 위치: 호주 / 건축가: Jørn Utzon
5. 그 건축가는 '오렌지'에서 영감을 얻었다.
동대문 디자인 플라자
6. 위치: 한국 / 건축가: Zaha Hadid
7. 그 건축가는 자연에서 곡선을 가져왔다.
8. 그곳은 서울의 인기 있는 관광 명소이다.

Word Power

1. The store has _____ _____ _____ , _____ it _____ many people.

2. Namsan is _____ _____ _____ _____ in Seoul.

3. I _____ _____ a world _____ _____ .

4. She used her _____ _____ _____ the story.

1. 그 가게는 재미있는 물품이 많아서, 많은 사람들을 끈다.
2. 남산은 서울의 인기 있는 관광 명소이다.
3. 나는 물이 없는 세상은 상상할 수 없다.
4. 그녀는 그 이야기를 쓰기 위해 상상력을 발휘했다.

Think and Write

1. I _____ _____ Boram Middle School _____ Suwon.

2. My school _____ _____ _____ _____ .

3. It also has a _____ _____ , a _____ and a _____ _____ .

4. The garden _____ _____ _____ _____ the school building.

5. We _____ some _____ there _____ we _____ have fresh food.

6. My _____ _____ is the bench _____ _____ _____ .

7. I love _____ there and _____ _____ my friends.

8. I _____ my school _____ _____ .

1. 나는 수원에 있는 보람 중학교에 다닌다.
2. 우리 학교는 4층짜리 건물을 가지고 있다.
3. 우리 학교에는 또한 넓은 운동장, 체육관, 작은 정원이 있다.
4. 정원은 학교 건물 옥상에 있다.
5. 우리는 신선한 음식을 먹을 수 있도록 그곳에 채소를 기른다.
6. 내가 가장 좋아하는 장소는 커다란 나무 아래에 있는 벤치이다.
7. 나는 그곳에 앉아서 친구들과 이야기하는 것을 아주 좋아한다.
8. 나는 우리 학교를 아주 좋아한다.

※ **다음 우리말을 영어로 쓰시오.**

After You Read

The Sagrada Familia
1. 위치: 스페인 / 건축가: Antoni Gaudi
➡ _____

2. 그것의 아름다운 높은 기둥은 나무처럼 보인다.
➡ _____

3. 그 건축가는 자연의 아름다움을 실내로 가져왔다.
➡ _____

The Sydney Opera House
4. 위치: 호주 / 건축가: Jørn Utzon
➡ _____

5. 그 건축가는 '오렌지'에서 영감을 얻었다.
➡ _____

Dongdaemun Design Plaza
6. 위치: 한국 / 건축가: Zaha Hadid
➡ _____

7. 그 건축가는 자연에서 곡선을 가져왔다.
➡ _____

8. 그곳은 서울의 인기 있는 관광 명소이다.
➡ _____

Word Power

1. 그 가게는 재미있는 물품이 많아서, 많은 사람들을 끈다.
➡ _____

2. 남산은 서울의 인기 있는 관광 명소이다.
➡ _____

3. 나는 물이 없는 세상은 상상할 수 없다.
➡ _____

4. 그녀는 그 이야기를 쓰기 위해 상상력을 발휘했다.
➡ _____

Think and Write

1. 나는 수원에 있는 보람 중학교에 다닌다.
➡ _____

2. 우리 학교는 4층짜리 건물을 가지고 있다.
➡ _____

3. 우리 학교에는 또한 넓은 운동장, 체육관, 작은 정원이 있다.
➡ _____

4. 정원은 학교 건물 옥상에 있다.
➡ _____

5. 우리는 신선한 음식을 먹을 수 있도록 그곳에 채소를 기른다.
➡ _____

6. 내가 가장 좋아하는 장소는 커다란 나무 아래에 있는 벤치이다.
➡ _____

7. 나는 그곳에 앉아서 친구들과 이야기하는 것을 아주 좋아한다.
➡ _____

8. 나는 우리 학교를 아주 좋아한다.
➡ _____

※ 다음 영어를 우리말로 쓰시오.

01 solar

02 average

03 blood

04 spot

05 probably

06 smash

07 complete

08 scenery

09 article

10 completely

11 abroad

12 serve

13 distance

14 enemy

15 species

16 surface

17 fool

18 forecast

19 octopus

20 wonder

21 million

22 surround

23 communicate

24 temperature

25 monster

26 clam

27 mop

28 nearby

29 breathe

30 calculate

31 discover

32 tightly

33 tool

34 vacuum

35 give up

36 go without

37 in a line

38 be full of

39 melt away

40 in the end

41 be covered with

42 this time of year

43 be different from

※ 다음 우리말을 영어로 쓰시오.

01 적 _____

02 지방 _____

03 해외에, 해외로 _____

04 피 _____

05 둘러싸다 _____

06 평균의, 보통의 _____

07 완전히 _____

08 경치, 풍경 _____

09 발견하다 _____

10 거리 _____

11 완성하다 _____

12 기사 _____

13 마침내 _____

14 예측, 예보 _____

15 수면, 표면 _____

16 조개 _____

17 추측하다 _____

18 때려 부수다, 깨뜨리다 _____

19 100만; 수많은 _____

20 대걸레로 닦다 _____

21 경이, 경탄; 궁금하다 _____

22 인근의, 가까운 곳의 _____

23 (입으로) 불다 _____

24 속이다; 바보 _____

25 진공청소기로 청소하다 _____

26 도구 _____

27 계산하다 _____

28 괴물 _____

29 문어 _____

30 아마 _____

31 태양의 _____

32 온도, 기온 _____

33 단단히, 꽉 _____

34 숨을 쉬다 _____

35 ~로 덮여 있다 _____

36 포기하다 _____

37 마침내, 결국 _____

38 차츰 사라지다 _____

39 한 줄로 _____

40 잠들다 _____

41 ~ 없이 지내다 _____

42 ~로 가득 차다 _____

43 ~와 다르다 _____

※ 다음 영영풀이에 알맞은 단어를 <보기>에서 골라 쓴 후, 우리말 뜻을 쓰시오.

1 _____ : the number 1,000,000: _____

2 _____ : the area around the North Pole: _____

3 _____ : to send out air from the mouth: _____

4 _____ : to finish making or doing something: _____

5 _____ : to move air into and out of your lungs: _____

6 _____ : to break something into many pieces: _____

7 _____ : a very large mammal that lives in the sea: _____

8 _____ : the amount of space between two places or things: _____

9 _____ : the upper layer of an area of land or water: _____

10 _____ : to trick someone into believing something that is not true: _____

11 _____ : to find a number, answer, etc. by using mathematical processes: _____

12 _____ : a piece of equipment you use with your hands for a particular task: _____

13 _____ : a statement about what you think is going to happen in the future: _____

14 _____ : a sea creature with a soft round body and eight long arms: _____

15 _____ : a set of animals or plants that have similar characteristics to each other: _____

16 _____ : to jump into water, especially with your arms and head going in first: _____

species	whale	octopus	calculate
smash	Arctic	tool	million
dive	distance	fool	surface
forecast	blow	breathe	complete

※ 다음 우리말과 일치하도록 빈칸에 알맞은 말을 쓰시오.

> **Listen and Speak 1 A**

B: We're _____ _____ _____ _____ the mountain.

G: I _____ _____ _____ this mountain is.

B: _____ _____ 2,000m _____.

G: Wow! This is a really _____ _____.

B: Yes, it is. Let's _____ _____.

B: 우리는 산 정상에 거의 다 왔어.
G: 나는 이 산이 얼마나 높은지 궁금해.
B: 이 산은 높이가 약 2,000미터야.
G: 우와! 정말 높은 산이구나.
B: 응, 맞아. 계속 올라가자.

> **Listen and Speak 1 B**

B: Look _____ the baby penguins _____ TV. They're so cute.

G: Yes, but they _____ very _____ out there.

B: Yeah, the South Pole _____ _____ _____ _____ _____ Earth.

G: I wonder _____ _____ _____ _____ there.

B: The _____ temperature _____ about -58℃ _____ July and -26℃ _____ December.

G: Oh, _____, July is _____ _____ December there. Interesting!

B: Yes. _____ very cold there, it _____ snow much.

G: That's _____, _____!

B: TV에 나온 아기 펭귄들을 봐. 아주 귀여워.
G: 응, 하지만 그들은 저곳에서 매우 추워 보여.
B: 응, 남극은 지구에서 가장 추운 곳이야.
G: 그곳이 얼마나 추운지 궁금해.
B: 평균 기온이 7월에는 약 섭씨 영하 58도이고, 12월에는 약 섭씨 영하 26도야.
G: 오, 그러면 그곳은 12월보다 7월이 더 춥구나. 흥미롭다!
B: 응. 비록 그곳은 매우 춥지만 눈은 많이 내리지 않아.
G: 그것도 흥미롭다!

> **Listen and Speak 1 C**

1. A: We're _____ here.

   B: Yes, I'm so _____. Let's _____ _____.

   A: I _____ _____ the bus stop is.

   B: It's _____ _____ _____ the _____ _____.

   A: You're right. _____ go.

2. A: We're _____ _____.

   B: Yes, I'm so excited. Let's _____ _____.

   A: I _____ _____ _____ _____ _____ is.

   B: It's _____ the library.

   A: You're _____. Let's go.

3. A: We're finally here.

   B: Yes, I'm so excited. _____ look around.

   A: _____ _____ _____ Green Park _____.

   B: It's _____ _____ the school.

   A: You're right. _____ _____.

1. A: 마침내 다 왔어.
   B: 맞아, 매우 신나. 둘러보자.
   A: 나는 버스 정류장이 어디에 있는지 궁금해.
   B: 경찰서 앞에 있어.
   A: 맞아. 가자.

2. A: 마침내 다 왔어.
   B: 맞아, 매우 신나. 둘러보자.
   A: 나는 안내 센터가 어디에 있는지 궁금해.
   B: 도서관 뒤에 있어.
   A: 맞아. 가자.

3. A: 마침내 다 왔어.
   B: 맞아, 매우 신나. 둘러보자.
   A: 나는 Green Park가 어디에 있는지 궁금해.
   B: 학교 옆에 있어.
   A: 맞아. 가자.

Listen and Speak 2 A

B: The weather is _____ nice _____.

G: Yeah. How _____ _____ _____ _____ _____ this afternoon?

B: Good idea. Can you _____ the _____?

G: Oh, no! The weather _____ _____ _____ _____ _____ in the afternoon.

B: Let's go _____ _____, then.

Listen and Speak 2 B

B: Sumin, what are you going _____ _____ on Sunday?

G: I'm going to _____ _____. Do you want to _____ _____?

B: I'd love to. _____ _____ _____ _____ _____ go?

G: I'm _____ _____ _____ to Namsan.

B: Oh, the _____ there is so beautiful _____ _____ _____ year.

G: Right. _____ _____ _____ _____ _____ _____ _____ red _____ _____ now.

B: Great. _____ _____ does the shortest hiking course _____?

G: _____ _____ _____ _____ _____ about two hours.

B: Okay, see you _____ Sunday!

Listen and Speak 2 C

1. A: _____ are you _____?

   B: I'm _____ the newspaper.

   A: Is there _____ _____?

   B: _____ _____ _____ _____ _____ _____ _____ a new planet.

2. A: What are you doing?

   B: I'm reading _____ _____.

   A: Is there _____ _____?

   B: _____ _____ _____ _____ a whale family _____ _____ _____ _____ _____ _____.

Real Life Talk Watch a Video

Suji: _____ _____ this picture!

Tony: Wow! The _____ are walking _____ _____ _____ _____ the desert.

Suji: Yeah. The desert looks very _____ and _____.

Tony: I _____ _____ _____ _____ _____ _____ _____ water in the desert.

Suji: Let's find _____ on the Internet.

Tony: Okay. _____ _____ _____ they can go about two weeks _____ _____.

Suji: Wow, that's amazing! _____ _____ really _____ animals.

Tony: I want to _____ _____ _____ in the desert someday.

수지: 이 사진을 봐!
Tony: 우와! 낙타들이 사막에서 한 줄로 걸어가고 있네.
수지: 응. 사막은 매우 덥고 건조해 보여.
Tony: 낙타들이 사막에서 물 없이 얼마나 오래 지낼 수 있는지 궁금해.
수지: 인터넷에서 찾아보자.
Tony: 그래. 인터넷 정보에 따르면 낙타는 물 없이 2주 정도 갈 수 있대.
수지: 우와, 굉장하다! 낙타는 정말 흥미로운 동물이구나.
Tony: 나는 언젠가 사막에서 그들과 함께 여행하고 싶어.

Real Life Talk Step 2

1. **A:** _____ is the _____ _____ on Earth?

   B: I thinks it's the _____ _____.

   A: _____ _____ _____ _____ _____ it is.

   B: The book _____ the _____ _____ of the South Pole is _____ -49°C.

   A: That's _____!

2. **A:** Which planet is the _____ in the _____ _____?

   B: I thinks it's _____.

   A: _____ _____ _____ _____ _____ it is.

   B: _____ _____ _____ Jupiter is over 11 _____ _____ Earth.

   A: That's amazing!

3. **A:** Where is the _____ _____ _____ Earth?

   B: I thinks it's the Sahara Desert.

   A: I wonder _____ _____ _____ _____.

   B: The newspaper _____ the temperature of the Sahara Desert can _____ _____ _____ 50°C.

   A: That's _____!

1. A: 지구에서 가장 추운 곳이 어디니?
   B: 남극이라고 생각해.
   A: 나는 그곳이 얼마나 추운지 궁금해.
   B: 책에 따르면 남극의 평균 온도가 섭씨 영하 49도래.
   A: 굉장하다!

2. A: 태양계에서 가장 큰 행성이 어느 것이니?
   B: 목성이라고 생각해.
   A: 나는 그것이 얼마나 큰지 궁금해.
   B: 인터넷에 따르면 목성은 지구보다 11배 이상 크다고 해.
   A: 굉장하다!

3. A: 지구에서 가장 더운 사막이 어디게?
   B: 사하라 사막이라고 생각해.
   A: 나는 그곳이 얼마나 더운지 궁금해.
   B: 신문에 따르면 사하라 사막 온도가 섭씨 50도까지 이룰 수 있다고 해.
   A: 굉장하다!

※ 다음 우리말에 맞도록 대화를 영어로 쓰시오.

Listen and Speak 1 A

B: _____

G: _____

B: _____

G: _____

B: _____

B: 우리는 산 정상에 거의 다 왔어.
G: 나는 이 산이 얼마나 높은지 궁금해.
B: 이 산은 높이가 약 2,000미터야.
G: 우와! 정말 높은 산이구나.
B: 응, 맞아. 계속 올라가자.

Listen and Speak 1 B

B: _____

G: _____

B: _____

G: _____

B: _____

G: _____

B: _____

G: _____

B: TV에 나온 아기 펭귄들을 봐. 아주 귀여워.
G: 응, 하지만 그들은 저곳에서 매우 추워 보여.
B: 응, 남극은 지구에서 가장 추운 곳이야.
G: 그곳이 얼마나 추운지 궁금해.
B: 평균 기온이 7월에는 약 섭씨 영하 58도이고, 12월에는 약 섭씨 영하 26도야.
G: 오, 그러면 그곳은 12월보다 7월이 더 춥구나. 흥미롭다!
B: 응. 비록 그곳은 매우 춥지만 눈은 많이 내리지 않아.
G: 그것도 흥미롭다!

Listen and Speak 1 C

1. A: _____

   B: _____

   A: _____

   B: _____

   A: _____

2. A: _____

   B: _____

   A: _____

   B: _____

   A: _____

3. A: _____

   B: _____

   A: _____

   B: _____

   A: _____

1. A: 마침내 다 왔어.
   B: 맞아, 매우 신나. 둘러보자.
   A: 나는 버스 정류장이 어디에 있는지 궁금해.
   B: 경찰서 앞에 있어.
   A: 맞아. 가자.

2. A: 마침내 다 왔어.
   B: 맞아, 매우 신나. 둘러보자.
   A: 나는 안내 센터가 어디에 있는지 궁금해.
   B: 도서관 뒤에 있어.
   A: 맞아. 가자.

3. A: 마침내 다 왔어.
   B: 맞아, 매우 신나. 둘러보자.
   A: 나는 Green Park가 어디에 있는지 궁금해.
   B: 학교 옆에 있어.
   A: 맞아. 가자.

Listen and Speak 2 A

B: _____

G: _____

B: _____

G: _____

B: _____

B: 바깥 날씨가 아주 좋아.

G: 응. 오늘 오후에 소풍 갈래?

B: 좋은 생각이야. 날씨를 확인해 주겠니?

G: 오, 안 돼! 일기 예보에 따르면 오후에 비가 올 거래.

B: 그러면 다음에 가자.

Listen and Speak 2 B

B: _____

G: _____

B: _____

G: _____

B: _____

G: _____

B: _____

G: _____

B: _____

B: 수민아, 일요일에 무엇을 할 거니?

G: 나는 등산을 갈 거야. 나와 함께 가겠니?

B: 그러고 싶어. 어디로 가고 싶니?

G: 나는 남산에 가려고 생각 중이야.

B: 오, 매년 이맘때 그곳 경치는 아주 아름다워.

G: 맞아. 지금 빨간 단풍잎으로 덮여 있다고 들었어.

B: 좋아. 가장 짧은 등산 코스는 얼마나 걸리니?

G: 인터넷 정보에 따르면 약 두 시간 정도 걸린대.

B: 알겠어, 일요일에 봐!

Listen and Speak 2 C

1. A: _____

   B: _____

   A: _____

   B: _____

2. A: _____

   B: _____

   A: _____

   B: _____

1. A: 뭐 하고 있니?
   B: 신문을 읽는 중이야.
   A: 흥미로운 것이 있니?
   B: 이 기사에 따르면 과학자들이 새로운 행성을 발견했대.

2. A: 뭐 하고 있니?
   B: 신문을 읽는 중이야.
   A: 흥미로운 것이 있니?
   B: 이 기사에 따르면 고래 가족이 동해에서 발견됐대.

Real Life Talk Watch a Video

Suji: _____

Tony: _____

Suji: _____

Tony: _____

Suji: _____

Tony: _____

Suji: _____

Tony: _____

수지: 이 사진을 봐!

Tony: 우와! 낙타들이 사막에서 한 줄로 걸어가고 있네.

수지: 응. 사막은 매우 덥고 건조해 보여.

Tony: 낙타들이 사막에서 물 없이 얼마나 오래 지낼 수 있는지 궁금해.

수지: 인터넷에서 찾아보자.

Tony: 그래. 인터넷 정보에 따르면 낙타는 물 없이 2주 정도 갈 수 있대.

수지: 우와, 굉장하다! 낙타는 정말 흥미로운 동물이구나.

Tony: 나는 언젠가 사막에서 그들과 함께 여행하고 싶어.

Real Life Talk Step 2

1. **A:** _____

   B: _____

   A: _____

   B: _____

   A: _____

2. **A:** _____

   B: _____

   A: _____

   B: _____

   A: _____

3. **A:** _____

   B: _____

   A: _____

   B: _____

   A: _____

1. A: 지구에서 가장 추운 곳이 어디니?
   B: 남극이라고 생각해.
   A: 나는 그곳이 얼마나 추운지 궁금해.
   B: 책에 따르면 남극의 평균 온도가 섭씨 영하 49도래.
   A: 굉장하다!

2. A: 태양계에서 가장 큰 행성이 어느 것이니?
   B: 목성이라고 생각해.
   A: 나는 그것이 얼마나 큰지 궁금해.
   B: 인터넷에 따르면 목성은 지구보다 11배 이상 크다고 해.
   A: 굉장하다!

3. A: 지구에서 가장 더운 사막이 어디게?
   B: 사하라 사막이라고 생각해.
   A: 나는 그곳이 얼마나 더운지 궁금해.
   B: 신문에 따르면 사하라 사막 온도가 섭씨 50도까지 이룰 수 있다고 해.
   A: 굉장하다!

※ 다음 우리말과 일치하도록 빈칸에 알맞은 것을 골라 쓰시오.

1 _____ the _____
A. Sea   B. Under

2 _____ of our _____ is _____ by _____.
A. covered   B. two-thirds   C. oceans   D. planet

3 They are _____ of _____ and are home to _____ of _____.
A. millions   B. wonder   C. species   D. full

4 _____ day, we are _____ _____ _____ about them.
A. things   B. every   C. new   D. learning

5 _____ _____ _____ about some interesting _____ animals.
A. find   B. sea   C. out   D. let's

6 _____ _____
A. Dreams   B. Sweet

7 Can you _____ _____ these _____ are _____ in the picture?
A. whales   B. what   C. guess   D. doing

8 It _____ _____ they are standing _____ in a _____.
A. like   B. up   C. looks   D. group

9 But they are _____ _____!
A. sleeping   B. actually

10 Humpback whales _____ _____ their _____ _____ they sleep.
A. while   B. stand   C. tails   D. on

11 They _____ _____ the _____.
A. near   B. surface   C. sleep

12 _____ they are not fish, they _____ to come _____ to _____.
A. breathe   B. since   C. up   D. need

13 _____, they don't _____ _____ completely.
A. asleep   B. also   C. fall

14 When they _____ up, they come out of the water for a _____ _____ and dive back _____ the sea.
A. wake   B. breath   C. deep   D. into

15 _____ Your _____
A. Meal   B. Enjoy

16 If you think fish are not _____, _____ a _____ _____ the tuskfish.
A. smart   B. look   C. take   D. at

1 바다 아래에

2 우리 행성의 3분의 2는 대양들로 덮여 있다.

3 대양들은 신기한 것으로 가득 차 있고 수많은 종의 서식지이다.

4 매일 우리는 그들에 관한 새로운 것들을 배우고 있다.

5 몇몇 흥미로운 바다 동물들을 알아보자.

6 좋은 꿈 꿔라

7 여러분은 그림 속 이 고래들이 무엇을 하고 있는지 추측할 수 있는가?

8 그들이 무리를 지어 서 있는 것처럼 보인다.

9 그러나 그들은 실제로는 잠을 자고 있다!

10 혹등고래들은 잠을 자는 동안 꼬리로 서 있다.

11 그들은 수면 근처에서 잠을 잔다.

12 그들은 물고기가 아니기 때문에 숨을 쉬기 위해 위로 나올 필요가 있다.

13 또한 그들은 완전히 잠들지 않는다.

14 그들은 잠에서 깨면 심호흡을 하러 물 밖으로 나왔다가 바다로 다시 뛰어든다.

15 맛있게 먹어라

16 만약 물고기가 똑똑하지 않다고 생각한다면 'tuskfish'를 보아라.

17 This small fish _____ favorite food is _____ uses a _____ to _____ them.

    A. tool   B. open   C. clams   D. whose

18 Clams usually _____ under the sand, so they _____ be _____ _____.

    A. easily   B. hide   C. discovered   D. cannot

19 The tuskfish _____ on the sand _____ a _____ _____.

    A. until   B. blows   C. appears   D. clam

20 The _____ is _____ _____, _____ the fish cannot eat it.

    A. so   B. closed   C. clam   D. tightly

21 But the tuskfish _____ _____ _____.

    A. up   B. give   C. doesn't

22 It _____ the clam _____ a _____.

    A. against   B. smashes   C. rock

23 _____ the _____, the clam _____ and dinner is _____.

    A. end   B. served   C. opens   D. in

24 One, Two, _____, _____!

    A. Jump   B. Three

25 You have _____ seen a bird _____ _____ to the sea to _____ a fish.

    A. catch   B. probably   C. down   D. fly

26 But have you ever _____ a fish _____ _____ _____ the water to catch a bird?

    A. out   B. seen   C. of   D. jump

27 Well, birds _____ to be _____ when a _____ trevally is _____.

    A. careful   B. have   C. around   D. giant

28 This fish can _____ _____ _____ 170cm and 80kg.

    A. up   B. grow   C. to

29 But don't _____ _____ _____ _____ you.

    A. fool   B. let   C. size   D. its

30 This _____ is _____ and _____.

    A. smart   B. fish   C. quick

31 It can _____ a _____ bird and _____ its speed and _____.

    A. distance   B. spot   C. calculate   D. flying

32 When the bird _____ _____, the giant trevally _____ out of the water and _____ it.

    A. jumps   B. flies   C. catches   D. nearby

17 가장 좋아하는 먹이가 조개인 이 작은 물고기는 조개를 열기 위해 도구를 사용한다.

18 조개는 대개 모래 아래에 숨어 있어서 쉽게 발견할 수 없다.

19 'tuskfish'는 조개가 나타날 때까지 모래에 입김을 분다.

20 조개가 단단히 닫혀 있어서 물고기는 이것을 먹을 수 없다.

21 그러나 'tuskfish'는 포기하지 않는다.

22 'tuskfish'는 돌에 조개를 내리친다.

23 마침내 조개가 열리고 밥상이 차려진다.

24 하나, 둘, 셋, 뛰어라!

25 여러분은 아마 새가 물고기를 잡기 위해 바다로 날아 내려가는 것을 본 적이 있을 것이다.

26 그러나 물고기가 새를 잡기 위해 물 밖으로 뛰어오르는 것을 본 적이 있는가?

27 자, 새들은 'giant trevally'가 주변에 있을 때 조심해야 한다.

28 이 물고기는 170센티미터에 80킬로그램까지 자랄 수 있다.

29 그러나 그 크기에 속지 마라.

30 이 물고기는 빠르고 똑똑하다.

31 이것은 날고 있는 새를 발견하고 그 새의 속도와 거리를 계산할 수 있다.

32 새가 근처에 날고 있을 때, 'giant trevally'는 물 밖으로 뛰어올라 새를 잡는다.

※ 다음 우리말과 일치하도록 빈칸에 알맞은 말을 쓰시오.

1 _____ the _____

2 _____ of our planet _____ _____ _____ oceans.

3 They _____ _____ _____ wonder and are home to _____ _____ _____.

4 Every day, we are learning _____ _____ about them.

5 _____ _____ _____ about some interesting _____ _____.

6 _____ Dreams

7 Can you guess _____ _____ _____ _____ _____ in the picture?

8 It _____ _____ they are standing up _____ _____ _____.

9 But they are _____ _____!

10 Humpback whales _____ _____ _____ _____ _____ _____ _____.

11 They sleep _____ _____ _____ _____.

12 _____ they are not fish, they _____ _____ _____ _____ _____ _____.

13 Also, they don't _____ _____ _____.

14 When they wake up, they come out of the water _____ _____ _____ _____ and _____ _____ _____ the sea.

15 _____ Your _____

16 If you think fish are not smart, _____ _____ _____ _____ the tuskfish.

1 바다 아래에

2 우리 행성의 3분의 2는 대양들로 덮여 있다.

3 대양들은 신기한 것으로 가득 차 있고 수많은 종의 서식지이다.

4 매일 우리는 그들에 관한 새로운 것들을 배우고 있다.

5 몇몇 흥미로운 바다 동물들을 알아보자.

6 좋은 꿈 꿔라

7 여러분은 그림 속 이 고래들이 무엇을 하고 있는지 추측할 수 있는가?

8 그들이 무리를 지어 서 있는 것처럼 보인다.

9 그러나 그들은 실제로는 잠을 자고 있다!

10 혹등고래들은 잠을 자는 동안 꼬리로 서 있다.

11 그들은 수면 근처에서 잠을 잔다.

12 그들은 물고기가 아니기 때문에 숨을 쉬기 위해 위로 나올 필요가 있다.

13 또한 그들은 완전히 잠들지 않는다.

14 그들은 잠에서 깨면 심호흡을 하러 물 밖으로 나왔다가 바다로 다시 뛰어든다.

15 맛있게 먹어라

16 만약 물고기가 똑똑하지 않다고 생각한다면 'tuskfish'를 보아라.

17 This small fish _____ _____ _____ is clams uses a tool to _____ them.

18 Clams usually _____ under the sand, so they _____ _____ _____ _____.

19 The tuskfish _____ on the sand _____ a clam _____.

20 The clam _____ _____ _____, so the fish cannot eat it.

21 But the tuskfish doesn't _____ _____.

22 It _____ the clam _____ a rock.

23 _____ _____ _____, the clam opens and dinner _____ _____.

24 One, Two, Three, _____!

25 You _____ probably _____ a bird _____ _____ to the sea to catch a fish.

26 But _____ you _____ _____ a fish _____ _____ _____ _____ _____ to catch a bird?

27 Well, birds _____ _____ be careful when a giant trevally _____ _____.

28 This fish can grow _____ _____ 170cm and 80kg.

29 But don't _____ its size _____ you.

30 This fish is _____ _____ _____.

31 It can _____ a flying bird and _____ its _____ and _____.

32 When the bird flies _____, the giant trevally _____ out of the water and _____ it.

17 가장 좋아하는 먹이가 조개인 이 작은 물고기는 조개를 열기 위해 도구를 사용한다.

18 조개는 대개 모래 아래에 숨어 있어서 쉽게 발견할 수 없다.

19 'tuskfish'는 조개가 나타날 때까지 모래에 입김을 분다.

20 조개가 단단히 닫혀 있어서 물고기는 이것을 먹을 수 없다.

21 그러나 'tuskfish'는 포기하지 않는다.

22 'tuskfish'는 돌에 조개를 내리친다.

23 마침내 조개가 열리고 밥상이 차려진다.

24 하나, 둘, 셋, 뛰어라!

25 여러분은 아마 새가 물고기를 잡기 위해 바다로 날아 내려가는 것을 본 적이 있을 것이다.

26 그러나 물고기가 새를 잡기 위해 물 밖으로 뛰어오르는 것을 본 적이 있는가?

27 자, 새들은 'giant trevally'가 주변에 있을 때 조심해야 한다.

28 이 물고기는 170센티미터에 80킬로그램까지 자랄 수 있다.

29 그러나 그 크기에 속지 마라.

30 이 물고기는 빠르고 똑똑하다.

31 이것은 날고 있는 새를 발견하고 그 새의 속도와 거리를 계산할 수 있다.

32 새가 근처에 날고 있을 때, 'giant trevally'는 물 밖으로 뛰어올라 새를 잡는다.

※ 다음 문장을 우리말로 쓰시오.

1 ▶ Under the Sea

➡ _____

2 ▶ Two-thirds of our planet is covered by oceans.

➡ _____

3 ▶ They are full of wonder and are home to millions of species.

➡ _____

4 ▶ Every day, we are learning new things about them.

➡ _____

5 ▶ Let's find out about some interesting sea animals.

➡ _____

6 ▶ Sweet Dreams

➡ _____

7 ▶ Can you guess what these whales are doing in the picture?

➡ _____

8 ▶ It looks like they are standing up in a group.

➡ _____

9 ▶ But they are actually sleeping!

➡ _____

10 ▶ Humpback whales stand on their tails while they sleep.

➡ _____

11 ▶ They sleep near the surface.

➡ _____

12 ▶ Since they are not fish, they need to come up to breathe.

➡ _____

13 ▶ Also, they don't fall asleep completely.

➡ _____

14 ▶ When they wake up, they come out of the water for a deep breath and dive back into the sea.

➡ _____

15 ▶ Enjoy Your Meal

➡ _____

16 If you think fish are not smart, take a look at the tuskfish.

➡ _____

17 This small fish whose favorite food is clams uses a tool to open them.

➡ _____

18 Clams usually hide under the sand, so they cannot be easily discovered.

➡ _____

19 The tuskfish blows on the sand until a clam appears.

➡ _____

20 The clam is closed tightly, so the fish cannot eat it.

➡ _____

21 But the tuskfish doesn't give up.

➡ _____

22 It smashes the clam against a rock.

➡ _____

23 In the end, the clam opens and dinner is served.

➡ _____

24 One, Two, Three, Jump!

➡ _____

25 You have probably seen a bird fly down to the sea to catch a fish.

➡ _____

26 But have you ever seen a fish jump out of the water to catch a bird?

➡ _____

27 Well, birds have to be careful when a giant trevally is around.

➡ _____

28 This fish can grow up to 170cm and 80kg.

➡ _____

29 But don't let its size fool you.

➡ _____

30 This fish is quick and smart.

➡ _____

31 It can spot a flying bird and calculate its speed and distance.

➡ _____

32 When the bird flies nearby, the giant trevally jumps out of the water and catches it.

➡ _____

※ 다음 괄호 안의 단어들을 우리말에 맞도록 바르게 배열하시오.

1 (the / Under / Sea)
➡ _____

2 (of / two-thirds / our / is / planet / by / covered / oceans.)
➡ _____

3 (are / they / of / full / and / wonder / home / are / millions / to / species. / of)
➡ _____

4 (day, / every / are / we / new / learning / about / them. / things)
➡ _____

5 (find / let's / about / out / interesting / some / animals. / sea)
➡ _____

6 (Dreams / Sweet)
➡ _____

7 (you / can / what / guess / whales / these / doing / are / the / in / picture?)
➡ _____

8 (looks / it / they / like / standing / are / in / up / group. / a)
➡ _____

9 (they / but / actually / are / sleeping!)
➡ _____

10 (whales / humpback / on / stand / tails / their / they / while / sleep.)
➡ _____

11 (sleep / they / the / near / surface.)
➡ _____

12 (they / since / not / are / fish, / need / they / come / to / to / up / breathe.)
➡ _____

13 (they / also, / fall / don't / completely. / asleep)
➡ _____

14 (they / when / up, / wake / come / they / of / out / water / the / a / for / breath / deep / and / back / dive / the / into / sea.)
➡ _____
_____

15 (Your / Meal / Enjoy)
➡ _____

16 (you / if / fish / think / not / are / smart, / a / take / at / look / tuskfish. / the)
➡ _____

---

1 바다 아래에

2 우리 행성의 3분의 2는 대양들로 덮여 있다.

3 대양들은 신기한 것으로 가득 차 있고 수많은 종의 서식지이다.

4 매일 우리는 그들에 관한 새로운 것들을 배우고 있다.

5 몇몇 흥미로운 바다 동물들을 알아보자.

6 좋은 꿈 꿔라

7 여러분은 그림 속 이 고래들이 무엇을 하고 있는지 추측할 수 있는가?

8 그들이 무리를 지어 서 있는 것처럼 보인다.

9 그러나 그들은 실제로는 잠을 자고 있다!

10 혹등고래들은 잠을 자는 동안 꼬리로 서 있다.

11 그들은 수면 근처에서 잠을 잔다.

12 그들은 물고기가 아니기 때문에 숨을 쉬기 위해 위로 나올 필요가 있다.

13 또한 그들은 완전히 잠들지 않는다.

14 그들은 잠에서 깨면 심호흡을 하러 물 밖으로 나왔다가 바다로 다시 뛰어든다.

15 맛있게 먹어라

16 만약 물고기가 똑똑하지 않다고 생각한다면 'tuskfish'를 보아라.

17 (small / this / whose / fish / food / favorite / clams / is / a / uses / to / tool / them. / open)

➡ _____

18 (usally / clams / under / hide / sand, / the / they / so / be / cannot / discovered. / easily)

➡ _____

19 (tuskfish / the / on / blows / sand / the / a / until / appears. / clam)

➡ _____

20 (clam / the / closed / is / tightly, / the / so / cannot / fish / it. / eat)

➡ _____

21 (the / but / doesn't / is / tuskfish / up. / give)

➡ _____

22 (smashes / it / clam / the / a / against / rock.)

➡ _____

23 (the / end, / in / clam / the / and / opens / is / dinner / served.)

➡ _____

24 (Two, / One, / Jump! / Three,)

➡ _____

25 (have / you / seen / probably / bird / a / down / fly / the / to / to / sea / a / catch / fish.)

➡ _____

26 (have / but / ever / you / a / seen / jump / fish / of / out / water / the / to / a / catch / bird?)

➡ _____

27 (birds / well, / to / have / careful / be / a / when / trevally / giant / around. / is)

➡ _____

28 (fish / this / grow / can / to / up / 80kg. / and 170cm)

➡ _____

29 (don't / but / its / let / fool / size / you.)

➡ _____

30 (fish / this / quick / is / smart. / and)

➡ _____

31 (can / it / a / spot / bird / flying / and / its / calculate / speed / distance. / and)

➡ _____

32 (the / when / flies / bird / nearby, / giant / the / jumps / trevally / of / out / water / the / catches / and / it.)

➡ _____
_____

---

17 가장 좋아하는 먹이가 조개인 이 작은 물고기는 조개를 열기 위해 도구를 사용한다.

18 조개는 대개 모래 아래에 숨어 있어서 쉽게 발견할 수 없다.

19 'tuskfish'는 조개가 나타날 때까지 모래에 입김을 분다.

20 조개가 단단히 닫혀 있어서 물고기는 이것을 먹을 수 없다.

21 그러나 'tuskfish'는 포기하지 않는다.

22 'tuskfish'는 돌에 조개를 내리친다.

23 마침내 조개가 열리고 밥상이 차려진다.

24 하나, 둘, 셋, 뛰어라!

25 여러분은 아마 새가 물고기를 잡기 위해 바다로 날아 내려가는 것을 본 적이 있을 것이다.

26 그러나 물고기가 새를 잡기 위해 물 밖으로 뛰어오르는 것을 본 적이 있는가?

27 자, 새들은 'giant trevally'가 주변에 있을 때 조심해야 한다.

28 이 물고기는 170센티미터에 80 킬로그램까지 자랄 수 있다.

29 그러나 그 크기에 속지 마라.

30 이 물고기는 빠르고 똑똑하다.

31 이것은 날고 있는 새를 발견하고 그 새의 속도와 거리를 계산할 수 있다.

32 새가 근처에 날고 있을 때, 'giant trevally'는 물 밖으로 뛰어올라 새를 잡는다.

※ 다음 우리말을 영어로 쓰시오.

1 바다 아래에

➡ _____

2 우리 행성의 3분의 2는 대양들로 덮여 있다.

➡ _____

3 대양들은 신기한 것으로 가득 차 있고 수많은 종의 서식지이다.

➡ _____

4 매일 우리는 그들에 관한 새로운 것들을 배우고 있다.

➡ _____

5 몇몇 흥미로운 바다 동물들을 알아보자.

➡ _____

6 좋은 꿈 꿔라

➡ _____

7 여러분은 그림 속 이 고래들이 무엇을 하고 있는지 추측할 수 있는가?

➡ _____

8 그들이 무리를 지어 서 있는 것처럼 보인다.

➡ _____

9 그러나 그들은 실제로는 잠을 자고 있다!

➡ _____

10 혹등고래들은 잠을 자는 동안 꼬리로 서 있다.

➡ _____

11 그들은 수면 근처에서 잠을 잔다.

➡ _____

12 그들은 물고기가 아니기 때문에 숨을 쉬기 위해 위로 나올 필요가 있다.

➡ _____

13 또한 그들은 완전히 잠들지 않는다.

➡ _____

14 그들은 잠에서 깨면 심호흡을 하러 물 밖으로 나왔다가 바다로 다시 뛰어든다.

➡ _____

15 맛있게 먹어라

➡ _____

16 만약 물고기가 똑똑하지 않다고 생각한다면 'tuskfish'를 보아라.

➡ _____

17 가장 좋아하는 먹이가 조개인 이 작은 물고기는 조개를 열기 위해 도구를 사용한다.

➡ _____

18 조개는 대개 모래 아래에 숨어 있어서 쉽게 발견할 수 없다.

➡ _____

19 'tuskfish'는 조개가 나타날 때까지 모래에 입김을 분다.

➡ _____

20 조개가 단단히 닫혀 있어서 물고기는 이것을 먹을 수 없다.

➡ _____

21 그러나 'tuskfish'는 포기하지 않는다.

➡ _____

22 'tuskfish'는 돌에 조개를 내리친다.

➡ _____

23 마침내 조개가 열리고 밥상이 차려진다.

➡ _____

24 하나, 둘, 셋, 뛰어라!

➡ _____

25 여러분은 아마 새가 물고기를 잡기 위해 바다로 날아 내려가는 것을 본 적이 있을 것이다.

➡ _____

26 그러나 물고기가 새를 잡기 위해 물 밖으로 뛰어오르는 것을 본 적이 있는가?

➡ _____

27 자, 새들은 'giant trevally'가 주변에 있을 때 조심해야 한다.

➡ _____

28 이 물고기는 170센티미터에 80킬로그램까지 자랄 수 있다.

➡ _____

29 그러나 그 크기에 속지 마라.

➡ _____

30 이 물고기는 빠르고 똑똑하다.

➡ _____

31 이것은 날고 있는 새를 발견하고 그 새의 속도와 거리를 계산할 수 있다.

➡ _____

32 새가 근처에 날고 있을 때, 'giant trevally'는 물 밖으로 뛰어올라 새를 잡는다.

➡ _____

※ 다음 우리말과 일치하도록 빈칸에 알맞은 말을 쓰시오.

After You Read A. Read and Correct

1. I _____ _____ _____ today.

2. _____ of our planet _____ _____ _____ oceans.

3. They are home to _____ _____ _____.

4. _____ _____ _____ _____ _____ about sea animals.

5. _____ _____, humpback whales _____ _____ _____ _____ _____ they sleep, and they sleep _____ _____ _____.

1. 나는 오늘 바다에 대해 배웠다.
2. 우리 행성의 3분의 2는 대양들로 덮여 있다.
3. 그것들은 수많은 종의 서식지이다.
4. 바다 동물들에 관한 많은 흥미로운 사실들이 있다.
5. 예를 들어, 혹등고래들은 잠을 자는 동안 꼬리로 서 있고, 그들은 수면 근처에서 잠을 잔다.

Word Power

1. He found a _____ _____ _____ _____ the car.

2. I can _____ you _____ _____ _____.

3. _____ _____ _____ _____ his cute looks.

4. Experience _____ even _____ _____.

1. 그는 차를 주차하기 좋은 장소를 발견했다.
2. 나는 관중 속에서 너를 발견할 수 있다.
3. 그의 귀여운 외모에 속지 마라.
4. 경험은 바보조차도 현명하게 만든다.

Think and Write Step 3

1. My _____ _____: Beluga whale

2. I _____ _____ the beluga _____.

3. It lives in _____ _____ _____. It has _____ _____ _____.

4. It _____ _____ fish and _____.

5. _____ _____ _____ about the beluga whale is _____ it is _____ _____ _____ _____.

6. _____ _____ people _____ _____ the _____ _____ _____.

7. _____ it _____ _____, it is _____.

8. But when it _____ _____, its body _____ _____!

9. I want to see this animal _____ _____ _____ _____!

1. 나의 재미있는 동물: 벨루가 고래
2. 저는 벨루가 고래를 소개할게요.
3. 벨루가 고래는 북극해에 살아요. 둥근 머리를 가졌어요.
4. 벨루가 고래는 주로 물고기와 조개를 먹어요.
5. 벨루가 고래에 관한 흥미로운 사실은 온몸이 하얗다는 거예요.
6. 그것이 사람들이 벨루가 고래를 흰고래라고 부르는 이유예요.
7. 벨루가 고래는 태어날 때, 회색이에요.
8. 그러나 다 자라면, 몸은 하얀색이 돼요!
9. 저는 제 눈으로 이 동물을 보고 싶어요!

※ 다음 우리말을 영어로 쓰시오.

After You Read A. Read and Correct

1. 나는 오늘 바다에 대해 배웠다.
➡ _____

2. 우리 행성의 3분의 2는 대양들로 덮여 있다.
➡ _____

3. 그것들은 수많은 종의 서식지이다.
➡ _____

4. 바다 동물들에 관한 많은 흥미로운 사실들이 있다.
➡ _____

5. 예를 들어, 혹등고래들은 잠을 자는 동안 꼬리로 서 있고, 그들은 수면 근처에서 잠을 잔다.
➡ _____

Word Power

1. 그는 차를 주차하기 좋은 장소를 발견했다.
➡ _____

2. 나는 관중 속에서 너를 발견할 수 있다.
➡ _____

3. 그의 귀여운 외모에 속지 마라.
➡ _____

4. 경험은 바보조차도 현명하게 만든다.
➡ _____

Think and Write Step 3

1. 나의 재미있는 동물: 벨루가 고래
➡ _____

2. 저는 벨루가 고래를 소개할게요.
➡ _____

3. 벨루가 고래는 북극해에 살아요. 둥근 머리를 가졌어요.
➡ _____

4. 벨루가 고래는 주로 물고기와 조개를 먹어요.
➡ _____

5. 벨루가 고래에 관한 흥미로운 사실은 온몸이 하얗다는 거예요.
➡ _____

6. 그것이 사람들이 벨루가 고래를 흰고래라고 부르는 이유예요.
➡ _____

7. 벨루가 고래는 태어날 때, 회색이에요.
➡ _____

8. 그러나 다 자라면, 몸은 하얀색이 돼요!
➡ _____

9. 저는 제 눈으로 이 동물을 보고 싶어요!
➡ _____

※ 다음 영어를 우리말로 쓰시오.

01 protect

02 active

03 contribute

04 merchant

05 due

06 unbelievable

07 mistake

08 dynamite

09 fault

10 graduate

11 headline

12 appreciate

13 describe

14 article

15 heart attack

16 including

17 regret

18 graduation

19 habit

20 invention

21 actually

22 inventor

23 shocked

24 opinion

25 disappointed

26 originally

27 participate

28 audience

29 normal

30 award

31 perfect

32 spill

33 mistakenly

34 stomachache

35 give up

36 put off

37 think of A as B

38 take eyes off

39 catch one's breath

40 rather than

41 keep in touch

42 take part in

43 describe A as B

※ 다음 우리말을 영어로 쓰시오.

01 보통의, 정상적인 _____

02 의견 _____

03 사실 _____

04 기술하다, 묘사하다 _____

05 잘못 _____

06 졸업하다 _____

07 고맙게 생각하다 _____

08 ~을 포함해서 _____

09 완벽한 _____

10 충격을 받은 _____

11 보호하다, 지키다 _____

12 감동시키다 _____

13 관객 _____

14 상인 _____

15 후회; 후회하다 _____

16 실망한, 낙담한 _____

17 실수, 잘못 _____

18 습관 _____

19 상, 시상 _____

20 실수로 _____

21 쏟아지다, 쏟다 _____

22 ~하기로 되어 있는, 예정된 _____

23 원래는, 처음에는 _____

24 기여하다, 공헌하다 _____

25 몹시, 깊이, 매우 _____

26 발명품 _____

27 기사 _____

28 (신문 기사 등의) 표제 _____

29 복통 _____

30 심장 마비 _____

31 믿을 수 없는, 믿기 어려운 _____

32 다이너마이트 _____

33 졸업(식) _____

34 신뢰하다, 믿다 _____

35 지각하다 _____

36 놀라서 _____

37 미루다, 연기하다 _____

38 ~에 참가하다 _____

39 ~보다는 _____

40 포기하다 _____

41 안 자다, 깨어 있다 _____

42 연락하고 지내다 _____

43 A를 B라고 생각하다 _____

※ 다음 영영풀이에 알맞은 단어를 <보기>에서 골라 쓴 후, 우리말 뜻을 쓰시오.

1 _____ : a powerful explosive: _____

2 _____ : to flow over the edge of a container: _____

3 _____ : to be grateful for something: _____

4 _____ : to explain about something: _____

5 _____ : to feel sorry or unhappy about something: _____

6 _____ : to gain a goal or point in a sport or game: _____

7 _____ : a thing or an idea that has been invented: _____

8 _____ : to help to cause something to happen: _____

9 _____ : a person who sells products in large amounts: _____

10 _____ : expected at or planned for a certain time: _____

11 _____ : a ceremony at which degrees or diplomas are given out: _____

12 _____ : difficult or impossible to believe: _____

13 _____ : the group of people who have gathered to watch or listen to something:
   _____

14 _____ : the title written in large letters over a story in a newspaper:
   _____

15 _____ : to cause someone to feel an emotion and especially sadness or sympathy:
   _____

16 _____ : to give information about something via newspaper, TV or radio:
   _____

보기			
report	describe	move	score
due	regret	unbelievable	dynamite
audience	appreciate	headline	invention
merchant	contribute	graduation	spill

※ 다음 우리말과 일치하도록 빈칸에 알맞은 말을 쓰시오.

Listen and Speak 1 A

G: Mike, why _____ _____ _____ _____ class?

B: I had a bad _____.

G: Oh, no! _____ you _____ now?

B: Yeah. I _____ _____ _____ _____ last night.

Listen and Speak 1 B

G: Jiho, what's _____? You look _____.

B: Yeah. I _____ _____ _____ last night.

G: Did you _____ computer games _____?

B: No, _____ this time. I _____ _____ _____ my history project.

G: Is it _____ today?

B: Yeah. I _____ _____ _____ _____ _____ the _____ _____.

G: Hmm, I understand. I often have _____ _____ problem.

B: Really? Well, let's _____ _____ _____ our bad _____.

Listen and Speak 1 C

1. A: What's _____?
   B: I _____ _____ _____ the rain.
   A: Oh, I'm _____ _____ _____ that.
   B: I should _____ _____ an umbrella.

2. A: _____ wrong?
   B: I _____ the test.
   A: Oh, I'm sorry to _____ _____.
   B: I _____ _____ _____ _____ _____.

3. A: What's _____?
   B: I _____ my bike.
   A: Oh, I'm sorry _____ _____ that.
   B: _____ _____ _____ _____ it.

4. A: What's wrong?
   B: I _____ _____ _____ school.
   A: Oh, I'm _____ _____ _____ _____ _____.
   B: I _____ _____ _____ _____ _____ _____.

G: Mike, 왜 수업에 늦었니?
B: 배가 많이 아팠어.
G: 오, 저런! 지금은 괜찮니?
B: 응. 어젯밤 덜 먹었어야 했어.

G: 지호야, 무슨 일이니? 너 피곤해 보여.
B: 응. 어젯밤에 늦게까지 깨어 있었어.
G: 너 또 컴퓨터 게임을 했니?
B: 아니, 이번엔 아니야. 나는 역사 과제를 끝내야 했어.
G: 그 과제가 오늘까지니?
B: 응. 나는 마지막 순간까지 미루지 말았어야 했어.
G: 음, 이해해. 나도 종종 같은 문제를 겪어.
B: 정말? 음, 우리의 나쁜 습관을 바꾸도록 노력하자.

1. A: 무슨 일 있니?
   B: 오, 비를 맞았어.
   A: 안됐구나.
   B: 나는 우산을 가져왔어야 했어.

2. A: 무슨 일 있니?
   B: 시험에 떨어졌어.
   A: 오, 안됐구나.
   B: 나는 공부를 열심히 했어야 했어.

3. A: 무슨 일 있니?
   B: 자전거를 잃어버렸어.
   A: 오, 안됐구나.
   B: 나는 사슬로 묶어놨어야 했어.

4. A: 무슨 일 있니?
   B: 학교에 늦었어.
   A: 오, 안됐구나.
   B: 나는 일찍 일어났어야 했어.

Listen and Speak 2 A

G: Jinsu, what are you _____ _____ _____ _____ the vacation?

B: I'm going to read _____ _____ books. _____ _____ you?

G: I'm _____ _____ _____ my grandparents in Busan.

B: Sounds great. I _____ _____ _____ a wonderful vacation.

G: 진수야, 방학 동안 무엇을 할 거니?
B: 나는 책을 많이 읽을 거야. 너는 어떠니?
G: 나는 부산에 계신 조부모님을 방문할 계획이야.
B: 좋구나. 멋진 방학을 보내길 바라.

Listen and Speak 2 B

G: Jaemin, are you _____ _____ the singing contest?

B: Well, _____ _____ _____ _____ _____, Tina.

G: Why? I _____ you really _____ _____ _____ _____ the contest.

B: I don't think I'm a _____ _____.

G: Come on. You're _____ _____ _____ _____.

B: Do you really _____ _____?

G: Of _____. You have a really nice _____.

B: Thank _____ _____ so, I'll _____ _____.

B: _____ _____ _____ the contest.

G: 재민아, 노래 경연 대회에 나갈 준비는 됐니?
B: 음, 포기할까 생각 중이야, Tina.
G: 왜? 나는 네가 그 대회에 정말로 참가하고 싶어 한다고 생각했어.
B: 나는 내가 노래를 잘하는 것 같지 않아.
G: 그러지 말고. 너는 내가 아는 노래를 가장 잘하는 사람이야.
B: 정말로 그렇게 생각하니?
G: 물론이지. 너는 정말 멋진 목소리를 가졌어.
B: 그렇게 말해 줘서 고마워. 최선을 다해 볼게.
G: 네가 대회에서 우승하기를 바라.

Listen and Speak 2 C

1. A: What _____ you _____ _____ do tomorrow?

   B: I'm _____ _____ _____ in the school festival.

   A: Great! I _____ _____ _____ the _____.

   B: Thanks. I _____ _____, too.

2. A: What are you going to do tomorrow?

   B: I'm _____ _____ _____ soccer.

   A: Great! I _____ _____ _____ _____ _____.

   B: Thanks. I hope so, _____.

3. A: What are you going to do tomorrow?

   B: I'm going to _____ _____ the _____ _____.

   A: Great! _____ _____ _____ _____ the contest.

   B: Thanks. _____ _____ _____, too.

1. A: 너는 내일 무엇을 할 계획이니?
   B: 학교 축제에서 노래 부를 거야.
   A: 멋지네! 나는 네가 청중을 감동시키기를 바라.
   B: 고마워. 나도 그러길 바라.

2. A: 너는 내일 무엇을 할 계획이니?
   B: 축구를 할 거야.
   A: 멋지네! 나는 네가 득점하기를 바라.
   B: 고마워. 나도 그러길 바라.

3. A: 너는 내일 무엇을 할 계획이니?
   B: 연설 대회에 참가할 거야.
   A: 멋지네! 나는 네가 대회에서 우승하기를 바라.
   B: 고마워. 나도 그러길 바라.

Real Life Talk Watch a Video

Minho: Linda, what are you _____?

Linda: I'm reading _____ _____ from my classmates.

Minho: Oh, it _____ _____ they had _____ _____ _____ _____ to you.

Linda: Many of them _____ _____ they like my _____.

Minho: That's nice. What _____?

Linda: _____ _____ _____ said I didn't _____ _____ _____ _____ them.

Minho: That's not your _____. You were always _____.

Linda: Yeah, but I _____ _____ _____ _____ _____ _____ my classmates.

Minho: You still have time _____ _____.

Linda: You're _____.

Minho: I _____ _____ _____ _____ _____ your classmates _____ _____.

Linda: Thanks. _____ _____ _____ _____, too.

Minho: Linda, 무엇을 읽고 있니?

Linda: 나는 학급 친구들에게 받은 졸업 메시지를 읽고 있어.

Minho: 오, 친구들이 너에게 할 말이 많은 것 같구나.

Linda: 그들 중 많은 친구들이 나의 미소를 좋아한다고 적었어.

Minho: 멋지네. 그 외에는?

Linda: 그들 중 몇몇은 내가 그들과 충분히 어울리지 않았다고 말했어.

Minho: 그건 네 잘못이 아니야. 너는 항상 바빴잖아.

Linda: 응, 하지만 나는 학급 친구들과 더 많은 시간을 보냈어야 했어.

Minho: 졸업 후에도 여전히 시간이 있어.

Linda: 네 말이 맞아.

Minho: 네가 졸업 후에도 학급 친구들과 계속 연락하기를 바라.

Linda: 고마워. 나도 그러길 바라.

Real Life Talk Step 2

1. A: I _____ _____ we're _____ soon.

   B: Yeah. Is _____ _____ you _____ about your middle school life?

   A: Yes. I _____ _____ _____ _____ _____ _____ _____.

   B: Well, you _____ _____ _____ _____ _____ in high school.

   A: I _____ you're right.

   B: I _____ _____ _____ _____ _____ in classes in high school.

2. A: I can't _____ _____ _____ _____ soon.

   B: Yeah. Is there _____ _____ _____ _____ _____ your middle school life?

   A: Yes. I _____ _____ _____ _____ _____ many school events.

   B: Well, you have a _____ _____ in high school.

   A: I _____ you're _____.

   B: I _____ _____ _____ _____ _____ many school events in high school.

1. A: 우리가 곧 졸업하는 것을 믿을 수 없어.

   B: 응. 중학교 생활에서 네가 후회하는 것이 있니?

   A: 응. 나는 수업에서 적극적이었어야 했어.

   B: 음, 너는 고등학교에서 다시 한 번 기회가 있어.

   A: 네 말이 맞는 것 같아.

   B: 고등학교에서는 네가 수업에서 적극적이기를 바라.

2. A: 우리가 곧 졸업하는 것을 믿을 수 없어.

   B: 응. 중학교 생활에서 네가 후회하는 것이 있니?

   A: 응. 나는 학교 행사에 많이 참여했어야 했어.

   B: 음, 너는 고등학교에서 다시 한 번 기회가 있어.

   A: 네 말이 맞는 것 같아.

   B: 고등학교에서는 네가 많은 학교 행사에 참여하기를 바라.

※ 다음 우리말에 맞도록 대화를 영어로 쓰시오.

 해석

Listen and Speak 1 A

G: _____

B: _____

G: _____

B: _____

G: Mike, 왜 수업에 늦었니?
B: 배가 많이 아팠어.
G: 오, 저런! 지금은 괜찮니?
B: 응. 어젯밤 덜 먹었어야 했어.

Listen and Speak 1 B

G: _____

B: _____

G: _____

B: _____

G: _____

B: _____

G: _____

B: _____

G: 지호야, 무슨 일이니? 너 피곤해 보여.
B: 응. 어젯밤에 늦게까지 깨어 있었어.
G: 너 또 컴퓨터 게임을 했니?
B: 아니, 이번엔 아니야. 나는 역사 과제를 끝내야 했어.
G: 그 과제가 오늘까지니?
B: 응. 나는 마지막 순간까지 미루지 말았어야 했어.
G: 음, 이해해. 나도 종종 같은 문제를 겪어.
B: 정말? 음, 우리의 나쁜 습관을 바꾸도록 노력하자.

Listen and Speak 1 C

1. A: _____

   B: _____

   A: _____

   B: _____

2. A: _____

   B: _____

   A: _____

   B: _____

3. A: _____

   B: _____

   A: _____

   B: _____

4. A: _____

   B: _____

   A: _____

   B: _____

1. A: 무슨 일 있니?
   B: 오, 비를 맞았어.
   A: 안됐구나.
   B: 나는 우산을 가져왔어야 했어.

2. A: 무슨 일 있니?
   B: 시험에 떨어졌어.
   A: 오, 안됐구나.
   B: 나는 공부를 열심히 했어야 했어.

3. A: 무슨 일 있니?
   B: 자전거를 잃어버렸어.
   A: 오, 안됐구나.
   B: 나는 사슬로 묶어놨어야 했어.

4. A: 무슨 일 있니?
   B: 학교에 늦었어.
   A: 오, 안됐구나.
   B: 나는 일찍 일어났어야 했어.

Listen and Speak 2 A

G: _____

B: _____

G: _____

B: _____

G: 진수야, 방학 동안 무엇을 할 거니?
B: 나는 책을 많이 읽을 거야. 너는 어떠니?
G: 나는 부산에 계신 조부모님을 방문할 계획이야.
B: 좋구나. 멋진 방학을 보내길 바라.

Listen and Speak 2 B

G: _____

B: _____

G: _____

B: _____

G: _____

B: _____

G: _____

B: _____

B: _____

G: 재민아, 노래 경연 대회에 나갈 준비는 됐니?
B: 음, 포기할까 생각 중이야, Tina.
G: 왜? 나는 네가 그 대회에 정말로 참가하고 싶어 한다고 생각했어.
B: 나는 내가 노래를 잘하는 것 같지 않아.
G: 그러지 말고. 너는 내가 아는 노래를 가장 잘하는 사람이야.
B: 정말로 그렇게 생각하니?
G: 물론이지. 너는 정말 멋진 목소리를 가졌어.
B: 그렇게 말해 줘서 고마워. 최선을 다해 볼게.
G: 네가 대회에서 우승하기를 바라.

Listen and Speak 2 C

1. A: _____

   B: _____

   A: _____

   B: _____

2. A: _____

   B: _____

   A: _____

   B: _____

3. A: _____

   B: _____

   A: _____

   B: _____

1. A: 너는 내일 무엇을 할 계획이니?
   B: 학교 축제에서 노래 부를 거야.
   A: 멋지네! 나는 네가 청중을 감동시키기를 바라.
   B: 고마워. 나도 그러길 바라.

2. A: 너는 내일 무엇을 할 계획이니?
   B: 축구를 할 거야.
   A: 멋지네! 나는 네가 득점하기를 바라.
   B: 고마워. 나도 그러길 바라.

3. A: 너는 내일 무엇을 할 계획이니?
   B: 연설 대회에 참가할 거야.
   A: 멋지네! 나는 네가 대회에서 우승하기를 바라.
   B: 고마워. 나도 그러길 바라.

Real Life Talk Watch a Video

Minho: _____

Linda: _____

Minho: _____

Linda: _____

Minho: _____

Linda: _____

Minho: _____

Linda: _____

Minho: _____

Linda: _____

Minho: _____

Linda: _____

Minho: Linda, 무엇을 읽고 있니?
Linda: 나는 학급 친구들에게 받은 졸업 메시지를 읽고 있어.
Minho: 오, 친구들이 너에게 할 말이 많은 것 같구나.
Linda: 그들 중 많은 친구들이 나의 미소를 좋아한다고 적었어.
Minho: 멋지네. 그 외에는?
Linda: 그들 중 몇몇은 내가 그들과 충분히 어울리지 않았다고 말했어.
Minho: 그건 네 잘못이 아니야. 너는 항상 바빴잖아.
Linda: 응, 하지만 나는 학급 친구들과 더 많은 시간을 보냈어야 했어.
Minho: 졸업 후에도 여전히 시간이 있어.
Linda: 네 말이 맞아.
Minho: 네가 졸업 후에도 학급 친구들과 계속 연락하기를 바라.
Linda: 고마워. 나도 그러길 바라.

Real Life Talk Step 2

1. **A:** _____

   B: _____

   A: _____

   B: _____

   A: _____

   B: _____

2. **A:** _____

   B: _____

   A: _____

   B: _____

   A: _____

   B: _____

1. A: 우리가 곧 졸업하는 것을 믿을 수 없어.
   B: 응. 중학교 생활에서 네가 후회하는 것이 있니?
   A: 응. 나는 수업에서 적극적이었어야 했어.
   B: 음, 너는 고등학교에서 다시 한 번 기회가 있어.
   A: 네 말이 맞는 것 같아.
   B: 고등학교에서는 네가 수업에서 적극적이기를 바라.

2. A: 우리가 곧 졸업하는 것을 믿을 수 없어.
   B: 응. 중학교 생활에서 네가 후회하는 것이 있니?
   A: 응. 나는 학교 행사에 많이 참여했어야 했어.
   B: 음, 너는 고등학교에서 다시 한 번 기회가 있어.
   A: 네 말이 맞는 것 같아.
   B: 고등학교에서는 네가 많은 학교 행사에 참여하기를 바라.

※ 다음 우리말과 일치하도록 빈칸에 알맞은 것을 골라 쓰시오.

1 _____ Will You _____ _____ ?
　A. Be　　　　　B. How　　　　　C. Remembered

2 It was _____ a _____ _____ .
　A. normal　　　B. just　　　　　C. morning

3 Alfred Nobel _____ _____ his _____ _____ read the newspaper.
　A. chair　　　B. in　　　　C. to　　　　D. sat

4 _____ he was drinking his coffee, a _____ _____ his _____ : *The Merchant of Death, Alfred Nobel, Is Dead.*
　A. headline　　B. eye　　　C. while　　　D. caught

5 "_____ ? What is _____ ?"
　A. this　　　　B. what

6 Reading the _____ , he _____ his cup _____ _____ .
　A. surprise　　B. article　　C. dropped　　D. in

7 His coffee _____ all _____ his clothes and desk, but he couldn't _____ his eyes _____ the newspaper.
　A. take　　　B. spilled　　C. off　　　D. over

8 The _____ was about _____ _____ _____ !
　A. death　　　B. article　　C. own　　　D. his

9 It said Nobel had _____ in France _____ a _____ _____ .
　A. attack　　B. died　　C. heart　　D. from

10 "Oh _____ _____ ! Am I _____ ?"
　A. dead　　　B. goodness　　C. my

11 _____ his _____ , Nobel _____ _____ .
　A. kept　　B. catching　　C. reading　　D. breath

12 Soon, he became _____ _____ _____ .
　A. shocked　　B. even　　C. more

13 The article _____ him _____ the _____ of dynamite and _____ dangerous objects for war.
　A. as　　B. other　　C. described　　D. inventor

14 It said that he had _____ _____ from the _____ of _____ .
　A. deaths　　B. become　　C. others　　D. rich

15 He _____ _____ his _____ .
　A. eyes　　B. believe　　C. couldn't

16 It was _____ that dynamite was _____ _____ his many _____ .
　A. inventions　　B. true　　C. one　　D. of

1 당신은 어떻게 기억될까요?

2 그저 평범한 아침이었다.

3 Alfred Nobel은 신문을 읽기 위해 의자에 앉았다.

4 커피를 마시는 동안 한 기사 제목이 그의 눈길을 끌었다. "죽음의 상인, Alfred Nobel 사망하다"

5 "뭐라고? 이게 뭐지?"

6 기사를 읽으며 그는 놀라서 컵을 떨어뜨렸다.

7 커피가 그의 옷과 책상 온 곳에 쏟아졌지만 그는 신문에서 눈을 뗄 수 없었다.

8 기사는 그 자신의 죽음에 관한 것이었다!

9 기사에는 Nobel이 심장 마비로 프랑스에서 죽었다고 쓰여 있었다.

10 "오, 이럴 수가! 내가 죽었다고?"

11 숨을 고른 후, Nobel은 계속 읽었다.

12 곧, 그는 훨씬 더 충격을 받게 되었다.

13 기사는 그를 전쟁에 쓰이는 다이너마이트와 다른 위험한 물건의 발명가로 기술했다.

14 기사에는 그가 다른 사람들의 죽음으로 인해 부유해졌다고 쓰여 있었다.

15 그는 자신의 눈을 믿을 수 없었다.

16 다이너마이트가 그의 많은 발명품 중 하나인 것은 사실이었다.

17 But he never _____ that the world would _____ _____ him _____ "the merchant of death."

    A. as   B. imagined   C. of   D. think

18 Nobel _____ _____ _____.

    A. deeply   B. was   C. disappointed

19 "_____ _____ this _____?"

    A. be   B. could   C. how

20 _____ is _____!

    A. unbelievable   B. This

21 I'm not a _____ _____ _____.

    A. death   B. merchant   C. of

22 I want to be _____ a _____ _____.

    A. remembered   B. different   C. in   D. way

23 I want to _____ _____ as a person who made the _____."

    A. world   B. be   C. better   D. remembered

24 He decided _____ _____ _____ about him.

    A. people's   B. to   C. opinions   D. change

25 In 1888, a French _____ _____ _____ Alfred Nobel's _____.

    A. death   B. mistakenly   C. newspaper   D. reported

26 The person _____ _____ _____ was his brother, Ludvig.

    A. died   B. had   C. actually   D. who

27 _____ _____ the report, _____, Nobel decided to do something to _____ to the world.

    A. however   B. thanks   C. contribute D. to

28 In 1895, he _____ to _____ his money _____ _____ the Nobel Prize.

    A. to   B. decided   C. create   D. use

29 _____, there were _____ _____ _____.

    A. awards   B. originally   C. five   D. only

30 A _____ _____ was _____ in 1968.

    A. added   B. sixth   C. award

31 Today, when we _____ of Alfred Nobel, we think of the Nobel Prize, _____ _____ _____.

    A. than   B. think   C. rather   D. dynamite

---

17 하지만 그는 세상이 그를 '죽음의 상인'으로 생각할 거라고는 결코 상상하지 못했다.

18 Nobel은 몹시 실망했다.

19 "어떻게 이럴 수가 있지?

20 이건 믿을 수 없어!

21 나는 죽음의 상인이 아니야.

22 나는 다르게 기억되고 싶어.

23 나는 세상을 더 좋게 만든 사람으로 기억되고 싶어."

24 그는 자신에 대한 사람들의 견해를 바꾸기로 결심했다.

25 1888년에, 한 프랑스 신문에서 실수로 Alfred Nobel의 죽음을 보도했다.

26 실제로 죽은 사람은 Alfred Nobel의 형인 Ludvig였다.

27 하지만 그 보도 덕분에, Nobel은 세상에 공헌하기 위해 무언가를 하기로 결심했다.

28 1895년에, 그는 자신의 돈을 노벨상을 만드는 데 사용하기로 결정했다.

29 원래 다섯 종류의 상만 있었다.

30 여섯 번째 상은 1968년에 추가되었다.

31 오늘날 우리가 Alfred Nobel을 생각할 때, 우리는 다이너마이트보다는 노벨상을 떠올린다.

Step2

※ 다음 우리말과 일치하도록 빈칸에 알맞은 것을 골라 쓰시오.

1 _____ Will You _____ _____?

2 It was _____ a _____ _____.

3 Alfred Nobel _____ _____ _____ _____ _____ _____ the newspaper.

4 _____ he was drinking his coffee, a _____ _____ _____ _____: *The Merchant of Death, Alfred Nobel, Is Dead.*

5 "_____? What is this?"

6 _____ the article, he dropped his cup _____ _____.

7 His coffee _____ all over his clothes and desk, but he couldn't _____ _____ _____ _____ the newspaper.

8 The article was _____ _____ _____ _____!

9 It said Nobel _____ _____ in France _____ _____ _____ _____.

10 "Oh _____ _____! Am I dead?"

11 _____ _____ _____, Nobel _____ _____.

12 Soon, he became _____ _____ _____.

13 The article _____ him _____ the inventor of dynamite and _____ _____ _____ for war.

14 It said that he _____ _____ _____ from the _____ _____ _____.

15 He _____ _____ his eyes.

16 _____ was true _____ dynamite was _____ _____ _____ _____ _____.

1 당신은 어떻게 기억될까요?

2 그저 평범한 아침이었다.

3 Alfred Nobel은 신문을 읽기 위해 의자에 앉았다.

4 커피를 마시는 동안 한 기사 제목이 그의 눈길을 끌었다. "죽음의 상인, Alfred Nobel 사망하다"

5 "뭐라고? 이게 뭐지?"

6 기사를 읽으며 그는 놀라서 컵을 떨어뜨렸다.

7 커피가 그의 옷과 책상 온 곳에 쏟아졌지만 그는 신문에서 눈을 뗄 수 없었다.

8 기사는 그 자신의 죽음에 관한 것이었다!

9 기사에는 Nobel이 심장 마비로 프랑스에서 죽었다고 쓰여 있었다.

10 "오, 이럴 수가! 내가 죽었다고?"

11 숨을 고른 후, Nobel은 계속 읽었다.

12 곧, 그는 훨씬 더 충격을 받게 되었다.

13 기사는 그를 전쟁에 쓰이는 다이너마이트와 다른 위험한 물건의 발명가로 기술했다.

14 기사에는 그가 다른 사람들의 죽음으로 인해 부유해졌다고 쓰여 있었다.

15 그는 자신의 눈을 믿을 수 없었다.

16 다이너마이트가 그의 많은 발명품 중 하나인 것은 사실이었다.

17 But he never imagined that the world would _____ _____ him _____ "the _____ _____ _____."

18 Nobel was _____ _____.

19 "_____ could this _____?

20 This is _____!

21 I'm not a _____ _____ _____.

22 I want to be remembered _____ _____ _____ _____.

23 I want to _____ _____ _____ a person who made _____ _____ _____."

24 He decided _____ _____ _____ _____ about him.

25 In 1888, a French newspaper _____ _____ Alfred Nobel's death.

26 The person _____ _____ _____ _____ was his brother, Ludvig.

27 _____ _____ the report, however, Nobel _____ _____ do something to _____ _____ the world.

28 In 1895, he decided to use his money _____ _____ the Nobel Prize.

29 _____, there were _____ _____ _____.

30 A _____ _____ was _____ in 1968.

31 Today, when we _____ _____ Alfred Nobel, we think of the Nobel Prize, _____ _____ dynamite.

17 하지만 그는 세상이 그를 '죽음의 상인'으로 생각할 거라고는 결코 상상하지 못했다.

18 Nobel은 몹시 실망했다.

19 "어떻게 이럴 수가 있지?

20 이건 믿을 수 없어!

21 나는 죽음의 상인이 아니야.

22 나는 다르게 기억되고 싶어.

23 나는 세상을 더 좋게 만든 사람으로 기억되고 싶어."

24 그는 자신에 대한 사람들의 견해를 바꾸기로 결심했다.

25 1888년에, 한 프랑스 신문에서 실수로 Alfred Nobel의 죽음을 보도했다.

26 실제로 죽은 사람은 Alfred Nobel의 형인 Ludvig였다.

27 하지만 그 보도 덕분에, Nobel은 세상에 공헌하기 위해 무언가를 하기로 결심했다.

28 1895년에, 그는 자신의 돈을 노벨상을 만드는 데 사용하기로 결정했다.

29 원래 다섯 종류의 상만 있었다.

30 여섯 번째 상은 1968년에 추가되었다.

31 오늘날 우리가 Alfred Nobel을 생각할 때, 우리는 다이너마이트보다는 노벨상을 떠올린다.

※ 다음 문장을 우리말로 쓰시오.

1 How Will You Be Remembered?

➡ _____

2 It was just a normal morning.

➡ _____

3 Alfred Nobel sat in his chair to read the newspaper.

➡ _____

4 While he was drinking his coffee, a headline caught his eye: *The Merchant of Death, Alfred Nobel, Is Dead.*

➡ _____

5 "What? What is this?"

➡ _____

6 Reading the article, he dropped his cup in surprise.

➡ _____

7 His coffee spilled all over his clothes and desk, but he couldn't take his eyes off the newspaper.

➡ _____

8 The article was about his own death!

➡ _____

9 It said Nobel had died in France from a heart attack.

➡ _____

10 "Oh my goodness! Am I dead?"

➡ _____

11 Catching his breath, Nobel kept reading.

➡ _____

12 Soon, he became even more shocked.

➡ _____

13 The article described him as the inventor of dynamite and other dangerous objects for war.

➡ _____

14 It said that he had become rich from the deaths of others.

➡ _____

15 He couldn't believe his eyes.

➡ _____

16 It was true that dynamite was one of his many inventions.

➡ _____

17 But he never imagined that the world would think of him as "the merchant of death."

➡ _____

18 Nobel was deeply disappointed.

➡ _____

19 "How could this be?

➡ _____

20 This is unbelievable!

➡ _____

21 I'm not a merchant of death.

➡ _____

22 I want to be remembered in a different way.

➡ _____

23 I want to be remembered as a person who made the world better."

➡ _____

24 He decided to change people's opinions about him.

➡ _____

25 In 1888, a French newspaper mistakenly reported Alfred Nobel's death.

➡ _____

26 The person who had actually died was his brother, Ludvig.

➡ _____

27 Thanks to the report, however, Nobel decided to do something to contribute to the world.

➡ _____

28 In 1895, he decided to use his money to create the Nobel Prize.

➡ _____

29 Originally, there were only five awards.

➡ _____

30 A sixth award was added in 1968.

➡ _____

31 Today, when we think of Alfred Nobel, we think of the Nobel Prize, rather than dynamite.

➡ _____

※ 다음 괄호 안의 단어들을 우리말에 맞도록 바르게 배열하시오.

1 (Will / How / Be / You / Remembered?)
➡ _____

2 (was / it / a / just / morning. / normal)
➡ _____

3 (Nobel / Alfred / in / sat / chair / his / read / to / newspaper. / the)
➡ _____

4 (he / while / drinking / was / coffee, / his / headline / a / his / caught / eye: / *Merchant* / *The* / *Death,* / *of* / *Nobel,* / *Alfred* / *Dead.* / *Is*)
➡ _____
_____

5 ("what? // this?" / is / what)
➡ _____

6 (the / reading / article, / dropped / he / cup / his / surprise. / in)
➡ _____

7 (coffee / his / all / spilled / his / over / clothes / desk, / and / he / but / take / couldn't / his / eyes / the / off / newspaper.)
➡ _____
_____

8 (article / the / about / was / own / his / death!)
➡ _____

9 (said / it / had / Nobel / in / died / from / France / heart / a / attack.)
➡ _____

10 (my / "oh / goodness! // I / am / dead?")
➡ _____

11 (his / catching / breath, / kept / Nobel / reading.)
➡ _____

12 (he / soon, / even / became / shocked. / more)
➡ _____

13 (article / the / him / described / the / as / of / inventor / dynamite / other / and / objects / dangerous / war. / for)
➡ _____
_____

14 (said / it / he / that / become / had / from / rich / deaths / the / others. / of)
➡ _____

15 (couldn't / he / believe / eyes. / his)
➡ _____

16 (was / it / that / true / was / dynamite / of / one / his / inventions. / many)
➡ _____

1 당신은 어떻게 기억될까요?

2 그저 평범한 아침이었다.

3 Alfred Nobel은 신문을 읽기 위해 의자에 앉았다.

4 커피를 마시는 동안 한 기사 제목이 그의 눈길을 끌었다. "죽음의 상인, Alfred Nobel 사망하다"

5 "뭐라고? 이게 뭐지?"

6 기사를 읽으며 그는 놀라서 컵을 떨어뜨렸다.

7 커피가 그의 옷과 책상 온 곳에 쏟아졌지만 그는 신문에서 눈을 뗄 수 없었다.

8 기사는 그 자신의 죽음에 관한 것이었다!

9 기사에는 Nobel이 심장 마비로 프랑스에서 죽었다고 쓰여 있었다.

10 "오, 이럴 수가! 내가 죽었다고?"

11 숨을 고른 후, Nobel은 계속 읽었다.

12 곧, 그는 훨씬 더 충격을 받게 되었다.

13 기사는 그를 전쟁에 쓰이는 다이너마이트와 다른 위험한 물건의 발명가로 기술했다.

14 기사에는 그가 다른 사람들의 죽음으로 인해 부유해졌다고 쓰여 있었다.

15 그는 자신의 눈을 믿을 수 없었다.

16 다이너마이트가 그의 많은 발명품 중 하나인 것은 사실이었다.

17 (he / but / imagined / never / the / that / would / world / of / think / as / him / merchant / "the / death." / of)

➡ _____

_____

18 (was / Nobel / disappointed. / deeply)

➡ _____

19 (could / "how / be? / this)

➡ _____

20 (is / this / unbelievable!)

➡ _____

21 (not / I'm / merchant / a / death. / of)

➡ _____

22 (want / I / be / to / remembered / a / in / way. / different)

➡ _____

23 (want / I / be / to / as / remembered / person / a / made / who / world / the / better.")

➡ _____

24 (decided / he / change / to / opinions / people's / him. / about)

➡ _____

25 (1888, / in / newspaper / French / a / reported / mistakenly / Nobel's / Alfred / death.)

➡ _____

26 (person / the / had / who / died / actually / his / was / Ludvig. / brother,)

➡ _____

27 (to / thanks / report, / the / Nobel / however, / to / decided / something / do / contribute / to / the / to / world.)

➡ _____

_____

28 (1895, / in / decided / he / use / to / money / his / create / to / Nobel / the / Prize.)

➡ _____

29 (there / originally, / only / were / awards. / five)

➡ _____

30 (sixth / a / was / award / in / added / 1968.)

➡ _____

31 (when / today, / think / we / Alfred / of / we / Nobel, / of / think / the / Prize, / Nobel / than / rather / dynamite.)

➡ _____

_____

17 하지만 그는 세상이 그를 '죽음의 상인'으로 생각할 거라고는 결코 상상하지 못했다.

18 Nobel은 몹시 실망했다.

19 "어떻게 이럴 수가 있지?

20 이건 믿을 수 없어!

21 나는 죽음의 상인이 아니야.

22 나는 다르게 기억되고 싶어.

23 나는 세상을 더 좋게 만든 사람으로 기억되고 싶어."

24 그는 자신에 대한 사람들의 견해를 바꾸기로 결심했다.

25 1888년에, 한 프랑스 신문에서 실수로 Alfred Nobel의 죽음을 보도했다.

26 실제로 죽은 사람은 Alfred Nobel의 형인 Ludvig였다.

27 하지만 그 보도 덕분에, Nobel은 세상에 공헌하기 위해 무언가를 하기로 결심했다.

28 1895년에, 그는 자신의 돈을 노벨상을 만드는 데 사용하기로 결정했다.

29 원래 다섯 종류의 상만 있었다.

30 여섯 번째 상은 1968년에 추가되었다.

31 오늘날 우리가 Alfred Nobel을 생각할 때, 우리는 다이너마이트보다는 노벨상을 떠올린다.

※ **다음 우리말을 영어로 쓰시오.**

1 당신은 어떻게 기억될까요?

➡ _____

2 그저 평범한 아침이었다.

➡ _____

3 Alfred Nobel은 신문을 읽기 위해 의자에 앉았다.

➡ _____

4 커피를 마시는 동안 한 기사 제목이 그의 눈길을 끌었다. "죽음의 상인, Alfred Nobel 사망하다"

➡ _____
_____

5 "뭐라고? 이게 뭐지?"

➡ _____

6 기사를 읽으며 그는 놀라서 컵을 떨어뜨렸다.

➡ _____

7 커피가 그의 옷과 책상 온 곳에 쏟아졌지만 그는 신문에서 눈을 뗄 수 없었다.

➡ _____

8 기사는 그 자신의 죽음에 관한 것이었다!

➡ _____

9 기사에는 Nobel이 심장 마비로 프랑스에서 죽었다고 쓰여 있었다.

➡ _____

10 "오, 이럴 수가! 내가 죽었다고?"

➡ _____

11 숨을 고른 후, Nobel은 계속 읽었다.

➡ _____

12 곧, 그는 훨씬 더 충격을 받게 되었다.

➡ _____

13 기사는 그를 전쟁에 쓰이는 다이너마이트와 다른 위험한 물건의 발명가로 기술했다.

➡ _____

14 기사에는 그가 다른 사람들의 죽음으로 인해 부유해졌다고 쓰여 있었다.

➡ _____

15 그는 자신의 눈을 믿을 수 없었다.

➡ _____

16 다이너마이트가 그의 많은 발명품 중 하나인 것은 사실이었다.

➡ _____

17 하지만 그는 세상이 그를 '죽음의 상인'으로 생각할 거라고는 결코 상상하지 못했다.

➡ _____

18 Nobel은 몹시 실망했다.

➡ _____

19 "어떻게 이럴 수가 있지?

➡ _____

20 이건 믿을 수 없어!

➡ _____

21 나는 죽음의 상인이 아니야.

➡ _____

22 나는 다르게 기억되고 싶어.

➡ _____

23 나는 세상을 더 좋게 만든 사람으로 기억되고 싶어."

➡ _____

24 그는 자신에 대한 사람들의 견해를 바꾸기로 결심했다.

➡ _____

25 1888년에, 한 프랑스 신문에서 실수로 Alfred Nobel의 죽음을 보도했다.

➡ _____

26 실제로 죽은 사람은 Alfred Nobel의 형인 Ludvig였다.

➡ _____

27 하지만 그 보도 덕분에, Nobel은 세상에 공헌하기 위해 무언가를 하기로 결심했다.

➡ _____

28 1895년에, 그는 자신의 돈을 노벨상을 만드는 데 사용하기로 결정했다.

➡ _____

29 원래 다섯 종류의 상만 있었다.

➡ _____

30 여섯 번째 상은 1968년에 추가되었다.

➡ _____

31 오늘날 우리가 Alfred Nobel을 생각할 때, 우리는 다이너마이트보다는 노벨상을 떠올린다.

➡ _____

※ 다음 우리말과 일치하도록 빈칸에 알맞은 말을 쓰시오.

After You Read A. Read and Correct

1. WORLD NEWS / _____ 13, 1888

2. _____ _____ _____ _____, Alfred Nobel, Is _____

3. Alfred Nobel _____ yesterday _____ France _____ _____ _____ _____.

4. He _____ _____ and _____ _____ _____ for war.

5. He _____ _____ from _____ _____ _____ _____ _____.

6. He _____ _____ _____ the deaths of _____ _____ _____.

7. The world will _____ him _____ " _____ _____ _____ _____ _____."

1. 세계 뉴스 / 1888년 4월 13일
2. 죽음의 상인, Alfred Nobel 사망하다
3. Alfred Nobel이 어제 프랑스에서 심장마비로 사망했다.
4. 그는 전쟁에 쓰이는 다이너마이트와 다른 위험한 물건들을 발명했다.
5. 그는 다른 사람들의 죽음으로 인해 부유해졌다.
6. 그는 수천 명의 사람들의 죽음에 대해 책임이 있다.
7. 세상은 그를 "죽음의 상인"으로 기억할 것이다.

Word Power

1. Tim _____ _____ _____ _____ the beach.

2. Thomas Edison made _____ 1,000 _____ in _____ _____.

3. Who is _____ _____ of _____ _____?

1. Tim은 특별한 해변용 신발을 발명했다.
2. Thomas Edison은 일생 동안 천 개 이상의 발명품을 만들었다.
3. 비행기의 발명가는 누구인가?

Think and Write Step 2

1. _____ _____ this year, I'm glad _____ I _____ money _____ _____ in Africa.

2. I did this _____ I wanted _____ _____ _____ _____ for children _____ _____.

3. _____ _____ money, I didn't buy snacks _____ _____ _____.

4. I _____ _____ _____ _____ UNICEF.

5. Before I donated, I sometimes _____ _____ _____ _____.

6. Now I _____ _____ _____ _____.

7. I'm _____ _____ _____.

1. 올해를 뒤돌아보니, 나는 아프리카의 아이들에게 돈을 기부해서 기쁘다.
2. 나는 어려움에 처한 아이들의 상황을 변화시키고 싶었기 때문에 기부를 했다.
3. 돈을 모으기 위해, 나는 한 달 동안 간식을 사지 않았다.
4. 나는 그 돈을 유니세프에 기부했다.
5. 나는 기부하기 전에는 가끔 접시에 음식을 남겼다.
6. 이제 나는 내 음식을 정말 고맙게 여긴다.
7. 나는 내 자신이 자랑스럽다.

※ 다음 우리말을 영어로 쓰시오.

After You Read A. Read and Correct

1. 세계 뉴스 / 1888년 4월 13일
   ➡ _____

2. 죽음의 상인, Alfred Nobel 사망하다
   ➡ _____

3. Alfred Nobel이 어제 프랑스에서 심장마비로 사망했다.
   ➡ _____

4. 그는 전쟁에 쓰이는 다이너마이트와 다른 위험한 물건들을 발명했다.
   ➡ _____

5. 그는 다른 사람들의 죽음으로 인해 부유해졌다.
   ➡ _____

6. 그는 수천 명의 사람들의 죽음에 대해 책임이 있다.
   ➡ _____

7. 세상은 그를 "죽음의 상인"으로 기억할 것이다.
   ➡ _____

Word Power

1. Tim은 특별한 해변용 신발을 발명했다.
   ➡ _____

2. Thomas Edison은 일생 동안 천 개 이상의 발명품을 만들었다.
   ➡ _____

3. 비행기의 발명가는 누구인가?
   ➡ _____

Think and Write Step 2

1. 올해를 뒤돌아보니, 나는 아프리카의 아이들에게 돈을 기부해서 기쁘다.
   ➡ _____

2. 나는 어려움에 처한 아이들의 상황을 변화시키고 싶었기 때문에 기부를 했다.
   ➡ _____

3. 돈을 모으기 위해, 나는 한 달 동안 간식을 사지 않았다.
   ➡ _____

4. 나는 그 돈을 유니세프에 기부했다.
   ➡ _____

5. 나는 기부하기 전에는 가끔 접시에 음식을 남겼다.
   ➡ _____

6. 이제 나는 내 음식을 정말 고맙게 여긴다.
   ➡ _____

7. 나는 내 자신이 자랑스럽다.
   ➡ _____

※ 다음 영어를 우리말로 쓰시오.

01	solution		21	comfortable
02	after		22	shake
03	clear		23	drawer
04	health condition		24	story
05	land		25	yell
06	appear		26	driverless
07	select		27	by -ing
08	bathroom		28	step in
09	press		29	feel like
10	special		30	be tired of
11	brightly		31	come back
12	rub		32	stop -ing
13	scan		33	remind A to 동사원형
14	usual		34	give a presentation
15	shower		35	on top of
16	whisper		36	pay for
17	sensor		37	print out
18	shine		38	send A to B
19	future		39	thanks to ~
20	grocery		40	don't have to 동사원형

※ 다음 우리말을 영어로 쓰시오.

01 빛나다, 비추다 _____

02 나타나다 _____

03 (건물의) 층 _____

04 일상의, 늘 먹던 것 _____

05 욕실 _____

06 맑게[투명하게] 하다;
   투명한, 맑은 _____

07 특별한 _____

08 미래 _____

09 식료품 및 잡화 _____

10 건강 상태 _____

11 센서, 감지기 _____

12 내려앉다, 착륙하다 _____

13 누르다 _____

14 ~ 후에 _____

15 문지르다, 비비다 _____

16 흔들리다, 흔들다 _____

17 운전자가 필요 없는 _____

18 정밀 검사[촬영]하다 _____

19 밝게 _____

20 선택하다 _____

21 서랍 _____

22 샤워실, 샤워 _____

23 속삭이다 _____

24 소리치다, 외치다 _____

25 편안한, 안락한 _____

26 해결책 _____

27 ~에 발을 디디다 _____

28 ~인 것처럼 느끼다 _____

29 돌아오다 _____

30 ~에 싫증이 나다 _____

31 ~의 값을 지불하다 _____

32 ~함으로써 _____

33 ~의 꼭대기에 _____

34 ~할 필요가 없다 _____

35 ~을 멈추다 _____

36 발표를 하다 _____

37 (프린트로) 출력하다 _____

38 ~ 덕분에 _____

39 A에게 ~할 것을 상기시키다 _____

40 A를 B에게 보내다 _____

※ 다음 영영풀이에 알맞은 단어를 <보기>에서 골라 쓴 후, 우리말 뜻을 쓰시오.

1 _____ : a level of a building; a floor: _____

2 _____ : to produce bright light: _____

3 _____ : to return to the ground or another surface after a flight: _____

4 _____ : to choose someone or something from a group: _____

5 _____ : a room with a sink and toilet and usually a bathtub or shower: _____

6 _____ : feeling physically relaxed, without pain or other unpleasant feelings: _____

7 _____ : food and other goods sold in a grocery store or at a supermarket: _____

8 _____ : to start to be seen, to arrive, or to exist in a place, especially suddenly: _____

9 _____ : to push a button, switch, etc. to make a machine start, a bell ring, etc.: _____

10 _____ : to speak or say something very quietly, using your breath rather than your voice: _____

11 _____ : to choose something or someone by thinking carefully about which is the best, most suitable, etc.: _____

12 _____ : a device that can react to light, heat, pressure, etc. in order to make a machine, etc. do something or show something: _____

13 _____ : to shout or say something very loudly, especially because you are frightened, angry, or excited: _____

14 _____ : a box that slides into and out of a piece of furniture such as a desk and that is used to store things: _____

15 _____ : to move your hand, or something such as a cloth, backwards and forwards over a surface while pressing firmly: _____

16 _____ : to move suddenly from side to side or up and down, usually with a lot of force, or to make something or someone do this: _____

보기			
yell	select	drawer	bathroom
whisper	shine	press	sensor
rub	comfortable	shake	grocery
appear	story	select	land

※ 다음 우리말과 일치하도록 빈칸에 알맞은 것을 골라 쓰시오.

1 _____ the _____
　A. Future　　　　B. Picture

2 _____ 7 _____
　A. a.m.　　　　B. it's

3 The bed _____ and Minji Kim _____, "Five more _____!"
　A. yells　　　B. minutes　　　C. shakes

4 The bed _____.
　A. shaking　　　B. stops

5 _____, Minji's mom _____ on a screen on the wall and says, "You're _____ to be _____ for school!"
　A. late　　　B. appears　　　C. suddenly　　　D. going

6 Minji _____ her _____ and _____, "_____ the windows."
　A. eyes　　　B. clear　　　C. rubs　　　D. says

7 The dark windows _____ clear and the sun _____ _____ them.
　A. through　　　B. brightly　　　C. become　　　D. shines

8 In the bathroom, a red _____ _____ Minji's _____.
　A. scans　　　B. body　　　C. light

9 A _____ says, "54 kilograms. Your _____ _____ is _____."
　A. excellent　　　B. voice　　　C. condition　　　D. health

10 When she _____ in the shower, water comes _____ from the _____ and _____.
　A. sides　　　B. steps　　　C. out　　　D. top

11 After her shower, _____ air _____ _____ and _____ her.
　A. dries　　　B. warm　　　C. out　　　D. comes

12 When she _____ _____, a drawer opens _____ today's _____.
　A. out　　　B. with　　　C. gets　　　D. clothes

13 In the _____, her father _____, "Good morning, Honey. What do you want _____ _____?"
　A. kitchen　　　B. for　　　C. says　　　D. breakfast

14 Minji _____, "The _____, please."
　A. usual　　　B. says

15 Mr. Kim _____ a _____ buttons on the _____ _____.
　A. presses　　　B. machine　　　C. few　　　D. cooking

16 The _____ _____ _____ some bacon, eggs and bread.
　A. prints　　　B. machine　　　C. out

17 Mr. Kim _____ goodbye and _____ _____ the door.
　A. rushes　　　B. says　　　C. out

18 A few minutes _____, Minji's father _____ on a screen and _____, "I _____ my glasses!"
　A. shouts　　　B. forgot　　　C. later　　　D. appears

19 Ms. Kim _____ and _____, "No _____. I'll _____ a drone to your office."
　A. send　　　B. smiles　　　C. problem　　　D. answers

1 미래를 상상하다

2 오전 7시이다.

3 침대가 흔들리고 김민지가 "5분만 더!"라고 소리를 지른다.

4 침대가 흔들기를 멈춘다.

5 갑자기, 민지의 엄마가 벽 스크린에 나타나 말한다. "학교에 늦겠구나!"

6 민지는 눈을 비비며 "창문을 투명하게 해 줘."라고 말한다.

7 어두운 창문이 투명해지며 창문으로 햇살이 밝게 비춘다.

8 욕실에서 빨간 빛이 민지의 몸을 정밀 검사한다.

9 목소리가 "54킬로그램. 건강 상태가 매우 좋습니다."라고 말한다.

10 그녀가 샤워실 안에 발을 디디자, 물이 위와 양측에서 나온다.

11 샤워 후에, 따뜻한 공기가 나와 그녀를 말린다.

12 그녀가 나가자, 서랍이 열리며 오늘의 옷이 나타난다.

13 부엌에서 민지의 아빠가 "좋은 아침이구나, 얘야. 아침으로 무엇을 먹고 싶니?"라고 말한다.

14 민지는 "늘 먹던 걸로 주세요."라고 말한다.

15 아빠가 요리 기계의 버튼 몇 개를 누른다.

16 기계는 베이컨, 달걀, 빵을 만들어 낸다.

17 아빠는 작별 인사를 하고 문 밖으로 급히 나간다.

18 몇 분 후에, 민지의 아빠가 스크린에 나타나 소리친다. "안경을 깜빡했어요!"

19 민지의 엄마가 미소 지으며 답한다. "괜찮아요. 드론을 당신의 사무실로 보낼게요."

20 Mr. Kim _____, "_____ a _____!"
A. million   B. says   C. thanks

21 Ms. Kim and Minji _____ _____ a _____ _____ car.
A. flying   B. get   C. driverless   D. into

22 They _____ _____ chairs _____ a table.
A. around   B. comfortable   C. in   D. sit

23 Ms. Kim _____ the car window to _____ the _____ this week.
A. select   B. touches   C. groceries   D. for

24 She _____ for them _____ _____ her finger on a _____.
A. putting   B. pays   C. sensor   D. by

25 They _____ _____ _____ her house.
A. be   B. will   C. to   D. delivered

26 The car _____ at Minji's school _____ of a 150-_____ building.
A. top   B. lands   C. story   D. on

27 Today Minji will _____ a _____ Dona, a student _____ America.
A. with   B. give   C. in   D. presentation

28 But Minji _____ _____ _____ to America.
A. to   B. doesn't   C. have   D. go

29 _____ _____ a VR classroom, they will feel _____ they are in the _____ classroom.
A. to   B. like   C. same   D. thanks

30 _____ Minji's family _____ _____ home, dinner is _____.
A. ready   B. back   C. when   D. comes

31 They eat and _____ _____ their _____.
A. talk   B. day   C. about

32 After a _____ dinner, the cleaning robot _____ the table and _____ the _____.
A. washes   B. delicious   C. clears   D. dishes

33 Minji says, "I _____ a game _____ _____ today. Do you want to _____?"
A. called   B. play   C. learned   D. chess

34 _____ _____.
A. agrees   B. everyone

35 A _____ chess _____ _____ the table.
A. on   B. board   C. 3-D   D. appears

36 They have _____ _____ _____.
A. fun   B. of   C. lots

37 _____ Minji goes to bed, she _____ to her _____.
A. before   B. whispers   C. right   D. watch

38 "_____ Daddy _____ his _____ tomorrow."
A. take   B. remind   C. glasses   D. to

20 민지의 아빠가 "정말 고마워요!" 라고 말한다.

21 민지의 엄마와 민지는 운전자가 필요 없는 비행 자동차에 탄다.

22 두 사람은 탁자 주변의 편안한 의자에 앉는다.

23 민지의 엄마가 이번 주 식료품을 선택하기 위해 자동차 창문을 터치한다.

24 그녀는 센서에 손가락을 대서 식료품 값을 지불한다.

25 식료품은 집으로 배달될 것이다.

26 자동차는 150층 빌딩의 꼭대기에 있는 민지의 학교에 내린다.

27 오늘 민지는 미국에 있는 학생 Dona와 함께 발표를 할 것이다.

28 하지만 민지가 미국에 갈 필요는 없다.

29 VR(가상 현실) 교실 덕분에, 그들은 같은 교실에 있는 것처럼 느낄 것이다.

30 민지의 가족이 집에 돌아오자 저녁이 준비된다.

31 그들은 식사를 하며 그 날에 관해 이야기한다.

32 맛있는 저녁 식사 후에, 청소 로봇이 탁자를 치우고 설거지를 한다.

33 민지가 "오늘 체스라고 불리는 놀이를 배웠어요. 해 보실래요?"라고 말한다.

34 모두가 동의한다.

35 탁자 위에 삼차원 체스판이 나타난다.

36 그들은 아주 즐거운 시간을 보낸다.

37 민지는 자러 가기 직전에, 자신의 손목시계에 속삭인다.

38 "아빠께 내일 안경을 가져가시라고 상기시켜 드려."

※ 다음 우리말과 일치하도록 빈칸에 알맞은 말을 쓰시오.

1 _____ the _____

2 _____ 7 a.m.

3 The bed _____ and Minji Kim _____, "_____ _____ _____!"

4 The bed _____ _____.

5 Suddenly, Minji's mom _____ on a screen on the wall and says, "You're going to _____ _____ _____ school!"

6 Minji _____ _____ _____ and says, "_____ the windows."

7 The dark windows _____ _____ and the sun _____ _____ through them.

8 In the bathroom, a red light _____ _____ _____.

9 A _____ says, "54 kilograms. Your _____ _____ is excellent."

10 When she _____ _____ the shower, water _____ _____ _____ the _____ and _____.

11 After her shower, warm air _____ _____ and _____ her.

12 When she _____ _____, a drawer opens _____ _____ _____.

13 In the kitchen, her father says, "Good morning, Honey. What do you want _____ _____?"

14 Minji says, "_____ _____, please."

15 Mr. Kim _____ _____ _____ buttons _____ the cooking machine.

16 The machine _____ _____ some bacon, eggs and bread.

17 Mr. Kim says goodbye and _____ _____ the door.

---

1 미래를 상상하다

2 오전 7시이다.

3 침대가 흔들리고 김민지가 "5분만 더!"라고 소리를 지른다.

4 침대가 흔들기를 멈춘다.

5 갑자기, 민지의 엄마가 벽 스크린에 나타나 말한다. "학교에 늦겠구나!"

6 민지는 눈을 비비며 "창문을 투명하게 해 줘."라고 말한다.

7 어두운 창문이 투명해지며 창문으로 햇살이 밝게 비춘다.

8 욕실에서 빨간 빛이 민지의 몸을 정밀 검사한다.

9 목소리가 "54킬로그램. 건강 상태가 매우 좋습니다."라고 말한다.

10 그녀가 샤워실 안에 발을 디디자, 물이 위와 양측에서 나온다.

11 샤워 후에, 따뜻한 공기가 나와 그녀를 말린다.

12 그녀가 나가자, 서랍이 열리며 오늘의 옷이 나타난다.

13 부엌에서 민지의 아빠가 "좋은 아침이구나, 얘야. 아침으로 무엇을 먹고 싶니?"라고 말한다.

14 민지는 "늘 먹던 걸로 주세요."라고 말한다.

15 아빠가 요리 기계의 버튼 몇 개를 누른다.

16 기계는 베이컨, 달걀, 빵을 만들어 낸다.

17 아빠는 작별 인사를 하고 문 밖으로 급히 나간다.

18 _____ _____ _____ _____, Minji's father appears on a screen and shouts, "I _____ my glasses!"

19 Ms. Kim smiles and answers, "No problem. I'll _____ _____ _____ _____ your office."

20 Mr. Kim says, "Thanks _____ _____!"

21 Ms. Kim and Minji get into a _____ _____ _____.

22 They sit _____ _____ _____ _____ a table.

23 Ms. Kim touches the car window _____ _____ the _____ for this week.

24 She _____ _____ them _____ _____ her finger _____ _____ _____.

25 They _____ _____ _____ to her house.

26 The car _____ at Minji's school on top of a _____ building.

27 Today Minji will _____ _____ _____ _____ _____ Dona, a student in America.

28 But Minji _____ _____ _____ go to America.

29 _____ _____ a VR classroom, they will _____ _____ they are in the _____ _____.

30 When Minji's family _____ _____ home, dinner _____ _____.

31 They eat and _____ _____ their day.

32 After a _____ _____, the cleaning robot clears the table and _____ _____ _____.

33 Minji says, "I learned a game _____ _____ today. Do you want _____ _____?"

34 Everyone _____.

35 A _____ _____ _____ _____ on the table.

36 They have _____ _____ _____.

37 Right before Minji goes to bed, she _____ _____ her watch.

38 "_____ Daddy _____ _____ his glasses tomorrow."

18 몇 분 후에, 민지의 아빠가 스크린에 나타나 소리친다. "안경을 깜빡했어요!"

19 민지의 엄마가 미소 지으며 답한다. "괜찮아요. 드론을 당신의 사무실로 보낼게요."

20 민지의 아빠가 "정말 고마워요!"라고 말한다.

21 민지의 엄마와 민지는 운전자가 필요 없는 비행 자동차에 탄다.

22 두 사람은 탁자 주변의 편안한 의자에 앉는다.

23 민지의 엄마가 이번 주 식료품을 선택하기 위해 자동차 창문을 터치한다.

24 그녀는 센서에 손가락을 대서 식료품 값을 지불한다.

25 식료품은 집으로 배달될 것이다.

26 자동차는 150층 빌딩의 꼭대기에 있는 민지의 학교에 내린다.

27 오늘 민지는 미국에 있는 학생 Dona와 함께 발표를 할 것이다.

28 하지만 민지가 미국에 갈 필요는 없다.

29 VR(가상 현실) 교실 덕분에, 그들은 같은 교실에 있는 것처럼 느낄 것이다.

30 민지의 가족이 집에 돌아오자 저녁이 준비된다.

31 그들은 식사를 하며 그 날에 관해 이야기한다.

32 맛있는 저녁 식사 후에, 청소 로봇이 식탁을 치우고 설거지를 한다.

33 민지가 "오늘 체스라고 불리는 놀이를 배웠어요. 해 보실래요?"라고 말한다.

34 모두가 동의한다.

35 탁자 위에 삼차원 체스판이 나타난다.

36 그들은 아주 즐거운 시간을 보낸다.

37 민지는 자러 가기 직전에, 자신의 손목시계에 속삭인다.

38 "아빠께 내일 안경을 가져가시라고 상기시켜 드려."

※ 다음 문장을 우리말로 쓰시오.

1 Picture the Future

➡ _____

2 It's 7 a.m.

➡ _____

3 The bed shakes and Minji Kim yells, "Five more minutes!"

➡ _____

4 The bed stops shaking.

➡ _____

5 Suddenly, Minji's mom appears on a screen on the wall and says, "You're going to be late for school!"

➡ _____

6 Minji rubs her eyes and says, "Clear the windows."

➡ _____

7 The dark windows become clear and the sun shines brightly through them.

➡ _____

8 In the bathroom, a red light scans Minji's body.

➡ _____

9 A voice says, "54 kilograms. Your health condition is excellent."

➡ _____

10 When she steps in the shower, water comes out from the top and sides.

➡ _____

11 After her shower, warm air comes out and dries her.

➡ _____

12 When she gets out, a drawer opens with today's clothes.

➡ _____

13 In the kitchen, her father says, "Good morning, Honey. What do you want for breakfast?"

➡ _____

14 Minji says, "The usual, please."

➡ _____

15 Mr. Kim presses a few buttons on the cooking machine.

➡ _____

16 The machine prints out some bacon, eggs and bread.

➡ _____

17 Mr. Kim says goodbye and rushes out the door.

➡ _____

18 A few minutes later, Minji's father appears on a screen and shouts, "I forgot my glasses!"
➡ _____

19 Ms. Kim smiles and answers, "No problem. I'll send a drone to your office."
➡ _____

20 Mr. Kim says, "Thanks a million!"
➡ _____

21 Ms. Kim and Minji get into a driverless flying car.
➡ _____

22 They sit in comfortable chairs around a table.
➡ _____

23 Ms. Kim touches the car window to select the groceries for this week.
➡ _____

24 She pays for them by putting her finger on a sensor.
➡ _____

25 They will be delivered to her house.
➡ _____

26 The car lands at Minji's school on top of a 150-story building.
➡ _____

27 Today Minji will give a presentation with Dona, a student in America.
➡ _____

28 But Minji doesn't have to go to America.
➡ _____

29 Thanks to a VR classroom, they will feel like they are in the same classroom.
➡ _____

30 When Minji's family comes back home, dinner is ready.
➡ _____

31 They eat and talk about their day.
➡ _____

32 After a delicious dinner, the cleaning robot clears the table and washes the dishes.
➡ _____

33 Minji says, "I learned a game called chess today. Do you want to play?"
➡ _____

34 Everyone agrees.
➡ _____

35 A 3-D chess board appears on the table.
➡ _____

36 They have lots of fun.
➡ _____

37 Right before Minji goes to bed, she whispers to her watch.
➡ _____

38 "Remind Daddy to take his glasses tomorrow."
➡ _____

※ 다음 괄호 안의 단어들을 우리말에 맞도록 바르게 배열하시오.

1 (the / Future / Picture)
➡ _____

2 (7 / it's / a.m.)
➡ _____

3 (bed / the / and / shakes / Kim / Minji / yells, / more / "five / minutes!")
➡ _____

4 (bed / the / shaking. / stops)
➡ _____

5 (Minji's / suddenly, / appears / mom / a / on / screen / the / on / wall / says, / and / "you're / to / going / be / for / late / school!")
➡ _____

6 (rubs / Minji / eyes / her / says, / and / the / "clear / windows.")
➡ _____

7 (dark / the / become / windows / and / clear / sun / the / brightly / shines / them. / through)
➡ _____

8 (the / in / bathroom, / red / a / scans / light / body. / Minji's)
➡ _____

9 (voice / a / says, / kilograms. / "54 // health / your / is / condition / excellent.")
➡ _____

10 (she / when / in / steps / shower, / the / comes / water / from / out / top / the / sides. / and)
➡ _____

11 (her / after / shower, / air / warm / out / comes / her. / and / dries)
➡ _____

12 (she / when / out, / gets / drawer / a / with / opens / clothes. / today's)
➡ _____

13 (the / in / kitchen, / father / her / says, / morning, / "good / Honey. // do / what / you / for / want / breakfast?")
➡ _____

14 (says, / Minji / usual, / "the / please.")
➡ _____

15 (Kim / Mr. / a / presses / buttons / few / the / on / machine. / cooking)
➡ _____

16 (machine / the / out / prints / bacon, / some / and / bread. / eggs)
➡ _____

17 (Kim / Mr. / goodbye / says / and / out / rushes / door. / the)
➡ _____

18 (few / a / later, / minutes / father / Minji's / appears / a / on / and / screen / shouts, / forgot / "I / glasses!" / my)
➡ _____

19 (Kim / Ms. / answers, / and / smiles / probelm. / "no // send / I'll / drone / a / your / to / office.")
➡ _____

1 미래를 상상하다

2 오전 7시이다.

3 침대가 흔들리고 김민지가 "5분만 더!"라고 소리를 지른다.

4 침대가 흔들기를 멈춘다.

5 갑자기, 민지의 엄마가 벽 스크린에 나타나 말한다. "학교에 늦겠구나!"

6 민지는 눈을 비비며 "창문을 투명하게 해 줘."라고 말한다.

7 어두운 창문이 투명해지며 창문으로 햇살이 밝게 비춘다.

8 욕실에서 빨간 빛이 민지의 몸을 정밀 검사한다.

9 목소리가 "54킬로그램. 건강 상태가 매우 좋습니다."라고 말한다.

10 그녀가 샤워실 안에 발을 디디자, 물이 위와 양측에서 나온다.

11 샤워 후에, 따뜻한 공기가 나와 그녀를 말린다.

12 그녀가 나가자, 서랍이 열리며 오늘의 옷이 나타난다.

13 부엌에서 민지의 아빠가 "좋은 아침이구나, 얘야. 아침으로 무엇을 먹고 싶니?"라고 말한다.

14 민지는 "늘 먹던 걸로 주세요."라고 말한다.

15 아빠가 요리 기계의 버튼 몇 개를 누른다.

16 기계는 베이컨, 달걀, 빵을 만들어 낸다.

17 아빠는 작별 인사를 하고 문 밖으로 급히 나간다.

18 몇 분 후에, 민지의 아빠가 스크린에 나타나 소리친다. "안경을 깜빡했어요!"

19 민지의 엄마가 미소 지으며 답한다. "괜찮아요. 드론을 당신의 사무실로 보낼게요."

20 (Kim / Mr. / says, / a / million!" / "thanks)
➡ _____

21 (Kim / Ms. / and / get / Minji / a / into / flying / driverless / car.)
➡ _____

22 (sit / they / comfortable / in / around / chairs / table. / a)
➡ _____

23 (Kim / Ms. / the / touches / car / to / window / select / groceries / the / this / for / week.)
➡ _____

24 (pays / she / them / for / putting / by / finger / her / on / sensor. / a)
➡ _____

25 (will / they / delivered / be / her / to / house.)
➡ _____

26 (car / the / at / lands / school / Minji's / top / on / a / of / building. / 150-story)
➡ _____

27 (Minji / today / give / will / with / presentation / a / Dona, / student / a / America. / in)
➡ _____

28 (Minji / but / have / doesn't / go / to / America. / to)
➡ _____

29 (to / thanks / VR / a / classroom, / will / they / like / feel / they / in / are / same / the / classroom.)
➡ _____

30 (Minji's / when / comes / family / home, / back / is / dinner / ready.)
➡ _____

31 (eat / they / talk / and / their / about / day.)
➡ _____

32 (a / after / dinner, / delicious / cleaning / the / clears / robot / table / the / washes / and / dishes. / the)
➡ _____

33 (says, / Minji / learned / "I / game / a / chess / called / today. // you / do / to / want / play?")
➡ _____

34 (agrees. / everyone)
➡ _____

35 (3-D / a / board / chess / on / appears / table. / the)
➡ _____

36 (have / they / fun. / of / lots)
➡ _____

37 (before / right / goes / Minji / bed, / to / whispers / she / her / to / watch.)
➡ _____

38 (Daddy / "remind / take / to / glasses / his / tomorrow.")
➡ _____

20 민지의 아빠가 "정말 고마워요!" 라고 말한다.

21 민지의 엄마와 민지는 운전자가 필요 없는 비행 자동차에 탄다.

22 두 사람은 탁자 주변의 편안한 의자에 앉는다.

23 민지의 엄마가 이번 주 식료품을 선택하기 위해 자동차 창문을 터치한다.

24 그녀는 센서에 손가락을 대서 식료품 값을 지불한다.

25 식료품은 집으로 배달될 것이다.

26 자동차는 150층 빌딩의 꼭대기에 있는 민지의 학교에 내린다.

27 오늘 민지는 미국에 있는 학생 Dona와 함께 발표를 할 것이다.

28 하지만 민지가 미국에 갈 필요는 없다.

29 VR(가상 현실) 교실 덕분에, 그들은 같은 교실에 있는 것처럼 느낄 것이다.

30 민지의 가족이 집에 돌아오자 저녁이 준비된다.

31 그들은 식사를 하며 그 날에 관해 이야기한다.

32 맛있는 저녁 식사 후에, 청소 로봇이 식탁을 치우고 설거지를 한다.

33 민지가 "오늘 체스라고 불리는 놀이를 배웠어요. 해 보실래요?"라고 말한다.

34 모두가 동의한다.

35 탁자 위에 삼차원 체스판이 나타난다.

36 그들은 아주 즐거운 시간을 보낸다.

37 민지는 자러 가기 직전에, 자신의 손목시계에 속삭인다.

38 "아빠께 내일 안경을 가져가시라고 상기시켜 드려."

※ 다음 우리말을 영어로 쓰시오.

1 미래를 상상하다

➡ _____

2 오전 7시이다.

➡ _____

3 침대가 흔들리고 김민지가 "5분만 더!"라고 소리를 지른다.

➡ _____

4 침대가 흔들기를 멈춘다.

➡ _____

5 갑자기, 민지의 엄마가 벽 스크린에 나타나 말한다. "학교에 늦겠구나!"

➡ _____

_____

6 민지는 눈을 비비며 "창문을 투명하게 해 줘."라고 말한다.

➡ _____

7 어두운 창문이 투명해지며 창문으로 햇살이 밝게 비춘다.

➡ _____

8 욕실에서 빨간 빛이 민지의 몸을 정밀 검사한다.

➡ _____

9 목소리가 "54킬로그램. 건강 상태가 매우 좋습니다."라고 말한다.

➡ _____

10 그녀가 샤워실 안에 발을 디디자, 물이 위와 양측에서 나온다.

➡ _____

11 샤워 후에, 따뜻한 공기가 나와 그녀를 말린다.

➡ _____

12 그녀가 나가자, 서랍이 열리며 오늘의 옷이 나타난다.

➡ _____

13 부엌에서 민지의 아빠가 "좋은 아침이구나, 얘야. 아침으로 무엇을 먹고 싶니?"라고 말한다.

➡ _____

14 민지는 "늘 먹던 걸로 주세요."라고 말한다.

➡ _____

15 아빠가 요리 기계의 버튼 몇 개를 누른다.

➡ _____

16 기계는 베이컨, 달걀, 빵을 만들어 낸다.

➡ _____

17 아빠는 작별 인사를 하고 문 밖으로 급히 나간다.

➡ _____

18 몇 분 후에, 민지의 아빠가 스크린에 나타나 소리친다. "안경을 깜빡했어요!"

➡ _____

19 민지의 엄마가 미소 지으며 답한다. "괜찮아요. 드론을 당신의 사무실로 보낼게요."

➡ _____

20 민지의 아빠가 "정말 고마워요!"라고 말한다.

➡ _____

21 민지의 엄마와 민지는 운전자가 필요 없는 비행 자동차에 탄다.

➡ _____

22 두 사람은 탁자 주변의 편안한 의자에 앉는다.

➡ _____

23 민지의 엄마가 이번 주 식료품을 선택하기 위해 자동차 창문을 터치한다.

➡ _____

24 그녀는 센서에 손가락을 대서 식료품 값을 지불한다.

➡ _____

25 식료품은 집으로 배달될 것이다.

➡ _____

26 자동차는 150층 빌딩의 꼭대기에 있는 민지의 학교에 내린다.

➡ _____

27 오늘 민지는 미국에 있는 학생 Dona와 함께 발표를 할 것이다.

➡ _____

28 하지만 민지가 미국에 갈 필요는 없다.

➡ _____

29 VR(가상 현실) 교실 덕분에, 그들은 같은 교실에 있는 것처럼 느낄 것이다.

➡ _____

30 민지의 가족이 집에 돌아오자 저녁이 준비된다.

➡ _____

31 그들은 식사를 하며 그 날에 관해 이야기한다.

➡ _____

32 맛있는 저녁 식사 후에, 청소 로봇이 식탁을 치우고 설거지를 한다.

➡ _____

33 민지가 "오늘 체스라고 불리는 놀이를 배웠어요. 해 보실래요?"라고 말한다.

➡ _____

34 모두가 동의한다.

➡ _____

35 탁자 위에 삼차원 체스판이 나타난다.

➡ _____

36 그들은 아주 즐거운 시간을 보낸다.

➡ _____

37 민지는 자러 가기 직전에, 자신의 손목시계에 속삭인다.

➡ _____

38 "아빠께 내일 안경을 가져가시라고 상기시켜 드려."

➡ _____

MEMO

영어 기출 문제집

2학기 전과정

적중100 plus

2학기

정답 및 해설

동아 | 이병민

중 3

적중100

영어 기출 문제집

적중 100

2학기

정답 및 해설

동아 | 이병민

중 3

Lesson 5

Believe in Yourself

시험대비 실력평가 p.08

01 ③   02 ③   03 ④   04 ⑤
05 ②   06 ①

01 ③에는 'ing'가, 나머지 보기의 빈칸에는 'ed'가 어울린다. 감정을 나타내는 동사의 형용사형으로 주어가 감정을 느끼는 주체일 경우에는 과거분사 형태를 쓰고, 주어가 감정의 대상인 경우에는 현재분사(동사원형-ing) 형태를 쓴다. ① 그들은 뱀을 무서워했다. ② 그녀는 뉴스를 듣고 충격을 받았다. ③ 그의 이야기는 항상 흥미롭다. ④ 나는 그를 직접 봐서 신이 난다. ⑤ 그는 시험 결과에 실망했다.

02 ① surprised: 놀란, 놀라는 / 나는 그가 경기에서 이겨서 놀랐다. ② bored: 지루해하는 / 그녀는 음악뿐만 아니라 미술에도 지루해한다. ③ scared: 무서워하는, 겁먹은 → thrilled: 아주 신이 난 / 그들이 금메달을 따냈다는 소식에 모두들 신이 났다. ④ worried: 걱정하는 / 나는 내일 영어 시험이 걱정된다. ⑤ excited: 신이 난 , 흥분한 / 아이들은 선물에 신이 나 있었다.

03 ④ 는 비교급 강조 부사로 '한층'의 뜻이다.

04 look after: ~를 돌보다, 살피다 take care of: ~를 돌보다 / 당신이 없을 때 아이들은 누가 돌볼 것인가요?

05 '매우 신이 나고 행복한'을 나타내는 단어는 thrilled(황홀해하는, 아주 신이 난)이다.

06 (A) turn A into B: A를 B로 바꾸다 / 그는 곧 그의 꿈을 현실로 바꿨다. (B) take part in: ~에 참가하다 / 그들은 부산 국제영화제에 참석하기 위해 부산에 갔다.

서술형 시험대비 p.09

01 ⓑ going → go, ⓒ work → working
02 (1) boring   (2) shocking   (3) amazing   (4) scared
03 into
04 (1) step by step   (2) known as   (3) out, (t)une
    (4) (F)rom then on, take   (5) patience   (6) (j)ourney
05 afford

01 ⓐ how to 동사원형: ~하는 방법, 어떻게 ~할지 / 그것을 어떻게 하는지 내게 보여 줄 수 있니? ⓑ can't afford to 동사원형: ~을 할 형편이 못되다 / 우리가 올 여름에는 해외로 갈 형편이 안 된다. ⓒ look forward to (동)명사: ~를 기대하다, 고대하다 / 나는 너와 일하기를 기대하고 있다.

02 감정을 나타내는 동사의 형용사형으로 주어가 감정을 느끼는 주체일 경우에는 과거분사 형태를 쓰고, 주어가 감정의 대상인 경우에는 현재분사(동사원형-ing) 형태를 쓴다. (1) boring: 재미없는, 지루한 / 그 쇼는 아주 지루했다. (2) shocking: 충격적인 / 그 소식은 모든 사람들에게 충격적이었다. (3) amazing: 놀라운 / 그의 새로운 책은 정말 놀랍다! (4) scared: 무서워하는, 겁먹은 / Mike는 너무 겁먹어서 번지 점프를 할 수 없었다.

03 be made into ~: ~로 만들어지다 / 소설 '미녀와 야수'가 영화로 만들어졌다. turn A into B: A를 B로 바꾸다 / 서울 도심에 위치한 광화문 광장이 스케이트장으로 바뀌었다. put ~ into practice: ~을 실행에 옮기다 / 그녀는 자신의 새 아이디어를 실행에 옮기기로 결심했다.

04 (1) step by step: 점차로, 차근차근, 하나씩 (2) be known as: ~로 알려지다 (3) out of tune: 음이 맞지 않는 (4) from then on: 그때부터 계속 take care of: ~를 돌보다 (5) patience: 인내심 (6) journey: 여행

05 afford: ~할 형편이 되다 / 어떤 것의 비용을 지불할 수 있는 / 나는 그들이 어떻게 그렇게 비싼 휴일을 보낼 형편이 되었는지 모르겠다.

교과서 Conversation

핵심 Check p.10~11

1 looking forward to
2 going
3 (B) → (A) → (C)
4 I'd love to, but I have to do my homework.
5 love to, but I can't
6 (D) → (B) → (C) → (A)

교과서 대화문 익히기

Check(√) True or False p.12~13

1 T   2 F   3 F   4 F   5 F   6 T   7 F   8 T

Listen and Speak 1 A

to, looking forward, excited to, See you on

Listen and Speak 1 B

what are / reading, about, named / who was born without / even won / was made into, going to / I'm really looking forward to / on

Listen and Speak 1 C

1. What's / excited, I'm going to travel / really looking forward to

2. look happy / learn to fly / I'm really looking, to flying

3. going on / so excited, I'm going / looking forward to watching

Listen and Speak 2 A

finish / difficult / interesting, too / help me with / I'd love to, have to take care of

Listen and Speak 2 B

take part in / how to play / I've played / Can you play / but I can't / sorry to hear / cheer for

Listen and Speak 2 C

1. going to do / want to / but I can't, have to / next time

2. are you going to / join me / I'd love to, to visit / next time

Real Life Talk Watch a Video

What are you going / watch / it about / about a boy who became / looking forward to watching / interesting / watched / want to join / but I can't, volunteer / next

Real Life Talk Step 2

1. I'm going to watch, to watching / fun / love to, but I can't, my face painted

2. going to do next / at, I'm really looking, playing it / Sounds / I'd love to, but

01 ①   02 ②   03 ②, ④

01 숙제를 도와달라는 B의 요청에 G가 거절하면서, 남동생을 돌봐야 한다고 이유를 말하고 있다. 그러므로 빈칸에는 거절하는 표현인 'I'd love to, but I can't.'가 들어가는 것이 적절하다.

02 B는 드론을 날리는 것을 배우는 것에 대해 신나고 있으므로, 이에 대한 기대를 표현하는 ②가 빈칸에 들어가는 것이 적절하다. be interested in: ~에 흥미가 있다 look forward to (동)명사: ~를 기대하다, 고대하다 be good at: ~을 잘하다

03 'I'm looking forward to (동)명사 ~.'는 '나는 ~하기를 기대한다.'라는 뜻으로, 기대를 나타낼 때 사용하는 표현이다. 'I'm looking forward to (동)명사 ~.' 대신 쓸 수 있는 표현으로, 'I can't wait to 동사원형 ~.', 'I'm excited about (동)명사 ~.' 등이 있다.

01 ④   02 ④, ⑤   03 ①, ③   04 ③

05 ③   06 ②   07 ⑤   08 ③

09 ②   10 watch → watching

01 주어진 문장은 '그의 이야기가 영화로 만들어졌어.'란 의미이다. 이후에 그 영화의 제목을 물어보는 'What's the title?'이 나와야 하므로 ④에 들어가는 것이 적절하다.

02 'I'm looking forward to (동)명사 ~.'는 '나는 ~하기를 기대한다.'라는 뜻으로, 기대를 나타낼 때 사용하는 표현이다. to는 전치사로 뒤에 명사 또는 동명사(-ing)를 쓴다. 'I'm looking forward to (동)명사 ~.' 대신 쓸 수 있는 표현으로, 'I can't wait to ~.'가 있는데 'can't wait to' 다음에는 동사원형을 써야 한다.

03 ② 여자아이는 영화 제목을 알고 있었다. ④ 지호는 토요일에 Jim Abbott에 관한 영화를 볼 것이다. ⑤ 여자아이는 Jim Abbott이 오른손이 없이 태어난 사람이라고 대답했다.

04 help A with B: A가 B하는 것을 돕다

05 ⓐ에는 수학이 어렵다는 말에 동의를 하고 이어서 흥미롭다는 말을 하고 있으므로 역접을 나타내는 but이 어울린다. ⓑ 'I'd love to, but I can't.'는 '그리고 싶지만, 할 수 없어.'라는 뜻으로 상대방의 제안을 거절할 때 사용할 수 있는 표현이다.

06 ① 민호는 남동생이 있다. (소녀는 남동생이 있다.) ② 소녀는 민호가 숙제하는 것을 도울 수 없다. ③ 민호는 수학이 쉽다고 생각한다. (민호는 수학이 어렵다고 생각한다.) ④ 소녀는 수학이 재미있지 않고 어렵다고 생각한다. (소녀는 수학이 어렵지만 재미있다고 생각한다.) ⑤ 민호는 수학 숙제를 끝냈다. (못 끝냈다.)

07 인사동에 같이 가자고 제안하는 말에 'Sure.'로 수락한 다음에 곧바로 'I'd love to, but I can't.'로 거절하는 말을 하는 것은 어색하다.

08 ⓐ, ⓑ, ⓔ, ⓕ가 빈칸에 들어갈 수 있다. 빈칸 (A)에는 뮤지컬을 같이 보러 가자고 제안하는 말에, 거절하며 주말에 자원봉사 활동이 있다고 말하는 것이 어울린다. 상대방의 제안을 거절할 때 사용할 수 있는 표현으로는 'I'd love to, but I can't.', 'I'm sorry, but I can't.', 'I'm afraid I can't.', 'I'll take a rain check.', 'I wish I could, but I have to ~.', 'Your suggestion sounds great, but ~.' 등이 있다.

09 ① 뮤지컬 Billy Elliot은 무엇에 관한 내용인가?(유명한 무용수가 된 한 소년에 관한 내용이다.) ② 얼마나 오래 Linda

는 자원봉사 활동을 했는가? ③ Jason Kim이 나온 뮤지컬을 Linda는 언제 보았는가?(작년) ④ 이번 주말에 Tony는 무엇을 할 것인가?(뮤지컬 Billy Elliot을 볼 것이다.) ⑤ Billy Elliot에서 누가 주연 배우인가?(Jason Kim)

10 'I'm looking forward to (동)명사 ~.'에서 to는 전치사로 뒤에 명사 또는 동명사(-ing)를 쓴다.

서술형 시험대비   p.21

01 (A) named   (B) to watching
02 but I can't
03 of
04 (E), I'd love to, but I can't.
05 I'm looking forward to watching it.

01 (A) named는 동사 name(이름 짓다)의 과거분사형으로 '이름이 ~인'의 의미를 가지며, 앞의 명사 baseball player를 수식하고 있다. (B) 'I'm looking forward to ~.'는 앞으로 일어날 일에 대한 기대를 표현할 때 사용하는 표현으로, '나는 ~하기를 기대한다'라는 의미이며 to 뒤에는 명사나 동명사가 온다.

02 'I'd love to, but I can't.'는 '그리고 싶지만, 할 수 없어.'라는 뜻으로 상대방의 제안을 거절할 때 사용할 수 있는 표현이다.

03 take care of: ~를 돌보다

04 뮤지컬을 보러 가자는 말에, 이번 주말에 자원봉사 활동이 있다고 말했으므로, 거절하는 것이 어울린다. 그러므로 'Of course.(물론이지.)'라는 제안에 승낙하는 말을 'I'd love to, but I can't.(그리고 싶지만, 할 수 없어.)'로 바꾸는 것이 적절하다.

05 'I'm looking forward to (동)명사 ~.'는 '나는 ~하기를 기대한다.'라는 뜻으로, 기대를 나타낼 때 사용하는 표현이다. to는 전치사로 뒤에 명사 또는 동명사(-ing)를 쓴다.

교과서
Grammar

핵심 Check   p.22~23

1 If I were you, I would wait a little longer.
2 (1) how to use
  (2) where to park

시험대비 기본평가   p.24

01 (1) have → had   (2) will → would
  (3) know → knew   (4) will → would
02 ③   03 ④
04 I did not know whom I should thank for the gift.

01 문제에서 모든 문장이 가정법 문장이라고 했고, 모든 문장의 구조는 '가정법과거' 형태이므로, 조건절의 동사를 과거로, 주절의 조동사도 과거형으로 고치는 것이 적절하다.

02 'why+to부정사'는 쓰이지 않으므로 'I can't find the reason why I should stay here.' 정도로 쓰는 것이 적절하다.

03 주절에 조동사의 과거형이 나왔으므로, 가정법 문장이다. 내용상 be동사의 과거형이 필요한데, 일반적으로 가정법과거에서 be동사의 과거형은 were를 쓴다.

04 '의문사+to부정사'는 '의문사+주어+should[can]+동사원형'으로 바꿔 쓸 수 있다. 내용상 should가 적절하다.

시험대비 실력평가   p.25~27

01 ④   02 ①   03 ②   04 ⑤
05 ③   06 ①   07 ③   08 ②
09 (1) were   (2) had   (3) how   (4) to go   10 ④
11 (1) how they should[can] write
  (2) when I should[can] bring
  (3) what I should[can] do
12 ⑤   13 ②, ④   14 ②   15 ③
16 (1) If it snowed all night, I would not leave tomorrow morning.
  (2) My mom taught me how to bake cookies.
17 (1) will → would   (2) what → how

01 가정법 문장이라면 will을 would로, 직설법 문장이라면 occurred를 occurrs로 쓰는 것이 적절하다.

02 'cook the eggs'로 목적어가 나와 있으므로 목적어로 쓰일 수 있는 것은 적절하지 않으며 'why to부정사'는 쓰지 않는다.

03 주절에 would가 나와 있고 내용상 가정법으로 보아야 하므로 have를 had로 고치는 것이 적절하다.

04 목적어 it이 있으므로 what이 아니라 how나 where 등이 나와야 하거나 it을 삭제해야 한다.

05 ①번과 ④번은 가정법 전환이 잘못된 이상한 문장이며, ②번은 과거의 상황이므로 가정법 과거완료가 필요하고, ⑤번은 직설법의 인과관계가 반대로 표현되었다.

06 ①번은 부사적 용법으로 쓰였고 주어진 문장과 나머지는 명사적 용법으로 쓰였다.

07 가정법과거 시제의 문장으로 쓴다. 'If I had a time machine'으로 종속절을 쓰고 주절에 조동사의 과거형 could를 쓰는 것에 유의한다.

08 'where to buy(어디에서 사야 할지)'가 found out의 목적어가 되도록 한다.

09 (1), (2) 주절에 조동사의 과거형이 나왔으므로, 가정법 문장이다. (3) ride의 목적어로 'a bicycle'이 있으므로 what을 쓸 수 없다. (4) '의문사+to부정사'가 적절하다.

10 가정법과거의 문장들이다. If절에는 동사의 과거형을, 주절에는 조동사의 과거형을 쓰는 것이 적절하다. Were it not for water and air = If there were no water and air = Without water and air = But for water and air

11 '의문사+to부정사'는 '의문사+주어+should/can+동사원형'으로 바꾸어 쓸 수 있다.

12 가정법과거 문장은 현재시제의 직설법으로 바꿔 쓸 수 있다. 가정법은 반대로 가정하는 것이므로 부정하는 것이 서로 바뀌는 것에 주의한다.

13 내용상 그들이 만나는 것이므로 목적어가 필요 없어 what과 which는 적절하지 않고 'why+to부정사'는 쓰지 않는다.

14 옳은 문장은 ⓒ, ⓔ 2개이다. ⓐ have → had, ⓑ will → would, ⓓ going → to go ⓕ exciting → excited ⓖ scare → scared

15 '~가 없다면'이라는 가정법 표현은 'If there were no ~'로 나타낸다. If there were no computers = If it were not for computers = Were it not for computers = Without computers = But for computers

16 (1) 주절에 would가 있는 가정법과거 문장이다. snows를 snowed로 고치는 것이 적절하다. (2) '의문사+to부정사'의 어순이 적절하다.

17 (1) 가정법과거는 'If+주어+were/동사의 과거형 ~, 주어+조동사의 과거형(would/should/could/might)+동사원형 …'의 형태이다. will을 would로 고치는 것이 적절하다. (2) play의 목적어로 chess가 나와 있으므로 what을 쓸 수 없고 내용상 how로 고치는 것이 적절하다.

🦉 서술형 시험대비 p.28~29

01 If he knew my address, he would send me a letter.

02 I told him when to feed the dog.

03 (1) If it were not for

(2) Were it not for

(3) If there were no

(4) But for

(5) As there is

04 which guitar to buy

05 sang

06 where to go

07 spoke, could be

08 (1) If I were Superman, I would save people in danger.

(2) If he didn't have a cold, he could go shopping with me.

(3) No one knew how to play musical instruments.

(4) Can you tell me which train to take?

09 amazed → amazing / am → were / will → would

10 (1) If I were a bird, I would fly.

(2) If it rained, I would put on the boots.

(3) If she had enough eggs, she could bake bread for her family.

(4) If I had a magic carpet, I would travel all around the world.

11 (1) where I should put the eggs

(2) how I can use this camera

(3) when they should take action

12 (1) has → had

(2) taking → to take

01 가정법과거 시제의 문장으로 쓴다. 'If he knew my address'로 종속절을 쓰고 주절에 조동사의 과거형 would를 쓰는 것에 유의한다.

02 'when to feed(언제 먹이를 줄지)'가 told의 직접목적어가 되도록 한다.

03 '불의가 없다면 인간은 정의를 알지 못할 것이다.(헤라클레이토스)'라는 뜻이다. 가정법 과거의 경우, Without = If it were not for = Were it not for = If there were no = But for이다.

04 의문사 which가 의문형용사로 쓰여 '의문형용사+명사+to부정사' 형태로 사용된 경우이다.

05 가정법과거는 'If+주어+were/동사의 과거형 ~, 주어+조동사의 과거형(would/should/could/might)+동사원형 …'의 형태이다.

06 '의문사+to부정사'를 이용한다.

07 가정법과거는 현재 사실과 반대되는 가정을 나타낼 때 사용하므로 직설법 문장을 가정법으로 나타낼 수 있다.

08 (1), (2) '가정법과거를 이용한다. (3) '의문사+to부정사'를 이용한다. (4) 의문사 which를 의문형용사로 사용하여 'which+명사+to부정사' 형태를 이용한다.

09 주어가 It이므로 amazing이 되어야 하며 내용상 가정법과거가 되어야 하므로 'If+주어+were/동사의 과거형 ~, 주어+조동사의 과거형(would/should/could/might)+동사원형 …'의 형태로 나타내야 한다.

10 직설법현재 문장을 가정법과거 문장으로 바꿀 때, 종속절에는 동사의 과거형을, 주절에는 '조동사의 과거형+동사원형'을 쓰는 것에 유의한다.

11 '의문사+to부정사'는 '의문사+주어+should[can]+동사원형'으로 바꿔 쓸 수 있다.

12 (1) 가정법과거에서 종속절에는 동사의 과거형을 쓴다. (2) '의문사+to부정사' 형태가 적절하다.

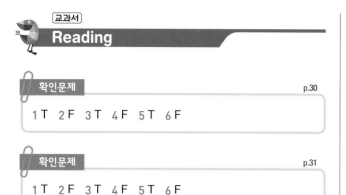

Reading

확인문제   p.30

1 T 2 F 3 T 4 F 5 T 6 F

확인문제   p.31

1 T 2 F 3 T 4 F 5 T 6 F

교과서 확인학습 A   p.32~33

01 Trash, Music
02 Tears of joy
03 thrilled
04 were, would fly
05 look around
06 The other members
07 has just finished, giving us a big hand
08 ever expected
09 It has been
10 I'm a violinist
11 Why is it called
12 are made of, from
13 That's why
14 are from
15 a huge landfill
16 itself
17 Many of us
18 many hopes and dreams
19 began to change
20 an environmental educator
21 teach us music
22 only a few
23 couldn't afford to
24 give up
25 with objects from the landfill
26 named, put, into practice
27 made, from
28 turned, into
29 another problem
30 how to play
31 how to read
32 with great patience
33 Step by step
34 the first piece of music
35 out of tune
36 the most beautiful music
37 felt a new hope
38 From then on
39 some great news
40 were going to have
41 hundreds of people
42 our music
43 sends us trash, send back music

교과서 확인학습 B   p.34~35

1 From Trash to Music

2 Tears of joy are rolling down my cheeks.

3 I'm so happy and thrilled.

4 If I were a bird, I would fly.

5 I look around.

6 The other members in my orchestra are hugging one another.

7 Our concert has just finished and everyone is standing and giving us a big hand.

8 None of us ever expected that this day would come.

9 It has been a long journey.

10 My name is Andrea and I'm a violinist in the Recycled Orchestra.

11 Why is it called the Recycled Orchestra?

12 It's because our musical instruments are made of objects from a landfill.

13 That's why it's also known as the Landfill Harmonic Orchestra.

14 Most of us in the orchestra are from Cateura, a small town in Paraguay.

15 There is a huge landfill in our town.

16 Some people even say that Cateura itself is a giant landfill.

17 Many of us are poor.

18 There weren't many hopes and dreams in our town.

19 Everything began to change, however, when we met Favio Chávez.

20 Favio was an environmental educator and a musician.

21 He wanted to teach us music, but there was a big problem.

22 There were only a few musical instruments in the whole town.

23 We couldn't afford to buy new ones.

24 But Favio didn't give up.

25 He said that we could make musical instruments with objects from the landfill.

26 A talented man named Nicholas was able to put this idea into practice.

27 He made violins from oil drums.

28 He turned water pipes into flutes.

29 We had another problem.

30 No one knew how to play musical instruments.

31 We didn't even know how to read music.

32 Favio taught us with great patience.

33 Step by step, we began to make some sounds on our instruments.

34 I still remember the first piece of music that we played.

35 It was very short and mostly out of tune.

36 But it was the most beautiful music to us.

37 We felt a new hope in our hearts.

38 From then on, we gathered to practice every day.

39 One day, Favio told us some great news.

40 We were going to have a concert, a real concert!

41 And here we are now in front of hundreds of people.

42 They love our music.

43 The world sends us trash, but we send back music!

시험대비 실력평가

p.36~39

01 (A) thrilled   (B) are   (C) giving

02 If I were a bird, I would fly.

03 ②, ⑤   04 ⑤   05 ④

06 by → as   07 ③   08 ones

09 we could make musical instruments with objects from the landfill

10 ④   11 ③   12 ②   13 ⑤

14 ④   15 ②   16 landfill

17 ③, ⑤   18 ③

19 온 마을에 악기가 단지 몇 개뿐이었고, 새 악기를 살 형편도 아니었던 것

20 buying → to buy   21 ①, ④, ⑤

22 in tune → out of tune   23 ②   24 ③

01 (A) 감정을 나타내는 동사는 수식받는 명사가 감정을 느끼게 되는 경우에 과거분사를 써야 하므로 thrilled가 적절하다. (B) 주어가 The other members이므로 수의 일치를 시켜 복수 동사 are로 쓰는 것이 적절하다. (C) standing과 병렬구문을 이루도록 giving으로 쓰는 것이 적절하다.

02 현재 사실에 반대되는 내용을 가정하고 있으므로, 가정법과거로 쓰는 것이 적절하다.

03 ⓑ와 ②, ⑤: 완료 용법, ①, ④: 계속 용법, ③: 경험 용법

04 그들 중 아무도 이 날이 올 거라고 예상하지 못했다. ④ applaud: 박수를 치다, 갈채를 보내다

05 앞에 나오는 내용과 상반되는 내용이 뒤에 이어지므로 however가 가장 적절하다. ① 대신에, ② 그러므로, ③ 즉[말하자면], ⑤ 게다가

06 be known as: ~로 알려져 있다, be known by: ~에 의해 알 수 있다

07 이 글은 'Andrea가 속한 오케스트라는 Recycled Orchestra라고 불리는데, 그 이유는 그들의 악기들이 파라과이의 작은 마을인 카테우라의 거대한 쓰레기 매립지에서 나온 물건들로 만들어졌기 때문'이라는 내용의 글이므로, 주제로는 ③번 '오케스트라가 Recycled Orchestra라고 불리는 이유'가 적절하다. ① description: (~이 어떠한지에 대한) 서술[기술/묘사/표현]

08 one/ones: 앞에 이미 언급했거나 상대방이 알고 있는 사람·사물을 가리킬 때 명사의 반복을 피하기 위해 사용, ⓐ의 ones는 앞 문장의 musical instruments를 가리킨다.

09 with objects from the landfill: 쓰레기 매립지의 물건들로

10 이 글은 'Favio 선생님이 Nicholas 아저씨의 도움으로 쓰레기 매립지의 물건들로 악기를 만드는' 내용의 글이므로, 제목으로는 ④번 '쓰레기를 악기로'가 적절하다.

11 마을에 무슨 악기가 있었는지는 알 수 없다. ① He was an environmental educator and a musician. ② He wanted to teach music. ④ With objects from the landfill. ⑤ A talented man named Nicholas.

12 ⓐ with patience = patiently: 인내심 있게, ⓑ on: ('수단'을 나타내어) ~으로[~에]

13 '우리에게 또 다른 문제가 있었다. 아무도 악기를 연주할 줄 몰랐다. 우리는 심지어 악보를 읽는 방법도 알지 못했다.'는 말로 미루어, 앞에 올 내용으로는 '악기를 구하는 어려움'이 적절하다.

14 'Cateura의 어린이들이 연주했던 첫 곡이 무엇이었는지'는 대답할 수 없다. ① No, there wasn't. ② No, there wasn't. ③ Favio did. ⑤ They thought it was the most beautiful music.

15 주어진 문장의 It에 주목한다. ②번 앞 문장에서 물어보고 있는 '오케스트라가 Recycled Orchestra라고 불리는 이유'를 가리키므로 ②번이 적절하다.

16 landfill: 쓰레기 매립지, 매우 많은 양의 쓰레기가 묻혀 있는 크고 깊은 구멍

17 ⓐ와 ③, ⑤: 재귀대명사의 강조 용법(재귀대명사가 주어, 목적어 등과 동격으로 쓰여 뜻을 강조하는 용법, 생략 가능), ①, ②, ④: 재귀 용법(재귀대명사가 타동사, 전치사 등의 목적어로 쓰이는 경우)

18 ⓐ put ~ into practice: ~을 실행에 옮기다, ⓑ turn A into B: A를 B로 바꾸다

19 (A) 다음에 이어지는 내용을 쓰는 것이 적절하다.

20 afford는 to부정사를 목적어로 취하는 동사이다.

21 step by step = gradually = by degrees = little by little: 점차로, 차근차근, 하나씩, ② 나란히, ③ 자주, 매번

22 '연주했던 첫 곡은 매우 짧고 대부분은 음이 맞지 않았다'고 해야 하므로, 'in tune'을 'out of tune'으로 고치는 것이 적절하다. in tune: 곡조[음]가 맞는, out of tune: 음이 맞지 않는

23 ⓒ와 ①, ③, ④: 부사적 용법, ②, ⑤: 명사적 용법

24 이 글은 '악기를 연주할 줄도 모르고 악보를 읽는 방법도 알지 못했던 단원들이 어려운 훈련 과정을 거쳐 마침내 공연을 하게 되는 과정'에 관한 글이므로, 주제로는 ③번 '공연을 하게 되기까지의 힘든 과정'이 적절하다.

01 a big hand

02 As[Because, Since] I am not a bird, I don't fly.

03 (A) joy   (B) none

04 That's why it's also known as the Landfill Harmonic Orchestra.

05 is → are

06 (A) the Recycled Orchestra   (B) a landfill

07 named

08 we could make musical instruments with objects from the landfill

09 (A) oil drums   (B) water pipes

10 (A) musical instruments   (B) talented

11 we should[could]

12 We were going to have a concert, a real concert!

13 hundred → hundreds

01 give a big hand: 큰 박수를 보내다, clap: 박수를 치다, enthusiastically: 열광적으로

02 가정법과거는 현재 사실과 반대되는 가정을 나타낼 때 사용하는 것이므로, 직설법으로 고칠 때 현재시제로 고치는 것이 적절하다.

03 공연이 이제 막 끝났고 글쓴이는 '기뻐서' 울고 있다. 청중들이 박수를 보내고 있고 오케스트라의 단원들 중 '아무도' 이 날이 올 거라고 예상하지 '못했다.' weep for joy: 기뻐서 울다, applaud: 박수를 치다, 갈채를 보내다

04 That's why ~: 그것이 ~한 이유이다, be known as: ~로 알려지다

05 주어가 'Most of us'이므로 수의 일치를 시켜 복수 동사 are로 고치는 것이 적절하다.

06 그 오케스트라의 악기들이 쓰레기 '매립지'에서 나온 물건들로 만들어지기 때문에 사람들은 그 오케스트라를 'Recycled Orchestra' 또는 Landfill Harmonic Orchestra로 부른다.

07 'Nicholas라는 이름의' 남자라고 해야 하므로 과거분사 named로 쓰는 것이 적절하다. named Nicholas는 주어인 A talented man을 수식한다.

08 '우리가 쓰레기 매립지의 물건들로 악기를 만들 수 있다'는 것을 가리킨다.

09 그는 '기름통'으로 바이올린을, 그리고 '수도관'으로 플루트를 만들었다.

10 Favio 선생님은 쓰레기 매립지의 물건들로 '악기'를 만들 수 있다는 생각을 한 환경 교육가이자 음악가였고, Nicholas는 Favio 선생님의 생각을 실행에 옮길 수 있었던 '재능이 많은' 사람이었다.

11 의문사+to부정사 = 의문사+주어+should[can]+동사원형

12 '우리가 공연을, 진짜 공연을 하게 될 것이었다!'를 가리킨다.

13 hundreds of: 수백의, 수백 명의

01 ①   02 ③   03 take part

04 made   05 ③   06 excited

07 ⑤   08 ⑤

09 the man who[that] was born without a right hand

10 ④   11 ⑤   12 ③

13 (C) – (B) – (A) – (D)   14 ③   15 ⑤

16 ②   17 how to contact

18 were[was], would make

19 (1) we should read   (2) I should do

    (3) to contact   (4) to leave   (5) which, to take

20 played, could win

21 (1) when to take out

    (2) which dress to wear

    (3) whom to meet

22 ③   23 ②   24 ②

25 There were only a few musical instruments in the whole town.

26 ⑤   27 ②   28 ②, ④   29 ③

01 talented: 재능 있는 / 그녀는 사진작가일 뿐만 아니라 재능 있는 음악가이기도 하다.

02 cheer for: 응원하다 / 그들은 그들이 좋아하는 팀과 선수들을 응원한다.

03 participate in: 참가하다, 참여하다 take part in: ~에 참가하다 / 그들은 그가 그 행사에 참가하기를 기대했다.

04 be made of: ~로 만들어지다 / 그것들은 고대 그리스신전들처럼 돌로 만든 것이 아니다. be made into ~: ~로 만들어지다 / 그녀의 베스트셀러는 곧 TV 미니 시리즈로 만들어질 것이다. made from: ~로 만든 / 많은 생산품들이 수작업보다는 기계로 제작된다.

05 'I'm looking forward to의 to는 전치사로 뒤에 명사 또는 동명사(-ing)를 쓴다. ③을 제외한 모든 보기는 to 뒤에 동명사가 나왔다. ① What do you say to 동명사 ~?: ~에 대해 어떻게 생각해? / 오늘 밤 외식하는 거 어때? ② prefer A to B: B보다 A를 더 좋아하다 / 나는 등산보다 걷기를 더 좋아한다. ③ be used to 동사원형: ~하기 위해 사용되다 / 싱크대를 청소하기 위해 무엇을 써야 하니? ④ adjust to 동명사: ~에 적응하다 / 그녀는 혼자 사는 것에 적응하는 데 한참이 걸렸다. ⑤ when it comes to 동명사: ~에 관해서는, ~에 관한 한 / 치과에 가는 일이라면 난 정말 겁쟁이가 돼.

06 사람이 흥분하는 것으로 과거분사형의 형용사가 올바르다.

07 ⑤ 보라가 공연에서 기타를 연주해 본 적이 있는지는 알 수 없다.

08 지호가 Jim Abbott에 관한 영화를 토요일에 같이 보자고 제안하는 말에, 소녀가 'Sure.(물론이지.)'로 대답하면서 토요일에 보자고 말하는 것이 어울리므로 ⑤가 적절하다.

09 who는 주격 관계대명사로, 'who was born without a right hand'가 'the man'을 수식하고 있다. who 대신에 that을 사용할 수 있다. be born: 태어나다 without: ~ 없이

10 주어진 문장은 '어제 체육 수업 중에 손을 다쳤어.'로 노래하는 동안 기타를 쳐 줄 수 없는 이유이므로, 거절을 나타내는 'I'd love to, but I can't.' 다음에 들어가는 것이 적절하다.

11 take part in: ~에 참가하다

12 (B) 'have p.p.'는 과거의 특정 시점에서 시작된 일이 현재까지 계속되고 있음을 나타내는 현재완료 형태로, 여기서는 계속적 용법으로 사용되고 있다. for+숫자+시간 단위: ~동안 (C) while: ~하는 동안

13 (C) 오늘 오후에 무엇을 할 것인지 질문하고 (B) 축구를 할 거라 대답 하면서 같이 하자고 제안하자 (A) 거절하며, 조부모님 댁에 방문해야 한다고 대답한다. (D) 상대방은 그럼 다음번에 같이 하자고 말한다.

14 ③번의 if는 간접의문문에 쓰였지만 나머지는 모두 가정법의 조건절을 이끌고 있다.

15 the dress가 wear의 목적어로 나와 있으므로 what을 when 등으로 고치거나 the dress를 삭제해야 한다.

16 가정법과거는 'If+주어+were/동사의 과거형 ~, 주어+조동사의 과거형+동사원형 …'의 형태로 나타낸다.

17 how to contact: 어떻게 연락할지

18 가정법과거에는 조건절에 동사의 과거형이 나오고 주절에는 '조동사의 과거형(would/should/could/might)+동사원형'이 나온다. 'be'동사는 주어의 인칭 및 수와 무관하게 'were'를 쓰지만, 구어체에서는 주어가 'I' 또는 3인칭 단수인 경우 'was'를 쓰기도 한다.

19 (1)~(4) 의문사+to부정사 = 의문사+주어+should/can+동사원형 (5) 의문사 which가 의문형용사로 쓰여 to부정사와의 사이에 명사가 올 수 있다.

20 가정법과거는 'If+주어+were/동사의 과거형 ~, 주어+조동사의 과거형(would/should/could/might)+동사원형 …'의 형태이다.

21 (1), (3) 의문사+to부정사 = 의문사+주어+should/can+동사원형 (2) 의문사 which가 의문형용사로 쓰여 to부정사와의 사이에 명사가 올 수 있다.

22 ③번은 '오케스트라가 Recycled Orchestra로 불리는 이유'를 가리키고, 나머지는 다 'Recycled Orchestra'를 가리킨다.

23 huge: 거대한, 막대한, 엄청난, tiny: 작은, 조그마한

24 ②번 다음 문장의 He에 주목한다. 주어진 문장의 Favio를 받고 있으므로 ②번이 적절하다.

25 a few는 '약간의, 몇 개의'라는 뜻의 수량형용사로 셀 수 있는 명사 앞에 위치한다.

26 Nicholas는 기름통으로 '바이올린'을 만들었고 수도관으로 '플루트'를 만들었다.

27 바로 앞 문장에서 '그들은 우리의 음악을 사랑한다.'라고 했으므로, 세상은 우리에게 쓰레기를 보내지만, 우리는 '음악'을 돌려보낸다고 하는 것이 적절하다. ④ garbage: 쓰레기

28 (A)와 ②, ④: 명사적 용법, ①, ⑤: 부사적 용법, ③: 형용사적 용법

29 (B)와 ③: (부사) (쉬지 않고) 계속하여, ① (전치사) ~ 위에 (무엇의 표면에 닿거나 그 표면을 형성함을 나타냄), ② (전치사), (요일, 날짜, 때를 나타내어) ~에, ④ (전치사), ~하자마자 [~한 즉시], ⑤ (전치사), [소속] ~의 일원으로

단원별 예상문제   p.48~51

01 ①   **02** ④   **03** ①   **04** ②

05 ②   **06** ⑤   **07** look forward to

08 ⓐ who/that   ⓑ watched

09 I'm really looking forward to flying a drone in the park.

10 (B) → (D) → (A) → (C)   **11** award

12 I'm really looking forward to watching it.

13 ③

14 (1) If she had a flying carpet, she could travel all over the world. / As she doesn't have a flying carpet, she can't travel all over the world.

(2) If it snowed a lot, I would ski in the mountains. / Since it doesn't snow a lot, I won't ski in the mountains.

(3) He taught us how to use the machine. / He taught us how we should use the machine.

15 ③, ④

16 Because their musical instruments are made of objects from a landfill.

17 ③   **18** ④   **19** environmental

20 musical instruments   **21** ②

22 No one knew how to play musical instruments.

23 ①, ⑤

---

01 ①은 반의어 관계이지만 이외의 보기들은 동의어 관계이다. ① bored: 지루해하는, thrilled: 아주 신이 난 ② award: 상, prize: 상 ③ journey: 여행, trip: 여행, 소풍 ④ mostly: 대부분, 일반적으로, mainly: 주로, 대개는 ⑤ take care of: 돌보다, look after: 돌보다, 살피다

02 put ~ into practice: ~을 실행에 옮기다 / 그들이 제안한 것을 실행에 옮겨야 할 때였다.

03 give a big hand: 큰 박수를 보내다 / 그들에게 큰 박수를 보내 주시지 않겠습니까?

04 a few+셀 수 있는 명사: 약간의, 몇 개의 / 나는 그 가게에서 몇 가지를 샀다.

05 제목을 묻지는 않았다. (A) What are you going to do this weekend?(이번 주말에 뭐 할 거니?) (B) What is it about?(무슨 내용이니?) (C) Who is the main actor?(주연 배우가 누구니?) (D) Do you want to join me?(나와 함께 가고 싶니?)

06 'I'd love to, but I can't.'는 '그러고 싶지만, 할 수 없어.'라는 뜻으로 상대방의 제안을 거절할 때 사용할 수 있는 표현이다. 그러므로 제안하는 말인 'Do you want to join me?(나와 함께 가고 싶니?)'의 대답이 될 수 있으므로 ⑤가 적절하다.

07 look forward to (동)명사: ~를 기대하다, 고대하다 / 당신이 그것을 즐길 것이라고 생각해서 그것이 일어나기를 바라다

08 ⓐ 선행사 'a boy'를 주격 관계대명사절인 'who became a famous dancer'가 수식하고 있다. who 대신에 관계대명사 that을 사용할 수 있다. ⓑ last year(작년)라는 시간의 부사구 때문에 과거시제를 써야 한다. 또한 흐름상 뮤지컬을 연주하는 것이 아니라 보는 것이 적절하므로 watched가 적절하다.

09 look forward to (동)명사: ~를 기대하다, 고대하다

10 수학 숙제를 끝냈는지 질문하자 (B) 아직 못 끝냈다고 대답하며, 수학이 어렵다고 말한다. (D) 수학이 어렵다는 것에 동의하면서, 하지만 동시에 흥미롭다고 말한다. (A) 그러면 수학 숙제를 도와줄 수 있는지 묻자 (C) 거절을 하면서 남동생을 돌봐야 한다고 거절의 이유를 말해준다.

11 award: 상 / 어떤 것을 잘해서 누군가에게 주어지는 상이나 증명서

12 'I'm looking forward to ~.'는 앞으로 일어날 일에 대한 기대를 말할 때 사용하는 표현으로, '나는 ~하기를 기대한다.'의 의미이며 to 다음에는 명사나 동명사가 온다.

13 ① If I knew the truth, I would tell it to you. ② If there were no corn, there would be no frozen pizza. ④ Were it not for trade unions, wages would not be so high as they are. ⑤ But for his idleness, he would be a good man.

14 (1), (2) 가정법과거 문장은 현재시제의 직설법으로 바꿔 쓸 수 있다. (3) '의문사+to부정사'는 '의문사+주어+should+동사원형'으로 바꿔 쓸 수 있다.

15 ③ The message will tell you whom to contact. ④ Do you want to know how to make friends?

16 그들의 악기들이 쓰레기 매립지에서 나온 물건들로 만들어지기 때문이다.

17 ⓐ와 ③: 물건, 물체, ① 목적, 목표, ② 반대하다(동사), ④ 목적어, ⑤ [사고·감정·행동 등의] 대상, objects of

consideration: 고려의 대상이 되는 것들

18 파라과이의 작은 마을인 카테우라에는 거대한 쓰레기 매립지가 있고 몇몇 사람들은 심지어 카테우라 자체가 거대한 쓰레기 매립지라고 말한다고 했을 뿐이므로, '카테우라가 거대한 쓰레기 매립지'라는 말은 옳지 않다.

19 environment의 형용사형이 되어야 한다.

20 '악기'를 가리킨다.

21 주어진 문장의 'we began to make some sounds'에 주목한다. ②번 앞 문장에서 Favio 선생님이 엄청난 인내심으로 우리를 가르쳐주신 결과 '우리가 악기로 어떤 소리를 만들어 내기 시작한' 것이므로 ②번이 적절하다.

22 how to+동사원형: ~하는 방법, 어떻게 ~할지

23 ⓑ와 ①, ⑤: 관계대명사, ②와 ④: 동격의 접속사(뒤에 완전한 문장이 이어짐.) ③ 그(앞에서 말한 사람이나 사물·말하는 이나 듣는 이가 이미 알고 있는 사람이나 사물을 가리킬 때 씀)(지시형용사)

서술형 실전문제
p.52~53

01 (f), I'd love to, but I can't. → Sure. 또는 OK.

02 (1) I'm really looking forward to riding a horse.
   (2) I can't wait to ride a horse.

03 (1) I'd love to, but I can't.
   (2) I'm sorry, but I can't.

04 (1) As I don't have a time machine, I won't go back in time and meet King Sejong.
   (2) I don't have a better camera, so I can't take better photos.
   (3) If she were not working, she could go to a movie with Jack.
   (4) Were he in Seoul today, he would come to my house.
   (5) Without people to be governed, there could be no government.

05 (1) They want to know how people decide how much they can eat.
   (2) I don't know which one I should say first.
   (3) The most important grammar rule to master is when to use "I" and when to use "me."

06 Why do they(people) call it the Recycled Orchestra?

07 itself   08 (A) because (B) objects (C) why

09 the first piece of music that we played

10 so that, colud[might], in order that, could[might]

01 'Can I join you?(나도 너와 함께 해도 될까?)'란 질문에, 'I'd love to, but I can't.(그러고 싶지만, 안 돼.)'로 대답하고, 토요일에 보자는 것을 어울리지 않는다. 그러므로 함께해도 된다는 긍정의 대답과 어울린다.

02 기대를 나타낼 때 사용하는 표현으로 'I'm looking forward to (동)명사 ~.(나는 ~하기를 기대한다.)', 'I can't wait to 동사원형 ~.(나는 ~하는 것이 기다려져.)' 등이 있다.

03 상대방의 제안에 거절하는 말에는 'I'd love to, but I can't.', 'I'm sorry, but I can't.', 'I'm afraid I can't.', 'Your suggestion sounds great, but ~.' 등이 있다.

04 (1)~(3) 가정법과거 문장은 현재시제의 직설법으로 바꿔 쓸 수 있다. (4) 가정법으로 고친 후, if를 생략하고 were를 문두에 쓰고 도치시킨다. (5) if there were no = if it were not for = were it not for = without = but for

05 '의문사+to부정사'는 '의문사+주어+should[can]+동사원형'으로 바꿔 쓸 수 있다.

06 they[people]를 능동태의 주어로 하여 고치는 것이 적절하다.

07 강조 용법(재귀대명사가 주어, 목적어 등과 동격으로 쓰여 뜻을 강조하는 용법, 생략 가능)의 재귀대명사를 쓰는 것이 적절하다.

08 (A) 오케스트라가 Recycled Orchestra라고 불리는 이유는 악기들이 쓰레기 매립지에서 나온 물건들로 만들어지기 '때문'이라고 해야 하므로 because가 적절하다. It's because ~: 그것은 ~ 때문이다. (B) 악기들이 쓰레기 매립지에서 나온 '물건들'로 만들어졌다고 해야 하므로 objects가 적절하다. object: 물건, 물체, (욕망, 연구, 관심 등의) 대상, subject: (논의 등의) 주제, (다뤄지고 있는) 문제, 학과, 과목, (C) '그것이 오케스트라가 Landfill Harmonic Orchestra로도 알려진 이유'라고 해야 하므로 why가 적절하다. That's why ~: 그것이 ~한 이유이다

09 '우리가 연주했던 첫 곡'을 가리킨다.

10 부사적 용법(목적)을 나타내는 to부정사는 so that ~ may(can) 또는 in order that ~ may(can)로 바꿔 쓸 수 있다.

창의사고력 서술형 문제   p.54

|모범답안|

01 I'm looking forward to / I'd love to, but I can't.

02 (1) If he had enough time, he would visit us.
    (2) If it were not rainy, I would go swimming.
    (3) If I had a car, I would not have to walk.
    (4) Without the fog, flights would not be delayed.

03 (A) Admiral Yi Sun-sin
    (B) you never gave up in difficult situations
    (C) saved   (D) with only 12 ships
    (E) how to make geobukseon

단원별 모의고사   p.55~59

01 ⑤   02 ①
03 (1) looking (2) turned (3) afford (4) take
04 (1) (o)ne another (2) (c)heer for (3) few
    (4) take part (5) able to (6) give, a big hand
05 (B) → (A) → (D) → (C)   06 ④   07 ③
08 I can't wait to watch it.   09 (A) in (B) for
10 ④   11 ②   12 ②   13 ③
14 (1) Please tell me where I should park my car.
    (2) He hasn't decided when he should leave for America.
    (3) I'm trying to decide what I should take with me.
15 ②   16 ④
17 (1) If she were[was] an adult, she would travel all around the world.
    (2) If I were[was] a king, I would give people presents.
    (3) How to start is the most important part of all.
    (4) I don't know what to do if there were[was] a fire in the building.
    (5) Could you tell me where to park?
18 ④   19 ⑤   20 ②   21 ①, ③, ④
22 (A) only a few (B) violins (C) flutes   23 ③
24 The world sends us trash, but we send back music!
25 ④

---

01 frightened: 두려워하는 scared: 무서워하는, 겁먹은

02 (A) That's why ~: 그것이 ~한 이유이다. / Simon은 너를 좋아해. - 그것이 그가 너와 있고 싶어하는 이유야. (B) how to 동사원형: ~하는 방법, 어떻게 ~할지 / 커피 추출기를 어떻게 사용하는지 아세요?

03 (1) look forward to (동)명사: ~를 기대하다, 고대하다 / 나는 그와 일하는 것을 기대하고 있다. (2) turn A into B: A를 B로 바꾸다 / 그 왕자는 마녀에 의해 개구리가 되었다. (3) can't afford to 동사원형: ~을 할 형편이 못되다 / 우리는 새 컴퓨터를 살 여유가 없다. 왜냐하면 너무 비싸기 때문이다. (4) take care of: ~를 돌보다 / 난 그녀에 대해 걱정하지 않아요. 그녀는 스스로를 돌볼 수 있어요.

04 (1) one another: 서로 (2) cheer for: 응원하다 (3) a few+셀 수 있는 명사: 약간의, 몇 개의 (4) take part in: ~에 참가하다 (5) be able to 동사원형: ~할 수 있다 (6) give a big hand: 큰 박수를 보내다

05 (B) 상대방이 행복해 보인다고 말하면서, 무슨 일 때문에 기분이

11

좋은지 질문하자 (A) Jackson의 콘서트를 볼 것이라고 대답한다. (D) 좋겠다고 말하자 (C) Jackson의 콘서트를 볼 것이 기대된다고 말한다.

06 주어진 문장은 제목을 물어보는 질문으로, 'Our Hero'로 대답할 수 있으므로 ④가 적절하다.

07 was won → won ⓐ named는 동사 name(이름 짓다)의 과거분사형으로 '이름이 ~인'의 의미를 가지며, 앞의 명사 'baseball player'를 수식하고 있다. ⓑ bear: 낳다 be born: 태어나다 ⓒ tried와 won은 접속사 and로 연결되어 있다. won은 win(이기다)의 과거형이다. ⓓ be made into ~: ~로 만들어지다 ⓔ be going to 동사원형: ~할 것이다

08 'I'm looking forward to (동)명사 ~.'는 '나는 ~하기를 기대한다.'라는 뜻으로, 기대를 나타낼 때 사용하는 표현이다. 'I'm looking forward to (동)명사 ~.' 대신 쓸 수 있는 표현으로, 'I can't wait to ~'가 있는데 'can't wait to' 다음에는 동사원형을 써야 한다.

09 (A) take part in: ~에 참가하다 (B) for+숫자+시간 단위: ~ 동안

10 빈칸 (C)에는 대회에서 노래하는 동안 기타를 쳐 줄 수 있는지 묻는 물음에 대한 대답으로, 어제 체육 수업 중에 손을 다쳤다는 말이 뒤에 나오므로 못 친다는 대답이 적절하다. 상대방의 제안을 거절할 때 사용할 수 있는 표현으로는 'I'd love to, but I can't.', 'I wish I could, but I have to ~.' 등이 있다.

11 ① Alex는 기타를 칠 수 있는가? (네) ② 몇 시에 수민이를 응원하러 Alex가 대회에 갈 것인가? ③ 얼마 동안 Alex가 기타를 배웠는가? (3년) ④ 수민이는 무슨 대회에 참여할 예정인가? (노래대회) ⑤ 왜 Alex는 대회에서 기타를 연주할 수 없는가? (어제 체육 수업에서 손을 다쳐서.)

12 (A) A가 'Sounds fun.'이라고 하고 있으므로 행진을 볼 것을 기대하는 표현이 어울린다. 'I'm looking forward to (동)명사 ~.'는 '나는 ~하기를 기대한다.'라는 뜻으로, 기대를 나타낼 때 사용하는 표현이다. (B) A가 '그때 페이스페인팅을 하러 간다.'고 하고 있으므로 못 간다고 말하는 것이 어울린다. 거절하는 'I'd love to, but I can't.(그러고 싶지만, 할 수 없어.)'가 적절하다.

13 ③ 내가 의사이기 때문에, 아픈 사람들을 도울 수 있다. ①, ②, ④, ⑤ 내가 의사라면, 아픈 사람들을 도울 수 있을 텐데. (내가 의사가 아니기 때문에, 아픈 사람들을 도울 수 없다.)

14 '의문사+to부정사'는 '의문사+주어+should[can]+동사원형'으로 바꿔 쓸 수 있다.

15 ②번의 if는 간접의문문으로 명사절을 이끄는 접속사이며, 나머지는 모두 가정법의 조건절을 이끄는 종속접속사이다.

16 If there were no ~ = If it were not for ~ = Were it not for ~ = Without ~ = But for ~

17 (1), (2) '만약 ~라면 …할 텐데'라는 뜻으로, 현재 사실을 반대로 가정하거나 실현 가능성이 없는 일에 대해서 가정할 때 사용하는 가정법과거로 'If+주어+were/동사의 과거형 ~, 주어+조동사의 과거형(would/should/could/might)+동사원형 …'의 형태로 쓴다. (3)~(5) '의문사+to부정사'는 'what/when/where/how/which/who(m)+to부정사'의 형태로 쓰이며, 문장 속에서 주어, 목적어, 보어 역할을 하는 명사구로 사용된다.

18 오케스트라가 Recycled Orchestra라고 불리는 이유가 악기들이 '쓰레기 매립지'에서 나온 물건들로 만들어지기 때문이라고 하는 것이 적절하다. ① 공장, ③ 작업장, ⑤ 악기점

19 ⓑ와 ⑤: 전치사, [역할·자격·기능·성질 따위를 나타내어] ~으로(서)(의), ① 접속사, [이유·원인] ~이므로, ~ 때문에, ② 전치사, 예를 들면, ~처럼[같이](= such as, like), ③ [보통 'as ~ as ...'로 형용사·부사 앞에서] …와 같은 정도로, 마찬가지로 (as ~ as ...에서, 앞의 as가 지시부사, 뒤의 as는 접속사), ④ 접속사, [비례] ~함에 따라, ~할수록

20 ⓐ objects from the landfill: 쓰레기 매립지의 물건들, ⓑ 재료를 이용하여 다른 물건으로 만드는 경우, 전치사 from을 사용한다.

21 (A)와 ②, ⑤: 명사적 용법, ①, ④: 부사적 용법, ③: 형용사적 용법

22 비록 온 마을에 악기가 '단지 몇 개뿐'이었고 새 악기를 살 형편도 아니었지만, Cateura의 어린이들은 Favio 선생님과 Nicholas 아저씨 덕분으로 '바이올린'과 '플루트'와 같은 악기들을 가질 수 있었다.

23 이 글은 '악기를 연주할 줄도 모르고 악보를 읽는 방법도 알지 못했던 단원들이 어려운 훈련 과정을 거쳐 마침내 공연을 하게 되는 과정'에 관한 글이므로, 어울리는 속담으로는 '고진감래'가 적절하다. ③번은 '제때의 한 땀(은 나중의 아홉 땀을 던다) (문제를 즉각 처리하면 훨씬 더 수월하게 해결할 수 있다는 뜻)', 나머지는 다 '고진감래'를 나타내는 속담이다. ④ 고생 끝에 낙이 온다.

24 sends trash to us도 sends us trash와 같은 뜻이지만, 10 단어로 영작하기 위해 4형식으로 쓰는 것이 적절하다. send back: 돌려보내다

25 그들이 연주했던 첫 곡은 매우 짧고 대부분은 음이 맞지 않았다. in tune: 곡조[음]가 맞는

Make the World Beautiful

01 ⑤	02 ①	03 ⑤	04 ②
05 ④	06 ③	07 ①	

01 ①, ④는 '-ation'을 붙여 명사형으로 만들 수 있고 ②, ③은 '-ion'을 붙여 명사형으로 만들 수 있다. ① inspire: 영감을 주다 inspiration: 영감 ② express: 표현하다 expression: 표현 ③ attract: 끌다 attraction: 매력 ④ imagine: 상상하다 imagination: 상상 ⑤ move: 움직이다 movement: 움직임

02 reserve: 예약하다 book: 예약하다, 예매하다 / 두 명 자리를 예약하고 싶습니다.

03 ① 그 미술관은 모네의 그림을 전시할 것이다. ② 그들은 그의 음악이 사람들에게 영감을 주고 사람들을 감동시킨다고 생각한다. ③ 그들은 그가 버는 돈으로는 살아갈 수가 없다. ④ 이 도자기 접시들에는 아름답고 섬세한 꽃무늬가 있다. ⑤ obvious: 분명한, 명백한 / 오염을 줄이는 명백한 방법은 차를 덜 쓰는 것이다.

04 ① book, book: 예약하다, 예매하다 / 더 낮은 가격을 원한다면 내일까지 예약을 해야 할 것이다. ② Remind, remind: 상기시키다, 생각나게 하다 / 오늘밤에 우유를 사야 할 것을 상기시켜 줘. ③ protects, protect: 보호하다 / 덮개는 기계를 먼지로부터 보호한다. ④ allowed, allow: 허락하다, 허가하다 / 시험에서 사전이 허락되나요? ⑤ captured, capture: 담아내다, 표현[포착]하다 / 그 강도 사건은 경찰 비디오 카메라에 포착되었다.

05 since then: 그때부터 / 나는 학교를 1995년에 떠났다, 그리고 그때부터 런던에서 살았다.

06 enough to 동사원형: ~할 만큼 충분히 / 날씨는 소풍을 가기에 충분히 좋았다.

07 capture 담아내다, 포착하다 / 말이나 이미지를 이용하여 매우 정확하게 어떤 것을 묘사하거나 설명하다

01 inspiration 02 to   03 if
04 (1) (e)xhibited   (2) (o)bvious
05 (1) She reminded him of the last time they had met.
    (2) Would you show me around?

(3) Getting close to Busan, I can't wait to see my parents.
(4) Did you thank Edith for the present?
06 (1) column   (2) sign   (3) architect   (4) content

01 접미사는 독립된 단어 뒤에 붙어서 그 단어의 의미와 품사를 변형시킨다. '-ation'은 명사형 접미사로 특정 동사 뒤에 붙으면 그 단어는 명사로 의미와 품사가 바뀐다. / imagine: 상상하다 imagination: 상상력 inspire: 영감을 주다 inspiration: 영감

02 be allowed to 동사원형: ~하도록 허가되다 / 학생들은 수업 중에 먹어서는 안 된다. try to 동사원형: ~하려고 노력하다 / 그녀는 울지 않도록 애를 쓰고 있었다.

03 if: 만약 ~라면 / 만약 네가 더 열심히 공부했더라면, 시험에 통과했을 텐데. Do you mind if ~?: ~해도 됩니까? / 당신에게 한 가지만 더 물어봐도 됩니까?

04 (1) display: 전시하다, exhibit: 전시하다 / 그의 그림은 지역 미술 전시관에서 전시되어 왔다. (2) evident: 명백한, obvious: 분명한, 명백한 / 회사가 재정적인 어려움에 처해 있었다는 것이 명백했다.

05 (1) remind A of B: A에게 B를 상기시키다 (2) show A around: A를 구경시켜 주다 (3) I can't wait to ~: 어서 ~하고 싶다 (4) Thank you for ~: ~에 대하여 감사하다

06 (1) column: 기둥 / 돌기둥이 사원을 떠받치고 있다 (2) sign: 표지판 / 그들은 그 모든 위험 표지판들에도 불구하고 수영을 했다. (3) architect: 건축가, 설계자 / 건축가가 새 사무실 설계도를 그리고 있다. (4) contents: (복수형으로) 내용물, 안에 든 것 / 나레이터가 시각 장애인을 위해 화면의 내용을 소리 내어 읽어 준다.

Conversation

1 Thank you for inviting me to your birthday party.
2 You're not allowed to fish here.
3 (B) → (C) → (A)

교과서 대화문 익히기

1 T   2 F   3 F   4 T   5 T   6 F   7 F   8 F

Listen and Speak 1 A

for inviting me to, glad, are

Listen and Speak 1 B

is leaving in / hope / Which, most / most / the most / liked walking, cool / glad to hear / for showing me around / pleasure, Have

Listen and Speak 1 C

1. Thank you for / welcome, pleasure

2. How / for recommending / welcome, pleasure

3. How was / for helping me make / my pleasure

Listen and Speak 2 A

You're not allowed to / where / stand / I'll put it

Listen and Speak 2 B

for, are on sale / book, away / left / Let's get / do you mind if / says that, not allowed to bring, under / problem / add, is / can't wait to see

Listen and Speak 2 C

1. You're not allowed / sign

2. not allowed to fly / check the sign

3. You're not allowed to / check the sign

Real Life Talk Watch a Video

Thank you for visiting, opened, has exhibited, famous artworks, remind you of, take pictures of, you're not allowed to, let's start

Real Life Talk Step 2

1. Can I ask / Am I allowed to / You're not allowed to drink / for

2. Can I ask you a question / Am I allowed to touch / You're not allowed to touch / for understanding

Check up Dialogue Champion

for helping me finish / pleasure

01 ③, ④　　02 left　　03 ④

01 Lisa가 생일이며, B가 생일 초대를 받았다. 그러므로 B는 Lisa의 생일파티에 초대해 줘서 고맙다는 말을 하는 것이 어울린다. 'Thank you for ~.'는 '~해 주셔서 감사합니다.'라는 뜻으로 고마움을 나타낼 때 사용하는 표현이다. 이와 바꿔 쓸 수 있는 표현으로는 'I appreciate ~.', 'I'm very thankful/grateful to you for ~.' 등이 있다.

02 '남겨진 표'라는 의미로 수동의 의미를 나타내는 과거분사가 적절하다.

03 접속사 But으로 보아 빈칸에는 남동생을 데려가는 것에 대해 긍정의 답이 들어가야 적절하다. 요청을 승낙할 때 mind는 '꺼리

다'의 뜻이므로 부정어(not)를 써서 승낙을 표현한다.

01 ③	02 ④	03 ②	04 ③
05 ②	06 ⑤	07 ⑤	08 ③
09 ③	10 ③	11 ④	

01 'I liked the folk village most.(민속촌이 가장 좋았어.)'라고 말하고 있으므로, 어디가 가장 좋았는지 묻는 것이 어울린다.

02 'Thank you for ~.'는 '~해 주셔서 감사합니다.'라는 뜻으로 고마움을 나타낼 때 사용하는 표현이다. 전치사 for 뒤에는 감사하는 이유가 오는데 보통 명사나 동명사의 형태로 쓴다. show A around: A를 구경시켜 주다

03 ① 수민이가 Daniel에게 마을을 구경시켜줬다. ③ 민속촌 ④ 5분 후 ⑤ 수민이는 민속촌을 갔다.

04 ⓒ 허락을 요청하는 말에 'You're right.(네 말이 맞아.)'는 어울리지 않는다. ⓓ 'Do you mind if ~?'에서 'mind'는 '꺼리다'라는 의미이기 때문에 'Of course'라고 답하면 '물론(꺼려한다)'의 의미로 'Go ahead.(그렇게 해.)'와 어울리지 않는다.

05 (B) 영화에 대해 어땠는지 질문을 하자 (A) 좋았다며 추천해 준 것에 대해 고마움을 표현하고 (C) 감사의 인사에 대해 '천만에.'라고 대답한다.

06 주어진 문장에서 there는 'an umbrella stand outside(밖에 우산꽂이)'이므로 ⑤가 적절하다.

07 'There is an umbrella stand outside.(밖에 우산꽂이가 있어요.)'의 답으로 보아, 우산을 안에 못 가지고 들어가므로 어디에 놓아야 하는지 질문하는 것이 어울린다.

08 접속사 But으로 볼 때, 남동생을 데려가는 것이 좋지만 8세 미만의 어린이들은 데려오지 못한다고 말하는 것이 어울리므로 ③이 적절하다.

09 'Do you mind if 주어 동사?'는 '내가 ~해도 될까?'라는 뜻으로 상대방에게 허락을 구하거나 요청할 때 사용하는 표현이다. mind 다음에는 if나 동명사의 형태가 올 수 있다.

10 ③은 ~을 …한 상태로 있게 하다의 의미로 사용되었고 이외의 보기들은 과거분사로 '남겨진'의 의미로 사용되었다. ① 뒤에 남겨진 사람들은 낮은 산소로 살아 남지 못하고 죽을 것입니다. ② 그들은 여전히 6경기가 남아 있다. ③ 그 경험은 그녀의 마음에 평생 지워지지 않는 상처를 남겼다. ④ 남겨진 문제가 있나요? ⑤ 그는 남겨진 많은 돈을 가지고 있다.

11 ① 10살 남자아이가 세계 음악 콘서트에 들어가는 것이 가능한가? (가능하다) ② 언제 그들은 세계 음악 콘서트를 볼 수 있나? (11월 5일) ③ 얼마나 많은 사람들이 세계 음악 콘서트에 갈 것인가? (3명) ④ 학생 표는 얼마인가? (학생 2명과 어린이 1명의 표 전체 값만 25달러라고 언급되어 있다.) ⑤ 어떤 표를 살 것인가? (세계 음악 콘서트의 표)

01 for   02 (A) is leaving (B) Of course

03 Thank you for showing me around.

04 Am I allowed to touch the artwork?

05 Thank you for helping me make a cake.

06 to bring

01 (A) 'Thank you for ~.'는 '~해 주셔서 감사합니다.'라는 뜻으로 고마움을 나타낼 때 사용하는 표현이다. 전치사 for 뒤에는 감사하는 이유가 오는데 보통 명사나 동명사의 형태로 쓴다. (B) 여기서 for는 전치사로 '~을 위해'의 의미로 사용됐다.

02 (A) 정해져 있는 가까운 미래에 대해서 말할 때 leave 동사의 경우 현재진행형(be동사+동사ing)을 사용할 수 있다. in+시간: (시간의 경과를 나타내어) ~ 후에 (B) 'I did.'의 대답으로 볼 때 긍정의 대답이 나와야 적절하다.

03 'Thank you for ~.'는 '~해 주셔서 감사합니다.'라는 뜻으로 고마움을 나타낼 때 사용하는 표현이다. show A around: A를 구경시켜 주다

04 'Am I allowed to 동사원형 ~?'은 '내가 ~하는 것이 허용될까요?'의 의미로, 어떤 행동을 하기 전에 허가 여부를 물을 때 쓰는 표현이다.

05 'Thank you for ~.'는 '~해 주셔서 감사합니다.'라는 뜻으로 고마움을 나타낼 때 사용하는 표현이다. help는 목적어와 목적격보어의 관계가 능동이면, 목적격보어로 원형부정사나 to부정사를 쓴다.

06 어떤 행동이 허락되지 않음을 알려 줄 때는 'You're not allowed to ~.'라고 표현하며 '~하는 게 허용되지 않는다.'라는 의미이다.

교과서
Grammar

핵심 Check   p.78~79

1 (1) that   (2) so that

2 (1) old enough   (2) to see   (3) for you

시험대비 기본평가   p.80

01 ⑤

02 (1) smart enough   (2) enough
    (3) so that   (4) so that

03 ①

04 (1) You should keep milk in a fridge so that it stays fresh.

(2) The mouse is small enough to go through the hole.

01 'so that'은 '~하기 위해서', '~하고자', '~하도록'의 의미로 '목적'이나 '의도'를 나타낸다.

02 (1), (2) '형용사/부사+enough to+동사원형'의 형태로, '~하기에 충분히 …한[하게]'이라는 의미를 갖고 어떤 일을 하기에 충분한 정도를 나타낼 때 쓴다. (3) '우리는 오래된 옷들을 기부할 수 있을지라도 모았다.'는 말은 어색하다. '목적'이나 '의도'를 나타내는 'so that'이 적절하다. (4) 'so that' 앞에 콤마(,)가 있고, '결과'의 부사절을 이끄는 '그래서, 그러므로'의 의미인 'so that'이 적절하다.

03 형용사 big을 뒤에서 수식하면서 '형용사/부사+enough to+동사원형'의 형태로 쓰이는 말로 enough가 적절하다.

04 (1) 일반적으로 '주절+so that+주어+can/may(조동사)+동사원형(또는 현재시제) ~'의 형태로 쓰여, 'so that'은 '~하기 위해서', '~하고자', '~하도록'의 의미로 '목적'이나 '의도'를 나타낸다. (2) '형용사/부사+enough to+동사원형'의 형태로, '~하기에 충분히 …한[하게]'이라는 의미를 갖고 어떤 일을 하기에 충분한 정도를 나타낼 때 쓴다.

시험대비 실력평가   p.81~83

01 ②   02 ③   03 ①   04 ⑤

05 (1) that   (2) as   (3) order   (4) enough
    (5) too   (6) enough

06 ③   07 ②   08 ⑤   09 enough

10 ②   11 ④

12 (1) that, could[might]   (2) so hard that   13 ④

14 (1) We must improve the work environment in order that everyone can work efficiently. 또는 We must improve the work environment in order for everyone to work efficiently.

(2) Jihun saved money so that he could donate it to the poor.

(3) He is fast enough to cross the finish line first.

(4) I don't think she's smart enough to get a job.

15 ②, ③   16 ⑤

17 We deliver lunch to the elderly on Sundays so that they can feel happy.

01 He noted every detail so as to fix the scene in his mind.

02 I was foolish enough to spend the money I had saved.

03 첫 번째 빈칸에는 '~하기 위해서', '~하도록'이라는 의미의 '목적'이나 '의도'를 나타내는 'so that'의 so가 적절하다. 두 번째 빈칸에는 '형용사/부사+enough to+동사원형'의 'to부정사'가

적절하다.

04 so that이 이끄는 절이 목적을 나타내는 경우, '(so as) to+동사원형', 'in order to+동사원형', 'in order that+주어+can/may ~'로 바꾸어 쓸 수 있다.

05 (1) '~하기 위해서', '~하도록'이라는 의미의 '목적'을 나타내도록 that이 적절하다. (2) '목적'을 나타내는 'so that ~ can …'은 주절과 종속절의 주어가 같은 경우, 'so as to부정사'로 바꿔 쓸 수 있다. (3) '목적'을 나타내는 'so that ~ may …'은 'in order that ~ may …'으로 바꿔 쓸 수 있다.' (4) '형용사/부사+enough to+동사원형'의 'enough'가 적절하다. (5) 'too+형용사/부사+to+동사원형'의 'too'가 적절하다. (6) '형용사/부사+enough to+동사원형'의 'enough'가 적절하다.

06 '형용사/부사+enough to+동사원형'의 형태로 so가 아닌 enough가 되는 것이 적절하다.

07 (A) 'so that ~ can …'은 주절과 종속절의 주어가 같은 경우 'so as to부정사'로 바꿔 쓸 수 있다. (B) 'so+형용사[부사]+that+주어+can …(매우 ~해서 …할 수 있는)'은 '형용사+enough to …(…할 정도로 충분히 ~한)'로 바꿔 쓸 수 있다.

08 'so that ~ can …'은 'in order that ~ can …'으로 바꿔 쓸 수 있으며, 주절과 종속절의 주어가 같은 경우 '(in order[so as]) to부정사'로 바꿔 쓸 수 있다.

09 'We're so old that we can look after ourselves.'나, 'We're old enough to look after ourselves.'로 쓸 수 있다.

10 일반적으로 '주절+so that+주어+can/may+동사원형 ~'의 형태로 쓰여, '~하기 위해서', '~하고자', '~하도록'의 의미로 '목적'이나 '의도'를 나타낸다.

11 '형용사/부사+enough to+동사원형'의 형태가 적절하다.

12 'so that'은 '목적'을 나타내고 'so+형/부+that+주어 can[can't]'은 '결과'를 나타낸다.

13 'so+형용사[부사]+that+주어+can't'는 '너무 ~해서 …할 수 없다'라는 의미이며, 'too+형용사[부사]+to부정사'(…하기에 너무 ~한)로 바꿔 쓸 수 있다.

14 (1) for 뒤에 완전한 절이 나오므로 for를 that으로 고쳐 'in order that'으로 쓰거나 'in order for+의미상의 주어+to부정사'로 쓰는 것이 적절하다. (2) 'so as to+부정사' 형태나 'so that+절'의 형태로 써야 하므로 as를 삭제해야 한다. (3) enough는 '형용사+enough' 형태로 쓰이므로 'fast enough'로 고치는 것이 적절하다. (4) '형용사/부사+enough to+동사원형'의 형태가 적절하다.

15 ② The drill is strong enough to bore through solid rock. ③ I blend tea so as to obtain a nice flavor. 또는 I blend tea so that I can obtain a nice flavor.

16 '형용사/부사+enough to+동사원형'의 형태로 '~하기에 충분히 …한[하게]'이라는 의미를 갖고 어떤 일을 하기에 충분한 정도를 나타낼 때 쓴다.

17 'so that'은 '~하기 위해서', '~하고자', '~하도록'의 의미로 '목

적'이나 '의도'를 나타낸다. so that 다음에 목적이 될 수 있는 'they can feel happy'를 쓴다.

🦉 서술형 시험대비
p.84~85

01 (1) He drinks plenty of water (in order[so as]) to stay healthy.
(2) Go early (in order[so as]) to get a good seat.
(3) The story touched her softly enough to fill her with happiness.
(4) Is it too late to cancel my order?
(5) This book is too difficult for me to read.

02 (1) Yumi swims every morning so that she can stay healthy.
(2) We wore running shoes so that we could go jogging together.

03 (1) The boy is not tall enough to reach the top shelf.
(2) His speech was clear enough to convey his point of view.
(3) She studied so hard that she often had nosebleeds.
(4) All the materials were ready, so that we could start to work immediately.

04 (1) so fast for me following → too fast for me to follow
(2) so generous to he could → generous enough to

05 (1) so kind that she could help
(2) kind enough to help

06 (1) not to get wet
(2) so that she did not get wet
(3) so as not to get wet

07 (1) She is clever enough to solve the problem.
(2) John saved money (so as[in order]) to buy a new bike. / John saved money so that he could[might] buy a new bike.
(3) He spoke loudly so[in order] that everyone could[might] hear him.

08 (1) Mina is smart enough to solve the math problem. 또는 Mina is so smart that she can solve the math problem.
(2) She learned French so that she could help her husband with his work. 또는 She learned French so as to help her husband with his work.

---

01 '(1) 'so that'은 주절과 종속절의 주어가 같은 경우 '(in order[so as]) to부정사'로 바꿔 쓸 수 있다. (2) 'in order

---

that'은 주절과 종속절의 주어가 같은 경우 '(in order[so as]) to부정사'로 바꿔 쓸 수 있다. (3) 'so+형용사/부사+that+주어 +can+동사원형'은 '형용사/부사+enough+to+동사원형'으로 바꿔 쓸 수 있다. (4) 'so+형용사/부사+that+주어+can't+동사 원형'은 'too+형용사/부사+to+동사원형'으로 바꿔 쓸 수 있다. (5) 주절의 주어와 다르므로 의미상의 주어로 'for me'를 쓰고 목적어 it은 생략해야 하는 것에 주의한다.

02 so that은 '목적'이나 '의도'를 나타내어 일반적으로 '주절+so that+주어+can/will(조동사)+동사원형 ~'의 형태로 쓰인다.

03 (1), (2) '형용사/부사+enough to+동사원형'은 '~하기에 충분 히 …한[하게]'이라는 의미로 어떤 일을 하기에 충분한 정도를 나타낼 때 쓴다. (3) so와 that 사이에 수식어가 오면, '너무 ~ 해서 결국 …하다'라는 뜻이 된다. (4) 'so that'은 '결과'의 부사 절을 이끌어 '그래서, 그러므로'의 의미를 갖는 접속사로 쓰이기 도 하는데, 대개 앞에 쉼표(,)가 온다.

04 (1) so+형용사[부사]+that+주어+can't …(너무 ~해서 …할 수 없는) = too+형용사[부사]+to부정사(…하기에 너무 ~한) (2) so+형용사[부사]+that+주어+can … = 형용사+enough to …

05 'so+형용사[부사]+that+주어+can …'은 '형용사+enough to …'로 바꿔 쓸 수 있다.

06 so that은 '목적'이나 '의도'를 나타내어, 일반적으로 '주절+so that+주어+can/may+동사원형[또는 현재시제] ~'의 형태로 쓰 인다. '(so as) to+동사원형'을 쓸 수도 있다. not은 to부정사 앞에 쓴다.

07 (1) '형용사+enough to …(…할 정도로 충분히 ~한)'는 'so+ 형용사[부사]+that+주어+can …(매우 ~해서 …할 수 있는)' 으로 바꿔 쓸 수 있다. (2), (3) so that은 '목적'이나 '의도'를 나타낸다. 일반적으로 '주절+so that+주어+can/may+동사원 형[또는 현재시제] ~'의 형태로 쓰인다. 주절과 종속절의 주어가 같은 경우 '(in order[so as]) to부정사'로 바꿔 쓸 수 있다.

08 (1) 형용사+enough to … = so+형용사[부사]+that+주어 +can … (2) 'so that ~ can …'은 'in order that ~ can …' 으로 바꿔 쓸 수 있으며, 주절과 종속절의 주어가 같은 경우 '(in order[so as]) to부정사'로 바꿔 쓸 수 있다.

교과서
Reading

확인문제	p.86

1 T 2 T 3 F 4 T 5 F

확인문제	p.87

1 T 2 F 3 T 4 F 5 T 6 F

교과서 확인학습 A
p.88~89

01 Meets
02 Art imitates nature
03 ideas, inspirations
04 the natural world
05 pleasing to the eyes
06 For example
07 Isn't it
08 strong enough to protect
09 looks like an egg
10 Such a building
11 has inspired
12 in Spain
13 one of the most famous churches
14 beautiful tall columns
15 don't they
16 used the shape of trees
17 brought, indoors
18 what inspired
19 so obvious
20 added his imagination
21 what inspired him
22 the waves in the ocean, a sailing boat
23 came from
24 closely
25 the peels
26 are shone, more clearly
27 What about
28 Have, been to
29 looks like
30 the curved lines, so that
31 Thanks to, tourist attraction
32 As, capture the beauty
33 Nature meets city
34 were, would, choose

교과서 확인학습 B
p.90~91

1 Nature Meets City
2 Have you heard of the expression, "Art imitates nature"?
3 Many artists get their ideas and inspirations from the world around them.
4 This is because the natural world is a beautiful place.
5 The shapes in nature are very pleasing to the eyes.
6 For example, look at the egg on the left.
7 Isn't it beautiful?
8 It is round and delicate, yet strong enough to protect its contents.
9 Can you imagine a building that looks like an egg?
10 Such a building actually exists in London.
11 Nature has inspired many architects around the world.
12 This is the Sagrada Familia in Spain.
13 It is one of the most famous churches in the world.
14 Look at the beautiful tall columns inside the church.

15 They look like trees, don't they?

16 The famous architect, Antoni Gaudi, used the shape of trees in the Sagrada Familia.

17 That's how he brought the beauty of nature indoors.

18 In the first two examples, we can easily see what inspired the architect.

19 But in the next example from Australia, this is not so obvious.

20 Jørn Utzon, the architect of the Sydney Opera House, took a shape from nature and added his imagination.

21 Can you guess what inspired him?

22 Many people think that it is the waves in the ocean or a sailing boat.

23 But interestingly, the inspiration came from an orange.

24 Look at the roof closely.

25 Can you see the peels of an orange?

26 When orange lights are shone on the building, you can see the peels more clearly.

27 What about Korea?

28 Have you ever been to Dongdaemun Design Plaza in Seoul?

29 Many people think that the building looks like a giant spaceship.

30 But the architect, Zaha Hadid, took the curved lines from nature so that city people could enjoy them.

31 Thanks to its special design, it has become a popular tourist attraction in Seoul.

32 As you can see, many buildings try to capture the nature of nature in their design.

33 They are perfect examples of "Nature meets city."

34 If you were an architect, what would you choose from nature?

시험대비 실력평가
p.92~95

01 ④   02 Many artists get their ideas and inspirations from the world around them.   03 ③
04 How about Korea?   05 ④   06 people living in the country → city people 또는 the country → the city   07 It is one of the most famous churches in the world.   08 outdoors → indoors
09 nature   10 (A) columns (B) the shape of trees
11 ②   12 ①, ④   13 ③   14 the

curved lines from nature   15 (A) Korea[Seoul] (B) Zaha Hadid (C) from nature (D) popular tourist attraction
16 ④   17 In the first two examples
18 ③   19 (A) his imagination (B) an orange
20 ②   21 the beautiful tall columns (inside the church) 22 ④   23 ⑤   24 ②
25 orange lights are shone

01 앞의 내용의 예가 나오고 있으므로 For example이 가장 적절하다. ② 그러므로, ③ 즉[말하자면], ⑤ 게다가

02 앞 문장의 내용을 가리킨다.

03 자연의 형태는 눈에 보기에 매우 좋다고 했으므로, 달걀의 형태는 아름답다고 하는 것이 적절하다.

04 What about ~? = How about ~?: ~은 어떤가?

05 ⓑ와 ④: ~하다시피, ~와 같이, ① 때, ② ~이긴 하지만(양보), ③ ~이기 때문에(이유), ⑤ ~함에 따라, ~할수록(비례)

06 동대문 디자인 플라자의 건축가는 '도시 사람들'이 즐길 수 있도록 자연에서 곡선을 가져왔다.

07 one of the+최상급+복수 명사: 가장 ~한 … 중의 하나

08 성당의 기둥에 나무의 형태를 사용한 것은 자연의 아름다움을 '실내로' 가져온 것에 해당하므로, outdoors를 indoors로 고치는 것이 적절하다.

09 세계의 많은 건축가들은 '자연'에 의해 영감을 받아 왔다.

10 Antoni Gaudi가 성당에 '나무의 형태'를 사용했기 때문에 사그라다 파밀리아 성당 안에 있는 아름다운 높은 '기둥들'은 나무처럼 보인다.

11 주어진 문장의 This에 주목한다. ②번 앞 문장의 내용을 받고 있으므로 ②번이 적절하다.

12 ⓐ와 ①, ④: 부사적 용법, ②, ⑤: 명사적 용법, ③: 형용사적 용법

13 이 글은 '많은 예술가들이 그들의 아이디어와 영감을 그들 주변의 세상에서 얻는다.'는 내용의 글이므로, 주제로는 ③번 '예술은 자연을 모방한다.'가 적절하다.

14 '자연에서 가져온 곡선'을 가리킨다.

15 (A) 위치: 한국(또는 서울), (B) 건축가: Zaha Hadid, (C) 그 건축가는 '자연에서' 곡선을 가져왔다. (D) 그곳은 서울의 '인기 있는 관광 명소'이다.

16 '동대문 디자인 플라자가 언제 서울의 인기 있는 관광 명소가 되었는지'는 대답할 수 없다. ① They think that the building looks like a giant spaceship. ② Zaha Hadid. ③ From nature. ⑤ They try to capture the beauty of nature.

17 '서수+기수'의 순서로 쓰는 것이 적절하다.

18 ⓑ closely: 자세히, ① 주의 깊게, ② 꼼꼼하게, ④ 철저히, ⑤ 자세하게, 상세하게, ③ 대략

19 시드니 오페라 하우스의 건축가인 Jørn Utzon은 자연에서 형태를 가져와 '자신의 상상력'을 더했고, 그에게 영감을 준 것은

'오렌지'였다.

20 the way how와 같이 선행사와 관계부사를 함께 쓸 수 없다.

21 '(교회 안에 있는) 아름다운 높은 기둥들'을 가리킨다.

22 사그라다 파밀리아 성당이 '언제 지어졌는지는' 알 수 없다. ① In Spain. ② Antoni Gaudi. ③ They look like trees. ⑤ He used the shape of trees.in tune.

23 ⓐ come from: ~에서 비롯되다, ⓑ shine on: ~에 비추다

24 '앞의 두 예시에서 우리는 무엇이 건축가에게 영감을 주었는지 쉽게 알 수 있다'고 했으므로, 앞에 올 내용으로는 '무엇이 건축가에게 영감을 주었는지를 명확하게 보여주는 두 예시'가 적절하다.

25 '오렌지색 조명이 건물을 비추면', 오렌지 껍질 이미지를 더 명확하게 볼 수 있다.

서술형 시험대비   p.96~97

01 enough strong → strong enough

02 a building that looks like an egg

03 (A) beautiful   (B) many artists

04 columns   05 don't they

06 (A) using the shape of trees   (B) look like trees

07 inspiration   08 vague → obvious

09 바다의 파도나 돛단배

10 (A) Australia   (B) Jørn Utzon   (C) an orange

11 (A) been   (B) looks like   (C) capture

12 Thanks to its special design, it has become a popular tourist attraction in Seoul.

13 will → would

14 (A) the beauty of nature   (B) Nature meets city

---

01 형용사/부사+enough to+동사원형: '~하기에 충분히 …한(하게)'

02 '달걀처럼 생긴 건물'을 가리킨다.

03 자연계는 '아름다운' 곳이기 때문에 '많은 예술가들'에게 아이디어와 영감을 준다.

04 기둥, (건축) 똑바로 서 있고 구조물을 떠받치기 위해 사용되는 높은 수직의 원통형의 구조물들

05 앞의 문장이 긍정문이면 부가의문문은 부정문으로 쓰는 것이 적절하다.

06 그는 '나무의 형태를 사용하여' 사그라다 파밀리아 성당 안에 있는 아름다운 높은 기둥을 '나무처럼 보이게' 만듦으로써 자연의 아름다움을 실내로 가져왔다.

07 그 '영감'은 오렌지에서 비롯되었다고 해야 하므로, inspired의 명사 형태로 쓰는 것이 적절하다.

08 하지만 호주의 다음 예시에서는 이것이 그다지 '명확하지' 않다

고 해야 하므로, vague를 obvious[apparent/distinct 등]로 고치는 것이 적절하다. not을 생략하는 것도 가능하다. vague: 모호한, 애매한

09 the waves in the ocean or a sailing boat

10 (A) 위치: 호주, (B) 건축가: Jørn Utzon, (C) 그 건축가는 '오렌지'에서 영감을 얻었다.

11 (A) '서울의 동대문 디자인 플라자에 가 본 적이 있는가?'라고 해야 하므로 been이 적절하다. have been to:~에 가 본 적이 있다, have gone to: ~에 가버렸다(지금 여기에 없다, 주어로는 3인칭만 가능함.), (B) 뒤에 명사가 나오므로 looks like가 적절하다. look like+명사, look+형용사: ~처럼 보이다, (C) 디자인에 자연의 아름다움을 '담아내려고 한다'고 해야 하므로 capture가 적절하다. capture: 담아내다, 표현하다, 포착하다, release: 풀어 주다, 석방하다, 놓아 주다

12 thanks to ~: ~ 덕분에

13 가정법 과거: 'If+주어+동사의 과거형 ~, 주어+조동사의 과거형+동사원형'이므로, 'will'을 'would'로 고치는 것이 적절하다.

14 디자인에 '자연의 아름다움'을 담아내려고 하는 많은 건물들은 '자연이 도시를 만나다'의 완벽한 예이다.

영역별 핵심문제   p.99~103

01 ④   02 ①   03 ③   04 ①

05 ⑤   06 do you mind if I bring my little brother?

07 ①   08 for   09 ⑤   10 ①

11 ②   12 Thank you for understanding.

13 ②   14 ①   15 ⑤

16 (1) Sumi is brave enough to go into the Ghost House.

   (2) The dog is too big to get through the small window.

   (3) Tom went to bed early so that he could[might] get up early.

   (4) Minsu turned on the radio so as to listen to the baseball game.

   (5) The training must be planned systematically in order that it should be effective.

17 ③   18 ②   19 ④   20 ②

21 (A) because   (B) pleasing   (C) strong enough

22 The world around them.   23 what inspired him

24 close → closely   25 ④   26 ④

27 ②   28 a 4-story building   29 ③

---

01 <보기>의 단어는 동사와 명사의 관계이다 arrive: 도착하다 arrival: 도착 ④번은 명사와 형용사의 관계이다. nature: 자연 natural: 자연의, 자연적인 ① inspire: 영감을 주다 inspiration: 영감 ② attract: 끌다 attraction: 매력

③ refuse: 거절하다 refusal: 거절 ⑤ imitate: 모방하다 imitation: 모방. 접미사는 독립된 단어 뒤에 붙어서 그 단어의 의미와 품사를 변형시킨다. '-ion'과 '-ation'은 명사형 접미사로 특정 동사 뒤에 붙으면 그 단어는 명사로 의미와 품사가 바뀐다. 그 외에 동사를 명사로 바꾸는 접미사는 '-ment', '-ure', '-al', '-y' 등이 있다.

02 wave 파도, 물결 / 바다의 표면을 가로질러 움직이는 수면의 도드라지는 선

03 closely: 자세하게 / 형사는 대답을 기다리며 그를 면밀히 살폈다.

04 on sale: 판매 중인, 할인 중인 / Stephen King의 새로운 소설이 다음 주에 판매될 것이다.

05 ⓐ book, Let's 동사원형: ~하자(권유) ⓑ left, left는 과거분사로 앞의 tickets를 수식하며 '남겨진'이다. ⓒ that, that 이하는 says의 목적어이다. ⓓ to bring, be allowed to: ~하도록 허가되다 ⓔ to see, I can't wait to ~: 너무 ~하고 싶다

06 do you mind if ~?: ~해도 됩니까? bring: 데려오다, 데려가다

07 'Since then'이 '그 때부터'의 의미이므로, 그 때라고 말할 수 있는 시간 정보가 먼저 나와야 한다. 주어진 문장에서 in 1995을 then으로 말할 수 있으므로, ①이 적절하다.

08 'Thank you for ~.'는 '~해 주셔서 감사합니다.'라는 뜻으로 고마움을 나타낼 때 사용하는 표현이다. 전치사 for 뒤에는 감사하는 이유가 오는데 보통 명사나 동명사의 형태로 쓴다.

09 remind A of B: A에게 B를 상기시키다

10 ① 이 미술관에 얼마나 많은 작품들이 전시되어 있는가? ② 학생들은 어디에 있는가? (미술관) ③ 학생들은 작품의 사진을 찍을 수 있는가? (네) ④ 학생들은 미술관에서 무엇을 볼 예정인가? (미술 책에 실린 유명한 작품) ⑤ 언제 미술관이 문을 열었는가? (1995년)

11 질문을 해도 되는지 묻는 말에 (B) 무슨 질문인지 묻고 (C) 탄산음료를 먹어도 되는지 물어보니 (A) 안 된다고 대답해 준다. (D) 이에 알겠다고 대답한다.

12 'Thank you for ~.'는 '~해 주셔서 감사합니다.'라는 뜻으로 고마움을 나타낼 때 사용하는 표현이다. understand: 이해하다

13 'too+형용사[부사]+to부정사(…하기에 너무 ~한)'는 'so+형용사[부사]+that+주어+can't ...(너무 ~해서 …할 수 없는)'로 바꿔 쓸 수 있다.

14 'so that ~ can ...'은 'in order that ~ can ...'으로 바꿔 쓸 수 있다.

15 'I went to Seoul Station in the heavy rain so as to meet my mother.' 또는 'I went to Seoul Station in the heavy rain so that I could meet my mother.'가 되어야 한다.

16 (1) 'so+형용사[부사]+that+주어+can ...'은 '형용사+enough to ...'로 바꿔 쓸 수 있다. (2) 'so+형용사[부사]+that+주어+can't ...'는 'too+형용사[부사]+to부정사'로 바꿔 쓸 수 있다. (3) so that이 이끄는 절이 목적을 나타내어

'~하기 위해서, ~하도록'이라는 의미를 나타낸다. (4) 'so that ~ can ...'은 주절과 종속절의 주어가 같은 경우 'so as to부정사'로 바꿔 쓸 수 있다. (5) 'so that ~ 조동사 …'은 'in order that ~ 조동사 …'로 바꿔 쓸 수 있다.

17 so that은 '목적'이나 '의도'를 나타내며, 일반적으로 '주절+so that+주어+조동사+동사원형[또는 현재시제] ~'의 형태로 쓰인다.

18 콤마(,) 다음에 오는 so (that)은 '그래서, 그 결과'라는 의미를 나타낸다.

19 '형용사/부사+enough to+동사원형'은 '~하기에 충분히 …한 [하게]'이라는 의미로 어떤 일을 하기에 충분한 정도를 나타낼 때 쓴다.

20 ⓐ와 ②, ⑤: 경험 용법, ①, ④: 계속 용법, ③: 완료 용법

21 (A) 뒤에 절(주어+동사)이 나오므로 because가 적절하다. because of+명사구, (B) 감정을 나타내는 동사는 감정을 유발할 때 현재분사를 쓰는 것이 적절하므로 pleasing이 적절하다. (C) 내용물을 보호할 만큼 '충분히 튼튼하다'고 해야 하므로 strong enough가 적절하다.

22 '그들(많은 예술가들) 주변의 세상'이 그들에게 아이디어와 영감을 준다.

23 앞 문장의 '무엇이 그에게 영감을 주었는지'를 가리킨다.

24 동사를 수식하므로 부사로 고치는 것이 적절하다. close(형용사): 가까운, 철저한, 면밀한

25 실제로 Jørn Utzon에게 영감을 준 것은 '오렌지'였다.

26 주어진 문장의 They에 주목한다. ④번 앞 문장의 'many buildings'를 받고 있으므로 ④번이 적절하다.

27 이 글은 '서울의 동대문 디자인 플라자와 같은 많은 건물들이 디자인에 자연의 아름다움을 담아내려고 하고 있고, 이 건물들은 '자연이 도시를 만나다'의 완벽한 예가 된다.'는 내용의 글이므로, 제목으로는 ②번 '디자인에 자연의 아름다움을 담아내려고 하는 많은 건물들'이 적절하다.

28 건물이 몇 층으로 되어 있는지, 주로 그 층수에 대해서 말할 때에는 'story'를 사용하는 것이 적절하다.

29 '보람중학교 정원에 무슨 채소를 재배하는지'는 대답할 수 없다. ① It is in Suwon. ② It is on top of the school building. ④ They grow them so that they can have fresh food. ⑤ The writer loves sitting there and talking with friends.

단원별 예상문제 p.104~107

01 ⑤   02 (c)ontents   03 ③   04 (p)icked
05 ④   06 ④   07 ③   08 it says that you are not allowed to bring children under 8.
09 book   10 ①   11 I can't wait to see the

---

20 정답 및 해설

concert!   **12** ①   **13** ③

14 (1) She studies several languages so[in order] that she can[may] be a tour guide.

    (2) Sumin is so tall that he can get on the ride.

    (3) The sand was so hot that I couldn't walk on it.

15 ④   **16** ②, ⑤   **17** ④   **18** ③

19 ③   **20** shined → shone   **21** ③

22 tourist attraction   **23** ③, ④

24 many buildings

01 <보기>의 단어는 반의어 관계이다. indoors: 실내로, 실내에, outdoors: 야외에. ⓐ와 ⓔ는 반의어 ⓑ, ⓒ, ⓓ는 동의어 관계이다. ⓐ lend: 빌려주다, borrow: 빌리다 ⓑ delicate: 부서지기 쉬운, fragile: 깨지기 쉬운 ⓒ actually: 실제로, indeed: 정말로 ⓓ allow: 허락하다, permit: 허락하다 ⓔ natural: 자연적인, artificial: 인공적인

02 contents: 내용물, 안에 든 것 / 어떤 것 속에 들어 있는 것 / 그 교재는 기초적인 내용을 다루고 있다.

03 (A) take pictures of ~: ~의 사진을 찍다 / 방문객들은 모형을 만지고 사진을 찍을 수 있습니다. (B) right away: 즉시, 당장 / 더 이상 시장 점유율을 뺏기기 전에 지금 당장 뭔가를 시작해야 한다.

04 pick: 고르다, (꽃을) 꺾다 / 그 호텔이 이 지역에서 가장 작은 호텔로 선정되었다. Amy는 어제 한 다발의 야생화들을 꺾었다.

05 Lisa의 생일로, B가 Lisa에게 생일선물인 꽃을 주는 것이 어울리므로 ④가 적절하다.

06 (A) 'Thank you for ~.'는 '~해 주셔서 감사합니다.'라는 뜻으로 고마움을 나타낼 때 사용하는 표현이다. 전치사 for 뒤에는 감사하는 이유가 오는데 보통 명사나 동명사의 형태로 쓴다. invitation은 명사로 뒤에 me를 목적어로 받을 수 없기 때문에 동명사 형태인 inviting이 와야 한다. (B) 자신의 파티에 와줘서 기쁨을 표현하고 있다.

07 '세계 음악 콘서트'의 표가 판매 중으로, 온라인으로 표를 예매하는 상황에서, 11월 5일의 표가 남아 있다고 말하니, 상대방이 'Sounds good.(잘됐다).'라고 반응하며 2장을 예매하자고 말하는 것이 어울리므로 ③이 적절하다.

08 표지판이나 안내문 등에 쓰인 내용을 말해줄 때는 'It says (that)+내용'으로 말한다. 'You're not allowed to ~.'는 '~하는 게 허용되지 않는다.'라는 뜻으로 하지 말아야 할 행동을 말할 때 사용하는 표현이다.

09 book: 예약하다, 예매하다 / 미래의 어떤 시간을 위해 예약하다

10 ⓐ is → are, the tickets가 복수 주어이므로 are가 적절하다.

11 I can't wait to ~: 너무 ~하고 싶다

12 (B) 드론을 날리면 안 된다고 말하니 (A) 몰랐다고 대답한다. (C) 표지판을 확인하라는 말에 (D) 알겠다고 대답한다.

13 ③ The problem is so difficult that you can't solve it. 'so+형용사[부사]+that+주어+can't ...'는 '너무 ~해서 …할 수 없다'라는 의미이며, 'too+형용사[부사]+to부정사' (…하기에 너무~한)로 바꿔 쓸 수 있다.

14 (1) 목적을 나타내므로 '(in order[so as]) that'로 바꿔 쓸 수 있다. (2) so+형용사[부사]+that+주어+can ... = 형용사[부사]+enough+to부정사 (3) so+형용사[부사]+that+주어+can't ... = too+형용사[부사]+to부정사. 주어가 다를 경우 to부정사의 의미상의 주어를 'for+목적격'으로 나타낸다.

15 ④는 결과, 나머지는 모두 목적을 나타낸다.

16 ⓐ와 ②, ⑤: 기둥, 원주, ⑤ Corinthian: 코린트식, ①과 ④: (신문의) 특정 기고란, ③ (이동 중인 사람들이나 차량이 길게 늘어선) 줄

17 이 글은 'Antoni Gaudi가 사그라다 파밀리아 성당에 나무의 형태를 사용함으로써 자연의 아름다움을 실내로 가져왔다.'는 내용의 글이므로, 제목으로는 ④번 'Gaudi는 자연의 아름다움을 실내로 가져왔다.'가 적절하다.

18 사그라다 파밀리아 성당은 세계에서 가장 유명한 성당이 아니라, '세계에서 가장 유명한 성당 중의 하나'이다.

19 주어진 문장의 him에 주목한다. ③번 앞 문장의 Jørn Utzon을 받고 있으므로 ③번이 적절하다.

20 오렌지색 조명이 건물을 '비추면'이라고 해야 하므로, shined를 shone으로 고치는 것이 적절하다. shine-shined-shined: 윤[광]을 내다, 닦다, shine-shone-shone: 빛나다, 반짝이다, 비추다

21 '시드니 오페라 하우스의 형태에 건축가가 언제 자신의 상상력을 더했는지'는 알 수 없다. ① No, it isn't. ② Jørn Utzon. ④ They think that it is the waves in the ocean or a sailing boat. ⑤ It came from an orange.

22 tourist attraction: 관광 명소, 관광객들이 방문하는 흥미 있는 장소

23 ⓐ와 ③, ④: 경험 용법, ①, ⑤: 완료 용법, ②: 계속 용법

24 '많은 건물들'을 가리킨다.

🦉 서술형 실전문제   p.108~109

01 You're not allowed to fish here.

02 ④ Of course. → Not at all.

03 (1) We collected old clothes [in order / so as] to donate them.

    (2) He practices singing very hard so[in order] that he can[may] be a singer.

        (3) The ladder is so tall that I can reach the shelf.

        (4) Mike is so weak that he cannot lift the box.

  04 (1) in order that   (2) in[so] order[as] to

        (3) enough to   (4) too hot to

  05 what inspired the architect

  06 Can you guess what inspired him?

  07 (A) the waves in the ocean   (B) a sailing boat

  08 nature / Nature   09 to enjoy

  10 Its special design

|모범답안|

  01 am I allowed to go out and watch a movie with
        my friend / You are not allowed to go out

  02 (1) This bag is big enough to carry many books.

        (2) I went to bed early (so as/in order) to get up
              early.

        (3) She studied hard (so as/in order) to pass the
              exam.

        (4) The coffee is too hot to drink.

  03 (A) Boram Middle School (B) 4-story
        (C) small garden (D) some vegetables
        (E) the bench

01 'You're not allowed to ~.'는 '~하는 게 허용되지 않는다.'라
  는 뜻으로 하지 말아야 할 행동을 말할 때 사용하는 표현이다.
  미술관이나 도서관 등 공공장소에서의 금지 사항을 말할 때 자
  주 쓰이는 표현이다. fish: 낚시하다

02 mind는 '꺼리다'의 뜻으로 Yes는 거절을 의미하고, No는 수
  락을 의미한다. 수락할 때 'No, I don't mind.', 'Not at all.',
  'No, go ahead.', 'Of course not.' 등을 사용할 수 있다.

03 (1), (2) '목적'을 나타내는 to부정사 또는 'in order to', 'so
  as to' 등의 표현은 'so[in order] that+주어+조동사'로 바꿔
  쓸 수 있다. (3) so+형용사[부사]+that+주어+can ... = 형용
  사[부사]+enough+to부정사. 주어가 다를 경우 to부정사의 의
  미상의 주어를 'for+목적격'으로 나타낸다. (4) so+형용사[부
  사]+that+주어+can't ... = too+형용사[부사]+to부정사.

04 (1), (2) 'so that ~ can ...'은 'in order that ~ can ...'으
  로 바꿔 쓸 수 있으며, 주절과 종속절의 주어가 같은 경우 '(in
  order[so as]) to부정사'로 바꿔 쓸 수 있다. (3), (4) 'so+형
  용사[부사]+that+주어+can …'은 '형용사+enough to ...'로
  바꿔 쓸 수 있으며, 'so+형용사[부사]+that+주어+can't ...'는
  'too+형용사[부사]+to부정사'로 바꿔 쓸 수 있다. (4)번의 경우
  주절과 종속절의 주어가 다르지만 일반인이 주어이므로 따로 밝
  혀 쓰지 않아도 된다.

05 '무엇이 건축가에게 영감을 주었는지'를 가리킨다.

06 'Can you guess what inspired him?'은 Yes/No로 대답할
  수 있으므로, 의문사를 앞으로 보내어 What can you guess
  inspired him?이라고 쓰지 않도록 조심해야 한다.

07 시드니 오페라 하우스의 건축가는 '바다의 파도'나 '돛단배'에서
  영감을 받은 것이 아니라 오렌지에서 영감을 받았다.

08 많은 건물들이 디자인에 '자연'의 아름다움을 담아내려고 한다.
  이 건물들은 "자연'이 도시를 만나다'의 완벽한 예이다.

09 so that ~ can은 부사적 용법(목적)의 to부정사로 바꿀 수 있
  다. 이때 주어를 to부정사의 의미상의 주어(for+목적격)로 바꾸
  는 것이 적절하다.

10 '서울의 동대문 디자인 플라자의 특별한 디자인'이 그곳을 서울의
  인기 있는 관광 명소로 만들어 준다.

  01 ②   02 ⑤   03 ③

  04 (1) curved   (2) (e)xpression

        (3) (r)ecommend   (4) (i)nspiration

  05 ④   06 most   07 ⑤   08 ①, ③

  09 ⑤   10 let me remind you of a basic rule

  11 Thank you for visiting our art museum.

  12 You're allowed to bring your umbrella inside. →
        You're not allowed to bring your umbrella inside.

  13 (1) We planted some trees in a park so that they
              could keep the air clean. 또는 We planted
              some trees in a park for them to keep the air
              clean.

        (2) I saved money in order that I could buy a
              present for my grandma. 또는 I saved money in
              order to buy a present for my grandma.

        (3) The bag is big enough to carry two soccer
              balls.

        (4) This place is too cold for people to live. 또는
              This place is so cold that people can't live.

  14 (1) She practices hard so that she can prepare for
              the contest.

        (2) The tea is too hot to drink.

  15 ③   16 ①, ③, ④

  17 (1) 그녀는 건강을 유지하기 위해 규칙적으로 조깅했다. /
              so that은 '~하기 위해서', '~하도록'의 의미로 '목적'
              을 나타낸다.

        (2) 그녀는 규칙적으로 조깅해서 건강을 유지할 수
              있었다. / so와 that 사이에 수식어가 오면, '너무 ~

01 Am I allowed to ~?: ~해도 됩니까? be allowed to: ~하도
  록 허가받다

해서 결국 …하다'라는 뜻이 된다.

18 ② **19** why → because **20** ①

21 ④ **22** ⑤

23 The famous architect, Antoni Gaudi, used the shape of trees in the Sagrada Familia.

24 ⑤ **25** the waves in the ocean or a sailing boat → an orange **26** ④ **27** ⑤

---

01 architect 건축가, 설계자 / 건물을 설계하는 사람

02 giant: 거대한; 거인 / 조심해라. 숲이 거대한 뱀과 거미로 가득 차 있다.

03 ① imitate, imitate: 모방하다 / 그는 그가 들은 어떠한 소리든 모방할 수 있는 독특한 능력을 가지고 있다. ② chose, choose: 선택하다 / 그는 말할 때, 단어를 주의 깊게 골랐다. ③ feeds, feed: 먹이를 주다 / 우리가 떠나 있을 때 내 여동생이 고양이들에게 먹이를 준다. ④ Add, add: 추가하다 / 전체에 10%를 더해라. ⑤ check, check: 확인하다 / 미스터리를 푸는 첫 번째 규칙은 사실을 확인하는 것이다.

04 (1) curved: 곡선 모양의, 굽은 (2) expression: 표현 (3) recommend: 추천하다 (4) inspiration: 영감

05 감사에 답하는 표현으로는 'You're welcome.(천만에요.)', 'Don't mention it.(별말씀을요.)', 'It's my pleasure.(제 기쁨이에요.)', 'No problem. (뭘요.)' 'Anytime.(언제든지요.)' 등이 있다. 'I appreciate ~.'는 감사할 때 사용하는 표현이다.

06 가장 좋아하는 것을 물어볼 때 최상급 most를 사용해 'Which ~ do you like most?(어떤 ~가 가장 좋아?)'로 물어 볼 수 있다.

07 walk around: 돌아다니다 show A around: A를 구경시켜 주다

08 대화에서 in은 '~ 후에'의 의미로 사용했다. ① 연극은 몇 시간 후에 시작한다. ② 밝은 노란색 꽃들이 늦여름에 나타난다. ③ 우리는 한 시간 후에 돌아올 것이다. ④ Shaw는 1927년 처음 러시아를 방문했다. ⑤ 그는 10월에 은퇴했다.

09 (A) since는 '~ 이래로'의 뜻으로, 과거에 일어난 일이 현재까지 영향을 미칠 때 쓰는 현재완료(have+p.p)와 잘 어울린다. since then: 그때부터 (B) 사진을 찍을 수 있다는 내용과 만져서는 안 된다는 말은 서로 상반되는 내용으로 접속사 but이 적절하다.

10 let은 사역동사로 목적어와 목적격보어의 관계가 능동이면, 목적격보어로 동사원형을 사용해야 한다. remind A of B: A에게 B를 상기시키다

11 'Thank you for ~.'는 '~해 주서서 감사합니다.'라는 뜻으로 고마움을 나타낼 때 사용하는 표현이다. 전치사 for 뒤에는 감사하는 이유가 오는데 보통 명사나 동명사의 형태로 쓴다.

12 'You're not allowed to ~.'는 '~하는 게 허용되지 않는다.'라

는 뜻으로 하지 말아야 할 행동을 말할 때 사용하는 표현이다. 'You're allowed to ~'를 사용하면 허용되는 바를 얘기하므로, 우산을 밖에 있는 우산꽂이에 놓으라는 말과 어울리지 않는다.

13 (1) 'so that+절' 또는 'so as to부정사'가 되어야 한다. (2) 'in order that+절' 또는 'in order to부정사'가 되어야 한다. (3) '형용사+enough'의 어순이 적절하다. (4) 'too+형용사[부사]+to부정사'나 'so+형용사[부사]+that+주어+can't ...'가 되어야 한다.

14 (1) '주절+so that+주어+조동사+동사원형 ~'의 형태로 so that은 '목적'이나 '의도'를 나타낸다. (2) too+형용사/부사+to+동사원형: 너무 ~해서 …할 수 없다, …하기에는 너무 ~하다

15 Additional funding will be required in order for the bridge to be completed. 주절과 부사절의 주어가 다른 경우 서로 다른 주어를 나타내야 하는데 to부정사의 경우 'for+목적격'으로 쓴다.

16 ② as → so ⑤ as to → that ⑥ too → so ⑦ talking → to talk

17 'so that+주어+can ...'과 'so+형용사[부사]+that+주어+can ...'의 차이를 구별한다.

18 '많은 예술가들이 그들의 아이디어와 영감을 그들 주변의 세상에서 얻는다.'고 했으므로, 예술이 자연을 '모방한다.'고 하는 것이 적절하다. ① 영감을 주다, ③ 생산하다, ④ 영향을 주다, ⑤ ~의 용기를 북돋우다, 격려하다

19 This(결과) is because+원인, This(원인) is why+결과

20 이때의 yet은 접속사로 '그러나'의 뜻이다.

21 주어진 문장의 They에 주목한다. ④번 앞 문장의 the beautiful tall columns를 가리키므로 ④번이 적절하다.

22 문맥상 '나무의 형태를 사용했다'가 되어야 한다.

23 '유명한 건축가인 Antoni Gaudi가 사그라다 파밀리아 성당에 나무의 형태를 사용한 것'을 가리킨다.

24 위 글은 'Jørn Utzon은 자연에서 형태를 가져와 자신의 상상력을 더하여 시드니 오페라 하우스를 건축했고, 그에게 영감을 준 것은 오렌지였다'는 내용의 글이므로, 주제로는 ⑤번 '무엇이 시드니 오페라 하우스의 건축가에게 영감을 주었나?'가 적절하다.

25 시드니 오페라 하우스의 건축가인 Jørn Utzon이 형태를 가져온(영감을 받은) 자연은 '바다의 파도나 돛단배'가 아니라 '오렌지'였다.

26 이 특별한 디자인 '덕분에', 동대문 디자인 플라자는 서울의 인기 있는 관광 명소가 되었다고 하는 것이 적절하다. ①: ~에도 불구하고, ②, ⑤: ~에 더하여, ③: ~ 대신에

27 많은 건물들이 디자인에 '자연'의 아름다움을 담아내려고 한다.

Lesson 7

Feel the Wonder

시험대비 실력평가   p.120

01 ④   02 ②   03 ⑤   04 ④
05 ①

01 하나의 단어가 품사에 따라 완전히 다른 의미를 갖는 경우가 있다. land는 동사로는 '착륙하다'를, 명사로는 '땅'을 뜻한다. ④번은 명사로, 나머지 보기들은 동사로 사용되고 있다. ① 비행기가 공항에 착륙했다. ② 새가 물 위에 착륙했다. ③ 조종사가 가까스로 비행기를 안전하게 착륙시켰다. ④ 이 마을의 땅은 농사 짓기에 좋다. ⑤ 지금 착륙을 위해 들어오는 비행기 한 대가 있다.

02 ① camel: 낙타 / 사람들이 동물원에서 낙타를 구경하고 있다. ② complete: 완성하다 / 학생들은 그 과정을 마쳐야만 한다. ③ abroad: 해외에, 해외로 / Katya는 다음 달에 해외로 처음 여행을 갈 것이다. ④ 나의 부모님은 가끔 내가 적인 것처럼 대한다. ⑤ article: 기사 / 이 기사는 내가 신문에서 오려낸 거야.

03 ① from, be different from: ~와 다르다 / 런던은 대부분의 유럽의 도시들과는 다르다. ② up, give up: 포기하다 / 우리는 30분 동안 열쇠를 찾느라 시간을 보냈고, 결국 포기하고 집에 갔다. ③ away, melt away: 차츰 사라지다 / 아이스 호텔은 완전히 녹아서 강으로 흘러 들어갈 것입니다. ④ with, be covered with: ~로 덮여 있다. / 그의 책상은 책과 서류로 뒤덮여 있었다. ⑤ in, in a line: 한 줄로 / 그들은 한 줄로 늘어선 차들 속에 갇혀 있었다.

04 landscape: 풍경 scenery: 경치, 풍경 • 언덕에서 그는 평화로운 풍경을 내려다보았다.

05 Arctic: 북극 (지방) the area around the North Pole 북극의 주변 지역

서술형 시험대비   p.121

01 smash   02 (1) (n)earby   (2) (f)orecast   (3) finally
(4) tightly   03 record   04 (f)ool
05 (1) spotted   (2) blow[blowing]   (3) Diving   (4) served
06 (1) The weather is very changeable at this time of year.
   (2) There will be a chance for parents to look around the school.

01 smash: 때려 부수다, 깨뜨리다 / 무언가를 많은 조각으로 깨뜨리다 smash A against B: A를 B에 내리치다 / 그들은 바위에 조개가 깨져서 열릴 때까지 조개류를 세게 반복적으로 부딪친다.

02 (1) nearby: 인근에, 가까운 곳에 (2) forecast: 예측, 예보 (3) finally: 마침내 (4) tightly: 단단히, 꽉

03 하나의 단어가 품사에 따라 완전히 다른 의미를 갖는 경우가 있다. record: (동) 녹음하다 (명) 기록 • 그녀는 스튜디오에서 신곡을 녹음하고 있다. • 그녀는 올림픽 기록을 세웠다.

04 fool: (동) 속이다 (명) 바보 / • TV 뉴스가 충분한 정보를 제공할 거라고 생각하는 사람은 바보다. • 너는 나를 속일 수 없어. 나는 그가 이미 너에게 돈을 주었다는 것을 알아.

05 (1) spot: 발견하다, 찾아내다 / 나는 방금 전에 우리 뒤에 있는 경찰차를 발견했다. (2) blow: (입으로) 불다 / 나는 그녀가 커피를 식히기 위해서 커피를 부는 것을 보았다. (3) dive: 뛰어들다, 다이빙하다 / 절벽에서 다이빙하는 것은 위험하다. (4) serve: (음식을) 제공하다, 차려 주다 / 티케이크는 버터와 같이 뜨겁게 제공되어야 한다.

06 (1) at this time of year: 이맘때는, 이맘때쯤이면 (2) look around: 둘러보다

[교과서]
Conversation

핵심 Check   p.122~123

1 (1) I wonder where the museum is.
  (2) I wonder how long the Amazon River is.
2 (1) The Internet says   (2) The book says
3 ③

교과서 대화문 익히기

Check(√) True or False   p.124~125

1 F   2 T   3 T   4 F   5 F   6 T   7 T   8 F

교과서 확인학습
p.127~129

Listen and Speak 1 A
almost at / wonder how high / It's about / keep going

Listen and Speak 1 B
at, on / look / is the coldest place on / how cold it is

/ average, is, in, in / then, colder than / Although it's, doesn't / interesting

Listen and Speak 1 C

1. finally / excited, look around / wonder where / in front of
2. finally here / wonder where the information center / behind
3. I wonder where, is / next to

Listen and Speak 2 A

so / about going on a picnic / check / forecast says it'll be rainy / another time

Listen and Speak 2 B

to do / join me / Where do you want to / thinking of going / scenery, this time of / I heard that it's covered with / How long, take / The Internet says it takes / on

Listen and Speak 2 C

1. What, doing / anything interesting / This article says scientists have discovered
2. the newspaper / anything interesting / This article says, was seen in the East Sea

Real Life Talk Watch a Video

Check out / camels, in a line in / wonder how long camels can go / out / The Internet says / Camels are, interesting / travel with them

Real Life Talk Step 2

1. Where / I wonder how cold / says, average temperature, about / amazing
2. solar system / I wonder how big / The Internet says, times bigger than
3. on / how hot it is / says / reach up to

시험대비 기본평가　　　　　　　　　　　p.130

01 ②　　　02 ④　　　03 ①

01 'I wonder ~.'는 '나는 ~이 궁금하다.'라는 뜻으로 어떤 것에 대해 궁금할 때 사용하는 표현이다. wonder 다음에는 의문사절이나 if/whether절이 온다. 형용사 'curious(궁금한, 호기심이 많은)'를 사용해서 'I'm curious ~.'로 궁금한 점을 나타내는 표현을 할 수 있다.

02 '~ says (that) ...'(~에 따르면 ⋯이다)는 어딘가에서 보거나 들은 내용을 상대방에게 보고하거나 전달할 때 사용하는 표현이다. 동사 'say'는 '~라고 말하다'는 뜻으로 흔히 사용되지만, 여기서는 '~라고 되어[쓰여] 있다, ~라고 나와 있다, (글, 표지판 등이) 나타내다, ~에 따르면 ⋯이다' 등의 의미로 사용되었다.

03 궁금증을 표현할 때 '~를 궁금해하다'라는 의미를 가진 동

사 wonder를 이용하여 'I wonder ~.'라고 말한다. 궁금증을 나타내는 다른 표현으로 'I'm curious about ~.', 'I don't know why ~.' 'Can you tell me more about ~?', 'I'm interested to know ~.', 'I'd like to know ~.', 'I wish I knew ~.' 등으로 바꿔 사용할 수 있다.

시험대비 실력평가　　　　　　　　　　p.131~132

01 ①	02 going	03 ⑤	04 ②
05 ③	06 (A) says　(B) away		07 ⑤
08 ④	09 (a) on　(b) than		10 ③
11 ⑤			

01 'I wonder ~.'는 '나는 ~이 궁금하다.'라는 뜻으로 어떤 것에 대해 궁금할 때 사용하는 표현이다.

02 keep -ing: 계속 ~하다

03 ① 산 정상에 도착하기 위해서, 그들은 2시간 정도 올라가야 한다.(산 정상까지 얼마의 시간이 남았는지 정보가 나와 있지 않다.) ② 소년은 산이 얼마나 높은지 모른다.(산 높이를 물어보는 질문에 소년이 2,000미터라고 대답했다.) ③ 그들은 그들이 올라가고 있는 산이 높지 않다고 생각한다.(높다고 생각했다.) ④ 그들은 막 정상에 도착했다.(도착하지 못 했다.) ⑤ 소녀는 산이 얼마나 높은지 알기를 원한다.

04 세상에서 가장 높은 산에 대해 궁금증을 나타내는 말에는 높이를 말하는 ②번의 '인터넷에 따르면 그것은 약 8,850m라고 해.'가 적절하다.

05 누가 노래를 불렀는지 궁금해하는 말에 인터넷에 따르면 Jack이 노래를 썼다고 말하는 것은 어색하다.

06 (A) '~ says (that) ...'(~에 따르면 ⋯이다)는 어딘가에서 보거나 들은 내용을 상대방에게 보고하거나 전달할 때 사용하는 표현이다. (B) melt away: 차츰 사라지다

07 마지막에 G가 말하고 있는 'That's interesting, too!'의 That이 가리키는 것이 주어진 문장이므로 주어진 문장(비록 그곳은 매우 춥지만 눈은 많이 내리지 않아.)은 ⑤번에 들어가는 것이 적절하다.

08 'I wonder ~.'는 '나는 ~이 궁금하다.'라는 뜻으로 어떤 것에 대해 궁금할 때 사용하는 표현이다. wonder 다음에는 의문사절이나 if/whether절이 온다. 궁금증을 나타내는 다른 표현으로 'I'm curious about ~.', 'I don't know why ~.', 'Can you tell me more about ~?', 'I'd like to know ~.', 등으로 바꿔 사용할 수 있다.

09 (a) on Earth: 지구상에서, (b) 비교급+than

10 ① 남극은 얼마나 추운가?(7월에 약 섭씨 영하 58도이고, 12월에는 약 섭씨 영하 26도이다.) ② 그들은 TV에서 무엇을 보고 있는가?(아기 펭귄들) ③ 남극의 연평균 기온은 몇 도인가? (대화에서 7월과 12월의 온도가 나와 있고, 연평균 기온은 나와 있

지 않았다.) ④ 어디가 지구에서 가장 추운 곳인가? (남극) ⑤ 남극에서 눈이 많이 내리는가?(많이 내리지 않는다.)

11 일요일에 무엇을 할 것인지 질문을 하자 (C) 등산을 갈 거라 말하며, 같이 가자고 제안하자 (D) 그러고 싶다고 대답하며 어디로 가는지 질문한다. (B) 남산에 가려고 생각 중이라고 대답하자 (A) 이맘때 그 곳 경치가 아름답다고 말하니, 맞다고 하며 단풍잎으로 덮여 있다고 말한다.

서술형 시험대비　　　　　　p.133

01 out　　　02 how long

03 camels　　04 (A) says (B) takes

05 I heard that it is covered with red autumn leaves now.

06 I wonder where Green Park is.

01 check out: (흥미로운 것을) 살펴보다, 확인하다 find out: 찾아내다, (조사하여) 발견하다

02 'The Internet says they can go about two weeks without water.(인터넷 정보에 따르면 낙타는 물 없이 2주 정도 갈 수 있대.)'를 볼 때 얼마나 오래 가는지 질문하는 것이 적절하므로 의문사 'how long'이 어울린다.

03 수지가 낙타가 흥미로운 동물이라고 말하는 것에 이어서 Tony가 언젠가 사막에서 그들과 함께 여행하고 싶다고 말하고 있으므로 them이 가리키는 것은 낙타이다.

04 (A) 'The Internet says ~.'는 '인터넷에 따르면.'라는 뜻으로 어딘가에서 보거나 들은 내용을 상대방에게 보고하거나 전달할 때 사용하는 표현이다. (B) take: (얼마의 시간이) 걸리다

05 어떤 내용을 들어서 알고 있음을 표현할 때 'I heard that+주어+동사 ~.'의 형태로 말할 수 있다. heard 대신에 현재완료 형태인 'have heard'를 사용할 수도 있다. be covered with: ~로 덮여 있다 autumn leaves: 단풍

06 궁금증을 표현할 때 '~를 궁금해 하다'라는 의미를 가진 동사 wonder를 이용하여 'I wonder ~.'라고 말한다. I wonder 뒤에는 간접의문문의 어순인 '의문사(where)+주어(Green Park)+동사(is)'의 순서로 문장을 쓴다.

교과서
Grammar

핵심 Check　　　　　　p.134~135

1 (1) whose　(2) of which

2 (1) I think we should wait until tempers have cooled.
(2) Give me your hand while we cross the road.

시험대비 기본평가　　　　　　p.136

01 ④　　　02 ①　　　03 ②

04 (1) when　(2) after　(3) until

01 뒤에 명사가 이어지는 소유격 관계대명사가 필요한 자리이다. 선행사가 'This small fish'이므로 of which나 whose를 쓴다. of which를 쓸 경우에는 이어지는 명사에 the가 붙어야 한다는 것에 주의한다.

02 첫 문장과 두 번째 문장이 '인과' 관계나 '역접'의 관계 등이 보이지 않으므로 '~하는 동안'을 의미하는 while이 가장 적절하다.

03 두 문장에서 공통되는 것이 'the woman'과 'Her'이므로 소유격 부분을 소유격 관계대명사로 전환하여 쓴다. 선행사가 사람으로 'of which'는 쓸 수 없으므로 'whose'가 적절하다.

04 (1) 문맥상 when이 적절하다. (2) 문맥상 after가 적절하다. (3) 문맥상 until이 적절하다.

시험대비 실력평가　　　　　　p.137~139

01 ③　　　02 ⑤　　　03 I met a girl whose name is the same as mine. 04 Be quiet while I'm speaking.　05 ①　　06 ③　　07 of which price → of which the price　　08 ②

09 ④　　10 ⑤　　11 ③　　12 ②

13 ⑤　　14 ①　　15 (1) whose　(2) whose

(3) of which　(4) while　(5) are　(6) until　16 ④, ⑤

01 '그 다큐멘터리는 그것에서 자신들의 생활이 묘사된 노동자들 사이에서 많은 불쾌감을 자아냈다.'는 문장이다. 사람이 선행사인 경우 소유격 관계대명사는 whose만 가능하다.

02 '암컷은 알이 부화할 때까지 알을 품는다.' 문맥상 after를 until로 바꾸는 것이 적절하다.

03 관계대명사의 소유격이 있으므로 선행사 a girl 뒤에 whose name을 배열하는 것이 적절하다.

04 '~하는 동안'이라는 뜻을 가진 시간을 나타내는 부사절을 이끄는 접속사 while이 있으므로 'Be quiet'으로 명령문을 쓰고, 접속사 while을 쓴 후, 'I'm speaking.'을 쓴다.

05 뒤에 명사가 이어지는 소유격 관계대명사가 필요하며, 사람이 선행사인 경우에는 whose만 가능하다.

06 '~한 후에'를 의미하는 시간의 접속사 after를 쓰는 것이 적절하다.

07 of which의 경우 이어지는 명사에 the를 붙여야 한다. 또는 of which 대신 whose를 써도 된다.

08 ⓐ, ⓒ, ⓔ는 whose, ⓑ, ⓓ는 of which를 써야 한다. 사람이 선행사일 경우에는 소유격 관계대명사는 whose만 쓰며, 사물이 선행사일 경우에는 whose와 of which 둘 다 가능하며, of which를 쓸 경우에는 명사에 정관사가 붙는다.

09 ④번에서 until은 '~까지'의 뜻이므로 '~할 때'를 의미하는

when으로 바꾸는 것이 적절하다.

10 ⑤는 의문대명사의 소유격으로 쓰였다. 앞에 선행사가 없으며 정관사가 없는 것이 특징이다. 그 외에는 모두 선행사의 소유격 관계대명사 whose이다.

11 ③ I usually go to the gym during my lunch hour. while은 접속사로 다음에 '주어+동사'가 이어지지만 during은 전치사로 명사(구)가 이어진다. 각각 ① 시간(~ 전에), ② 조건 (~한다면), ④ 이유(~ 때문에), ⑤ 양보(~일지라도)의 접속사이다.

12 ②번은 선행사 the beluga whale 뒤에 소유격 관계대명사가 알맞게 쓰였다. ① of which roof → whose roof 또는 of which the roof, ③ of which the hobby → whose hobby, ④ the → 삭제, ⑤ roof of which → the roof of which 또는 whose roof

13 '그녀는 이름이 Mark인 남자를 만났다.'라는 문장이다. His name을 대신하는 소유격 관계대명사 whose를 사용해서 하나의 문장으로 만드는 것이 적절하며, of which는 선행사가 사람인 경우에는 쓰지 않는다. whose 뒤에 정관사 the를 함께 쓰지 않는다.

14 War must be a word whose meaning has to disappear from our understanding. 또는 War must be a word the meaning of which[of which the meaning] has to disappear from our understanding.이 알맞다.

15 (1) 선행사가 사물이므로 'whose'나 'of which'를 쓸 수 있지만 'of which'를 쓸 경우 the가 명사 앞에 붙는다. (2) 뒤에 명사가 이어지고 완전한 절이 나오므로 소유격 관계대명사 whose가 적절하다. (3) 뒤에 the tail이 나오므로 of which 가 적절하다. whose 다음에는 정관사가 있는 명사가 이어질 수 없다. (4) while은 접속사로 다음에 '주어+동사'가 이어지지만 during은 전치사로 명사(구)가 이어진다. (5) 시간의 접속사가 이끄는 부사절에서는 미래의 의미일지라도 현재시제를 쓴다. (6) 내용상 부사절을 이끄는 until이 적절하다.

16 선행사가 사물이므로 'whose+명사'나 'of which+the+명사' 또는 'the+명사+of which'의 형태로 쓸 수 있지만 'of which' 를 쓸 경우 보통 the가 명사 앞에 붙으며, whose를 쓸 경우 the 를 명사 앞에 쓸 수 없다.

서술형 시험대비 p.140~141

01 (1) Tony has seen the girl whose hair is red.
    (2) They are private businesses whose main focus is making money.
    (3) Humpback whales stand on their tails while they sleep.
    (4) As soon as we arrived on the island, we were eager to explore.

02 (1) I met my friend while I was on my way to school.
    (2) You will be instructed where to go as soon as the plane is ready.
    (3) He grew and grew until he was taller than his father.
    (4) You must be careful when you are handling chemicals.

03 (1) I have a cup the color of which[of which the color] is blue.
    (2) I could not solve the science problem the solution of which[of which the solution] was very difficult.
    (3) I want to enter an international school the students of which[of which the students] come from many countries.
    (4) Years ago I happened to get a very old-looking jar the owner of which[of which the owner] is not known up to now.

04 (1) the → 삭제 (2) owner → the owner
    (3) which → of which (4) who → whose
    (5) whose → who (6) who → whose

05 of which the top[the top of which] is covered with

06 While Jinsu was talking with Mark

07 (1) The tuskfish blows on the sand until a clam appears.
    (2) You can select the album the cover of which you'd like to change.
    (3) Humanity can be quite cold to those whose eyes see the world differently.

01 소유격 관계대명사 whose와 시간을 나타내는 접속사 등에 유의하여, 주어진 단어들을 적절히 배열한다.

02 while(~하는 동안에), as soon as(~하자마자), until(~까지), when(~할 때) 등의 접속사가 시간을 나타내는 부사절을 이끌도록 쓴다.

03 소유격 관계대명사가 필요한데, which를 이용하라고 했고 선행사가 사물이므로 'the+명사+of which' 또는 'of which+the+명사'의 어순으로 연결한다.

04 어색한 단어를 하나만 찾아야 하므로, 관계대명사의 쓰임에 주의해서 찾아 적절하게 고치도록 한다. (5)번은 소유격이 아니라 주격 관계대명사를 써야 하는 것에 유의한다.

05 선행사는 the mountain이고, the top이 있으므로 관계대명사 소유격 whose를 쓸 수 없다. of which를 써서 'the top of which'나 'of which the top'을 써야 한다. 산이 눈으로 덮인 것이므로 cover를 'be covered with'로 변형시켜야 함에도 유의한다.

06 '~하는 동안'은 접속사 While로 나타내고 6 단어이므로 진행형을 이용하여, 'was talking with'로 표현하는 것에 유의한다.

07 (1) '~까지'를 의미하는 until을 추가한다. (2) 주어진 어휘에 cover of가 있으므로, 'the cover of which'로 표현해야 하므로 the와 which를 추가한다. (3)은 선행사가 those로 사람이므로 관계대명사 whose를 써야 하므로 whose를 추가한다.

확인문제　　　　　　　　　　　　p.142

1 T　2 F　3 T　4 F　5 T　6 F

확인문제　　　　　　　　　　　　p.143

1 T　2 F　3 T　4 F　5 T　6 F

교과서 확인학습 A　　　　　　p.144~145

01 Under	02 Two-thirds
03 millions of species	04 new things
05 Let's find out	06 Sweet
07 what these whales are doing	
08 in a group	09 actually
10 stand on their tails	11 near the surface
12 need to come up	13 fall asleep
14 for a deep breath	15 Enjoy
16 take a look at	17 whose favorite food
18 cannot be easily discovered	
19 until, appears	20 is closed tightly
21 give up	22 smashes, against
23 is served	24 Jump
25 fly down	26 jump out of the water
27 is around	28 up to
29 let, fool	30 quick and smart
31 spot, calculate	32 nearby, jumps, catches

교과서 확인학습 B　　　　　　p.146~147

1 1 Under the Sea

2 Two-thirds of our planet is covered by oceans.

3 They are full of wonder and are home to millions of species.

4 Every day, we are learning new things about them.

5 Let's find out about some interesting sea animals.

6 Sweet Dreams

7 Can you guess what these whales are doing in the picture?

8 It looks like they are standing up in a group.

9 But they are actually sleeping!

10 Humpback whales stand on their tails while they sleep.

11 They sleep near the surface.

12 Since they are not fish, they need to come up to breathe.

13 Also, they don't fall asleep completely.

14 When they wake up, they come out of the water for a deep breath and dive back into the sea.

15 Enjoy Your Meal

16 If you think fish are not smart, take a look at the tuskfish.

17 This small fish whose favorite food is clams uses a tool to open them.

18 Clams usually hide under the sand, so they cannot be easily discovered.

19 The tuskfish blows on the sand until a clam appears.

20 The clam is closed tightly, so the fish cannot eat it.

21 But the tuskfish doesn't give up.

22 It smashes the clam against a rock.

23 In the end, the clam opens and dinner is served.

24 One, Two, Three, Jump!

25 You have probably seen a bird fly down to the sea to catch a fish.

26 But have you ever seen a fish jump out of the water to catch a bird?

27 Well, birds have to be careful when a giant trevally is around.

28 This fish can grow up to 170cm and 80kg.

29 But don't let its size fool you.

30 This fish is quick and smart.

31 It can spot a flying bird and calculate its speed and distance.

32 When the bird flies nearby, the giant trevally jumps out of the water and catches it.

시험대비 실력평가　　　　　　p.148~151

01 are → is	02 oceans	03 ④	04 is closed
05 clams		06 gives up eating it → doesn't give up (eating it)	07 ②
08 (A) are (B) uses　(C) give up		09 a rock	10 As

[Because/Since]   11 ①, ③, ④   12 ②

13 (A) jumps   (B) catches   14 clams

15 It smashes the clam against a rock.

16 It blows on the sand until a clam appears.

17 ③   18 ①, ③   19 sleepy → asleep

20 ③   21 ⑤   22 ⑤   23 ②

24 ②   25 ④

01 '부분이나 분수를 나타내는 말+단수명사'는 단수로 취급해야 하므로 are를 is로 고치는 것이 적절하다.

02 They는 앞 문장의 'oceans'를 가리킨다.

03 몇몇 흥미로운 바다 동물들을 알아보자고 했으므로, 뒤에 올 내용으로는 '몇몇 흥미로운 바다 동물들에 대한 이야기들'이 적절하다.

04 조개가 단단히 '닫혀 있다'고 해야 하므로 'is closed'로 쓰는 것이 적절하다.

05 '조개'를 가리킨다.

06 조개가 단단히 닫혀 있어서 tuskfish가 그것을 먹을 수 없을 때, 그 물고기는 '(그것을 먹는 것을) 포기하지 않는다.'

07 appears는 자동사이므로 수동태로 쓸 수 없다.

08 (A) 명사 fish는 단수형과 복수형이 동일한 단어인데, a fish는 단수 취급, fish는 복수 취급하므로 are가 적절하다. (B) 주어인 fish 앞에 This small이 있으므로 단수 취급하여 uses가 적절하다. (C) 그러나 tuskfish는 '포기하지 않는다'고 해야 하므로 give up이 적절하다. give up: 포기하다, keep trying: 계속 노력하다

09 tuskfish는 조개가 단단히 닫혀 있어서 먹을 수 없을 때 포기하지 않고 돌에 조개를 내리친다고 했으므로, 조개를 열기 위해 사용한 도구는 '돌'이라고 하는 것이 적절하다.

10 so는 '그래서, 그 결과'라는 뜻의 접속사인데, so를 생략하는 경우에는 이유를 나타내는 접속사 As[Because/Since]로 문장을 시작하는 것이 적절하다.

11 ⓐ와 ①, ③, ④: 현재분사, ②, ⑤: 동명사

12 이 글은 'giant trevally가 물 밖으로 뛰어올라 새를 잡는' 것에 관한 글이므로, 주제로는 ②번 'giant trevally는 새를 잡기 위해 물 밖으로 뛰어오르는 물고기이다'가 적절하다.

13 새가 근처에 날고 있을 때, giant trevally가 물 밖으로 '뛰어올라' 새를 '잡기' 때문이다.

14 '조개'를 가리킨다.

15 smash A against B: A를 B에 내리치다

16 그것(tuskfish)은 조개가 나타날 때까지 모래에 입김을 분다.

17 ⓐ in a group: 한 무리를 이루어, ⓑ on their tails: 꼬리로, on: 무엇에 기대거나 받쳐져 있음을 나타냄(on one foot: 한 발로)

18 ⓒ와 ①, ③: 부사적 용법, ②, ⑤: 명사적 용법, ④: 형용사적 용법

19 '동작을 나타내는 자동사+형용사'는 become의 뜻이 된다. asleep: 잠이 든, 자고 있는, fall asleep: 잠들다

20 이 글은 'giant trevally가 물 밖으로 뛰어올라 새를 잡는' 것에 관한 글이므로, 제목으로는 ③번 '하나, 둘, 셋, 뛰어라!'가 적절하다.

21 ⓑ와 ⑤: (특정한 수·정도 등)까지 (less than), ① ~하고 있는 (doing), ② ~의 책임인, ~에게 달려 있는, ③ ~할 수 있는(육체적으로나 정신적으로), 너 이 일을 할 능력이 있니? ④ (특정한 위치·시점)까지 (until)

22 'giant trevally가 날고 있는 새의 속도와 거리를 어떻게 계산할 수 있는지'는 대답할 수 없다. ① Yes, there is. ② It can grow up to 170cm and 80kg. ③ Yes, it is. ④ It can spot a flying bird.

23 이 글은 'humpback whale들의 잠을 자는 모습과 그들의 심호흡'에 관한 내용의 글이므로, 제목으로는 ②번 '좋은 꿈 꿔라'가 적절하다.

24 주어진 문장의 But에 주목한다. ②번 앞 문장의 내용과 상반되는 내용이 뒤에 이어지므로 ②번이 적절하다.

25 'humpback whale'들은 '완전히 잠들지 않는다.'

🦉 **서술형 시험대비**   p.152~153

01 Two-thirds of our planet

02 with   03 millions of species

04 Can you guess what these whales are doing in the picture?

05 (A) while (B) near (C) to breathe

06 (A) out of the water (B) dive back

07 (1) in order that (2) so that

08 to jump → jump[jumping]

09 (A) quick and smart (B) size

10 the bird   11 whose   12 is served

13 the tuskfish[this small fish] cannot discover them easily.

14 (A) smashes (B) against

01 Two-thirds는 '3분의 2'를 나타내는 분수 표현이며 분자는 기수로, 분모는 서수로 쓴다.

02 be full of = be filled with

03 '수많은 종'을 가리킨다.

04 'what these whales are doing in the picture'는 동사 guess의 목적어로, '의문사+주어+동사'의 어순으로 쓰인 간접의문문이다.

05 (A) 뒤에 '주어+동사'가 이어지므로 while이 적절하다. while+주어+동사, during+기간을 나타내는 명사, (B) 수면 '근처에서'라고 해야 하므로 near가 적절하다. near: (거리상으

로) ~에서 가까이(전치사), nearby: 인근의, 가까운 곳의(형용사), the nearby surface처럼 주로 명사 앞에 씀), 인근에, 가까운 곳에(부사), (C) '숨을 쉬기 위해' 위로 나올 필요가 있다고 해야 하므로 to breathe가 적절하다.

06 혹등고래는 물고기가 아니기 때문에 잠에서 깨면 심호흡을 하러 '물 밖으로' 나왔다가 바다로 '다시 뛰어든다.'

07 부사적 용법의 목적을 나타내는 to부정사는 'in order that ~ can[may]'이나 'so that ~ can[may]'을 사용하여 복문으로 고치는 것이 적절하다.

08 지각동사 see+목적어+동사원형/현재분사: (목적어)가 ~하는 것을 보다

09 비록 giant trevally가 170센티미터에 80킬로그램까지 자랄 수 있지만 그것은 '빠르고 똑똑하다.' 그러므로, 그 '크기'에 속지 않는 것이 좋을 것이다. 왜냐하면 새가 근처에 날고 있을 때, 그것은 날고 있는 새를 발견하고 그 새의 속도와 거리를 계산하고 그 새를 잡기 위해 물 밖으로 뛰어오르기 때문이다.

10 '새'를 가리킨다.

11 소유격 관계대명사 whose로 쓰는 것이 적절하다.

12 밥상이 '차려진다'고 해야 하므로 'is served'로 쓰는 것이 적절하다.

13 생략된 'by the tuskfish[this small fish]'의 'the tuskfish[this small fish]'를 주어로 사용하여 능동태로 고치는 것이 적절하다.

14 조개가 모래로부터 나타날 때, 그것은 단단히 닫혀 있다. 그러면 tuskfish는 그것을 열기 위해 '돌에 조개를 내리친다.' smash A against B: A를 B에 내리치다

영역별 핵심문제 p.155~159

01 ②, ④, ⑤ 02 wonder 03 ① 04 ③
05 I wonder how high this mountain is. 06 ①
07 ④ 08 ③ 09 forecast 10 ⑤
11 in 12 The Internet says they can go about two weeks without water. 13 ②
14 ① 15 ⑤ 16 ④ 17 whose night view is wonderful 18 ③ 19 ②
20 ④ 21 breath 22 ③, ④ 23 to breathe 25 ④ 25 This small fish whose favorite food is clams uses a tool to open them.
26 ② 27 ①, ⑤ 28 ④
29 because → why 30 (A) gray[grey] (B) white

---

01 spot은 동사로 '발견하다, 찾아내다'의 뜻이며, 명사로는 '장소, 위치'이다. ⓑ, ⓒ는 '장소, 위치' ⓐ, ⓓ, ⓔ는 '발견하다, 찾아내다'의 의미로 사용되었다. ⓐ 만약에 엄마와 아빠가 오시는 것을 발견한다면, 나에게 경고해 줘. ⓑ 주차할 장소를 찾느라 약

20분이 걸렸다. ⓒ 이곳은 멈춰서 쉬기에 좋은 장소처럼 보인다. ⓓ 만약에 네가 운이 좋다면, 너는 사슴 한 마리 혹은 두 마리를 발견할 것이다. ⓔ 이 개미들은 비교적 찾기 쉽다.

02 wonder: (명) 경이, 경탄, 놀라움 (동) 궁금하다 • 가끔 그는 왜 그의 아버지가 그를 싫어하는지 궁금했다. • 타지마할의 경관은 우리를 경탄으로 가득 채웠다.

03 average: (명) 평균 (형) 평균의 / 3, 8, 10의 평균은 7이다.

04 (A) be full of: ~로 가득 차다 • 부엌은 연기로 가득 찼다. (B) this time of year: 이맘때는, 이맘때쯤이면 • 보스턴은 이맘때쯤이면 매우 아름답다.

05 궁금증을 표현할 때 '~를 궁금해하다'라는 의미를 가진 동사 wonder를 이용하여 'I wonder ~.'라고 말한다. I wonder 뒤에는 간접의문문의 어순인 '의문사(how high)+주어(this mountain)+동사(is)'의 순서로 문장을 쓴다.

06 숫자 앞의 about은 '대략, 약'의 의미이다.

07 주어진 문장은 '정말 높은 산이구나.'로, 상대방의 말에 맞다고 하는 'Yes, it is.'와 연결될 수 있으므로 ④가 적절하다.

08 주어진 문장은 상대방에게 날씨를 확인해 달라고 요청하는 말이며, 다음에 날씨를 확인하고 일기 예보에 따르면 오후에 비가 올 것이라는 말하는 내용이 나오는 것이 자연스러우므로 ③번이 적절하다.

09 forecast: 예측, 예보 / 당신이 생각하기에 미래에 무엇이 일어날지에 대한 언급

10 ⓐ 오늘 오후에 날씨는 어떤가?(비가 온다) ⓑ 누가 일기 예보를 확인했는가?(G) ⓒ 그들은 무슨 요일에 소풍을 갈 예정인가?(다음에 가자고 말했지 정확히 언제 가자고 말하지 않았다.) ⓓ 지금 바깥 날씨가 좋은가?(네) ⓔ 누가 소풍을 가자고 제안했는가?(G)

11 in a line: 한 줄로, in+장소: ~에서

12 '~가 …라고 말하다'라는 의미의 '주어+say(s)+that+주어+동사 ~.' 구문을 이용해 주어가 한 말인 that절의 내용을 상대방에게 보고하거나 전해줄 수 있다. 이때 접속사 that은 생략 가능하다. about: 대략, 약 without: ~ 없이

13 <보기>와 ②의 when은 시간의 접속사로 쓰였다. ① 관계부사 ③ 의문부사 ④ 대명사 ⑤ 명사

14 <보기>와 ①의 whose는 관계대명사의 소유격이다. 나머지는 모두 의문사로 '누구의'라는 의미로 사용되었다.

15 나에게는 '아빠가 유명한 배우인 친구가 있다.'는 문장이다. 선행사가 사람이므로 관계대명사의 소유격 whose를 사용해서 하나의 문장으로 만드는 것이 적절하다.

16 '꼬리가 매우 짧은 개를 봐라.'라는 문장이다. 선행사가 사람이므로 관계대명사의 소유격 'of which'나 'whose'를 사용해서 하나의 문장으로 만드는 것이 적절하며, 'of which'를 쓸 경우 정관사 the가 있어야 함에 주의한다.

17 5 단어이므로 소유격 관계대명사 whose를 활용하여, 'whose

night view'로 표현하는 것에 유의한다.

18 가장 어울리는 의미의 접속사를 찾는다. '비가 그칠 때까지 여기서 기다리자.'라는 의미가 가장 적절하다.

19 ② Linda lost her husband when she was 40. 보통 접속사 when은 '바로 그 때(at that time)'의 상황이나 동작을 나타낼 때 사용하고 접속사 while은 특정하게 길이가 있는 기간을 나타낼 때 쓰며 '동시에 일어나는(happening at the same time)' 상황이나 동작을 나타낼 때 사용한다. 남편과 사별하는 것은 한순간의 일이므로 while과는 어울리지 않는다.

20 문장의 의미에 맞게 적절한 접속사를 찾는다. (A) 그는 여행을 하는 동안 책을 썼다. (B) 그는 나를 보자마자 도망쳤다. (C) 그의 엄마는 청소를 끝낸 후에 꽃을 탁자 위에 놓았다.

21 '심호흡을 하라'라고 해야 하므로, breathe의 명사 breath를 쓰는 것이 적절하다. a deep breath: 심호흡

22 (A)와 ③, ④: [이유를 나타내어] ~이므로, ~이니까(접속사), ①, ⑤: [종종 계속을 나타내는 완료형의 동사를 가진 주절 뒤에서] ~한 이래(죽), ~한 때부터 내내(접속사), ② 그 이래(부사)

23 그들은 잠에서 깨면 '숨을 쉬기 위해' 물 밖으로 나오려고 그렇게 한다.

24 이 글은 'tuskfish가 가장 좋아하는 먹이인 조개를 열기 위해 도구를 사용하는 것'에 관한 글이므로, 제목으로는 ⑤번 '맛있게 먹어라'가 적절하다.

25 선행사인 This small fish 다음에 소유격 관계대명사 whose를 쓰는 것이 적절하다.

26 ② '이 작은 물고기는' 조개를 열기 위해 도구를 사용한다고 했으므로, tuskfish는 '작은 물고기'라는 것을 알 수 있다.

27 ⓐ와 ①, ⑤: 경험 용법, ② 계속 용법, ③ 결과 용법, ④ 완료 용법

28 ④는 '날고 있는 새'를 가리키고, 나머지는 다 'giant trevally'를 가리킨다.

29 벨루가 고래는 온몸이 하얗기 때문에 사람들이 벨루가 고래를 흰고래라고 부른다고 해야 하므로, because를 why로 고치는 것이 적절하다. That's why+결과, That's because+이유

30 벨루가 고래는 태어날 때, '회색'이지만, 다 자라면, 몸이 '하얀색'이 된다. (A)에는 'The beluga whale is born'이라는 1형식 문장에 형용사 gray를 유사보어로 사용하여 답하는 것이 적절하다.

단원별 예상문제
p.160~163

01 ⓐ, ⓓ와 ⓑ, ⓒ, ⓔ   02 ⑤
03 (1) Arctic (2) breathe   04 out   05 ②
06 I wonder how cold it is.   07 ③   08 ⓐ July
ⓑ December   09 I wonder how cold it is there.
10 ②   11 ①   12 The Internet says it

---

takes about two hours.   13 ③
14 (1) whose (2) of which (3) who (4) whose
(5) of which (6) which
15 ③   16 ④   17 don't let its size fool
you   18 ①   19 ①   20 ④
21 ⑤   22 ③   23 ④

---

01 land는 동사로는 '착륙하다, 떨어지다'의 의미이며, 명사로는 '땅'의 의미로 사용된다. ⓐ와 ⓓ는 '착륙하다'로, ⓑ, ⓒ, ⓔ는 '땅'의 의미로 사용되었다. ⓐ 그것은 공이 어디에 떨어지는지 보여준다. ⓑ 그들의 여정은 그들을 많은 외국의 땅으로 이끌었다. ⓒ 그들은 시골로 이사 가서 약간의 땅을 샀다. ⓓ 그는 비행기가 착륙하는 소리를 듣지 못했다. ⓔ 비행기가 땅으로 내려갔는지 바다로 내려갔는지는 명확하지 않다.

02 tightly: 단단히, firmly: 단단히 • 대문이 잠겼고, 모든 창문이 단단히 닫혀 있다.

03 (1) Arctic: 북극 (지방) (2) breathe: 숨을 쉬다

04 check out: (흥미로운 것을) 살펴보다, 확인하다 • 저희 새 매장에서 가격들을 한번 살펴보세요! find out: 찾아내다, (조사하여) 발견하다 • 그 회의가 몇 시에 시작하는지 알아 볼 수 있어요? out of: ~ 밖으로 • 창 밖으로 기대지 마.

05 temperature: 온도, 기온

06 궁금증을 표현할 때 '~를 궁금해하다'라는 의미를 가진 동사 wonder를 이용하여 'I wonder ~.'라고 말한다. wonder 다음에는 의문사절이나 if/whether절이 온다. 여기서는 의문사절인 '의문사+주어+동사'를 사용하였다.

07 (A) 펭귄들이 귀엽다는 것과 그것들이 추워 보인다는 내용은 접속사 'but(하지만)'으로 연결될 수 있다. (B) '매우 춥지만, 눈은 많이 내리지 않아.'가 내용상 어울리므로 although가 적절하다. although: 비록 ~일지라도, ~이긴 하지만

08 7월이 약 섭씨 영하 58도이고, 12월은 약 섭씨 영하 26도이므로, 7월이 12월보다 춥다.

09 궁금증을 표현할 때 '~를 궁금해하다'라는 의미를 가진 동사 wonder를 이용하여 'I wonder ~.'라고 말한다. I wonder 뒤에는 간접의문문의 어순인 '의문사(how cold)+주어(it)+동사(is)'의 순서로 문장을 쓴다.

10 주어진 문장은 '어디로 가고 싶니?'로 이 질문에 대한 대답으로 가고 싶은 장소가 나오는 것이 어울리므로, 장소를 말하고 있는 'I'm thinking of going to Namsan.(나는 남산에 가려고 생각 중이야.)'이 대답이 될 수 있다. 그러므로 주어진 문장은 ②에 들어가야 알맞다.

11 (A) 'I'm thinking of ~.'는 '나는 ~할까 생각 중이다'라는 뜻으로 of 뒤에 동명사를 취해 의도나 계획을 나타낼 때 쓰는 표현

31

이다. (B) 어떤 내용을 들어서 알고 있음을 표현할 때 'I heard that+주어+동사 ~.'의 형태로 말할 수 있다. heard 대신에 현재완료형의 형태인 have heard를 사용할 수도 있다. (C) be covered with: ~로 덮여 있다

12 'The Internet says ~.'는 '인터넷에 따르면 ~'이라는 뜻으로 어딘가에서 보거나 들은 내용을 상대방에게 보고하거나 전달할 때 사용하는 표현이다. take: (얼마의 시간이) 걸리다 about: 대략, 약

13 He won't rest until he finds her. 시간의 접속사가 이끄는 부사절에서는 미래의 의미일지라도 현재시제를 쓴다.

14 (1), (4)는 소유격 관계대명사 whose가 적절하다. (2), (5)는 내용상 소유격이 필요한데, 정관사 the가 있으므로 'of which'가 적절하다. (3)은 주격 관계대명사 who가 적절하다. (6)은 전치사 for의 목적어 자리에 쓰인 관계대명사로 which가 적절하다.

15 ⓐ와 ③: 접속사, ① 지시형용사, ② 지시부사, ④ 지시대명사, ⑤ 관계대명사

16 '문어가 어떻게 피부색을 바꿀 수 있는지'는 알 수 없다. ① It lives on the ocean floor. ② It usually eats small fish. ③ It can change the color of its skin to hide from its enemies. ⑤ It shoots out dark black ink and swims away.

17 사역동사(let)+목적어+동사원형: '(목적어)가 ~하도록 허락하다', fool: '속이다, 기만하다'

18 글의 첫 부분에서 '여러분은 아마 새가 물고기를 잡기 위해 바다로 날아 내려가는 것을 본 적이 있을 것'이라고 했다.

19 ⓐ out of: ~에서 밖으로, ~의 밖으로, ⓑ into: ~ 안으로

20 이 글은 'humpback whale들의 잠을 자는 모습과 그들의 심호흡'에 관한 내용의 글이므로, 주제로는 ④번 'humpback whale들은 어떻게 잠을 자고 호흡하는가?'가 적절하다.

21 주어진 문장의 But에 주목한다. ⑤번 앞 문장의 내용과 상반되는 내용이 뒤에 이어지므로 ⑤번이 적절하다.

22 ⓐ와 ①, ④: 부사적 용법, ②: 형용사적 용법, ③, ⑤: 명사적 용법

23 'tuskfish가 조개를 여는데 얼마나 오래 걸리는지'는 대답할 수 없다. ① Its favorite food is clams. ② They usually hide under the sand. ③ It blows on the sand until a clam appears. ⑤ To open the clam.

![owl] **서술형 실전문제**　　　　　p.164~165

01 (1) I wonder how long the shortest hiking course takes.

(2) I'm curious (about) how long the shortest hiking course takes.

02 (1) This article says scientists have discovered a new planet.

(2) According to this article, scientists have discovered a new planet.

03 I wonder how long can camels go without water in the desert. → I wonder how long camels can go without water in the desert.

04 (1) I interviewed a man whose dream is to climb Baekdusan.

(2) The cat whose name[the name of which, of which the name] is Molly is sitting on the table.

05 (1) You have to finish your homework before you go to bed.

(2) Tom waited in front of the door until someone came out.

06 they don't fall asleep completely

07 bottom of the sea → surface

08 (A) fish　(B) a deep breath

09 (A) fly　(B) nearby　(C) out of

10 to fool　　11 spot

01 'I wonder ~.'는 '나는 ~이 궁금하다.'라는 뜻으로 어떤 것에 대해 궁금할 때 사용하는 표현이다. 궁금증을 나타내는 다른 표현으로 curious를 사용해 'be[become] curious about ~'으로 나타낼 수 있다.

02 '~ says (that) ...'(~에 따르면 …이다)는 어딘가에서 보거나 들은 내용을 상대방에게 보고하거나 전달할 때 사용하는 표현이다. '~에 따르면'이라는 뜻으로 'according to'를 사용할 수 있다. *article: 기사

03 궁금증을 표현할 때 '~를 궁금해 하다'라는 의미를 가진 동사 wonder를 이용하여 'I wonder ~.'라고 말한다. wonder 다음에는 의문사절(의문사+주어+동사)이 나올 수 있다.

04 (1) a man이 선행사이므로, 사람을 선행사로 하는 소유격 관계대명사 whose를 이용하여 두 문장을 연결하는 것이 적절하다.
(2) The cat이 선행사이므로, 소유격 관계대명사 whose나 'of which'를 활용한다.

05 (1) 잠자리에 들기 전에 숙제를 끝내라고 하는 것이 적절하다.
(2) 누군가가 나올 때까지 기다렸다고 하는 것이 적절하다.

06 fall asleep: 잠들다

07 humpback whale들은 '수면' 근처에서 잠을 잔다.

08 그들은 '물고기'가 아니기 때문에, 잠에서 깨면 '심호흡'을 하러 물 밖으로 나올 필요가 있다.

09 (A) '지각동사 see+목적어+동사원형: (목적어)가 ~하는 것을 보다'라고 해야 하므로 fly가 적절하다. (B) 새가 '근처에' 날고

있을 때라고 해야 하므로 nearby가 적절하다. nearby: 인근에, 가까운 곳에(부사), 인근의, 가까운 곳의(형용사), the nearby surface처럼 주로 명사 앞에 씀, nearly: 거의, (C) giant trevally는 물 '밖으로' 뛰어올라 새를 잡는다고 해야 하므로 out of가 적절하다.

10 사역동사(let)+목적어+동사원형 = allow+목적어+to부정사: (목적어)가 ~하도록 허락하다

11 spot: 발견하다, 찾아내다, 어떤 것 또는 어떤 사람을 주목하다, 알아채다

창의사고력 서술형 문제
p.166

|모범답안|

01 I wonder what this is. / The Internet says it is / I'm curious where it is.

02 (A) in the Arctic Ocean (B) a round head
(C) fish and clams (D) it is white all over
(E) gray (F) white

01 I wonder ~: 나는 ~이 궁금하다. ~ says (that) …: ~에 따르면 …이다

단원별 모의고사
p.167~171

01 ⑤

02 (1) nearby (2) friendly (3) completely (4) finally

03 ④

04 (1) was full (2) go on a picnic (3) grow up to
(4) millions of

05 (A) → (C) → (D) → (B)

06 I wonder where the bus stop is.

07 in front of 08 going

09 (1) The weather forecast says it'll be rainy in the afternoon.
(2) According to the weather forecast, it'll be rainy in the afternoon.

10 the scenery there is so beautiful this time of year

11 ③   12 ③   13 ①   14 ⑤

15 I have a friend whose hobby is to play basketball.

16 When he comes back home, he will call his father.

17 (1) Charlotte is a wise spider whose best friend is Wilbur. 또는 Charlotte is a wise spider of which the best friend is Wilbur.
(2) The girl whose dress is yellow is Bora.
(3) I'll take care of your dog while you are away.

18 ⑤   19 ③

---

20 (A) the surface (B) their tails (C) completely

21 breathe → breath   22 ⑤   23 ②

24 the clam

25 have you ever seen a fish jump out of the water to catch a bird?

26 ②

27 one hundred and seventy centimeters and eighty kilograms

---

01 (A) fall asleep: 잠들다 • 아까 커피를 많이 마셔서 지금은 잠들 수 없다. (B) keep -ing: 계속해서 ~하다 • 중요한 것은 계속 시도하는 것이다.

02 (1) nearby: 인근에, 가까운 곳에 / 나는 인근에 있는 작은 가게에 갔었어. (2) friendly: 친절한 / 호텔 직원들이 매우 친절하고 도움이 많이 되었다. (3) completely: 완전히 / 나는 오늘이 그의 생일이라는 것을 완전히 잊었다. (4) 우리는 마침내 한밤중에 집에 도착했다.

03 ① take, take: (얼마의 시간이) 걸리다 / 이것은 얼마나 걸릴 거야? ② surrounded, surround: 둘러싸다 / 너는 포위되었다! 무기를 내려놓아라. ③ hide, hide: 숨다, 숨기다 / 그녀가 도착하지 않자 그는 실망감을 감추기가 어려웠다. ④ smashed, smash: 때려 부수다, 깨뜨리다 ⑤ calculate, calculate: 계산하다 / 아무리 계산해도 3천 원이 빈다.

04 (1) be full of: ~로 가득 차다 (2) go on a picnic: 소풍가다 (3) grow up to: 자라서 ~이 되다 (4) millions of: 수백만의

05 (A) 무엇을 하고 있는지 질문을 하자 (C) 신문을 읽고 있다고 대답한다. (D) 신문에서 흥미로운 것이 있는지 질문하자 (B) 고래 가족이 동해에서 발견되었다는 것을 얘기해준다.

06 'I wonder ~.'는 '나는 ~이 궁금하다.'라는 뜻으로 어떤 것에 대해 궁금할 때 사용하는 표현이다. wonder 다음에는 의문사절이나 if/whether절이 온다. 여기서는 '의문사(where)+주어(the bus stop)+동사(is)'인 의문사절을 wonder의 목적어로 사용한다.

07 버스 정류장은 경찰서 앞에 있다. in front of: ~ 앞에

08 How about -ing?: ~하는 것이 어떠니?

09 '~ says (that) …'(~에 따르면 …이다)는 어딘가에서 보거나 들은 내용을 상대방에게 보고하거나 전달할 때 사용하는 표현이다. 동사 'say'는 '~라고 말하다'는 뜻으로 흔히 사용되지만, 여기에서는 '~라고 되어[쓰여] 있다, ~라고 나와 있다, (글, 표지판 등이) 나타내다'라는 뜻으로 사용되었다. '~에 따르면'이라는 뜻으로 'according to'를 사용할 수 있다. weather forecast: 일기 예보

10 scenery: 경치, 풍경 this time of year: 이맘때는, 이맘때쯤

이면

11 be covered with: ~로 덮여 있다

12 ⓐ 수민이는 어디를 갈 예정인가?(남산) ⓑ 남산에는 얼마나 많은 하이킹 코스가 있는가?(모른다.) ⓒ 어디서 남자아이가 한강의 가장 짧은 코스를 찾는가?(한강이 아니라 남산이다.) ⓓ 무슨 요일에 그들은 만날 것인가?(일요일) ⓔ 수민이는 이번 일요일에 무엇을 할 예정인가?(등산을 갈 것이다.)

13 during은 다음에 명사(구)가 이어지고, while은 다음에 절(주어+동사)이 이어진다.

14 ① who → whose, ② of which → whose, ③ of whose → whose, ④ window → the window

15 소유격 관계대명사 whose를 활용한다.

16 시간의 접속사가 이끄는 부사절에서는 미래의 의미일지라도 현재 시제를 쓴다.

17 (1) 뒤에 명사가 이어지고 완전한 절이 나오므로 소유격 관계대명사로 whose 또는 'of which'를 쓴다. (2) 선행사가 The girl로 사람일 때, 소유격 관계대명사는 whose만 가능하다. (3) 시간의 접속사가 이끄는 부사절에서는 미래의 의미일지라도 현재시제를 쓴다.

18 ① the 생략 ② of which price → whose price 또는 of which the price ③ will be → is ④ as soon as → until

19 ③ exactly: 정확히, ⓐ와 ①, ②, ④, ⑤: 실제로는

20 혹등고래들은 '꼬리로' 선 채로 '수면' 근처에서 잠을 자며, 그들은 '완전히' 잠들지 않는다.

21 breathe는 동사이므로 명사형인 breath로 고쳐야 한다.

22 'humpback whale들이 심호흡을 하러 얼마나 자주 물 밖으로 나오는지'는 알 수 없다. ① No, they don't. sleep on one's side: 옆으로 누워서 자다, ② No, they aren't. ③ Because they are not fish. ④ They come out of the water for a deep breath and dive back into the sea.

23 이 글은 'tuskfish가 가장 좋아하는 먹이인 조개를 열기 위해 도구를 사용하는 것'에 관한 글이므로, 주제로는 ②번 'tuskfish는 조개를 열기 위해 도구를 사용하는 똑똑한 물고기이다'가 적절하다.

24 '조개'를 가리킨다.

25 have you ever seen: 현재완료 경험 용법, 지각동사 see+목적어+동사원형: (목적어)가 ~하는 것을 보다

26 주어진 문장의 its size에 주목한다. ②번 앞 문장의 내용을 받고 있으므로 ②번이 적절하다.

27 hundred 다음에는 보통 and를 넣어서 읽고, 쓸 때는 cm과 kg이라고 써도, 읽을 때는 centimeters와 kilograms라고 읽는 것이 적절하다.

Up to You

시험대비 실력평가   p.176

| 01 ①, ④ | 02 ② | 03 ③ | 04 ④, ⑤ |
| 05 ③ | 06 ③ | 07 ④ | |

01 ①, ④번은 동사 뒤에 행위자를 나타내는 접미사 '-er'을 붙여 명사형으로 만들 수 있다. ① produce: 생산하다 producer: 생산자 ② invent: 발명하다 inventor: 발명가 ③ protect: 보호하다 protector: 보호자 ④ educate: 교육하다 educator: 교육자 ⑤ collect: 모으다 collector: 수집가

02 ① contribute: 기여하다, 공헌하다 / 모든 사람들이 토론에 참여해 주시기 바랍니다. ② should have+과거분사: ~했어야 했다 / 그는 더 조심했어야 했다. ③ including: 포함해서 / 뷔페식 아침식사를 포함해서 1박에 150달러입니다. ④ active: 활동적인, 적극적인 / 그녀는 지역 정치에 적극 관여하고 있다. ⑤ describe: 기술하다, 묘사하다 / 내 심정은 말로는 다 표현할 수 없다.

03 report: 보도하다 / 신문, TV 또는 라디오를 통해서 무언가에 관한 정보를 주다

04 주어진 문장에서 move는 '(남을) 감동시키다'의 의미로 사용하여 '그러한 친절함에 의해 나는 깊이 감동받았다.'로 해석된다. ① 그들은 꽤 자주 집을 이사한다. ② 그녀는 빠르게 문으로 이동했다. ③ 자동차를 이동시켜 줄 수 있나요? ④ 이 이야기들은 나를 놀라게 했으며 감동시켰다. ⑤ 그의 연설은 청중에게 감동을 주어 눈물을 자아냈다.

05 be grateful for: ~에 감사하다 appreciate: 감사하다 / 도와주셔서 감사합니다

06 thanks to 명사: ~ 덕분에 / 오늘은 좋은 날씨 덕분에 일찍 도착했다.

07 rather than: ~보다는 / 그는 새로운 규칙을 받아들이기 보다는 그만두기로 결정했다.

서술형 시험대비   p.177

01 winner   02 (p)articipate
03 catch   04 keep
05 (d)ynamite, (h)eadline, (m)erchant
   (1) headline   (2) merchant   (3) dynamite
06 (1) His new book is due to be published next year.
   (2) The film is described as a highly charged thriller.

34 정답 및 해설

(3) I won't make the same mistake again.

(4) It was fine until we got caught in the rain at the picnic.

01 '-or'은 '~하는 사람(행위자)'이라는 의미를 만들어 주는 접미사이다. '-or'과 더불어 동사 뒤에 붙여 행위자를 나타내는 명사형 접미사에는 '-er'이 있다. act: 연기하다, actor: 연기자, win: 우승하다, winner: 우승자

02 engage in: ~에 참가하다 participate in: ~에 참가하다 / 전교생이 자원봉사에 참가해야 한다.

03 catch one's breath: 숨을 고르다 / 숨을 고르기 위해서 Clark 는 앉아야 했다. catch one's eye: 눈길을 끌다 / 내 눈길을 끄는 몇몇 그림들이 있다.

04 keep in touch: 연락하고 지내다 / 너 그와 계속 연락하고 지내니? keep -ing: 계속해서 ~하다 / 왜 계속 그런 식으로 말해?

05 (1) headline: (신문 기사 등의) 표제 / 신문 기사에 큰 글씨로 쓰여진 제목 / 오늘 신문 헤드라인 보셨어요? (2) merchant: 상인 / 대량으로 상품을 파는 사람 / 그 상인은 중국에서 산 물품에 관세를 냈다. (3) dynamite: 다이너마이트 / 강력한 폭약, 폭발물 / 그들은 큰 돌들을 깨기 위해 다이너마이트를 이용했다.

06 (1) due: ~하기로 되어 있는, 예정된 (2) describe A as B: A 를 B로 기술하다, 묘사하다 (3) make a mistake: 실수하다 (4) get caught in the rain: 비를 만나다

[교과서] Conversation

핵심 Check
p.178~179

1 (1) I should have studied hard.

(2) I should not have been late for school.

2 ②

교과서 대화문 익히기

Check(√) True or False
p.180~181

1 F 2 T 3 T 4 T 5 F 6 F 7 T 8 F

교과서 확인학습
p.183~185

Listen and Speak 1 A

were you late for / stomachache / Are / should have eaten

Listen and Speak 1 B

up, tired / stayed up late / again / not, had to / due / shouldn't have put it off until / the same / try to change, habits

Listen and Speak 1 C

1. wrong / got caught in / sorry to / have taken

2. What's / failed / hear that / should have studied hard

3. lost / I should have chained

4. was late for / should have got up early

Listen and Speak 2 A

going to do during / lots of, about / visit / hope you have

Listen and Speak 2 B

ready for / I'm thinking of giving up / wanted to take part in / good singer / the best singer I know / think so / voice / you for saying, do my best / I hope you win

Listen and Speak 2 C

1. going to sing / hope you move, audience / hope so

2. hope you score a goal

3. participate in / I hope you win / I hope so

Real Life Talk Watch a Video

graduation / looks like, a lot to say / wrote that / else / Some of them, hang out enough with / fault, should have spent more time with / after graduation / hope you keep in touch with / I hope so

Real Life Talk Step 2

1. can't believe / there anything, regret / should have been active / have a second chance / guess / hope you are active

2. believe we're graduating / anything you regret about / should have taken / guess, right / hope you take part in

시험대비 기본평가
p.186

01 ②   02 ①   03 ③

01 B는 학교 축제에서 노래를 부를 거라고 말하고 있다. A는 B가 노래를 불러서 청중을 감동시키는 것을 희망하는 표현을 할 수 있다. move: (남을) 감동시키다

02 'should have 과거분사'는 '~했어야 했는데 (하지 못했다.)'의 의미로 후회를 표현할 때 쓰는 표현이다. 'I should have+과거분사 ~.'는 'I'm sorry I didn't[wasn't] ~.' 또는 'I regret that I didn't[wasn't] ~.'로 바꿔 쓸 수 있다.

03 (C) 내일 무엇을 할지 예정에 대해 질문을 하자 (A) 상대방은 연설 대회에 참가할 것이라고 대답한다. (B) 멋지다고 말하며, 대회에서 우승하기를 기원하는 말을 덧붙인다. (D) 이에 대해 고마움을 표현하고 자신도 우승하기를 바란다고 말한다.

01 어젯밤에 늦게까지 깨어 있었다는 B의 말에 또 컴퓨터 게임을 했는지 물어보자, 이번에는 아니라는 대답과 함께 역사 과제를 끝내야 했다는 말을 하는 것이 어울리며 'Is it due today?'에서 it은 'my history project'를 가리키는 것이므로 ③이 적절하다.

02 'should not have+과거분사'는 '~하지 말았어야 했는데 (해 버렸다)'의 의미이다. 위의 대화에서 지호가 역사 과제를 마지막 순간까지 미루지 말았어야 했다는 말이 어울리므로 ②가 적절하다. put off: 미루다, 연기하다

03 지호와 G 둘 다 과제를 마지막 순간까지 미루는 문제를 가지고 있으므로, 우리의 나쁜 습관을 바꾸도록 노력하자고 말하고 있는 ⑤번이 빈칸에 어울린다.

04 곧 졸업하는 것에 대해 놀라움을 표현하고, (C) 상대방의 의견에 동의하면서 중학교 생활에서 후회하는 것이 있는지 질문한다. (A) 그렇다고 대답하며 학교 행사에 많이 참여 했어야 했다고 말한다. (B) 고등학교에서 다시 한 번 기회가 있다고 말하자 (D) 그 의견에 동의한다.

05 주어진 문장은 노래 경연 대회에 나가는 것을 포기하려고 하는 재민에게 '너는 내가 아는 노래를 가장 잘하는 사람이야.'라고 말하고 있는 문장이다. 또한 'Do you really think so?'에서 so가 받는 것은 주어진 문장의 내용이므로, 주어진 문장은 ④에 들어가는 것이 적절하다.

06 give up: 포기하다

07 A가 시드니에 많이 가 본 적이 있다고 했는데 A가 언젠가 시드니를 방문할 수 있기를 기원하는 말을 하는 것은 어색하다.

08 주어진 문장의 That은 Linda가 친구들과 충분히 어울리지 않았다는 내용으로 ③이 적절하다.

09 them은 앞에 언급된 my classmates(나의 학급 친구들)을 의미한다.

10 'Some of them said I didn't hang out enough with them.(그들 중 몇몇은 내가 그들과 충분히 어울리지 않았다고 말했어.)'이라고 하고 있으므로 Linda의 친구들은 Linda가 친구들과 많은 시간을 보내지 않았다고 생각한다.

01 밑줄 친 문장은 '어젯밤에 덜 먹었어야 했어.'의 의미로 '어젯밤에 더 먹지 말았어야 했어.'와 같으므로 less 대신에 more를 사용해서 문장을 만들 수 있다. 'should have 과거분사'는 '~했어야 했는데 (하지 못했다.)'의 의미로 후회를 표현할 때 사용하는 표현이며 'should not have+과거분사'는 '~하지 말았어야 했는데 (해 버렸다.)'의 의미이다.

02 (A) be ready for ~: ~의 준비가 되다 (B) I'm thinking of ~: '나는 ~할까 생각 중이다'라는 뜻으로 of 뒤에 동명사를 취해 의도나 계획을 나타낼 때 쓰는 표현이다.

03 'I hope you ~.'는 '나는 네가 ~하기를 바란다[희망한다].'라는 뜻으로 상대방에게 기원하는 말을 할 때 쓸 수 있는 표현이다. win: 이기다 contest: 대회

04 stay up: 안 자다, 깨어 있다

05 지금 '~하지 말아야 한다'의 의미가 아니라 과거에 '숙제를 마지막 순간까지 미루지 말았어야 했다'로 사용해야 하므로, 'should not have+과거분사(~하지 말았어야 했는데 (해 버렸다.))'를 사용해야 한다.

06 'I should have+과거분사 ~.'는 '나는 ~했어야 했다.'라는 뜻으로 과거 사실에 대한 후회를 표현할 때 사용한다. active: 적극적인

01 ①

02 (1) Reading　(2) Not knowing　(3) had　(4) visited

03 ⑤

04 (1) Watching TV, she ate dinner.

　(2) The article said Alfred Nobel had died in France from a heart attack.

01 접속사 없이 '주어+동사'가 이어지고 있으므로 빈칸에는 '접속사+주어+동사'의 역할을 할 수 있는 현재분사로(내가 늦은 것은 능동의 의미이므로) 분사구문이 되어야 한다.

02 (1) 접속사가 없으므로 '접속사+주어+동사'의 역할을 할 수 있는 Reading이 적절하다. (2) 분사구문의 부정은 분사 앞에 'not'이나 'never'를 쓴다. (3) 도착한 것이 그가 떠난 다음이므로 떠난 것을 과거완료로 나타내는 것이 적절하다. (4) 과거완료는 'had+과거분사'의 형태로, 과거 이전에 일어난 일이 과거의 어느 시점까지 영향을 미칠 때 쓴다.

03 돈을 가져간 것이 실토한 것보다 앞서므로 과거완료로 나타내는 것이 적절하다.

04 (1) Watching을 '접속사+주어+동사'의 역할을 하는 분사로 하여 알맞게 배열한다. (2) 프랑스에서 죽은 것이 기사가 쓰여진 것보다 앞선 시제이므로 과거완료로 나타내는 것이 적절하다.

01 ③　　02 ④　　03 ①　　04 ②

05 (1) had already left　(2) had done　(3) had never been　(4) Running　(5) talking　(6) knowing

06 ⑤　　07 ②　　08 Being　　09 ③

10 ④　　11 Mom had bought for me

12 ②　　13 ④　　14 (1) he was　(2) she was

15 had　　16 ③　　17 ①

01 washes라는 동사가 있고 접속사가 없으므로 listens를 listening으로 분사구문으로 만들어야 한다. She washes away the fatigue of the day listening to music.

02 주어진 문장과 ④번은 결과 용법이다. ①, ② 계속 ③ 경험 ⑤ 완료

03 뒤에 left라는 동사가 있고 접속사가 없으므로 thought를 thinking으로 바꿔 분사구문으로 만들어야 한다. 분사구문이 문장의 중간에 삽입된 형태이다.

04 첫 번째 빈칸에는 접속사가 없으므로 '접속사+주어+동사'의 역할을 할 수 있는 feeling이 적절하다. 두 번째 빈칸에는 밤에 비가 온 것이 앞선 시제이므로 'had rained'가 적절하다.

05 (1) '도착했을 때 이미 떠난 것'이므로 '완료'를 나타내는 과거완료가 적절하다. (2) '자신이 한 짓에 대해 용서를 구했다.'라는

뜻으로 용서를 구하는 시점 이전에 한 것이므로 과거완료가 적절하다. (3) 'Until last week'이 있으므로 그때까지의 경험을 나타내는 과거완료가 적절하다. (4) 접속사가 없으므로 '접속사+주어+동사'의 역할을 할 수 있는 분사구문으로 쓰는 것이 적절하다. (5) 분사구문의 뜻을 명확히 하기 위해 접속사 While을 생략하지 않고 남겨둔 경우이다. (6) 분사구문의 부정은 분사 앞에 'not'이나 'never'를 쓴다.

06 '접속사+주어+동사'의 부사절을 분사구문으로 바꾸어 쓸 수 있다. 이때, 분사구문의 뜻을 명확히 하기 위해 접속사를 생략하지 않기도 하지만 주어를 생략하지는 않는다.

07 We talked about what had happened the previous week. 말하는 시점인 과거보다 더 앞선 시점인 지난주에 일어난 일이므로 과거완료로 쓰는 것이 적절하다.

08 한 문장으로 쓰면 'Because[As] I was nervous, I forgot my lines at the school musical.'이고, 분사구문으로 바꾸면 'Because[As] I was'를 현재분사 Being으로 써야 한다.

09 Sam이 도착한 것은 과거로 쓰고, '가고 없었다'는 '결과'의 의미를 나타내기 위해서는 과거완료의 '결과'로 쓰는 것이 적절하다.

10 'Because she was tired, she came back home early.'를 분사구문으로 바르게 바꾼 것은 ④번이다.

11 사준 것이 잃어버린 것보다 먼저이고 현재 갖고 있지 않은 결과까지 나타내려면 과거완료로 쓰는 것이 적절하다.

12 주어진 문장과 ②번은 '이유'를 나타낸다. ① 양보, ③ 시간, ④ 동시동작, ⑤ 조건

13 주어진 문장과 ④번은 '완료'를 나타낸다. ①, ③ 경험, ② 결과, ⑤ 계속

14 부사절에서 주어가 주절의 주어와 같을 때 '주어+be동사'를 생략할 수 있으며 이것은 분사구문으로 고쳤을 때 being을 생략하고 접속사를 남겨둔 것과 같다.

15 before나 after가 있는 경우 시간의 순서가 분명하기 때문에 흔히 대과거를 나타내는 과거완료 대신에 과거로 쓰기도 한다.

16 부사절과 주절의 주어가 다를 때는 부사절의 주어를 생략하지 않으며 이것을 독립분사구문이라고 한다.

17 '집에 열쇠를 둔 것'이 '그것을 알아차린' 시점보다 앞서므로 알아차린 주절은 과거로 쓰고, 열쇠를 둔 것은 과거완료로 쓰는 것이 적절하다.

01 (1) Getting up too late, I missed the school bus.

　(2) Talking on the phone, he watered the plants.

　(3) Having a problem, ask the teacher.

　(4) Knowing it was wrong, she wouldn't change it.

　(5) Not having any money, I couldn't buy a bike.

　(6) The weather being good, we'll eat out.

02 (1) They couldn't find the treasure because[as,

since] Mr. Joe had hidden it under the sea.

(2) When[As] I arrived at home, Lucky had already fallen asleep.

03 (1) Seen from the mountains, the landscape is green and beautiful.

(2) Being sick, I had to stay home all day.

(3) She had just finished her task when the teacher came in.

(4) They ran to the platform, but the train had just gone.

04 (1) disappointing → disappointed

(2) Taking → Having taken

05 had never been   06 Arriving

07 (1) Leaving right now, you won't miss the train. / If you leave right now, you won't miss the train.

(2) Running to me, she waved her hand. / As she ran to me, she waved her hand.

(3) He had studied Chinese for two years before he went to China.

08 (1) My grandmother had been ill for five days when I visited her.

(2) The ground was covered with snow because it had snowed during the night.

(3) Walking in the park, he met an old friend.

(4) It getting so cold outside, the rain changed into snow.

(5) Made of thick trees, the doors looked unbreakable.

(6) Having eaten dinner, he was not hungry.

01 '접속사+주어+동사'로 이루어진 부사절의 주어가 주절의 주어와 일치할 때 접속사와 주어를 생략하고 동사를 분사(동사원형+-ing)로 만든다. (1) '이유', (2) '동시동작' (3) '조건' (4) '양보' (5) 분사구문의 부정은 분사 앞에 'not'이나 'never'를 쓴다. (6) 주절의 주어와 부사절의 주어가 다르므로 주어를 생략하면 안 된다.(독립분사구문)

02 의미상 어울리는 접속사를 사용하여 한 문장으로 쓰되, 먼저 일어난 사건을 과거완료를 이용하여 쓴다.

03 (1) 과거분사로 시작되는 분사구문은 being이 생략된 것으로 수동의 의미를 갖는다. (2) 현재분사가 분사구문을 이끌도록 한다. (3) 일을 끝마친 것이 앞선 시점이므로 과거완료의 '완료'로 나타낸다. (4) 이미 기차가 출발해서 탈 수 없었으므로 '결과'를 나타내는 과거완료를 이용한다.

04 (1) '실망한'이라는 '수동'의 의미가 되어야 하므로 과거분사 disappointed로 고쳐야 한다. (2) 부사절의 시제가 주절보다 앞선 경우에는 완료분사구문으로 쓴다. 'After he had taken his holiday, he came back refreshed.'를 분사구문으로 고친 것이다.

05 '~에 가 본 적이 없었다'라는 경험을 나타내기 위해서는 과거완료로 쓰는 것이 적절하다. have been to: ~에 가 본 적이 있다

06 'When he arrived ~'를 부사구문으로 고쳐 쓴다.

07 (1), (2) '접속사+주어+동사'로 이루어진 부사절의 주어가 주절의 주어와 일치할 때 접속사와 주어를 생략하고 동사를 분사(동사원형+-ing)로 만들어서 분사구문으로 바꿔 쓴다. (3) 2년 동안 계속 공부했으므로 '계속'을 나타내는 과거완료를 쓴다.

08 (1) 뒤에 'for five days'라는 기간이 나오므로 'had been ill'로 '계속'을 나타내는 것이 적절하다. (2) '밤에 눈이 와서 땅이 눈으로 덮인 것'이므로 눈이 온 것을 과거완료로 쓰고, 눈으로 덮인 것을 과거로 쓰는 것이 적절하다. (3) 산책하는 것은 능동이므로 현재분사를 쓰는 것이 적절하다. (4) 주절의 주어와 부사절의 주어가 다르므로 독립분사구문으로 써야 한다. (5) Being이 생략된 분사구문으로, '만드는' 것이 아니라 '만들어진' 것이므로 Making을 Made로 고쳐야 한다. (6) 시제가 앞서므로 완료분사구문으로 써야 한다.

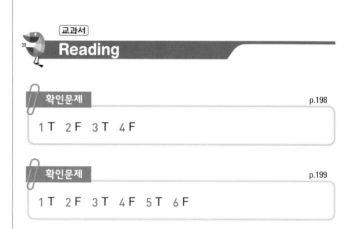

교과서 Reading

확인문제   p.198

1 T 2 F 3 T 4 F

확인문제   p.199

1 T 2 F 3 T 4 F 5 T 6 F

교과서 확인학습 A   p.200~201

01 How, Be Remembered   02 normal morning

03 sat in his chair   04 caught his eye

06 in surprise   07 take his eyes off

08 his own death   09 from a heart attack

10 my goodness   11 Catching his breath

12 even more shocked   13 described, as

14 had become rich   15 couldn't believe

16 one of his many inventions

17 think of, as   18 disappointed

19 How   20 unbelievable

21 merchant of death   22 in a different way

23 be remembered, the world better

24 to change people's opinions

25 mistakenly

26 who had actually died

27 Thanks to, contribute to   28 to create

29 only five awards   30 sixth award

31 rather than

1 How Will You Be Remembered?

2 It was just a normal morning.

3 Alfred Nobel sat in his chair to read the newspaper.

4 While he was drinking his coffee, a headline caught his eye: *The Merchant of Death, Alfred Nobel, Is Dead.*

5 "What? What is this?"

6 Reading the article, he dropped his cup in surprise.

7 His coffee spilled all over his clothes and desk, but he couldn't take his eyes off the newspaper.

8 The article was about his own death!

9 It said Nobel had died in France from a heart attack.

10 "Oh my goodness! Am I dead?"

11 Catching his breath, Nobel kept reading.

12 Soon, he became even more shocked.

13 The article described him as the inventor of dynamite and other dangerous objects for war.

14 It said that he had become rich from the deaths of others.

15 He couldn't believe his eyes.

16 It was true that dynamite was one of his many inventions.

17 But he never imagined that the world would think of him as "the merchant of death."

18 Nobel was deeply disappointed.

19 "How could this be?

20 This is unbelievable!

21 I'm not a merchant of death.

22 I want to be remembered in a different way.

23 I want to be remembered as a person who made the world better."

24 He decided to change people's opinions about him.

25 In 1888, a French newspaper mistakenly reported Alfred Nobel's death.

26 The person who had actually died was his brother, Ludvig.

27 Thanks to the report, however, Nobel decided to do something to contribute to the world.

28 In 1895, he decided to use his money to create the Nobel Prize.

29 Originally, there were only five awards.

30 A sixth award was added in 1968.

31 Today, when we think of Alfred Nobel, we think of the Nobel Prize, rather than dynamite.

01 ④   02 ②   03 ⑤   04 The article   05 ②   06 ③

07 (A) dynamite   (B) the merchant of death   08 as a person who made the world better   09 He decided to change people's opinions about him.

10 ⑤   11 was added   12 ②

13 from   14 ②, ③, ⑤   15 ②, ③   16 who 또는 that   17 disappointing → disappointed

18 ⑤   19 ④   20 ③   21 ①

22 ③   23 (A) mistakenly (B) actually (C) A sixth award was added   24 ⑤

01 ⓐ와 ④: ~하고 있는 동안에(접속사), ① 잠깐 동안(명사), ②, ⑤: [주절 뒤에서 반대·비교·대조를 나타내어] 그런데, 한편(으로는)(접속사), ③ (시간을) 빈둥빈둥 보내다(동사)

02 ② 중반부의 "What? What is this?"와 'he dropped his cup in surprise'를 통해 'embarrassed and confused'를 찾을 수 있다. embarrassed; 당황스러운, confused: 혼란스러워 하는, ① nervous: 불안해[초조해]하는, anxious: 불안해하는, ③ disappointed: 실망한, depressed: 우울한, ⑤ ashamed: 부끄러운

03 '그는 신문에서 눈을 뗄 수 없었다.'고 했다. ignore: 무시하다

04 It은 앞 문장의 'The article'을 가리킨다.

05 very는 원급을 강조하고, ⓑ와 나머지는 비교급을 강조한다.

06 ⓒ와 ③: 대과거 용법(과거에 일어난 두 가지 일 중 더 먼저 일어난 일을 나타냄.), ①, ⑤: 경험 용법, ②, ④: 계속 용법

07 Nobel은 전쟁에 쓰이는 '다이너마이트'와 다른 위험한 물건들을 발명함으로써 부자가 되었지만, 그것들은 많은 사람들을 죽일 수 있었기 때문에 기사에서 그를 '죽음의 상인'으로 기술했다.

08 '다르게' 기억되고 싶다는 것은 '세상을 더 좋게 만든 사람으로' 기억되고 싶다는 것을 가리킨다.

09 decide는 to부정사를 목적어로 취하는 동사이다.

10 사람들이 Nobel을 세상을 더 좋게 만든 사람으로 기억한 것이 아니라, Nobel 자신이 세상을 더 좋게 만든 사람으로 기억되고 싶다고 했을 뿐이다.

11 여섯 번째 상이 '추가되었다'고 해야 하므로 수동태로 쓰는 것이 적절하다.

12 이 글은 '한 프랑스 신문의 실수로 인한 보도 덕분에, Nobel이 세상에 공헌하기 위해 무언가를 하기로 결심하고 자신의 돈을 노벨상을 만드는 데 사용하기로 결정했다'는 내용의 글이므로, 제목으로는 ②번 '실수가 귀중한 결과로 이어졌다!'가 적절하다.

13 ⓐ die from: ~으로 죽다, ⓑ from: [원인·이유] ~으로 인해

14 (A)와 ②, ③, ⑤: 현재분사, ①, ④: 동명사

15 (B) think of/regard/look upon/see A as B: A를 B로 생각하다[여기다] ② respect: 존경하다 ③ discuss: 상의[의논/논의]하다

16 주격 관계대명사 'who' 또는 'that'을 쓰는 것이 적절하다.

17 감정을 나타내는 동사의 분사가 형용사로 쓰일 때, 감정을 느끼게 되는 경우에 과거분사를 써야 하므로 disappointed로 고치는 것이 적절하다.

18 (B)와 ①, ②, ③, ④: [역할·자격·기능·성질 따위를 나타내어] ~으로, ⑤: 예를 들면 ~와[같은](= such as, like)

19 '이건 믿을 수 없어! 나는 죽음의 상인이 아니야.'라는 Nobel의 말로 미루어, 앞에 올 내용으로는 'Nobel이 죽음의 상인으로 언급되었다'가 적절하다.

20 ⓐ in surprise: 놀라서, ⓑ off: [분리·이탈] ~으로부터, ~에서 떨어져; ~에서 벗어나, can't take one's eyes off ~: ~에서 눈을 뗄 수 없다

21 ①번 다음 문장의 a headline에 주목한다. 주어진 문장의 the newspaper의 headline을 가리키는 것이므로 ①번이 적절하다.

22 앞에 나오는 내용과 상반되는 내용이 뒤에 이어지므로 however가 가장 적절하다. ② 그 결과, ④ 즉[말하자면], ⑤ 게다가, 더욱이

23 (A) '실수로' Alfred Nobel의 죽음을 보도했다고 해야 하므로 mistakenly가 적절하다. mistakenly: 실수로, purposely: 고의로, (B) '실제로' 죽은 사람이라고 해야 하므로 actually가 적절하다. actually: 실제로, accidentally: 우연히, 뜻하지 않게, (C) '여섯 번째 상이 추가되었다'고 해야 하므로 A sixth award was added가 적절하다. A sixth award: 여섯 번째 상

24 '왜 상을 한 개 더 더했는지'는 알 수 없다. ① In 1888. ② No. ③ He decided to use his money to create the Nobel Prize. ④ Originally, there were only five awards.

🦉 **서술형 시험대비**　　　　　　　　　　p.208~209

01 As → Is
02 "죽음의 상인, Alfred Nobel 사망하다"라는 기사 제목
03 As[When] he read the article
04 headline
05 the world would think of him as "the merchant of death
06 Nobel's brother → Nobel

07 (A) more shocked　(B) the deaths of others
08 be remembered
09 (A) deeply　(B) unbelievable　(C) to change
10 merchant
11 (A) disappointed　(B) the world better
12 ⓐ eighteen eighty-eight　ⓑ eighteen ninety-five
　　ⓒ nineteen sixty-eight
13 (A) the Nobel Prize　(B) dynamite
14 Ludvig

01 'The Merchant of Death'와 'Alfred Nobel'은 동격이므로 Are를 Is로 고치는 것이 적절하다.

02 this는 앞 문장의 'The Merchant of Death, Alfred Nobel, Is Dead'라고 적힌 headline을 가리킨다.

03 접속사 As[When]를 사용하여 고치는 것이 적절하다.

04 신문의 '기사 제목'을 읽고 놀랐기 때문이다.

05 think of A as B: A를 B로 생각하다[여기다]

06 기사에는 'Nobel'이 심장 마비로 프랑스에서 죽었다고 쓰여 있었다.

07 기사에서 Nobel이 '다른 사람들의 죽음'으로 인해 부유해졌다고 말하면서, 그를 전쟁에 쓰이는 다이너마이트와 다른 위험한 물건의 발명가로 기술했기 때문에 Nobel은 훨씬 '더 충격을 받게' 되었다.

08 '기억되고 싶다'고 해야 하므로 수동태로 쓰는 것이 적절하다.

09 (A) '몹시' 실망했다고 해야 하므로 deeply가 적절하다. deep: 깊은; (깊이가) 깊게, deeply: (대단히·몹시의 뜻으로) 깊이[크게], (B) '이건 믿을 수 없어!'라고 해야 하므로 unbelievable이 적절하다. reasonable: 타당한, 합리적인, unbelievable: 믿을 수 없는, 믿기 어려운, (C) decide는 to부정사를 목적어로 취하는 동사이므로 to change가 적절하다.

10 대량으로 상품을 사거나 파는 사람, 특히 상품을 수입하고 수출하는 사람, merchant: (상품을 대규모로 매매하는) 상인, (특히) 무역상

11 Nobel은 죽음의 상인이라고 언급되어서 몹시 '실망했고', 그래서 사람들이 자신을 '세상을 더 좋게' 만든 사람으로 기억해주기를 원했다.

12 연도는 두 자리씩 끊어 읽고, 십 단위와 단 단위 사이에 보통 하이픈을 쓰는 것이 적절하다.

13 오늘날 우리가 Alfred Nobel을 생각할 때, 우리는 '다이너마이트'보다는 '노벨상'을 떠올린다. B rather than A = B more than A: A라기보다는 B

14 실제로 죽은 사람은 Alfred Nobel의 형인 'Ludvig'였다.

01 ①   02 ④   03 ②

04 unbelievable   05 I'm thinking of giving up

06 (A) take   (B) do   07 ③

08 (A) late   (B) to change   09 due

10 I shouldn't have put it off until the last moment.

11 ③

12 I should have spent more time with my classmates.

13 ③   14 ⑤   15 It being   16 ⑤

17 (1) When Mina returned home, her brother had eaten all her cookies.

  (2) When the waiter finally arrived with the food, the guests had already left the restaurant.

18 (1) Though[Although] it's a thrilling movie

  (2) Because[As] I felt hungry

  (3) If you turn left

19 ⓓ, ⓔ, ⓗ   20 deaths   21 ②

22 The person who had actually died was his brother, Ludvig.

23 ②, ⑤   24 (A) contribute to   (B) the Nobel Prize

25 ⑤   26 ④   27 ③   28 ②

29 ②

---

01 disappointed: 실망한, 낙담한 / 나는 내가 부정적이어서 실망스럽다.

02 create: 창조하다, 만들어 내다 / 그 새로운 공장은 400개가 넘는 일자리를 만들어 낼 것이라고 예상된다.

03 (A) give it a try: 시도하다 / 어렵겠지만 한번 해 볼게요. (B) put off: 미루다, 연기하다 / 그 경기는 날씨가 나빠서 내일까지 미뤄졌다.

04 unbelievable: 믿을 수 없는, 믿기 어려운 / 우리는 파리에서 믿기 어려울 정도로 멋진 시간을 보냈다.

05 'I'm thinking of ~'는 '나는 ~할까 생각 중이다'라는 뜻으로 of 뒤에 동명사를 취해 의도나 계획을 나타낼 때 쓰는 표현이다. give up: 포기하다

06 (A) take part in: ~에 참가하다 (B) do one's best: 최선을 다하다

07 노래 경연대회에 나가는 Jaemin에게 Tina는 Jaemin이가 대회에서 우승하기를 기원하는 말을 할 수 있다.

08 (A) stay up: 안 자다, 깨어 있다 late: 늦게 lately: 최근에 (B) try to 동사원형: ~하기 위해 노력하다, try 동사ing: 시험 삼아 ~해 보다

09 due: ~하기로 되어 있는[예정된] / 어떤 특정한 때 예정되어 있거나 계획된

10 should not[shouldn't] have+과거분사: ~하지 말았어야 했다, put off: 미루다, 연기하다

11 주어진 문장의 뜻은 '그 외에는?'의 의미로 졸업 메시지에 많은 친구가 Linda의 미소를 좋아한다 말을 썼다는 말에, 상대방이 '그 외에는?'이라고 말하고 'Some of them said I didn't hang out enough with them.(그들 중 몇몇은 내가 그들과 충분히 어울리지 않았다고 말했어.)'을 이어서 얘기하는 것이 적절하다.

12 should have+과거분사: ~했어야 했다 spend+시간+with ~: ~와 시간을 보내다

13 When I got up, she had already gone to work. 일어나기 전에 이미 가버린 것이므로 일어난 것은 과거로, 가버린 것은 과거완료로 써야 한다.

14 주어진 문장은 '이유'를 나타내는 분사구문이다.

15 'As it was ~'를 부사구문으로 고쳐 쓴다. 주절의 주어와 부사절의 주어가 다르므로 주어를 생략하면 안 된다.(독립분사구문)

16 'As he had not told the truth the previous day, he fell in danger.'를 분사구문으로 쓴 것이므로 telling을 'having told'로 고쳐야 한다.

17 과거완료는 과거보다 한 시제 앞서는 대과거를 나타낼 수 있으므로 앞서는 사건을 과거완료로 쓴다.

18 (1) 내용상 '양보'의 부사절이 적절하다. (2) 내용상 '이유'의 부사절이 적절하다. (3) 내용상 '조건'의 부사절이 적절하다.

19 ⓐ Read → Reading ⓑ Being not → Not being ⓒ Seeing → Seen ⓕ has → had ⓖ stayed → had stayed, had returned → returned

20 수천 명의 사람들의 '죽음'에 대해 책임이 있다고 하는 것이 적절하다. be responsible for: ~에 대해 책임이 있다, ~의 원인이 되다

21 위 글은 '(신문,잡지의) 기사'이다. ③ 수필, ⑤ (책,연극,영화 등에 대한) 논평[비평], 감상문

22 주격 관계대명사 who가 주어 The person을 수식하도록 쓰는 것이 적절하다.

23 ⓑ와 ②, ⑤: 명사적 용법, ①, ④: 형용사적 용법, ③: 부사적 용법

24 한 프랑스 신문의 부정확한 보도 덕분에, Nobel이 세상에 '공헌하기' 위해 무언가를 하기로 결심하고 자신의 돈을 '노벨상'을 만드는 데 사용하기로 결정했다.

25 ⓐ와 ⑤: 때, ① 조건, ②와 ④: 양보, ③ 이유

26 '글쓴이가 UNICEF에 얼마나 많은 돈을 기부했는지'는 대답할 수 없다. ① The writer donated money to children in Africa. ② Because the writer wanted to make a difference for children in need. ③ The writer didn't buy snacks for a month. ⑤ Now the writer really appreciate his or her meals.

27 주어진 문장의 It에 주목한다. ③번 앞 문장의 The article을 받고 있으므로 ③번이 적절하다.

41

28 이 글은 '자신을 '죽음의 상인'이라고 묘사한 기사를 읽고 Nobel이 충격을 받게 되는 내용'의 글이므로, 제목으로는 ②번 '오, 이럴 수가! 내가 '죽음의 상인'이라고?'가 적절하다.

29 ② 숨을 고른 후, Nobel은 '계속 기사를 읽었다.'

단원별 예상문제   p.216~219

01 ③   02 ③   03 (t)ook
04 (1) graduation   (2) director
05 shouldn't have got up   06 ⑤   07 out
08 ④   09 (A) that   (B) after   10 ⑤
11 (A) to finish   (B) have put it off   12 ①
13 ②, ④   14 had just left   15 ②
16 had become
17 (A) dead   (B) shocked   (C) objects   18 ④
19 in order that, might[could] create
20 Because he wanted to honor people who made the world better.
21 ②   22 ③, ⑤   23 ②   24 ①

01 <보기>의 단어의 관계는 동의어 관계이다. move: 감동시키다, touch: 감동을 주다 ⓒ, ⓓ는 동의어 관계이며 이외의 보기는 반의어 관계이다. ⓐ active: 활동적인, inactive: 활동이 없는 ⓑ including: ~을 포함해서, excluding: ~을 제외하고 ⓒ normal: 보통의, ordinary: 보통의 ⓓ decide: 결정하다, determine: 결정하다 ⓔ satisfied: 만족한, dissatisfied: 불만족한

02 (A) be over: 끝나다 / 우리가 도착했을 때쯤에는 그 모임이 끝났다. (B) get caught in: ~에 사로잡히다 / 교통체증에 걸리면 우리는 3시간이 걸릴 것이다.

03 take eyes off: 눈을 떼다 / 그녀는 나를 흘끗 보기 위해 길에서 눈을 뗐다. take part in: ~에 참가하다 / 약 2만 4천 명이 이 마라톤 대회에 참가하였다.

04 (1) graduate: 졸업하다 graduation: 졸업(식) / 그것은 내가 Oxford 대학을 2019년에 졸업한 후 잡은 첫 직장이었다. (2) direct: 감독하다 director: 감독 / 그는 이 영화의 미술 감독이다.

05 should have 과거분사: ~했어야 했다 should not have 과거분사: ~하지 말았어야 했다 early: 일찍, late: 늦게

06 (C) 방학 동안 무엇을 할 건지 진수한테 물어보자 (D) 책을 많이 읽을 것이라고 대답하며, 상대방의 방학 동안의 계획을 물어본다. (B) 부산에 계신 조부모님을 방문할 계획이라고 대답한다. (A) 멋진 방학을 보내길 바란다고 기원하는 말을 한다.

07 hang out: 많은 시간을 보내다

08 'should have 과거분사'는 '~했어야 했는데 (하지 못했다.)'의 의미로 후회를 표현할 때 쓰는 표현이다. spend: (시간을) 보내다[들이다]

09 (A) write의 목적어로 that절이 적절하다. 명사절을 연결하는 접속사 that 다음에는 완전한 문장이 나온다. (B) 민호가 'I hope you keep in touch with your classmates after graduation.(네가 졸업한 후에도 학급 친구들과 계속 연락하기를 바라.)'이라고 말하는 것을 볼 때 졸업 후에도 여전히 시간이 있다고 말하는 것이 어울린다.

10 지호가 마지막 순간까지 과제를 미루지 말아야 했는데 미룬 것에 대해 후회를 나타내는 말을 하고 있다. 주어진 문장에서 'the same problem'이 마지막 순간까지 미루는 것을 의미하므로 ⑤가 적절하다.

11 (A) have to 동사원형: ~해야 한다 (B) should not have 과거분사: ~하지 말았어야 했다 put off: 미루다, 연기하다

12 ① 그들의 나쁜 습관을 어떻게 바꿀 것인가?(언급되지 않았다.) ② 역사 과제의 마감은 언제인가?(오늘) ③ Jiho는 어떻게 보이는가?(피곤해 보인다.) ④ 그들이 바꿔야 하는 나쁜 습관은 무엇인가? (마지막 순간까지 일을 미루는 것) ⑤ 지난밤에 Jiho는 무엇을 했는가?(역사 과제를 끝냈다.)

13 ② Walked → Walking ④ 분사구문에서 의미를 분명히 하기 위해 분사 앞에 접속사를 쓰는 경우도 있지만 주절의 주어와 같은 부사절의 주어를 쓰지는 않는다.

14 '버스가 막 떠난 것'으로 '완료'를 나타내는 과거완료로 쓰는 것이 적절하다.

15 ② When Tom opened the door, Alex had already watered the plants.

16 기사가 쓰인 것보다 부유해진 것이 더 먼저 일어난 일이므로 과거완료 시제 (had+과거분사)로 쓰는 것이 적절하다.

17 (A) die는 수동태로 쓸 수 없는 동사이므로 dead가 적절하다. (B) 감정을 나타내는 동사의 분사가 형용사로 쓰일 때, 감정을 느끼게 되는 경우에 과거분사를 써야 하므로 shocked가 적절하다. (C) 다른 위험한 '물건'들이라고 해야 하므로 objects가 적절하다. object: 물건, 물체, subject: (논의 등의) 주제, 과목

18 ⓑ와 ④: 가주어, ① 가목적어, ② 비인칭주어(거리), ③ 그것 (앞에 이미 언급되었거나 현재 이야기되고 있는 사물·동물을 가리킴), ⑤ 비인칭주어(막연한 상황)

19 목적을 나타내는 to부정사는 in order that 주어 may[can]을 사용하여 복문으로 고치는 것이 적절하다.

20 '세상을 더 좋게 만든 사람들을 존경해주기 위해서'였다.

21 ② 노벨상은 해마다 물리학, 화학, 생리학 및 의학, 문학, 평화, 경제학의 여섯 부문의 수상자에게 메달과 상장, 상금을 수여하며, 경제학상의 경우, 1968년에 신설되어 1969년부터 상을 수

여했다.

22 그 보도 '덕분에'라고 해야 하므로, ③번 Thanks to와 ⑤번 Because of가 적절하다. ① ~ 대신에, ② ~에도 불구하고, ④ ~에 더하여, ~뿐 아니라

23 이 글은 '한 프랑스 신문의 실수로 인한 보도 덕분에, Nobel이 세상에 공헌하기 위해 무언가를 하기로 결심하고 자신의 돈을 노벨상을 만드는 데 사용하기로 결정했다'는 내용의 글이므로, 주제로는 ②번 '부정확한 보도가 Nobel로 하여금 세상에 공헌하기 위해 무언가를 하기로 결심하게 만들었다'가 적절하다.

24 1888년에, 한 프랑스 신문에서 '실수로' Alfred Nobel의 죽음을 보도했다. on purpose: 고의로[일부러], ⑤ come to one's mind: 생각이 나다, 생각이 떠오르다

서술형 실전문제 p.220~221

01 I hope you take part in many school events

02 (1) I ought to have eaten less last night.
   (2) I regret (that) I didn't eat less last night.
   (3) I'm sorry (that) I didn't eat less last night.

03 ④ must have spent → should have spent

04 (1) Because[As] he was sick, he went to see a doctor.
   (2) You will get a perfect result if you follow these instructions.
   (3) There being no bus left, I had to walk home.
   (4) He goes to work by train every morning, coming home the same way.

05 (1) had become   (2) had changed

06 had died   07 After he caught his breath

08 Nobel   09 made a decision

10 we think of the Nobel Prize, rather than dynamite

11 Alfred Nobel

01 B가 '너는 고등학교에서 다시 한 번 기회가 있어.'라고 말하는 것을 볼 때 빈칸에는 학교 행사에 많이 참여하는 것을 기원하는 말을 하는 것이 적절하다. take part in: ~에 참가하다

02 'should have 과거분사'는 '~했어야 했는데 (하지 못했다)'의 의미로 후회를 표현할 때 사용하는 표현이다. 비슷한 표현으로 'I regret that 주어+과거동사 ~.', 'I feel sorry that 주어+과거 동사 ~.', 'I ought to have 과거분사 ~.'가 있다.

03 'must have p.p.'는 과거에 대한 강한 추측을 나타내어 '~이었음에 틀림없다'의 의미로 사용한다. 흐름상 학급 친구들과 더 많은 시간을 보냈어야 했다며 후회하는 표현이 어울리므로 must가 아니라 should를 사용해야 한다.

04 (1) 의미상 '이유'를 나타내는 분사구문이다. (2) 의미상 '조건'

을 나타내는 분사구문이다. (3) 주절의 주어와 다르므로 독립분사구문으로 바꾼다. (4) 의미상 '연속상황'을 나타내는 분사구문으로 바꾼다.

05 (1) 기사에 쓰여진 내용은 이미 일어난 사건이므로 said의 목적어인 that절은 과거완료로 쓴다. (2) 발견한 것은 이미 변한 것이므로 that절을 과거완료로 쓴다.

06 기사가 쓰인 것보다 죽은 것이 더 먼저 일어난 일이므로 과거완료 시제인 had died로 쓰는 것이 적절하다.

07 '숨을 고른 후'라고 해야 하므로, 접속사 After를 사용하여 고치는 것이 적절하다.

08 'Nobel'을 가리킨다.

09 decide = make a decision

10 B rather than A: A라기보다는 B

11 1888년에, 한 프랑스 신문에서 실수로 'Alfred Nobel'이 죽었다고 보도했지만, 실제로 죽은 사람은 Alfred Nobel의 형인 Ludvig였다.

창의사고력 서술형 문제 p.222

|모범답안|

01 (1) Having nothing to do, I went for a walk to the park.
   (2) Being tired, I came back home early.
   (3) Not being fish, they need to come up to breathe.
   (4) Walking on the street, I saw a famous movie star.

02 (A) donated money to children in Africa
   (B) make a difference for children in need
   (C) buy snacks for a month (D) my meals
   (E) myself

단원별 모의고사 p.223~226

01 ②   02 unbelievable

03 (1) spent, gave   (2) hang   (3) stay

04 (1) in   (2) (h)ope, keep, touch
   (3) made, mistake   (4) (t)hink of, as

05 (A) tired   (B) due   (C) change

06 I shouldn't have put it off until the last moment.

07 ④   08 ④   09 ①, ③

10 (C)–(A)–(B)–(D)   11 graduation

12 I hope you keep in touch with your classmates after graduation.

13 (1) When I woke up this morning, the rain had

already stopped.

(2) The article said Alfred Nobel had died in France from a heart attack.

(3) Being late for school, Ann ran to catch the school bus.

14 (1) When I got home, I found someone had broken into our house.

(2) They had finished the pizza before their friends arrived.

(3) Eating popcorn, he watched TV.

(4) Turning to the right, you will find the flower shop.

15 ①, ④

16 Catching his breath, Nobel kept reading.

17 ③　　　　18 (A) death　(B) imagined　19 ①

20 ③　　　　21 It was added in 1968.

22 participated in the tree planting program　23 ⑤

---

01 be late for ~: ~에 늦다 / 그녀는 매일 직장에 지각한다. be ready for ~: ~의 준비가 되다 / 그렇게 오래 걷고 난 우리는 모두 한잔하고 싶은 생각이 간절했다.

02 unbelievable: 믿을 수 없는, 믿기 어려운 / 그들은 똑같이 그녀에게 놀랐다. 그녀가 그들 중 많은 이들과 같은 나이라는 것이 믿을 수 없었다.

03 (1) spend: (시간을) 보내다[들이다] give up: 포기하다 / 우리는 열쇠를 찾으려고 30분을 보냈고, 결국 포기하고 집에 갔다. (2) hang out: 많은 시간을 보내다 / 나는 종종 커피숍에서 시간을 보낸다. (3) stay up: 안 자다, 깨어 있다 / Josh는 밤새도록 피곤하지 않고 깨어 있을 수 있다.

04 (1) in surprise: 놀라서 (2) hope: 희망하다 keep in touch: 연락하고 지내다 (3) make a mistake: 실수하다 (4) think of A as B: A를 B라고 생각하다

05 (A) 지호는 어젯밤에 늦게까지 깨어 있었으므로 피곤해 보일 것이다. tired: 피곤한 (B) due: ~하기로 되어 있는, 예정된 (C) 지호가 마지막 순간까지 할 일을 미루고, G도 종종 같은 문제를 가지고 있다고 말하는 것으로 보아 나쁜 습관을 바꾸도록 노력하자고 말하는 것이 어울린다.

06 should not have 과거분사: ~하지 말았어야 했다 put off: 미루다, 연기하다 until: ~까지

07 ⓐ for, be ready for ~: ~할 준비가 되다 ⓑ of, think of ~을 생각하다 ⓒ up, give up: 포기하다 ⓓ in, take part in: ~에 참가하다 ⓔ for, thank you for ~: ~에 대해 감사하다

08 ④ Of course not. → Of course. Tina가 아는 노래를 가장 잘하는 사람이 재민이고, 멋진 목소리를 가졌다고 말하는 것으

로 보아 물론이라고 대답하는 것이 어울린다.

09 재민이는 Tina가 아는 노래를 가장 잘하는 사람이라고 언급되어 있지만 구체적으로 어떤 종류의 노래를 잘 하는지에 대해서는 나와 있지 않다. 또한 노래 대회가 언제인지도 언급되지 않고 있다.

10 무엇을 읽고 있는지 물어보는 질문에 (C) 학급 친구들에게 받은 졸업 메시지를 읽고 있다고 대답한다. (A) 메시지를 본 민호가 친구들이 Linda에게 할 말이 많은 것 같다고 말하자 (B) 졸업 메시지에 쓰여진 친구들이 Linda의 미소를 좋아한다는 내용을 얘기해 준다. (D) 멋지다고 칭찬하며 그 외에 다른 어떤 내용이 있는지 질문한다.

11 graduation 졸업(식) / 학위나 졸업장이 주어지는 의식

12 'I hope you ~.'는 '나는 네가 ~하기를 바란다[희망한다].'라는 뜻으로 상대방에게 기원하는 말을 할 때 쓸 수 있는 표현이다. keep in touch: 연락하고 지내다 after: ~ 후에

13 (1) 일어났을 때 이미 비가 멈췄다는 것은 어색하며 비가 이미 멈춘 '완료'의 의미를 나타내도록 과거완료로 쓰는 것이 적절하다. (2) 이미 죽었다는 것을 기사로 쓰는 것이므로 죽었다는 내용이 과거완료가 되어야 한다. (3) 접속사가 없으므로 'Ann was'를 being으로 바꾸어 분사구문으로 만든다.

14 (1) '결과'를 나타내는 과거완료를 이용한다. (2) '완료'를 나타내는 과거완료를 이용한다. (3) '동시동작'의 분사구문을 이용한다. (4) '조건'의 분사구문을 이용한다.

15 ① Being nervous on the stage, the actor forgot his lines. ④ Jimmy borrowed some money because he had lost his bag.

16 After he caught his breath를 분사구문으로 고쳐 Catching his breath라고 쓰는 것이 적절하다. catch one's breath: 숨을 고르다, keep+동사-ing: 계속 ~하다

17 ⓑ와 ③: 진주어에 해당하는 명사절을 이끄는 접속사, ① 보어절을 이끄는 접속사, ②와 ④: 목적절을 이끄는 접속사, ⑤ 동격절을 이끄는 접속사

18 그가 죽은 뒤에 세상이 그를 '죽음'의 상인으로 생각할 것임을 깨달았고, 그는 그럴 것이라고는 결코 '상상하지' 못했기 때문이다.

19 주어진 문장의 who had actually died에 주목한다. ①번 앞 문장의 내용과 상반되는 내용을 말하는 것이므로 ①번이 적절하다.

20 ⓐ와 ②, ⑤: 부사적 용법, ①, ④: 명사적 용법, ③: 형용사적 용법

21 여섯 번째 상은 1968년에 추가되었다.

22 '나무 심기 프로그램에 참가한 것'을 가리킨다.

23 글쓴이가 나무에 관심을 가지지 않았던 것은 나무 심기 프로그램에 참가하기 전이고, 현재는 '나무들이 우리에게 정말 중요하다는 것을 알고 있다.'

Picture the Future

교과서 Reading

1 T 2 F 3 T 4 F

1 T 2 F 3 F 4 T 5 F

교과서 확인학습 A p.232~233

01 Picture
02 It's
03 shakes, Five more minutes
04 stops shaking
05 appears, be late for
06 Clear
07 become clear
08 scans Minji's body
09 health condition
10 comes out from
11 comes, dries
12 with today's clothes
13 for breakfast
14 The usual
15 presses, on
16 prints out
17 rushes out
18 A few minutes later
19 send a drone to
20 a million
21 driverless flying car
22 in comfortable chairs
23 to select
24 by putting, on a sensor
25 will be delivered
26 150-story
27 give a presentation with
28 doesn't have to
29 Thanks to, feel like
30 is ready
31 talk about
32 washes the dishes
33 called chess
34 agrees
35 3-D chess board
36 lots of fun
37 whispers to
38 Remind, to take

교과서 확인학습 B p.234~235

1 Picture the Future

2 It's 7 a.m.

3 The bed shakes and Minji Kim yells, "Five more minutes!"

4 The bed stops shaking.

5 Suddenly, Minji's mom appears on a screen on the wall and says, "You're going to be late for school!"

6 Minji rubs her eyes and says, "Clear the windows."

7 The dark windows become clear and the sun shines brightly through them.

8 In the bathroom, a red light scans Minji's body.

9 A voice says, "54 kilograms. Your health condition is excellent."

10 When she steps in the shower, water comes out from the top and sides.

11 After her shower, warm air comes out and dries her.

12 When she gets out, a drawer opens with today's clothes.

13 In the kitchen, her father says, "Good morning, Honey. What do you want for breakfast?"

14 Minji says, "The usual, please."

15 Mr. Kim presses a few buttons on the cooking machine.

16 The machine prints out some bacon, eggs and bread.

17 Mr. Kim says goodbye and rushes out the door.

18 A few minutes later, Minji's father appears on a screen and shouts, "I forgot my glasses!"

19 Ms. Kim smiles and answers, "No problem. I'll send a drone to your office."

20 Mr. Kim says, "Thanks a million!"

21 Ms. Kim and Minji get into a driverless flying car.

22 They sit in comfortable chairs around a table.

23 Ms. Kim touches the car window to select the groceries for this week.

24 She pays for them by putting her finger on a sensor.

25 They will be delivered to her house.

26 The car lands at Minji's school on top of a 150-story building.

27 Today Minji will give a presentation with Dona, a student in America.

28 But Minji doesn't have to go to America.

29 Thanks to a VR classroom, they will feel like they are in the same classroom.

45

30 When Minji's family comes back home, dinner is ready.

31 They eat and talk about their day.

32 After a delicious dinner, the cleaning robot clears the table and washes the dishes.

33 Minji says, "I learned a game called chess today. Do you want to play?"

34 Everyone agrees.

35 A 3-D chess board appears on the table.

36 They have lots of fun.

37 Right before Minji goes to bed, she whispers to her watch.

38 "Remind Daddy to take his glasses tomorrow."

서술형 실전문제
p.236~238

01 (u)sual 02 of

03 (1) story (2) comfortable (3) clear

04 (1) He couldn't finish college because of his bad health condition.

(2) A man suddenly appeared from behind a tree.

(3) The moon shone brightly in the sky.

05 (R)emind

06 ⓐ to read → reading, ⓒ By use → By using

07 driverless 08 ⑤

09 (1) It is right before Minji goes to bed that she whispers to her watch.

(2) It is water that[which] comes out from the top and sides.

(3) It is a few buttons that[which] Mr. Kim presses on the cooking machine.

(4) It is on top of a 150-story building that[where] the car lands.

10 Do you have a client named Peters?

11 be delivered

12 (A) a drone (B) his office

13 She pays for them by putting her finger on a sensor.

14 150-stories → 150-story

15 need not 16 a VR classroom

17 to shake → shaking 18 the windows

19 (A) scans (B) clothes (C) a few

20 Warm air comes out and dries her.

21 drawer

01 usual: 일상의, 늘 하는; 늘 먹던 것 / 그녀는 늘 하는 온갖 변명들을 늘어놓았다. 늘 먹던 걸로 주세요.

02 be tired of ~: ~에 싫증이 나다 / 우리는 그가 전화하는 것을 기다리는 것에 싫증이 났다. on top of: ~의 꼭대기에 / 그 집은 언덕 꼭대기에 위치해 있다.

03 (1) story: (건물의) 층 / 그의 사무실은 30층 건물의 꼭대기 층에 있다. (2) comfortable: 편안한, 안락한 / 침대가 너무 편하고 따뜻해서 일어나고 싶지 않았다. (3) clear: 치우다 / 식탁 치우는 거 거들어 줄래?

04 (1) health condition: 건강 상태 (2) appear: 나타나다 (3) shine: 빛나다, 비추다

05 remind A to 동사원형: A에게 ~할 것을 상기시키다 / 누군가가 그들이 해야만 하는 것을 기억하게 만들다 / 나에게 오늘 밤 우유를 살 것을 상기시켜 줘.

06 ⓐ stop 동명사: ~하기를 멈추다 / 나는 읽기를 멈추고 불을 껐다. ⓑ thanks to 명사: ~ 덕분에 / 최근의 호우 덕택에 가뭄이 가셨다. ⓒ by 동사ing: ~함으로써 / 인터넷을 사용함으로써 너는 쇼핑을 집에서 할 수 있다.

07 driverless: 운전자가 필요 없는

08 조동사가 있는 문장의 수동태는 '조동사+be+과거분사'의 형태로 나타낸다.

09 'It ~ that ...' 강조 구문으로 강조하며, 'It is/was ~ that ...'의 형태로, 강조하고자 하는 부분을 'It is/was'와 that 사이에 넣고, 나머지 부분을 that 뒤에 쓴다. 또한 'It ~ that ...' 강조 구문에서 강조하는 대상이 사람일 때는 that 대신에 who[whom], 사물이나 동물일 때는 which로 바꿔 쓸 수 있으며, 시간 또는 장소의 부사(구/절)일 경우, when(시간) 또는 where(장소)로 바꿔 쓸 수 있다.

10 named가 뒤에서 a client를 수식하도록 쓴다. 앞에 'who is' 가 생략된 형태로 볼 수 있다.

11 식료품이 집으로 '배달될' 것이라고 해야 하므로 수동태로 써야 하고, 조동사 수동태는 '조동사+be+과거분사'의 형태로 쓰는 것이 적절하다.

12 민지의 엄마가 '그의 사무실로' 안경과 함께 '드론'을 보낼 것이다.

13 by+동사-ing: ~함으로써

14 150-story는 '150층의, 150층짜리'라는 뜻으로 두 개의 단어가 하이픈(-)으로 연결된 복합 형용사이며, '층'을 나타내는 명사 story를 '단수'로 쓰는 것이 적절하다.

15 don't/doesn't have to+동사원형 = don't/doesn't need to+동사원형 = need not+동사원형: ~할 필요가 없다, need not 에서 need가 조동사이므로 'needs not'으로 쓰지 않도록 주의해야 한다.

16 'VR(가상 현실) 교실' 덕분에, 그들이 같은 교실에 있는 것처럼

느끼는 것이 가능할 것이다.

17 침대가 '흔들기를' 멈춘다고 해야 하므로 to shake를 shaking으로 고치는 것이 적절하다. stop ~ing: ~하기를 그만두다, stop+to부정사: ~하기 위해 멈추다(to부정사의 부사적 용법 목적)

18 '창문'을 가리킨다.

19 (A) 민지의 몸을 '정밀 검사한다'라고 해야 하므로 scans가 적절하다. scan: 정밀 검사[촬영]하다, skip: 깡충깡충 뛰다, 건너뛰다, (B) 오늘의 '옷'이 나타난다고 해야 하므로 clothes가 적절하다. cloths: cloth(옷감, 직물)의 복수, clothes: 옷, 의복, (C) 버튼 '몇 개'라고 해야 하므로 a few가 적절하다. a few+복수명사, a little+셀 수 없는 명사

20 샤워 후에는, '따뜻한 공기가 나와 그녀를 말린다.'

21 박스 같은 형태로 물건들을 안에 넣도록 디자인된 책상, 상자 또는 다른 가구의 부분, drawer: 서랍

단원별 예상문제　　　　　　p.239~242

01 (1) on　(2) for　(3) out　(4) to
02 ②　　　　　03 ⑤　　　　　04 ③
05 (1) (t)ired of　(2) Remind, to　(3) stopped (t)alking
06 ③　　　　　07 ②　　　08 Pressing the button
09 will be decorated
10 (Being) Tired after a long walk, Minji went to bed early.
11 (1) Appearing on a screen on the wall, Minji's mom says, "You're going to be late for school!"
　(2) As[Because/Since] she was late, she hurried to work.
　(3) If you are an architect, what will you choose from nature?
12 (1) This movie will be loved by many teens.
　(2) The environment should not be destroyed (by us).
　(3) The fruit can be made into delicious jam (by them).
　(4) What you promised has to be delivered (by you).
13 ⓐ, ⓓ, ⓔ　14 ③
15 the groceries (for this week)
16 I learned a game which[that] is called chess today.
17 ②　　　　　18 ①　　　　　19 The usual, please.
20 ③　　　　　21 ③, ⑤
22 is appeared → appears　23 ④

01 (1) on top of: ~의 꼭대기에 / 그 탑은 언덕 꼭대기에 위치해 있다. (2) pay for: ~의 값을 지불하다 / 현실은 이 사업에 지불

할 충분한 돈이 없다는 것이다. (3) print out: (프린트로) 출력하다 / 이 문서를 출력해 주시겠어요? (4) send A to B: A를 B에 보내다 / 그는 수십 개의 장미를 그의 여자친구에게 생일날 보냈다.

02 ②의 영영풀이는 yell의 영영풀이이다. ① select: 선택하다 / 어떤 것이나 누군가를 무엇이 최선인지, 가장 적절한지 등에 관해 조심스러운 생각으로 고르다 ② whisper: 속삭이다 / to speak or say something very quietly, using your breath rather than your voice 목소리보다는 숨을 사용해서 매우 조용하게 말하다 yell: 소리치다, 외치다 / to shout or say something very loudly, especially because you are frightened, angry, or excited 특히 겁이 나거나, 화나거나, 흥분해서 매우 크게 소리치거나 말하다 ③ press: 누르다 / 기계가 시작하거나, 종이 울리도록 하기 위해서 버튼이나 스위치 등을 누르다 ④ shine: 빛나다, 비추다 / 밝은 빛이 생기게 하다 ⑤ appear: 나타나다 / 특히 갑자기 보이거나, 도착하거나, 어느 장소에 존재하기 시작하다

03 select: 선택하다 choose: 고르다, 선택하다 / 부모들이 배우는 데 어려움을 가진 아이들을 위한 올바른 학교를 고르는 것은 중요하다.

04 ③은 'ful', 나머지는 모두 'less'가 들어간다. ① careless: 부주의한 / 사고가 나는 데는 부주의한 운전자 한 명만 있으면 된다. ② driverless: 운전자가 필요 없는 / 회사는 현재 운전자가 필요 없는 차를 실험 중이다. ③ harmful: 해로운 / 흡연은 건강에 해로운 효과를 준다. ④ useless: 쓸모없는 / 그것에 대해 걱정해 봐야 소용없다. ⑤ endless: 끝없는 / 음악은 많은 사람에게 한없는 즐거움의 원천이 된다.

05 (1) be tired of ~: ~에 싫증이 나다 (2) remind A to 동사원형: A에게 ~할 것을 상기시키다 (3) stop 동명사: ~ 하기를 멈추다

06 (A) give a presentation: 발표를 하다 / 나는 발표하기 위해 얼마나 시간이 있는지 항상 묻는다. (B) step: 서다, (발을) 디디다 / 문 앞에 서면 문이 저절로 열립니다.

07 ② word → words / a few+복수명사(긍정), few+복수명사(부정), a little+셀 수 없는 명사(긍정), little+셀 수 없는 명사(부정)

08 'If you press the button, ~'을 분사구문으로 만든다.

09 장식되어야 하는 것이므로 수동태를 이용하고 '조동사+be+과거분사'의 형태로 쓴다.

10 민지가 피곤하게 된 것으로 수동의 의미이므로 과거분사 Tired가 되어야 한다.

11 (1) '연속동작'의 분사구문으로 쓴다. (2) 내용상 '이유'의 부사절이 적절하다. (3) 내용상 '조건'의 부사절이 적절하다.

12 (1) 조동사가 있는 문장의 수동태는 '조동사+be+과거분사'의 형태로 나타낸다. (2) 부정문의 경우 '조동사+not+be+과거분사'의 형태로 나타낸다. (3) 일반인이 주어일 경우 'by+목적격'을 생략할 수 있다. (4) 수동태로 바꿀 때 주어가 단수로 바뀌므로 'have to'를 'has to'로 써야 하는 것에 주의한다.

13 ⓑ today → today's ⓒ is appeared → appears ⓕ catching → to catch

14 ③번 다음 문장의 them에 주목한다. 주어진 문장에서 Ms. Kim이 선택한 식료품을 가리키므로 ③번이 적절하다.

15 민지의 엄마가 선택한 '이번 주 식료품'을 가리킨다.

16 주격 관계대명사와 be동사(which[that] is)가 생략되어 있다. 요즘에도 체스라고 불리는 것이므로 생략된 부분의 시제를 '현재시제'로 쓰는 것이 적절하다.

17 이 글은 '미래 사회에서 민지의 가족이 저녁 시간을 보내는 모습'을 보여주는 글이므로, 주제로는 ②번 '미래의 삶의 한 장면'이 적절하다.

18 ⓐ for breakfast: 아침식사로, ⓑ 요리 기계에 버튼이 부착되어 있는 것이므로 on이 적절하다.

19 usual 일상의, 늘 하는; 늘 먹던 것

20 민지가 옷을 고르기 위해 서랍을 여는 것이 아니라, 서랍이 열리며 오늘의 옷이 나타난다.

21 ⓐ와 ③, ⑤: 동명사, ①, ②, ④: 현재분사

22 appear는 수동태로 쓸 수 없는 자동사이므로, is appeared를 appears로 고치는 것이 적절하다.

23 '민지가 엄마에게 뭐라고 말하는지'는 대답할 수 없다. ① It shakes. ② No, she yells, "Five more minutes!", instantly: 즉시, 즉각, ③ She appears on a screen on the wall and says, "You're going to be late for school!" ⑤ She says, "Clear the windows."

교과서 파헤치기

Lesson 5

01 아무도 ~않다	02 바다	03 ~할 형편이 되다
04 재능 있는	05 지루해하는	06 구르다, 굴러가다
07 무서워하는, 겁먹은		08 걱정하는
09 신이 난, 흥분한	10 응원하다	11 연설
12 여행	13 쓰레기 매립지	
14 대부분, 일반적으로		15 나타나다
16 놀란, 놀라는	17 황홀해하는, 아주 신이 난	
18 전쟁, 전투	19 곡, 곡조, 선율	20 교육자
21 환경의	22 인내심	23 상
24 악기	25 공연	26 존경하다
27 거대한	28 볼, 뺨	29 붙이다
30 제목	31 쓰레기	32 운동, 체육관
33 무인 항공기	34 오케스트라, 관현악단	
35 응원하다	36 그때부터	37 ~를 돌보다
38 포기하다	39 ~에 참가하다	40 서로
41 큰 박수를 보내다	42 ~을 실행에 옮기다	
43 음이 맞지 않는		

01 drone	02 educator	03 performance
04 respect	05 giant	06 landfill
07 mostly	08 afford	09 appear
10 none	11 cheek	12 award
13 battle	14 violinist	15 thrilled
16 worried	17 surprised	18 talented
19 bored	20 trash	21 patience
22 stick	23 roll	24 scared
25 environmental	26 cheer	27 excited
28 speech	29 still	30 tune
31 gym class	32 journey	33 parade
34 musical instrument		35 give up
36 be known as	37 take part in	38 cheer for
39 from then on	40 one another	41 be made of
42 take care of	43 put ~ into practice	

1 talented, 재능 있는   2 afford, ~할 형편이 되다
3 thrilled, 황홀해하는, 아주 신이 난
4 step by step, 점차로, 차근차근, 하나씩
5 cheek, 볼, 뺨   6 practice, 실행, 실천
7 scared, 무서워하는, 겁먹은   8 roll, 구르다, 굴러가다
9 landfill, 쓰레기 매립지   10 trash, 쓰레기
11 award, 상   12 look forward to, ~를 기대하다, 고대하다
13 patience, 인내심   14 tune, 곡, 곡조, 선율
15 orchestra, 오케스트라, 관현악단   16 bored, 지루해하는

Listen and Speak 1 A

Welcome to, looking forward to playing, excited to, See you on

Listen and Speak 1 B

what are, reading / reading, about, named / who was born without / even won / was made into, going to watch / I'm really looking forward to watching / join / on

Listen and Speak 1 C

1. What's, on / excited, I'm going to travel / sounds / really looking forward to
2. look happy / excited, learn to fly / I'm really looking, to flying
3. look happy, going on / so excited, I'm going / looking forward to watching, performance

Listen and Speak 2 A

finish, math homework / difficult / interesting, too / help me with / I'd love to, have to take care of

Listen and Speak 2 B

going to take part in / how to play, right / I've played, for / Can you play, while / but I can't, hurt, gym class / sorry to hear / cheer for

Listen and Speak 2 C

1. going to do / want to / but I can't, have to / next time
2. are you going to / going to, join me / I'd love to, to visit / next time

Real Life Talk Watch a Video

What are you going / going to watch / it about / about a boy who became / looking forward to watching / interesting, main actor / watched, last year / want to join / but I can't, volunteer / next

Real Life Talk Step 2

1. are, going to / I'm going to watch, looking forward to watching / fun / love to, but I can't, my face

49

painted
2. going to do next / at, I'm really looking forward, playing it / Sounds / to join / I'd love to, but, longest

Listen and Speak 1 A

B: Hey, Bora. Welcome to our rock band.

G: Thanks. I'm looking forward to playing in a concert with you.

B: We're excited to have a new guitar player.

G: Yeah. See you on Friday.

Listen and Speak 1 B

G: Jiho, what are you reading?

B: I'm reading a book about baseball player named Jim Abbott.

G: Oh, the man who was born without a right hand?

B: That's right. He tried really hard and even won the MVP award.

G: Yeah. His story was made into a movie. I'm going to watch it this Saturday.

B: Really? What's the title?

G: *Our Hero*. I'm really looking forward to watching it.

B: Can I join you?

G: Sure. See you on Saturday.

Listen and Speak 1 C

1. A: You look happy today. What's going on?
   B: I'm so excited. I'm going to travel to Jeju-do.
   A: That sounds great!
   B: Yes. I'm really looking forward to riding a horse.

2. A: You look happy today. What's going on?
   B: I'm so excited. I'm going to learn to fly a drone.
   A: That sounds great!
   B: Yes. I'm really looking forward to flying a drone in the park.

3. A: You look happy today. What's going on?
   B: I'm so excited. I'm going to see Jackson's concert.
   A: That sounds great!
   B: Yes. I'm really looking forward to watching Jackson's performance.

Listen and Speak 2 A

G: Minho, did you finish the math homework?

B: Not yet. Math is difficult.

G: Yes, but it's interesting, too.

B: Then can you help me with my math homework?

G: I'd love to, but I can't. I have to take care of my brother.

Listen and Speak 2 B

G: Alex, I'm going to take part in a singing contest next Monday.

B: That's great, Sumin!

G: You know how to play the guitar, right?

B: Yes, I've played the guitar for 3 years.

G: Great. Can you play the guitar while I sing in the contest?

B: I'd love to, but I can't. I hurt my hand in gym class yesterday.

G: Oh! I'm sorry to hear that.

B: Thanks. But I'll be there to cheer for you.

Listen and Speak 2 C

1. A: What are you going to do this afternoon?
   B: I'm going to ride my bike. Do you want to join me?
   A: I'd love to, but I can't. I have to do my homework.
   B: Okay, then next time.

2. A: What are you going to do this afternoon?
   B: I'm going to play soccer. Do you want to join me?
   A: I'd love to, but I can't. I have to visit my grandparents.
   B: Okay, then next time.

Real Life Talk Watch a Video

Linda: Hi, Tony! What are you going to do this weekend?

Tony: I'm going to watch the musical, *Billy Elliot*.

Linda: *Billy Elliot*? What is it about?

Tony: It's about a boy who became a famous dancer. I'm looking forward to watching it.

Linda: Sounds interesting. Who is the main actor?

Tony: Jason Kim. He's a great dancer.

Linda: He's my favorite actor. I watched his musical last year.

Tony: Oh, really? Do you want to join me?

Linda: I'd love to, but I can't. I have volunteer work this weekend.

Tony: Okay. Maybe next time!

Real Life Talk Step 2

1. A: What are you going to do first?
   B: I'm going to watch a parade at 10:30. I'm really looking forward to watching it.
   A: Sounds fun.
   B: Do you want to join me?
   A: Yes, I'd love to. / I'd love to, but I can't. I'm

going to get my face painted at that time.

2. A: What are you going to do next?

B: I'm going to play a water balloon game at 12:30. I'm really looking forward to playing it.

A: Sounds fun.

B: Do you want to join me?

A: Yes, I'd love to. / I'd love to, but I can't. I'm going to have the longest hot dog at that time.

본문 TEST Step 1 p.11~13

01 Trash to Music

02 Tears, joy, rolling down

03 so happy, thrilled 04 were, would fly

05 look around

06 other, hugging one another

07 has, finished, giving, hand

08 None, ever expected, would

09 has been, long journey 10 name, a violinist in

11 Why is it called

12 because, made of, from

13 why, also known as

14 Most, us, are from

15 There, huge landfill, town

16 even, itself, giant landfill 17 Many, us, poor

18 weren't many hopes, dreams

19 began, change, however, met

20 an environmental educator, musician

21 teach us music, problem

22 only, few, instruments, whole

23 couldn't afford to, ones 24 didn't give up

25 with objects from, landfill

26 named, put, into practice 27 made, from, drums

28 turned, into flutes

29 had another problem

30 No, how to play 31 even, how to read

32 with great patience

33 by step, sounds, instruments

34 remember, piece, music, played

35 short, mostly out, tune

36 the most beautiful music

37 felt, new hope, hearts

38 From then on, gathered

39 One, some great news

40 were going to have

41 front, hundreds of people

42 love our music

43 sends us trash, back

본문 TEST Step 2 p.14~16

01 Trash, Music

02 Tears of joy, rolling down

03 thrilled 04 were, would fly

05 look around

06 The other members, one another

07 has just finished, giving us a big hand

08 None, ever expected 09 It has been, journey

10 I'm a violinist 11 Why is it called

12 because, are made of, from, landfill

13 That's why, known as 14 Most of, are from

15 a huge landfill 16 itself, giant landfill

17 Many of us, poor

18 many hopes and dreams

19 began to change, however

20 an environmental educator, musician

21 teach us music

22 only a few, whole town 23 couldn't afford to

24 give up

25 with objects from the landfill

26 named, was able to put, into practice

27 made, from 28 turned, into

29 another problem 30 how to play

31 how to read

32 taught, with great patience

33 Step by step

34 the first piece of music, played

35 mostly out of tune

36 the most beautiful music 37 felt a new hope

38 From then on, gathered to practice

39 some great news

40 were going to have

41 front, hundreds of people

42 our music

43 sends us trash, send back music

본문 TEST Step 3 p.17~19

1 쓰레기를 음악으로

2 기쁨의 눈물이 내 볼에 흘러내리고 있다.

3 나는 정말 기쁘고 황홀하다.

4 내가 새라면, 날아오를 텐데.

5 나는 주변을 본다.

6 우리 오케스트라의 다른 단원들은 서로 껴안고 있다.

7 우리의 공연은 이제 막 끝났고 모든 사람들이 서서 우리에게 큰 박수를 보내고 있다.

8 우리 중 아무도 이 날이 올 거라고 예상하지 못했다.

9 긴 여정이었다.

10 내 이름은 Andrea이고 나는 Recycled Orchestra의 바이올리니스트이다.

11 오케스트라가 왜 Recycled Orchestra라고 불리냐고?

12 그것은 우리의 악기들이 쓰레기 매립지에서 나온 물건들로 만들어지기 때문이다.

13 그것이 오케스트라가 Landfill Harmonic Orchestra로도 알려진 이유이다.

14 오케스트라의 우리들 대부분은 파라과이의 작은 마을인 카테우라 출신이다.

15 우리 마을에는 거대한 쓰레기 매립지가 있다.

16 몇몇 사람들은 심지어 카테우라 자체가 거대한 쓰레기 매립지라고 말한다.

17 우리들 중 많은 이들이 가난하다.

18 우리 마을에는 꿈과 희망이 많지 않았다.

19 그러나 우리가 Favio Chávez 선생님을 만났을 때 모든 것이 바뀌기 시작했다.

20 Favio 선생님은 환경 교육가이자 음악가였다.

21 그는 우리에게 음악을 가르치고 싶어 했지만, 큰 문제가 있었다.

22 온 마을에 악기가 단지 몇 개뿐이었다.

23 우리는 새 악기를 살 형편도 아니었다.

24 그러나 Favio 선생님은 포기하지 않았다.

25 그는 우리가 쓰레기 매립지의 물건들로 악기를 만들 수 있다고 말했다.

26 재능이 많은 Nicholas 아저씨가 이 생각을 실행에 옮길 수 있었다.

27 그는 기름통으로 바이올린을 만들었다.

28 그는 수도관을 플루트로 바꾸었다.

29 우리에게 또 다른 문제가 있었다.

30 아무도 악기를 연주할 줄 몰랐다.

31 우리는 심지어 악보를 읽는 방법도 알지 못했다.

32 Favio 선생님은 엄청난 인내심으로 우리를 가르쳤다.

33 점차로, 우리는 악기로 어떤 소리를 만들어 내기 시작했다.

34 나는 아직도 우리가 연주했던 첫 곡을 기억한다.

35 그 곡은 매우 짧고 대부분은 음이 맞지 않았다.

36 그러나 그것은 우리에게 가장 아름다운 곡이었다.

37 우리는 마음속에 새로운 희망을 느꼈다.

38 그때부터, 우리는 매일 연습을 하기 위해 모였다.

39 어느 날, Favio 선생님은 우리에게 엄청난 소식을 말해 줬다.

40 우리는 공연을, 진짜 공연을 하게 될 것이었다!

41 그리고 여기 우리는 지금 수백 명의 사람들 앞에 있다.

42 그들은 우리의 음악을 사랑한다.

43 세상은 우리에게 쓰레기를 보내지만, 우리는 음악을 돌려보낸다!

1 From Trash to Music

2 Tears of joy are rolling down my cheeks.

3 I'm so happy and thrilled.

4 If I were a bird, I would fly.

5 I look around.

6 The other members in my orchestra are hugging one another.

7 Our concert has just finished and everyone is standing and giving us a big hand.

8 None of us ever expected that this day would come.

9 It has been a long journey.

10 My name is Andrea and I'm a violinist in the Recycled Orchestra.

11 Why is it called the Recycled Orchestra?

12 It's because our musical instruments are made of objects from a landfill.

13 That's why it's also known as the Landfill Harmonic Orchestra.

14 Most of us in the orchestra are from Cateura, a small town in Paraguay.

15 There is a huge landfill in our town.

16 Some people even say that Cateura itself is a giant landfill.

17 Many of us are poor.

18 There weren't many hopes and dreams in our town.

19 Everything began to change, however, when we met Favio Chávez.

20 Favio was an environmental educator and a musician.

21 He wanted to teach us music, but there was a big problem.

22 There were only a few musical instruments in the whole town.

23 We couldn't afford to buy new ones.

24 But Favio didn't give up.

25 He said that we could make musical instruments with objects from the landfill.

26 A talented man named Nicholas was able to put this idea into practice.

27 He made violins from oil drums.

28 He turned water pipes into flutes.

29 We had another problem.

30 No one knew how to play musical instruments.

31 We didn't even know how to read music.

32 Favio taught us with great patience.

33 Step by step, we began to make some sounds on our instruments.

34 I still remember the first piece of music that we played.

35 It was very short and mostly out of tune.

36 But it was the most beautiful music to us.

37 We felt a new hope in our hearts.

38 From then on, we gathered to practice every day.

39 One day, Favio told us some great news.

40 We were going to have a concert, a real concert!

41 And here we are now in front of hundreds of people.

42 They love our music.

43 The world sends us trash, but we send back music!

After You Read B

1. feel

2. feel thrilled, just performed, first concert

3. Why, called

4. That's because, musical instruments are made of, from a landfill

5. amazing

6. None of, how to play musical instruments, with great patience

7. wonderful story

Think and Write

1. Dear Admiral

2. respect, because, gave up in difficult situations

3. saved, country

4. It, that, won, with only 12 ships

5. If, had, would go to meet

6. like to ask, how to make

7. my hero

8. Sincerely

Project Step 3

1. bottle shaker

2. To make, a bottle, buttons

3. Clean, put, in the bottle

4. Close, decorate it

5. can also put different things like, it

6. Different, different sounds

7. Listen to, group's bottle shaker

After You Read B

1. Reporter: Congratulations! How do you feel now?

2. Andrea: I feel thrilled. We just performed our first concert.

3. Reporter: Why is the orchestra called the Recycled Orchestra?

4. Andrea: That's because our musical instruments are made of objects from a landfill.

5. Reporter: That's amazing.

6. Andrea: Yeah. None of us knew how to play musical instruments, but Favio taught us with great patience.

7. Reporter: That is a wonderful story.

Think and Write

1. Dear Admiral Yi Sun-sin,

2. I'm Sumin. I really respect you because you never gave up in difficult situations.

3. You saved the country and the people.

4. It was amazing that you won the battle with only 12 ships.

5. If I had a time machine, I would go to meet you!

6. I'd like to ask you how to make geobukseon.

7. You're my hero. Thank you.

8. Sincerely yours, Sumin

Project Step 3

1. This is a bottle shaker.

2. To make it, you need a bottle and buttons.

3. Clean the bottle and put the buttons in the bottle.

4. Close the bottle and decorate it.

5. You can also put different things like rice or sand in it.

6. Different items make different sounds.

7. Listen to my group's bottle shaker.

단어 TEST Step 1 p.28

01 총, 전체의 02 표현 03 먹이를 주다

04 관광 명소 05 파도, 물결 06 보호하다

07 상기시키다, 생각나게 하다 08 건축가, 설계자

09 빌려주다 10 영감

11 미술품, 예술품, 예술작품 12 자세하게

13 즐거운, 기분 좋은 14 기둥

15 섬세한, 부서지기 쉬운 16 실제로, 정말로

17 아름다움 18 전시하다 19 자연적인

20 분명한, 명백한 21 (과일·채소의) 껍질

22 존재하다 23 모방하다 24 기본적인

25 거대한; 거인 26 (복수형으로) 내용물, 안에 든 것

27 곡선 모양의, 굽은 28 상상력 29 형태

30 예약하다, 예매하다

31 담아내다, 표현[포착]하다 32 영감을 주다

33 지붕 34 추천하다 35 ~하려고 노력하다

36 A에게 B를 구경시켜 주다 37 너무 ~하고 싶다!

38 ~할 만큼 충분히 39 (할인) 판매중이다

40 ~처럼 보이다 41 그런 식으로 ~하다.

42 ~에 대하여 감사하다. 43 ~해도 됩니까?

단어 TEST Step 2 p.29

01 lend 02 expression 03 artwork

04 basic 05 actually 06 exist

07 feed 08 folk village 09 architect

10 exhibit 11 recommend 12 beauty

13 delicate 14 remind 15 curved

16 imitate 17 inspiration 18 closely

19 pick 20 wet 21 stick

22 imagination 23 book 24 giant

25 wave 26 capture 27 spaceship

28 nature 29 protect 30 shape

31 obvious 32 peel 33 total

34 inspire 35 hear of ~ 36 be allowed to ~

37 enough to ~ 38 be on sale 39 That's how ~.

40 try to ~ 41 I can't wait to ~!

42 show A around B

43 Do you mind if ~?

단어 TEST Step 3 p.30

1 architect, 건축가, 설계자 2 indoors, 실내로, 실내에

3 curved, 곡선 모양의, 굽은 4 exist, 존재하다

5 book, 예약하다, 예매하다 6 delicate, 부서지기 쉬운

7 imitate, 모방하다 8 wave, 파도, 물결

9 contents, 내용물, 안에 든 것 10 spaceship, 우주선

11 imagination, 상상력 12 elect, 선출하다

13 exhibit, 전시하다 14 column, 기둥

15 pick, (꽃, 과일 등을) 꺾다 16 capture, 담아내다, 포착하다

대화문 TEST Step 1 p.31~33

Listen and Speak 1 A

for inviting me to / pleasure, glad / are / beautiful

Listen and Speak 1 B

is leaving in / hope / course / Which place, most / folk village most / the most popular place / liked walking, cool / glad to hear / for showing me around / pleasure, Have

Listen and Speak 1 C

1. Thank you for lending / welcome, pleasure

2. How / for recommending / welcome, pleasure

3. How was / for helping me make / welcome, my pleasure

Listen and Speak 2 A

You're not allowed to bring / where, put / stand outside / I'll put it

Listen and Speak 2 B

for, are on sale / Let's book, away / left / Let's get / do you mind if / says that, not allowed to bring, under / problem / add, total price is / can't wait to see

Listen and Speak 2 C

1. You're not allowed to feed / sign over there

2. not allowed to fly / check the sign

3. You're not allowed to pick / check the sign

Real Life Talk Watch a Video

Thank you for visiting, opened, Since, has exhibited, famous artworks, famous artworks, let, remind you of, take pictures of, you're not allowed to touch, let's start

Real Life Talk Step 2

1. Can I ask / Am I allowed to / You're not allowed to drink / for understanding

2. Can I ask you a question / Am I allowed to touch / You're not allowed to touch / for understanding

for helping me finish / welcome, pleasure

대화문 TEST Step 2 p.34~36

Listen and Speak 1 A

B: Hi, Lisa. Thank you for inviting me to your birthday party.

G: My pleasure. I'm glad you could come.

B: These flowers are for you. Happy birthday!

G: They are beautiful! Thank you.

Listen and Speak 1 B

B: Sumin, my train is leaving in five minutes.

G: I hope you enjoyed your trip, Daniel.

B: Of course, I did.

G: Which place did you like most in my town?

B: I liked the folk village most.

G: Yeah, it's the most popular place here.

B: I really liked walking around in hanbok. I looked really cool.

G: I'm glad to hear that.

B: Thank you for showing me around.

G: It was my pleasure. Have a safe trip.

Listen and Speak 1 C

1. A: How was the book?

   B: It was great. Thank you for lending me the book.

   A: You're welcome. It was my pleasure.

2. A: How was the movie?

   B: It was great. Thank you for recommending the movie.

   A: You're welcome. It was my pleasure.

3. A: How was your mom's birthday party?

   B: It was great. Thank you for helping me make a cake.

   A: You're welcome. It was my pleasure.

Listen and Speak 2 A

M: Excuse me. You're not allowed to bring your umbrella inside.

G: Oh, where should I put it?

M: There is an umbrella stand outside.

G: Okay, I'll put it there. Thank you.

Listen and Speak 2 B

B: The tickets for the World Music Concert are on sale now.

G: Really? Let's book the tickets online right away.

B: Okay. Let's see.... There are still tickets left for November 5th.

G: Sounds good. Let's get two student tickets.

B: Oh, do you mind if I bring my little brother?

G: Not at all. But it says that you are not allowed to bring children under 8.

B: No problem. He's 10.

G: Okay, I'll add one child ticket. The total price is 25 dollars.

B: Great.

G: I can't wait to see the concert!

Listen and Speak 2 C

1. A: Excuse me. You're not allowed to feed the birds here.

   B: I'm sorry. I didn't know that.

   A: Please check the sign over there.

   B: Okay. Thank you.

2. A: Excuse me. You're not allowed to fly a drone.

   B: I'm sorry. I didn't know that.

   A: Please check the sign over there.

   B: Okay. Thank you.

3. A: Excuse me. You're not allowed to pick flowers.

   B: I'm sorry. I didn't know that.

   A: Please check the sign over there.

   B: Okay. Thank you.

Real Life Talk Watch a Video

W: Hello, students! Thank you for visiting our art museum. This museum opened in 1995. Since then, it has exhibited many famous artworks. Today, you will see some famous artworks from the art books. Before we begin the tour, let me remind you of a basic rule. You can take pictures of the artworks, but you're not allowed to touch them. Now let's start the tour.

Real Life Talk Step 2

1. A: Excuse me. Can I ask you a question?

   B: Sure, what is it?

   A: Am I allowed to drink soda?

   B: Sorry. You're not allowed to drink soda here.

   A: Okay, I see.

   B: Thank you for understanding.

2. A: Excuse me. Can I ask you a question?

   B: Sure, what is it?

   A: Am I allowed to touch the artwork?

   B: Sorry. You're not allowed to touch the artwork here.

   A: Okay, I see.

   B: Thank you for understanding.

A: Thank you for helping me finish my project.

B: You're welcome. It was my pleasure.

본문 TEST Step 1   p.37~38

01 Nature Meets

02 heard, expression, Art imitates

03 artists, ideas, inspirations, around

04 because, natural world, place

05 shapes, pleasing to, eyes

06 For example, look, left   07 Isn't it

08 delicate, enough, protect, contents

09 imagine, looks like, egg

10 Such a, actually exists

11 has inspired, architects around

12 This, in Spain

13 one, most famous churches

14 beautiful tall columns inside

15 look like, don't they

16 famous architect, used, shape

17 how, brought, beauty, indoors

18 examples, easily, what inspired

19 example from, so obvious

20 took, shape, added, imagination

21 guess what inspired

22 waves, ocean, sailing boat

23 interestingly, inspiration came from

24 Look, roof closely   25 see, peels, orange

26 shone, peels more clearly 27 What about

28 Have, ever been to

29 looks like, giant spaceship

30 curved lines, so that

31 Thanks to, tourist attraction

32 As, capture, beauty, nature

33 perfect examples, Nature meets

34 were, would, choose, nature

본문 TEST Step 2   p.39~40

01 Nature Meets

02 Have, heard, Art imitates nature

03 ideas, inspirations, around

04 the natural world

05 pleasing to the eyes   06 For example, look at

07 Isn't it

08 strong enough to protect

09 imagine, looks like an egg

---

10 Such a building, exists

11 has inspired, architects   12 in Spain

13 one of the most famous churches

14 beautiful tall columns inside

15 look like, don't they

16 famous architect, used the shape of trees

17 how, brought, beauty, indoors

18 examples, what inspired   19 so obvious

20 architect, added his imagination

21 what inspired him

22 the waves in the ocean, a sailing boat

23 interestingly, came from   24 roof closely

25 the peels

26 are shone, peels more clearly

27 What about   28 Have, been to

29 looks like, giant spaceship

30 the curved lines, so that

31 Thanks to, popular tourist attraction

32 As, capture the beauty   33 Nature meets city

34 were, architect, would, choose

본문 TEST Step 3   p.41~42

1 자연이 도시를 만나다

2 "예술은 자연을 모방한다"라는 표현을 들어 본 적이 있는가?

3 많은 예술가들이 그들의 아이디어와 영감을 그들 주변의 세상에서 얻는다.

4 이것은 자연계가 아름다운 곳이기 때문이다.

5 자연의 형태는 눈에 보기에 매우 좋다.

6 예를 들면 왼쪽의 달걀을 봐라.

7 아름답지 않은가?

8 그것은 둥글고 부서지기 쉽지만 내용물을 보호할 만큼 충분히 튼튼하다.

9 달걀처럼 생긴 건물을 상상할 수 있는가?

10 이러한 형태의 건물이 런던에는 실제로 존재한다.

11 자연은 세계의 많은 건축가에게 영감을 주어 왔다.

12 이것은 스페인에 있는 사그라다 파밀리아 성당이다.

13 그것은 세계에서 가장 유명한 성당 중의 하나이다.

14 교회 안에 있는 아름다운 높은 기둥을 봐라.

15 기둥은 나무처럼 보인다, 그렇지 않은가?

16 유명한 건축가인 Antoni Gaudi는 사그라다 파밀리아 성당에 나무의 형태를 사용했다.

17 그것이 그가 자연의 아름다움을 실내로 가져온 방법이다.

18 앞의 두 예시에서 우리는 무엇이 건축가에게 영감을 주었는지 쉽게 알 수 있다.

19 하지만 호주의 다음 예시에서는 이것이 그다지 명확하지 않다.

20 시드니 오페라 하우스의 건축가인 Jørn Utzon은 자연에서 형태를 가져와 자신의 상상력을 더했다.

21 무엇이 그에게 영감을 주었는지 추측할 수 있는가?

22 많은 사람들은 그것이 바다의 파도나 돛단배라고 생각한다.

23 하지만 흥미롭게도, 그 영감은 오렌지에서 비롯되었다.

24 지붕을 자세히 봐라.

25 오렌지의 껍질 형태가 보이는가?

26 오렌지색 조명이 건물을 비추면, 껍질 이미지를 더 명확하게 볼 수 있다.

27 한국은 어떤가?

28 서울의 동대문 디자인 플라자에 가 본 적이 있는가?

29 많은 사람들은 이 건물이 거대한 우주선처럼 보인다고 생각한다.

30 하지만 건축가인 Zaha Hadid는 도시 사람들이 즐길 수 있도록 자연에서 곡선을 가져왔다.

31 이 특별한 디자인 덕분에, 동대문 디자인 플라자는 서울의 인기 있는 관광 명소가 되었다.

32 보는 바와 같이 많은 건물들이 디자인에 자연의 아름다움을 담아내려고 한다.

33 이 건물들은 '자연이 도시를 만나다'의 완벽한 예이다.

34 만약 당신이 건축가라면, 자연에서 무엇을 선택할 것인가?

1 Nature Meets City

2 Have you heard of the expression, "Art imitates nature"?

3 Many artists get their ideas and inspirations from the world around them.

4 This is because the natural world is a beautiful place.

5 The shapes in nature are very pleasing to the eyes.

6 For example, look at the egg on the left.

7 Isn't it beautiful?

8 It is round and delicate, yet strong enough to protect its contents.

9 Can you imagine a building that looks like an egg?

10 Such a building actually exists in London.

11 Nature has inspired many architects around the world.

12 This is the Sagrada Familia in Spain.

13 It is one of the most famous churches in the world.

14 Look at the beautiful tall columns inside the church.

15 They look like trees, don't they?

16 The famous architect, Antoni Gaudi, used the shape of trees in the Sagrada Familia.

17 That's how he brought the beauty of nature indoors.

18 In the first two examples, we can easily see what inspired the architect.

19 But in the next example from Australia, this is not so obvious.

20 Jørn Utzon, the architect of the Sydney Opera House, took a shape from nature and added his imagination.

21 Can you guess what inspired him?

22 Many people think that it is the waves in the ocean or a sailing boat.

23 But interestingly, the inspiration came from an orange.

24 Look at the roof closely.

25 Can you see the peels of an orange?

26 When orange lights are shone on the building, you can see the peels more clearly.

27 What about Korea?

28 Have you ever been to Dongdaemun Design Plaza in Seoul?

29 Many people think that the building looks like a giant spaceship.

30 But the architect, Zaha Hadid, took the curved lines from nature so that city people could enjoy them.

31 Thanks to its special design, it has become a popular tourist attraction in Seoul.

32 As you can see, many buildings try to capture the nature of nature in their design.

33 They are perfect examples of "Nature meets city."

34 If you were an architect, what would you choose from nature?

After You Read

1. Location, Architect

2. Its beautiful tall columns, like

3. brought, beauty of nature indoors

4. Australia, Architect

5. was inspired by

6. Location, Architect

7. took the curved lines from

8. a popular tourist attraction

Word Power

1. many interesting items, so, attracts
2. a popular tourist attraction
3. can't imagine, without water
4. imagination to write

Think and Write

1. go to, in
2. has a 4-story building
3. large playground, gym, small garden
4. is on top of
5. grow, vegetables, so that, can
6. favorite place, under the big tree
7. sitting, talking with
8. like, very much

구석구석지문 TEST Step 2   p.48

After You Read

1. Location: Spain / Architect: Antoni Gaudi
2. Its beautiful tall columns look like trees.
3. The architect brought the beauty of nature indoors.
4. Location: Australia / Architect: Jørn Utzon
5. The architect was inspired by an orange.
6. Location: Korea / Architect: Zaha Hadid
7. The architect took the curved lines from nature.
8. It is a popular tourist attraction in Seoul.

Word Power

1. The store has many interesting items, so it attracts many people.
2. Namsan is a popular tourist attraction in Seoul.
3. I can't imagine a world without water .
4. She used her imagination to write the story.

Think and Write

1. I go to Boram Middle School in Suwon.
2. My school has a 4-story building.
3. It also has a large playground, a gym and a small garden.
4. The garden is on top of the school building.
5. We grow some vegetables there so that we can have fresh food.
6. My favorite place is the bench under the big tree.
7. I love sitting there and talking with my friends.
8. I like my school very much.

단어 TEST Step 1   p.49

01 태양의	02 평균의, 보통의	03 피
04 발견하다, 찾아내다		05 아마
06 때려 부수다, 깨뜨리다		07 완성하다
08 경치, 풍경	09 기사	10 완전히
11 해외에, 해외로	12 (음식을) 제공하다, 차려 주다	
13 거리	14 적	15 (분류상의) 종
16 수면, 표면	17 속이다, 기만하다; 바보	
18 예측, 예보	19 문어	
20 경이, 경탄, 놀라움; 궁금하다		
21 100만; 100만의, 수많은		22 둘러싸다
23 소통하다	24 온도, 기온	25 괴물
26 조개	27 대걸레로 닦다	
28 인근의, 가까운 곳의 인근에, 가까운 곳에		29 숨을 쉬다
30 계산하다	31 발견하다	32 단단히, 꽉
33 도구	34 진공청소기로 청소하다	
35 포기하다	36 ~ 없이 지내다	37 한 줄로
38 ~로 가득 차다	39 차츰 사라지다	40 마침내, 결국
41 ~로 덮여 있다	42 이맘때는, 이맘때쯤이면	
43 ~와 다르다		

단어 TEST Step 2   p.50

01 enemy	02 fat	03 abroad
04 blood	05 surround	06 average
07 completely	08 scenery	09 discover
10 distance	11 complete	12 article
13 finally	14 forecast	15 surface
16 clam	17 guess	18 smash
19 million	20 mop	21 wonder
22 nearby	23 blow	24 fool
25 vacuum	26 tool	27 calculate
28 monster	29 octopus	30 probably
31 solar	32 temperature	33 tightly
34 breathe	35 be covered with	
36 give up	37 in the end	38 melt away
39 in a line	40 fall asleep	41 go without
42 be full of	43 be different from	

단어 TEST Step 3   p.51

1 million, 100만, 수많은   2 Arctic, 북극 (지방)
3 blow, (입으로) 불다   4 complete, 완성하다
5 breathe, 숨을 쉬다   6 smash, 때려 부수다, 깨뜨리다

7 whale, 고래　8 distance, 거리　9 surface, 수면, 표면

10 fool, 속이다, 기만하다　11 calculate, 계산하다

12 tool, 도구　13 forecast, 예측, 예보

14 octopus, 문어　15 species, (분류상의) 종

16 dive, 뛰어들다, 다이빙하다

대화문 TEST Step 1

p.52~54

Listen and Speak 1 A

almost at the top of / wonder how high / It's about, high / high mountain, keep going

Listen and Speak 1 B

at, on / look, cold / is the coldest place on / how cold it is / average, is, in, in / then, colder than / Although it's, doesn't / interesting, too

Listen and Speak 1 C

1. finally / excited, look around / wonder where / in front of, police station / Let's

2. finally here / look around / wonder where the information center / behind / right

3. Let's / I wonder where, is / next to / Let's go

Listen and Speak 2 A

so, outside / about going on a picnic / check, weather / forecast says it'll be rainy / another time

Listen and Speak 2 B

to do / go hiking, join me / Where do you want to / thinking of going / scenery, this time of / I heard that it's covered with, autumn leaves / How long, take / The Internet says it takes / on

Listen and Speak 2 C

1. What, doing / reading / anything interesting / This article says scientists have discovered

2. the newspaper / anything interesting / This article says, was seen in the East Sea

Real Life Talk Watch a Video

Check out / camels, in a line in / hot, dry / wonder how long camels can go without / out / The Internet says, without water / Camels are, interesting / travel with them

Real Life Talk Step 2

1. Where, coldest place / South Pole / I wonder how cold / says, average temperature, about / amazing

2. biggest, solar system / Jupiter / I wonder how big / The Internet says, times bigger than

3. hottest desert on / how hot it is / says, reach up to / amazing

대화문 TEST Step 2

p.55~57

Listen and Speak 1 A

B: We're almost at the top of the mountain.

G: I wonder how high this mountain is.

B: It's about 2,000m high.

G: Wow! This is a really high mountain.

B: Yes, it is. Let's keep going.

Listen and Speak 1 B

B: Look at the baby penguins on TV. They're so cute.

G: Yes, but they look very cold out there.

B: Yeah, the South Pole is the coldest place on Earth.

G: I wonder how cold it is there.

B: The average temperature is about -58℃ in July and -26℃ in December.

G: Oh, then, July is colder than December there. Interesting!

B: Yes. Although it's very cold there, it doesn't snow much.

G: That's interesting, too!

Listen and Speak 1 C

1. A: We're finally here.

   B: Yes, I'm so excited. Let's look around.

   A: I wonder where the bus stop is.

   B: It's in front of the police station.

   A: You're right. Let's go.

2. A: We're finally here.

   B: Yes, I'm so excited. Let's look around.

   A: I wonder where the information center is.

   B: It's behind the library.

   A: You're right. Let's go.

3. A: We're finally here.

   B: Yes, I'm so excited. Let's look around.

   A: I wonder where Green Park is.

   B: It's next to the school.

   A: You're right. Let's go.

Listen and Speak 2 A

B: The weather is so nice outside.

G: Yeah. How about going on a picnic this afternoon?

B: Good idea. Can you check the weather?

G: Oh, no! The weather forecast says it'll be rainy in the afternoon.

B: Let's go another time, then.

Listen and Speak 2 B

B: Sumin, what are you going to do on Sunday?

G: I'm going to go hiking. Do you want to join me?

B: I'd love to. Where do you want to go?

G: I'm thinking of going to Namsan.

B: Oh, the scenery there is so beautiful this time of year.

G: Right. I heard that it's covered with red autumn leaves now.

B: Great. How long does the shortest hiking course take?

G: The Internet says it takes about two hours.

B: Okay, see you on Sunday!

Listen and Speak 2 C

1. A: What are you doing?

B: I'm reading the newspaper.

A: Is there anything interesting?

B: This article says scientists have discovered a new planet.

2. A: What are you doing?

B: I'm reading the newspaper.

A: Is there anything interesting?

B: This article says a whale family was seen in the East Sea.

Real Life Talk Watch a Video

Suji: Check out this picture!

Tony: Wow! The camels are walking in a line in the desert.

Suji: Yeah. The desert looks very hot and dry.

Tony: I wonder how long camels can go without water in the desert.

Suji: Let's find out on the Internet.

Tony: Okay. The Internet says they can go about two weeks without water.

Suji: Wow, that's amazing! Camels are really interesting animals.

Tony: I want to travel with them in the desert someday.

Real Life Talk Step 2

1. A: Where is the coldest place on Earth?

B: I thinks it's the South Pole.

A: I wonder how cold it is.

B: The book says the average temperature of the South Pole is about -49°C.

A: That's amazing!

2. A: Which planet is the biggest in the solar system?

B: I thinks it's Jupiter.

A: I wonder how big it is.

B: The Internet says Jupiter is over 11 times bigger than Earth.

A: That's amazing!

3. A: Where is the hottest desert on Earth?

B: I thinks it's the Sahara Desert.

A: I wonder how hot it is.

B: The newspaper says the temperature of the Sahara Desert can reach up to 50°C.

A: That's amazing!

본문 TEST Step 1   p.58~59

01 Under, Sea

02 Two-thirds, planet, covered, oceans

03 full, wonder, millions, species

04 Every, learning new things

05 Let's find out, sea   06 Sweet Dreams

07 guess what, whales, doing

08 looks like, up, group   09 actually sleeping

10 stand on, tails while   11 sleep near, surface

12 Since, need, up, breathe   13 Also, fall asleep

14 wake, deep breath, into   15 Enjoy, Meal

16 smart, take, look at

17 whose, clams, tool, open

18 hide, cannot, easily discovered

19 blows, until, clam appears

20 clam, closed tightly, so   21 doesn't give up

22 smashes, against, rock

23 In, end, opens, served   24 Three, Jump

25 probably, fly down, catch   26 seen, jump out of

27 have, careful, giant, around

28 grow up to   29 let its size fool

30 fish, quick, smart

31 spot, flying, calculate, distance

32 flies nearby, jumps, catches

본문 TEST Step 2   p.60~61

01 Under, Sea

02 Two-thirds, is covered by

03 are full of, millions of species

04 new things

05 Let's find out, sea animals

06 Sweet

07 what these whales are doing

08 looks like, in a group   09 actually sleeping

10 stand on their tails while they sleep

11 near the surface

12 Since, need to come up to breathe

13 fall asleep completely

14 for a deep breath, dive back into

15 Enjoy, Meal   16 take a look at

17 whose favorite food, open

18 hide, cannot be easily discovered

19 blows, until, appears   20 is closed tightly

21 give up   22 smashes, against

23 In the end, is served   24 Jump

25 have, seen, fly down

26 have, ever seen, jump out of the water

27 have to, is around   28 up to

29 let, fool   30 quick and smart

31 spot, calculate, speed, distance

32 nearby, jumps, catches

---

27 자, 새들은 'giant trevally'가 주변에 있을 때 조심해야 한다.

28 이 물고기는 170센티미터에 80킬로그램까지 자랄 수 있다.

29 그러나 그 크기에 속지 마라.

30 이 물고기는 빠르고 똑똑하다.

31 이것은 날고 있는 새를 발견하고 그 새의 속도와 거리를 계산할 수 있다.

32 새가 근처에 날고 있을 때, 'giant trevally'는 물 밖으로 뛰어올라 새를 잡는다.

본문 TEST Step 3   p.62~63

1 바다 아래에

2 우리 행성의 3분의 2는 대양들로 덮여 있다.

3 대양들은 신기한 것으로 가득 차 있고 수많은 종의 서식지이다.

4 매일 우리는 그들에 관한 새로운 것들을 배우고 있다.

5 몇몇 흥미로운 바다 동물들을 알아보자.

6 좋은 꿈 꿔라

7 여러분은 그림 속 이 고래들이 무엇을 하고 있는지 추측할 수 있는가?

8 그들이 무리를 지어 서 있는 것처럼 보인다.

9 그러나 그들은 실제로는 잠을 자고 있다!

10 혹등고래들은 잠을 자는 동안 꼬리로 서 있다.

11 그들은 수면 근처에서 잠을 잔다.

12 그들은 물고기가 아니기 때문에 숨을 쉬기 위해 위로 나올 필요가 있다.

13 또한 그들은 완전히 잠들지 않는다.

14 그들은 잠에서 깨면 심호흡을 하러 물 밖으로 나왔다가 바다로 다시 뛰어든다.

15 맛있게 먹어라

16 만약 물고기가 똑똑하지 않다고 생각한다면 'tuskfish'를 보아라.

17 가장 좋아하는 먹이가 조개인 이 작은 물고기는 조개를 열기 위해 도구를 사용한다.

18 조개는 대개 모래 아래에 숨어 있어서 쉽게 발견할 수 없다.

19 'tuskfish'는 조개가 나타날 때까지 모래에 입김을 분다.

20 조개가 단단히 닫혀 있어서 물고기는 이것을 먹을 수 없다.

21 그러나 'tuskfish'는 포기하지 않는다.

22 'tuskfish'는 돌에 조개를 내리친다.

23 마침내 조개가 열리고 밥상이 차려진다.

24 하나, 둘, 셋, 뛰어라!

25 여러분은 아마 새가 물고기를 잡기 위해 바다로 날아 내려가는 것을 본 적이 있을 것이다.

26 그러나 물고기가 새를 잡기 위해 물 밖으로 뛰어오르는 것을 본 적이 있는가?

본문 TEST Step 4·Step 5   p.64~67

1 1 Under the Sea

2 Two-thirds of our planet is covered by oceans.

3 They are full of wonder and are home to millions of species.

4 Every day, we are learning new things about them.

5 Let's find out about some interesting sea animals.

6 Sweet Dreams

7 Can you guess what these whales are doing in the picture?

8 It looks like they are standing up in a group.

9 But they are actually sleeping!

10 Humpback whales stand on their tails while they sleep.

11 They sleep near the surface.

12 Since they are not fish, they need to come up to breathe.

13 Also, they don't fall asleep completely.

14 When they wake up, they come out of the water for a deep breath and dive back into the sea.

15 Enjoy Your Meal

16 If you think fish are not smart, take a look at the tuskfish.

17 This small fish whose favorite food is clams uses a tool to open them.

18 Clams usually hide under the sand, so they cannot be easily discovered.

19 The tuskfish blows on the sand until a clam appears.

20 The clam is closed tightly, so the fish cannot eat it.

21 But the tuskfish doesn't give up.

22 It smashes the clam against a rock.

23 In the end, the clam opens and dinner is served.

24 One, Two, Three, Jump!

25 You have probably seen a bird fly down to the sea to catch a fish.

26 But have you ever seen a fish jump out of the water to catch a bird?

27 Well, birds have to be careful when a giant trevally is around.

28 This fish can grow up to 170cm and 80kg.

29 But don't let its size fool you.

30 This fish is quick and smart.

31 It can spot a flying bird and calculate its speed and distance.

32 When the bird flies nearby, the giant trevally jumps out of the water and catches it.

구석구석지문 TEST Step 1
p.68

After You Read A. Read and Correct

1. learned about oceans
2. Two-thirds, is covered by
3. millions of species
4. There are many interesting facts
5. For example, stand on their tails while, near the surface

Word Power

1. good spot to park
2. spot, in the audience
3. Don't be fooled by
4. makes, fool wise

Think and Write

1. Fun Animal
2. will introduce, whale
3. the Arctic Ocean, a round head
4. usually eats, clams
5. An interesting fact, that, white all over
6. That's why, call it, white whale
7. When, is born, gray
8. grows up, becomes white
9. with my own eyes

구석구석지문 TEST Step 2
p.69

After You Read A. Read and Correct

1. I learned about oceans today.
2. Two-thirds of our planet is covered by oceans.
3. They are home to millions of species.
4. There are many interesting facts about sea animals.
5. For example, humpback whales stand on their tails while they sleep, and they sleep near the surface.

Word Power

1. He found a good spot to park the car.
2. I can spot you in the audience.
3. Don't be fooled by his cute looks.
4. Experience makes even fool wise.

Think and Write

1. My Fun Animal: Beluga whale
2. I will introduce the beluga whale.
3. It lives in the Arctic Ocean. It has a round head.
4. It usually eats fish and clams.
5. An interesting fact about the beluga whale is that it is white all over.
6. That's why people call it the white whale.
7. When it is born, it is gray.
8. But when it grows up, its body becomes white!
9. I want to see this animal with my own eyes!

단어 TEST Step 1　　　　　　　　　　p.70

01 보호하다, 지키다　02 활동적인, 적극적인

03 기여하다, 공헌하다　　　　04 상인

05 ~하기로 되어 있는, 예정된

06 믿을 수 없는, 믿기 어려운　　07 실수, 잘못

08 다이너마이트　09 잘못　　10 졸업하다

11 (신문 기사 등의) 표제　　　12 고맙게 생각하다

13 기술하다, 묘사하다　　　　14 기사

15 심장 마비　　16 ~을 포함해서　17 후회; 후회하다

18 졸업(식)　19 습관　　20 발명품

21 사실　　22 발명가　　23 충격을 받은

23 의견　　24 실망한, 낙담한　25 원래, 처음에는

26 참가하다　27 관객　　28 보통의, 정상적인

29 상, 시상　30 완벽한

31 쏟아지다, 흐르다, 쏟다　　32 실수로

33 복통　　34 포기하다　　35 미루다, 연기하다

36 A를 B라고 생각하다　　　　37 눈을 떼다

38 숨을 고르다　39 ~보다는　40 연락하고 지내다

41 ~에 참가하다　42 A를 B로 기술하다, 묘사하다

단어 TEST Step 2　　　　　　　　　　p.71

01 normal　　02 opinion　　03 actually

04 describe　05 fault　　　06 graduate

07 appreciate　08 including　09 perfect

10 shocked　11 protect　　12 move

13 audience　14 merchant　15 regret

16 disappointed　17 mistake　18 habit

19 award　　20 mistakenly　21 spill

22 due　　　23 originally　24 contribute

25 deeply　26 invention　27 article

28 headline　29 stomachache　30 heart attack

31 unbelievable　32 dynamite　33 graduation

34 trust　　35 be late for　36 in surprise

37 put off　38 take part in　39 rather than

40 give up　41 stay up　　42 keep in touch

43 think of A as B

단어 TEST Step 3　　　　　　　　　　p.72

1 dynamite, 다이너마이트　2 spill, 쏟아지다, 흐르다, 쏟다

3 appreciate, 고맙게 생각하다

4 describe, 기술하다, 묘사하다　5 regret, 후회하다

6 score, 득점하다　7 invention, 발명품

8 contribute, 기여하다, 공헌하다　9 merchant, 상인

10 due, ~하기로 되어 있는, 예정된　11 graduation, 졸업(식)

12 unbelievable, 믿을 수 없는, 믿기 어려운

13 audience, 관객　14 headline, (신문 기사 등의) 표제

15 move, 감동시키다　16 report, 보도하다

대화문 TEST Step 1　　　　　　　　　　p.73~75

Listen and Speak 1 A

were you late for / stomachache / Are, okay / should have eaten less

Listen and Speak 1 B

up, tired / stayed up late / play, again / not, had to finish / due / shouldn't have put it off until, last moment / the same / try to change, habits

Listen and Speak 1 C

1. wrong / got caught in / sorry to hear / have taken

2. What's / failed / hear that / should have studied hard

3. wrong / lost / to hear / I should have chained

4. was late for / sorry to hear that / should have got up early

Listen and Speak 2 A

going to do during / lots of, What about / planning to visit / hope you have

Listen and Speak 2 B

ready for / I'm thinking of giving up / thought, wanted to take part in / good singer / the best singer I know / think so / course, voice / you for saying, do my best / I hope you win

Listen and Speak 2 C

1. are, going to / going to sing / hope you move, audience / hope so

2. going to play / hope you score a goal / too

3. participate in, speech contest / I hope you win / I hope so

Real Life Talk Watch a Video

reading / graduation messages / looks like, a lot to say / wrote that, smile / else / Some of them, hang out enough with / fault, busy / should have spent more time with / after graduation / right / hope you keep in touch with, after graduation / I hope so

Real Life Talk Step 2

1. can't believe, graduating / there anything, regret / should have been active in classes / have a second chance / guess / hope you are active

2. believe we're graduating / anything you regret about / should have taken part in / second chance / guess, right / hope you take part in

Listen and Speak 1 A

G: Mike, why were you late for class?

B: I had a bad stomachache.

G: Oh, no! Are you okay now?

B: Yeah. I should have eaten less last night.

Listen and Speak 1 B

G: Jiho, what's up? You look tired.

B: Yeah. I stayed up late last night.

G: Did you play computer games again?

B: No, not this time. I had to finish my history project.

G: Is it due today?

B: Yeah. I shouldn't have put it off until the last moment.

G: Hmm, I understand. I often have the same problem.

B: Really? Well, let's try to change our bad habits.

Listen and Speak 1 C

1. A: What's wrong?

    B: I got caught in the rain.

    A: Oh, I'm sorry to hear that.

    B: I should have taken an umbrella.

2. A: What's wrong?

    B: I failed the test.

    A: Oh, I'm sorry to hear that.

    B: I should have studied hard.

3. A: What's wrong?

    B: I lost my bike.

    A: Oh, I'm sorry to hear that.

    B: I should have chained it.

4. A: What's wrong?

    B: I was late for school.

    A: Oh, I'm sorry to hear that.

    B: I should have got up early.

Listen and Speak 2 A

G: Jinsu, what are you going to do during the vacation?

B: I'm going to read lots of books. What about you?

G: I'm planning to visit my grandparents in Busan.

B: Sounds great. I hope you have a wonderful vacation.

Listen and Speak 2 B

G: Jaemin, are you ready for the singing contest?

B: Well, I'm thinking of giving up, Tina.

G: Why? I thought you really wanted to take part in the contest.

B: I don't think I'm a good singer.

G: Come on. You're the best singer I know.

B: Do you really think so?

G: Of course. You have a really nice voice.

B: Thank you for saying so, I'll do my best.

B: I hope you win the contest.

Listen and Speak 2 C

1. A: What are you going to do tomorrow?

    B: I'm going to sing in the school festival.

    A: Great! I hope you move the audience.

    B: Thanks. I hope so, too.

2. A: What are you going to do tomorrow?

    B: I'm going to play soccer.

    A: Great! I hope you score a goal.

    B: Thanks. I hope so, too.

3. A: What are you going to do tomorrow?

    B: I'm going to participate in the speech contest.

    A: Great! I hope you win the contest.

    B: Thanks. I hope so, too.

Real Life Talk Watch a Video

Minho: Linda, what are you reading?

Linda: I'm reading graduation messages from my classmates.

Minho: Oh, it looks like they had a lot to say to you.

Linda: Many of them wrote that they like my smile.

Minho: That's nice. What else?

Linda: Some of them said I didn't hang out enough with them.

Minho: That's not your fault. You were always busy.

Linda: Yeah, but I should have spent more time with my classmates.

Minho: You still have time after graduation.

Linda: You're right.

Minho: I hope you keep in touch with your classmates after graduation.

Linda: Thanks. I hope so, too.

Real Life Talk Step 2

1. A: I can't believe we're graduating soon.

    B: Yeah. Is there anything you regret about your middle school life?

    A: Yes. I should have been active in classes.

    B: Well, you have a second chance in high school.

    A: I guess you're right.

B: I hope you are active in classes in high school.

2. A: I can't believe we're graduating soon.

B: Yeah. Is there anything you regret about your middle school life?

A: Yes. I should have taken part in many school events.

B: Well, you have a second chance in high school.

A: I guess you're right.

B: I hope you take part in many school events in high school.

01 How, Be Remembered   02 just, normal morning

03 sat in, chair to

04 While, headline caught, eye

05 What, this

06 article, dropped, in surprise

07 spilled, over, take, off

08 article, his own death

09 died, from, heart attack   10 my goodness, dead

11 Catching, breath, kept reading

12 even more shocked

13 described, as, inventor, other

14 become rich, deaths, others

15 couldn't believe, eyes

16 true, one of, inventions

17 imagined, think of, as

18 was deeply disappointed   19 How could, be

20 This, unbelievable   21 merchant of death

22 remembered in, different way

23 be remembered, world better

24 to change people's opinions

25 newspaper mistakenly reported, death

26 who had actually died

27 Thanks to, however, contribute

28 decided, use, to create

29 Originally, only five awards

30 sixth award, added

31 think, rather than dynamite

01 How, Be Remembered   02 just, normal morning

03 sat in his chair to read

04 While, headline caught his eye

05 What   06 Reading, in surprise

07 spilled, take his eyes off

08 about his own death

09 had died, from a heart attack

10 my goodness

11 Catching his breath, kept reading

12 even more shocked

13 described, as, other dangerous objects

14 had become rich, deaths of others

15 couldn't believe

16 It, that, one of his many inventions

17 think of, as, merchant of death

18 deeply disappointed   19 How, be

20 unbelievable   21 merchant of death

22 in a different way

23 be remembered as, the world better

24 to change people's opinions

25 mistakenly reported

26 who had actually died

27 Thanks to, decided to, contribute to

28 to create

29 Originally, only five awards

30 sixth award, added

31 think of, rather than

1 당신은 어떻게 기억될까요?

2 그저 평범한 아침이었다.

3 Alfred Nobel은 신문을 읽기 위해 의자에 앉았다.

4 커피를 마시는 동안 한 기사 제목이 그의 눈길을 끌었다. "죽음의 상인, Alfred Nobel 사망하다"

5 "뭐라고? 이게 뭐지?"

6 기사를 읽으며 그는 놀라서 컵을 떨어뜨렸다.

7 커피가 그의 옷과 책상 온 곳에 쏟아졌지만 그는 신문에서 눈을 뗄 수 없었다.

8 기사는 그 자신의 죽음에 관한 것이었다!

9 기사에는 Nobel이 심장 마비로 프랑스에서 죽었다고 쓰여 있었다.

10 "오, 이럴 수가! 내가 죽었다고?"

11 숨을 고른 후, Nobel은 계속 읽었다.

12 곧, 그는 훨씬 더 충격을 받게 되었다.

13 기사는 그를 전쟁에 쓰이는 다이너마이트와 다른 위험한 물건의 발명가로 기술했다.

14 기사에는 그가 다른 사람들의 죽음으로 인해 부유해졌다고 쓰여 있었다.

15 그는 자신의 눈을 믿을 수 없었다.

16 다이너마이트가 그의 많은 발명품 중 하나인 것은 사실이었다.

17 하지만 그는 세상이 그를 '죽음의 상인'으로 생각할 거라고는 결코 상상하지 못했다.

18 Nobel은 몹시 실망했다.

19 "어떻게 이럴 수가 있지?

20 이건 믿을 수 없어!

21 나는 죽음의 상인이 아니야.

22 나는 다르게 기억되고 싶어.

23 나는 세상을 더 좋게 만든 사람으로 기억되고 싶어."

24 그는 자신에 대한 사람들의 견해를 바꾸기로 결심했다.

25 1888년에, 한 프랑스 신문에서 실수로 Alfred Nobel의 죽음을 보도했다.

26 실제로 죽은 사람은 Alfred Nobel의 형인 Ludvig였다.

27 하지만 그 보도 덕분에, Nobel은 세상에 공헌하기 위해 무언가를 하기로 결심했다.

28 1895년에, 그는 자신의 돈을 노벨상을 만드는 데 사용하기로 결정했다.

29 원래 다섯 종류의 상만 있었다.

30 여섯 번째 상은 1968년에 추가되었다.

31 오늘날 우리가 Alfred Nobel을 생각할 때, 우리는 다이너마이트보다는 노벨상을 떠올린다.

본문 TEST Step 4 - Step 5   p.85~88

1 How Will You Be Remembered?

2 It was just a normal morning.

3 Alfred Nobel sat in his chair to read the newspaper.

4 While he was drinking his coffee, a headline caught his eye: *The Merchant of Death, Alfred Nobel, Is Dead.*

5 "What? What is this?"

6 Reading the article, he dropped his cup in surprise.

7 His coffee spilled all over his clothes and desk, but he couldn't take his eyes off the newspaper.

8 The article was about his own death!

9 It said Nobel had died in France from a heart attack.

10 "Oh my goodness! Am I dead?"

11 Catching his breath, Nobel kept reading.

12 Soon, he became even more shocked.

13 The article described him as the inventor of dynamite and other dangerous objects for war.

14 It said that he had become rich from the deaths of others.

15 He couldn't believe his eyes.

---

16 It was true that dynamite was one of his many inventions.

17 But he never imagined that the world would think of him as "the merchant of death."

18 Nobel was deeply disappointed.

19 "How could this be?

20 This is unbelievable!

21 I'm not a merchant of death.

22 I want to be remembered in a different way.

23 I want to be remembered as a person who made the world better."

24 He decided to change people's opinions about him.

25 In 1888, a French newspaper mistakenly reported Alfred Nobel's death.

26 The person who had actually died was his brother, Ludvig.

27 Thanks to the report, however, Nobel decided to do something to contribute to the world.

28 In 1895, he decided to use his money to create the Nobel Prize.

29 Originally, there were only five awards.

30 A sixth award was added in 1968.

31 Today, when we think of Alfred Nobel, we think of the Nobel Prize, rather than dynamite.

구석구석지문 TEST Step 1   p.89

After You Read A. Read and Correct

1. APRIL
2. The Merchant of Death, Dead
3. died, in, from a heart attack
4. invented dynamite, other dangerous objects
5. became rich, the deaths of others
6. is responsible for, thousands of people
7. remember, as, the merchant of death

Word Power

1. invented special shoes for
2. over, inventions, his life
3. the inventor, the plane

Think and Write Step 2

1. Looking back, that, donated, to children
2. because, to make a difference, in need
3. To save, for a month
4. donated the money to
5. left food on my plate
6. really appreciate my meals
7. proud of myself

After You Read A. Read and Correct

1. WORLD NEWS / APRIL 13, 1888
2. The Merchant of Death, Alfred Nobel, Is Dead
3. Alfred Nobel died yesterday in France from a heart attack.
4. He invented dynamite and other dangerous objects for war.
5. He became rich from the deaths of others.
6. He is responsible for the deaths of thousands of people.
7. The world will remember him as "the merchant of death."

Word Power

1. Tim invented special shoes for the beach.
2. Thomas Edison made over 1,000 inventions in his life.
3. Who is the inventor of the plane?

Think and Write Step 2

1. Looking back this year, I'm glad that I donated money to children in Africa.
2. I did this because I wanted to make a difference for children in need.
3. To save money, I didn't buy snacks for a month.
4. I donated the money to UNICEF.
5. Before I donated, I sometimes left food on my plate.
6. Now I really appreciate my meals.
7. I'm proud of myself.

Lesson S

01 해결책
02 ~ 후에
03 맑게[투명하게] 하다; 투명한, 맑은
04 건강 상태
05 내려앉다, 착륙하다; 육지, 땅
06 나타나다
07 선택하다
08 욕실
09 누르다
10 특별한
11 밝게
12 문지르다, 비비다
13 정밀 검사[촬영]하다
14 일상의, 늘 하는; 늘 먹던 것
15 샤워실, 샤워
16 속삭이다
17 센서, 감지기
18 빛나다, 비추다
19 미래
20 식료품 및 잡화
21 편안한, 안락한
22 흔들리다, 흔들다
23 서랍
24 (건물의) 층
25 소리치다, 외치다
26 운전자가 필요 없는
27 ~함으로써
28 ~에 발을 디디다
29 ~인 것처럼 느끼다
30 ~에 싫증이 나다
31 돌아오다
32 ~하기를 멈추다
33 A에게 ~할 것을 상기시키다
34 발표를 하다
35 ~의 꼭대기에
36 ~의 값을 지불하다
37 (프린트로) 출력하다
38 A를 B에게 보내다
39 ~ 덕분에
40 ~할 필요가 없다

01 shine
02 appear
03 story
04 usual
05 bathroom
06 clear
07 special
08 future
09 grocery
10 health condition
11 sensor
12 land
13 press
14 after
15 rub
16 shake
17 driverless
18 scan
19 brightly
20 select
21 drawer
22 shower
23 whisper
24 yell
25 comfortable
26 solution
27 step in
28 feel like
29 come back
30 be tired of ~
31 pay for
32 by -ing
33 on top of
34 don't have to 동사원형
35 stop -ing
36 give a presentation
37 print out
38 thanks to ~
39 remind A to 동사원형
40 send A to B

1 story, (건물의) 층   2 shine, 빛나다, 비추다
3 land, 착륙하다   4 select, 선택하다   5 bathroom, 욕실
6 comfortable, 편안한   7 grocery, 식료품 및 잡화

8 appear, 나타나다　9 press, 누르다

10 whisper, 속삭이다　11 select, 선택하다

12 sensor, 센서, 감지기　13 yell, 소리치다, 외치다

14 drawer, 서랍　15 rub, 문지르다, 비비다

16 shake, 흔들다

01 Picture, Future　02 It's, a.m.

03 shakes, yells, minutes　04 stops shaking

05 Suddenly, appears, going, late

06 rubs, eyes, says, Clear

07 become, shines brightly, through

08 light scans, body

09 voice, health condition, excellent

10 steps, out, top, sides

11 warm, comes out, dries

12 gets out, with, clothes

13 kitchen, says, for breakfast

14 says, usual

15 presses, few, cooking machine

16 machine prints out　17 says, rushes out

18 later, appears, shouts, forgot

19 smiles, answers, problem, send

20 says, Thanks, million

21 get into, driverless flying

22 sit in comfortable, around

23 touches, select, groceries for

24 pays, by putting, sensor　25 will be delivered to

26 lands, on top, story

27 give, presentation with, in　28 doesn't have to go

29 Thanks to, like, same

30 When, comes back, ready　31 talk about, day

32 delicious, clears, washes, dishes

33 learned, called chess, play　34 Everyone agrees

35 3-D, board appears on　36 lots of fun

37 Right before, whispers, watch

38 Remind, to take, glasses

01 Picture, Future　02 It's

03 shakes, yells, Five more minutes

04 stops shaking　05 appears, be late for

06 rubs her eyes, Clear

07 become clear, shines brightly

08 scans Minji's body

09 voice, health condition

10 steps in, comes out from, top, sides

11 comes out, dries

12 gets out, with today's clothes

13 for breakfast　14 The usual

15 presses a few, on　16 prints out

17 rushes out

18 A few minutes later, forgot

19 send a drone to　20 a million

21 driverless flying car

22 in comfortable chairs around

23 to select, groceries

24 pays for, by putting, on a sensor

25 will be delivered　26 lands, 150-story

27 give a presentation with　28 doesn't have to

29 Thanks to, feel like, same classroom

30 comes back, is ready　31 talk about

32 delicious dinner, washes the dishes

33 called chess, to play　34 agrees

35 3-D chess board appears　36 lots of fun

37 whispers to　38 Remind, to take

1 미래를 상상하다

2 오전 7시이다.

3 침대가 흔들리고 김민지가 "5분만 더!"라고 소리를 지른다.

4 침대가 흔들기를 멈춘다.

5 갑자기, 민지의 엄마가 벽 스크린에 나타나 말한다. "학교에 늦겠구나!"

6 민지는 눈을 비비며 "창문을 투명하게 해 줘."라고 말한다.

7 어두운 창문이 투명해지며 창문으로 햇살이 밝게 비춘다.

8 욕실에서 빨간 빛이 민지의 몸을 정밀 검사한다.

9 목소리가 "54킬로그램. 건강 상태가 매우 좋습니다."라고 말한다.

10 그녀가 샤워실 안에 발을 디디자, 물이 위와 양측에서 나온다.

11 샤워 후에, 따뜻한 공기가 나와 그녀를 말린다.

12 그녀가 나가자, 서랍이 열리며 오늘의 옷이 나타난다.

13 부엌에서 민지의 아빠가 "좋은 아침이구나, 얘야. 아침으로 무엇을 먹고 싶니?"라고 말한다.

14 민지는 "늘 먹던 걸로 주세요."라고 말한다.

15 아빠가 요리 기계의 버튼 몇 개를 누른다.

16 기계는 베이컨, 달걀, 빵을 만들어 낸다.

17 아빠는 작별 인사를 하고 문 밖으로 급히 나간다.

18 몇 분 후에, 민지의 아빠가 스크린에 나타나 소리친다. " 안경을 깜빡했어요!"

19 민지의 엄마가 미소 지으며 답한다. "괜찮아요. 드론을 당신의 사무실로 보낼게요."

20 민지의 아빠가 "정말 고마워요!"라고 말한다.

21 민지의 엄마와 민지는 운전자가 필요 없는 비행 자동차에 탄다.

22 두 사람은 탁자 주변의 편안한 의자에 앉는다.

23 민지의 엄마가 이번 주 식료품을 선택하기 위해 자동차 창문을 터치한다.

24 그녀는 센서에 손가락을 대서 식료품 값을 지불한다.

25 식료품은 집으로 배달될 것이다.

26 자동차는 150층 빌딩의 꼭대기에 있는 민지의 학교에 내린다.

27 오늘 민지는 미국에 있는 학생 Dona와 함께 발표를 할 것이다.

28 하지만 민지가 미국에 갈 필요는 없다.

29 VR(가상 현실) 교실 덕분에, 그들은 같은 교실에 있는 것처럼 느낄 것이다.

30 민지의 가족이 집에 돌아오자 저녁이 준비된다.

31 그들은 식사를 하며 그 날에 관해 이야기한다.

32 맛있는 저녁 식사 후에, 청소 로봇이 식탁을 치우고 설거지를 한다.

33 민지가 "오늘 체스라고 불리는 놀이를 배웠어요. 해 보실래요?"라고 말한다.

34 모두가 동의한다.

35 탁자 위에 삼차원 체스판이 나타난다.

36 그들은 아주 즐거운 시간을 보낸다.

37 민지는 자러 가기 직전에, 자신의 손목시계에 속삭인다.

38 "아빠께 내일 안경을 가져가시라고 상기시켜 드려."

1 Picture the Future

2 It's 7 a.m.

3 The bed shakes and Minji Kim yells, "Five more minutes!"

4 The bed stops shaking.

5 Suddenly, Minji's mom appears on a screen on the wall and says, "You're going to be late for school!"

6 Minji rubs her eyes and says, "Clear the windows."

7 The dark windows become clear and the sun shines brightly through them.

8 In the bathroom, a red light scans Minji's body.

9 A voice says, "54 kilograms. Your health condition is excellent."

10 When she steps in the shower, water comes out from the top and sides.

11 After her shower, warm air comes out and dries her.

12 When she gets out, a drawer opens with today's clothes.

13 In the kitchen, her father says, "Good morning, Honey. What do you want for breakfast?"

14 Minji says, "The usual, please."

15 Mr. Kim presses a few buttons on the cooking machine.

16 The machine prints out some bacon, eggs and bread.

17 Mr. Kim says goodbye and rushes out the door.

18 A few minutes later, Minji's father appears on a screen and shouts, "I forgot my glasses!"

19 Ms. Kim smiles and answers, "No problem. I'll send a drone to your office."

20 Mr. Kim says, "Thanks a million!"

21 Ms. Kim and Minji get into a driverless flying car.

22 They sit in comfortable chairs around a table.

23 Ms. Kim touches the car window to select the groceries for this week.

24 She pays for them by putting her finger on a sensor.

25 They will be delivered to her house.

26 The car lands at Minji's school on top of a 150-story building.

27 Today Minji will give a presentation with Dona, a student in America.

28 But Minji doesn't have to go to America.

29 Thanks to a VR classroom, they will feel like they are in the same classroom.

30 When Minji's family comes back home, dinner is ready.

31 They eat and talk about their day.

32 After a delicious dinner, the cleaning robot clears the table and washes the dishes.

33 Minji says, "I learned a game called chess today. Do you want to play?"

34 Everyone agrees.

35 A 3-D chess board appears on the table.

36 They have lots of fun.

37 Right before Minji goes to bed, she whispers to her watch.

38 "Remind Daddy to take his glasses tomorrow."

MEMO

MEMO

2학기 전과정

적중100 plus

영어 기출 문제집

정답 및 해설

동아 | 이병민

적중 1◌◌ + 특별부록

Plan B

우리학교
최신기출

동아 · 이병민 교과서를 배우는

학교 시험문제 분석 · 모음 · 해설집

전국단위 학교 시험문제 수집 및 분석
출제 빈도가 높은 문제 위주로 선별
문제 풀이에 필요한 상세한 해설

중3-2
영어

동아 · 이병민

적중 **1OO** + 특별부록

Plan B

우리학교
최신기출

중3-2
영어

동아 · 이병민

◎ 선택형 문항의 답안은 컴퓨터용 수정 싸인펜을 사용하여 OMR 답안지에 바르게 표기하시오.
◎ 서술형 문제는 답을 답안지에 반드시 검정 볼펜으로 쓰시오.
◎ 총 29문항 100점 만점입니다. 문항별 배점은 각 문항에 표시되어 있습니다.

[충북 ○○중]

01 다음 중 밑줄 친 단어의 쓰임이 <u>어색한</u> 것은?　　(2점)

① He is <u>worried</u> about his mom in the hospital.
② The TV program was very <u>bored</u>, so she turned it off.
③ He was even <u>scared</u> of walking home in the dark.
④ They were <u>surprised</u> to watch the news during the night.
⑤ Mr. Jackson was so <u>thrilled</u> while riding a roller coaster on Sunday.

[충북 ○○중]

02 다음 우리말을 주어진 〈조건〉에 맞게 영어로 쓰시오.　　(4점)

내가 너라면 그에게 사탕을 줄 텐데.

조건
1. 가정법을 사용할 것.
2. I, you, give, sweets를 포함할 것.
3. 전체 문장을 9단어를 사용해서 쓸 것.

→ _____

[경북 ○○중]

03 다음 빈칸에 들어갈 전치사가 차례대로 바르게 연결된 것은?　　(4점)

■ They looked _____ this place in detail.
(= 그들은 이 장소를 자세히 조사했다.)
■ She is looking _____ English words in the dictionary.
(= 그녀는 사전에서 영어 단어를 찾는 중이다.)
■ What are you looking _____, sir?
(= 무엇을 찾는 중이신가요, 손님?)
■ My mom told me to look _____ my brother all day long.
(= 엄마는 나에게 하루종일 나의 남동생을 돌보라고 말씀하셨다.)
■ He looks _____ his English teacher very much.
(= 그는 그의 영어 선생님을 매우 존경한다.)
■ Look _____ the sky over the window.
(= 창 너머의 하늘을 보아라.)
■ The clouds in the sky look _____ cotton candy.
(= 하늘의 구름이 솜사탕처럼 보인다.)

① at – into – like – after – up – up to – like
② into – up – like – for – after – up to – at
③ at – into – for – after – like – up to – up
④ for – up – like – at – after – up to – into
⑤ into – up – for – after – up to – at – like

[경기 ○○중]

04 다음 중 가정법과거 문장으로 옳은 것은?　　(3점)

① If I were a king, I would gave people presents.
② If he studies hard, he could pass the exam.
③ If it snowed a lot, I will ski in the mountain.
④ If I had a better camera, I could take better pictures.
⑤ If I be Superman, I could save many people in danger.

05 다음 문장에서 어법상 <u>어색한</u> 부분을 찾아서 한 단어만 고쳐 쓰시오. (4점)

(1) Can you teach me what to use the copy machine?

_____ → _____

(2) If the weather were nice, we will go outside.

_____ → _____

[7~8] 다음 대화를 읽고 물음에 답하시오.

A: Jiho, what are you reading?
B: I'm reading a book about a baseball player named Jim Abbott.
A: Oh, was he born without a right hand, wasn't he?
B: That's right. He tried really hard and even won the MVP award.
A: Yeah. His story was made into a movie. I'm going to watch it this Saturday.
B: Really? What's the title?
A: *Our Hero*. I'm really looking forward to ⓐ <u>watch</u> it.
B: Can I join you?
A: Sure. See you on Saturday.

07 위 대화의 밑줄 친 ⓐwatch의 알맞은 형태는? (3점)

① watch
② watched
③ watching
④ have watched
⑤ be watched

06 다음 중 짝지어진 대화가 <u>어색한</u> 것은? (3점)

① A: You're not allowed to take picture here.
  B: Sorry, I didn't know that.

② A: You're not allowed to bring your umbrella inside.
  B: Oh, where should I put it?

③ A: Can you play the guitar while I sing in the contest?
  B: I'd love to, but I can't. I've played the guitar for 3 years.

④ A: Thank you for helping me make a cake.
  B: It was my pleasure.

⑤ A: Are you going to travel to Jeju-do?
  B: Yes, I'm really looking forward to riding a horse.

08 위 대화의 내용과 일치하지 <u>않는</u> 것은? (3점)

① Jiho는 어떤 야구 선수에 관한 책을 읽고 있다.
② 그 야구 선수의 이름은 Jim Abbott이다.
③ Jim은 열심히 노력하여 MVP상을 받았다.
④ Jim의 이야기가 영화로 만들어질 예정이다.
⑤ 대화를 나누는 두 사람은 Our Hero를 함께 보러 가기로 했다.

09 다음 대화의 빈칸에 알맞은 표현을 주어진 단어들을 활용해서 쓰시오. (4점)

> A: You look happy today. What's up?
> B: I'm so excited. I'm going to travel to Jeju-do.
> A: That sounds good.
> B: Yes, I'm really _____.
> (look, forward, a horse)
> (나는 말을 타기를 학수고대하고 있어.)

→ _____

10 다음 (A), (B), (C)에 들어갈 의문사끼리 알맞게 짝지어진 것은? (4점)

> Sujin: Let's get ready for the party.
> Brian: Okay. Please tell me (A)_____ to stick the balloons.
> Sujin: Stick them on the door. I don't know (B)_____ to bring the birthday cake in.
> Brian: Bring it in when the lights are turned off.
> Sujin: Okay. I'm going to make some spaghetti. Do you know (C)_____ to cook spaghetti?
> Brian: Of course. You should boil water first.

	(A)	(B)	(C)
①	how	where	how
②	when	where	how
③	where	when	how
④	where	how	when
⑤	when	how	where

11 다음 두 문장의 의미가 같도록 할 때 빈칸에 알맞은 말이 순서 대로 짝지어진 것은? (3점)

> ■ As I am busy, I can't visit my parents.
> → If I _____ busy, I _____ my parents.

① am – can't visit
② am not – can visit
③ were – couldn't visit
④ were not – can visit
⑤ were not – could visit

12 다음 대화의 흐름에 맞게 ⓐ~ⓓ를 알맞은 순서로 묶은 것은? (3점)

> A: I'm going to take part in a singing contest next Monday.
> B: That's great!
>
> ⓐ I'd love to, but I can't. I hurt my hand in gym class yesterday.
> ⓑ Great. Can you play the guitar while I sing in the contest?
> ⓒ Yes, I've played the guitar for 3 years.
> ⓓ You know how to play the guitar, right?
>
> A: Oh, I'm sorry to hear that.
> B: Thanks. But I'll be there to cheer for you.

① ⓐ-ⓑ-ⓒ-ⓓ
② ⓒ-ⓐ-ⓓ-ⓑ
③ ⓒ-ⓓ-ⓐ-ⓑ
④ ⓓ-ⓒ-ⓐ-ⓑ
⑤ ⓓ-ⓒ-ⓑ-ⓐ

Linda: Tony! What are you going to do this weekend?

Tony: Hi, Linda. ⓐI'm going to watch the musical, *Billy Elliot*.

Linda: *Billy Elliot*? ⓑWhat is it about?

Tony: ⓒIt's about a boy who became a famous dancer. ⓓI'm look forward to watch it.

Linda: Sounds interesting. Who is the main actor?

Tony: Jason Kim. He's a great dancer.

Linda: He's my favorite actor. I watched his musical last year.

Tony: Oh, really? Do you want to join me?

Linda: I'd love to, but I can't. I have volunteer work this weekend.

Tony: Okay. Maybe next time!

[충북 ○○중]

13 위 대화의 ⓐ~ⓓ 중 어법상 <u>어색한</u> 문장을 하나 찾아, 올바르게 쓰시오. (4점)

정답: _____ → _____

[인천 ○○중]

14 위 대화의 내용과 일치하지 <u>않는</u> 것은? (3점)

① Tony plans to watch the musical, *Billy Elliot*.

② Jason Kim is the main actor of the musical, *Billy Elliot*.

③ The musical is about a boy who became a famous dancer.

④ Tony is a big fan of Jason Kim and he watched Jason's musical last year.

⑤ Linda wants to watch the musical, *Billy Elliot*, but she needs to do volunteer work this weekend.

[경북 ○○중]

15 다음 빈칸에 들어갈 의문사가 순서대로 연결된 것은? (4점)

- He's still in Seoul. He hasn't decided _____ to leave for America.
- What should I do next? Dad, please tell me _____ to do.
- I can't park here. Could you tell me _____ to park?

① when – what – how

② what – how – where

③ where – how – when

④ when – what – where

⑤ where – what – when

[인천 ○○중]

16 다음 대화의 빈칸 (A), (B)에 들어갈 알맞은 문장을 〈조건〉에 맞게 쓰시오. (6점)

Sujin: What are you going to do this weekend? How about watching a movie with me?

Brian: I'm sorry, but I can't. I have a cold.
(A)_____
(내가 감기에 걸리지 않았으면, 너와 영화를 볼 텐데.)

Sujin: That's too bad.
(B)_____
(내가 의사라면, 너를 도울 수 있을 텐데.)
I hope you get well soon.

Brian: Thanks. I'll take a rain check.

Sujin: OK. Take care. Bye.

┌─ 조건 ─
• 어법과 철자의 오류가 없어야 함.
• 괄호 안의 우리말을 영작할 것.
• 가정법과거 형태를 사용할 것.

(A) _____

(B) _____

ⓐTears of joy is rolling down my cheeks. I am so happy and thrilled. If I were a bird, I would fly. I look around. ⓑThe other member in my orchestra are hugging one another. ⓒOur concert have just finished and everyone is standing and giving us a big hand. None of us ever expected that (가)this day would come. ⓓIt is a long journey.

My name is Andrea and I'm a violinist in the Recycled Orchestra. (A) ⓔIt's because our musical instruments are made of objects from a landfill. (B) ⓕThat's why it is also known as the Landfill Harmonic Orchestra. (C) Most of us in the orchestra are from Cateura, a small town in Paraguay. (D) There is a huge landfill in our town. Some people even say that Cateura itself is a giant landfill. Many of us are poor. There weren't many hopes and dreams in our town. (E) Everything began to change, however, when we met Favio Chávez.

[충북 ○○중]

17 위 글의 밑줄 친 ⓐ~ⓕ 중 어법상 올바른 문장으로만 묶은 것은? (4점)

① ⓕ
② ⓔ, ⓕ
③ ⓑ, ⓔ
④ ⓒ, ⓔ, ⓕ
⑤ ⓐ, ⓑ, ⓓ

[경기 ○○중]

18 위 글의 필자의 심경으로 알맞은 것은? (3점)

① 슬픔
② 감격
③ 분노
④ 좌절
⑤ 지루함

[충북 ○○중]

19 위 글에서 언급되지 않은 것은? (3점)

① 글쓴이의 감정
② 글쓴이의 이름
③ 오케스트라의 명칭
④ 재활용 악기의 장점
⑤ 콘서트 후의 분위기

[경북 ○○중]

20 위 글의 밑줄 친 (가)this day의 내용으로 적절한 것은? (3점)

① 긴 여행을 끝내는 날
② 기쁨의 눈물이 흘러내리는 날
③ 내가 새가 되어서 주변을 날아다닌 날
④ 연주회를 마치고 사람들에게서 큰 박수를 받은 날
⑤ 유명한 오케스트라의 연주회에 단원들이 초대받은 날

[경기 ○○중]

21 위 글의 (A)~(E) 중 〈보기〉의 문장이 들어갈 위치로 가장 알맞은 것은? (3점)

보기
Why is it called the Recycled Orchestra?

① (A)
② (B)
③ (C)
④ (D)
⑤ (E)

22 위 글 다음에 올 내용은?

(3점)

① Favio의 악기 만들기

② 음악 교사가 된 Andrea

③ 멀리 이사를 가게 된 Andrea

④ Favio가 Cateura를 변화시킨 일

⑤ Andrea와 Favio가 학교를 세우기 시작한 것

23 위 글의 내용과 일치하지 않는 것은?

(3점)

① Cateura는 파라과이의 작은 마을이다.

② 몇몇 사람들은 Cateura 자체가 거대한 쓰레기 매립지라고 말한다.

③ Cateura의 사람들은 가난하지만, 꿈과 희망으로 가득 차 있었다.

④ Recycled Orchestra는 Landfill Harmonic Orchestra로도 알려져 있다.

⑤ Recycled Orchestra의 악기는 쓰레기 매립지에서 나온 물건들로 만들어졌다.

24 다음 문장에 대한 설명으로 옳지 않은 것은?

(4점)

■ If he knew my address, he would send me a letter.

① 과거 사실과 반대되는 상황을 가정하여 말하는 가정법과거 문장이다.

② If절에 동사 knew를 사용한 것은 올바르다.

③ would 대신 could를 써도 된다.

④ 그(he)는 내 주소를 모른다.

⑤ would를 생략할 수 없다.

[25~29] 다음 글을 읽고 물음에 답하시오.

Favio was an environmental educator and a musician. He wanted to teach us music, but there was a big problem. There were only a few musical instruments in the whole town. We couldn't afford to buy new ones, so we said, "(A)_____"

But Favio didn't give up. He said that we could make musical instruments with objects from the landfill. A talented man named Nicholas was able to put (B)this idea into practice. He made violins from oil drums. He turned water pipes into flutes.

We had ⓐanother problem. No one knew how to play musical instruments. We didn't even know how to read music. Favio taught us with great ⓑpatience. Step by step, we began to make some sounds on our instruments. I still remember the first piece of music that we played. It was very short and mostly ⓒout of tune. But it was the most ⓓterrible music to us. We felt a new hope in our hearts. From then on, we gathered to practice every day. One day, Favio told us some ⓔgreat news. We were going to have a concert, a real concert!

And here we are now in front of hundreds of people. They love our music. The world sends us trash, but we send back music!

25 위 글의 제목으로 가장 알맞은 것은?

(4점)

① The From Trash to Music

② The Concert with Trash

③ Children from a Trash Village

④ Favio: the Great Magician in the World

⑤ Unhappy People in South America

26 위 글의 밑줄 친 ⓐ~ⓔ 중 문맥상 알맞지 <u>않은</u> 것은? (3점)

① ⓐ   ② ⓑ   ③ ⓒ

④ ⓓ   ⑤ ⓔ

28 위 글의 밑줄 친 (B)가 의미하는 바로 적절한 것은? (4점)

① 악기를 살 돈이 없다.

② 악기 연주를 가르치고 싶다.

③ 쓰레기로 악기를 만들 수 있다.

④ 마을 전체에 악기가 몇 개 없다.

⑤ 음악을 가르치는 것을 포기하고 싶다.

27 위 글의 빈칸 (A)에 들어갈 말로 가장 적절한 것은? (3점)

① "If we had more people, we could make new musical instruments."

② "If we had a rich teacher, we could buy new musical instruments."

③ "If we had more patience, we could make new musical instruments."

④ "If we had more trash, we could make new musical instruments."

⑤ "If we had enough money, we could buy new musical instruments."

29 위 글의 내용과 일치하는 것은? (3점)

① Favio didn't want to teach his students music.

② After practicing every day, the students had a real concert in front of many people.

③ Because his students couldn't buy musical instruments, Favio didn't help them learn music.

④ Nicholas came up with the idea that the students could make instruments with objects from the landfill.

⑤ From the beginning, the members of the Recycled Orchestra played very beautiful and perfect music.

3학년 영어 2학기 중간고사(5과) 2회

문항수 : 선택형(26문항) 서술형(4문항) | 20 . . .

◎ 선택형 문항의 답안은 컴퓨터용 수정 싸인펜을 사용하여 OMR 답안지에 바르게 표기하시오.
◎ 서술형 문제는 답을 답안지에 반드시 검정 볼펜으로 쓰시오.
◎ 총 30문항 100점 만점입니다. 문항별 배점은 각 문항에 표시되어 있습니다.

01 다음 단어의 영영 풀이로 알맞지 <u>않은</u> 것은? (3점)

① thrilled: very excited and happy

② practice: easily broken or damaged

③ obvious: easy to see or understand

④ afford: to be able to pay for something

⑤ imitate: to copy somebody or something

02 다음 밑줄 친 부분의 표현이 <u>어색한</u> 것은? (2점)

① Tears of joy are <u>rolling down</u> my cheeks.
(흘러내린다)

② He is a bad singer. His singing is always <u>out of tune</u>. (음이 맞지 않는)

③ The famous pianist started to <u>read music</u> when she was four. (악보를 읽다)

④ Please <u>give a big arm</u> to the singers on the stage. (큰 박수를 보내다)

⑤ Scientists tried to <u>put the idea into practice</u>.
(그 아이디어를 실행에 옮기다)

03 다음 괄호 안의 단어와 〈보기〉의 의문사를 이용하여 문장을 완성하시오. (필요시 단어 추가) (5점)

┌─**보기**─────────────────────────┐
│ where / when / how / what / why │
└─────────────────────────────────┘

(1) What should I do next? Mom, please tell me
_____. (do)

(2) I can't live here anymore. Could you tell me
_____? (should)

04 다음 빈칸에 들어갈 말이 순서대로 바르게 짝지어진 것은? (3점)

┌─────────────────────────────────┐
│ • She went to the store _____ buy some │
│   ice cream. │
│ • I'm thinking about where _____ │
│   during the holiday. │
└─────────────────────────────────┘

① in order to - to go

② in order to - going

③ in order to - went

④ so as to - have gone

⑤ so as to - going

05 다음 대화의 빈칸에 들어갈 말로 알맞은 것은? (2점)

> A: Minho, did you finish the math homework?
> B: Not yet. Math is difficult.
> A: Yes, but it's interesting, too.
> B: Then can you help me with my math homework?
> A: _____ I have to take care of my brother.

① I'm so excited.
② Don't mention it.
③ Of course I can.
④ That sounds great.
⑤ I'd love to, but I can't.

06 다음 대화의 빈칸에 기대를 표현하는 말을 주어진 단어를 이용하여 완성하시오. (4점)

> A: You look happy today. What's up?
> B: I'm so excited. I'm going to travel to Jeju-do.
> A: That sounds good.
> B: Yes, I'm really _____.
> (look, ride, forward, a horse)

→ _____

[7~9] 다음 대화를 읽고 물음에 답하시오.

> (A)
> A: Alex, I'm going to take part in a singing contest next Monday.
> B: That's great, Sumin!
> A: You know how to play the guitar, right?
> B: Yes. I've played the guitar for 3 years.
> A: Great. Can you play the guitar while I sing in the contest?
> B: ⓐ_____ I hurt my hand in gym class yesterday.
> A: Oh! I'm sorry to hear that.
> B: Thanks. But I'll be there to cheer for you.
> *A: Sumin, B: Alex

> (B)
> Linda: Hi, Tony! What are you going to do this weekend?
> Tony: I'm going to watch the musical, *Billy Elliot*.
> Linda: *Billy Elliot*? What is it about?
> Tony: It's about a boy ⓑ_____ became a famous dancer. (그것은 유명한 댄서가 된 소년에 관한 거야.) I really want to watch it.
> Linda: Sounds interesting. Who is the main actor?
> Tony: Jason Kim. He's a great dancer.
> Linda: He's my favorite actor. I watched his musical last year.
> Tony: Oh, really? Do you want to join me?
> Linda: ⓒ_____ I have volunteer work this weekend.
> Tony: Okay. See you!

07 위 대화의 빈칸 ⓐ와 ⓒ에 들어갈 표현으로 적절하지 <u>않은</u> 것은? (3점)

① That sounds great.

② Maybe next time.

③ I'm afraid I can't.

④ I'd love to, but I can't.

⑤ I'd like to, but I can't.

[10~12] 다음 대화를 읽고 물음에 답하시오.

G: Jiho, what are you reading?

B: I'm reading a book about a baseball player whose name is Jim Abbott.

G: Oh, the man who was born without a right hand?

B: That's right. He tried really hard and even won the MVP award.

G: Yeah. His story was made into a movie. I'm going to watch it this Saturday.

B: Really? Nana, what's the title?

G: *Our Hero*. (가)_____

B: Can I join you?

G: Sure. See you on Saturday.

08 위 대화의 빈칸 ⓑ에 들어갈 단어로 알맞은 것은? (2점)

① who   ② which

③ what   ④ while

⑤ whose

09 위 대화의 (A)의 내용과 일치하는 것은? (3점)

① Alex hurt his hand while he was playing the guitar.

② Alex is going to participate in the singing contest next Monday.

③ Alex doesn't know how to play the guitar because he has never played it.

④ Alex wants to play the guitar while Sumin sings in the contest, but he can't.

⑤ Alex won't be at the place where the singing contest will be held since he hurt his hand.

10 위 대화의 내용과 일치하지 <u>않는</u> 것은? (3점)

① 지호는 어떤 야구 선수에 관한 책을 읽고 있다.

② Jim Abbott는 오른손이 없이 태어난 사람이다.

③ Jim Abbott는 훌륭한 선수였지만 수상 경력은 없다.

④ 나나는 Jim Abbott의 이야기가 영화로 제작된 것을 알고 있다.

⑤ 나나와 지호는 토요일에 함께 'Our Hero'라는 영화를 보려고 한다.

11 위 대화의 빈칸 (가)에 들어갈 말로 가장 <u>어색한</u> 것은?   (3점)

① I'm excited about it.

② You should watch it.

③ I can't wait to watch it.

④ It won't be nice to watch it.

⑤ I'm really looking forward to watching it.

12 위 대화를 읽고 알 수 <u>없는</u> 것은?   (3점)

① What's the title of the book that Jiho is reading?

② What problem was Jim Abbott born with?

③ Did Jim Abbott get the MVP award?

④ What is Jiho going to do this Saturday?

⑤ What is the movie, *Our Hero*, about?

13 다음 우리말을 주어진 〈조건〉에 맞게 영어로 쓰시오.   (4점)

> 내가 발명가라면 타임머신을 발명할 텐데.

조건
1. 가정법을 사용할 것.
2. inventor, invent, time machine을 포함할 것.
3. 전체 문장을 11단어를 사용해서 쓸 것.

→ _____

14 다음 대화의 빈칸에 들어갈 말이 순서대로 짝지어진 것은?   (3점)

> A: Let's get ready for the party.
> B: Okay. Please tell me _____ the balloons.
> A: Stick them on the door. I don't know _____ the birthday cake in.
> B: Bring it in when the lights are turned off.

① where to stick – when to bring

② where to stick – how to bring

③ when to stick – how to make

④ how to make – where to put

⑤ how to make – when to put

15 다음 문장을 가정법과거로 바꿔 쓰시오.   (6점)

(1) As I am not a bird, I can't fly.

→ _____

(2) As he doesn't know my address, he doesn't send me a letter.

→ _____

16 다음 중 어법상 <u>어색한</u> 것은? (3점)

① They didn't know where to go.

② I wanted to know why to go there.

③ He showed us what to see in this town.

④ We didn't know how to cook spaghetti.

⑤ Jenny found out where to buy the dress.

18 위 글의 밑줄 친 ⓐ~ⓔ 중 어법상 옳지 <u>않은</u> 것은? (4점)

① ⓐ   ② ⓑ   ③ ⓒ

④ ⓓ   ⑤ ⓔ

[17~18] 다음 글을 읽고 물음에 답하시오.

> Tears of joy are rolling down my cheeks. I'm so happy and ⓐ<u>thrilling</u>. If I ⓑ<u>were</u> a bird, I would fly. I look around. The other members in my orchestra are ⓒ<u>hugging</u> one another. Our concert has just finished and everyone is standing and (A)_____. ⓓ<u>None of us</u> ever expected that this day ⓔ<u>would</u> come. It has been a long journey.

17 위 글의 빈칸 (A)에 들어갈 표현으로 알맞은 것은? (3점)

> everyone is standing and (A)_____
> _____.
>
> (모든 사람들이 일어나서 우리에게 큰 박수를 보내고 있다.)

① give us a big hand

② give a big hand us

③ give a big hand to us

④ giving us a big hand

⑤ giving a big hand us

[19~23] 다음 글을 읽고 물음에 답하시오.

> My name is Andrea and I'm a violinist in the Recycled Orchestra. Why is it called the Recycled Orchestra? It's because ⓐ<u>our musical instruments made of objects from a landfill</u>. That's (A)_____ it's also known as the Landfill Harmonic Orchestra.
>
> ⓑ<u>Most of us in the orchestra is from Cateura, a small town in Paraguay</u>. There is a huge landfill in our town. Some people even say that Cateura (B)<u>itself</u> is a giant landfill. Many of us are poor. There weren't many hopes and dreams in our town. Everything began to change, however, when we met Favio Chávez.
>
> Favio was an environmental educator and a musician. ⓒ<u>He wanted to teach music us, but there was a big problem.</u> ⓓ<u>There were only a little musical instruments in the whole town.</u> ⓔ <u>We couldn't afford to buy new ones.</u> But Favio didn't give up. He said that we could make musical instruments with objects from the landfill.

19 위 글의 밑줄 친 부분 중, 어법상 옳은 것은? (4점)

① ⓐ   ② ⓑ   ③ ⓒ

④ ⓓ   ⑤ ⓔ

20 위 글의 빈칸 (A)에 들어갈 알맞은 단어는? (3점)

① who   ② why   ③ how

④ where   ⑤ when

21 위 글의 밑줄 친 (B)itself와 같은 용법으로 짝지어진 것은? (4점)

(a) I love <u>myself</u> very much.

(b) I <u>myself</u> finished this homework.

(c) He taught <u>himself</u> how to use this machine.

(d) This work <u>itself</u> is not difficult.

(e) My sister made this cake <u>herself</u>.

(f) They saw <u>themselves</u> in the mirror.

---

① (a), (d)

② (b), (d), (e)

③ (a), (b), (c), (e)

④ (b), (c), (d), (f)

⑤ (a), (b), (c), (d), (e), (f)

22 위 글의 내용을 바르게 이해하지 <u>못한</u> 사람은? (3점)

① 성재: Cateura is in Paraguay.

② 준혁: Many people in Cateura are poor.

③ 혜성: There is a huge landfill in Cateura.

④ 승빈: Many people in Cateura were full of dreams.

⑤ 범찬: Favio began changing everything about Cateura.

23 위 글의 내용과 일치하는 것은? (3점)

① 오케스트라의 악기는 거의 중고품이었다.

② Favio는 환경 교육자이자 음악가였다.

③ 단원들 중 일부만 카테우라 마을 출신이다.

④ Favio는 기부금을 모아 악기를 마련하기로 했다.

⑤ Favio는 카테우라 마을 사람들에게 환경의 중요성을 가르치고 싶어 했다.

[24~25] 다음 글을 읽고 물음에 답하시오.

Step by step, we began to make some sounds ⓐon our instruments. (A)나는 우리가 연주했던 음악의 첫 곡을 아직도 기억한다. It was very short and mostly ⓑout of tune. But it was the most beautiful music ⓒto us. (B)우리는 우리의 마음 속에서 새로운 희망을 느꼈다. ⓓTo then on, we gathered to practice every day. One day, (C)Favio는 우리에게 어떤 엄청난 소식을 말해 줬다. (D)우리는 진짜 콘서트를 가지려고 했다. And here we are now ⓔin front of hundreds of people. They love our music. (E)세상은 우리에게 쓰레기를 보낸다, 하지만 우리는 음악을 돌려보낸다.

[충북 ○○중]

24 위 글의 ⓐ~ⓔ 중, 알맞지 않은 것은? (3점)

① ⓐ ② ⓑ ③ ⓒ

④ ⓓ ⑤ ⓔ

[26~30] 다음 글을 읽고 물음에 답하시오.

ⓐMost of us in the orchestra is from Cateura, a small town in Paraguay. (A) There is a huge landfill in our town. (B) ⓑSome people even say that Cateura themselves is a giant landfill. (C) Many of us are poor. (D) ⓒThere weren't many hopes and dreams in our town. (E) Favio was an environmental educator and a musician. ⓓHe wanted to teach us music, but there were a big problem. ⓔThere were only a few musical instrument in the whole town. ⓕWe couldn't afford to buy new ones.

But Favio didn't give up. He said that we could make musical instruments with objects from the landfill. ⓖA talented man naming Nicholas was able to put this idea into practice. He made violins from oil drums. He turned water pipes into flutes. (가)_____. ⓗNo one knew how to playing musical instruments. Favio taught us music with great patience.

[충북 ○○중]

25 위 글의 (A)~(E)를 영어로 어색하게 옮긴 것은? (3점)

① (A) I still remember the first piece of music in that we played.

② (B) We felt a new hope in our hearts.

③ (C) Favio told us some great news.

④ (D) We were going to have a real concert.

⑤ (E) The world sends us trash, but we send back music.

[인천 ○○중]

26 위 글의 빈칸 (가)에 들어갈 말로 가장 적절한 것은? (3점)

① We made a big mistake.

② We had another problem.

③ We didn't know how to make musical instruments.

④ We suddenly became famous musicians in our town.

⑤ We were so talented that we could play beautiful music soon.

27 위 글의 (A)~(E) 중 다음 문장이 들어가기에 가장 적합한 곳은? (4점)

> Everything began to change, however, when we met Favio Chávez.

① (A)　　　② (B)　　　③ (C)

④ (D)　　　⑤ (E)

29 위 글에서 찾을 수 <u>없는</u> 단어의 뜻풀이는? (4점)

① to be able to pay for something

② an area where waste is buried under the ground

③ give something to a charity or other organizations

④ related to the natural conditions in which people, animals and plants live

⑤ the ability to stay calm and accept a delay or suffering

28 위 글의 내용과 일치하지 <u>않는</u> 것은? (3점)

① Favio는 환경 교육자이자 음악가이다.

② 글쓴이의 마을에는 거대한 쓰레기 매립지가 있다.

③ Favio는 음악을 가르칠 때, 인내심을 가지고 가르쳤다.

④ 플룻과 바이올린을 만든 사람은 Nicholas다.

⑤ Nicholas는 쓰레기 매립지 물건들로 악기를 만들 수 있다고 말했다.

30 위 글의 밑줄 친 ⓐ~ⓗ 중, 어법이 맞는 문장의 총 개수는? (4점)

① 0개　　　② 1개　　　③ 2개

④ 3개　　　⑤ 4개

3학년 영어 2학기 중간고사(6과) 1회

반		점수	
이름			

문항수 : 선택형(26문항) 서술형(4문항) | 20 . . .

◎ 선택형 문항의 답안은 컴퓨터용 수정 싸인펜을 사용하여 OMR 답안지에 바르게 표기하시오.
◎ 서술형 문제는 답을 답안지에 반드시 검정 볼펜으로 쓰시오.
◎ 총 30문항 100점 만점입니다. 문항별 배점은 각 문항에 표시되어 있습니다.

[경기 ○○중]

01 다음 밑줄 친 부분이 옳지 <u>않은</u> 문장은? (3점)

① Ghosts exist only in your <u>imagination</u>.
② The artist got his <u>inspiration</u> from nature.
③ The monkeys <u>imitate</u> my body movements.
④ The famous restaurants <u>attraction</u> many people.
⑤ Do you know the <u>expression</u>, "I have two left feet"?

[경북 ○○중]

02 다음 중 단어를 바르게 고른 사람은? (3점)

① 지은: Add the lemon (<u>peel</u> / feel) to the olive oil.
② 현승: The music is (pleasing / <u>pleased</u>) to the ears.
③ 혜진: I want to have a TV with a (curved / <u>curve</u>) screen.
④ 준섭: The (architect / <u>architecture</u>) built a tall building in the town.
⑤ 은혜: She drew her (<u>inspire</u> / inspiration) from her experiences.

[경북 ○○중]

03 다음 빈칸에 공통으로 들어갈 말로 알맞은 것은? (3점)

• If you _____ the concert tickets this month, you can get a 20% discount.
• *Holes* is a _____ by Louis Sachar in 1998.

① book   ② exhibit
③ allow   ④ capture
⑤ imitate

[인천 ○○중]

04 다음 중 짝지어진 대화가 가장 <u>어색한</u> 것은? (2점)

① A: We are finally here.
  B: Yes, I'm so excited. Let's look around.
② A: Thank you for lending me the book.
  B: You are welcome.
③ A: Thank you for inviting me to your party.
  B: My pleasure. I'm glad you could come.
④ A: Which place did you like most in my town?
  B: I want to visit Central Park most.
⑤ A: You are not allowed to bring your tennis racket.
  B: Oh, where should I put it?

05 다음 중 빈칸에 들어갈 말이 나머지와 <u>다른</u> 것은?   (3점)

① The boy is fast _____ to win the race.

② He is smart _____ to understand the problem.

③ The marble table is _____ heavy for me to carry.

④ This rice cake is big _____ for all of us to eat.

⑤ The weather is warm _____ for us to play outside.

07 다음과 같은 뜻이 되도록 주어진 단어들을 알맞게 배열한 것은?   (3점)

> Tom은 차를 운전할 수 있는 충분한 나이가 아니다.
> (Tom / enough / not / old / is / to / drive / a car)

① Tom drive a car is not enough to old.

② Tom is not enough old to drive a car.

③ Tom drive not old enough to a car is.

④ Tom is not old enough drive to a car.

⑤ Tom is not old enough to drive a car.

06 다음 두 문장의 의미가 같지 <u>않은</u> 것은?   (3점)

① Jim is too short to reach the top shelf.

= Jim is so short that he can't reach the top shelf.

② He asked me when he should take out the eggs.

= He asked me when to take out the eggs.

③ Tom studied hard in order to pass the test.

= Tom studied hard, so that he could pass the test.

④ If I were a doctor, I could help sick people.

= As I'm not a doctor, I can't help sick people.

⑤ The mouse is so small that it can go through the hole.

= The mouse is small enough to go through the hole.

08 다음 문장을 괄호 안의 주어진 표현을 사용하여 같은 의미의 문장으로 바꾸어 쓰시오.   (5점)

(1) The girl studied hard to pass the exam.

→ _____

   (so that)

(2) I wrote his name in my diary so that I wouldn't forget it.

→ _____

   (so as to)

09 다음 대화의 내용과 일치하지 <u>않는</u> 것은? (3점)

> A: The tickets for the World Music Concert are on sale now.
> B: Really? Let's book the tickets online right away.
> A: Okay. Let's see... There are still tickets left for November 5th.
> B: Sounds good. Let's get two student tickets.
> A: Oh, do you mind if I bring my little brother?
> B: Not at all. But it says that you are not allowed to bring children under 8.
> A: No problem. He's 10.
> B: Okay. I'll add one child ticket. The total price is 25 dollars.
> A: Great.
> B: I can't wait to see the concert!

① A의 남동생도 콘서트에 갈 것이다.

② 그들은 3장의 티켓을 예약할 것이다.

③ B는 콘서트에 갈 수 없을지도 모른다.

④ 그들은 11월 5일에 콘서트에 갈 것이다.

⑤ 8세 미만의 어린이들은 World Music Concert에 갈 수 없다.

10 다음 중 어법상 <u>어색한</u> 문장은? (3점)

① Please speak louder so that everyone can hear you.

② Tom goes to bed early so that he can got up early.

③ Yumi swims every morning so that she can stay healthy.

④ My father went to the airport so that he could pick up my sister.

⑤ Minsu turned on the radio so that he could listen to the baseball game.

11 다음과 같은 뜻이 되도록 주어진 단어들을 알맞게 배열한 것은? (3점)

> 그는 모든 사람들이 들을 수 있도록 큰 소리로 말했다.
> (He / loudly / so / everyone / spoke / that / hear / him / could)

① He spoke loudly so everyone that could hear him.

② He so spoke loudly that everyone could hear him.

③ He spoke so loudly everyone that could hear him.

④ He loudly so that everyone spoke could hear him.

⑤ He spoke loudly so that everyone could hear him.

12 다음 〈보기〉의 문장과 의미를 같게 만들 때 어법상 바른 것은? (3점)

> 보기
> Jimin practices hard so that he can win the contest.

① Jimin practices hard so as to win the contest.

② Jimin practices so hard that he could win the contest.

③ Jimin practices hard that he can win the contest.

④ Jimin practices hard in order to winning the contest.

⑤ Jimin practices hard in order that he win the contest.

13 다음 문장 전환 중 올바른 것은? (3점)

① John writes a book to be famous.
= John writes a book so to be famous.

② Eunchae exercises every day to be healthy.
= Eunchae exercises every day in order to being healthy.

③ He spoke loudly so that everybody could hear him.
= He spoke loudly to hear everybody.

④ They went to bed early so that they could get up early.
= They went to bed early to getting up early.

⑤ Teachers study hard to teach students well.
= Teachers study hard in order that students can teach well.

14 다음 우리말과 같은 의미가 되도록 괄호 안의 주어진 어구를 사용하여 영작하시오. (단어 추가 가능, 어형 변화 없음) (5점)

(1) 그 쥐는 그 구멍을 통과할 만큼 충분히 작지 않다.
(go through / enough / the hole)

→ _____

(2) 민호의 영어는 외국인과 이야기할 만큼 충분히 좋다.
(a foreigner / talk with / good / enough)

→ _____

15 다음 글에서 어법상 <u>어색한</u> 부분을 4군데 찾아 올바른 영어로 고쳐 쓰시오. (6점)

Jorn Utzon, the architect of the Sydney Opera House, took a shape from nature and added his imagine. Can you guess whose inspired him? Many people think that it is the waves in the ocean or a sailing boat. But interesting, the inspiration came from an orange. Look at the roof closely. Can you see the peels of an orange? When orange lights are shine on the building, you can see the peels more clearly.

(1) 어색한 표현: _____
올바르게 고친 표현: _____

(2) 어색한 표현: _____
올바르게 고친 표현: _____

(3) 어색한 표현: _____
올바르게 고친 표현: _____

(4) 어색한 표현: _____
올바르게 고친 표현: _____

[16~18] 다음 글을 읽고 물음에 답하시오.

Hello, students! ⓐThank you for visiting our art museum. This museum opened in 1995. ⓑSince then, (A)it has exhibited many famous artworks. ⓒToday, you will see some famous artworks from the art books. Before we begin the tour, let me remind you of a basic rule. ⓓYou can take pictures of the artworks, but you're not allowed to touch (B)them. ⓔYou can feel artworks by breaking them. Now let's start the tour.

16 위 글의 밑줄 친 부분 중, 흐름상 어색한 것은? (3점)

① ⓐ   ② ⓑ   ③ ⓒ
④ ⓓ   ⑤ ⓔ

18 위 글의 밑줄 친 (A)it와 (B)them이 가리키는 대상이 바르게 짝지어진 것은? (3점)

	(A)	(B)
①	1995	the art books
②	the tour	the art books
③	the tour	the artworks
④	this museum	pictures
⑤	this museum	the artworks

[19~20] 다음 글을 읽고 물음에 답하시오.

In the first two examples, we can ⓐeasily see what inspired the architect. But in the next example from Australia, (가)this is not so ⓑobviously. Jørn Utzon, the architect of the Sydney Opera House, took a shape from nature and added his imagination. Can you guess what inspired him? Many people think that it is the waves in the ocean or a sailing boat. But ⓒinterestingly, the inspiration came from an orange. Look at the roof ⓓclosely. Can you see the peels of an orange? When orange lights are shone on the building, you can see the peels more ⓔclearly.

17 위 글을 읽고 답을 알 수 없는 질문은? (2점)

① Who made this museum?
② When did this museum open?
③ What does this museum exhibit?
④ What are you allowed to do in this museum?
⑤ What are you not allowed to do in this museum?

19 위 글의 밑줄 친 (가)this가 가리키는 것은? (4점)

① a shape from nature
② the first two examples
③ the Sydney Opera House
④ what inspired the architect
⑤ the next example from Australia

20 위 글의 ⓐ~ⓔ 중 단어의 쓰임이 바르지 <u>않은</u> 것은? (3점)

① ⓐ ② ⓑ ③ ⓒ

④ ⓓ ⑤ ⓔ

22 위 글의 La Sangrada Familia에 대한 설명 중 내용과 <u>다른</u> 것은? (3점)

① Gaudi started work on it in 1884.

② It was Gaudi's most ambitious project.

③ Gaudi was hit by a tram in front of it.

④ Now it is the most visited attraction in Spain.

⑤ The construction often stopped because of lack of money.

[21~22] 다음 글을 읽고 물음에 답하시오.

ⓐLa Sagrada Familia, which Gaudi wanted to be a cathedral for everybody, especially the poor, was Gaudi's most ambitious project. He started work on it in 1884 and dedicated his entire life to it. ⓑTo Gaudi, who remained single all his life, the cathedral was like his family. In fact, it was in front of the cathedral where he was hit by a tram and died in 1926. ⓒDespite his dedication, the cathedral was finished when he died. The construction often stopped due to a shortage of money. The work was also slowed by his poor health and death of the people close to him. ⓓWork on La Sagrada Familia is still ongoing, and it is expected to be finished by 2030. Every year, ⓔmillions of people come to Barcelona to see it and now it is the most visited attraction in Barcelona.

21 위 글의 ⓐ~ⓔ 중, 글의 흐름상 내용이 <u>어색한</u> 것은? (4점)

① ⓐ ② ⓑ ③ ⓒ

④ ⓓ ⑤ ⓔ

[23~25] 다음 글을 읽고 물음에 답하시오.

What about Korea? Have you ever (A)[gone / been] to Dongdaemun Design Plaza in Seoul? Many people think that the building (B)[looks like / looks] a giant spaceship. But the architect, Zaha Hadid, took the curved lines from nature so that city people could enjoy them. Thanks (C)[to / for] its special design, it has become a popular tourist attraction in Seoul. As you can see, many buildings try (D)[capturing / to capture] the beauty of nature in their design. They are perfect examples of "_____." If you were an architect, what should you choose from nature?

23 위 글을 읽고 답할 수 없는 질문은? (3점)

① Where is Dongdaemun Design Plaza?

② What does Dongdaemun Design Plaza look like?

③ What did the architect of Dongdaemun Design Plaza bring from nature?

④ Who is the architect of Dongdaumun Design Plaza?

⑤ What is Dongdaemun Design Plaza used for?

24 위 글의 빈칸에 들어갈 알맞은 말은? (4점)

① Nature mood.

② Nature is great.

③ Nature meets city.

④ Nature is the mother.

⑤ Protect the nature around us.

25 위 글의 (A)~(D)에서 쓰임이 바른 것끼리 묶인 것은? (3점)

① been – looks – to – capturing

② gone – looks – for – to capture

③ been – looks like – to – to capture

④ gone – looks like – for – capturing

⑤ been – looks like – for – to capture

[26~30] 다음 글을 읽고 물음에 답하시오.

Have you heard of the expression, "Art imitates nature?" Many artists get their ideas and inspirations from the world around them. ⓐThis is because the natural world is a beautiful place. ⓑThe shapes in nature are very pleased to the eye. (A)_____, look at the egg on the left. Isn't it beautiful? (B)그것은 둥글고 부서지기 쉽지만 그것의 내용물을 보호할 만큼 충분히 튼튼하다. Can you imagine a building that looks like an egg? ⓒ Such a building actually exists in London.

Nature has inspired many architects around the world. This is the Sagrada Familia in Spain. ⓓIt is one of the most famous churches in the world. Look at the beautiful tall columns inside the church. They look like trees, don't they? The famous architect, Antoni Gaudi, used the shape of trees in the Sagrada Familia. ⓔThat's how he brought the beauty of nature indoors.

26 위 글의 밑줄 친 부분 중, 어법상 어색한 것은? (4점)

① ⓐ   ② ⓑ   ③ ⓒ

④ ⓓ   ⑤ ⓔ

27 위 글의 빈칸 (A)에 들어갈 말로 가장 적절한 것은? (3점)

① Instead
② However
③ Fortunately
④ In the end
⑤ For example

29 Which question CANNOT be answered? (3점)

① What has inspired many architects around the world?
② Where do many artists get their ideas and inspirations?
③ Which shape did Antoni Gaudi use in the Sagrada Familia?
④ How many columns are there inside the Sagrada Familia?
⑤ In which city can you see the building that looks like an egg?

28 위 글의 밑줄 친 (B)의 우리말과 같은 의미가 되도록 〈보기〉에 주어진 단어를 올바르게 배열하여 문장을 완성하시오. (4점)

보기

delicate / It / enough / its contents / round / strong / to protect / yet / and / is
(단어 추가 및 어형 변화 없음)

→ _____

_____

30 위 글의 내용과 일치하지 <u>않는</u> 것은? (3점)

① 자연은 건축가에게 영감을 준다.
② 사그라다 파밀리아 성당은 스페인에 위치한다.
③ 달걀처럼 생긴 건물은 실제로 런던에 존재한다.
④ 사그라다 파밀리아 성당은 세계에서 가장 화려한 성당이다.
⑤ Antoni Gaudi는 사그라다 파밀리아 성당 내부에 나무의 형태를 사용했다.

3학년 영어 2학기 중간고사(6과) 2회

반		점수	
이름			

문항수 : 선택형(26문항) 서술형(4문항)   20 . . .

◎ 선택형 문항의 답안은 컴퓨터용 수정 싸인펜을 사용하여 OMR 답안지에 바르게 표기하시오.

◎ 서술형 문제는 답을 답안지에 반드시 검정 볼펜으로 쓰시오.

◎ 총 30문항 100점 만점입니다. 문항별 배점은 각 문항에 표시되어 있습니다.

[경기 ○○중]

01 다음 영어 표현과 우리말 뜻이 옳지 <u>않은</u> 것은?   (2점)

① delicate: 부서지기 쉬운, 섬세한
② contents: 내용물
③ architect: 우주인
④ spaceship: 우주선
⑤ tourist attraction: 관광 명소

[충북 ○○중]

02 다음 〈보기〉는 어떤 4개의 단어에 대한 영영 풀이이다. 다음 중 〈보기〉의 단어 풀이에 해당하지 <u>않는</u> 단어는?   (3점)

[?]: easily broken or damaged
[?]: the things that are inside something
[?]: the ability to form pictures or ideas in your mind
[?]: something that gives you ideas about what to do or create

① obvious   ② delicate
③ contents   ④ inspiration
⑤ imagination

[서울 강남구 ○○중]

03 다음 중 밑줄 친 부분이 바르게 쓰인 것은?   (3점)

① The dress is <u>such pretty to</u> wear.
② The coffee is <u>too hot for to</u> drink.
③ This bag is <u>too small to</u> carry two balls.
④ Sumi isn't <u>old enough that</u> she can't drive a car.
⑤ He is <u>enough smart to</u> solve the math problem.

[경기 ○○중]

04 다음 주어진 우리말과 같은 뜻이 되도록 문장을 완성할 때 알맞지 <u>않은</u> 것은?   (2점)

그녀는 건강을 유지하기 위해 매일 아침 조깅을 한다.
→ She jogs every morning _____ _____.

① to stay healthy
② so as stay healthy
③ in order to stay healthy
④ so that she can stay healthy
⑤ in order that she can stay healthy

[인천 ○○중]

05 다음 Sam과 Emily의 저축 목적을 읽고, 〈조건〉에 맞게 빈칸을 완성하시오.   (4점)

조건
• 어법과 철자의 오류가 없어야 함.
• (1)번은 order, (2)번은 so 단어를 반드시 포함할 것.
• Sam과 Emily의 저축 목적을 바탕으로 주어진 영어 문장을 완성할 것.

(1) Sam saved money _____.
(Sam의 저축 목적: 아픈 사람들을 도와주기 위해)

(2) Emily saved money _____.
(Emily의 저축 목적: 새로운 핸드폰을 구매하기 위해)

06 다음 대화의 ⓐ~ⓓ에 들어갈 말로 적절하지 <u>않은</u> 것은? (3점)

> A: Sumin, my train is leaving in five minutes.
> B: I hope you enjoyed your trip, Daniel.
> A: ⓐ_____
> B: Which place did you like most in my town?
> A: ⓑ_____
> B: Yeah, it's the most popular place here.
> A: I really liked walking around in hanbok.
>   ⓒ_____
> B: I'm glad to hear that.
> A: ⓓ_____
> B: It was my pleasure. Have a safe trip.

① Of course, I did.
② I looked really cool.
③ I'm sorry to hear that.
④ I liked the folk village most.
⑤ Thank you for showing me around.

08 다음 중 우리말을 바르게 영작한 것은? (2점)

① 수진이는 건강을 유지하기 위해 매일 아침 수영을 한다.
→ Sujin swims every morning so that stay healthy.

② 그는 그 시험에 합격하기 위해 최선을 다했다.
→ He did his best, so that he could pass the test.

③ 아빠는 언니를 태우기 위해 공항에 가셨다.
→ My father went to the airport so as to he could pick up my sister.

④ 그녀는 가수가 되기 위해 매우 열심히 노래 연습을 한다.
→ She practices singing very hard in order that she can be a singer.

⑤ 우리는 기부하기 위해 헌 옷을 모았다.
→ We collected old clothes so that we can donate them.

07 다음 중 어법상 옳은 문장의 개수는? (3점)

> • My puppy is small enough of me to carry in my bag.
> • Minho's English is enough good to talk with a foreigner.
> • Sumi is brave enough to going into the Ghost house.
> • The boy is not tall enough to reach the top shelf.

① 0개   ② 1개   ③ 2개
④ 3개   ⑤ 4개

09 다음 단어들을 배열하여 자연스러운 문장을 만들 때, 다섯 번째로 오는 단어는? (3점)

> Jiho / hear / everyone / spoke / that / could / him / loudly / so

① so
② that
③ everyone
④ could
⑤ hear

10 다음 우리말과 뜻이 같도록 주어진 단어를 활용하여 문장을 완성하여 쓰시오. (8점)

(1) 그는 상자를 들 만큼 강하다. (lift)

→ He is _____ the box.

(2) 그 사다리는 선반 꼭대기에 닿을 만큼 길다. (reach, the top shelf)

→ The ladder is _____.

(3) 그녀는 차를 운전할 만큼 나이가 들지 않았다. (old, a car)

→ She is not _____.

(4) 그녀의 영어는 외국인과 이야기할 만큼 충분히 좋다. (talk with a foreigner)

→ Her English is _____.

11 다음 중 밑줄 친 부분이 올바른 문장은? (3점)

① The coffee is <u>too hot for to</u> drink.

② The box is <u>such enough to</u> take a cake.

③ The desk is <u>too small to</u> put a computer.

④ She is <u>enough clever to</u> solve the problem.

⑤ This car is <u>too small that</u> it can't carry four people.

12 다음 중 어법상 <u>어색한</u> 문장은? (3점)

① I studied hard so that I could pass the test.

② I left home early so that I could caught the bus.

③ My mother went to the airport to pick up my sister.

④ My father jogs every morning so that he can stay healthy.

⑤ Mike turned on the TV so that he could watch the basketball game.

13 다음 대화의 내용과 일치하는 것은? (3점)

Sally: Hi, Jiho. The tickets for the World Music Concert are on sale now.

Jiho: Let's see, Sally. There are still tickets left for October 5th.

Sally: Sounds good. Let's get two student tickets.

Jiho: Oh, do you mind if I bring my little brother?

Sally: Not at all. But it says that you are not allowed to bring children under 8.

Jiho: No problem. He's 10.

Sally: Okay, I'll add one child ticket. The total price is 25 dollars.

Jiho: Great.

Sally: I can't wait to see the concert!

① The tickets aren't left for October 5th.

② The World Music Concert is for all ages.

③ Sally's little brother will go to the concert.

④ Sally and Jiho will get the three student tickets.

⑤ Sally is looking forward to going to the concert.

14 다음 문장을 괄호 안의 주어진 표현을 사용하여 같은 의미의 문장으로 바꾸어 쓰시오. (4점)

(1) Mike saved money to buy a new bicycle.

→ _____

(so that)

(2) I turned on the TV so that I could watch the news.

→ _____

(so as to)

15 다음 글의 Boram Middle School에 대한 설명으로 가장 적절한 것은? (3점)

I go to Boram Middle School in Suwon. My school has a 4-story building. It also has a large playground, a gym and small garden. The garden is on top of the school building. We grow some vegetables there so that we can have fresh food. My favorite place is the bench under the big tree. I love sitting there and talking with my friends. I like my school very much.

① 우리 학교에는 네 가지 이야기가 있다.
② 학교 가장 위층에는 커다란 체육관이 있다.
③ 내가 좋아하는 장소는 나무로 만든 벤치이다.
④ 나는 교실에 앉아 친구들과 이야기 나누는 것을 좋아한다.
⑤ 학교 정원에서는 신선한 음식을 먹을 수 있도록 채소를 키운다.

16 다음 주어진 문장이 들어가기에 가장 적절한 곳은? (3점)

You can take pictures of the artworks, but you're not allowed to touch them.

W: Hello, students! Thank you for visiting our art museum. (A) This museum opened in 1995. (B) Since then, it has exhibited many famous artworks. (C) Today, you will see some famous artworks from the art books. (D) Before we start the tour, let me remind you of a basic rule. (E) Now let's start the tour.

① (A)   ② (B)   ③ (C)
④ (D)   ⑤ (E)

[17~20] 다음 글을 읽고 물음에 답하시오.

[I] Have you heard of the expression, "Art imitates nature"? Many artists get their ideas and inspirations from the world around them. This is because the natural world is a beautiful place. ⓐ The shapes in nature are very pleased to the eye. For example, look at the egg on the left. Isn't it beautiful? ⓑIt is round and delicate, yet enough strong to protect its contents. Can you imagine a building that looks like an egg? ⓒSuch a building actually exists in London.

Nature has inspired many architects around the world. This is the Sagrada Familia in Spain. ⓐIt is one of the most famous church in the world. Look at the beautiful tall columns inside the church. They look like trees, don't they? The famous architect, Antoni Gaudi, used the shape of trees in the Sagrada Familia. ⓔThat is how he brought the beauty of nature indoors.

[Ⅱ] In the first two examples, we can easily see what inspired the architect. But in the next example from Australia, this is not so (A)_____. Jørn Utzon, the architect of the Sydney Opera House, took a shape from nature and added his imagination. Can you guess what inspired him? Many people think that it is the waves in the ocean or a sailing boat. But interestingly, the (B)_____ came from an orange. Look at the roof closely. Can you see the peels of an orange? When orange lights are shone on the building, you can see the peels more clearly.

What about Korea? Have you ever been to Dongdaemun Design Plaza in Seoul? Many people think that the building looks like a giant spaceship. But the architect, Zaha Hadid, took the curved lines from nature so that city people could enjoy them. Thanks to its special design, it has become a popular tourist attraction in Seoul.

As you can see, many buildings try to capture the beauty of nature in their design. They are perfect examples of "Nature meets city." If you were an architect, what (C)_____ you choose from nature?

17 위 글의 내용과 일치하는 것은? (3점)

① The building that looks like an egg is in Paris.
② Antoni Gaudi used trees to make the columns.
③ Many architects have been influenced by nature.
④ All artists get their ideas from their imagination.
⑤ People enjoy the spaceship in Dongdaemun Design Plaza in Seoul.

18 위 글 [Ⅰ]의 ⓐ~ⓔ 중 어법상 잘못된 것만 고른 것은? (3점)

① ⓐ, ⓑ   ② ⓐ, ⓒ
③ ⓐ, ⓑ, ⓓ   ④ ⓑ, ⓓ, ⓔ
⑤ ⓒ, ⓓ, ⓔ

19 위 글 [Ⅱ]의 (A)~(C)에 들어갈 가장 적절한 단어는? (4점)

	(A)	(B)	(C)
①	clear	inspiration	would
②	clear	inspiration	will
③	unclear	inspire	would
④	obvious	inspire	would
⑤	obvious	inspiration	will

20 위 글을 바탕으로 건축물을 소개하는 표를 완성하고자 한다. 빈칸 (A)~(C)에 들어갈 말을 위 글에서 찾아 〈조건〉에 맞게 쓰시오. (6점)

> **조건**
> • 어법과 철자의 오류가 없어야 함.
> • (A)~(C) 모두 위 글에서 찾아 그대로 쓸 것.

	The Sagrada Familia	The Sydney Opera House	Dongdamun Design Plaza
•Country (Location)	Spain	(A)_____	Korea
•Architect	Antoni Gaudi	JØrn Utzon	Zaha Hadid
•What inspired the architect	(B)_____	the peels of an orange	(C)_____

(A) _____

(B) _____

(C) _____

21 위 글의 빈칸 ⓐ에 들어갈 말로 알맞은 것은? (3점)

① so that

② but

③ however

④ anyway

⑤ for example

22 위 글의 빈칸 ⓑ와 ⓒ에 들어갈 말이 순서대로 짝지어진 것은? (3점)

① As – As

② If – As

③ If – If

④ Such – As

⑤ As – If

[21~23] 다음 글을 읽고 물음에 답하시오.

What about Korea? Have you ever been to Dongdaemun Design Plaza in Seoul? Many people think that the building looks like a giant spaceship. But the architect, Zaha Hadid, took the curved lines from nature ⓐ_____ city people could enjoy them. Thanks to its special design, it has become a popular tourist attraction in Seoul.

ⓑ_____ you can see, many buildings try to capture the beauty of nature in their design. They are perfect examples of "Nature meets city." ⓒ_____ you were an architect, what would you choose from nature?

23 위 글의 내용과 일치하는 것은? (3점)

① Zaha Hadid is an architect who is inspired by nature.

② Korea does not have any examples of nature-inspired buildings.

③ Many people believe that Dongdaemun Design Plaza is a giant spaceship.

④ Tourists like to visit Dongdaemun Design Plaza since it has many attractive stores.

⑤ It is impossible for us to find buildings that try to bring the beauty of nature in their design.

Nature has ⓐ_____ many architects around the world. This is the Sagrada Familia in Spain. It is one of the ⓑ_____ famous ⓒ_____ in the world. Look at the beautiful tall columns inside the church. They look like trees, ⓓ_____ they? The famous architect, Antoni Gaudi, used the shape of trees in the Sagrada Familia. That's ⓔ _____ he brought the beauty of nature indoors.

In the first two examples, we can easily see what inspired the architect. But in the next example from Australia, this is not so (A)_____. Jørn Utzon, the architect of the Sydney Opera House, took a shape from nature and added his imagination. Can you guess what inspired him? Many people think that it is the waves in the ocean or a sailing boat. But interestingly, the inspiration came from an orange. Look at the roof closely. Can you see the peels of an orange? When orange lights are shone on the building, you can see the peels more clearly.

24 위 글의 빈칸 ⓐ~ⓔ에 들어갈 말로 알맞지 **않은** 것은? (3점)

① ⓐ - inspired

② ⓑ - most

③ ⓒ - churches

④ ⓓ - don't

⑤ ⓔ - why

25 위 글에 대한 내용으로 알맞지 **않은** 것은? (3점)

① 자연은 많은 건축가들에게 영감을 주었다.

② Antonio Gaudi는 Sagrada Familia 성당에 나무의 형태를 사용했다.

③ Sydney Opera House는 돛단배의 모습을 표현한 것이다.

④ Sydney Opera House는 오렌지에서 영감을 얻어 디자인했다.

⑤ Sydney Opera House는 Jørn Utzon이라는 건축가가 디자인했다.

26 위 글의 빈칸 (A)에 들어갈 단어의 영어 뜻풀이로 가장 적절한 것은? (4점)

① easy to see or understand

② the things that are inside something

③ the ability to form pictures or ideas in your mind

④ something that gives you ideas about what to do or create

⑤ to represent or describe something very accurately using words or image

27 위 글의 내용과 일치하는 것은? (3점)

① Nature often tries to imitate art in many ways.

② Humans always fail to catch the beauty of the nature by building structures.

③ There is an orange-shaped building in London, England.

④ Outside of the Sagrada Familia, you can see the columns that look like flowers.

⑤ Antoni Gaudi tried to capture the beauty of nature by building Sagrada Familia.

28 위 글의 밑줄 친 (A)them이 가리키는 것으로 알맞은 것은? (3점)

① the expression

② Many artists

③ their ideas

④ inspirations

⑤ the world

29 위 글의 빈칸 ⓐ∼ⓔ에 들어갈 말로 알맞지 <u>않은</u> 것은? (3점)

① ⓐ - heard

② ⓑ - pleased

③ ⓒ - For example

④ ⓓ - Isn't

⑤ ⓔ - Such

[28∼30] 다음 글을 읽고 물음에 답하시오.

Have you ⓐ_____ of the expression, "Art imitates nature"? Many artists get their ideas and inspirations from the world around (A)<u>them</u>. This is because the natural world is a beautiful place. The shapes in nature are very ⓑ_____ to the eye. ⓒ_____, look at the egg on the left. ⓓ_____ it beautiful? (B)그것은 둥글고 부서지기 쉽지만 그것의 내용물을 보호할 만큼 충분히 강하다. Can you imagine a building that looks like an egg? ⓔ_____ a building actually exists in London.

30 위 글의 (B)의 우리말과 같은 뜻이 되도록 〈보기〉의 단어들을 배열할 때 다섯 번째 오는 것은? (4점)

> **보기**
>
> delicate / contents / yet / round / and / enough to / its / protect / strong

→ It is _____.

① its   ② yet

③ and   ④ strong

⑤ enough to

3학년 영어 2학기 중간고사(7과) 1회

문항수 : 선택형(29문항)   서술형(1문항)   20 . . .

◎ 선택형 문항의 답안은 컴퓨터용 수정 싸인펜을 사용하여 OMR 답안지에 바르게 표기하시오.
◎ 서술형 문제는 답을 답안지에 반드시 검정 볼펜으로 쓰시오.
◎ 총 30문항 100점 만점입니다. 문항별 배점은 각 문항에 표시되어 있습니다.

[서울 강남구 ○○중]

01 다음 중 빈칸에 들어갈 단어가 나머지 넷과 <u>다른</u> 것은? (3점)

① The boy _____ dog is very big is Tom.
② Shrek is a monster _____ is always friendly.
③ I have a friend _____ hobby is playing baseball.
④ BTS is a popular idol group _____ fan club name is ARMY.
⑤ My sister _____ favorite subject is math hates English.

[경기 ○○중]

02 다음 두 문장의 빈칸에 공통으로 들어갈 알맞은 것은? (3점)

> • I have a watch _____ price is 9,000 won.
> • I met a girl _____ name is the same as mine.

① who   ② that   ③ whom
④ which   ⑤ whose

[서울 마포구 ○○중]

03 다음 중 두 단어의 관계가 나머지와 <u>다른</u> 하나는? (4점)

① allow : let   ② book : borrow
③ book : reserve   ④ imitate: mimic
⑤ join : participate

[충북 ○○중]

04 다음 중 밑줄 친 부분이 어법상 <u>어색한</u> 것은? (3점)

① He visited the temple <u>which</u> was built in 1800.
② My sister met a boy <u>who</u> hobby is swimming.
③ Son Heungmin, <u>who</u> is a soccer player, is my role model.
④ The person <u>who</u> pulled your hair must be your son.
⑤ I still remember the first piece of music <u>that</u> we played.

[서울 강남구 ○○중]

05 다음 중 우리말로 바르게 해석한 것은? (4점)

① Did you stay up all night?
   → 너 밤새 안 잤니?
② I keep in touch with my old friend.
   → 나는 내 옛 친구와 연락이 안 된다.
③ Where do you want to hang out today?
   → 너 오늘 어디에서 공부하고 싶니?
④ I'll have a piece of pizza rather than cake.
   → 나는 피자를 먹고 나서 케이크를 먹을 거야.
⑤ We had to put off our soccer game.
   → 우리는 우리의 축구 경기를 취소해야만 했다.

06 다음 중 어법상 옳지 <u>않은</u> 것은? (3점)

① The boy whose hair is red is Mark.

② I saw a dog which tail is very short.

③ She met the man whose name is Homin.

④ I like the girl whose hobby is playing the piano.

⑤ The man whose painting is in the museum is my uncle.

07 다음 대화의 내용과 일치하는 것은? (3점)

> W: Look at the baby penguins on TV. They're so cute.
> M: Yes, but they look very cold out there.
> W: Yeah, the South Pole is the coldest place on Earth.
> M: I wonder how cold it is there.
> W: The average temperature is about -58℃ in July and -26℃ in December.
> M: Oh, really? That's interesting!
> W: Also, though it's very cold there, it doesn't snow much.
> M: That's interesting, too!
> *M: man, W: woman

① They are watching a picture of penguins.

② The North Pole is the coldest on Earth.

③ The woman wants to know about the temperature in the South Pole.

④ July is colder than December in the South Pole.

⑤ It snows a lot in the South Pole.

08 다음 대화의 빈칸 (A), (B)에 들어갈 알맞은 단어로 짝지어진 것은? (4점)

> 보기
>
> A: Which planet is the biggest in our solar system?
> B: I think it's Jupiter.
> A: I (A)_____ (B)_____ big it is.
> B: The Internet says Jupiter is over 11 times bigger than Earth.
> A: That's amazing!

	(A)	(B)
①	think	why
②	know	how
③	think	how
④	wonder	which
⑤	wonder	how

09 다음 중 짝지어진 대화가 <u>어색한</u> 것은? (3점)

① A: You got caught in the rain.

　B: I should not have taken an umbrella.

② A: Why were you late for class?

　B: I had a bad stomachache.

③ A: I wonder where the bus stop is.

　B: It's in front of the police station.

④ A: Are you ready for the singing contest?

　B: I'm thinking of giving up.

⑤ A: What is the longest river in the world?

　B: I think it's the Amazon river.

10 다음 문장의 밑줄 친 (A)~(C)와 용법이 같은 관계대명사를 〈보기〉에서 찾아 고른 것은? (4점)

- The book (A)that I read yesterday was boring.
- The man (B)whose wallet was stolen called the police.
- The students (C)who are late will clean the classroom.

> 보기
- The girls ⓐwho we met are Chinese.
- That is the reporter ⓑwhose article I read.
- He is the boy ⓒwho received the gold medal.
- Do you have anyone ⓓwho you can depend on?
- The person ⓔwho is looking at you is my father.
- I'm going to wear the tie ⓕwhich I bought yesterday.

	(A)	(B)	(C)
①	ⓐ, ⓑ	ⓒ, ⓓ	ⓔ, ⓕ
②	ⓐ, ⓓ	ⓑ, ⓒ	ⓔ, ⓕ
③	ⓐ, ⓕ	ⓑ, ⓓ	ⓒ, ⓔ
④	ⓐ, ⓓ, ⓔ	ⓑ	ⓒ, ⓕ
⑤	ⓐ, ⓓ, ⓕ	ⓑ	ⓒ, ⓔ

11 다음 글의 (A)~(C)에 들어갈 접속사로 가장 적절한 것은? (3점)

Humpback whales stand on their tails (A)_____ they sleep. They sleep near the surface. (B)_____ they are not fish, they need to come up to breathe. Also, they don't fall asleep completely. When they wake up, they come out of the water (C)_____ they can breathe. After a deep breath, they dive back into the sea.

	(A)	(B)	(C)
①	because	After	that
②	when	Since	so that
③	while	Because	though
④	unless	As soon as	until
⑤	as	If	when

12 다음 중 어법상 옳은 문장을 2개 고르면? (3점)

① Shrek is a friendly monster that body is green.

② I met a girl whose name is the same as mine.

③ We know a boy which favorite subject is music.

④ She will wait here until the concert will be over.

⑤ Mike called her back as soon as he saw her message.

13 다음 대화의 내용과 일치하지 <u>않는</u> 것은? (3점)

> Suji: Check out this picture!
>
> Tony: Wow! The camels are walking in a line in the desert.
>
> Suji: Yeah. The desert looks very hot and dry.
>
> Tony: I wonder how long camels can go without water in the desert.
>
> Suji: Let's find out on the Internet.
>
> Tony: Okay. The Internet says they can go about two weeks without water.
>
> Suji: Wow, that's amazing! Camels are really interesting animals.
>
> Tony: I want to travel with them in the desert someday.

① Suji와 Tony는 사진을 보고 있다.

② 사막은 매우 덥고 건조해 보인다.

③ Tony는 낙타와 사막을 여행한 적이 있다.

④ 낙타들은 한 줄로 사막을 걷고 있다.

⑤ 낙타들은 물 없이 2주 동안 사막에서 살 수 있다.

[14~15] 다음 글을 읽고 물음에 답하시오.

> One, Two, Three, Jump!
>
> You have probably seen a bird fly down to the sea to catch a fish. But have you ever seen a fish jump out of the water to catch a bird? Well, birds have to be careful when a giant trevally is around. This fish can grow up to 170cm and 80kg. But don't let its size fool you. This fish is quick and smart. (A)_____ When the bird flies nearby, the giant trevally jumps out of the water and catches it.

14 위 글의 내용상 주어진 질문에 대한 답이 바르지 <u>않은</u> 것은? (4점)

① What does the giant trevally eat?

→ It eats only other big fish.

② How big does the giant trevally grow?

→ It can grow up to 170cm and 80kg.

③ What can the giant trevally calculate?

→ It can calculate the flying bird's speed and distance.

④ Why shouldn't you be fooled by the giant trevally's size?

→ Because it is quick and smart.

⑤ How does the giant trevally catch the bird?

→ It jumps out of the water and catches the bird when it flies nearby.

15 위 글의 빈칸 (A)에 들어갈 문장으로 가장 적절한 것은? (3점)

① The bird can fly really fast.

② It can calculate the size of a bird.

③ It can spot fish that are hiding behind rocks.

④ It can calculate how many birds are flying around.

⑤ It is smart enough to calculate the speed and distance of a flying bird.

16 다음 중 어법상 올바른 문장은? (3점)

① I saw a dog which tail is very short.

② I have some friends who they like English.

③ Shrek is a monster whose wife is Fiona.

④ She is the girl whom can finish it.

⑤ The boy whose I ate lunch with was Tom.

[18~21] 다음 글을 읽고 물음에 답하시오.

You have probably seen a bird ⓐ<u>fly down</u> to the sea to catch a fish. But have you ever seen a fish jump out of the water to catch a bird? Well, birds have to be careful when a giant trevally is ⓑ<u>around</u>. This fish can grow up to 170cm and 80kg. But don't let its size (A)<u>fool</u> you. This fish is ⓒ<u>quick</u> and smart. It can spot a flying bird and calculate ⓓ<u>their speed and distance</u>. When the bird flies ⓔ<u>nearby</u>, the giant trevally jumps out of the water and catches it.

18 위 글의 밑줄 친 ⓐ~ⓔ 중 어법상 옳지 <u>않은</u> 것은? (3점)

① ⓐ   ② ⓑ   ③ ⓒ

④ ⓓ   ⑤ ⓔ

---

17 다음 빈칸 ⓐ에 공통으로 들어갈 말로 가장 알맞은 것은? (4점)

Tsunami waves are not very ⓐ_____ in deep water although they travel fast. People in boats may ride over the waves without even noticing them. However, when the waves approach land and the water becomes shallow, the waves slow down and get bigger and bigger. People who saw the tsunami in 2004 said that the waves were almost 30 meters ⓐ_____.

① high

② large

③ strong

④ shallow

⑤ dangerous

---

19 According to the passage above, which of the following is true? (3점)

① All birds can catch small fish in the sea.

② Birds don't have to be careful when the giant trevally is nearby.

③ Only a few trevallies grow up to 170cm and 80kg.

④ People cannot be fooled by the giant trevally's size and speed.

⑤ Giant trevally is very smart because it can calculate flying birds' speed and distance.

20 위 글의 밑줄 친 (A)fool과 같은 의미로 쓰인 문장은? (3점)

① I felt a <u>fool</u> when I realized my mistake.

② He is <u>fool</u> enough to come to me for help.

③ Don't be such a <u>fool</u>.

④ The <u>fool</u> doesn't know that these promises are never kept.

⑤ Be a smart eater and don't be <u>fooled</u> by the advertisement.

[22~25] 다음 글을 읽고 물음에 답하시오.

If you think fish are not smart, take a look at the tuskfish. This small fish (A)<u>whose</u> favorite food is clams (가)<u>use</u> a tool to open them. Clams usually hide under the sand, so they cannot be easily discovered. The tuskfish blows on the sand ⓐ_____ a clam appears. The clam is closed tightly, so the fish cannot eat it. But the tuskfish doesn't give up. It smashes the clam against a rock. In the end, the clam opens and dinner is (나)<u>serve</u>.

---

21 위 글의 giant trevally에 대한 내용과 일치하지 <u>않는</u> 것은? (3점)

① 새를 잡는다.

② 빠르고 똑똑하다.

③ 170cm에 80kg까지 자랄 수 있다.

④ 물 밖으로 뛰어올라 사냥을 한다.

⑤ 수면에 앉은 새를 잡을 수 있다.

---

22 위 글의 빈칸 ⓐ에 들어갈 말과 다음 문장의 빈칸에 들어갈 말이 같은 것은? (3점)

① I wonder _____ you can help me.

② I have known her _____ she was born.

③ They will wait for the train _____ it arrives.

④ He wanted to be a singer _____ he was young.

⑤ Tony lost his phone _____ he was playing soccer.

23 위 글을 읽고 답할 수 <u>없는</u> 것은? (3점)

① Where do the clams hide?

② Why does the tuskfish use a tool?

③ What is the tuskfish's favorite food?

④ How does the tuskfish open the clams?

⑤ Why does the tuskfish like clams?

24 위 글의 (A)whose와 용법이 같은 것을 〈보기〉에서 있는 대로 고른 것은? (3점)

보기

ⓐ Could you tell me <u>whose</u> that hat is?

ⓑ <u>Whose</u> pizza was the most delicious?

ⓒ My son <u>whose</u> major was English is a teacher.

ⓓ <u>Whose</u> responsibility is it to take care of the child?

ⓔ Harry potter is an unusual boy <u>whose</u> parents are magicians.

① ⓐ, ⓓ

② ⓑ, ⓒ

③ ⓒ, ⓔ

④ ⓐ, ⓑ, ⓒ

⑤ ⓒ, ⓓ, ⓔ

25 위 글의 (가), (나)에 주어진 각각의 단어를 알맞게 변형하여 〈조건〉에 맞게 빈칸을 채우시오. (5점)

조건

• 어법과 철자의 오류가 없어야 함.

• 주어진 단어의 형태를 변형할 수 있음.

(가) _____

(나) _____

[26~30] 다음 글을 읽고 물음에 답하시오.

Can you guess (가)_____ in the picture? ⓐ It looks like they are standing up in a group. ⓑ Humpback whales stand on their tails (A)[while / during] they sleep. ⓒ They sleep (B)[near / nearly] the surface. ⓓ (나)<u>Since</u> they are not fish, they need to come up to breathe. ⓔ Also, they don't fall (C)[sleepy / asleep] completely. When they wake up, they come out of the water for a deep breath and dive back into the sea.

26 위 글의 흐름에 맞게 빈칸 (가)에 들어갈 말을 고르면? (3점)

① how are these whales doing

② what these whales are doing

③ these whales are doing what

④ what are these whales doing

⑤ how do these whales something

29 위 글의 밑줄 친 (나)와 같은 의미로 쓰인 것은? (3점)

① He's worked for this company <u>since</u> 2017.

② He's been collecting stamps <u>since</u> he was ten.

③ My brother has changed a lot <u>since</u> his graduation.

④ It's been over seven months <u>since</u> I had the accident.

⑤ The man couldn't dig in the ground <u>since</u> it was too dark.

27 위 글의 괄호 (A), (B), (C) 안에서 어법에 맞는 표현으로 가장 적절한 것은? (4점)

	(A)	(B)	(C)
①	while	near	asleep
②	while	near	sleepy
③	while	nearly	asleep
④	during	nearly	asleep
⑤	during	nearly	sleepy

28 위 글의 ⓐ~ⓔ 중 아래의 문장이 들어가기에 가장 적절한 곳은? (4점)

But they are actually sleeping!

① ⓐ   ② ⓑ   ③ ⓒ

④ ⓓ   ⑤ ⓔ

30 위 글의 내용상 humpback whales에 대한 설명으로 일치하지 않는 것은? (3점)

① 수면 근처에서 잠을 잔다.

② 완전히 잠들지는 않는다.

③ 물고기의 한 종류로 거대하다.

④ 숨을 쉬기 위해 물 밖으로 나온다.

⑤ 잠을 자는 동안 꼬리로 서 있다.

3학년 영어 2학기 중간고사(7과) 2회

문항수 : 선택형(28문항) 서술형(2문항) 20 . . .

◎ 선택형 문항의 답안은 컴퓨터용 수정 싸인펜을 사용하여 OMR 답안지에 바르게 표기하시오.
◎ 서술형 문제는 답을 답안지에 반드시 검정 볼펜으로 쓰시오.
◎ 총 30문항 100점 만점입니다. 문항별 배점은 각 문항에 표시되어 있습니다.

[서울 강남구 ○○중]

01 다음 중 밑줄 친 단어의 쓰임이 <u>어색한</u> 것은? (3점)

① Is this a good <u>spot</u> to hide?

② The beautiful sights <u>spot</u> many tourists.

③ I can <u>spot</u> my boyfriend from a long distance.

④ This is my favorite <u>spot</u> to relax and drink coffee.

⑤ The goal is to <u>spot</u> the difference between these pictures.

[서울 강남구 ○○중]

02 다음 <보기>의 분수를 영어로 바르게 읽은 것은? (3점)

> **보기**
>
> 3/4

① three four

② third of four

③ three fourths

④ three and fourth

⑤ third of fourth

[서울 마포구 ○○중]

03 다음 빈칸에 알맞은 단어를 <보기>에서 골라 쓸 때 사용되지 <u>않는</u> 것은? (4점)

> • Giving a hug is a(n) _____ of love.
> • According to the weather _____, it will be sunny tomorrow.
> • The _____ of the bed was made of wood.
> • I'll be busy tomorrow. Can we meet on Friday _____?

① base   ② expression   ③ forecast

④ hurry   ⑤ instead

[경기 ○○중]

04 다음 중 밑줄 친 관계대명사가 바르게 쓰인 것은? (3점)

① The pill <u>whom</u> I took made me sleepy.

② I met a couple <u>whom</u> just got married.

③ I remember the girl <u>whose</u> we met in Italy.

④ I met a man <u>who</u> wife is an English teacher.

⑤ Did you find the book <u>which</u> you were looking for?

05 다음 대화의 빈칸에 들어갈 말로 가장 알맞은 것은? (3점)

> B: The weather is so nice outside.
> G: Yeah. How about going on a picnic this afternoon?
> B: Good idea. Can you check the weather?
> G: On, no! The weather forecast says it'll be rainy in the afternoon.
> B: _____

① We're finally here.

② You're right. Let's go.

③ Let's go another time, then.

④ I can't agree with you more.

⑤ It look very cold out there.

06 다음 중 어법상 <u>어색한</u> 문장은? (3점)

① I wonder where is the bus stop.

② Experience makes even fools wise.

③ We had dinner after we watched a movie.

④ Can you spot the difference between these two pictures?

⑤ Tom waited in front of the door until someone came out.

07 다음 괄호 안에 주어진 접속사를 사용하여 두 문장을 한 문장으로 연결했을 때 <u>어색한</u> 것은? (4점)

① We had dinner.
  We watched a movie. (after)
→ We had dinner after we watched a movie.

② Emily met many foreigners.
  She was in Paris. (while)
→ Emily met many foreigners while she was in Paris.

③ Jane mopped the floor.
  It looked very shiny. (after)
→ After Jane mopped the floor, it looked very shiny.

④ Yongchan will grow up.
  He will be a scientist. (when)
→ When Yongchan will grow up, he will be a scientist.

⑤ You have to finish your homework.
  You go to bed. (before)
→ Before you go to bed, you have to finish your homework.

Jisung: I think fish are not so smart.

Yumi: That's not true. You should take a look at the tuskfish.

Jisung: Tuskfish? I have never heard of it before.

Yumi: Well, it's a small fish whose favorite food is clams.

Jisung: How can a fish eat clams?

Yumi: The tuskfish blows on the sand under the sea until they find a clam, and then, uses a tool to open it.

Jisung: Fish using tools? Is that possible?

Yumi: It throws the clam very hard against a rock until the clam opens or breaks. Finally, the clam opens and dinner is served.

Jisung: Wow! That is so amazing! You're right. The tuskfish is a very smart fish after all!

[서울 강남구 ○○중]

08 위 대화의 주제로 알맞은 것은? (4점)

① The size of the tuskfish

② Fish that are not smart

③ Favorite food of the tuskfish

④ How clams hide under the sea

⑤ A smart fish using tools for food

[서울 강남구 ○○중]

09 위 대화의 내용과 일치하는 것은? (3점)

① Yumi는 Jisung의 말에 동의하지 않는다.

② Jisung은 tuskfish에 대해 들어 본 적이 있다.

③ Yumi는 tuskfish에 대해서 새로 알게 되었다.

④ Jisung은 모든 물고기가 똑똑하다고 생각한다.

⑤ Yumi는 Jisung에게 tuskfish에 대해 물어보고 있다.

[경기 ○○중]

10 다음 중 어법상 옳지 않은 것은? (4점)

① When he was a child, he lived in Busan.

② I learned French after I moved to Paris.

③ I met my friend while I was on my way to school.

④ When she will come back home, she will call her dad.

⑤ You have to finish your homework before you go to bed.

[경기 ○○중]

11 다음 글의 괄호 (A)~(C) 안에서 어법에 맞는 어구로 가장 적절한 것은? (4점)

I love my girlfriend so much. I can do anything for her. When she (A)[asks / will ask] me for help, I will do it with pleasure. We will get married as soon as we (B)[graduate / will graduate] from the university. We (C)[buy / will buy] a house when we have enough money.

	(A)	(B)	(C)
①	asks	graduate	buy
②	will ask	will graduate	will buy
③	asks	graduate	will buy
④	will ask	graduate	buy
⑤	asks	will graduate	buy

12 다음 짝지어진 대화가 가장 자연스러운 것은? (3점)

① A: How have you been?

　　B: I've been to Jeju-do.

② A: I wonder where the bus stop is.

　　B: Yes, it is full of wonder.

③ A: You're not allowed to fly a drone here.

　　B: You're welcome. I didn't know that.

④ A: Thank you for recommending me the movie.

　　B : It is my pleasure.

⑤ A: I had a fight with my friend.

　　B: That's why you look upset. I'm glad to hear that.

13 다음 글의 ⓐ~ⓔ 중 어법상 어색한 것은? (3점)

Sweet Dreams

Can you guess ⓐwhat these whales are doing in the picture? ⓑIt looks like they are standing up in a group. But they are actually sleeping! ⓒHumpback whales stand on their tails while they sleep. They sleep near the surface. ⓓSince they are not fish, they need to come up to breath. ⓔAlso, they don't fall asleep completely. When they wake up, they come out of the water for a deep breath and dive back into the sea.

① ⓐ　　　　② ⓑ　　　　③ ⓒ

④ ⓓ　　　　⑤ ⓔ

[14~17] 다음 글을 읽고 물음에 답하시오.

Two-thirds of our planet is covered by oceans. (A)바다는 신기한 것으로 가득 차 있고 수많은 종의 서식지이다. Every day, we are learning new things about them. Let's find out about some interesting sea animals.

Sweet Dreams

Can you guess what these whales are doing in the picture? It looks like they are standing up in a group. But they are actually sleeping! Humpback whales stand on their tails while they sleep. They sleep near the surface. Since they are not fish, they need to come up to breathe. Also, they don't fall asleep completely. When they wake up, they come out of the water for a deep breath and dive back into the sea.

Enjoy Your Meal

If you think fish are not smart, take a look at the tuskfish. (B)(가장 좋아하는 먹이가 조개인 이 작은 물고기는) uses a tool to open ⓐthem. Clams usually hide under the sand, so ⓑthey cannot be easily discovered. The tuskfish blows on the sand until a clam appears. The clam is closed tightly, so the fish cannot eat ⓒit. But the tuskfish doesn't give up. ⓓIt smashes the clam against a rock. In the end, ⓔthe clam opens and dinner is served.

14 위 글의 밑줄 친 문장 (A)를 〈보기〉의 단어들을 모두 사용하여 만들 때, ★에 알맞은 것은? (3점)

> 보기
>
> to / millions / species / home / of

> Oceans are full of wonder and are _____ _____ _(★)_ _____ _____.

① to ② millions
③ species ④ home
⑤ of

15 위 글의 밑줄 친 @~@ 중, 가리키는 대상이 <u>다른</u> 것은? (3점)

① @ ② ⓑ ③ ⓒ
④ ⓓ ⑤ ⓔ

16 위 글을 읽고 답할 수 <u>없는</u> 것은? (4점)

① Where do humpback whales sleep?
② How does the tuskfish discover clams?
③ When is the tuskfish's favorite time to eat?
④ How much of the planet is covered by oceans?
⑤ Why do humpback whales sleep near the surface?

17 위 글의 괄호 안의 밑줄 친 우리말 (B)와 같도록 주어진 단어들을 바르게 배열하여 문장으로 쓰시오. (4점)

> whose, this small fish, is, food, favorite, clams

→ _____

[18~21] 다음 글을 읽고 물음에 답하시오.

You have probably seen a bird fly down to the sea to catch a fish. But have you ever (A)_____ a fish jump out of the water to catch a bird? Well, birds have to be careful when a giant trevally is around. @<u>This fish</u> can grow up to 170cm and 80kg. But don't let its size (가)<u>fool</u> you. ⓑ<u>This fish</u> is quick and smart. ⓒ<u>It</u> can spot a flying bird and calculate its speed and distance. When the bird flies nearby, ⓓ<u>the giant trevally</u> jumps out of the water and catches ⓔ<u>it</u>.

18 위 글의 빈칸 (A)에 들어갈 말로 알맞은 것은? (3점)

① see ② seeing ③ seen
④ to see ⑤ saw

19 위 글의 밑줄 친 @~@ 중 가리키는 것이 <u>다른</u> 것은? (3점)

① @ ② ⓑ ③ ⓒ
④ ⓓ ⑤ ⓔ

20 위 글의 giant trevally에 관한 내용과 일치하지 <u>않는</u> 것은?

(3점)

① 물 밖에서 새의 먹이가 된다.

② 물 밖으로 뛰어오를 수 있다.

③ 170cm까지 자랄 수 있다.

④ 무게가 80kg까지 나가기도 한다.

⑤ 날고 있는 새의 속도와 거리를 계산할 수 있다.

21 위 글의 (가)fool과 쓰임이 같은 문장을 <u>모두</u> 고르면? (정답 3개)

(4점)

① Experience makes even <u>fools</u> wise.

② Don't be <u>fooled</u> by his cute looks.

③ You can't <u>fool</u> me with that excuse.

④ He tries to <u>fool</u> people about his age.

⑤ I felt like a <u>fool</u> when I lost my phone again.

[22~25] 다음 글을 읽고 물음에 답하시오.

If you think fish are not smart, take a look at the tuskfish. This small fish (A)_____ favorite food is clams uses a tool to open them. Clams usually hide under the sand, so they cannot be easily discovered. The tuskfish blows on the sand (B)_____ a clam appears. The clam is closed tightly, so the fish cannot eat ⓐ<u>it</u>. But the tuskfish doesn't give up. It smashes the clam (C)_____ a rock. In the end, the clam opens and dinner is served.

22 위 글의 빈칸 (A)에 들어갈 말로 알맞은 것은? (3점)

① who

② that

③ whose

④ which

⑤ whom

23 위 글의 빈칸 (B)에 들어갈 말로 가장 알맞은 것은? (3점)

① after

② until

③ because

④ while

⑤ when

24 위 글의 빈칸 (C)에 들어갈 말로 알맞은 것은? (3점)

① against

② hide

③ forward

④ across

⑤ backward

25 위 글의 밑줄 친 ⓐ가 가리키는 말을 쓰시오. (3점)

→ _____

Can you guess (가)what these whales are doing in the picture? It looks like they are standing up in a group. But they are actually sleeping! Humpback whales stand on their tails while they sleep. They sleep near the surface. ⓐSince they are not fish, they need to come up ⓑbreathe. Also, they don't fall asleep completely. When they wake up, they come out of the water for a deep breath and dive back into the sea.

[충북 ○○중]

26 위 글의 밑줄 친 (가)와 용법이 같게 쓰인 것은? (4점)

① What he said to me was really true.

② The result was different from what I expected.

③ That's what happens when you get careless.

④ I don't know what is in the box.

⑤ What he brought for me was a bunch of flowers.

[경기 ○○중]

27 위 글의 밑줄 친 ⓐSince와 의미가 같은 것은? (3점)

① I have known her since she was a child.

② He has not been at home since Christmas.

③ Since 2019, he has won every competition.

④ It has been ten years since the war ended.

⑤ Since you were late, your teacher got angry.

[경기 ○○중]

28 위 글의 밑줄 친 ⓑbreathe의 형태로 알맞은 것은? (3점)

① breathe

② breathed

③ breath

④ to breathe

⑤ breathing

[경기 ○○중]

29 위 글의 주제로 가장 적절한 것은? (4점)

① What humpback whales eat

② How humpback whales sleep

③ Where humpback whales live

④ The way humpback whales swim

⑤ Why humpback whales are disappearing

[경기 ○○중]

30 위 글의 혹등고래(humpback whale)에 관한 내용과 일치하지 않는 것은? (3점)

① 물고기가 아니다.

② 꼬리로 서서 잠을 잔다.

③ 해수면 가까이에서 잠을 잔다.

④ 잠을 잘 때 깊은 숙면을 취한다.

⑤ 해수면 밖에서 호흡을 해야 한다.

3학년 영어 2학기 중간고사(8과) 1회

문항수 : 선택형(29문항) 서술형(1문항)　　　20 ． ． ．

◎ 선택형 문항의 답안은 컴퓨터용 수정 싸인펜을 사용하여 OMR 답안지에 바르게 표기하시오.

◎ 서술형 문제는 답을 답안지에 반드시 검정 볼펜으로 쓰시오.

◎ 총 30문항 100점 만점입니다. 문항별 배점은 각 문항에 표시되어 있습니다.

[경기 ○○중]

01 다음 영어 표현과 우리말 뜻이 알맞게 짝지어진 것은? (3점)

① spill: 섞다

② describe: 나누다

③ mistakenly: 일부러

④ rather than ~: ~ 덕분에

⑤ contribute: 공헌하다

[울산 ○○중]

02 다음 중 빈칸 어느 곳에도 들어갈 수 없는 단어는 무엇인가? (3점)

- The _____ of the river was calm.
- I'll _____ how much money we need.
- I want to _____ fresh air.
- We were _____ at her death.
- We learn from the _____ of others.

① shocked

② mistakes

③ calculate

④ regret

⑤ breathe

[서울 강남구 ○○중]

03 다음 빈칸에 들어갈 대답으로 적절하지 <u>않은</u> 것은? (3점)

A: Is there anything you regret about your middle school life?

B: _____

① Yes. I should have read many English books.

② Yes. I should have been on time to school every day.

③ Yes. I didn't take part in any of my school events.

④ No. I did my best on almost everything during the school years.

⑤ No. I regret riding my bicycle to school instead of taking the bus.

[서울 강남구 ○○중]

04 다음 짝지어진 문장의 의미를 같게 만들 때 어법상 바른 것은? (3점)

① After she lost the game, she felt upset.

= Lost the game, she felt upset.

② Because I was nervous, I forgot my lines.

= I being nervous, I forgot my lines.

③ If you turn to the right, you will find the shop.

= Turning to the right, you found the shop.

④ While he listened to music, he watered the plants.

= While listening to music, he watered the plants.

⑤ As I didn't do my homework, I had to stay at home.

= Doing not my homework, I had to stay at home.

05 다음 대화에 이어질 것을 순서대로 나열한 것은? (4점)

Minho: Linda, what are you reading?
Linda: Oh, Minho. I'm reading graduation messages from my classmates.

(A)
Minho: That's nice. What else?
Linda: Some of them said I didn't hang out enough with them.

(B)
Minho: Oh, it looks like they had a lot to say to you.
Linda: Many of them wrote that they like my smile.

(C)
Minho: I hope you keep in touch with your classmates after graduation.
Linda: Thanks. I hope so, too.

(D)
Minho: That's not your fault. You were always busy.
Linda: Yeah, but I should have spent more time with my classmates.

(E)
Minho: You still have time after graduation.
Linda: You're right.

① (B)-(A)-(D)-(E)-(C)
② (B)-(A)-(E)-(C)-(D)
③ (C)-(A)-(E)-(B)-(D)
④ (D)-(E)-(A)-(B)-(C)
⑤ (D)-(A)-(E)-(B)-(C)

06 다음 대화의 빈칸에 알맞지 않은 것은? (3점)

A: How long does the shortest hiking course take?
B: _____ it takes about two hours.

① This book says
② This article says
③ The Internet says
④ I never say that
⑤ According to the Internet,

07 다음 대화 중 자연스럽지 않은 것은? (3점)

① A: I was late for school this morning.
   B: You should have gotten up earlier.
② A: I got caught in the rain.
   B: You should have taken an umbrella.
③ A: I lost my new bike yesterday.
   B: You should have chained it tightly.
④ A: I failed the final exam.
   B: You should have studied much harder.
⑤ A: I had a bad stomachache. I ate too much last night.
   B: You should have eaten more.

08 다음 대화의 밑줄 친 부분의 의도로 가장 알맞은 것은? (3점)

> A: What are you going to do tomorrow?
> B: I'm going to have a job interview.
> A: Great! I hope you pass the interview.
> B: Thanks. I hope so, too.

① 경고하기

② 기원하기

③ 도움을 요청하기

④ 과거의 일을 후회하기

⑤ 미래의 일을 계획하기

09 다음 밑줄 친 부분이 어법상 바르게 쓰인 것을 모두 고른 것은? (4점)

> (A) I went to bed after I had watched TV.
> (B) I had played baseball after I ate dinner.
> (C) I found that I had left my key at home.
> (D) I study English and had read a book every night.
> (E) When I returned home, my dog had eaten all my cookies.

① (A), (B)

② (A), (C), (E)

③ (B), (D), (E)

④ (A), (C), (D), (E)

⑤ (A), (B), (C), (D), (E)

10 다음 중 어법상 올바른 문장은? (3점)

① Mike was sick in bed for a week when I visited him.

② He had stayed up late last night.

③ I had gone to school after I took a shower quickly.

④ Katie arrived at the theater at 5 o'clock, but the play had already begun.

⑤ When she came back home, she found that someone stole the diamond ring.

11 다음 중 과거완료 시제를 활용한 문장 중 어법상 어색한 것은? (3점)

① When I got to the store, it had already closed.

② She had lost the bag that her father bought for her.

③ My brother had already eaten pizza when I came back home.

④ We knew about Tony because we had met him before.

⑤ There had been a cute cat in my house before I was born.

12 다음 〈보기〉에서 어법상 맞는 문장을 있는 대로 고른 것은?

(4점)

> **보기**
>
> A: Where is his hometown?
> B: He was born in Busan and he still lives there. ⓐHe has lived there for 15 years.
>
> A: Did you enjoy the play?
> B: No, I couldn't. ⓑWhen I arrived at the theater, the play had already ended.
>
> A: Why did Jimmy borrow money?
> B: ⓒHe had borrowed money because he lost his wallet.
>
> A: Why are you so angry?
> B: I couldn't eat pizza. ⓓMy friends already finished it before I had arrived.
>
> A: I heard you visited your grandmother. How was she?
> B: Not good. ⓔMy grandmother had been ill for five days when I visited her.
>
> A: What did the newspaper report about the car accident?
> B: ⓕIt said that the accident had happened at the corner of the school.

① ⓐ, ⓑ, ⓔ

② ⓐ, ⓑ, ⓒ, ⓔ

③ ⓐ, ⓑ, ⓔ, ⓕ

④ ⓐ, ⓑ, ⓒ, ⓔ, ⓕ

⑤ ⓐ, ⓑ, ⓓ, ⓔ, ⓕ

13 다음 중 〈보기〉의 문장이 들어갈 곳으로 가장 적절한 것은?

(3점)

> **보기**
>
> Thanks to the report, however, Nobel decided to do something to contribute to the world.

> In 1888, a French newspaper mistakenly reported Alfred Nobel's death. (A) The person who had actually died was his brother, Ludvig. (B) In 1895, he decided to use his money to create the Nobel Prize. (C) Originally, there were only five awards. A sixth award was added in 1968. (D) Today, when we think of Alfred Nobel, we think of the Nobel Prize, rather than dynamite. (E)

① (A)   ② (B)   ③ (C)

④ (D)   ⑤ (E)

14 다음 밑줄 친 동사를 알맞게 변형하시오.

(5점)

> (A) <u>Save</u> by the firefighter, they felt happy.
> (B) <u>Pick</u> up my kids at school, I drove to the shopping mall.
> (C) <u>Bite</u> by a monkey, he screamed as loudly as he could.

(A) _____

(B) _____

(C) _____

15 다음 〈보기 1〉의 빈칸에 들어갈 알맞은 말을 〈보기 2〉에서 골라 바르게 짝지은 것은? (4점)

┌─ 보기 1 ─────────────────────────┐
(A) I learned French _____ I moved to Paris.

(B) She will wait here _____ the class is over.

(C) He ran home _____ he got the message.

(D) Mr. Kim met many movie stars _____ he worked near Hollywood.
└──────────────────────────────────┘

┌─ 보기 2 ─────────────────────────┐
ⓐ when   ⓑ while   ⓒ if   ⓓ until

ⓔ though   ⓕ as soon as
└──────────────────────────────────┘

   (A) (B) (C) (D)

① ⓐ   ⓓ   ⓕ   ⓑ

② ⓑ   ⓕ   ⓒ   ⓔ

③ ⓒ   ⓐ   ⓓ   ⓔ

④ ⓓ   ⓑ   ⓒ   ⓕ

⑤ ⓔ   ⓕ   ⓑ   ⓒ

16 다음 밑줄 친 ⓐ~ⓔ 중 글의 흐름상 어색한 문장은? (4점)

┌──────────────────────────────────┐
Ants live in large groups called colonies. ⓐHundreds of ants live in each colony. Each ant has its own job. Together the ants help their colony grow. ⓑMost ant colonies are in the ground. A colony has many cozy little rooms.

Most ants in a colony are worker ants. They find food, care for the baby ants, and make the colony bigger. ⓒWorker ants are very weak. A single worker ant can carry something 20 times heavier than its own weight. That would be the same as a person being able to lift an elephant! ⓓIf a worker ant finds food that is too big to carry, other worker ants help. ⓔWhile they work, they communicate in order to share information about food or to get help from others.
└──────────────────────────────────┘

① ⓐ   ② ⓑ   ③ ⓒ

④ ⓓ   ⑤ ⓔ

I bought star-shaped pieces of paper for my students. On each star, I wrote a short message, beginning with "You are a star because ..."

One of my students, Lucy, showed slow progress during the year. She was smart in her own way, though. On her star, I wrote, "You are a star because you are smart and you can do anything you put your mind to. Don't forget that."

After I gave out the stars, Lucy approached me, holding her star in her hand. She was crying. "Mr. Porter, do you think I am smart?" was her question. I was the first person to tell her that in her life. The thought had never even crossed her mind until she read that star. It was by far the single greatest moment in my life. The stars were definitely worth my time.

[울산 ○○중]

17 위 글의 글쓴이의 직업은? (3점)

① 작가

② 교사

③ 과학자

④ 예술가

⑤ 정치인

[울산 ○○중]

18 위 글의 내용과 일치하는 것은? (3점)

① Lucy는 1년이 지나자 발전을 보였다.

② 글쓴이는 삼각형 모양의 메모지를 구입했다.

③ 글쓴이를 제외하면 Lucy에게 그녀가 똑똑하다고 말해준 사람이 없었다.

④ Lucy는 사실 자신이 영리하다는 것을 알고 있었다.

⑤ 글쓴이는 Lucy의 성적을 보고 포기하기로 마음 먹었다.

Dear Chris,

Two weeks ago, I moved to a new middle school. I have been feeling like a stranger ever since. The most difficult thing about school is making friends. I often have lunch in the school cafeteria by myself. Sometimes, I want to skip lunch rather than feel lonely and miserable. I cannot just let my school life go on like this. What should I do? I need your advice.

- Nick

Dear Nick,

You need to keep this simple rule in mind: you should make the first move. When you see people having lunch, go and ask if you can sit with them. Then, start a light conversation about the weather, a TV show or school life. You may be afraid of being rejected but people are nicer than you think. Think positive!

In order to make new friends, you have to give a good impression of yourself. Make sure you have a smile on your face at all times. Your smile will bring you many chances to make new friends. Good luck.

- Chris

[울산 ○○중]

19 위 글의 Nick이 글을 쓴 목적은? (3점)

① to reply to Chris

② to finish a project

③ to ask for advice

④ to look for a new club

⑤ to thank Chris

20 Which piece of advice did Chris not give to Nick? (3점)

① Think positive.

② You should move first.

③ Have a smile on your face at all times.

④ Try to give a good impression of yourself.

⑤ Always bring a serious topic like politics.

22 위 글의 흐름상 빈칸 (A)~(C)에 들어갈 단어가 옳게 짝지어진 것은? (4점)

	(A)	(B)	(C)
①	truly	actually	Originally
②	purposely	really	At first
③	mistakenly	truly	Finally
④	purposely	mistakenly	Totally
⑤	mistakenly	actually	Originally

[21~24] 다음 글을 읽고 물음에 답하시오.

After reading the newspaper, ⓐNobel was deeply disappointed.

"How could this be? This is unbelievable! I'm not a merchant of death. ⓑI want to be remembered as a person who made the world better."

ⓒHe decided to change people's opinions about him.

In 1888, a French newspaper (A)_____ reported Alfred Nobel's death. The person who had (B)_____ died was his brother, Ludvig. Thanks to the report, however, Nobel decided to do something to contribute to the world. ⓓIn 1895, he decided to use his money to create the Nobel Prize. (C)_____, there were only five awards. A sixth award was added in 1968. Today, when we think of Alfred Nobel, ⓔwe think that the Nobel Prize, rather than dynamite.

23 위 글의 내용상 주어진 질문에 대한 답이 바르지 않은 것은? (3점)

① What is the name of Nobel's brother?

→ His name is Ludvig.

② Which newspaper reported Nobel's death?

→ A French newspaper.

③ How did Nobel feel after reading the article?

→ He was very disappointed.

④ How many awards were there in Nobel Prize in 1895?

→ There were six awards.

⑤ After the report, what did Nobel decide to do?

→ He decided to do something to contribute to the world.

21 위 글의 밑줄 친 ⓐ~ⓔ 중 어법상 어색한 것은? (3점)

① ⓐ   ② ⓑ   ③ ⓒ

④ ⓓ   ⑤ ⓔ

24 위 글의 내용과 일치하지 <u>않는</u> 것은? (3점)

① Nobel은 죽음의 상인이라는 오명을 싫어했다.

② Nobel은 자신에 대한 사람들의 의견을 바꾸고 싶었다.

③ 1888년 한 프랑스 신문은 실수로 노벨의 죽음을 보도했다.

④ Nobel은 노벨상을 만들기 위해 자신의 재산을 썼다.

⑤ 노벨상이 처음 만들어질 당시, 상의 종류는 6가지였다.

25 위 글의 주인공의 심경으로 알맞은 것은? (3점)

① shocked

② happy

③ pleased

④ bored

⑤ thrilled

[26~30] 다음 글을 읽고 물음에 답하시오.

It was just a normal morning. Alfred Nobel sat in his chair to read the newspaper. While he was ⓐdrink his coffee, a headline ⓑcatch his eye: *The Merchant of Death, Alfred Nobel, Is Dead.*

"What? What is this?"

ⓒRead the article, he dropped his cup in surprise. His coffee spilled all over his clothes and desk, but he couldn't take his eyes off the newspaper.

The article was about his own death! It said Nobel had died in France from a heart attack.

"Oh my goodness! Am I dead?"

ⓓCatch his breath, Nobel kept ⓔread. Soon, he became even more shocked. The article described him as the inventor of dynamite and other dangerous objects for war. It said that he had become rich from the deaths of others. He couldn't believe his eyes. It was true that dynamite was one of his many inventions. But he never imagined that the world would think of him as (A)_____.

26 위 글의 흐름상 빈칸 (A)에 들어갈 알맞은 말은? (3점)

① a reporter

② a rich merchant

③ the merchant of death

④ the merchant of peace

⑤ the inventor who loved peace

27 위 글을 읽고, 〈보기〉의 괄호에 글의 내용과 일치하면 T, 일치하지 <u>않으면</u> F라고 쓸 때 바르게 짝지어진 것은? (4점)

> 보기
> • Nobel made many people rich.
>   (_____)
> • The newspaper reported Nobel's death.
>   (_____)
> • Nobel invented many things, including dynamite.
>   (_____)

① F - T - T
② F - F - T
③ T - T - F
④ T - T - T
⑤ F - F - F

28 위 글의 밑줄 친 ⓐ~ⓔ의 단어를 어법에 맞게 고칠 때 형태가 바르지 <u>않은</u> 것은? (3점)

① ⓐ drinking
② ⓑ catching
③ ⓒ Reading
④ ⓓ Catching
⑤ ⓔ reading

29 위 글의 내용과 일치하는 것은? (3점)

① Alfred Nobel은 부유한 상인이 되고 싶었다.
② Alfred Nobel은 가족들과 산책 중이었다.
③ Alfred Nobel은 앉아서 과학 잡지를 읽고 있었다.
④ Alfred Nobel은 옷과 책상에 커피를 쏟았다.
⑤ Alfred Nobel은 심장마비로 갑자기 죽었다.

30 다음은 위 글의 Alfred Nobel이 읽은 신문 기사이다. 빈칸 부분에 들어갈 표현으로 알맞지 <u>않은</u> 것은? (4점)

> WORLD NEWS
> APRIL 13, 1888
> **Alfred Nobel Is Dead**
> Alfred Nobel died in France from a ⓐ
> _____.
> He invented ⓑ_____ and other dangerous objects for ⓒ_____. He became ⓓ
> _____ from the deaths of others. He is responsible for the ⓔ_____ of thousands of people.

① ⓐ - heart attack
② ⓑ - dynamite
③ ⓒ - peace
④ ⓓ - rich
⑤ ⓔ - deaths

정답 및 해설

Lesson 5 (중간)

---

01 ②　**02** If I were you, I would give him sweets.　**03** ⑤

04 ④　**05** (1) what → how (2) will → would　**06** ③　**07** ③

08 ④　**09** looking forward to riding a horse　**10** ③　**11** ⑤

12 ⑤　**13** ⓓ, I'm looking forward to watching it.　**14** ④

15 ④

16 (A) If I didn't have a cold, I would watch a movie with you.

　　(B) If I were[was] a doctor, I could help you.

17 ②　**18** ②　**19** ④　**20** ④　**21** ①　**22** ④　**23** ③　**24** ①

25 ①　**26** ④　**27** ⑤　**28** ③　**29** ②

---

01 감정을 나타내는 형용사를 사용할 때, 주어가 감정을 느끼는 주체일 경우, 감정을 나타내는 형용사는 과거분사 형태로 쓰고, 주어가 감정의 대상인 경우, 현재분사(동사원형+~ing) 형태로 쓴다.

02 현재 사실과 반대되는 가정을 나타낼 때, 'If+주어+were/동사의 과거형 ~, 주어+조동사의 과거형(would/should/could/might)+동사원형 ….' 형식의 가정법과거를 쓰며, '만약 ~라면, …할 텐데.'로 해석한다.

03 look into: ~를 조사하다 / look up: ~를 찾아보다 / look for: ~를 찾다 / look after: ~를 돌보다 / look up to: ~를 존경하다 / look at: ~를 보다 / look like ~처럼 보이다

04 현재 사실과 반대되는 가정을 나타낼 때, 'If+주어+were/동사의 과거형 ~, 주어+조동사의 과거형(would/should/could/might)+동사원형 ….' 형식의 가정법과거를 쓰며, '만약 ~라면, …할 텐데.'로 해석한다.

05 (1) use의 목적어로 the copy machine이 있으므로 what을 쓸 수 없고 내용상 how로 쓰는 것이 적절하다. (2) 가정법과거는 'If+주어+were/동사의 과거형 ~, 주어+조동사의 과거형(would/should/could/might)+동사원형 ...'의 형태이다.

06 "내가 대회에서 노래를 부를 때 기타를 연주해 줄 수 있니?"라는 A의 질문에 대해 "그리고 싶지만 안 돼. 난 기타를 3년 동안 연주해 왔어."라는 B의 대답은 흐름상 자연스럽지 않다.

07 "I'm looking forward to ~."는 '나는 ~하기를 기대한다.'라는 뜻으로, 기대를 나타낼 때 사용하는 표현이다. to는 전치사로 뒤에 명사 또는 동명사(-ing)를 쓴다.

08 위 대화에 따르면, 야구 선수 Jim Abbott의 이야기는 이미 영화로 만들어졌다.

09 "I'm looking forward to ~."는 '나는 ~하기를 기대한다.'라는

뜻으로, 기대를 나타낼 때 사용하는 표현이다. to는 전치사로 뒤에 명사 또는 동명사(-ing)를 쓴다.

10 '의문사+to+동사원형'은 문장에서 주어, 목적어, 보어의 역할을 할 수 있으며, 동사의 목적어로 자주 쓰인다. 이때 해석은 의문사에 따라 '무엇을(what)/언제(when)/어디서(where)/어떻게(how) ~를 해야 할지'라고 해석한다.

11 현재 사실과 반대되는 가정을 나타낼 때, 'If+주어+were/동사의 과거형 ~, 주어+조동사의 과거형(would/should/could/might)+동사원형 …. 형식의 가정법과거를 쓰며, '만약 ~라면, …할 텐데.'로 해석한다.

12 A가 다음주 월요일에 노래 대회에 나갈 예정이라고 말하자 B는 잘됐다고 대답하고, A는 B에게 기타 연주하는 법을 아는지 물어본다. B는 3년 동안 기타를 연주해 왔다고 대답하고, A는 노래 대회에서 자신이 노래를 부를 때 기타를 연주해 줄 수 있는지 물어본다. B는 어제 체육 시간에 손을 다쳐서 해줄 수 없다고 대답하고 A는 유감을 표현하는 순서로 이어지는 것이 대화의 흐름상 가장 자연스럽다.

13 "I'm looking forward to ~."는 '나는 ~하기를 기대한다.'라는 뜻으로, 기대를 나타낼 때 사용하는 표현이다. to는 전치사로 뒤에 명사 또는 동명사(-ing)를 쓴다.

14 Jason Kim의 팬이고 작년에 그의 뮤지컬을 본 사람은 Tony가 아니라 Linda이다.

15 '의문사+to+동사원형'은 문장에서 주어, 목적어, 보어의 역할을 할 수 있으며, 동사의 목적어로 자주 쓰인다. 이때 해석은 의문사에 따라 '무엇을(what)/언제(when)/어디서(where)/어떻게(how) ~를 해야 할지'라고 해석한다.

16 현재 사실과 반대되는 가정을 나타낼 때, 'If+주어+were/동사의 과거형 ~, 주어+조동사의 과거형(would/should/could/might)+동사원형 ….' 형식의 가정법과거를 쓰며, '만약 ~라면, …할 텐데.'로 해석한다.

17 ⓐ is → are / ⓑ member → members / ⓒ have just finished → has just finished / ⓓ is → has been으로 고쳐야 어법상 적절한 문장이 된다.

18 첫 문단에서 화자는 기쁨의 눈물을 흘렸다고 언급되어 있다. 따라서 필자의 심경으로 가장 적절한 것은 ② '감격'이다.

19 ④ '재활용 악기의 장점'에 대한 내용은 위 글에서 언급된 바 없다.

20 위 글의 문맥상 '이런 날'이 가리키는 것은 연주회를 마치고 사람들이 큰 박수를 오케스트라 단원들에게 보낸 날을 의미한다.

21 '왜 재활용 오케스트라라고 불리는가?'라는 문장이 들어가기에 가장 적절한 곳은 오케스트라의 이름이 지어진 이유에 대해서 설명하고 있는 곳 앞인 (A)이다.

22 위 글의 마지막 문장에서 모든 것은 Favio Chávez 선생님을 만나고 난 뒤 변했다고 언급되었다. 따라서 위 글의 뒤에 올 내용으로

가장 적절한 것은 ④ 'Favio가 Cateura를 변화시킨 일'이다.

23 위 글에 따르면, Cateura 마을에는 희망도 꿈도 없었다고 ("There weren't many hopes and dreams in our town.") 한다.

24 가정법과거형 문장은 현재 사실과 반대되는 가정을 할 때 쓰는 형식으로 '만약 ~라면, …할 텐데.'로 해석한다.

25 위 글에서는 Favio Chávez 선생님이 Cateura 마을에서 사람들을 모아 쓰레기로 버려졌던 악기를 재활용해 오케스트라를 만들고 연주를 할 수 있게 도와준 내용에 대해서 이야기하고 있다. 따라서 위 글의 제목으로 가장 적절한 것은 ① From Trash to Music (쓰레기에서 음악으로)이다.

26 ⓓterrible은 문맥상 ⓓterrific으로 고치는 것이 자연스럽다.

27 위 글의 빈칸 (A)에는 Favio Chávez 선생님이 학생들이 새 악기를 살 수 있는 돈이 없다는 것을 알고 난 뒤 하는 말이 들어간다. 따라서 빈칸에 가장 적절한 말은 ⑤ "If we had enough money, we could buy new musical instruments."(우리가 충분한 돈이 있다면 새로운 악기를 살 수 있을 텐데.)이다.

28 (B)'이 아이디어'가 의미하는 것은 문맥상 쓰레기로 악기를 만드는 것이다.

29 위 글에 따르면, 학생들은 쓰레기를 재활용해서 만든 악기를 갖고 열심히 연습한 끝에, 사람들 앞에서 진짜 연주회를 열 수 있었다고 한다.

Lesson 5 (중간) 2회

01 ② 02 ④
03 (1) what to do / (2) where I should live   04 ①   05 ⑤
06 looking forward to riding a horse   07 ①   08 ①   09 ④
10 ③   11 ④   12 ①
13 If I were[was] an inventor, I would invent a time machine.
14 ①
15 (1) If I were[was] a bird, I could fly.
　　(2) If he knew my address, he would send me a letter.
16 ②   17 ④   18 ①   19 ⑤   20 ②   21 ②   22 ④   23 ②
24 ④   25 ①   26 ②   27 ⑤   28 ⑤   29 ③   30 ③

01 practice는 '연습', '연습하다'라는 뜻을 가진 단어이다.

02 큰 박수를 보내다'라는 뜻의 표현은 'give a big hand' 이다.

03 '의문사+to+동사원형'은 문장에서 주어, 목적어, 보어의 역할을 할 수 있으며, 동사의 목적어로 자주 쓰인다. 이때 해석은 의문사에 따라 '무엇을(what)/언제(when)/어디서(where)/어떻게(how) ~를 해야 할지'라고 해석한다. 「의문사+to부정사」는 「의문사+주어+should+동사원형」으로 바꿔 쓸 수 있다.

04 in order to: ~하기 위해서 / where to go: 어디를 가야 할지

05 B가 수학 숙제를 푸는 것을 도와달라고 말했고, 이에 A는 남동생을 돌봐야 한다고 대답한다. 따라서 빈칸에 들어갈 말로 가장 적절한 것은 ⑤ I'd love to, but I can't.(그리고 싶지만 안 돼.)이다.

06 "I'm looking forward to ~."는 '나는 ~하기를 기대한다.'라는 뜻으로, 기대를 나타낼 때 사용하는 표현이다. to는 전치사로 뒤에 명사 또는 동명사(-ing)를 쓴다.

07 대화의 흐름상 ⓐ와 ⓒ에는 상대방의 요청을 거절하는 표현이 들어가는 것이 적절하다. 따라서 빈칸에 들어갈 말로 적절하지 않은 것은 ① That sounds great.(그거 좋게 들린다.)이다.

08 빈칸 ⓑ에는 선행사 a boy를 수식하는 형용사절을 이끄는 관계대명사 who가 들어가는 것이 어법상 적절하다.

09 위 대화 (A)의 내용에 따르면, Alex는 수민이가 대회에서 노래를 부르는 동안 기타를 연주하고 싶지만 손을 다쳐서 그럴 수 없다고 제안을 거절하고 있다.

10 Jim Abbott는 MVP 상을 받기도 했다고 지호가 언급했다.

11 위 대화의 흐름상 나나가 야구 선수 Jim Abbott에 관한 영화를 보기를 기대하고 있는 표현이 들어가는 것이 적절하다.

12 ① 책의 제목에 대해서는 위 대화에서 언급된 바 없다.

13 현재 사실과 반대되는 가정을 나타낼 때, 'If+주어+were/동사의 과거형 ~, 주어+조동사의 과거형(would/should/could/might) +동사원형 ….' 형식의 가정법과거를 쓰며, '만약 ~라면, …할 텐데.'로 해석한다.

14 '의문사+to+동사원형'은 문장에서 주어, 목적어, 보어의 역할을 할 수 있으며, 동사의 목적어로 자주 쓰인다. 이때 해석은 의문사에 따라 '무엇을(what)/언제(when)/어디서(where)/어떻게(how) ~를 해야 할지'라고 해석한다.

15 현재 사실과 반대되는 가정을 나타낼 때, 'If+주어+were/동사의 과거형 ~, 주어+조동사의 과거형(would/should/could/might) +동사원형 ….' 형식의 가정법과거를 쓰며, '만약 ~라면, …할 텐데.'로 해석한다.

16 '의문사+to+동사원형'은 문장에서 주어, 목적어, 보어의 역할을 할 수 있으며, 동사의 목적어로 자주 쓰인다. 이때 해석은 의문사에 따라 '무엇을(what)/언제(when)/어디서(where)/어떻게(how) ~를 해야 할지'라고 해석한다. 사용되는 의문사에는 how, what, when, where 등이 있으며, why는 쓰이지 않는다.

17 '큰 박수를 보내다'라는 뜻의 표현은 'give one a big hand'라고 쓴다. 또한 이 경우 현재진행형이 쓰였으므로 동사 give는 giving으로 쓰는 것이 어법상 적절하다.

18 ⓐthrilling은 thrilled로 고치는 것이 어법상 적절하다.

19 ⓐ made of → are made of / ⓑ is → are / ⓒ teach music us → teach us music / ⓓ a little → a few로 고쳐야 어법상 적절한 문장이 된다.

20 (A) 앞에서는 왜 재활용 오케스트라라는 이름이 붙여졌는지에 대해서 설명하고 있다. 따라서 빈칸에는 ② why가 들어가는 것이 가장 적절하다.

21 (B)itself는 '그 자체'라는 뜻으로 사용된 강조 용법의 재귀대명사이다. 이와 쓰임이 같은 것은 (b) myself, (d) itself, (e) herself이다.

22 위 글에 따르면, Cateura 마을의 많은 사람들은 희망과 꿈이 없었다고 한다.

23 위 글에 따르면, Favio 선생님은 환경 교육자이자 음악가('Favio was an environmental educator and a musician')였다고 언급되어 있다.

24 ⓓTo는 From으로 고치는 것이 어법상 적절하다.

25 (A) I still remember the first piece of music in that we played.는 I still remember the first piece of music that we played.라고 고치는 것이 어법상 적절하다.

26 위 글의 흐름상, 악기를 살 수 없어서 쓰레기를 재활용해서 악기를 만들었지만, 학생들이 연주를 하는 방법을 모른다는 또 다른 문제가 있었다는 문장이 들어가는 것이 흐름상 가장 적절하다.

27 '그러나 우리가 Favio Chávez 선생님을 만났을 때 모든 것이 바뀌기 시작했다.'라는 문장이 들어가기에 가장 적절한 곳은 Favio Chávez 선생님을 만나기 전과 후에 대해서 설명하고 있는 (E)이다.

28 쓰레기 매립지 물건들로 악기를 만들 수 있다고 말한 것은 Favio 선생님이다.

29 '자선단체나 기관에 어떤 것을 주다'('give something to a charity or other organizations')라는 영영 풀이가 가리키는 것은 donate이다.

30 ⓐ is → are / ⓑ themselves → itself / ⓓ were → was / ⓔ instrument → instruments / ⓖnaming → named / ⓗ how to playing → how to play로 고쳐야 어법상 적절한 문장이 된다.

Lesson 6 (중간)

01 ④ **02** ① **03** ① **04** ④ **05** ③ **06** ③ **07** ⑤
08 (1) The girl studied hard so that she could pass the exam.
　　(2) I wrote his name in my diary so as not to forget it.
09 ③ **10** ② **11** ⑤ **12** ① **13** ⑤
14 (1) The[That] mouse is not[isn't] small enough to go through the hole. (2) Minho's English is good enough to talk with a foreigner.
15 (1) imagine → imagination / (2) whose → what /
　　(3) interesting → interestingly / (4) shine → shone

---

16 ⑤ **17** ① **18** ⑤ **19** ④ **20** ② **21** ③ **22** ④ **23** ⑤
24 ③ **25** ③ **26** ② **27** ⑤
28 It is round and delicate, yet strong enough to protect its contents.
29 ④ **30** ④

01 명사 attraction은 동사 attract로 바꿔 써야 어법상 적절하다.

02 pleasing: 기쁘게 하는 / curved: 곡선으로 된 /
architect: 건축가 / inspiration: 영감

03 book: 예약하다; 책

04 "내 동네에서 어느 장소가 가장 좋았니?"라는 A의 질문에 대해 "난 센트럴 파크를 가장 가고 싶어."라는 B의 대답은 흐름상 자연스럽지 않다.

05 ③의 빈칸에는 too가 들어가는 것이 문맥상 적절하다. 나머지 빈칸에는 enough가 들어가는 것이 문맥상 적절하다.

06 Tom studied hard in order to pass the test.는 Tom studied hard so that he could pass the test.으로 고치는 것이 어법상 적절하다.

07 「형용사/부사+enough to+동사원형」은 '~하기에 충분히 …한〔하게〕'이라는 의미로 어떤 일을 하기에 충분한 정도를 나타낼 때 쓴다.

08 so that이 이끄는 절이 목적을 나타내어 '~하기 위해서, ~하도록'이라는 의미를 나타낸다. 목적을 나타낼 때 「(so as) to+동사원형」, 「in order to+동사원형」, 「in order that+주어+can/may ~」를 쓸 수도 있다.

09 B는 콘서트에 갈 것이라고 A에게 말했다.

10 so that he can got up early는 so that he can get up early로 바꿔 쓰는 것이 어법상 적절하다.

11 so that이 이끄는 절이 목적을 나타내어 '~하기 위해서, ~하도록'이라는 의미를 나타낸다. so that이 이끄는 절의 동사는 주로 can/could 또는 will/would와 함께 쓰거나 단순 현재 시제로 쓴다.

12 so that이 이끄는 절이 목적을 나타내어 '~하기 위해서, ~하도록'이라는 의미를 나타낸다. 목적을 나타낼 때 「(so as) to+동사원형」, 「in order to+동사원형」, 「in order that+주어+can/may ~」를 쓸 수도 있다.

13 They went to bed early so that they could get up early.를 의미가 같은 문장으로 바꾸면, They went to bed early to get up early.가 된다.

14 「형용사/부사+enough to+동사원형」은 '~하기에 충분히 …한〔하게〕'이라는 의미로 어떤 일을 하기에 충분한 정도를 나타낼 때 쓴다.

15 (2) whose의 뒤에는 항상 명사가 붙는다. / (4) 수동형이므로

shine의 과거분사 shone으로 바꾸는 것이 적절하다.

16 ⓔYou can feel artworks by breaking them.(예술작품을 망가뜨림으로써 그것들을 느낄 수 있습니다.)라는 문장은 미술관 방문의 기본 규칙을 설명하고 있는 글의 흐름에는 어색하다.

17 ① Who made this museum?(이 박물관은 누가 만들었는가?)에 대해서는 위 글에서 언급되어 있지 않다.

18 문맥상 (A) 대명사 it은 단수명사인 this museum을 가리킨다. / (B) 대명사 them은 복수명사인 the artworks를 가리킨다.

19 문맥상 (가)this는 앞 문장의 'what inspired the architect'(무엇이 건축가에게 영감을 주었는지)를 가리킨다.

20 ⓑobviously는 형용사인 obvious로 고치는 것이 문맥상 적절하다.

21 ⓒDespite his dedication, the cathedral was finished when he died.는 흐름상 Despite his dedication, the cathedral was not finished when he died.로 고치는 것이 적절하다.

22 '현재 그것은 바르셀로나에서 가장 많이 방문하는 관광 명소'('now it is the most visited attraction in Barcelona.')라고 언급되어 있다.

23 ⑤ What is Dongdaemun Design Plaza used for?(동대문 디자인 플라자는 무엇에 사용되고 있는가?)에 대해서는 위 글에서 언급되어 있지 않다.

24 위 글에서 동대문 디자인 플라자 건물 뿐만 아니라 많은 도시의 디자인들이 자연의 아름다움을 담기 위해 노력한다고 언급하고 있다. 따라서 ③ Nature meets city.가 빈칸에 가장 적절하다.

25 (A) have been to ~: ~에 가 본 적이 있다 / (B) look like: ~처럼 보이다 / (C) Thanks to ~: ~의 덕택으로 / (D) try to ~: ~하려고 노력하다

26 ⓑThe shapes in nature are very pleased to the eye.는 The shapes in nature are very pleasing to the eye.로 고치는 것이 어법상 적절하다.

27 위 글에서 자연의 형태들이 눈에 즐거움을 준다고 말하면서 달걀을 예로 들고 있다. 따라서 빈칸에 들어갈 말로 가장 적절한 것은 ⑤ For example(예를 들어)이다.

28 주어진 우리말에 따라 단어들을 배열하면 It is round and delicate, yet strong enough to protect its contents.가 된다.

29 ④ How many columns are there inside the Sagrada Familia?(사그라다 파밀리아 성당 안에는 몇 개의 기둥이 있는가?)에 대해서는 위 글에서 언급된 바 없다.

30 사그라다 파밀리아 성당은 세계에서 가장 유명한 성당이라고('It is one of the most famous churches in the world') 언급되어 있다.

Lesson 6 (중간)

01 ③ **02** ① **03** ③ **04** ②
05 (1) in order to help sick people
　　(2) so that she could buy a new handphone
06 ③ **07** ② **08** ④ **09** ②
10 (1) strong enough to lift
　　(2) long enough to reach the top shelf
　　(3) old enough to drive a car
　　(4) good enough to talk with a foreigner
11 ③ **12** ② **13** ⑤
14 (1) Mike saved money so that he could buy a new bicycle.
　　(2) I turned on the TV so as to watch the news.
15 ⑤ **16** ⑤ **17** ③ **18** ③ **19** ①
20 (A) Australia / (B) the shape of trees / (C) the curved lines from nature
21 ① **22** ⑤ **23** ① **24** ⑤ **25** ③ **26** ① **27** ⑤ **28** ②
29 ② **30** ④

01 architect는 '건축가'라는 뜻을 갖는 단어이다.

02 순서대로 delicate(섬세한) / contents(내용물) / imagination(상상력) / inspiration(영감)이 주어진 영영 풀이로 가장 적절하다.

03 「형용사/부사+enough to+동사원형」은 '~하기에 충분히 …한[하게]'이라는 의미로 어떤 일을 하기에 충분한 정도를 나타낼 때 쓴다. 한편 「too+형용사/부사+to+동사원형」은 '너무 ~해서 …할 수 없다, …하기에는 너무 ~하다'라는 의미를 나타낸다.

04 목적을 나타낼 때 「(so as) to+동사원형」, 「in order to+동사원형」, 「in order that+주어+can/may ~」를 쓸 수 있다.

05 so that이 이끄는 절이 목적을 나타내어 '~하기 위해서, ~하도록'이라는 의미를 나타낸다. 목적을 나타낼 때 「(so as) to+동사원형」, 「in order to+동사원형」, 「in order that+주어+can/may ~」를 쓸 수 있다.

06 ⓐ Of course, I did. / ⓑ I liked the folk village most. / ⓒ I looked really cool. / ⓓ Thank you for showing me around.이 들어가는 것이 흐름상 가장 적절하다.

07 of → for / enough good → good enough / enough to going → enough to go로 고쳐야 어법상 적절한 문장이 된다.

08 ① so that → so as to / ② He did his best, so that → He did his best so that / ③ so as to → so that / ⑤ can → could 로 고쳐야 어법상 적절한 문장이 된다.

09 주어진 단어들을 배열하면 'Jiho spoke loudly so that everyone could hear him.'이 된다.

10 「형용사/부사+enough to+동사원형」은 '~하기에 충분히 …한

〔하게〕'이라는 의미로 어떤 일을 하기에 충분한 정도를 나타낼 때 쓴다.

11 「형용사/부사+enough to+동사원형」은 '~하기에 충분히 …한 〔하게〕'이라는 의미로 어떤 일을 하기에 충분한 정도를 나타낼 때 쓴다. 한편 「too+형용사/부사+to+동사원형」은 '너무 ~해서 …할 수 없다, …하기에는 너무 ~하다'라는 의미를 나타낸다.

12 ② I left home early so that I could caught the bus.는 I left home early so that I could catch the bus.로 고치는 것이 어법상 적절하다.

13 Sally는 "I can't wait to see the concert!"라고 말한 바 있다.

14 so that이 이끄는 절이 목적을 나타내어 '~하기 위해서, ~하도록'이라는 의미를 나타낸다. 목적을 나타낼 때 「(so as) to+동사원형」, 「in order to+동사원형」, 「in order that+주어+can/may ~」를 쓸 수 있다.

15 위 글에 따르면, '학교 정원에서는 신선한 음식을 먹을 수 있도록 채소를 키운다'('We grow some vegetables there so that we can have fresh food.')고 언급되어 있다.

16 '예술 작품들의 사진을 찍어도 되지만, 그것들을 만지는 것은 안 됩니다.'라는 문장이 들어가기에 가장 적절한 곳은 미술관 방문의 기본적인 규칙을 설명한다고 말하고 있는 문장 다음인 (E)이다.

17 위 글에 따르면, 많은 건축가들은 자연에서 영감을 얻는다고 ('Nature has inspired many architects around the world.') 언급되어 있다.

18 ⓐ pleased → pleasing / ⓑ enough strong to → strong enough to / ⓓ church → churches 로 고쳐야 어법상 적절한 문장이 된다.

19 (A) clear: 분명한 / (B) inspiration: 영감 / (C) what would you choose from nature?: 자연에서 무엇을 선택할 거니?

20 (A) 시드니 오페라 하우스는 Australia에 있으며, (B) 사그라다 파밀리아 성당은 나무의 형태에서 영감을 받았다고 한다. 또한 (C) 동대문 디자인 플라자는 자연의 곡선에서 영감을 받았다고 언급되어 있다.

21 so that이 이끄는 절이 목적을 나타내어 '~하기 위해서, ~하도록'이라는 의미를 나타낸다. so that이 이끄는 절의 동사는 주로 can/could 또는 will/would와 함께 쓰거나 단순 현재 시제로 쓴다.

22 ⓑ As you can see: 당신이 볼 수 있듯이 / ⓒ If you were an architect: 당신이 건축가라면

23 Zaha Hadid는 자연에서 영감을 받아 동대문 디자인 플라자를 건축했다고 언급되어 있다.

24 ⓔ why는 의문사 how로 바꿔 쓰는 것이 어법상 적절하다.

25 Sydney Opera House는 돛단배의 모습을 표현한 것이 아니라 오렌지에서 영감을 받아서 지었다고('interestingly, the inspiration came from an orange') 언급되어 있다.

26 빈칸 (A)에 들어갈 단어로 가장 적절한 것은 obvious이다.

27 가우디와 같은 건축가들은 자연의 아름다움을 담기 위해 노력했다고 언급되어 있다.

28 대명사 (A)them이 가리키는 것은 앞에서 언급된 복수명사인 Many artists이다.

29 ⓑ pleased는 pleasing으로 고치는 것이 어법상 적절하다.

30 주어진 단어들을 우리말에 맞게 배열하면, 'It is round and delicate, yet strong enough to protect its contents.'가 된다.

Lesson 7 (기말) ^{1회}

01 ②	02 ⑤	03 ②	04 ②	05 ①	06 ②	07 ④	08 ⑤
09 ①	10 ⑤	11 ②	12 ②, ⑤	13 ③	14 ①	15 ⑤
16 ③	17 ①	18 ④	19 ⑤	20 ⑤	21 ⑤	22 ③	23 ⑤
24 ③	25 (가) uses / (나) served	26 ②	27 ①	28 ②
29 ⑤	30 ③

01 ②의 빈칸에는 어법상 that 또는 which가 들어가는 것이 자연스럽다. 나머지 빈칸에는 소유격 관계대명사 whose가 들어가는 것이 어법상 적절하다.

02 빈칸에는 선행사가 사람 또는 사물이며 소유격인 (대)명사 대신에 쓰는 소유격 관계대명사 whose가 들어가는 것이 어법상 가장 적절하다.

03 ② book과 borrow는 각각 '예약하다', '빌리다'라는 뜻을 가진 단어들이다. 나머지 단어들은 모두 동의어나 유의어 관계에 있는 단어들이다.

04 ②who는 소유격 관계대명사인 whose로 고치는 것이 어법상 적절하다.

05 ② '난 내 옛 친구와 계속 연락을 취한다.' / ③ '넌 오늘 어디서 놀고 싶니?' / ④ '나는 케이크보다는 오히려 피자를 먹을 거야.' / ⑤ '우리는 우리의 축구 경기를 미뤄야 했다.'로 고쳐야 어법상 적절한 문장이 된다.

06 ②which는 소유격 관계대명사인 whose로 고치는 것이 어법상 적절하다.

07 위 대화에 따르면, 남극의 온도는 7월에는 영하 58도, 12월에는 영하 26도라고 한다.

08 "I wonder ~."는 '나는 ~이 궁금하다.'라는 뜻으로 어떤 것에 대해 궁금할 때 사용하는 표현이다. 위 대화에서는 목성이 얼마나 큰지 궁금하다고 말하고 있으므로 빈칸 (B)에는 의문사 how가 들어가는 것이 자연스럽다.

09 "너 비를 맞았구나."라는 A의 말에 대해 "우산을 가져오지 말았어

야 하는데."라는 B의 대답은 흐름상 자연스럽지 않다.

10 (A)는 사물인 선행사를 수식하는 목적격 관계대명사, (B)는 소유격 관계대명사, (C)는 사람인 선행사를 수식하는 주격 관계대명사이다. 따라서 이와 쓰임이 같은 것은 (A)는 ⓐ, ⓓ, ⓕ / (B)는 ⓑ / (C)는 ⓒ, ⓔ이다.

11 (A) when: ~할 때 / (B) since: ~이기 때문에 / (C) so that+주어+동사: ~하기 위해서

12 ① that → whose / ③ which → whose / ④ will be → is

13 위 대화의 내용에 따르면, Tony는 언젠가 낙타와 사막을 여행하고 싶다고 언급했다.

14 위 글에 따르면, giant trevally는 새를 먹이로 먹기 위해 물에서 뛰어올라 새를 잡아 먹는다고 한다.

15 위 글에서 giant trevally는 빠르고 똑똑하다고 말하면서, 물에서 뛰어올라 날아가는 새를 잡아 먹을 수 있다고 한다. 따라서 빈칸에 들어갈 말로 가장 적절한 것은 ⑤ It is smart enough to calculate the speed and distance of a flying bird.(그것은 날아가는 새의 속도와 거리를 계산할 수 있을 만큼 충분히 똑똑하다.)이다.

16 ① which → whose / ② who they → who / ④ whom → who / ⑤ whose → whom

17 위 글에서는 쓰나미 파도에 대해서 이야기하고 있다. 따라서 문맥상 빈칸에 들어갈 말로 가장 적절한 것은 ① high이다.

18 ⓓtheir speed and distance는 its speed and distance로 고쳐야 어법상 적절하다.

19 위 글에 따르면, giant trevally는 먹이인 새들을 잡기 위해 날아가는 새의 속도와 거리를 계산할 줄 알 정도로 똑똑하다고 언급되어 있다.

20 (A)fool은 '속이다', '기만하다'라는 뜻으로 사용되었다. 이와 쓰임이 같은 문장은 ⑤ Be a smart eater and don't be fooled by the advertisement.(똑똑하게 드시고 광고에 속지 마세요.)이다.

21 수면에 앉은 새가 아니라 날아가는 새를 잡을 수 있다고 언급되어 있다.

22 밑줄 친 ⓐ에는 문맥상 until이 들어가는 것이 가장 자연스럽다. ① if, ② since, ④ when, ⑤ while이 들어가는 것이 자연스럽다.

23 ⑤ Why does the tuskfish like clams?에 대해서는 위 글에서 언급된 바 없다.

24 (A)whose는 소유격 관계대명사로 사용되었다. 따라서 이와 쓰임이 같은 것은 ⓒ, ⓔ이다.

25 (가) 문장에서 주어는 단수형인 This small fish이므로 동사는 uses가 되어야 한다. / (나) 문장에서 dinner(저녁식사)가 제공되는 것이므로 수동형 동사인 (is) served가 되어야 어법상 적절하다.

26 간접의문문은 문장 내에서 주어 또는 보어, 목적어로 사용되며 '의문사+주어+동사'의 형식으로 쓴다. 따라서 빈칸에 들어갈 말로 가장 적절한 것은 what these whales are doing이다.

27 (A) while: ~하는 동안에 / (B) near: ~ 근처에 / (C) fall asleep: 잠들다

28 '그러나 그들은 사실 자고 있는 것이다!'라는 문장이 들어가기에 가장 적절한 곳은 집단으로 서 있는 것처럼 보이지만 사실은 자고 있는 상태라고 이야기하고 있는 ⓑ이다.

29 (나)since는 '~이기 때문에'라는 뜻으로 사용되었다. 이와 쓰임이 같은 것은 ⑤ The man couldn't dig in the ground since it was too dark.(너무 어두웠기 때문에 그 남자는 땅을 팔 수 없었다.)이다.

30 위 글에 따르면, humpback whales는 물고기의 한 종류가 아니라서 호흡을 하기 위해 수면으로 올라와야 한다고 언급되어 있다.

Lesson 7 (기말)

2회

01 ②	**02** ③	**03** ④	**04** ⑤	**05** ③	**06** ①	**07** ④	**08** ⑤
09 ①	**10** ④	**11** ③	**12** ④	**13** ④	**14** ②	**15** ④	**16** ③

17 This small fish whose favorite food is clams

18 ③	**19** ⑤	**20** ①	**21** ②,③,④	**22** ③	**23** ②	**24** ①

25 the clam | **26** ④ | **27** ⑤ | **28** ④ | **29** ② | **30** ④

01 spot은 동사일 때 '발견하다', '알아채다'라는 뜻을 갖는 단어이다. ②spot은 문맥상 attract로 바꿔 쓰는 것이 더 자연스럽다.

02 분수를 표현할 때, 분자는 기수로, 분모는 서수로 쓴다.

03 위에서부터 순서대로, expression(표현), forecast(예보), base(기반), instead(대신에)가 들어가는 것이 문맥상 가장 자연스럽다.

04 ① whom → which / ② whom → who / ③ whose → who[whom] / ④ who → whose로 고쳐야 어법상 적절한 문장이 된다.

05 위 대화에서는 날씨가 좋아 소풍을 가기로 했지만 일기 예보를 확인해 보니 비가 온다고 말하고 있다. 따라서 빈칸에 들어갈 말로 가장 적절한 것은 ③ Let's go another time, then.(그럼 다음에 가자.)이다.

06 ① where is the bus stop → where the bus stop is로 고쳐야 어법상 적절한 문장이 된다.

07 시간을 나타내는 접속사가 이끄는 부사절에서는 미래의 의미일지라도 현재 시제를 쓴다. 따라서 ④의 두 문장을 when을 이용해 한 문장으로 만들면 When Yongchan grows up, he will be a scientist.가 된다.

08 위 대화에서는 tuskfish가 어떻게 먹이인 조개를 도구를 사용해서

먹는지에 대해서 이야기하고 있다. 따라서 위 대화의 주제로 가장
적절한 것은 ⑤ A smart fish using tools for food(먹이를 구하
기 위해 도구를 이용하는 똑똑한 물고기)이다.

09 위 대화에 따르면, 유미는 지성이가 물고기는 똑똑하지 않은 것 같
다고 생각한다는 말에 그것은 사실이 아니라고("That's not
true.") 대답했다.

10 ④ When she will come back home → When she comes
back home으로 고쳐야 어법상 적절한 문장이 된다.

11 시간을 나타내는 접속사가 이끄는 부사절에서는 미래의 의미일지
라도 현재 시제를 쓴다. 따라서 (A)~(C) 안에 asks / graduate /
will buy가 들어가는 것이 가장 적절하다.

12 영화를 추천해 줘서 고맙다는 A의 말에 대해 "오히려 제가 기쁩니
다."라는 B의 대답이 가장 흐름상 자연스럽다.

13 ⓓSince they are not fish, they need to come up to breath.
는 ⓓSince they are not fish, they need to come up to
breathe.로 바꿔 써야 어법상 적절하다.

14 우리말에 맞게 주어진 단어들을 배열하면, Oceans are full of
wonder and are home to millions of species.가 된다.

15 ⓓIt은 the tuskfish를 가리킨다. 나머지는 모두 the clam을 가
리킨다.

16 ③ When is the tuskfish's favorite time to eat? (tuskfish가
먹이를 먹기에 가장 좋아하는 때는 언제인가?)에 대한 내용은 위
글에서 언급된 바 없다.

17 소유격 관계대명사 whose는 선행사가 사람 또는 사물이며 소유
격인 (대)명사 대신에 쓰며, whose가 이끄는 관계대명사절은 형
용사 역할로 바로 앞의 선행사를 수식한다

18 현재완료 시제가 사용되었으므로 ③ seen이 들어가는 것이 어법
상 가장 적절하다.

19 ⓔit은 the bird를 가리킨다. 나머지는 모두 the giant trevally
를 가리킨다.

20 위 글에 따르면, giant trevally는 우리가 알고 있는 것과는 반대
로 새를 먹이로 삼기 때문에 물 밖으로 뛰어올라 새를 잡는다고 언
급되어 있다.

21 (가)fool은 '속이다', '기만하다'라는 뜻으로 사용되었다. 이와 쓰
임이 같은 것은 ② Don't be fooled by his cute looks.(그의 귀
여운 외모에 속지 마라.) / ③ You can't fool me with that
excuse.(너는 그 변명으로 나를 속일 수 없다.) / ④ He tries to
fool people about his age.(그는 그의 나이에 대해서 사람들을
속이려고 한다.)이다.

22 빈칸 (A)에는 선행사가 사람 또는 사물이며 소유격인 (대)명사 대
신에 쓰는 소유격 관계대명사 whose가 들어가는 것이 어법상 가
장 적절하다.

23 글의 흐름상 until(~할 때까지)이 들어가는 것이 가장 자연스럽다.

24 smash A against B'는 'A를 B에 내리치다'라는 뜻이다.

25 ⓐit은 the clam을 가리킨다.

26 (가)what은 간접의문문을 이끄는 의문사이다. 이와 쓰임이 같은
것은 ④이다.

27 ⓐSince는 '~이기 때문에'라는 뜻으로 사용되었다. 이와 쓰임이
같은 것은 ⑤ Since you were late, your teacher got angry.
(네가 늦었기 때문에, 너의 선생님이 화가 나셨다.)이다.

28 ⓑbreathe는 문맥상 '호흡하기 위해'가 되어야 적절하다. 따라서
to부정사의 부사적 용법을 사용해 to breathe가 되는 것이 자연스
럽다.

29 위 글에서는 humpback whales의 수면 방법에 대해서 이야기
하고 있다. 따라서 위 글의 주제로 가장 적절한 것은 ② How
humpback whales sleep(humpback whales는 어떻게 자는
가)이다.

30 위 글에 따르면, humpback whale(혹등고래)는 잠을 잘 때 완전
히 잠들지는 않는다('they don't fall asleep completely.')고
언급되어 있다.

Lesson 8 (기말)

1회

01 ⑤	02 ④	03 ⑤	04 ④	05 ①	06 ④	07 ⑤	08 ②
09 ②	10 ④	11 ②	12 ③	13 ②			
14 (A) Saved (B) Picking (C) Bitten			15 ①	16 ③	17 ②		
18 ③	19 ⑤	20 ⑤	21 ⑤	22 ⑤	23 ④	24 ⑤	25 ①
26 ③	27 ①	28 ②	29 ④	30 ③			

01 spill: 흘리다 / describe: 묘사하다 / mistakenly: 실수로 /
rather than ~: ~이기보다는 오히려

02 빈칸 위에서부터 순서대로, stream(흐름), calculate(계산하다),
breathe(호흡하다), shocked(충격 받은), mistakes(실수)가 들
어가는 것이 문맥상 가장 적절하다.

03 A는 B에게 중학교 생활에서 후회되는 것이 있냐고 물어 보았다.
이에 No. I regret riding my bicycle to school instead of
taking the bus.(아뇨, 전 버스를 타는 대신에 자전거로 통학한 것
을 후회해요.)라는 대답은 문맥상 적절하지 않다.

04 ① Lost the game → Losing the game / ② I being
nervous → Being nervous / ③ you found the shop → you
will find the shop / ⑤ Doing not my homework → Not
doing my homework

05 민호가 Linda에게 무엇을 읽고 있냐고 물어보았고, Linda는 반
친구들이 써 준 졸업 메시지를 읽고 있다고 대답했다. 이에 민호는
친구들이 Linda에게 할 말이 많은 것 같다고 대답하고 Linda는
친구들이 자신의 미소가 좋았다고 이야기하고 있다고 대답한다.
민호가 또 무슨 내용이 써 있냐고 물어보자, Linda는 몇몇 친구들

정답 및 해설 **7**

이 자신과 충분히 놀지 못했다고 썼다고 대답한다. 민호는 그것이 Linda의 잘못이 아니라고 말하면서 Linda가 바빴다고 한다. 이에 Linda는 친구들과 더 많은 시간을 보냈어야 한다고 후회한다. 민호는 졸업 후에도 시간이 있다고 말하고 Linda는 그렇다고 대답한다. 또한 민호가 졸업 후에도 친구들과 연락하고 지내기를 바란다고 말하고 Linda는 자신도 그러기를 바란다고 말하는 순서로 이어지는 것이 대화 흐름상 가장 자연스럽다.

06 A가 B에게 가장 짧은 등산 코스는 시간이 얼마나 걸리냐고 물어보고 있다. 이에 대한 B의 대답으로 적절하지 않은 것은 ④ I never say that(난 절대 ~라고 말하지 않아.)이다.

07 어젯밤에 너무 많이 먹어서 심한 복통이 있었다는 A의 말에 대해 "넌 더 먹었어야 해."라는 B의 대답은 흐름상 자연스럽지 않다.

08 'I hope ~'는 어떤 일에 대해 기원하는 표현이다.

09 (B) I had played baseball after I ate dinner. → I played baseball after I had eaten dinner. / (D) I study English and had read a book every night. → I study English and read a book every night.

10 ① was → had been / ② had stayed → stayed / ③ had gone → went / ⑤ stole → had stolen

11 ② She had lost the bag that her father bought for her.는 She lost the bag that her father had bought for her.로 고치는 것이 어법상 적절하다.

12 ⓒHe had borrowed money because he lost his wallet. → He borrowed money because he had lost his wallet. / ⓓ My friends already finished it before I had arrived. → My friends had already finished it before I arrived.로 고쳐야 어법상 적절한 문장이 된다.

13 '그러나, 보도 덕분에, Nobel은 세계에 공헌할 수 있는 일을 하고자 결심했다.'라는 문장이 들어가기에 가장 적절한 곳은 1895년에 노벨상을 만들기로 결심했다고 하는 (B)이다.

14 분사구문은 「접속사+주어+동사」로 이루어진 부사절을 분사를 포함하는 부사구로 표현한 것으로 시간, 이유나 원인, 조건 등을 나타낸다. 분사구문은 접속사와 주어를 생략하고 현재분사나 과거분사로 시작한다. (A), (C)는 수동의 의미이므로 과거분사를 쓴다.

15 (A) when: ~할 때 / (B) until: ~할 때까지 / (C) as soon as: ~하자마자 / (D) while: ~하는 동안

16 ⓒWorker ants are very weak.는 문맥상 ⓒWorker ants are very strong.으로 바꾸는 것이 자연스럽다.

17 위 글에 따르면, 글쓴이는 자신의 학생들을 위해 별 모양으로 된 종이를 샀다고 언급했다. 따라서 글쓴이의 직업으로 가장 적절한 것은 ②교사이다.

18 글쓴이는 Lucy에게 똑똑하다는 말을 해준 사람이 자신이 처음(I was the first person to tell her that in her life.)이라고 언급

19 위 글에서 Nick은 전학 간 학교에서 친구를 사귀는 데 어려움을 겪고 있어서 이에 대한 조언이 필요하다고 말하고 있다. 따라서 Nick이 글을 쓴 목적으로 가장 적절한 것은 ③ to ask for advice(충고를 구하기 위해)이다.

20 위 글에 따르면, ⑤ Always bring a serious topic like politics.(항상 정치와 같은 심각한 주제를 꺼내라.)라는 조언은 언급되어 있지 않다.

21 ⓔwe think that the Nobel Prize, rather than dynamite.는 we think of the Nobel Prize, rather than dynamite.로 고치는 것이 어법상 적절하다.

22 (A) mistakenly: 실수로 / (B) actually: 사실은 / (C) Originally: 원래는

23 위 글에 따르면, 노벨상에는 1895년에는 5개의 부문만 있었다고 한다.

24 위 글에 따르면, 노벨상이 처음 만들어질 당시, 상의 종류는 5가지였다고 한다.

25 위 글에서 주인공은 죽지 않았지만 신문에서 자신이 죽었다고 보도하는 것을 발견했다. 따라서 주인공의 심경으로 가장 적절한 것은 ① shocked이다.

26 위 글에 따르면, 노벨은 사람들이 자신을 '죽음의 상인'이라고 생각한다는 것을 상상도 못했다고 한다.

27 위 글에 따르면, 노벨은 다이너마이트를 발명해 부유해졌으며, 신문은 노벨의 죽음을 보도했다.

28 ⓑ는 catching이 아니라 caught가 들어가는 것이 문맥상 적절하다.

29 위 글에 따르면, Alfred Nobel은 죽지 않았지만 신문에서 자신이 죽었다고 보도한 것을 발견했고, 이에 옷과 책상에 커피를 쏟았다.

30 ⓒ에는 peace가 아니라 war(전쟁)가 들어가는 것이 문맥상 적절하다.